THE
Ufa
Story

Klaus Kreimeier

THE

Ufa
Story

A History of Germany's Greatest Film Company

1918–1945

Translated by Robert and Rita Kimber

HILL AND **WANG**

A DIVISION OF FARRAR, STRAUS AND GIROUX

NEW YORK

Translation copyright © 1996 by Hill and Wang
All rights reserved
Originally published in German under the title *Die Ufa-Story: Geschichte eines Filmkonzerns*
by Carl Hanser Verlag, München Wien, 1992
Printed in the United States of America
Published simultaneously in Canada by HarperCollinsCanadaLtd
Designed by Fritz Metsch
First edition, 1996

Library of Congress Cataloging-in-Publication Data
Kreimeier, Klaus.
[Ufa-story. English]
The Ufa story : a history of Germany's greatest film company,
1918–1945 / Klaus Kreimeier ; translated by Robert and Rita Kimber.
p. cm.
Includes bibliographical references and index.
1. UFA—History. 2. Motion picture industry—Germany—History.
I. Title.
PN1999.U35K713   1996   384'.8'0943—dc20   96-7201   CIP

AUTHOR'S
ACKNOWLEDGMENTS

Hans Abich, Gerd Albrecht, Petrus Bartelsman, Christoph Buchwald, Thomas Elsaesser, Lothar Fend, Cornelia Fleer, Heinrich Gräfenstein, Hanns Groessel, Alfred Hirschmeier, Alfred Hürmer, Wolfgang Jacobsen, Kurt Johnen-Bühler, Friedrich P. Kahlenberg, Joachim Klinger, Heinz Klunker, Ute Kreimeier, Peter Latta, Hermine Marxová, Wolfgang Mühl-Benninghaus, Friedrich Karl Pflughaupt, Hans Helmut Prinzler, Karl Prümm, Paul Püschel, Carl Raddatz, Helmut Regel, Gaby Scherer, Heide Schlüpmann, Wolfram Schütte, Eberhard Spiess, Zdenek Stáblat, Werner Sudendorf, Wolfgang Theis, Jürgen Habakuk Traber, Heinz Trenczak, Karsten Visarius.

CONTENTS

Photographs follow pp. 152 and 280.

THE
Ufa
Story

Fade In

U F A was a major German film company, one of the most important movie studios in the world. Its name calls up a host of memories, and even today—depending on your age and temperament—it may evoke either a dreamy mood or a sharp aesthetic antidote to dreaminess, bitter derision or a bout of nostalgia.

Ufa: Didn't it mark "the great era of German film"? Wasn't it the birthplace of German stars who could hold their own with the great American, French, and Italian screen stars? A cinematic paradise whose movie theaters resembled palaces and cathedrals and added an element of electrifying splendor to Germany's urban culture? A film factory spread out over several square miles that contained Europe's largest studios and had room outdoors where any number of dream cities and fantasy landscapes could take shape simultaneously?

Ufa was all that and more, far more than just a business. It was Germany's imperial purveyor of magical images. Ufa's films, its stars, its advertising strategies, its palatial theaters and its gala premieres are part and parcel of German dreams and nightmares in the first half of this century. And if that is so, we should be able to see in the images it created the era's internal contradictions, the alternatives it had, and the better possibilities it wasted and betrayed.

From Ernst Lubitsch to Veit Harlan, from Erich Ludendorff to Alfred Hugenberg to Joseph Goebbels, from Henny Porten to Lilian Harvey and Marlene Dietrich and on to Zarah Leander and Hildegard Knef, from the lively, experimental studio of the Weimar years to the National Socialist, state-owned company, and then to its questionable "dismantling" in the Adenauer years: Ufa's history is German cultural history, a mix of politics and economics, science and technology, mass madness and mass dreams, kitsch, commerce, and art all stirred together in a complex, self-contradictory, and explosive brew.

To tell Ufa's history is also to tell a history of war and big money and those who invested their money both in war and in the art of film. Ufa's victory march is bracketed between two of Germany's most disastrous defeats: Verdun and Stalingrad. It began with nine hundred field theaters for the Imperial Office of Photography and Film, and it ended on January 30, 1945, in the fort of La Rochelle with the premiere of *Kolberg*, a film designed to encourage German forces and the German people to fight to the bitter end. The problem is clearly this: Culture may go to rack and ruin in wartime, but its history is not wholly absorbed by the history of war. Sometimes cultural history—especially the history of film—shows film to be the continuation of war by other means.

The history of big money and those who possessed it is an ambiguous one. In Germany, nothing comes to pass—neither triumph nor tragedy—without the backing of the German Bank, and it was the German Bank that presided over Ufa's birth in 1917 and at its funeral in 1962, when what was left of the firm was sold to the Bertelsmann Publishing Group. But though cinematic culture may be financed by banks, the history of Germany's culture and film is not identical with that of the German Bank. Financial and industrial magnates invested millions in films in the 1920s. They helped to produce worldwide successes and enormous flops. Ufa wanted to overwhelm Hollywood with vast sums of money, and the ironic result was that it had to accept credit from the Americans and become dependent on them. Its artists, directors, and stars often had heads of their own, and more complex ideas of what should be done with all that money than the money managers did. The history of images and of ideas does not necessarily coincide with corporate history.

No sooner had Ufa been founded at the orders of the Army Supreme Command than it was caught up in the maelstrom of the November Revolution. Was 1918 the end of the world or the dawning of a new era? The masses took to the streets and appeared on the screen. Max Reinhardt put mass scenes on the stage; in Tempelhof, Lubitsch made overblown historical films for Ufa; and out on the heaths of the Mark Brandenburg, Joe May conjured up all the continents of the earth for his megalomaniacal travel and adventure films.

A propaganda factory became a flourishing economic enterprise. Inflation, Germany's boycott of foreign films, and a huge popular demand for movies meant that the stockholders made money hand over fist. German films soon became hits in the United States. Ufa started to compete with Hollywood, with France's Pathé and Gaumont, and with Italy's film paradise Cinecittà. The company's directors and executives dreamed of German film hegemony. Its writers, directors, actors, cameramen, and set designers conjured up magical worlds in Tempelhof and Neubabelsberg, producing film fantasies throughout the 1920s, symphonies of weightless matter, of light, shadow, and iridescent movement. This was the world of Fritz Lang and Friedrich Wilhelm Murnau and the brilliant producer Erich Pommer, also the world of their technical magicians: film-obsessed architects like Robert Herlth and Walter Röhrig, camera virtuosos like Carl Hoffmann and Karl Freund. With the help of the hydraulic stage, the camera crane, the arc lamp, and the curving backdrop that allowed for receding horizons, the old story of the journey from hell to heaven by way of the world took on new form.

Dr. Mabuse, Die Nibelungen (The Nibelungs), Faust, Varieté (Variety), Der blaue Engel (The Blue Angel), and *Frau im Mond (Woman in the Moon)* were enduring masterpieces. But also, time and again, there were *Fridericus Rex* and perennial potboilers for quick consumption. Ballroom fantasies and wax figures, heavyweight Teutonic dramas and "sophisticated comedies" (German style), operettas and orgies of disaster, Marlene Dietrich and also (a little later) Kristina Söderbaum. The artists dreamed of a guild like the ones that had united the builders of medieval cathedrals, of a great "company of intellectuals," and had no inkling that power-hungry politicians like Alfred Hugenberg and Joseph Goebbels had long been eager to usurp for their own purposes what others had created. Sometimes reluctantly and sometimes lusting for big profits, Ufa emulated Germany's aggressive patriotism. It became a citadel of the German National People's Party, and when the time was ripe, it was taken over by the National Socialists. Jews, who had supplied the firm's intellectual resources ever since its founding, were ignominiously driven out, but most of the "German" stars stayed, and they stayed German: Henny Porten, Luise Ullrich, and Ilse Werner, Emil Jannings and Hans Albers, Gustav Fröhlich and Carl Raddatz. These men and women represented a typology of German longings and role models over four decades. They thought, spoke, and felt German until—as in Renate Müller's case—their hearts broke. They were the company's serfs (Willy Fritsch was a prime example). And under Goebbels they became "soldiers of art."

Ufa embodied discipline and a penchant for spectacle, both drill and ballet. Its love of ornamentation was a matter of both choice and obligation. Its theaters combined a chaos of styles with an architecture that induced the proper mood—Egyptian or Indian temples, elements of Wilhelmine, Art Nouveau, and Bauhaus styles mixed together with reckless abandon in façades, sumptuous halls, and eclectic "stage shows." When Hitler's will triumphed, Ufa and its theaters provided megalomaniacal productions and propaganda on behalf of death. In 1939 Ufa went to war and died in it.

Combining artistic inspiration with obedience to its new masters, Ufa stayed in step with the Wehrmacht and the SA, but it would still occasionally harken back to its anarchistic beginnings—to the circus, the variety hall, and the nickelodeon. Propaganda agency and do-it-yourself workshop, media giant, "guild" of film art, and retort of both beautiful and evil dreams—Ufa was all these things at once. And it was Germany's very German response to Hollywood.

Finally, Ufa was (and still remains today) a great symbolic construction, a super symbol. For the writers, theater people, painters, architects, and musicians who worked for it, it was the El Dorado of a new art form based on technology and capable of reaching and winning the masses. For its left-wing opponents it was—long before Axel Cäsar Springer and long before Adorno's and Horkheimer's analyses of the cultural industry—a stronghold of bourgeois media manipulation and an arsenal of reactionary power. For the National Socialists, it was a pedagogic institution devoted to "education for war." For Goebbels, it was a bordello and something like a playground for political adventurism. All in all, Ufa as a "propaganda instrument" was a Fascist wish projection.

After 1945, Ufa was a made-to-order enemy for the Allies, especially for American film companies. For this colossus blocked their access to the European film market. Now, they thought, it was their turn to make European profits.

But the story of Ufa's "dismantling" is only an epilogue, and Bertelsmann no more than a footnote to it. A company was disposed of; the symbols—the myth—remained.

Preview

Oₙ May 25, 1917, a special meeting, chaired by Colonel von Wrisberg,
took place in the Ministry of War in Berlin. Ministerial Director Le-
wald, Lieutenant Colonel von Haeften, and other high-ranking civilian and
military officials gathered to discuss a problem that could no longer be overlooked. The majority of Germans were dissatisfied with the monarchy in general and the ruling Hohenzollern dynasty and the person of Wilhelm II in
particular. The meeting stated the causes with admirable clarity and pressed
forward to solutions. The topic of discussion was "hostile, anti-monarchistic
efforts" against which measures were to be taken as soon as possible. Sub-
scribing to the doctrine that all was well but the public was inadequately
informed, the meeting determined that the Kaiser and his family had "to
be brought into closer personal contact with the people." Appropriate individuals, such as wounded officers, should be engaged "to give talks supportive of the monarchy," where possible "in formal settings." Given the
seriousness of the problem, the clergy and school officials should have "detailed and explicit instructions . . . because the extent of the danger [had]
not been understood everywhere in the country." Last but not least, the
German press had to do its part, conveying to the German people "in
words, but more importantly in images and films," a clear picture of "the
activities of the monarch and the members of his family in their rigorous
devotion to duty, in the simplicity of their way of life, in their actions on
the field of battle, their losses, etc."[1] Lieutenant Colonel von Haeften,
director of the military bureau of the Foreign Office, suggested founding a
Reich office for propaganda.

This conference on May 25 was one of many meetings of high-ranking
civilian and military authorities in the third year of the war. A year after
the "hell of Verdun" and a few weeks after the retreat of German troops
on the western front between Arras and Soissons to the Siegfried Line,

these members of the Prussian ruling elite called attention to serious errors and omissions on the psychological battlefield of propaganda. They had underestimated the impact of the modern mass media, they thought, and put them in the hands of the wrong people. Now, they appealed to wounded officers to lecture on behalf of the fatherland—which calls to mind instructors from the time of Frederick the Great—but references to "image and film" suggested a more modern means of education, pointing the way to a still uncertain media future. Acting on its patriotic impulses, the Wilhelmine military bureaucrats—naïve, pragmatic, and dictatorial—acceded to an experiment with modernity.

On July 4, 1917, Erich Ludendorff, since August 1916 First Quartermaster General to the Chief of the General Staff of the Field Army, sent a letter to the Ministry of War in which he described this experiment as a serious enterprise and gave it the blessing of the Supreme Command. This letter, which film literature likes to cite as the "founding document of Ufa," unites long-range strategic vision and shortsighted, goal-oriented narrow-mindedness in typically Prussian fashion. "The war has demonstrated the supremacy of picture and film as instruments of education and influence," it begins. "Unfortunately, our enemies have so thoroughly exploited their advantage in this area that we have suffered serious harm as a result."[2]

In 1917–18 Germany's political and military leaders, particularly Ludendorff, experimented with all the factors that had any possible bearing on the war, including some which existed only in their imaginations. They experimented, often against their better judgment, with the physical endurance of the soldiers on the western front and with the German people's yearning for peace. They gambled that the Western Allies' patience would run out; and with the Peace of Brest-Litovsk, they gambled on the weakness of the young Soviet Union. They toyed with voting reform, and the siege conditions Germans were forced to live under tested the efficacy of their domestic political control.

Modern technology accounted in no small measure for the failure of what were undoubtedly the most murderous of the Supreme Command's experiments, the three last offensives on the western front between March and August 1918, when large numbers of British tanks simply overran the German positions. By contrast, Germany had only halfheartedly experimented with modern technology. The U-boats sent so unscrupulously into action were, for example, as Sebastian Haffner has pointed out, "actually only diving boats and not true submarines. They had to surface constantly to recharge their batteries, and on the surface they were no match for even the smallest warship."[3]

The execution of the Supreme Command's plans for modern mass media took a similar course, another project born of modern times and spawned by the first war of mass destruction. Wildly inaccurate assessments and a disastrous tendency to risk the nation's destruction on all-or-nothing bets favored such experiments, and this legacy remained a heavy burden for Ufa in its future. "Once it became clear in the course of the First World War what kind of civilian role film could play, it was placed under house arrest," Paul Virilio has written. "Film production was subjected to a set of rules derived from methods of misinformation developed for wartime propaganda."[4] Born under Wilhelmine house arrest yet soon rebellious; motivated by the curiosity characteristic of its era, by hunger for life, and by the yearnings of the masses, yet always prepared to submit to rules bred of lies and self-deception—that is the central inconsistency at the heart of Ufa.

In Berlin in the 1890s the Busch Circus and its competition, the Schumann Circus on Schiffbauerdamm, staged neo-baroque water spectaculars featuring pantomime and dance and complete with nymphs, water sprites, and sea serpents. These shows owed their technical sophistication to stage technology imported from the United States. The circus soon gave way to "specialty theater," or what we would call variety shows; their mélange of song, cabaret, dance, acrobatics, and burlesque delighted turn-of-the-century Berlin audiences in the Metropol and the Apollo and, especially, the Winter Garden. The stars were dancers like Saharet, from Brazil, and Mata Hari, whom the French shot as a German spy in 1917 and whose name has become synonymous with political intrigue. She was born Margaretha Zelle in the Netherlands, and in 1927 Friedrich Feher made a film of her life for Berlin National-Film, *Mata Hari—Die rote Tänzerin* (*Mata Hari— The Red Dancer*), starring Magda Sonja and Fritz Kortner. In the movies everything was melted down and cast again: burlesque and acrobatics, water ballet, circus, and variety show.

The first public movie show in Germany was Max Skladanowsky's presentation of "living photographs" on November 1, 1895, as part of a variety program in the Winter Garden. The variety show and the circus were not only midwives to the movies; they also provided the backdrop, the atmosphere, the glitz, and the excitement that helped launch the movies in the world of mass entertainment.

Unlike the Lumières in France, who were successful factory owners, Skladanowsky was not an industrialist but a tinkerer, and the German tinkerer is a tragicomic figure. He had vague inklings of the twentieth century to come, yet the witches' spells and magic mirrors of the Romantic period held sway over his dreams. Skladanowsky and his brother Eugen, a circus performer, booking themselves as the Hamilton Brothers, had toured the German provinces with a late-Romantic mechanized spectacular whose "electromechanical effects" promised the public the pleasures of an all-inclusive artwork incorporating painting, a light show, amazing three-dimensionality, and mysterious sequences of movement.

It is not surprising that President Mankewitz of the German Bank showed no interest when Max Skladanowsky applied for a loan to finance further costly development of his cinematographic equipment. The banker thought he was dealing with a crackpot. Germany's most powerful financial institution would not make up for this misapprehension until it backed the founding of Ufa. But a little later, in 1896, Skladanowsky, using a camera he had financed himself, made a film about Alexanderplatz in Berlin, another one about Frederick the Great (played by Eugen), and various patriotic films like *Die Wachtparade marschiert Unter den Linden* (*The Guard Marches Down Unter den Linden*) and *Die Wache tritt ins Gewehr!* (*The Guard Goes into Action!*), which General von Ising, commandant of the Guard in Berlin, gave him permission to make. If, from the patriotic high points of Ufa's later history, we look back on these pioneer years, we see some of the basic elements of that history present even then, in vivid, miniature form.

In 1917, the year of Ufa's founding, all the railroad lines in Germany taken together added up to 65,000 kilometers (compared with 7,500 in 1850). The railroad had done more than revolutionize transportation and increase mobility. As a symbol of industrialization, a metallic beast that could devour time and space, it had changed human perception and behavior, altering the way people looked at life and the world. The pace and rhythm of early slapstick and early films reflected the stresses that propulsive industrial capitalism was imposing on society. From the beginning, movies were seismographic indicators of upheavals in the structure of society as well as in the human psyche and human consciousness. If the railroad ripped the nineteenth-century experience of reality out of the "intellectual and psychic verticality" of Victorian contemplation and oriented it to "the meaning of the horizontal"[5] and to the dizzying possibility of "interweaving" simultaneous events, so did the film's language of montage carry these possibilities to the outer limits of the imagination and give them vivid immediacy.

Early films were made by urbane bohemians and outsiders eager to experiment, the sensitive, nervous spirits of the age, tinkerers and visionaries with a keen business sense. They belonged to the first generation to grow up in electrified cities. Arc lights, which began illuminating the main business streets of European cities around 1880, did much to change the modes of perception of urban populations.[6] As early as 1900, Max Reinhardt revolutionized the theater with the use of spotlights and the revolving stage, and in 1920, with Reinhardt in mind, Hugo von Hofmannsthal summarized the change that the interaction between industrialization, "social sensuality," and the aesthetic avant-garde had brought about: "The generation that is shaping this epoch has, in contrast to the previous one, shifted its orientation to the sense of vision."[7] Reinhardt's electrical "impressionistic" stage was, by 1910, the school that early Ufa directors attended. Ernst Lubitsch played in many Reinhardt premieres in 1911–13, and F. W. Murnau had major roles in two very filmlike Reinhardt productions, Shakespeare's *Midsummer Night's Dream* and Karl Vollmoeller's *Mirakel (Miracle)*. (Lubitsch's opulent and richly staged ballet film *Sumurun* [*One Arabian Night*] in 1920, one of Ufa's first major productions, paid homage to Reinhardt and his aesthetic accomplishments, using light, movement, and "electrifying" sensuality in a way that was characteristic of Reinhardt's theater.)

"Art stood side by side with industry," Théophile Gautier wrote of the World's Fairs.[8] He could have said the same thing about film. Even before the invention of cinematography the World's Fairs achieved filmic, "horizontal" effects; they were the total-art works of their times. The one in Paris in 1900—with its fountains of electric light, new subway, racetrack for automobiles, conveyor belts, machine halls, and Asiatic, neo-baroque industrial pagodas—all this elevated the "horizontal" mode of perception to a programmatic level and promoted the idea of a world of montage. "Berlin is a wonderful, modern machine hall, an immense electrical motor that accomplishes innumerable complicated mechanical tasks with incredible precision, speed, and energy. Granted, this machine does not have a soul yet. The life of Berlin is the life of a cinematographic theater."[9] This is how Egon Friedell described the German capital in 1912, writing a kind of literary preview of the city as technological utopia—as seen in Fritz Lang's great Ufa film *Metropolis*.

An industrial fair held in 1896 glowed in electric light provided by the two market leaders in the German electrical industry, Siemens and AEG (Allgemeine Electricitäts-Gesellschaft). Siemens had a monopoly in the field of low-voltage technology and supplied the world with telephones. AEG, founded by Emil Rathenau (father of Walter Rathenau, who became Foreign Minister), built electrical power plants and was Germany's first major capitalist concern. Rathenau had lost large sums of money in the early 1870s as a manufacturer of machinery and got help to found AEG from the banker Carl Fürstenberg, whose star was rising in the Bleichröder banking house, the institution charged with administering 5 billion francs of French "war reparations" after the war of 1870–71. (France avenged itself in cinematography: the films alone that they sold to Germany before the First World War easily recouped those reparation payments.)

At first, however, the money flowed into the industrial boom, "cheap money that was used to finance innumerable factories and stockholding companies. The capital was consolidated into a few large banks, the industries into large concerns."[10] The electrical industry especially, which was so important for communications systems, tended to new consolidations.

The big credit institutes had, of course, made occasional sorties into show business in the nineteenth century. The collection of wax figures in the Grévin Museum in Paris, for example, was created in 1881 with the support of Crédit Lyonnais, the same bank that through the mediation of the Lyons industrialist Neyret helped the butcher's son Charles Pathé found film's first monopoly enterprise. But it took the increasing division of labor in the early film studios and the recognition of the social importance of the new medium to get the major banks involved and to encourage financial strategies on a grander scale.

Ferdinand Zecca, who used the film camera about 1900 to animate for Pathé the wax figures of the Grévin Museum in "dramatic" and "realistic" horror scenes, embodied the transition from one-man production to dream factory. "He began his career as a jack-of-all-trades and ended it as 'chief of staff,' so to speak, whose commands and arrangements were law for a whole team under him."[11] In 1905 Zecca became the chief executive of Pathé Frères, the French predecessor of all the later Ufa and Hollywood production chiefs and tycoons. With seed money of a million francs, which came from the coal mines of St. Etienne to the studios in Vincennes, "the metamorphosis of film from a small craftsman's business to an industry"[12] was accomplished.

Where an understanding of capital, an insistence on technical quality, an urge to expand, and a talent for organization all came together, the production structure of a major film company was present in embryonic form. In Germany, these talents were united in the ingenious businessman and inventor Oskar Messter. Between 1896 and 1917, he set the standards for a modern film industry, and his life's work fell like ripe fruit into the hands of Ufa's founders. From the outset, Messter made substantial profits, which spurred both his inventiveness and his compulsion to succeed. No sooner was his first mass-produced projector on the German market than he set about constructing a second camera that was more practical, worked faster, and had interchangeable lenses. For exposed film he built better developing and copying devices, and to save himself the cost of purchasing the Edison and Pathé films that dominated the market, he became a film producer. Because he had to get his wares into the theaters, he established his own distribution system. By 1896, Messter owned film theaters, and acting as his own advertising firm, he published illustrated handbills and mounted publicity efforts that were way ahead of their time. By the turn of the century, Messter's Projektions was already a "vertically" organized film company, a superbly functioning miniature empire with all its parts working in harmony.

Messter did not—as is often said in film literature—"invent" the Maltese cross, and disclaimed this attribution in his autobiography.[13] But he did perfect this little film-transport ratchet and thus significantly improve the sales of his projectors. Similarly, the Theater Unter den Linden that he took over in September 1896 was not Germany's first permanent movie theater, but it certainly was the first under professional management and with reliable projection equipment. And in November 1896 Messter established on Friedrichstrasse the first artificially illuminated film studio in Germany and the first in Berlin's "film district"-to-be. Then on Blücher-strasse came a "greenhouse" studio with a movable stage that could set the camera and the scenery in motion during shooting. And then in Berlin-Tempelhof Messter acquired the Literaria Studio from Pathé.

Messter also produced the first newsreels or, more precisely, the first newsreel-like film reports, experimenting with the "colorful material" of natural catastrophes and current events that later became the main ingredients of news film. His first reportage covered a flood in Silesia in early 1897 and was followed in March by a report on the celebration of Kaiser Wilhelm I's hundredth birthday. And in 1908 none other than Carl Froelich, who for almost half a century more would accompany political catastrophes with innumerable light comedies and entertainments, made a Messter news film at the scene of a massive elevated-train wreck.

In September 1914, when he was commissioned to make film reports on all the war fronts, Oskar Messter transformed his news films into "Messter weeklies." His copying studio worked furiously during the war: in 1916 and 1917 alone, it processed 4.5 million meters of film. Messter's invention of a fully automatic camera for airplanes also was an important contribution to the war effort. "Messter took for granted in the construction of this camera, which he called a 'picture sequencer,' that it would use rolls of film instead of the glass plates that had previously been used in aerial cameras."[14] Flight, as Paul Virilio has observed, became "a way of seeing or rather the very means of seeing itself."[15]

The origins of film, shaped by the times and containing the stuff of cultural revolution, are to be found in this coincidental meeting of war, industry, and modern "mass communications" and in the development of a new "mode of seeing"—a mode informed by inklings of catastrophe and by a new technology's demand for, and ability to deliver, authenticity. In a note that a Dr. Duisberg, an attaché with the German embassy in Christiana, sent to the Foreign Office in 1917 we find a wary prophecy of the medium's darker possibilities: "We must be on our guard. It is by no means a fantastic idea that film, accessible as it is now to subversives, is capable of inciting revolutions. . . . men have been given a new power they can use either to lead us into chaos or to bring new worlds into being."[16] In the "anarchist" period of the film industry this affinity for chaos and for new realms of fantasy was very prominent, and evoked, depending on one's social perspective, fascination or anxiety. In Messter's production methods and attitude to his métier, these untamed elements made themselves felt, and they lived on in the divided nature of Ufa.

The war on the international film front before 1914 showed some important differences from the political and military fronts. The leading position of the French firms was threatened first by the English, but a few years later the United States, Italy, and, of all countries, Denmark emerged as even more persistent rivals. The war altered this situation, but not until the founding of Ufa was Germany's inferiority complex about film alleviated, and thus Germans could feel adequate steps had been taken to remedy a national failing.

Pathé's executives had had the idea—for accelerating the company's expansion and modernizing the business—of terminating the previous practice of selling film copies to movie theaters and organizing distribution instead through lending companies, to which they granted exclusive rights. Ufa introduced new orders of magnitude and new modes of thought into these practices, but the radically monopolistic measures taken primarily by Pathé had set the stage for later structural development.

In its struggle for public favor, the early film industry developed that double nature that would determine its later course and, ultimately, its cultural fate in the century of the mass media. At the beginning, it reflected spontaneous, "tasteless," and anarchistic popular demands, but very soon it looked for the patronage of the educated classes, too, and wanted cultural and aesthetic confirmation from the bourgeoisie. Basic economic considerations forced a cultural orientation to the tastes of the educated middle class and gave rise, in France, to such ambitious but dubious enterprises as the *film d'art*, with its mechanical adoption of the rigid theatrical traditions of the Comédie Française. In Italy, the recognition of film by the culturally sophisticated upper classes was promoted by the bellicose imperialistic mood following Italy's annexations in North Africa and its campaign against Turkey in 1911–12. A decade before Fritz Lang's *The Nibelungs* (1924), Cines and Itala-Turin, the major Italian production companies, were turning out highly effective political propaganda in the guise of spectaculars.

The Danish Nordisk-Films played a part, too, in this European pattern. Established in 1906, primarily with the help of German banks, it was in large part absorbed eleven years later into the expanding Ufa empire, again at the behest of German bankers; but in its early years Nordisk moved aggressively and successfully into the Central European market. Ole Olsen, the pioneer of the Danish film industry, understood that he would have to look to the large and growing export market. In 1913, the film historian Toeplitz reports, Nordisk took in 1.5 million kroner in Berlin alone, a larger amount than Nordisk's start-up capital.[17] With a keen instinct for quality, the company made good use of its talented directors, notably Urban Gad and Viggo Larsen, who worked in Berlin studios during the war. Urban Gad was also an early theoretician. His concept of film as a dream vehicle with artistic standards, one that could transport people from their everyday dreary monotony to a paradise of unclouded happiness and exotic sensuality, became a staple of illusionistic strategy.[18]

Where Pathé and Gaumont, Cines in Rome, and Itala in Turin won positions of power and influence in ferocious competition and were blessed with a spontaneous expansiveness and the élan of determined industry pioneers, the first consolidation of energies in German film production came about—as we shall see in detail later—with the involvement of secret diplomacy and as a plot developed by bureaucrats, military men, and financiers with their backs to the wall. Comparing this with what happened in the United States, we can see vast and unbridgeable differences. In the first decade of this century, the American film industry clawed its way up "in a state of lawlessness reminiscent of the stories in many a film scenario."[19] The two leading companies, Biograph and Vitagraph, not only had to battle each other for market share but also had to combat the unlimited importation of European films and fend off swarms of plagiarists and profit-hungry adventurers in all sectors of the industry. "On the screen as in real life, corruption, deception, theft, and, often enough, violent crime were the rule of the day."[20] These Mafia circumstances and this Gold Rush atmosphere were ideal conditions for an aggressive, varied film culture hungry for reality and obsessed with fantasy. The 1908 attempt of the leading firms, aided by the Motion Picture Patents Company, to introduce some structure to the chaos was only a continuation, at a higher organizational level, of the dog-eat-dog competition. Eastman Kodak was now obliged to sell film only to companies within a new patent trust: Edison, Biograph, Vitagraph, and four others; all other producers, distributors, and theater owners had to take out licenses. This policy was strongly resisted by distributors, and antitrust laws eventually ended it, though even before that, it was doomed to failure by the independent producers who were in closer touch with the moods and tastes of the public and who were making more interesting, imaginative, and successful films.

Between 1912 and 1915, and in this atmosphere of ferocious competition and merciless exploitation, Hollywood arose in the land between the desert and the Pacific Ocean. Max Weinhaber called this film industry Babylon, which served producers in New York as both a playground and a studio with natural light, a "waiting room of destitution"; Arnold Hollriegel termed it "a rich, clean, whipped-cream sweet, picture-perfect, soulless city."[21]

In America the age of montage took violent, eruptive form. Its convulsions and harsh dissonances shaped everyday culture for the millions of immigrants streaming into the country. In 1913 there were 60,000 movie theaters worldwide, and the theatrical sector alone employed 75,000 people. In the United States there were 15,700 established movie theaters, in Germany, 2,900; and in those theaters every day almost 1.5 million visitors succumbed to the spell of the moving pictures.[22]

But in no other country of the world was cinematography so dramatically castigated as a "danger to the nation" and a symptom of general moral decline as in Germany, and in no other country did well-meaning reformers and custodians of good taste reflect so passionately about the taming and ennobling of the new medium. As early as 1910, church observers compiled statistics on what they considered the film industry's flouting of public morality and order. In 250 films, they counted no less than ninety-seven murders, fifty-one adulteries, nineteen seductions, thirty-five drunks, and twenty-five prostitutes.[23] The warning of the Catholic Teachers Association against "filth in word and picture"[24] was no more effective than the film censorship imposed in May 1906 by order of the Berlin Police Department, and these measures only served to hinder the development of a theoretical understanding of film and of its psychological and aesthetic potential. Neither the bans imposed by church and state nor academic reform efforts did anything to dampen the movie enthusiasm of the public, and especially of the urban masses.

The German production companies before Ufa—among them Vitascope, Messter, Deutsche Bioscop, and Münchner Kunstfilm—were intractable or at least indifferent to the Wilhelmine state's call to order. Patriotic commissioned productions like *Bunte Bilder von der Deutschen Flotte* (*Living Pictures of the German Fleet*, 1909) or the first U-boat film, *Pro Patria* (1910), remained the exceptions. At a time when Karl Brunner, Prussia's highest-ranking censorship official, set the tone in the ruling classes with his polemic *Der Kinematograph von heute—eine Volksgefahr* (*The Contemporary Cinematographer—A Danger to the Nation*), published by the Vaterländischer Schriftenverband (Writers' Association of the Fatherland), when the Deutscher Theaterverein (German Theater Association) mobilized itself—in vain—against stage actors who were flirting with film, and when even Kurt Tucholsky advocated strict censorship of film (in an essay "Hier gibt es keinen Kompromiss. Hier Kunst! Hier Kino!" ["There Can Be No Compromise: Art Here! Film There!"])[25]—even in such times German film producers insisted, with remarkable determination, on their basic right to offend and to overstep the boundaries of good taste. Nor were they lacking in an instinct for bizarre sorties against the spirit of the times, for the odd or eccentric aspects of their era. The trick that the shoemaker Wilhelm Voigt played on the police department at Köpenick in 1906, for example, was "filmed" three times that year (long before Richard Oswald made his successful film version of Zuckmayer's play *Der Hauptmann von Köpenick* [*The Captain of Köpenick*] in 1931). And Continental Kunstfilm in Berlin demonstrated a sense for the timely and for the widespread fascination with impending catastrophe when it released, only four months after the *Titanic* sank in 1912, its film *In Nacht und Eis* (*In Night and Ice*), billed as a "true-to-life drama of the sea based on authentic reports."

Another important pathbreaker for Ufa was Paul Davidson, the first German film entrepreneur who unhesitatingly entered into a pact with big capital. In Frankfurt/Main in 1906 he founded the Allgemeine Kinematographische Theatergesellschaft (General Cinematographic Theater Company), from which the first chain of movie theaters in Germany developed. In 1908 he assumed ownership of Germany's biggest film theater, the Union Theater on Berlin's Alexanderplatz. In 1909 he became executive director of Projektions Union, which produced its early films on the roof of its office building on Frankfurt's Kaiserstrasse. In 1912, the Union, the first stockholding company in the German film industry, doubled its capital stock of 500,000 gold marks, moved its headquarters to Berlin, set up production studios in Tempelhof, and went into distribution. Five years later, this Tempelhof film factory, like Oskar Messter's glass studios, became part of the Ufa empire; and the East Prussian businessman's son, Paul Davidson, who began his career as a traveling salesman peddling curtains and who was struck by show-business fever when he visited a "magic theater" in Paris, had a place in its executive offices.

In 1913, the last year before the war, German firms produced 353 films, a record, and ten times more than the industry had produced in 1910.[26] The famous Reinhardt actor Albert Bassermann had gone over to film, and under the direction of Max Mack he made for Vitascope a movie entitled *Der Andere* (*The Other*). Following the French *film d'art* model, it was designed to attract the educated public. Emil Jannings expressed the attitude of many actors who began to be drawn to film at this time but had to struggle against their own middle-class prejudices and against the blandishments of the conservative Theater Association:

> Filmmaking made a very strange impression on me. Superficial as the whole business was, I found that nothing stood in the way of the camera producing much more respectable results at some time in the future. So I stayed on the alert and waited for an opportunity. . . . Even though I could not have articulated this feeling then, I sensed in some hidden corner of my innermost self that the moving pictures posed an artistic challenge of global dimensions.[27]

In the Deutsche Bioscop studios, Paul Wegener, the first modern German film actor, joined forces with the Danish director Stellan Rye and the cameraman Guido Seeber to make the first real *auteur* film, *Der Student von Prag* (*The Student of Prague*), based on a book by Hanns Heinz Ewers. Henri Langlois called this work and Wegener's *Golem* of 1914 the "sources of Germany's national film art."[28] Wegener made this beginning possible: his gifts as an actor were important, but more important still were his camera sense and a highly developed awareness of the nature of movement and visual effects in film.

By 1913, Germany also had intellectuals who were giving serious thought to the artistic possibilities of film. In the face of powerful competition from abroad, a few creative businessmen, with great imagination and an even greater investment of energy, built up smoothly functioning studios and attended to the vital matters of distribution and theater acquisition. Intelligent authors, with antennae alert to the changing times, began to write for the films. On Berlin's boulevards, movie palaces with exotically styled façades welcomed their mass audiences. The industry stood on the verge of promising social, economic, and artistic development. But the war came instead, and the Royal Prussian Ministry of War and the Supreme Command emerged as the primary promoters of German film culture.

Looking back on the situation of Germany's film theaters at the outbreak of the war, the magazine *Der Kinematograph* wrote: "On August 1, the world stood still; it seemed as if everything would sink and disappear."[29] Producers, distributors, theater owners, and the public tumbled into a vacuum. From one day to the next, the import of films from France, the most important country in Europe for film, was cut off. Current film reports from the fronts were painfully lacking. While most Germans, caught up in the whirl "of these epoch-making, historical days,"[30] eagerly awaited news and visible proof of Germany's quick victories, cinematography was astonishingly inadequate for the task. Technically, politically, and psychologically unprepared for its work in this "national struggle," it waited for instructions from a propaganda agency inexperienced with film and otherwise unable to meet the demands on it.

On the home front, military and civilian officials were feverishly developing plans for centralizing war propaganda, apparently with the expectation that the entire film industry would more or less voluntarily submit. As it turned out, threats and extortion had to be applied. Ministerial Director Deutelmoser, after November 1916 chief of the intelligence division in the Foreign Office, planned to declare movie theaters that refused to show patriotic films "unnecessary to the fatherland"[31] and to shut them all down. The government frequently threatened to cut off electricity and coal deliveries to theater owners who would not "devote themselves wholeheartedly to the work of patriotic enlightenment."[32] On the other hand, precisely because of the coal and electricity shortages, other voices stressed the importance of film theaters to the war effort. In November 1917 the Ministry of War in Berlin circulated a statement to the Reich offices subordinate to it: "In addition to providing entertainment, the motion-picture theater promotes patriotism and makes the conduct of the war on land, at sea, and in the air visually accessible to the public."[33]

It is of no little importance to the development of the German film industry in general and Ufa in particular that the industrialists who had shown an early interest in film belonged to the radically conservative Pan-German Party or to groups that shared its ideology—in other words, to the camp that called for the enemy's unconditional surrender and for an unfettered policy of annexation. In December 1915, Chancellor Bethmann-Hollweg attacked the "unconscionable, parvenu intrigues of the insatiable

Pan-Germans" and the "unbridled annexation plans of heavy industry and the right-wing parties aligned with it."[34] He had in mind here the Rhenish-Westphalian industrial circles in which Alfred Hugenberg and Hugo Stinnes set the tone. Acting under their influence was Ludwig Klitzsch, a man who later was chief executive of Ufa. As early as 1912, as a young advertising man for the publisher Siegfried Weber and his Leipzig *Illustrirte Zeitung*, Klitzsch had been impressed with the advertising possibilities of film and had made suggestions for a "comprehensive campaign of cultural and business propaganda"[35] that would use the new medium. Most important, he learned early on to think in a centralized way in the interest of a national concentration of available energies and skills. On July 24, 1914, eight days before the outbreak of war, Klitzsch presented ideas of this nature to an audience of more than 120 leaders of business, industry, and trade. They responded by forming a Committee to Study the Possibility of a German Film and Photography Campaign Abroad. These gentlemen apparently thought the world and their own circumstances to be altogether in order.

Barely two years later, in April 1916, this committee met again in Berlin's Hotel Kaiserhof, now under wartime conditions, and Klitzsch spoke to the needs of the hour with appropriate militancy: "Our mission is not only to meet the armaments of our enemies with an equally strong defense but beyond that to forge weapons that will let us occupy a place in the sun and take possession of new territories." It was essential to cut off "the dreadful filth imposed upon us from abroad."[36] At the same time film had to be exploited to promote Germany's interests among the partially or totally uncivilized peoples of the world. The committee recommended founding a film company which would enjoy the special support of the government as well as of key economic institutions and the shipping lines.

In November 1916, at the initiative of Alfred Hugenberg, chairman of the Krupp board of directors, the Deutsche Lichtbild-Gesellschaft (DLG, German Motion Picture Company) was formed, and none other than Ludwig Klitzsch drafted its bylaws.[37] Hugenberg had earlier recruited Klitzsch for the board of his Deutsche Überseedienst (German Overseas Service). With the creation of the DLG, Krupp's chairman acquired the instrument he needed to take a hand in film politics during the war.

Despite the efforts of many individuals and the self-sacrificing work of many photographers and cameramen at the front, neither the DLG nor the Prussian War Ministry's Bild- und Filmamt (Bufa, Office of Photography and Film, formed in early 1917) could bring together diverse organizations and energies and respond effectively to the Allies' propaganda offensive.

Ludwig Klitzsch was on the verge of developing the DLG into an economically powerful enterprise, but his activities were recognized as maneuvers backed by Hugenberg and Rhenish-Westphalian heavy industry, and they evoked bitter resistance from other German commercial interests (especially the electronics, chemical, and shipping industries), which in competition with heavy industry regarded the Balkans and Asia Minor as favored sources of raw materials and as trading partners. The German Bank, which was closely allied with these commercial groups, was able to launch an extremely successful campaign against the DLG because the bank was able to align the film-related political interests of its backers with those of the Supreme Command.[38]

This analysis by the film historian Jürgen Spiker would seem to suggest that commercial interests competing with heavy industry thought that Hugenberg, with the help of the DLG, might lure away their sources of raw materials and their export markets in Asia Minor and the Balkans. And it is true that not only political leaders but also the business elite in Wilhelmine Germany had a remarkably materialistic, instrumentalist understanding of corporations, commerce, and zones of influence, an understanding that they applied uncritically to the film industry. The movie industry was looked upon and treated as if it were a mere lump of clay, susceptible to any and every conceivable form of manipulation. Klitzsch's ideas about film were just as materialistic and reflected ignorance of the medium and a vast cultural misunderstanding:

> We will never gain a foothold in foreign movie theaters with films on German industry, culture, and transportation. To do that, we will have to take into account the hunger of foreign movie audiences for sensationalism, a hunger that, viewed from our German perspective, seems to know no bounds. We have to surround the serious kernel of German propaganda films with the opulent trimmings of drama, comedy, and so forth, so that the foreign audiences will continue to swallow the initially quite alien kernel for the sake of the pleasing husk until they eventually become accustomed to the kernel and until the constantly dripping water has hollowed out the stone.[39]

In other words, he dismissed the public's passion for movies as "a hunger for sensationalism" that he could exploit and undermine. The essence of the medium he regarded as "trimmings" which he could use as bait. This media theory, defective at its core, had grave consequences for the future development of Ufa, notably when the National Socialists took it over and "refined" and "perfected" it.

Only a few officials, like retired State Minister Hentig, troubled themselves about "improving and promoting the moving-picture industry for patriotic purposes that serve the common good"[40] and tried to engage artists like Max Reinhardt and Paul Wegener. Efforts by German intellectuals to suggest ways to improve propaganda met with mistrust and rejection; such was the fate of an initiative from the Bund deutscher Gelehrter und Künstler

(League of German Scholars and Artists) in 1916 that was presented to the government by the writers Hermann Sudermann and Ludwig Fulda and the ethnologist Leo Frobenius, by Max Planck and the AEG chief, Walther Rathenau, among others. In their view, "public education should not be undertaken by government authorities but by neutral agencies to which no ulterior motives can be attributed. The representatives of the governmental agencies were presumably offended. They saw the suggestions of the League as an attack and responded accordingly."[41]

The general lack of long feature films in Germany, a lack that German distributors abroad complained of repeatedly, led to one of the first commissions granted to Ufa in late 1917: the production of a "major film" that would "illuminate contemporary life in Germany."[42] Gustav Meyrink, the author of *The Golem*, was given a lucrative contract to write the screenplay, but the course of events prevented realization of the project.

So it is that films produced by the Office of Photography and Film or commissioned by it (350 titles altogether) include only fourteen short or half-length feature films in the production of which German stage or film artists participated. The most important of them is *Das Tagebuch des Dr. Hart* (*The Diary of Dr. Hart*, 1917), starring Heinrich Schroth and Käthe Haack, which included scenes showing the work of military medics and was made by Davidson's Projektions Union; the cameraman was Carl Hoffmann. Paul Leni was the director.

The militarization of film after 1916 that culminated in the founding of Ufa was driven primarily by a man who later became president of the Reich Archives. As late as 1938 and after this man's death, the historian Friedrich Meinecke praised his "quick intellect," his "idealistic fervor," his "always lively but critically disciplined imagination," and the "extraordinary grace of his nature."[43] The man was Lieutenant Colonel Hans von Haeften, after July 1916 chief of the Military Office for Propaganda Abroad in the Foreign Office (and father of Werner Karl von Haeften, a colleague of Klaus von Stauffenberg, who joined with him in the July 20, 1944, attempt on Hitler's life). Although he had been attached to the Foreign Office, Haeften was clear from the outset that the only directives he would consider binding came from another quarter: "The head of this agency is an instrument of the chief of the general staff of the field army and takes orders and directions from him."[44] His conception of film management was consistent with that outlook: Bufa (the Office of Photography and Film), which was formed shortly after Haeften's appointment, would as a government "instrument of pictorial propaganda" be put under civilian control after the war, but during the war only military administration promised success:

Bufa would secure distribution channels in the occupied territories, take a defensive position against the Deutsche Lichtbild-Gesellschaft, supervise filming at the front for German newsreels, take over from 1918 on the distribution of Agfa supplies, supply foreign countries each week with pictures, cards, pamphlets, and films, and consolidate in its hands the censorship of all films for import and export.[45]

The militarization of German movies was expressed in terminology, too. Bufa had command over seven "film detachments," each of whose directors was called "Filmführer." There were nine hundred "front movie houses" in all of Europe, and "motion-picture officers" looked after military interests on the home front. Even film critics armed themselves to the teeth. The critic and Bufa screenplay author Hans Brennert had this to say after the premiere of the film *Unsere Helden an der Somme* (*Our Heroes on the Somme*) in the Tauentzien-Palast in January 1917:

> On orders from the Supreme Command, heroic cameramen from German film detachments brought back from the hell on the Somme, from the flaming ground of the Saint-Pierre-Vast forest, the first cinematographic documents of this grisly war. With steel helmets on their heads and cameras in hand, they traveled in the vehicles of the assault troops on their combat missions.[46]

The "iron film" (the title of another Bufa production) dominated the screen and claimed with its martial manner to have won over the public. Bufa censors also declared themselves judges of art and experts in film dramaturgy and quickly adopted the strident tone of military command:

> An order from the Minister of War communicated through the Royal High Command requires that all films whose superficiality and insipidness make them inappropriate for these serious times no longer be shown in cinema theaters. . . . Highly recommended, however, is the presentation of worthwhile films of a serious nature that are likely to maintain and encourage love of the fatherland and good morals. Disregard of this order can lead to disciplinary action and ultimately to the closing of a theater.[47]

"Worthwhile films of a serious nature" suggests the German obsession with tragedy, death, destruction, and self-destruction. But movies provide just the opposite: trash and intrigue, whores and crooks, humor and mad pranks. Between those two extremes lies an unbridgeable abyss. Both tendencies would be embodied in Ufa, and though time and again problematic attempts at uniting them were made, an organic synthesis was never achieved.

The founding of Ufa was a direct result of the unproductive and increasingly bitter rivalry between the Office of Photography and Film and the Deutsche Lichtbild-Gesellschaft. As a member of DLG's board, Alfred Hugenberg had been cleverly but inconspicuously pulling strings and had filled almost all the key positions in the company with heavy-industry representatives. (Hugenberg also took over August Scherl's newspaper company in

1916, and we can without hesitation regard his media policy in the First World War as preparation and practice for his assumption of power in Ufa in the late 1920s.) For its domestic work, Ludwig Klitzsch developed production guidelines for documentary, "instructional," and "educational" films: "Germany's landscapes, historic places, spas, and recreational resorts" were to be filmed, also "the achievements of German technology" and the "hygienic and social measures instituted by our major businesses."[48]

Open hostilities broke out when Bufa declared that the DLG was simply "a for-profit private enterprise"[49] and stressed its claim as the "sole central agency for education through photography and film." Hans von Haeften brought the matter to a head when he wondered whether the state or heavy industry should control Germany's propaganda effort, and asked the Foreign Office for support in overseeing DLG's activities in the Balkans and the Near East. Rumors set in circulation from the other side, claiming that Bufa was intent on nationalizing the entire film industry, led to similar inquiries in the Reichstag. The battle, in which Quartermaster General Ludendorff had in the meantime become embroiled, reached fever pitch in early June 1917, when Haeften complained that the DLG was "brutal, accomplished nothing, and under the pretext of idealistic endeavors kept constantly absorbing monies and organizations."[50]

Organizationally, Bufa was under the Supreme Command and the Military Division of the Foreign Office; it was financed primarily from propaganda funds from the military command, and though Haeften may have held a position in the Foreign Office, he was every inch Ludendorff's man. With the militarization of civilian life and the Supreme Command's rise to predominance in the final years of the war—Ludendorff had long been regarded as Germany's "secret dictator"—the stage was set, and a briefing Haeften gave the quartermaster general was decisive. Haeften's anti-DLG position impressed a military man who was mistrustful of all civilians. That there had to be a private firm "over which the government would have influence"[51] was conclusive. On July 4, 1917, Ludendorff wrote the letter that has gone down in film history as the "birth certificate of Ufa," and Lieutenant Colonel Hans von Haeften had prepared the way for it.

Erich Ludendorff was obviously convinced when he wrote to the Royal Ministry of War in Berlin that it was "absolutely necessary for a successful conclusion to the war that film be put to work with the highest priority everywhere where German influence is still possible."[52] He quickly came to a crucial issue: the activities of Nordisk in neutral foreign countries. If this Danish company was hostile toward Germany, it might greatly damage German interests. On the other hand, it could distribute films in Russia. "Assuming that the company's influence is carried out in a manner favorable to Germany, we can hardly begin to imagine what impact it could have, given the volatile mood currently prevailing in the Russian population." Accustomed to command (influence would be not exerted but "carried out," like an order), Ludendorff simply took the thinking behind the

Peace Treaty of Brest-Litovsk and applied it to Germany's propaganda effort. This propaganda would suggest to the Russian people, whose mood was not merely "volatile" but filled with crisis and revolution, that Germany's goals represented the best solution for Russia's foreign and domestic problems.

In the summer of 1917, Ludendorff had no eye for anything but the goals of victory and annexation that he himself and all conservatives were proclaiming, and this annexationist spirit dictated his solution to the problem of Nordisk: "The simplest and best thing to do is to purchase the major portion of Nordisk's stock." But first German film production would be unified so "that it could confront Nordisk as a united contractual power."

Mincing no words, the general called the film industry an "effective weapon of war" to be deployed against the propaganda of the Entente, in accordance with strategic considerations and utilizing all its energies. Ludendorff knew that only an absolute majority was required to control a firm, not "the purchase of all the shares." The company had to be bought, "but it must not become known that the state is the purchaser." So he recommended that the transaction be initiated "by a private institution (banking house) that is expert in its field, influential, experienced, reliable, and, most important of all, completely supportive of the government. . . . The negotiators must not have the slightest inkling of who the actual purchaser is."

Ludendorff closed his letter with a businessman's assessment of costs. Nordisk would cost about 20 million marks, the German film firms another 8 million. This was a mere pittance compared with the 100 million the Entente had appropriated for propaganda purposes in the last quarter alone, most of it for film activity. Ludendorff's final sentence was directed at the Finance Office: "I would add that these are investments on which a return can be expected."

The Ministry of War initially reacted to General Ludendorff's letter with great reserve. Still, Haeften was told to work out the details of the transaction with the Reich Treasury Office. In Karl Demeter's account, it was Haeften who, not wanting to see Ludendorff's "promising plan" fail, decided to enlist "private financial interests in the service of his cause," and secured the support of Emil Georg von Stauss, president of the German Bank.[53] But in his letter Ludendorff had already recommended including private institutions and had mentioned the banks. In any case, Stauss was the right man to help establish a mixed public-private enterprise.

According to Hans Traub, a conscientious chronicler of Ufa's history (if inclined to cast it in a favorable light), Major Alexander Grau, director of the press office in the Ministry of War, "in close cooperation with Haeften," carried out Ludendorff's "suggestion" and conducted preliminary negotiations with the German film companies. But Grau encountered difficulties in the Reich Treasury Office, and never succeeded in completely overcoming the reservations he encountered here. Some factions in the Treasury Office were for participating, some against. . . . Only when Grau and Haeften could assure the availability of private sources could they win partial concessions. . . . Grau and Haeften had won over the undersecretaries Helfferich and Kühlmann to Ludendorff's proposal. Both these men had close ties to the German Bank. Helfferich had been an executive of the bank. Kühlmann's father had been chief executive of the Anatolian Railroad, financed by the bank. These two introduced the idea to Emil Georg von Stauss, who then, with his financial expertise, gave it concrete form and shape. In a meeting arranged by Haeften, Stauss was able to present General Ludendorff with a clear plan. The German Bank now took an active, albeit invisible, role in the negotiations, which thus far had not been conducted in a businesslike way but now moved ahead more satisfactorily. Among the private parties already won over to the project were Prince Henkel von Donnersmarck and Robert Bosch. Both saw their participation less in terms of a profitable investment. Rather, they wanted to help establish what they considered a politically necessary enterprise. Given the capital required, however, no one could ignore the fact that investors who wanted a good return on their money would also be needed. The Ministry of War, the Treasury Office, and the German Bank therefore considered Ludendorff's suggestion to use the Nordische Filmgesellschaft's interest in the German film market as a way of gaining direct influence over the company and acquiring a commanding role in the most important German film factories.[54]

The government's share was set at 7 million marks. The German Bank and two private banking houses signed as trustees. At Ludendorff's suggestion, Stauss was appointed chairman of the board; also at the general's suggestion, Major Grau became an executive. Private and government interests were to be equally represented, and among the government's representatives the general again made his fine distinctions between civilians and military men.

Seen at a historical remove, the founding history of Ufa commands our attention for two reasons. First, it demonstrates the astonishing creativity of a political, economic, and military elite that in time of crisis could conjure up out of nothing a cultural production company of historically unprecedented magnitude. Second, it reveals just how disastrously wrong were the assessments made by the military and civilian planning staffs when they founded the company. Yet ironically, precisely those mistaken judgments enabled this remarkable focusing of energies to occur. When blindness to history and naïveté are in command, they can move mountains, but with the ever-present danger that once mountains have been set in motion, they may move in quite different directions than those originally planned for them.

Part
One

1.

Ludendorff's Golem and How It Came into the World

TH E official founding of Universum-Film AG took place on December 18, 1917, in the building of the Deputy General Staff, not far from the Reichstag. The celebration afterward was held in the Hotel Adlon. The newly created colossus had at its disposal the appreciable capital of 25 million marks. The first board of directors was made up of a respectable cross section of the Wilhelmine haute bourgeoisie, with especially strong representation from Prusso-German financial and industrial capital.

As Ludendorff had suggested, Emil Georg von Stauss of the German Bank was made chairman. Nominated as his deputies were State Councillor (ret.) Gerlach (a director of the Silesian mining company Henkel-Donnersmarck) and Robert Bosch, spokesman for the electrical industry. Other members were: Prince Guidotto von Henkel-Donnersmarck, Herbert M. Gutmann (Dresden Bank), Commercial Councillor Max von Wassermann (A. E. Wassermann banking house), Commercial Councillor Paul Mamroth (AEG), Privy Commercial Councillor Herman Frenkel (Jaquier and Securius banking house), Senior Governmental Councillor Dr. Wilhelm Cuno (Hamburg-America Line; later Reich Chancellor), Privy Senior Governmental Councillor Stimming (North German Lloyd), President Goldschmidt (Schwarz, Goldschmidt, banking house; later president of the National Bank), Consul Salomon Marx (the gramaphone company Karl Lindström), Karl Bratz (War Committee of the German Jute Trade), and Johannes Kiehl (vice president of the German Bank). The composition of the board successfully hid from the outside world the government's participation, which had been contractually established.[1] On February 14, 1918, Ufa was entered into the Registry of Commerce, its mission defined as "the operation of all branches of the film industry, specifically, the making of films, the renting of films, the operation of film theaters, and any form of manufacture or trade related to the film and motion-picture industry."[2]

Karl Bratz, representing the board, assumed a post in the central administration of the new firm, along with Major Grau and Paul Davidson of the
Union and Siegmund Jacob of the Frankfurter Film Company. The War
Ministry's delegate, Major Grau, retired from military service before the
end of the war to devote his energies to building up Ufa's cultural-film
division.

Successful early negotiations led to the hoped-for acquisition of the
German production, distribution, and theater holdings of Nordisk, as
well as of Messter and Union. For 10 million marks Ufa got not only
Nordisk's German production studio, Oliver Film; its distribution organization, Nordische Filmgesellschaft; and its film theaters but also exclusive rights to the use of Nordisk productions in Germany, Austria,
Hungary, Switzerland, Holland, and, later, Poland and the Balkans as
well. Ludendorff's strategic concept of establishing German control over
the "film supply" in Central Europe as well as in large parts of eastern
and southeastern Europe was thus realized, on paper at least. And even
though the Bolsheviks had come to power in Russia only a few weeks
earlier, the general could continue to dream his dream of influencing "the
volatile mood of the people" in the new Soviet Union. In August 1918,
Ufa's representative in St. Petersburg reported that the Soviet government
intended to "take annually from Ufa 210 films at 10 copies each." Plans
were also under way "for Ufa to make and develop Russian feature films
in Moscow."[3]

Nordisk, in any case, could consider itself saved. The company's devil-
may-care policy of expansion had left it in a difficult financial position
"from which it was liberated by Ufa."[4] Its business chief, David Oliver, was
engaged by Ufa as "the leading expert in the field" for an annual salary of
44,000 marks plus profit sharing.[5]

As the minutes of an Ufa executive committee meeting on January 15,
1918, reveal, the Messter company cost 5.3 million marks.[6] Along with
Messter, Ufa acquired important equipment companies: Messter Film and
Equipment in Vienna and Projection Machinery Construction in Berlin.
For a salary of 24,000 marks plus profit sharing, Messter himself was hired
as a technical adviser. For a majority interest in Paul Davidson's Union
company and its subsidiaries (e.g., Vitascope, which Davidson had taken
over in 1914) and fifty-six theaters throughout Germany, Ufa paid 1.11
million marks. For a salary of 30,000 marks, Davidson acted as an "adviser
for camerawork."[7] Payment to the firms was primarily in the form of Ufa
stock priced at a thousand marks per share. "Whatever shares did not go
to the film companies as payment were taken over by the government and
the private interests previously mentioned."[8]

In their first report Ufa executives offered a happy summary of their
work: the goal of all the negotiations preliminary to the founding had been
to consolidate

the film industry that represented, on the one hand, a vital economic enterprise with promising prospects and that guaranteed, on the other, that important tasks in the field of German propaganda and of German cultural and national education be carried out in the interest of the Reich government. In the private economic sector, the intent was to create a company in which the most important activities of the film industry, namely, production, distribution, and theater operation, would be adequately represented.[9]

Germany's largest film enterprise was not organized without some objections being raised. Ludwig Klitzsch, Hugenberg's viceroy in the DLG, considered it a "battle" waged by the Supreme Command, and presumably by the government as well, against the DLG and the iron and steel industry supporting it.[10]

Haeften and Major Grau had some fundamental disagreements, too. Haeften thought that after the war Ufa should remain under government control, exercised, of course, by Bufa. Grau favored the umbrella concept: Ufa would be made up of several independently functioning firms, among which Bufa could be included as a "purely military department." Ufa already had, he thought, an "almost governmental character."[11] Haeften was uneasy about this umbrella concept, and remarked that Ufa had taken over Messter's and other studios, as well as the important Geyer copying business; he no doubt feared his agency would suffer a similar fate.[12]

During the final year of the war, these conflicts between the Supreme Command and Bufa on the one hand and Ufa and the civilian government agencies on the other took clearer, sharper form. In August, Bufa asserted once again to the Foreign Office that it was the only "official central agency for propaganda." All negotiations with Ufa were not to be conducted directly but through Bufa.[13] A few days later, Minister of War Stein expressed in a circular the plausible fear that Ufa was tending "toward ever greater independence," though Bufa's control was essential. "Because this industry has developed very rapidly from small beginnings and has consequently bred certain questionable business practices, all questions relating to the film industry require thorough and professional supervision."[14] On the other hand, men in the Foreign Office questioned the rationale for Bufa's very existence. The agency was not making any money, they claimed, and was spending too much.[15] Meanwhile, the film people at Ufa had a fundamental mistrust of military agencies' ambitions to control their activities. Paul Davidson, for example, rejected Bufa's films in no uncertain terms, saying they were of "poor quality."[16]

At the same time, the old battle with DLG was still going on. When Grau suggested a cooperative effort between Ufa and DLG ("Our goals are the same after all"[17]), he met with a blunt refusal from Haeften, who recalled their earlier "unedifying negotiations." The "battle against DLG" that Klitzsch feared had in fact already been fought. After the war, the DLG became Deulig-Film; Bufa, after first being placed directly under the Ministry of War in January 1918, was then moved into the chancellor's office as the Reich Film Agency; in 1919, it went over to the Foreign Office and ultimately shriveled away into the film bureau of the Ministry of the Interior.

Ufa, an artificially created colossus, born of capital, clever negotiation, and patriotic delusions, had swept away everything before it. Private firms and state agencies fell victim to it. Economics and politics, military strategy, and vague ideas of a "reformed film industry" melted together in a gigantic structure of which the only thing that could be said with any certainty at the end of 1917 was that it existed. A drawing-board mentality deeply rooted in the Prussian bureaucracy had constructed Ufa, and now the hope was that this giant child would march off into the world behaving just the way the drawing-board design said it would, winning over people everywhere to Germany's war aims. Only a view of history fossilized in abstraction, occluded by reactionary emotions, and paired with an insensitivity to both the nature of film and the needs of the public could harbor such expectations.

On the other hand, Heinrich Fraenkel is surely correct when he says of the founding of Ufa:

> The vision that saw beyond the emergency of the moment and that took into consideration the company's development after the war proved just as correct as the liberal financing that was immediately provided. A "vertically organized" firm had been created with millions at its disposal and with its own production, its own distribution, its own theater chain, and, most important, its own branches and theaters in neutral foreign countries. This strong, independent position would prove to be a key factor in film history after the war.[18]

Ufa's position of power enabled the German film industry after 1918 to defend itself effectively against the film boycott of the victorious powers and to launch at least a short-lived offensive on the international markets. As Jerzy Toeplitz has written:

> The Weimar Republic inherited from the Wilhelmine era a powerful film company that for many years was decisive in shaping German film, that left an ideological imprint on the work of producers and directors, and that set the tone for the production of smaller, independent, and competing firms. Until Hitler's fall, the Ufa film factory dominated Germany.[19]

Yet a contradiction remains. The film historian H.-B. Heller touches on this when he asks:

> How did the literary intelligentsia react in the face of this obviously new direction in the socialization of film in Germany? And that at a time when

the contradiction between the medium and its uses had become clearly apparent? For whether film was welcomed with open arms or regarded as a phenomenon of cultural decline, the idea that it should be seen as an expression of modernity collapsed when confronted with the fact that in terms of ownership and control of power film bore the imprint of Wilhelmine imperialism.[20]

If we look at this contradiction from another perspective, we have to ask how film—bearing "the imprint of Wilhelmine imperialism" or, as Virilio put it, born under "house arrest" of the militarists—would react to modernism and its rejection of the past. This question bears not only on the relationship of the intelligentsia to film but also on that of the public to the life of the imagination, which film can stimulate, crush, or steer in disastrous directions. Ufa began under conditions that continued to affect the force field made up of capital, politics, film, and the public. The contradictions perpetuated themselves, and this apparently superpowerful, monolithic organization and its internal structure were shot through with those contradictions. Ufa marched out of the war that had given birth to it and into a peace for which it seemed to be a perfect match. But this peace was merely a continuation of war by other means. Universum-Film, Ludendorff's Golem, became one of those new and highly modern "other means."

2.

The Roofless House: The Movies and
Everyday Life During the War

IN 1917, Ernst Bloch described the image of Wilhelm II not only in propaganda but also in the political dreamworld of many of his subjects; it was a phantasmagoria in which history and mysticism had formed a kind of chemical compound. The Kaiser appeared to the people

> as the last ruler, as the latest and strongest in a direct line from Khosrow, Hadrian, Harun al Raschid, Justinian, Friedrich II, Louis the Sun King, a giant in the magic realms of nobility, court splendor, glorious remoteness, immovability, sublimity of ceremony, and Byzantine magic; even now, in his decline, all his brothers and ancestors since the most ancient days of Assyrian imperial glory welcomed him into their company.[1]

World cultures in a cross-section montage, a whirlwind tour through the ages with close-ups of their crowned heads: a cinematic phantasmagoria.

If Bloch's diagnosis is right, then there flourished in the fantasies of Germans loyal to the Kaiser a jungle of megalomania and mysticism. This had traditionally drawn its aesthetic impulses from the steamy, hothouse pomp of court and historical painting but also, since about 1910, from early epic films, especially Italian ones. After 1918, Ufa launched its own colossal productions in the style of films by Ambrosio, Pastrone, and others. The mounting flood of historical films in Germany could be attributed, as Lotte Eisner has written, "to the yearning for splendor and 'escape' of an impoverished people that has always loved the glitter of parades."[2] As the remnants of "Assyrian imperial glory" were shattered under the blows of the war, its legends let romantic blossoms flourish on the screen and in the heads of moviegoers.

After all, everyday life on the home front was depressing. "Germany is like a house with the roof torn off. The contours of the mammonistic, dynastic disaster lie exposed for all to see."[3] The monarchical pyramid, of which the Kaiser was the peak, was now a roofless house, too.

Modern technology and its accelerated pace, which had at first seemed fascinating, underwent redefinition on the battlefield and now seemed essentially hostile. "The rattle of machine-gun fire was the metronome setting a murderous new tempo, and the railroads rushed masses of humanity to the front with the strategy of bleeding the enemy to death."[4] Hunger and disease decimated the home front. For the summer of 1917 the mayor of Berlin had recorded a death rate "that drove the weekly statistics up to one and a half times normal levels and more, until the fall harvest brought an increase in the potato supply. Death was the harvester in the city's hospitals, and it did not let up until all the frail had fallen. The population in the insane asylums was cut in half."[5]

Death enjoyed a rich harvest, and so did the movies. During the war years, the number of movie houses in Berlin had risen from 195 (April 1914) to 312 (November 1918). The first film palaces had been built before the war: the Mozart Hall, the Cines-Theater (renamed the Ufa-Pavilion in 1920), the Marmorhaus (Marble House). Their architecture anticipated the eclectic splendor and bombastic elegance of the postwar era. The "gracefully ironic pathos, the erotically overloaded sacrilege, the rhythmically organized dissonance of solemnity and dance"[6] that a critic saw in the Cines-Theater became the key formal elements of the "Ufa style."

Completion of the Marmorhaus a year before the outbreak of the war marked cinematography's triumphal march into the well-to-do sections of west Berlin. Worn down by fear for relatives at the front and by worry about how to get through the next day, the Berliner who visited the Marmorhaus in the war years encountered a decor of sophisticated and capricious modernity, where colors clashed "cubistically, futuristically, symbolically, and secessionistically in the most daring combinations." It was a bizarre atmosphere of contrasts and calculated dissonances. "Pale-blue decor, tangles of lines, silver sculptures, painted monkeys, a bright red bar—everything whirled before our eyes."[7] For the opening night of May 1, 1913, the theater had been doused with the perfume Marguerite Carré from Bourgeois-Paris, which only added to the "steamy, bizarre dream-state" evoked by the lights and colors.

It was not the "better society" of west Berlin, however, but the proletarian and semiproletarian classes that still made up the majority of moviegoers. For them, the movies had always been—and became even more so—a refuge and hiding place from the gray reality of the street, a realm of wishes where the decor was less important than the chance to hide from the world and be at the same time both totally self-contained and transported beyond oneself. An emigrant from the land of reality, distressed, disillusioned, and often with an empty stomach, the moviegoer could "forget" what was going on "out there": the reality on the front, the Molochs in the munitions factories, the icy "turnip winter," the casualty notices in the newspapers. And he could repress what was coming and could not be ignored: defeat, the end of the monarchy, the re-evaluing of all values—the maelstrom into which he and everything he held dear had long since been drawn.

The expansive young film industry was obviously much more attractive to such working-class audiences than the "second" proletarian culture propagated by the Social Democratic educational leagues. The movies were a defense against the ascetic principle that not only guardians of bourgeois values but also ideologues of a revolutionary culture wanted to impose on workers. The sensuality of film opened up an escape from that "impoverished system of cultural values"[8] to which the proletarian was subjugated.

A plush and gilded foyer with crystal chandeliers served an additional function of allowing the visitor symbolic entrée into "better circles" (provided a worker could even afford the price of a ticket). But the movie itself, with its hallucinatory offerings and fascinating possibilities, offered a different kind of symbolic participation: a chance to live entirely by and for oneself, entirely outside the everyday world, to be drawn into the illuminated surface of the screen and "disappear" in it, to venture into a realm of experience lost to everyday consciousness, to enter another dimension of world and reality.

The longer the war lasted, the more insatiable German movie audiences became. Since 1914, distributors had been cut off from French and British products, soon thereafter from Italian films, and, starting in 1917, from American ones as well. The Supreme Command tried to break the hunger blockade with unlimited U-boat warfare, but the only measure to take against a film blockade was increased national production. In August 1914, 25 German production companies and distributors were competing against 47 foreign firms; by 1918, 130 German firms dominated the field.[9] The film industry was "Germanized," thanks to the founding of Ufa. At the same time, in one of those ironies of history, Germany's film patriotism was exhausted. "The war is no longer a novelty, and it has become painful to be reminded of it every day on the screen."[10]

The public preferred imaginary duels in urban jungles to the real war and its devastating slaughter. A particular favorite was the famous series of Stewart Webb detective films. Webb, an investigator and champion of the law modeled on Sherlock Holmes and characterized by a brutal and elegant style, had been created before the war by the perfectionist and highly successful producer and director Joe May and the actor Ernst Reicher. During the war, Max Landa as Joe Deebs continued this successful run of suspenseful, fast-paced, big-city thrillers. British detectives, dressed in tweeds and with the obligatory pipe clenched between their teeth, competed with films designed to inflame hatred against "perfidious Albion." The public abandoned the propagandists in droves. They simply laughed at them. Or frustrated—at best indifferent—they let wash over them propaganda for a war they had come to reject.

It has to be said of Henny Porten, who was the first great star of German film, who inspired the love of the moviegoing public and who knew how to return that love with warmth and feeling, who was ridiculed as a "ladies-magazine romantic" and glorified as a "Germanic diva," who still remains today a monument in German film history; of this Henny Porten, who never saw the inside of an acting school but who under her father's direction posed in 1907 for pantomimic "sound pictures" accompanied by opera music from blatting gramophones and soon became Oskar Messter's greatest attraction, of her it must emphatically be said that she was the legitimate child of all movie passions *and* of ebullient patriotic emotions as well. She played a poverty-stricken blind girl totally alone in the world who in the end experiences the joy of love; she played a minister's daughter; she played a mannequin who has to cope with high-society ladies and even with the devil himself; she played a "misunderstood" girl as charming as she was obstinate; and she played the home-loving "Claudi of Geislerhof." Measured by the standard of the public's approval, she was the only genuine heroine of the First World War (and the only genuinely German one). As able in tragedy as in comedy, sometimes tender, sometimes raging, sometimes melting with love, sometimes stubbornly rebellious in her defiance of adversity, she embodied all the tangled thoughts and emotions that filled the minds and hearts of war-weary Germans; embodied what they loved, what they dreamed of, and what they could relate to.

Not without reason does Oskar Kalbus stress how "brave" Henny Porten was when in 1916, as an unschooled actress, she held her own with Jannings in *Die Ehe der Luise Rohrbach* (*The Marriage of Luise Rohrbach*), and he calls her 1917 Messter film *Die Faust des Riesen* (*The Giant's Fist*), based on a novel by Rudolf Stratz and directed by Rudolf Biebrach, her "greatest wartime accomplishment." As hyperpatriotic film historians are wont to put it, however, she made her greatest sacrifice as a wife.

> Porten's husband [the actor and director Kurt Stark] was in the trenches at the front, in constant danger of his life, and the letters she received from him would elate the actress one day, worry her the next, allow her no emotional peace. And so it went, day after day, week after week, month after month. But Porten kept on working in the studio with great diligence and with a passionate commitment to this new art, playing both the lightest and heaviest of roles. Surely no easy matter for a recently married woman whose husband was face-to-face with the enemy. Then one day the long-feared telegram came: Her husband had been killed! He was dead![11]

Many years later, in a second marriage to a Jewish doctor, this widow put her career at risk and, in the era of Joseph Goebbels, staged one of the many political scandals of Ufa's history.

3.

The End of the World and
New Beginnings: The First Year of Ufa

1917–18: Abel Gance made his debut as a director in France with the Pathé production of *J'accuse*, and in Hollywood Metro brought out its first Rudolph Valentino film. Douglas Fairbanks founded his own production company, and in Austria Hubert Marischka sued Wiener Kunstfilm to have his name included in film credits. Charlie Chaplin, with his million-dollar annual salary the highest-paid film actor in the world, made *The Immigrant* for Mutual and a little later his antiwar film *Shoulder Arms!* for First National. In the title role of an American Dubarry film, Theda Bara created the vamp, and after America's entry into the war, films like *The Kaiser—Beast of Berlin* began appearing, prompting complaints from German consuls about this hostile "horror propaganda."

While all this was going on in the world, the fifth year of war dominating the German screen began, with films like *Anna dreht Granaten* (*Anna Makes Artillery Shells*) and *Die dicke Berta* (*Fat Berta*), which starred Anna Müller-Lincke as a peasant girl working in an arms factory and as a cook, "who, presented as a dance star at a private showing for war wounded, rejects the advances of an older playboy type to remain true to her fiancé in field uniform."[1]

The fiancé in field uniform cut a dashing figure not only in films but in illustrated magazines and light novels. He was the erotic hero of the epoch and the object of a "wartime nymphomania" (cited ten years later by Magnus Herschfeld's school of psychology as proof "that women react to the experience of war with a massive increase in libido"[2]).

1917–18: While traditional cultural institutions had to cut back, Ufa could have whatever it wanted. Samuel Fischer continued to publish contemporary novels with handsome title-page vignettes, but the covers were of cardboard and on the copyright page was the notice: "Printed during wartime on paper with wood-pulp content." Max Reinhardt's productions had to do without their usual decorative splendor; changing the lighting "was the only possible way to cover up the mediocre quality of substitute materials and fabrics."[3] But Ufa, the Supreme Command's cultural bastion created expressly for the war, was arming itself with impressive opulence for its peacetime tasks.

1917–18: While militarists and the armed forces continued to hope to forge Ufa into a weapon that would assure a peace favorable to Germany, the civilians in the company's leadership had taken control of it, and in the last year of the war they presented their production plans to the intelligence branch of the Foreign Office. Included were four films with Pola Negri, six films with Ossi Oswalda, eight with Henny Porten, four with Georg Alexander, six with Fern Andra, some "epic films" from Joe May's production, and more of the same. The fit of rage that overcame Ludendorff when the list was presented to him may well be apocryphal, but there is probably a certain truth to it. For the film civilians had marshaled their new projects without regard for the strategic planning of the general staff and as if their primary mission was for loose and fast living. "Typists and apprentices, salesgirls and post-office clerks dreamed of nothing but becoming film stars, while the stars themselves, on the screens of innumerable theaters and on millions of star postcards, became models for the fans who idolized them."[4]

The planners had not reckoned with this turn of events, thinking they could control this new instrument without having to concern themselves with its ambiguous nature and subversive qualities. General Ludendorff, preoccupied in 1918 with the military retreat and the collapse of his political authority, was fighting both in the field and as supreme cultural officer against modernity, against the twentieth century, and he was fighting a losing battle.

Germany was in turmoil; the political planners had gradually lost their grasp, and among actors, artists, and intellectuals, among producers and screenplay writers the dominant mood was one of nervousness, rebellion, and a tendency toward gleeful sarcasm. Ufa underwent a qualitative change. It behaved obstinately and irregularly, its irregularity in tune with history. "Ufa's leaders were looking further ahead than their military protectors were. In view of Germany's impending defeat, their main concern was to keep the young enterprise intact and to take what measures they could to ensure a favorable financial future in the coming years."[5] Bratz supposedly even established some secret contacts with Hollywood representatives while the war was going on. In the meantime, even more modern strategists were lurking in the background, waiting for the chance to take this glittering monster over for their own purposes.

Thanks to the merger policy so energetically promoted under the protection of the German Bank, Ufa from the start boasted a gallery of stars with big names and box-office appeal. From Davidson's Union company came the directors Ernst Lubitsch and Paul Wegener, and they brought their closest associates with them—the dramaturg Hanns Kräly and the film architect, actor, screenplay writer, and director Rochus Gliese; stars such as Asta Nielsen, Pola Negri, Ossi Oswalda, Erna Morena, Harry Liedtke, Victor Janson, Emil Jannings, Hans Junkermann, and many others. From Messter, the new company took the director and actor Viggo Larsen as well as Henny Porten, Bruno Decarli, Arnold Rieck, and other favorites. The production companies continued to work under their own names, but everything was consolidated under the umbrella of the Universum-Film AG.

The star contracts taken over from Nordisk, Union, and Messter were capital of inestimable value, an index of "exchange value," which, as Bächlin has observed, set "the price range for exceptional actors."[6] The contracts elevated the stars to extraterrestrial spheres in the eyes of the public and at the same time made them tradable, brand-name goods for producers. The star cult as part of a carefully crafted economic and psychological strategy had already been developed by Messter with Henny Porten and by Union with Asta Nielsen. With vastly greater means at its disposal, Ufa now paid the stars salaries that could compare with American ones. In January 1918, Der Kinematograph sounded the alarm about this special treatment afforded the stars:

> The salaries of actors rise from one film to the next and are climbing sky high! . . . On the one hand, actors of less than star rank and extras are treated arbitrarily and work in pitiable conditions, and on the other, the star system offers more than even opera prima donnas have ever been granted![7]

Heinrich Fraenkel has analyzed the exchange value of the early female stars, quite in keeping with the workings of the marketplace, by dismantling them into their body parts: "Ossi's legs, Pola's gleaming eyes, and Asta's slim figure" were the "assets" available at Ufa's founding.[8] This ungracious formulation is itself of course a late reflection of the cult of the female star, with its tendency to expose woman's sexuality to the public eye and —for the sake of visual desire vicariously fulfilled by the camera—to divide her body up into erogenous zones. The war encouraged and accelerated this to a great degree. It produced new female types—the woman working in a munitions factory or behind the front lines, the soldier's wife, the war bride, the nurse—who asserted their rights not only in daily economic life but also in the erotic sphere. The cultural historian Curt Moreck (who also wrote a notable moral history of film[9]) has argued that in the popular literature, popular theater, and on the variety stage of the prewar period three female types had their particular erotic modes: the "grande dame," the "half virgin," and the "Lulu type."[10] The erotic flair of these types was sometimes trivialized in wartime German films, sometimes given crass Germanic form, and sometimes romantically "ennobled" with subliminal ambivalence (such as Henny Porten embodied). But the founding of Ufa, which coincided with the general decline of wartime morale, allowed the three types to flourish again, in both sophisticated and demimondaine form—the licentious adulteress or vice-ridden flapper, the lascivious high-society lady and the man-destroying Lulu of Wedekind's invention.

Still, the erotic appeal of an actress like Asta Nielsen cannot be reduced, as Fraenkel suggested, to her "trim figure," nor can she be readily classified as one of Moreck's star types. The inestimable "capital" that she represented first for Union, then for the early Ufa, lay in her passionate nature and her radical humanity—factors that the standardized star system could not begin to comprehend. Those qualities were evident in the matchless physical and intellectual presence that enabled Nielsen to think with her eyes, to inform sensuality with intelligence. She developed, as Béla Balázs observed in 1924, "the great and complete mimetic dictionary of sensual love" and created an awareness that eroticism was "the true subject of film, the film material per se."

> Her eyes are the main thing here, not her body. . . . Her abstract slenderness has the effect of a single, twitching nerve with a twisted mouth and two burning eyes. . . . [She can] suggest obscene nudity *with her eyes*, and she can smile in a way that would oblige the police to ban the film as pornography.[11]

The eyes, not the body: Balázs touches here on an important secret of all film. As we will see later in Ufa's history, the great mimetic dictionary of sensual love would become impoverished, and we shall inquire into the reasons. But Hollywood and its female stars—from Mary Pickford to Marilyn Monroe—continued to contribute to this dictionary. Asta Nielsen never became *the* Ufa star type, and though her best films were made in Germany and with German directors (*Die freudlose Gasse* [*The Joyless Street*], Sofar-Film, G. W. Pabst, 1925; *Dirnentragodie* [*Harlot's Tragedy*], Pantomim-Film, Bruno Rahn, 1927), they were not made for Ufa. Ufa's capacity for cultural assimilation during its first decade was significant, but it is equally interesting to note the actors, writers, and other artists it employed but could not integrate, the ideas and obsessions it bought but could not make its own.

Far more predictable was the fixed capital that Ufa acquired with its ambitiously conceived purchasing offensive. In March 1918 Ufa took over the studio complex on Tempelhof's Oberlandstrasse: two immense glass buildings on grounds of almost a hundred thousand square meters. Literaria-Film, founded by the film manufacturer Alfred Duskes with additional backing supplied by Pathé, had built the first glass studio in 1913; it was soon followed on a neighboring lot by the second, built for Davidson's Union. They looked, it was said, like two "giant birdcages. . . . Light can flood in here from all sides, and one quickly sees immediately that these buildings serve the enterprise whose motto is 'Everything loves light and turns to the light.' "[12] In addition to the studios, the buildings contained workshops and stage materials, a copying lab, offices, and dressing rooms for the actors. A freight elevator linked the ground floor with the 800-square-meter studio, which contained trapdoors, water pools, and a mobile bridge crane.[13] Messter had acquired the Literaria glass house in 1917 and now brought it into the Ufa empire, which improved it and used it as headquarters until the company moved to Neubabelsberg.

For several decades, these first film glass houses had added a new element to the Berlin scene. Apparently weightless structures glittering in the sunlight and designed to bring daylight indoors, plainly constructed yet as inspiring as spaceships, they stood out among the stolid Wilhelmine buildings and signaled a new age. One saw them in Steglitz (the little Bolten-Baeckers studio, in which Krieger set up Ufa's cultural division in 1919) and on Stahnsdorfer Strasse in Babelsberg (the Deutsche Bioscop glass house built under the direction of Guido Seeber). The first film made in the latter was Asta Nielsen's Der Totentanz (The Dance of Death) in 1912. Bioscop had a second studio on Chausseestrasse. Duske's studio was at Blücherstrasse 12, and the Eiko studio—at 1,000 square meters the largest glass house in prewar Berlin—was in Marienfelde. In 1916, the American-born actress Fern Andra opened her own glass studio on Chausseestrasse. In a glass house in Weissensee Harry Piel made his Joe Deebs series for Joe May, and next door in the Lixie studio Ernst Reicher produced his Stuart Webb films. Messter had already worked with artificial light in 1896 on Friedrichstrasse before he built his first glass studio in the heart of Berlin in 1905. Still others stood in Lankwitz (Muto-Studio, 1907) and on the Teltow Canal (Treumann-Larsen, 1912), in Wedding (Rex Studio, owned from 1918 on by Lupu Pick, who made his "chamber films" Scherben [Shattered] and Sylvester [New Year's Eve] there), and on Belle Alliance-Platz (Vitascope; The Other was produced here in 1912). Glass buildings were put up anywhere on the sand of Mark Brandenburg or, as a crowning glory, so to speak, on top of office buildings in the center of the city, where they could still be seen long after film producers in the 1920s switched from daylight to floodlights.

The glass buildings of the film industry—architectural symbols of an art that reveals mysteries to the eye, opens a window on the world, and finds new perspectives—fit perfectly with the monumental functionalism that the Deutscher Werkbund (German Work League) had propagated before the war. The architect Walter Gropius, for example, had presented at the Work League exhibit of 1914 a new, "puristic" industrial architecture of glass and steel. AEG's turbine hall by Peter Behrens (1909) and his high-tension plant at Humboldthain (1910) modeled the transparent, "work-oriented, functional" lines that were repeated and literally mirrored in the glass film studios. The functional lines were, however, violated by other parts of the building, executed in a wide variety of styles, intended for backdrops in outdoor shots. An example is the copying lab next to the Bioscop studio in Neubabelsberg: "One part of the façade is Romanesque; another Gothic, another old German or Renaissance, and so on. Even the roof was covered with different tiles so that Italian or Spanish roofs as well as German ones would be available at any time for shooting."[14]

In the 1920s Ufa added a new dimension to studio architecture when it built in Neubabelsberg the largest film workshop in Europe, and in the sets for *Metropolis* Fritz Lang erected a late, hyperutopian monument to these functionalist, technological utopias of Walter Gropius and Bruno Taut. The ideologues of the Work League—and Fritz Lang after them—dreamed of "total revitalization." Lang was blind (as his models had been twenty years earlier) to the truth "that a Work League–inspired 'idealism of work' was less important in this process than strengthened monopoly capitalism."[15]

Ufa energetically pursued its vertical and horizontal expansion while the war was still on. With the Nordische Filmgesellschaft—now called Universum-Filmverleih (Universum Film Distribution)—a smoothly functioning distribution organization had fallen into the firm's hands. Its many theaters and the enlargement of that number fell to the Ufa-Theater-Betrieb (Ufa Theater Management), founded at the end of July 1918. When Ufa acquired the stock of the Winterfeld Bank for Trade and Real Estate, it got with it the Fatherland House (formerly the Piccadilly), an imposing, half-round, domed building on Potsdamer Platz, where it set up its central administrative offices in 1919. (In 1927 Ufa sold the building to the Aschinger concern and its Kempinski Restaurant.) The Ufa cultural-film division was founded in 1918 under the direction of Major Ernst Krieger.

The acquisition of May-Film, which Joe May and his wife, Mia, had built up together, quickly proved an important addition on the horizontal plane. Ufa engaged May for six years as an adviser, director, and dramaturge. His wife received a star's contract as an actress.

Mid-sized producers, distributors, and theater owners did not watch the expansion of Ufa with equanimity, however. At the end of February 1918 the Reich Association of German Motion Picture Theater Owners voiced its concerns "that the trusts will buy up the best theaters and thus deprive the owners of smaller theaters of their living."[16] Some theater owners took this a step further and demanded government concessions, a highly controversial idea throughout the industry because many feared that government concessions would bring with them government restrictions and pressures. A few weeks later the Association of Bavarian Cinematographic Interests resolved "to demand that motion-picture concessions be denied to corporate entities, for the negative impacts on the film industry that have resulted from the recent strong tendency to form trusts and concerns in it will inevitably bring about the annihilation of medium-sized operations in our business."[17] In view of a bill under discussion in the Reichstag concerning the showing of motion pictures, the Society of German Filmmakers in April 1918 addressed a memorandum to members of the Reichstag in which these worries were bluntly expressed.

A national law governing motion pictures would not be passed until May 1920. Until then the German film and theater industry was preoccupied with even more basic debates prompted by the end of the war and by the November revolution that ended the Wilhelmine monarchy. But filmmakers' worries about how the overall performance of the economy might affect them proved unfounded: annual production in 1919 climbed to 499 films, and in the following year to 545.

In 1918, a year of national bankruptcy for Germany, a lively, enterprising spirit was afoot throughout the entire film industry and not just at Ufa. In Munich, the MLK company (Münchener Lichtspielkunst, "Emelka") was founded; and outside the city, in Schwabing, the cornerstone was laid for Bavaria's big glass studio. In the last year of the war, 376 films were produced, an increase of more than 50 percent over the previous year. Hans Albers began his career with Deutsche Bioscop, and Lupu Pick directed his first film, *Der Weltspiegel* (*The Mirror of the World*), in 1918 for Rex. Carl Boese—who two years later in collaboration with Paul Wegener made a second Golem film, *Der Golem, wie er in die Welt kam* (*Golem, How He Came into the World*)—also began his career in 1918, making films for Deutsche Kolonialfilm and with support from the Colonial Office. Harry Piel plugged on with his detective and sensationalistic dramas, and Richard Oswald made not only the courageous "educational films" that made him famous (*Es werde Licht* [*Let There Be Light*], 1917–18; *Das Tagebuch einer Verlorenen* [*Diary of a Wayward Woman*], 1918), but also, with Anita Berber and Conrad Veidt in the lead roles, the comedy *Das Dreimäderlhaus* (*The House with Three Girls*). The Berlin police, still the highest-ranking censorship authority in the Reich, found the title *Diary of a Wayward Woman* and the introductory scenes to the film offensive; they allowed it to run with cuts and under the title *Das Tagebuch einer Toten* (*Diary of a Deceased Woman*); only after obligatory censorship was lifted in November 1918 did this film reach the theaters unabridged and with its original title.

By 1918 Messter, Union, and Nordisk were producing under Ufa's wing. Union brought out two Wegener films, both made in the glass studio on Oberlandstrasse: *Der fremde Fürst* (*The Foreign Prince*), a "drama of racial conflict," with Lyda Salmonova, Elsa Wagner, and Rochus Gliese; and the fairy-tale film *Der Rattenfänger von Hameln* (*The Pied Piper of Hamelin*), the outdoor scenes of which were shot in Bautzen and Hildesheim. Lotte Reiniger had drawn the silhouettes shown with the title and credits. (In 1926 Ufa included in its distribution program her *Die Abenteuer des Prinzen Achmed* [*The Adventures of Prince Achmed*], also made with silhouette cutouts in animated sequence, the first full-length animated feature in film history.)

With *The Student of Prague* (1913) and *The Golem* (1914) Wegener had introduced ambitious artistic goals and a conception of film work not unlike that of today's *auteur* moviemakers, and he had won over members of the literary intelligentsia to the new medium. His early recognition that the camera had to be "the real poet of film"[18] and his vision of "kinetic lyricism"[19] (developed in a 1916 lecture) anticipated the aesthetics of animated films and the "abstract films" of the 1920s. With his fairy-tale films during the war years—in addition to his Pied Piper film he made *Rübezahls Hochzeit* (*Rübezahl's Wedding*, 1916) and *Hans Trutz im Schlaraffenland* (*Hans Trutz on the Big Rock Candy Mountain*, 1917)—Wegener continued his efforts to let "the fantasy world of past centuries flow together with contemporary life."[20] He wanted to "kill off" in the viewer the everyday, common urban dweller and make him a child again, marveling at a pre-rational, fairy-tale world. H. B. Heller, citing his example, has noted a characteristic contradiction in this type of film: "In terms of its technical resources and its organizational form, film bore like no other medium the mark of highly developed capitalism, [yet the writers wanted] in most cases to create visually a pre-industrial world. They did so by creating an illusion that let the *viewer* forget the movie's technical base."[21]

It was not so much Wegener's artistic ambition as his stress on the concept of illusion, his neo-Romantic preference for pre-industrial visual worlds, and his anti-civilization bias that linked him with the ideological and emotional values that set Ufa on the path to becoming a German national company and a modern cathedral of German "inwardness." This kind of divided consciousness is part of the German intellectual legacy, a schizophrenia that becomes full-blown when united with the destructive principle. Wegener later accepted major roles in National Socialist propaganda films like *Hans Westmar* (directed by Franz Wenzler, 1933), *Der grosse König* (*The Great King*, Veit Harlan, 1942), and the Ufa film *Kolberg* (Veit Harlan, 1945). But even in 1918 he did not shrink from the current political scene when it seemed opportune to take part in it. Right after the war, at the behest of the Foreign Office, he wrote the screenplay for a one-act antiwar film, *Apokalypse*, which Rochus Gliese directed for Union and in which he, Ernst Deutsch, and Paul Hartmann played leading roles.

Union's other star director—Wegener's intellectual opposite, and the greatest stroke of luck in Ufa's early history—was the brilliantly eclectic Ernst Lubitsch. In 1918 he directed no less than seven films. From 1913 on, he had been involved either as an actor in or a director of about twenty Union productions, mainly one-act comedies set in a milieu familiar to him from his own home (the world of textile and shoe workers) and featuring Berlin types, bald humor, and heavy-handed situation comedy. The Reinhardt actor wove together and "ennobled" these still rough forms with an agile intellectuality, irony, and urbane flair, and with a chameleonlike talent for moving about among radically different film genres. Lubitsch was already developing his characteristic balance of emotion, mood, and stylistic gesture, as intelligent as it was artful, which has gone down in film history as the "Lubitsch touch." It did not reach its heights, however, until he went to Hollywood. Ufa was a stepping-stone in that direction.

While the war ground to an end and depression and defeatism spread in Germany, Lubitsch took leave of his stage career at the Apollo Theater, where a revue was playing called *Die Welt geht unter* (*The End of the World*). A revue mentality was widespread in the film industry, too, but fired with optimism. With Ufa's capital behind him, Lubitsch made the first of many expensive costume films: *Die Augen der Mumie Ma* (*The Eyes of the Mummy Ma*) and *Carmen* (*Gypsy Blood*), both starring Pola Negri and Harry Liedtke and both written by his friend and closest collaborator, Hanns Kräly. Pola Negri, a fiery dancer from Warsaw and a sex symbol and cult figure of the early cinema, describes in her memoirs the atmosphere in the Tempelhof studio:

> Although the world was going to pieces around us, Lubitsch and I enjoyed many hilariously funny moments as we worked together on films in those early days of Ufa. It may be that only in the Berlin of those times could we have flourished so successfully. The tragicomedy of life in Germany was our métier. Even our jokes had a doomsday quality to them.[22]

The completion of *Gypsy Blood* coincided with the end of an era:

> On the evening of November 8, 1918, we invited the press and the top officials of Ufa to a special pre-release showing of *Gypsy Blood* in the studio's previewing auditorium. Lubitsch was still working on the final editing. A new evening dress had been made for me for this showing, and the studio put on a champagne reception. None of us was paying much attention to the revolutionary events taking place around us. If you live on the edge of an abyss, you soon cease to be aware of it; and if the papers are filled with catastrophes day after day, you soon stop registering them. . . .
> My lamé dress was a glittering triumph that night. The champagne had been cooled perfectly, and it loosened tongues, filling the room with laughter, joking, and small talk. The studio orchestra played melodies from *Gypsy Blood* to put us in the right mood, conversation flowed as freely and ebulliently as the champagne, and even the gloomy premonitions of the bankers who had advanced Ufa credit were overwhelmed by the splendor of the gathering. We took our seats and the film began. There was applause at my first entrance. During the applause and for a moment afterward I heard a faint sound in the distance. It sounded—but that couldn't be—like rifle fire. I looked around to see if others had heard it,

too, but all I saw was intense concentration on the film, interrupted now and then by applause for certain effects achieved on the screen. . . .

The distant rifle fire came nearer now and was a constant accompaniment. Everyone had to have noticed it, but people continued to watch the screen, and no one acknowledged what he had heard with so much as a turn of his head. I huddled down in my seat, horrified by our calm self-preoccupation and the fact that we all knew what was going on but preferred to act as if nothing were happening. It was so much easier to shut one's eyes rather than ask questions. When the film was over, there was enthusiastic applause. Everyone stayed in the previewing hall, presumably to congratulate us but in reality because no one knew what else to do. The rifle fire continued.[23]

On that very night of November 8, revolution broke out in Berlin. Spartacists and government troops exchanged machine-gun fire. Pola Negri— or so she claimed fifty years later—stole out of the studio with the Ufa party still going on "as if everything in the world were in order." Perspiring heavily, she reached the closest subway station while stray bullets whined through the air. On November 9, the major Berlin factories spontaneously declared a general strike. In the garrisons, soldiers' soviets were elected, but they aligned themselves neither with the Spartacists nor with the left-wing USPD and the revolutionary cadres but with the majority Social Democrats under Ebert and Scheidemann. On November 10, the revolution was over. On that day, in the Busch Circus, a plenary assembly of the Berlin Workers' and Soldiers' Soviets elected a new, republican government. The monarchy had collapsed; the military aristocracy was stripped of power; the Kaiser went into exile in Holland.

But the dreams of the radical left came to naught. All the Germans had done, considerably later than everyone else, was to stage a middle-class revolution. *Gypsy Blood* premiered on December 20 in the Ufa Theater on Kurfürstendamm and was a smash hit with both the public and the press. "With this film," Herman Weinberg wrote, "his first great international success, Lubitsch put Germany on the world map of film."[24] The military Supreme Command, after every single one of its experiments had failed, yielded in the face of unhappy circumstances. Its historic project, however, Germany's greatest film factory, took form, grew, flourished, and moved to the rhythms of a new era.

4.

Lay Down Your Arms!
Cinema and Revolution

AT the end of 1918 and in the first weeks of 1919, revolution and cinema melted together into a dissonant harmony full of overlappings and internal contradictions.

> In spite of the bloody machine-gun duels between government troops and Spartacists in all parts of Berlin; in spite of the stray bullets that have taken the lives of many innocent bystanders; in spite of the urgent plea to citizens to stay off the streets; in spite of the strikes of the trolley and S-Bahn personnel; in spite of fearful rumors that race through the city like wildfire, blathering that the Bolsheviks mean to blow up the electric, gas, and water works; in spite of and in spite of—the movie palaces and theaters (as long as they are not in the combat zone . . .) go about their business unperturbed and are enjoying big audiences.[1]

Thus wrote Egon Jacobsohn in an essay published on January 15, 1919, the day that the celebrated Communists Karl Liebknecht and Rosa Luxemburg were murdered.

Harry Count Kessler, one of the keenest observers of his epoch, had thought in cinema terms when he passed through the Reichstag building on November 9:

> At the feet of the columns in the lobby, groups of soldiers and sailors are lying and standing on the thick red carpet. Rifles are stacked together; here and there men are sleeping stretched out full-length on benches—a film from the Russian Revolution, Tauric Palace under Kerensky.[2]

But the revolutionary events were reflected only faintly in German film. What was happening "out there" reached the minds of screenplay writers as through a heavy fog, and before appearing on the screen it underwent strange anamorphoses.

In Georg Jacoby's 1919 Union film *De Profundis*, Ellen Richter played a young nihilist who shoots down a Russian grand duke. Similar motifs appear in F. W. Murnau's second film, *Satanas*, made for Viktoria in the fall of 1919 in Neubabelsberg, under the overall artistic direction of Robert Wiene, with Conrad Veidt and Fritz Kortner in the lead roles. This episodic film took the viewer from the pharaohs to Lucretia Borgia and then, in the third part, abruptly into the German present. A student comes under the influence of Russian anarchists "who are in the habit of drinking innumerable cups of tea in a café." In his hometown, he rouses the masses to storm the castle, lets himself be drawn into atrocities, and goes mad. Lotte Eisner, writing on the basis of a detailed synopsis of this now lost film, says:

> It is perhaps characteristic of Murnau that he felt drawn to render a passage in Wiene's script in more detailed form: the scene of the actual revolt, which Murnau . . . brings to life with hastily penciled ideas, brief focusings on individual actors, and instructions on their actions. Still stuck in his mind are scenes from the revolution he had recently experienced.[3]

A decidedly bohemian visual outlook, a kind of coffeehouse perspective, is unmistakable in the view that German literati and artists took of revolutionary events. The Ullstein journalist Jacobsohn realized, after the occupation of the newspaper quarter by Spartacists in January 1919, that he was "homeless and unemployed," since the most important Berlin papers —the *Vossische Zeitung*, the *Berliner Morgenpost*, the *B.Z. am Montag*, the *Berliner Tageblatt*, and the *Berliner Lokalanzeiger*—could not appear. So he had time and leisure "to see all the films that are playing now."[4] "Come what would, the people wanted to be entertained," Herman Weinberg wrote decades later, "and film was the entertainment of the masses."[5]

Film reality and political reality sometimes intersected only to split apart again. For the young Fritz Lang, who was making *Halbblut* (*Half Blood*), his first feature film for Decla, in January 1919, the raw realities of politics literally proved an obstacle in his path. On the first day of filming, armed guards of the Spartacus League repeatedly stopped his car en route to the studio. Some Ufa board members apparently faced similar difficulties. The minutes of a board meeting scheduled for January 21 begin: "The chairman, Herr von Stauss, opened the meeting, welcoming the members present and observing that the difficult transportation situation had prevented a number of others from attending."[6] But Fritz Lang did not let Spartacus stand in his way: "It would have taken more than a revolution to keep me from directing my first film."[7] Two years later he drafted his first *Mabuse* film as a "picture of the times" and gave it documentary qualities; in the showdown episode there are shots whose "imagery intentionally recalls the tumultuous postwar months," one critic has written.[8]

The popular image of madcap Berlin and its cultural revolution neglects the depressed state of postwar society, the threat of economic collapse, and the decline in the "human factor" as a force for productivity. After 1871, Germany had hastily and belatedly become an industrial power, and now, after losing the war, it partially regressed to pre-industrial conditions. One analyst of German workers of that period, of their productivity, wages, and living conditions, has called them "unique beings" who had little in common with the English or American proletariat.[9] For lack of raw materials and energy, managers often shut down the machines and returned to hand work. Industrial workers suddenly found themselves thrown back to the wages, living conditions, and confining, oppressive ways of thought and life characteristic of the early nineteenth century. The ideological flip side of this economic misery was a glorification of the provincial idyll, of a dreamworld harking back to the "simple life" of pre-industrial and pre-revolutionary times. Capitalizing on these bucolic yearnings became a major project for Ufa.

In the confusing social scene—a discredited royal dynasty finally collapsed, cities rife with revolutionary impulses and reassessing old values, tentative first steps being taken by a democratic government supported by the working class, widespread economic and psychological depression linked with regression to pre-industrial modes of life and psychic orientations—in this diffuse picture the impassioned appeals of the intellectual avant-garde for peace and the brotherhood of all men seemed especially abstract and vague. Carlo Mierendorff wrote in November 1918:

> The times challenge us! We are at the end! We can no longer be quiet and let ourselves be carried along by events. For four years we took refuge from atrocities in ethereal poetry. . . . But now we are free. . . . Now we need to leap into the stream of history, to be active to the limits of our strength, and let nothing be torn from us. . . . We do not want to, nor can we, remain silent any longer. We are waiting for you, friends, for your warm hearts, your pure commitment! Jump in and muster your courage; search out directions, pathways, and goals. May an indomitable will to build a better future raise us on high and be our most devout watchword. Friends, take hold![10]

At this same time, Ufa published in *Der Kinematograph* an eight-page ad for Nordisk-Film's *Die Waffen nieder* (*Lay Down Your Arms*). It blithely mixed this kind of feverish pathos with a direct pitch for its film theaters:

> He who seizes the right moment, he is the right man! Cinema is the theater of the people! Lead the masses toward understanding. Help promote the idea of the League of Nations!
>
> Lay down your arms! is a cry heard throughout the world, the cry of every nation! Bright these words burn, brightly the flame of freedom leaps up after years of slaughter! *Lay Down Your Arms* (made by Nordisk) is the film of the day! The film for every theater!

Our desire is to make this film immediately available to everyone! Here Bertha von Suttner's warning cry is embodied in moving tragedy and gripping images! The film is finished! Never has Olaf Fönss acted so convincingly and with such profound feeling as in this film LAY DOWN YOUR ARMS! Sign this film up now. Clear the way for this work!

We are living under the sign of a new age! Our motto is *Pax Aeterna* —Eternal Peace.[11]

The gigantic capital letters were intended to make theater owners sign their contracts quickly, but like the pacifist manifestos and the expressionist lyrics of the time, they were also inspired by the spirit of a new age, by "visionary dramas announcing to a suicidal mankind the gospel of a new age of brotherhood,"[12] as Siegfried Krakauer has put it, though Ufa's management was inclined "to perpetuate on the screen the conservative and nationalist pattern set by the former regime."[13] Yet even in the last year of the war, the civilian leadership in Ufa had not only pulled back from the Supreme Command's propaganda mission but devoted the firm's energies, openly and without hindrance, to the pursuit of its business interests. After the war ended, those business ambitions were freed from ideological limits dictated by a political and military clique unfamiliar with the film industry. In the chaos of the times, they struck out on their own path, and it goes without saying that Ufa's program planners, staff, and ad writers were all affected by the same powerful ideas that were sweeping through German society: a universal yearning for peace and vague concepts of revolution and global brotherhood. Popular stars didn't require convincing to join in this campaign for a better world and for good box office. They were in tune with the times, shared the public mood, and wanted to become rich, in this respect, too, in sync with the public. Olaf Fönss, the Danish lead in *Lay Down Your Arms*, was a universally beloved screen hero after starring in Otto Rippert's *Homunculus* (1916), and his "romantic attire in the film [had] reportedly influenced the fashions of elegant Berlin."[14]

The chronicle of 1918–19 in the *Film Yearbook*, a sober, indeed, dry compilation of facts, doesn't begin to suggest the dramatic events and convolutions the industry experienced, though the events it so tersely records were far from insignificant. An immediate consequence of the revolution was the "demilitarization" of the Office of Photography and Film. Removed from the jurisdiction of the Supreme Command, it was placed under the Reich Chancellery, which now had to organize the government's film propaganda in a department of its own. In November 1918, eleven months after the founding of Ufa, the government's share in Ufa's financing was made public. In December, the Reichstag did away with film censorship—a measure that many censors apparently did not accept, for as late as April 1919 a debate on censorship took place in the national assembly, and the film industry sent a deputation to testify and to demand an end to the now illegal censorship the police were still imposing. In March 1919 the generally rebellious mood affected the inner workings of the film industry: theater owners held meetings to protest high rental prices, and a general strike temporarily shut down production. "It lasted a week," the *Film Yearbook* reported, "and stopped the unrealistic demands of certain overly radical elements."[15] In April 1919, new trouble brewed: "There is talk of socializing the film industry. The danger is particularly acute in Bavaria, where the imposition of concessions for all film enterprises is close to becoming a reality."[16] However, the new Weimar Republic's brutal disbanding of a nascent soviet republic in Bavaria with the use of army troops in the last days of April ended those anticapitalistic dreams, too.

The theories about socialization were, of course, remarkably primitive and displayed an amazing misunderstanding of the actual political situation. An unbridgeable abyss had opened up between theory and practice at a time when nearly every political and intellectual constituency—from Communists to "enlightened" conservatives, from esoteric poets to advocates of militant art—was working for radical changes. "This is more than a lost war," Walter Gropius wrote. "A world has come to an end. We must seek a radical solution to our problems."[17] In the Workers' Soviet for Art, under Gropius's leadership, and in the "November group," architects, painters, sculptors, and graphic artists fought covertly and overtly for a different, better world, issued calls to arms in the "battle against the established authorities and the academies," supported the idea of "masters' ateliers and apprentice workshops instead of academic instruction," and asked for "idealistic projects with ambitious goals."[18] The poet Rainer Maria Rilke welcomed this revolution, hoping that humanity would now finally turn over a new leaf, but by December 1918 he noted with resignation: "Under the pretense of a great upheaval, the old want of character persists."[19] Rilke's sober assessment was far closer to reality than the intellectual giddiness of the revolutionary enthusiasts, and it agreed with the warnings that Kurt Tucholsky issued in early 1919:

> If revolution meant only collapse, then we have witnessed one. But we cannot expect that the ruins will look any different from the old building. We have experienced failure and hunger, and those responsible have taken to their heels. . . . We are left with a Germany full of outrageous corruption, full of con men and sneaks, full of three times a hundred thousand devils, every one of whom claims for his own blackhearted self the right to remain untouched by the revolution.[20]

The old lack of character continued to rule the day, and of course, as it had in decades past, it portrayed itself as a pillar of the state, claimed that its dominance of political life was legitimate, and defended its threatened strongholds in culture and the arts.

Yet the failure of the revolution and the inadequate realization of its democratic goals did not mean a final outcome favoring reactionary forces, the old military and aristocratic ruling caste, and nationalistic, revanchist business factions. If the picture is to come clear for us of a mighty institution like Ufa, with influence over the public and a place in the border territory between business and culture, we need to understand the extremely ambivalent circumstances that shaped the Weimar Republic. The historian Peter Gay has characterized it as a "republic of outsiders," and stressed that for the first time marginal constituencies—democrats, cosmopolites, Jews—could assume influential positions in public life, the economy, the universities, and politics. "And it was that major change that gave the republic its peculiar and unique character. It was lively, often hectic, productive, but also vulnerable."[21] The republic's mode was that of a state of emergency, but "that should not be confused with lack of viability." Its first months showed what the republic was capable of. Quickly innumerable possibilities emerged, but they were soon betrayed. The Weimar Republic was a source of energy increasingly directed toward resolving basic internal conflicts, and it exhausted itself in the effort. "Weimar was the arena for a huge battle that by 1918–19 was more than a century old, a battle of the one Germany against the other."[22]

And Ufa took part in this battle—how could it be otherwise? Indeed, Ufa itself became an important secondary battleground, with the front lines spread in many directions, corresponding to the various forces controlling the company. Democrats, cosmopolites, and Jews had long made up the creative heart of the German film industry, and they provided the ferment in the new company, too. The emancipation of the firm from its Wilhelmine patrons not only was a victory of the civilian spirit, bourgeois business sense, and an openness to all manner of trade and traffic, but also enabled "outsiders" like Paul Davidson, Ernst Lubitsch, Joe May, Reinhold Schünzel, and, later, Erich Pommer, F. W. Murnau, and Fritz Lang to set the tone. They were not locked into political positions; many of them were, or professed to be, uninterested in politics. But they were all cosmopolitans, anti-provincial, affected by Berlin's edgy nervousness and its sense of the possibilities a technological civilization held out. Ufa was vulnerable to all the latent and obvious currents in German society, but its vulnerability did not mean it was doomed from its inception.

No one more clearly embodied "vulnerability" in the sense of fruitful aesthetic voluntarism and ideological scrupulousness than Ernst Lubitsch. In 1918 and 1919 Lubitsch made twelve films. With the exception of *Rausch* (*Intoxication*), based on a Strindberg play and produced for Argus-Film, they were all Union films and can be regarded as belonging to the early history of Ufa. Lubitsch's films reflect a time of upheaval. A great era was calling for great art, but Lubitsch pointed up the ridiculousness of the sublime. He pulled pretense down from its pedestal and shattered it into many small grotesques. A divided people and their spokesmen were calling for unity and cohesion, but Lubitsch passed sarcastic judgment on them and put his artificial film worlds together out of thousands of unrelated, conflicting details, each illuminating and unmasking the other. Absurdities and sly ironies were his trademarks. The bogus costume revues of the Wilhelmine era had no sooner gone out of style than Lubitsch, with Ufa's money, introduced grand-scale historical costume movies. Day after day Berlin's workers, driven by revolutionary fever, swarmed in the streets of downtown Berlin, on Potsdamer Platz, and in the city park, while Lubitsch—in *Madame Dubarry* (*Passion*)—had French Revolutionary masses marching around in artistic, ornamental patterns. And when foreign boycotts threatened to strangle the export of German films, Ufa was able, thanks to Lubitsch, to hold its own in international film production.

Ernst Lubitsch inspired disagreement, and he continues to do so today. Kracauer's vehement criticism of Lubitsch, for example, which has many imitators, is rooted in his rigorous adherence to the thesis that Germany's "secret history" can be read in the films of the Weimar Republic and that by uncovering the "inner dispositions" of the people as expressed in the medium of film Hitler's ascent and ascendancy can be understood.[23] Kracauer went about the writing of film history as if it were a kind of dark teleology. In his view, Weimar—its power constellations, its inner disposition, its cultural images and caricatures—drifted inevitably toward Fascism. But at the same time that he denies the role of chance and uncertainty in history, he denies its ambivalence and its multitudinous possibility, and so he concludes that underlying the events and their reflection in film was an inevitable fatal flaw. He has no difficulty in putting Lubitsch's "cynicism" and "nihilistic outlook on world affairs" in this category.[24]

At the other extreme, Lotte Eisner, who sees two of the "colorful ingredients" in the "Lubitsch touch" being Max Reinhardt's direction of actors and mass scenes and the keen wit of Jewish intellectuals, also judges too narrowly when she says that Lubitsch's sole intent in his "pseudo-historical costume films" was "to come up with comic traits and ridiculous incidents and situations that would amuse an undiscriminating public."[25] Responding to outraged foreign critics claiming that in *Passion* Lubitsch had made the history of *la grande nation*, and in *Anna Boleyn* (*Deception*) the heroic epoch of England, look ridiculous, she correctly objects that Ufa was much more interested in collecting foreign currencies than it was in insulting its neighbors. But she fails to recognize the radicalism of Lubitsch's dismantling of history and his subversive attacks on the lies that are an integral part of all pathos. As Lubitsch himself wrote in 1947, looking back on his costume films, he had tried to "de-opera-ize" the contemporary (especially Italian) film versions of history and to reduce grand gestures to their human essences. "I considered the intimate nuances just as important as the mass scenes, and I tried to mix the two."[26] Frieda Grafe perhaps comes closest to capturing the Lubitsch phenomenon when she writes that he was "a child of the inflation." "All his life he remained dependent on times of crisis. They inspired him to make his best films."[27] And Enno Patalas's summing up of Lubitsch's American comedies is relevant to certain elements of those earlier historical costume movies: "Lubitsch's cinema is not a cinema of revolt. But making use of the movement inherent in things as they are, it pushes them a little further along toward their own self-destruction."[28]

At Projektions-Union Lubitsch had assembled a team of very different talents and temperaments—much like the team that formed a little later around F. W. Murnau—and those divergent talents were a perfect match for his eclectic artistry. Foremost in this group was the writer Hanns Kräly, who wrote most of Lubitsch's screenplays and worked together with him in the United States until 1929. His cameraman from 1918 to 1922 was Theodor Sparkuhl; his set designer Kurt Richter (who had often worked with Ernst Stern, one of Max Reinhardt's outstanding stage designers).

As early as the war years, some of the regulars among Lubitsch's actors were Harry Liedtke as a "lover" and "youthful hero," Victor Janson as a "comic figure," and Margarete Kupfer in mother or governess roles. They were all limited at first by these established parts, but trained by Reinhardt and moving back and forth as they did between stage and film, they were ready to try anything new. This was the time when, according to Stefan Grossmann, editor of *Das Tage-Buch*, the Ufa director Paul Davidson was determined to win control over Berlin theater.

> Not only is Ufa reaching out now with Davidson's sure hand for Berlin's Grosses Schauspielhaus, but other theater directors, too, are seeking salvation with pilgrimages to Ufa's offices. . . . Berlin theater will become an appendage of the German film industry. Herr Davidson will decide whether the Deutsches Theater will retain the director Max Reinhardt.[29]

Ossi Oswalda played the flapper roles in Lubitsch's comedies until 1920 (after 1925 she became an Ufa star under Max Macks and remained one until the end of the silent-film era). Pola Negri was the female star of the "major dramatic films" like *The Eyes of the Mummy Ma*, *Gypsy Blood*, *Passion*, and *One Arabian Night*. In *Kohlhiesels Töchter* (*Kohlhiesel's Daughters*, 1920) Henny Porten played a double role, and in the same year she appeared in the title role in *Deception*. And then there was Asta Nielsen. In 1919 she had the lead in the "chamber film" *Intoxication*, and a year later she complained in the *Lichtbild-Bühne* with obvious reference to her experience with Lubitsch: "All the public wants is plot and thrill-packed films in the Yankee style. The artist is allowed no time for the full dramatic development of a role, and if such time is allowed during shooting, the director's scissors will cut away his best work as 'superfluous.' "[30] She was clearly vexed by Lubitsch's "American" lack of respect and his uncomplicated approach to great literature and great dramatic art.

H. H. Prinzler has called Lubitsch an "artist in Ufa's circus."[31] On September 18, 1919, Berlin's biggest movie theater, the Ufa-Palast am Zoo, opened with the premiere of *Passion*. "Huge demonstrations swept continuously through the Berlin streets at that time; similar throngs of aroused Parisians were unleashed in *Passion* to illustrate the French Revolution. Was it a revolutionary film?" asks Siegfried Kracauer. Of course not. "Instead of tracing all revolutionary events to their economic and ideal causes, it persistently presents them as the outcome of psychological conflicts. . . . *Passion* . . . reduces the Revolution to a derivative of private passions."[32]

But where did the border between "revolutionary" and "private" passions lie? What interest did Lubitsch of all people have—Lubitsch, a character actor and entertainer who had worked his way up from the Galician petit bourgeoisie of east Berlin and who now, finally, was working for Ufa and living well—what interest should he of all people have in subtleties like that?

If Ufa films were to be successful, they of course had to be in tune with the "private" passions of audiences numbering in the millions. After its experience with the Supreme Command, the company was as little interested in state commissions—whether from a Social Democratic government or any other—as was the government itself, which had just put an end to censorship. (Even Kracauer mistrusted the idea of a "revolutionary" film policy decreed by the government. The Socialists' bill that proposed nationalizing the film industry so as to dam the flood of sex films he regarded as an example of the "cleavage between the convictions of many socialists and their middle-class dispositions."[33])

It is possible that a recounting of the "cynical," "nihlistic" spectacles that Lubitsch conjured up on movie screens in 1918 and 1919 vis-à-vis an account of the events that occurred in the streets of Berlin can reveal the "inner" psychic state of Weimar. One day after the premiere of *Gypsy Blood* on December 20, 1918, in the Ufa Theater am Kurfürstendamm, an endless funeral procession from the Victory Column to Potsdamer Platz accompanied the coffins of Spartacists shot in street fighting. The coffins were carried on simple flatbed wagons driven by beer-wagon drivers in their work clothes, and above the black-clad procession waved a sea of red flags. Within a few weeks came the "bloody January" of 1919—and two Lubitsch premieres. The first was a farce, *Meyer aus Berlin* (*Meyer from Berlin*), shown in the Ufa theater on Nollendorfplatz on January 17, two days after the murders of Rosa Luxemburg and Karl Liebknecht. A week later on Kurfürstendamm came the comedy *Meine Frau, die Filmschauspielerin* (*My Wife the Movie Actress*) with Ossi Oswalda and Victor Janson. On January 17, the Ebert government took down the decorations on the Brandenburg Gate that had been put up to welcome home the troops from the front. The parade of the defeated regiments was over, and the Spartacus rebellions had been crushed; their leaders were dead. That evening Count Kessler suddenly realized, prompted by a visit to a cabaret, that it was not the government but a completely different, undefinable power that had absorbed the revolution, swallowed it up:

> Not until the revolution did I begin to comprehend the Babylonian, immeasurably deep, chaotic, and powerful aspect of Berlin. This aspect became evident in the fact that this immense movement within the even more immense ebb and flow of Berlin caused only small, local disturbances, as if an elephant had been stabbed with a penknife. It shook itself but then moved on as if nothing had happened.[34]

The throngs that poured into the movie theaters night after night, Ufa's opulent premieres, the sometimes elegant, sometimes crudely comic achievements of Ernst Lubitsch—these were all part and parcel of that immense "ebb and flow of Berlin," of the leviathanlike, voracious, everyday life of the city. It was this everyday life that gave Berliners their equanimity and armed them against the impositions of history. In a state of civil war, it protected them against the icy winds of global historical changes, which were giving free rein to passion but promising little security.

In the last days of 1918 and the first of 1919, "revolutionary" and "private" passions concurred in a way that no film plot, no cinematic saga, could surpass. On Christmas Eve, half Berlin's population had been out and about because "something" was expected to take place on the square in front of the bullet-riddled royal palace—a street battle, a speech by Karl Liebknecht. Government troops and rebelling sailors stood face to face while a stone's throw away a Christmas fair was going on as usual. Hand organs were playing on Friedrichstrasse; "street vendors were selling firecrackers, gingerbread cookies, and silver baubles; the jewelry shops on Unter den Linden, unconcerned about possible danger, were open, their brightly lit show windows sparkling in the night; on Leipziger Strasse, the Christmas crowds poured into the department stores as usual."[35] Then, about a week later, a grotesque little incident occurred that Hanns Kräly or Lubitsch might have dreamed up. Kessler wrote:

> The antique dealer Lippmann left for Holland yesterday morning with some valuables of the Empress and several sailors with whom he maintains a tender liaison. A little satyr play, because L. is able to perform this service for the Empress only by virtue of his relationship with sailors in the Executive Committee who stayed at his house during the revolution.[36]

Monarchist, revolutionary, and "private" passions—who can separate them out here?

"All of Berlin is a seething witches' cauldron in which violence and ideas bubble and stew together," said Kessler.[37] This cauldron was also cooking up a film industry with radical and banal nightmares, sentimentalities and vapidities, scandalous sex films and tear-jerking sagas of love and heartache.

In revolutionary Berlin, nightpieces in the style of *Caligarisme* and "expressionist" film flourished along with Ufa's historical costume dramas; this signaled to the world that in defeated Germany a film art was developing that was disquieting, intriguing, extremely varied, romantic, and thoroughly German.

The first postwar German film sold in the United States, for a price of $40,000, was the Ufa production *Madame Dubarry*, which premiered in New York on December 12, 1920, under the title *Passion*. Two weeks later *The New York Times* estimated the value of the rights at $500,000. The film's immense success confirmed the optimistic predictions made by unconventional American film entrepreneurs that one could "break through the blockade the public and the press had imposed against films from Germany."[38] In the following year, Lubitsch's films *Deception*, *Gypsy Blood*, and *One Arabian Night*—all Ufa productions—reached the American market and prepared the way a little later for other films, such as Robert Wiene's *Das Cabinet des Dr. Caligari* (*The Cabinet of Dr. Caligari*) and Paul Wegener's Golem film. Thus did German film establish a beachhead in the American market.

The hopes of the German revolution had been crushed; the right-wing Kapp putsch against the Republic had passed through Germans' awareness like a specter; and the new chief of the armed forces, Hans von Seeckt, was about to build up an army of 100,000 men. Such was the state of affairs when, in September 1920, President Friedrich Ebert, accompanied by two ministers, some undersecretaries and ministerial councillors, and several members of the Reichstag and the Berlin House of Representatives, staged an official visit to Ernst Lubitsch and his colleagues at Ufa's outdoor filming area in Tempelhof. *Deception* was in production, and on this particular day the coronation procession in front of Westminster Abbey was to be filmed with Emil Jannings and Henny Porten at the head of four thousand extras. Ufa had called in Karl Bratz and Paul Davidson to welcome the head of state, and Lubitsch was expected to pull out all the stops with his direction of crowd scenes. The *Film-Kurier* reported the next day:

> In workman's clothes, his neck free of a collar that might prevent him from using his voice at full force, and often raising the megaphone to his mouth, Lubitsch stood on a big lumber pile along with his assistant directors and camera crew . . . and issued commands to the crowd. The perspective on Westminster Abbey, the mass of people, and the procession with the clergy in full regalia, the knights-at-arms, the nobility and court ladies in all their splendor produced a colorful and lively scene that will not fail of its effect on celluloid.[39]

But what really happened we can learn from the writer Paul Eipper, who was present as a friend of the Porten family. At the sight of the waves of extras—four thousand unemployed workers stuck in English Renaissance costumes—Eipper thought how little it would take to turn them into a boiling sea. The coronation procession had just reached the church portals for the first time when the President and his entourage arrived. It must be said to his credit that he and his companions took their places very modestly on the hill beside Ufa's general staff and, like any other spectators, looked on with interest. But the unemployed workers forgot they were supposed to be English citizens in the time of Henry VIII and remembered instead the misery of their everyday lives. Groups formed and whispered among themselves, and Lubitsch bellowed more than usual. The assistant directors grew red in the face and yanked on the horses' reins, making the animals nervous, but all to no avail: As the procession returned and the crowd was supposed to pour through the city gates, driven along by King Henry's mounted guard, a chain of people formed in front of the gate, shouted "Down with Ebert!" and wouldn't let anyone behind them get through. Lubitsch had the presence of mind to film this genuine excitement but was then completely helpless. The four thousand people clumped together, and the shooting had to stop for the day. An incident that cost a quarter of a million and that never would have occurred if someone had only had wits enough not to keep the extras standing in the hot sun and with empty stomachs from seven in the morning until eleven.[40]

The agitation that so abruptly broke through the fictive framework of the production and into political reality probably had other, more profound social and political causes. After all, the displeasure of the extras was directed not against Ufa niggardliness but against Ebert himself, the highest representative of the Social Democratic power elite by whom millions of German workers already felt betrayed.

Deception cost about 8 million marks. The premiere in the Ufa-Palast am Zoo in December 1920, organized by the Berlin Press Association as a benefit showing, mollified some who were inclined to reproach Ufa for extravagance. Kurt Pinthus calculated in *Das Tage-Buch* that the proceeds from the sale of the American rights alone ($200,000, or 14 million marks) would more than cover production costs. He made no bones of his admiration for the crowd scenes, though he tempered his enthusiasm with a touch of irony: "Surely scenes of this kind can be staged so flawlessly only in Germany. I always have the feeling, with both Reinhardt and Lubitsch, that current theater and film are now reaping the benefits of the old militaristic age. Only a people accustomed to maneuvers can execute crowd scenes so perfectly."[41]

A year later, in the mountains of Goschen, when Lubitsch set Egyptian and Ethiopian armies marching against each other for his production *Das Weib des Pharao* (*The Loves of Pharaoh*), there was again trouble with the extras, who were striking for a hundred instead of sixty marks apiece "and would not return to work until the additional sums they demanded had been fetched from Berlin."[42] The extras were all unemployed workers hoping to earn a little extra to supplement their meager government welfare checks. "The incident is typical," commented *Der Kinematograph* in indignant tones reminiscent of the old ruling elite, and suggested that actual soldiers beef up the crowd scenes, though unfortunately, it added, the military was not at present allowed to participate in movies.

The "old militaristic age" was by no means a thing of the past. In July 1920 Count Kessler noticed a psychological shift in Germany. A "mood antagonistic toward France and for another war" was gaining ground.[43] Large numbers of people, in a nation accustomed to maneuvers, were standing at attention once again, ready once again to be stirred by parades, drill, and columns of disciplined marching troops. It is to Ufa's credit that in the well-orchestrated crowd scenes of its historical costume films, it provided, along with high entertainment value, an effective but fairly harmless outlet for the German love of martial pomp.

5.

Ufa Goes Abroad

TRAVEL movies that took Ufa's big audiences to all the corners of the globe soon followed its lavishly produced historical dramas. Since its founding, of course, the firm's activities abroad had sought neither more nor less than the establishment of a pan-European media empire of vast cultural diversity. At stake was control of film in Central Europe, cinematic hegemony in the countries bordering Germany and into Eastern Europe, and, finally, the creation of a European rival to Hollywood, whose films had already begun to conquer the international market during the war.

On April 12, 1918, Emil Georg von Stauss revealed to Ufa's executive committee plans to bring together under one company Ufa's foreign interests and those of the Deutsche Lichtbild-Gesellschaft. Ufa, of course, would have "exclusive control over all the combine's external activities, and it will form internally an independent foreign department with separate bookkeeping and accounting."[1] Sixty percent of the shares were to be allocated to Ufa, 30 percent to DLG (later increased to 35 percent), and 10 percent to Agfa. Seats on the board of directors were apportioned correspondingly: five members nominated by Ufa, three by DLG, and two by Agfa. In case of a tie vote, the chair, "elected from among the Ufa members," was empowered to decide the issue. The politics of power won out, too, in determining the fields of operations. DLG, the stepchild of heavy industry, suffered a humiliating defeat here: "This foreign branch will control activities everywhere abroad, including the Balkans, which the DLG originally wanted to see excepted because of its interests already established there."

Indeed, it went further than that. After consultation with the executive committee, Chairman Stauss stated "that in the national interest as well as in the expectation of commercial success, Ufa will aggressively assume control of the organization in Russia and in the Balkans." Ufa's management was authorized, "after a careful assessment," to invest 3 million marks in Eastern Europe, including Russia, to acquire motion-picture theaters that drew local and regional audiences. Karl Bratz, the jute manufacturer who represented the board in Ufa's administration, was instructed to go immediately to Bucharest, Sofia, and Constantinople "to initiate prelimi-nary organizational measures and particularly to secure appropriate theaters."

Two months later, at a meeting of June 13, the board authorized still larger sums. The 3 million marks originally earmarked for all of Eastern Europe were now reallocated to Ufa activities in Ukraine alone. Two million each for Russia and Poland were approved; 3 million for investments in Romania, Turkey, and the Caucasus; and another million for Finland. Western Europe was by no means neglected: 2 million were made available for Ufa acquisitions in Holland and Belgium and another 2 million for activities in Scandinavia.

At an executive committee meeting that same day, Stauss expressed in no uncertain terms the annexationist character of this ambitious policy: "In the discussion of foreign initiatives, the chairman stressed that our com-pany's shares should assure us not only a simple majority but the majority required by law or statue to ensure us complete control over the company, even in case of dissolution or merger."[2]

Political and military developments on the eastern front in the first half of 1918 might have seemed to justify such optimism. In February, Germany and Austria-Hungary in an alliance with Turkey concluded a "bread peace" with Ukraine: this was to secure for the Central Powers the "breadbasket of the East" and to force Russia to recognize the Ukrainian state. Trotsky consequently broke off the peace negotiations that had been in progress since the December before, but was obliged in March, after a renewed military advance by the Central Powers, to yield to Germany's terms dic-tated to him in the Treaty of Brest-Litovsk. The young Soviet Union not only agreed to economic concessions but also renounced any claims to Poland and the Baltic regions. In addition, it was obliged to recognize Fin-land and Ukraine as independent states. Then in May 1918 the Treaty of Bucharest obliged Romania to cede a large territory to Austria's ally Bulgaria and to guarantee Germany utilization of Romania's oil fields. The situation in the east and southeast seemed tailor-made to reawaken the enterprising spirit of German capital and to refocus its attention on markets it had believed lost.

Only a few months later the situation had changed decisively. In early November, with the war lost and revolution at home, the basis for Ufa's acquisition strategy in the Balkans was gone. At a November 4 meeting of the executive committee, Bratz asked that "the new factors posed by the unhappy result of the war for Germany be taken into account."[3] It had to be considered in the management of the firm's finances "that because of the blocking off of the Balkans and other areas where we have interests, income we had counted on will not be forthcoming." At a board meeting the next day, Bratz steered a clear course away from the propaganda commission of the Supreme Command. "Management has been intent on phasing out one-sided militaristic propaganda and shaping film enterprise abroad in such a way that it can work effectively for peace, for German culture, and for German industry and trade."[4] Given the turn of events, Bratz no doubt thought it useful to have it recorded in the minutes that Germany's largest film company was preparing its retreat from the military complex. He was giving voice to that well-known civilian, businessman's mistrust of military leadership, a mistrust that had already taken root in Ufa's board and management.

Still, at the end of 1919, Ufa's enterprises abroad showed a positive balance overall. The minutes of an executive committee meeting on December 30 note: "A point of particular interest that emerges from the figures is that the increase in value of our shares abroad exceeds by more than 5 million marks our losses on foreign commitments."[5]

However, that same Karl Bratz who was primarily responsible for the company's flourishing expansion abroad drew chairman Stauss's anger. Though his "indefatigable diligence" and "outstanding abilities" were beyond question,

> it has become increasingly clear that Herr Bratz's temperament is not well suited to the discipline necessary in a stockholding company. Apart from his failure to supply his management colleagues with adequate information and his disregard for orderly business procedures, his major fault is his readiness to take risks on his own authority.

What drew this criticism were operations Bratz had initiated in the United States. With the American agent Ben Blumenthal and Famous Players and Chaplin, Bratz had concluded contracts for distributing American films in Germany without giving Ufa's management the specific details. But his most serious transgression was violating a management resolution "to avoid under any circumstances" making contracts in foreign currencies. Stauss saw Bratz's freewheeling style as a threat to Ufa's future, but ever-increasing competition with Hollywood threatened, and for the time being, the delinquent remained in office; in subsequent years he would prove indispensable.

Ufa negotiated contracts with Moscow for supplying films in Ukraine, and through its subsidiary in Constantinople, the Balkan-Orient-Filmgesellschaft, it even put in an appearance in Turkey. With its investments in Apollo Film in Vienna, and Corvin Filmfabrik and Budapest Projektograph in Budapest, it gained influence in the Austrian and Hungarian markets.

Its foreign productions were also valuable to Ufa's growing distribution organization and its theaters, and it opened up new markets for its own films. In 1924, Ufa acquired a majority interest in the Westi-Film Società

Anonima Italiana in Rome (henceforth renamed Ufa-Film Società Anonima Italiana), and a significant interest in the Alliance Cinematographique Européenne in Paris. All in all, however, this impressive "expansion in all directions"[6] was soon to put the company in an extremely difficult financial position.

6.

Early Monumentalism: On the Way to Becoming a Major Film Power

"AN audience of millions that comes, lives, and disappears, that has no name and yet is there, that—on the move in its immense mass— will shape everything, and that we must therefore win control of. There is no other means but the cinema." Carlo Mierendorff, writer, editor of the political magazine *Das Tribunal*, and until 1933 press secretary to the Hessian Minister of the Interior Wilhelm Leuschner, wrote these words in 1920.[1] *Hätte ich das Kino!* (*If I Had the Cinema!*) was the title of a pamphlet of his that was later often quoted:

> *It expands into all the regions of the earth, reaches the remote corners of continents.*
> *A crystal ball, may the cinema span the entire globe.*
> *Gazing into the zenith, may the poles behold each other.*
> *May good and evil flash across the heavens, warning, doing battle.*
> *The last one-eyed man in the northern and southern hemispheres will not escape me.*
> *Whoever has the cinema will lift the world off its hinges.*

But it was not expressionist artists, literary visionaries, or leftist intellectuals who "had" the cinema. Some of them were part of its production machinery, but who *really* had control of German cinema? It was hardly the state, even though the state did reintroduce moderate censorship with the Reich Motion Picture Law of May 12, 1920, to discourage films that tended "to endanger public order or safety, to offend religious sensibilities, to have a brutalizing or demoralizing effect, or to endanger Germany's prestige or its relations with foreign states."[2] Apart from some socialist elements pressing for the nationalization of film production and the communalizing of theaters, the shifting government coalitions of the young Weimar Republic had no interest in direct control over the film industry.

This reluctance to get involved from the political quarter became very clear when in 1921 the government gave up—which is to say, gave back to the German Bank—the shares in Ufa that it had acquired in the Ludendorff era.

The reasons that prompted this move are documented in a memorandum that clearly illuminates the overall relationship between the state and the film industry. The author began by asserting that Ufa had become "very well organized," and able to offset "the harmful effects of contracts too hastily concluded with foreign firms." However, "given the general situation of the film industry, no profit could be expected in the next few years." The government's continuing influence on Ufa was desirable, although the company's "active propaganda effort" had been reduced. But Ufa's growing need for credit required an increase of capital from 25 to 100 million marks, and the Finance Ministry had said that was out of the question. It was therefore recommended "that the primary stockholder (or consortium) take over the Reich's interests and that the Reich withdraw completely from the enterprise." The primary stockholder was, of course, the German Bank. Through its agency, the government considered its influence "absolutely secure." If the bank would "assume a binding obligation to follow the government's instructions in certain respects," the government was prepared to unload its stock even "at its present below-par price, provided the government's goals can be achieved in that way."[3]

The transaction went off without a hitch. The governing coalitions in the next few years had no interest in issuing "instructions" on how Ufa should be managed, and the subjection of the film industry to strong government control was not a topic of discussion for many years—until Ufa's management itself brought that subjection about.

No group of people, much less any individual, had control over the German cinema in the early 1920s, neither the banks that backed the film companies nor their officers, who often sat on the companies' boards. Cinema was a great project into which heterogeneous entities poured their energies with differing influence, goals, and success. Among those entities the Universum-Film AG, only a few years old, had a position of uncontested leadership. It rightly claimed in its distribution catalogue for 1922–23:

> In its totality, Ufa is recognized as setting the standards in the European film industry, and it owes this reputation not only to its financial strength and superiority but even more to the systematic development of all its productive resources, the most important of which are its creative artists themselves.[4]

We should remember, however, that economic and political circumstances were hardly favorable to an expanding film industry. As early as 1919 skyrocketing prices throughout the economy affected film producers. Agfa's threatened price rise of 50 percent for raw film led to heated debate in the industry. The *Lichtbild-Bühne* published calculations that showed how Union's production costs per meter of negative film rose from 24 marks in 1917 to 69 marks in a year.[5] As a result of increased production costs—of course passed on to the distributors and theater owners—the latter decided in May 1920 to raise the price of the cheapest ticket to 2.50 marks. Enjoying movies—until now well within the financial capabilities of the working class—became expensive.

Rising wages as well as taxes and other state-imposed costs gave additional cause for worry. After weeks of negotiation, a wage contract for film-industry employees was hammered out in early May 1919, but by January 1920 the film union was demanding a 100 percent increase over the minimum wage previously agreed upon. In April it called a strike of the workers in the Berlin companies; and the Munich theater owners decided to strike when the city councillors there imposed heavy new tax demands on movie theaters (they reopened only after the city council said it would work out a compromise). Other government decrees, too, provoked determined resistance and had to be partially rescinded. In 1920, for example, the industry intervened to reduce to 2 percent an export tariff on exposed film originally set at 10 percent.

The politically imposed limitations on postwar exports seemed to affect producers less than distributors directly involved in foreign sales. In any case, the limitations prompted distributors in the German film industry to form an export association in mid-1920. On the other side, the victorious powers had seen to it that import regulations serving their interests were included in the 1919 Treaty of Versailles. "During the first six months after the peace treaty becomes effective, imports from countries of the allied and associated powers may not have higher tariffs imposed on them than were in effect on July 31, 1914. For 30 months after that, these terms will apply to all goods included in the German tariff agreement in effect on July 31, 1914."[6] So the blanket regulation was applied to film imports, too, and it was perceived in Germany, where the currency had been devalued and prices had rapidly risen, as part of a "humiliating, dictatorial" treaty. The German filmmakers' greatest fear, however, was that they would be undone by foreign competitors, to whom the treaty gave such a huge advantage. They therefore protested vigorously in late 1919, when foreign films were shown for the first time after the war in the occupied Rhineland. A year later, the Ministry of Commerce limited film imports to 15 percent of the total distributed in Germany. The percentage was of linear measure; the Ministry calculated that 180,000 meters of celluloid could be imported.

The film business was meanwhile adversely affected by other factors: an energy crisis and the turbulence associated with the right-wing Kapp putsch, which, the *Film Yearbook* of March 1920 noted, "temporarily interrupted the orderly conduct of film business."[7] A general strike, called in response to the putsch attempt, reduced to practically nothing the attendance at a film fair mounted for the first time in connection with the industrial fair in Leipzig. In November 1919, movie theaters in Kiel and other cities had been temporarily closed for lack of coal, and in Berlin showing times were reduced for the same reason.

Then there was the new motion-picture law, which made the entire industry uneasy; in June 1920 a heavily attended protest meeting took place in the Ufa-Palast am Zoo, primarily to protest the newly required barring of juveniles from film attendance. Then, too, the unrealistic debate about socializing the industry fueled heated discussions that were more disturbing than productive. The film industry had a far from united (defensive) front on this issue. Max Seckelsohn, for example, chairman of the film manufacturers' cartel, favored communalizing theaters—"owing to his membership in the USPD," as the *Yearbook* presumed[8]—and declared them ripe for socialization. In August 1919, the representative assembly of Baden passed a resolution calling for the nationalization of the film industry—but it was a declaration of intent that remained without consequences. Supported by the Berlin Chamber of Commerce, the associations guarding the interests of theater owners fought vigorously against any and all nationalization proposals; in May 1920 the Reichstag rejected several socialization bills. For lack of any new, realistic ideas, the debate was for all practical purposes dead.

Despite these irritations and threats, Ufa's capital accumulated and activities expanded briskly in the first postwar years. In October 1919, the decision was made to expand Bioscop—at the time under the artistic direction of Richard Oswald—to an enterprise worth 30 million marks. A little later, in March 1920, Bioscop merged with Decla, founded by Erich Pommer, to form Decla-Bioscop, the second-largest German film company and artistically the most interesting production studio of the early postwar period. (Shortly before this, Decla had absorbed Meinert-Film.) Increases in capital stock linked with takeovers of smaller firms occurred in Münchenchener Lichtspielkunst, too, and in the Deutsche Lichtbild-Gesellschaft, which changed its name to Deulig-Film in October 1920. Its chief executive, Ludwig Klitzsch, Alfred Hugenberg's energetic viceroy and later Ufa's chief executive, had for the time being withdrawn from the film business, however, to run the Scherl publishing concern.

Ufa, meanwhile, continued to pursue its policy of vertical expansion in a cautious yet purposeful manner. Messter, Union, and Nordisk were the foundation of the empire, but it was soon enlarged by the acquisition of other small and middle-sized firms: Bolten-Baeckers, Gloria, and Maxim. In 1920 Ufa took over Frankfurter-Film, a distributor, and thus made its own distribution company, Universum-Filmverleih, more competitive. Years later, Ufa also acquired Martin Dentler in Braunschweig, as well as its distributor, also the big copying facility of the Tempelhof Aktiengesellschaft für Filmfabrikation (Afifa).

The studios, too, increased and expanded. The production of monumental films gave the studios a fantastic atmosphere in which the ancient Orient mingled helter-skelter with the Italian Renaissance and yearnings for a utopian paradise blended with the nostalgia of a nation that had lost its colonies.

On the spacious grounds of the Ufa studio, whole palaces and exotic city streets sprang up. Imitations of the Palazzo Vecchio, the Palazzo degli Uffizi, the Loggia dei Lanzi, and other opulent buildings were constructed with fidelity to the originals. Space enough for ten to fifteen thousand extras allowed for mass scenes. Indian, Chinese, African, ancient Roman, and Babylonian wonders sprang up, too. With these films, Germany claimed its right, for the first time after its defeat, to be regarded as a major world film power.[9]

When Rudolf Oertel wrote those sentences in 1941, Germany's dreams of being a major world power had again become bloody reality, and once again her imperial yearnings, which in Ufa's exotic monumental films had been colored over with curiosity and a yen for far-off lands, were driving her toward a catastrophe unparalleled in history.

Ufa was indebted not only to Lubitsch for its first monumental films but also to May-Film, with whose acquisition Ufa also obtained a large studio in Weissensee and a tract of land in Woltersdorf.[10] Joe May—born in Vienna; his real name was Joseph Mandel—had been working in Germany since 1911. Kurt Pinthus called him a "universal film man," adding that his "determination and energy as a director, executive, and businessman have earned him a place in the progressive leadership of German film."[11] During the final months of the war, Ufa invested 750,000 marks in May's episodic three-part film *Veritas vincit*: this was in Kracauer's view "a gigantic nonentity which resorted to the theory of transmigration of souls to drag a love story through three pompously staged historic ages,"[12] but for Oskar Kalbus it "drew the attention of the entire world to the German film industry for the first time."[13] A year later May followed this by a film in no less than eight parts: *Die Herrin der Welt* (*The Mistress of the World*); directed by Uwe Jens Krafft and Karl Gerhardt under May's artistic supervision, it starred Mia May, Michael Bohnen, and Hans Mierendorff. "Near the Woltersdorf locks in the suburbs of Berlin, May bought about fifty acres of land with hills, valleys, woods, and a lake. Here he would construct China, America, Africa, half the world."[14] Ufa's strategy of economic expansion found a counterpart in its production strategy and in the global space-and-time adventures of its early monumental films.

In addition to buying entire companies or the majority of their stock, Ufa also used production contracts to bring producers under its control. It made production agreements of this type—on terms it dictated—with Cserepy-

Film (later the Film-Gesellschaft am Dönhoffplatz), the Fern-Andra Ver-triebsgesellschaft, Musia-Film, Gloria-Film, Ossi-Oswalda-Film, and Rex Film, founded by Lupu Pick. All these small firms, founded during and after the war, were in financial difficulties because of inflation. Association with Ufa assured them of survival, though of course it took away a measure of their independence. Thus it became increasingly difficult for prominent artists to escape Ufa's clutches. For example, in early 1921 Henny Porten was under contract with Lubitsch-Produktion to make *Die Bergkatze* (*The Mountain Cat*) but was trying to break that contract and accept a new one with Gloria-Film; the monopolistic acquisition policy of the industry leader made her an Ufa star once again.

Like all German film companies in these difficult years, Ufa was fighting for its life, but it fought under the motto that a good offense is the best defense. It took the offensive in expanding its bases of operations and in dealing with its competition, and it looked to the future and to the lucrative possibilities offered by foreign markets. At the end of 1919, the balance sheet of Ufa's distribution and theater organizations showed a clear profit of 8 million marks (it had been "only" 4.8 million in 1918).[15] The com-pany's "gigantomania," its drive to expand, and its penchant for doing things on a grand scale seemed a sound strategy for survival before inflation set in. Of course, its position was secure because of its (still) stable capital base and its vital ties to the German Bank.

When the Ministry of Finance unloaded its shares in 1921 and important shareholders like Prince Henkel von Donnersmarck and Robert Bosch put their Ufa stock on the market, the German Bank bought up the stock and averted a possible disaster for the company. But this also meant that "the company gradually became a purely German enterprise of a completely private nature."[16] According to one account, the policy of the German Bank and notably of its chief, Stauss, was driven by a kind of Nibelungen fidelity to Ufa and "the idea of national film production."[17]

That statement correctly expresses the truth that everything Germany's leading bank did was always attended by political considerations. And it is correct, too, that the bank's chief executive—"the leading figure in the German Bank between the wars"[18]—had clear political views. Stauss him-self may never have produced an Ufa film, nor did he ever personally or directly issue guidelines for Ufa's production planning. But the German Bank's majority interest in Ufa was not without influence. It was a formative element in the political and cultural power structure of the Weimar Re-public, as well as in that "battle of the one Germany against the other" that so dominated German politics and culture before 1933.

The American military government drew a portrait of Stauss after the Second World War, in the course of its investigations of the German Bank, and that portrait is admirably direct. Well before Hitler, it says, this man's outlook was characterized by "extreme nationalism and militarism."[19] Even before 1914, when his bank had persistently and successfully supported

German oil interests in Romania and the Near East, he was regarded as a "political banker." After 1918 Stauss made the financial resources of his bank available for the rebuilding of the German aircraft and aircraft-engine industries, and helped to found Lufthansa. After 1925, as a member of the boards of the Bayerische Motorenwerke (BMW) and Daimler-Benz, he developed a lively interest in German rearmament. "When he was elected to the German Reichstag in 1930," the U.S. military government's warrant continues,

> Stauss, still chief executive of the German Bank, aligned himself with the reactionary group of industrialists and financiers who gave Hitler financial support before his rise to power and then helped him take over the reins of government. By that time, Stauss was already a member of the NSDAP. He had personal contact with Hitler, Goebbels, and Schacht and was a good friend of Hermann Göring, who shared Stauss's interest in aviation. Hitler not only made Stauss vice president of the Reichstag but showered him later with honors and titles.[20]

Harry Kessler met Stauss on the evening of January 30, 1933, in the Hotel Kaiserhof and noted how he "boasted of his close relationship with Hitler. Hitler had promised to fulfill for him any wish Stauss brought to his attention."[21]

Stauss's involvement with Ufa was a small but fitting link in the chain of his varied political activities. The blending of economic and political power, the control over big industrial empires, the ties to the military complex, and the close contact with those who happened to be in political power at any given moment—all these may have fueled his desire for a "total" domination that included the complicated business of manipulating public consciousness and mood. The idea of "national film production," insofar as it intrigued him, had its logical roots in these other interests. BMW, Daimler-Benz, Lufthansa—why not Ufa, too? In the mentality of a Stauss the ideological schematic of the Supreme Command and battlefield philosophy à la Ludendorff was carried over intact. For a technocrat accustomed to the direct and directorial exercise of power, the idea of using Ufa as an instrument in the strategy of power politics and in the realization of his own political ambitions was obvious.

But complicated structures like film companies react to economic pressures and political directives only indirectly, which is to say, in complicated and very contradictory ways. Ufa's physiognomy, its astonishing productivity, and the dazzling variety of its movies in the early postwar years cannot be ascribed solely to its favorable finances, and even less to the German Bank, no matter what blanket judgments, like those Kracauer formed in 1947, continue to appear. For example,

> Ludendorff had the Ufa colossus hammered together out of different film companies and under the leadership of the German Bank in order to

counter the enemy's successful films with Germany's own film propaganda. The company was a holdover from the war and *continued, so to speak, to exist independently of the republic.* Its loyalty was not to [Germany] . . . but to its backers, the banks, and industry.[22]

Such a judgment is highly problematic. It overlooks the differentiated and often troubled accommodations made between economic power and productive forces in the "ideas business," the resistance, the attrition, the many ideological and psychological imponderables—all the factors that interfere so powerfully with a direct causal relation between economy and culture. Stauss and his close associates did not sit on the planning staff of Ufa or in its dramaturgical offices. They were in no position to issue orders to the directors or actors, or to the production directors, set designers, cameramen, or screenplay writers. For all their power, they were abstract rulers over an empire that was difficult to survey and recalcitrant by its very nature.

In 1921, when the German Bank took over the majority interest in Ufa's stock, Ufa's board elected Dr. Felix Kallmann as the new chief executive; he was a former executive of the Deutsche Gasglühlicht-Aktiengesellschaft (German Gaslight Co.). That year a merger began to take shape that would enrich the company with an unparalleled infusion of artistic and intellectual talent. In June, initially unsuccessful negotiations between Ufa's banks and Decla-Bioscop had broken off, but in October things began to move. Ufa published its balance sheets for its fiscal year (which ended in May) showing profits of about 8.5 million marks and capital stock of 25 million. Decla-Bioscop rejected a takeover bid from National-Film in July, and merger negotiations between National-Film and Ufa also proved fruitless. On October 11, however, Decla-Bioscop stockholders voted for a merger with Ufa, and in November, Ufa's stockholders approved management's balance sheet, gave its blessing to a dividend distribution of 12 percent, and approved the merger with Decla-Bioscop. Now nothing stood in the way of the two largest and most productive German film companies joining forces. The merger was formally sealed in June 1922 with the controlling interest in the new Decla-Bioscop now in the hands of Ufa, and Ufa became the assignee of the old Decla-Bioscop.[23]

After the merger with Decla-Bioscop, Ufa not only owned two new distribution companies with several branches but could also move into the Bioscop studios in Neubabelsberg. Soon the company expanded them, creating the legendary "Ufa film city," the company's major fortress in its competitive war against Hollywood. At the same time, Ufa took into its ranks still more of the elite of German film: the directors Ludwig Berger, Johannes Guter, Carl Froelich, Fritz Lang, F. W. Murnau, Robert Reinert, and Fritz Wendhausen; Germany's first modern production chief, Erich

Pommer; screenplay writers with the unlimited imagination of a Thea von Harbou and the genius of a Carl Mayer; highly talented architects like Robert Herlth, Walter Röhrig, Hermann Warm, Otto Hunte, Rochus Gliese, and Erich Czerwonski, all devoted to satisfying the eye of the camera; cameramen and pioneers of visual experimentation like Karl Freund, Carl Hoffmann, Axel Graatkjär, Fritz Arno Wagner, and Erich Waschneck; an army of beloved actors and actresses prominent in their specialties and ranging from Lil Dagover to Aud Egede Nissen and Grete Berger, from Agnes Straub to Gertrud Welcker, Paul Richter to Rudolf Klein-Rogge, Alfred Abel, Bernhard Goetzke, Paul Hartmann, Gustav von Wangenheim; Anton Edthofer to Werner Krauss and Hermann Thimig. Overnight, all of them were reunited under the roof of this huge company. This multitude of different talents and temperaments, which in the coming years made Ufa the liveliest film production company in Europe, troubled themselves little with whether the change in ownership had brought a "change in direction" or not.[24]

On October 7, 1921, a Decla-Bioscop film premiered simultaneously in the Ufa-Theater on Kurfürstendamm and in the Mozart Hall on Nollendorfplatz (here accompanied with music by Giuseppe Becce). With this film, Decla-Bioscop brought its era of independent production to a triumphant conclusion and at the same time displayed the dowry it was bringing to its union with Ufa. The film was Fritz Lang's *Der müde Tod* (*Destiny*), "a German folk song in six verses," based on a book by Lang's future wife, Thea von Harbou. The film contains Venetian, Near Eastern, and Chinese episodes (filmed by Fritz Arno Wagner as cameraman and staged outdoors in Neubabelsberg by Robert Herlth and Hermann Warm); Walter Röhrig constructed the buildings for the old German scene that frames the episodic flashbacks. Lil Dagover and Werner Janssen played the immortal lovers and Bernhard Goetzke the incarnation of Death. Other stars excelled in supporting roles: Max Adalbert and Hermann Picha, Georg John and Grete Berger, Eduard von Winterstein and Rudolf Klein-Rogge, Lothar Müthel, Lina Paulsen, and Paul Biensfeldt. This film went unappreciated by some critics, but it started Fritz Lang on his way to artistic success and evoked enthusiastic audience response, especially after its appearance in France: "You who believe in the future of cinema, see this movie! You who mistrust the cinema, you more than anyone else should see this film . . . for you will be the guest of a new muse, a guest of film!"[25]

Decla or Decla-Bioscop had produced some of Lang's early films: *Half Blood* (1919), the two-part *Die Spinnen* (*The Spiders*, 1919), *Harakiri* (1919), and *Die Vier um die Frau* (*Four Suitors, One Woman*, 1920–21). With the Robert Wiene films *The Cabinet of Dr. Caligari* (1919) and *Genuine* (1920) Decla or Decla-Bioscop had initiated that trend in early postwar cinematography that—with its plots borrowed from a dark romanticism, its demonic figures obsessed with power, its expressionistically conceived sets,

and its "magical" light-and-shadow directing—provided later interpreta-
tions with proof that the Germans had set out on a fascinating and dangerous path not only in their films but also in their wish projections and
delusionary ideas.

In early 1920 Decla devised for its Caligari film some unusual advertising
methods that broke new ground. On advertising pillars, in cafés, and in the
subway, posters with the challenge "You must become Caligari!" announced to the people of Berlin a film that the poet Ernst Angel called a
dive from overblown mysticism into the realm "of Protestant moral enlightenment."[26] That same year Decla tried out a "multimedia" marketing strategy that larger companies later made a key element in their business policy.
A contract with the publisher Ullstein stipulated that a number of Ullstein's
most successful adventure novels would be made into movies as "Uco-
films." An example is F. W. Murnau's *Schloss Vogelöd* (*Vogelöd Castle*),
which premiered in April 1921 in the Marmorhaus as the second Uco-Film.
Carl Mayer based the screenplay on a novel by Rudolf Stratz that was being
serialized at this same time in the Ullstein paper *Berliner Illustrieter*. The
premiere took place just before the last installment appeared. Literature of
a higher caliber underwent the same transformation, which was not simply
a matter of "making a book into a movie." Murnau's *Phantom*, based on
the novel of the same title by Gerhart Hauptmann, also appeared as an
Uco-Film. The Berlin premiere on November 13, 1922, in the Ufa-Palast
am Zoo, was staged as the film industry's homage to Hauptmann in celebration of his sixtieth birthday.

A little less than a year before the merger of Ufa and Decla-Bioscop, a
German-American tiff threw into relief the competition with Hollywood.
In December 1920 Paul Davidson terminated his contract with Ufa and
announced that he and Ernst Lubitsch would found their own production
company and, if interest was forthcoming, also work with the Americans.
The success in the United States of Lubitsch's *Passion* guaranteed that
such interest was indeed forthcoming, as were financially attractive offers
to the director and his leading performers Pola Negri, Emil Jannings, Paul
Wegener, and Harry Liedtke.

Samuel Rachman and Ben Blumenthal and their Hamilton Theatrical
Corporation had opened the way for the astonishing success of the Dubarry
movie, a quite exotic film for American tastes at the time. Adolph Zukor,
founder of the Famous Players company and a business ally of Rachman
and Blumenthal, had become aware of European talent and of the attractive possibilities of the European market, and in early 1921 he was instrumental in founding the European Film Alliance (EFA), with Paul Davidson
and Karl Bratz as its presidents. EFA remained no more than a marginal
note in the history of film, but it nevertheless made possible Lubitsch's
film *The Loves of Pharaoh*, and the departure of the Lubitsch team for the
United States initiated the first Ufa exodus to Hollywood.

In *Das Tage-Buch*, Leopold Schwarzschild gave a vivid account of the shaky beginnings of EFA and what happened thereafter:

> Sami Rachman, a former variety impresario from somewhere in Galicia, arrives alone and equipped with carte blanche and takes a suite in Berlin's finest hotel. . . . He makes new contracts, buys manuscripts, forbids Davidson and Lubitsch to enter their offices; he scolds, bribes, dresses down, deals under the table, fights with everybody, soon has seven lawyers hard at work on libel and civil suits, deliriously tosses money out the window, runs things so far into the ground that his American colleagues break with him and he is finally summoned back to the States, leaving total chaos in his wake. Mr. Blumenthal and his brother Ike appear to replace Rachman, and they announce that "a period of solid work" will now begin. But very little has been left to work with.[27]

Lubitsch was in the meantime already in the promised land. He, having

> completed *The Loves of Pharaoh*, had prudently traveled to America with Davidson before the Rachman ruckus and been assured there that his company would be totally independent of EFA and directly under the Hamilton Corporation. And so the world was surprised to learn that the only EFA film actually completed during that riotous period was ultimately not an EFA film at all.

Ufa's great subsequent successes could at first compensate for the loss suffered from Lubitsch's departure. But once Paramount and Metro-Goldwyn-Mayer advanced into the European market, it became clear how labile this construct of art and commerce, money and passion, business sense and avant-garde thinking that constituted Ufa actually was. Despite its "American" behavior, Ufa was born of European culture, and it attracted the theater people, writers, and visual artists of its time. But at the same time, it was vulnerable to "American" temptations: the almost religious belief that with more money everything could be done better; the priority of profit over culture; the tendency to tame by standardization the unpredictable product that is film. For several years Ufa kept these contradictions in admirable balance, thanks to an unsurpassed concentration of intelligence, artistic talent, and technical and organizational imagination that it never achieved again. So it was that the "great epoch of German film" before 1933 did indeed coincide with Ufa's early blossoming—a fact either suppressed or, just as questionably, apologetically glorified in film historiography. Ufa's economic power, all but complete political independence, and artistic resources assured German film the privilege of cultural autonomy for a short time—that is, before it became the object of American desire and, later, the instrument of Fascist experiments in national education.

7.

The Allure of Distant Lands:
Inflation and Expansion

"UNEMPLOYMENT, inflation, strikes, utility failures, and partisan battles held sway over country and city. . . . Shortages of coal and other factors precipitated such unfavorable conditions that many film theaters had to shut down, while others were converted into shelters for the unemployed."[1] Traditional film histories usually limit to summaries of this kind their comments on the actual situation during the years after the First World War with their extreme social and political conditions. And indeed, the astonishing rise of Ufa remains an abstract fact if considered apart from the context of everyday events. But parallel and contrasting montages will help us see that this mighty cultural empire developed in a context of impending societal breakdown and frightful mass suffering.

In October 1919 Bruno Stümke, editor of the *Berliner Tageblatt,* wrote an editorial, "Cinema, Cabaret, and the Housing Shortage." Alarmed by the report "that in recent days alone 615—that is, spelled out in words, six hundred and fifteen!—applications to open new movie theaters in Berlin had been made, he recommended that they be rejected on the grounds "that so-and-so many hundred thousand families are homeless and that the halls rented for such enterprises should immediately be made serviceable as shelters." Stümke went even further and asked whether the "thousands upon thousands of movie theaters" in Berlin and in Germany as a whole "really serve any pressing need. Why not invoke eminent domain?" *Der Kinematograph* was quick to make an angry response: "With a wave of the hand the gentleman dismisses an honorable trade and passes on to the order of the day."[2]

Stümke had not considered (and *Der Kinematograph* understandably did not mention either) that both urban and rural movie theaters were already providing many unemployed and homeless people with emergency shelter, places to sleep, and opportunities to warm themselves—provided they had the price of admission. For the subproletariat, and even more the workers, regular attendance at the movies had long since become an unaffordable luxury.

In November Harry Kessler published photographs from the slums in the north and east of the capital along with an appeal, "Children's Hell in Berlin," in which he called attention to the impending "destruction of a people":

> Hundreds of thousands of Germans, millions of German children are living in this kind of misery today. It has slowly crept upward—from the lumpenproletariat to the unemployed, from the unemployed to the small tradesmen and pensioners, from them up into the ranks of blue-collar and white-collar workers with middle-class incomes.[3]

For critical observers like Kessler the physical decline of so much of the population was not just a theoretical possibility. They saw a different reality than did the people of west Berlin, where new movie theaters were popping up out of the ground. In their judgment, "the German working people who were once so energetic and hardworking"[4] were literally dying, while the film industry flourished and looked for a new clientele with more disposable income.

Inflation had become the scourge of the entire country. With equal force it struck the just and the unjust, the rich and the poor, the exploiter and the exploited. Not even the new cathedrals of leisure were spared. "Following on the phase of Ufa's first expansion came a time of grave financial difficulties that began with the inflationary period. Ufa suffered greatly from the devastating effects of inflation."[5] Thus wrote Rita Lipschütz in 1932 in the first chronicle of the company. But a company like Ufa, capable of "securities substitution," as economists' jargon puts it, could respond to inflationary trends in a different way than a tradesman's shop or someone who had only his labor to sell. It could set into motion a complex machinery involving financial and stock manipulations to offset what was at first a creeping, then a galloping, currency devaluation and, where possible, even turn it to advantage.

"Encouraged by the company's essentially vigorous business"[6] Ufa's top management attempted to keep pace with the currency devaluations of 1921–23 with drastic infusions of capital. In the spring of 1921 capital stock had been increased from 25 million to 100 million marks. On the securities market, 65,000 new Ufa shares had been offered at 1,000 marks each, also 10,000 shares of preferred stock that gave their owners eight votes (later raised to twelve) in elections of directors, on proposed changes to the by-laws, and in case of a possible dissolving of the company. In November 1921, Ufa doubled its capital stock to 200 million marks, again by issuing new stock. Still another infusion in October 1923 raised capital to 300 million.

In the meantime, at the height of the inflation, the exchange rate for one dollar reached 4.2 billion marks, an astronomical number that reflected the situation of the ruined middle class, especially those with lifetime savings or small stock holdings—theirs was a devastating and ultimately incomprehensible fate. Anyone without real property—and that meant most Germans—was reduced to hopeless poverty. And when currency stabilization was finally instituted, it included forgiveness of debt for the owners of real property.

The introduction of the Rentenmark (the basic unit of currency in 1923–24) and a little later the Reichsmark (1924–48) put Ufa on a new, quite favorable financial basis. Its capital stock was set at 45 million marks; the value of 1,000-mark shares was lowered to 150; the 5,000-mark shares to 600. Its financial situation after the currency reform—in comparison with many businesses that went under—was relatively stable, and the financial difficulties after 1924 were not, or not primarily, attributable to inflation.

Inflation and film—this topic has often preoccupied film historians and prompted theories that one analyst has formulated thus:

> People went to the movies more often because there was nothing at home but hunger and cold. Some theaters were not heated, of course, but it's always warmer in a crowd, and in addition events on the screen enabled one to forget one's own troubles. In the inflation years, movie theaters became refuges for many tormented people. The producers, theater owners, and distributors consciously exploited this situation. They knew what spiritual nourishment to offer their starving audiences.[7]

The question of how "consciously" the film industry exploited this situation will have to remain unanswered here—but the lack of unity within the industry must be stressed. Theater owners fought with distributors over prices; distributors engaged in permanent guerrilla warfare against producers. And as for the "spiritual nourishment" that the industry offered its demoralized public, it cannot be explained solely on the basis of the economic situation. The traumatic experiences of loss and futility in those first years after the war and the political climate of the early Weimar Republic made for a mood that welcomed "diversion" but also needed reassurance and a lifting of spirits.

To the detriment of the "Weimar coalition," made up of the majority Socialists, the Democratic Party, and the Center, the Reichstag elections of June 6, 1920, heightened the already intense polarization between the camps of the right and the left. Ebert and Scheidemann's Social Democratic Party had neither the political élan nor the intellectual energies needed to transform the times and create the basis for a lasting democratic culture in Germany. Their petit-bourgeois, bureaucratic thinking, their readiness to cut deals with the forces of reaction, and the policeman's posture they assumed when faced with revolutionary or radically democratic impulses brought down on them in equal measure the scorn of the right and the hatred of the left.

With the support of army troops, police forces, and the radically right-wing Free Corps units, the SPD had put down the Spartacists, the Munich soviet republic, the Berlin workers' rebellion of 1920, the Communist uprising in central Germany in March 1921, and finally the Hamburg uprising of 1923. For its part, the overpowered left stared as if hypnotized at the trail of blood left behind by the Social Democratic policy of violence and fancied itself in the pose of tragic martyrdom. It seemed unable to break out of its revolutionary attitude and to join in the work of forming a sound democracy.

The state and social institutions, especially the armed forces and the judicial system, were deeply resistant to democratic efforts at reform and remained important supports for extreme reaction. The class justice of the Weimar Republic, with its fateful consequences for the political equilibrium of the body politic, has often been described. It is equally important to ask what effects it had on the form, content, and daily routine of public life; on Weimar's self-image and the history of consciousness; on the cultural projects of the republic—and on the republic *as* a cultural project.

Consciously or unconsciously, the millions of have-nots must have felt the repeated pattern that resolved social conflict in favor of the haves as a mockery. It weighed like a nightmare on Weimar's political and cultural life. It radicalized the losers and sent them in droves to demagogues and dream merchants in extremist camps.

"But a sense for politics surely cannot develop in an atmosphere of constant frustration or in the face of a conviction that everything is mere theater," Peter Gay has written.[8] That "high-level politics" was only a spectacle, a gigantic machination for the purpose of deceit was a belief held by many Germans even before 1914. Now, after the immense frustration of the lost war, it prevailed among great masses of the population. Quixotic political showmen of the ultra-right camp and East Prussian aristocrats with dangerous ambitions and egos big enough for the stage reinforced the sense that with the proclamation of the democratic Weimar constitution the curtain had gone up on a chaotic third-rate play. When the East Prussian official Wolfgang Kapp staged a putsch attempt in March 1920, Harry Kessler noted, "That all sounds more like tomfoolery than like serious history."[9] And when Kessler learned that Ludendorff had been part of the Kapp putsch, he wrote in utter dismay:

> The thought that political incompetence of these proportions determined in dictatorial fashion our fate from 1916 to 1918, in the most dreadful moment of German history, is devastating. . . . The present illuminates the past with a terrifying light. We fell victim not to great, unfortunate generals but to political idiots and confidence men. This escapade retro-

spectively besmirches our history. Ludendorff sinks to the level of a brilliant idiot savant who was at the same time a reckless gambler playing an
all-or-nothing game, the military equivalent of the "German professor"
who out of obsession with his subject sloughs off all ethical obligations,
indeed, abandons all reason, a tragicomic figure as the key player in events
that meant life or death for his country.[10]

This brilliant idiot savant and all-or-nothing gambler—who in November
1923 joined Adolf Hitler in leading the march against the government to
seize the Munich Field Marshal's Hall—had established Ufa in 1917 and
charged it with a political mission whose ideological objectives were, at the
least, not alien to the gentlemen on the board and to the world of Emil
Georg von Stauss. Ufa had become "civilian," but its governing board was
still dominated by that Wilhelmine political caste that even the judicious
historian Friedrich Meinecke had derided as a "Pan-German-militaristic-
conservative concern."[11]

Those responsible for the actual operations of Ufa were oriented differently. At the level of practical management they made the business, organizational, and artistic decisions. Their interests were primarily economic
and social, and to a greater or lesser degree cultural, and they no doubt
saw themselves as belonging to that sector of the haute bourgeoisie who
cares not at all for monarchy or republic but only to realize their particular
goals. As for the "operations staff," the personnel engaged in actual artistic
and technical work, this large group reflected all the ideological shadings
present in Weimar; a large minority was clearly sympathetic to the "anti-
bourgeois" camp, to the opposition of expressionist artists, and to the intellectual and proletarian left. Seen up close, Ufa was a colossus dressed in
motley, from whom just about everything but a unified program could be
expected.

Nor was Ufa, although centrally organized, a hermetically sealed economic power bloc. The mingled vertical and horizontal structures made for
decentralization and diversification. (Lipschütz defines as "horizontally"
structured those companies in which "the individual enterprises linked together turn out products at the same level of production." The premise of
a "vertical" structure is that "hierarchically organized individual and subordinate enterprises process their products and pass them on up to the next
production level for further processing."[12]) In Ufa's case and in other
German film companies as well, both organizational principles were employed.

> In one sense, Ufa is a combined enterprise, but at the same time it also
> comprises businesses at the same production level. The combination of
> . . . production, distribution, and theater operation is typical for the struc-
> ture of all German film companies. But along with these three main ele-
> ments Ufa also includes, through its ownership of Afifa, the link between

production and distribution, namely, the support industry that does film developing and copying.[13]

When Alfred Hugenberg acquired a majority interest in Ufa in 1927, I. G. Farben emerged as a major purchaser of Ufa stock and thus created an internal link between Ufa and film manufacture.

In the early 1920s the production, distribution, and theater operations united under the Ufa umbrella enjoyed a fairly high degree of independence. The production companies determined volume with almost complete autonomy, and as a rule they continued to favor the genres in which they were already established. Ufa made contracts with them covering a given production period, and paid out advances to them. "In exchange, the production companies were obliged to put their products at Ufa's disposal, and Ufa in turn placed the films in the hands of its distributors."[14]

The distributors that Ufa acquired maintained their existing business relationships and developed them further. Hansa Film, for example, which had originated in the Messter concern, continued under Ufa's direction to deal primarily in Messter films. Geographical criteria were also applied: films would be entrusted to several distributors who were each responsible for getting them into theaters in their areas.

Ufa's theater chain was centrally controlled by two subsidiary companies: the Union Theater Berlin and U. T. Provinzlichtspielhäuser Berlin. "These two companies either owned theaters outright or had a controlling interest in ones that were independent or belonged to other firms. The theaters enjoyed unlimited freedom in their internal administration (setting admission prices and so on)."[15]

In the 1920s, Ufa proved its worth on the international film market as a perfectly organized production and distribution organization, and that is what made it historically novel. The relative independence of individual companies on the three levels of organization guaranteed Ufa a large influence on the *dispersa publica* of the geographically, socially, and culturally diverse society of the Weimar Republic. Its managerial organization thus made it a complex processing system for widely differing public preferences, "contemporary moods," ideological currents, and emerging aesthetic patterns. It administered the (mass) culture of the republic in a way that served its own business interests. To speak of a dictatorship over mass taste, at least for the first half of the 1920s, is wide of the mark. The experiences of different operations flowed together profitably in Ufa's "big brain," which functioned primarily as an administrative center and focused on economic expansion.

The principle of allowing its subsidiaries autonomy was especially valuable in the theater sector. Independence of motion-picture theaters

permits better adaptation to local market conditions. It is difficult, if not impossible, for a central office to operate theaters advantageously. Their profitability is heavily influenced by what competing theaters are doing, which a remote central office can't keep abreast of. Ufa has consequently given its theater managers freedom regarding the selection and scheduling of films, the equipping of their theaters, and so on. Indeed, it has even left them as independent legal entities.[16]

In the production sector, many small firms were soon swallowed up by Ufa, and their films released under the Ufa name. The three big companies—Decla-Bioscop, Deulig, and Union—were so well known that they were allowed to produce under their own names. A year after the merger with Ufa, Murnau's *Die Austreibung* (*Driven from Home*)—the screenplay by Thea von Harbou was based on a play by Carl Hauptmann —still appeared in the theaters as a Decla-Bioscop film. Murnau's worldwide hit *Der letzte Mann* (*The Last Laugh*, 1924) was the first of his films to carry the Ufa production emblem. Even Fritz Lang's *The Nibelungs*, which has a reputation as the Ufa film par excellence, premiered in 1924 as a Decla-Bioscop production.

Given this complicated situation, all attempts to quantify Ufa's part in the total production of the early 1920s have to be evaluated with caution. Numbers alone carry very little weight. According to comprehensive (but not complete) catalogues compiled by Gerhard Lamprecht[17] it is certainly possible that of the 545 films produced in Germany in 1920 at least 57 can be attributed to the Ufa empire. In that number are included films done on production contracts with smaller firms like Cserépy, Greenbaum, and Gloria. In 1921, Ufa productions accounted for 59 out of 396 films; in 1922, 45 out of 252. These numbers, which show an increase in Ufa's percentage share, reflect, however, only the economic side of the firm's expansion. Given the relative independence of the firms taken over by Ufa, it is much harder to determine the growth of its cultural influence. The concept "Ufa film"—which later came to be seen as a sign of quality but also as the mark of a certain form of mass culture (seen positively by some, negatively by others)—must be applied with great discretion.

It was not just Ufa's films but also its theaters and the splendor of its premieres, of course, that helped the name "Ufa" acquire a special aura. Cultivated with a sure instinct for both business and the tastes of the times, the Ufa name was soon famous. With the one exception of *Romeo und Julia im Schnee* (*Romeo and Juliet in the Snow*), which premiered in the Mozart Hall and in the Ufa Theater am Kurfürstendamm, all of Lubitsch's films in 1920–22 (including two that he produced himself: *The Loves of Pharaoh* and *Die Flamme* [*Montmartre*]) premiered in the Ufa-Palast am Zoo, the company's royal palace.

In *One Arabian Night* (1920), a "Union-Film of Ufa," the master director and his company produced an early showpiece of opulent staging and direction. First brought to the stage as pantomime by Max Reinhardt in 1910, the screen version was an intoxicating fantasy event of early film that drew from the original Arabian fairy tale new experiences of perception. It poured out for a thirsting public overwhelming "abundance and contrast" (Fritz Engel), "richness, abundance, extravagance, improvisation" (Herbert Jhering).[18] Only Joe May's adventure film *Das indische Grabmal* (*The Indian Tomb*, 1921), which also premiered in the Ufa-Palast, could begin to compete with *One Arabian Night*, primarily thanks to a cast of stars that included Conrad Veidt, Erna Morena, Olaf Fönss, Mia May, Lya de Putti, Paul Richter, Berhard Goetzke, and Wilhelm Diegelmann.

What the public seemed to demand of cinema was an intensification of experience, and it found what it wanted with these exotic subjects and opulent staging. "We truly lived in the world of India for a few hours," wrote Oskar Kalbus about *The Indian Tomb*, "even after the lights went on again in the theater." And what fascinated him about Georg Jacoby's Union film *Der Mann ohne Namen* (*Man without a Name*) was how "over and over again only plot, one new thrill after another, varied events, and beautiful scenes"[19] overwhelmed the audience's senses. Commissioned by Ufa and made in 1920–21 on the basis of Ewald Gerhard Seeliger's novel *Peter Voss, der Millionendieb* (*Peter Voss, the Million-Dollar Thief*), *Man without a Name* starred Harry Liedtke, Georg Alexander, and Mady Christians and was filmed in the novel's original settings in Morocco and on the Dalmatian coast.

An intensification of experience meant sophisticated *trompe l'oeil* effects conveying authenticity and a convincing sense of physical presence.

> Moviegoers were spoiled early on. Where shortly after the war they had gaped wide-eyed at the splendid palaces of Indian maharajahs built in the sands of the Mark Brandenburg and at German extras made up to look like Malays and Negroes, they soon began to cast a critical eye on makeup and sets made of concrete. . . . So once the gold mark was stabilized, filmmakers started to travel to give their films the local color of distant lands.[20]

The movies became a vehicle for imaginary trips around the world. The stars embarked on these filmic journeys in a style sure to arouse the envy of the audiences that streamed into the cinema's temples of illusion. Ellen Richter, for example, producer of, and diva in, her own films, was reputed never to make a movie that didn't involve expensive trips abroad. Her husband, Willi Wolff, created the "world-travel film," and in the advertisements for them, the desires of the public, exotic images, and the stars' travel adventures all meld together in a collage of dream and reality that makes the head spin. Such was the case with the Ufa-distributed Ellen Richter and Willi Wolff film *Der Flug um den Erdball* (*Flight around the World*) of 1924–25. In its first part, it swept its audiences away to Ceylon by way of Paris; in the second, it took them from India to China and California and back to Europe via New York.

"These space-devouring films reveal how bitterly the average German resented his involuntary seclusion,"[21] Kracauer has written, suggesting that these films provided vicarious satisfaction of repressed desires for escape. "They naïvely satisfied," he continues, the viewer's "suppressed desire for expansion through pictures that enabled his imagination to reannex the world." The films served up their intercontinental panorama as a colorful muddle of improbable, fairy-tale elements—a let's-pretend, fictive jungle where the limits of time and space could be forgotten.

Im Kaleidoskop der Weltteile (In the Kaleidoscope of the Wide World)[22] and *Von sieben Meeren (Of the Seven Seas)*[23] were the titles of two travel books of the period that were bestsellers and written, interestingly enough, by screenwriters. In *Of the Seven Seas* Hanns Heinz Ewers drew together in letter form real and fictional adventures from two decades, and in an afterword the publisher called attention to the arbitrary and chaotic principle behind this kind of world annexation: Neither a chronological sequence of the letters nor a "geographical organization, as by regions of the world,"[24] had been used in the book. A random collage was the form most appropriate to the character of these adventures. A similar approach suggested the title of *In the Kaleidoscope of the Wide World* by Norbert Jacques, published by the German Book Club. The sometimes tacky language of this popular author repeatedly shows an oft-hidden aspect of the yen for distant lands: a craving for erotic expansion and a desire to break away from sexual repression and frustration. "The little city . . . wakes in me thoughts of a small woman in whom sweet passion lies asleep and though asleep still glows in her half-opened eyes."[25]

If there was any organizing principle at work in these travelogue films of Ufa's early years, it was that of the kaleidoscope, a device that to the disillusioned eye and starved imagination showed the world as a playground of infinite possibilities. The travel films were products of an inflationary age and offered a utopian counterimage to it: a realm beyond the confining reach of facts and beyond economics and politics as well. Germany's colonies had been lost, and the economic base for mass tourism was wholly lacking. But an unarticulated desire for the world and for reality was alive, and the bizarre images of the world which the movies provided helped to keep it alive.

8.

The Democratic Department Store:
Ufa Films in 1920–22

No study of the 1920s fails to mention the "hunger for amusement" that seized every class of people after the First World War, a novel longing—progressive in nature and "imbued with clearly democratizing tendencies."[1] "Democratization" meant a homogenizing and equalizing of social classes that—"from the bank director to the office clerk, from the diva to the typist"[2]—found common ground in their cultural needs and in their forms of aesthetic communication. Democratization also meant obliterating the borders between (serious) high culture and (vulgar) popular culture; raising the status of the mass media of radio, film, illustrated magazines, and records in relation to classical artistic and bourgeois educational institutions; "ennobling" jazz, the dance revue, the film comedy, and the hit song in relation to the art song, opera, ballet, the stage play, and "serious" literature. If the abyss "between extreme refinement and the crudest triviality" was to be bridged and art given an opportunity "to move gradually onto the level of a new, generally accessible art,"[3] then a special role in this process would obviously fall to the cinema, especially to the movies made by the large film companies.

The films that Ufa produced or distributed in the early 1920s displayed astonishing thematic and formal variety and presumed the existence of a mass audience that was educable but had widely differing needs. Relaxation and diversion were uppermost, but "intellectual nourishment" and "sublime emotions" were conceded a place.

Thematic impulses from "high culture" ran up against film's inherent tendency to trivialize everything that standards of good taste deemed serious, solemn, and "classical" and that therefore smacked of boredom. "In circles that insisted on distance and respectability, that kind of boredom was more welcomed than regretted."[4] As Erwin Panofsky wrote in 1934: "Surely commercial art always runs the risk of ending up a whore, but just as surely does noncommercial art run the risk of ending up an old maid."[5]

A writer like Thea von Harbou, for example, saw it as her mission to bridge this abyss. She did not consider it contradictory when in 1921 she and Fritz Lang wrote the screenplay for *The Indian Tomb* just a year after she had written scenarios based on tales of two saints: *Die heilige Simplicia* (*Saint Simplicia*), directed by Joe May, and *Das wandernde Bild* (*The Wandering Picture*), directed by the young Fritz Lang. In 1919 this much-sought-after writer had published with Ullstein a collector's edition of medieval legends[6] in which she recounted in prose as precious as it was flowery the lives of pious women of the Middle Ages, among them the life of Saint Simplicia. The contradiction was only one of subject matter, and Harbou reconciled it thanks to a well-developed talent for what she no doubt considered commercialism of a high cultural order. She made concessions in *The Indian Tomb* to yearnings for the monumental and the tropical, but she also understood how to use material to exploit a widespread enthusiasm for nationalistic, romanticized images of the Middle Ages, and for bigoted, sweetly sentimental religious fervor.

In companies like Ullstein and Ufa that dominated their markets, a sure instinct for popular taste was an integral part of capitalistic calculations. What Hermand and Trommler have said in another context could be applied here: "What was produced amounted without doubt to an increase in culture for the greatest possible number of people, but at the same time it produced an increase in nonculture." What was supposed to have entertained the masses "contributed just as much to their ideological stultification. For this reason most of this democratically intended culture was not so much popular in a positive sense as it was trivial in a negative one."[7]

Filmmakers were as little interested in "stultifying" their audiences as they were in a conscious effort to expand their knowledge or improve their taste, of course. And an essentially trivial quality is at the very heart of film's fascination—an urbane, "nervous," even aggressive vulgarity that film uses against the demands of bourgeois high culture.

The "pluralized" taste of a socially uprooted mass audience that was also given to "vagrant"[8] emotions found no echo in German high culture. Other efforts to wrest from the misery of the times a radically democratic or even "revolutionary" popular culture were failing; this offered a "market opening" for the commercial media to draw the public's diverse feelings together at focal points of entertainment and sentiment. It was in this vacuum that Ufa made its home, and the company's pluralistic program dealt in the stuff of dreams but remained conservative: its appeal was to the inner life of a nostalgic populace. Ufa's pluralism spurred the development of the language of cinematography and its self-confidence.

Because he adhered so rigorously to film's "material aesthetic," Paul Wegener was more successful than Thea von Harbou and the early Fritz Lang in capturing his fairy-tale worlds on film without cutting himself off from film's modernity and popularity and he did this in every capacity: as a director in *Golem, How He Came into the World* (with Carl Boese, 1920); as an actor, with Asta Nielsen, in *Vanina—Die Galgenhochzeit* (*Vanina—The Gallows Wedding*, directed by Arthur von Gerlach, 1922); and as a writer for *Der verlorene Schatten* (*The Lost Shadow*, directed by Rochus Gliese, 1920). These films were all made by Projektions Union and are generally categorized as "expressionist," even though their subject matter was drawn from nineteenth-century Romanticism (*Vanina* is based on a story by Stendhal, Gliese's film on one by Chamisso) or turn-of-the-century Neo-Romanticism (Gustav Meyrink).

The term "expressionism" applied to film is misleading if it suggests a tie to the Expressionism in the visual arts of the same period. Describing Hans Poelzig's sets for the Jewish ghetto in *The Golem*, Lotte Eisner speaks of a "gothic" style,[9] a term better used for the stylistic trappings and historical pretensions of films in the Caligari style. A gloomy, bizarre fantasy of "gothic tales," a partiality to the irrational, to psychological extremes, to the "night side" of life, and to the central themes of dark Romanticism— the Doppelgänger motif, the linking of insanity and crime, of psychiatry and terror—all these elements (present as late as 1926 in the "gothic" figure of the engineer Rotwang in Lang's *Metropolis*) harken back to an imaginary medieval era, to relics of preindustrial structures in the German (and European) psychic landscape. They appear in literature and the visual arts, too, but in film they found an authentic language and flourished spectacularly.

Kracauer sees subliminally at work in such films, especially *Vanina*, "the psychological causes and effects of tyranny."[10] Eisner explains the "mystery of dark corridors" and sinister labyrinths in *Vanina* and other films with reference to the German mentality, which, she suggests, values "becoming" above "being."[11] What can be said with certainty is that this "gothic" film style does not offer the possibility of salvation but seems confining, claustrophobic, psychically undigested, anxiety-producing. It expresses a rebellion of provinces and small cities against industrial culture and its superficial rationality.

Ufa saw things in much simpler terms: "The strength of the German film lies in fantastic drama," it claimed in its program magazine of 1921.[12] So the company satisfied the "German" penchant for dream (and trauma), for anti-realism and anti-naturalism, for denying the present. Though Ufa surely cultivated the irrational and trivialized the mystical, it did not turn away from contemporary reality. On April 27, 1922, Fritz Lang's Uco film *Dr. Mabuse, der Spieler* (*Dr. Mabuse, the Gambler*) premiered in the Ufa-Palast am Zoo. Lang wanted this film understood as a "picture of the times," a mirror of an endangered epoch, and it is a film in which, as Toeplitz has noted, fantasy and the documentary are woven together. The premiere coincided with an extremely precarious political moment for the Weimar Republic. Only a few days earlier, France's premier, Henri Poincaré, had threatened to initiate military action against Germany if it did not meet its obligations spelled out in the Treaty of Versailles. "The period after the First World War," Lang wrote years later, reflecting on the background of his Mabuse film, "was for Germany a period of deepest despair, of hysteria, cynicism, unrestrained vice. The most dreadful poverty existed side by side with immense new wealth. Berlin coined the word *Raffke*, or 'profiteer,' from *Zusammenraffen des Geldes* [raking in money]." Mabuse, Lang said, was the "prototype of this period."[13]

"Berlin is dancing," Harry Kessler wrote in his diary at about that time. In 1922, the war profiteers were dancing with the exploiters of inflation. In the meantime, the political superstructure had consolidated its position. The Social Democratic political elite was partially a new "proletarian ruling caste"; Kessler saw "the old Prussian discipline joining hands with a new socialistic one." The spirit of this group was bureaucratic and repressive, and it had moved into an ideological and actual bunker. "Noske sits there on Bendlerstrasse behind barbed wire and with a bodyguard of seven officers, fifteen NCOs, and fifty troops for his personal protection, like Nicholas II or Dionysius the Tyrant"—or Mabuse in his hideout. Old-guard nationalistic politicians, mourning the monarchy and at the same time fascinated by the stirring masses, fantasized in all seriousness that Germany's salvation could come only from a "monarchist–Social Democratic Bolshevism."[14] Philosophies, varied outlooks, political utopias could be had anywhere, a dime a dozen, and sometimes joined in the most unlikely alliances.

Mabuse, a criminal figure exerting a powerful fascination through the mass media, conquers such a society easily. Hitler, who was arrested in 1923 in Munich, didn't yet have it so easy. The Republic was still defending itself against extremists. The chance still existed for it to develop into a democratic community. But its films showed the dangers.

Mabuse was a popular mythic representation of an outsized *Raffke*, who, like a spider spinning a vast web, pursues an expansionist media policy. And worked into the film, too, were all the characteristics of a vulgarized, inanely superficial Nietzsche cult. The psychically crippled and Nietzsche-inspired heroes of "psychological novels" by Otto Julius Bierbaum or Felix Hollaender might have come up with the line that Countess Told addresses to D.A. Wenk: "I need life, sensation, adventure, the powerful breath of the unusual."

Mabuse supplied Germany's urbane and politically disoriented public with all these attitudes, and they were delivered in multimedia form, with a carefully crafted strategy. While Norbert Jacques's novel was appearing in installments in the *Berliner Illustriete*, Ullstein was preparing the book publication and Harbou was working on the screenplay for Uco-Production. The Lang–Harbou team continued to employ this multimedia strategy until

1932. Novels by successful writers (usually Harbou herself) Lang and Harbou would jointly rework into screenplays. Then Ullstein or Scherl would issue them as books, illustrated with studio stills, to coincide with the release of the film; and at the premiere Ufa would present signed copies bound in silk to guests who had received engraved invitations to the event. Already with the Mabuse film—which cost 15 million (inflation) marks to make and took almost four hours on two consecutive evenings to show— this machinery was functioning at peak efficiency: with the final installments of the novel, the *Berliner Illustrierte* used stills from the forthcoming film.

Dr. *Mabuse* resists classification as an "expressionist" film, and Lang himself explicitly rejected this label. It is equally impossible to assign any particular outlook, any political or philosophical position, to the film's main character. Mabuse embodies both the Enlightenment and a Counter-Enlightenment, terror from both the left and the right; a monster born of imperialism, he is driven by raging paranoia to destroy everything he brings under his control. Norbert Jacques saw in Lang's film an attempt to show "only motion, not the emotion behind it; to show only effects, not causes."[15] The overall effects mark Lang's Mabuse film as an authentic product of a disoriented era.

The company that produced this film kept its distance from Weimar's polarizing politics, its warring camps and fronts, already yearning for violent solutions to society's problems. Ufa was not yet an "ideological fortress." It was part of an urbane, pleasure-seeking world in which thousands of people and hundreds of newspapers and magazines representing a multitude of points of view set the tone every day.

As a newspaper city, Berlin was a catalyst that set off reactions among diverse temperaments, ideas, subjects, and currents. "A journalist can become anything," Stefan Grossmann wrote in *Das Tage-Buch* in 1922. "When I saw Mr. E. A. Dupont editing the news seven or eight years ago at Ullstein, curious about everything going on in the world and ready at a moment's notice to translate current events into large or small type, I never would have thought that this quick-thinking newspaperman would become one of the world's most able film directors."[16]

Dupont became one of Ufa's world-class stars with the production of *Variety* in 1925, and made no less than seven films between 1920 and 1922, all for Gloria, which Ufa took over in 1921. Among them was *Der weisse Pfau* (*The White Peacock*, 1920), which anticipated motifs that later appeared in *Variety* and was praised by critics for its style and its "American" staging. *Whitechapel* (1920), the critics said, demonstrated "that a film with crime and sensation as its subject matter can be sophisticated in a way that does not detract from its impact."[17] In 1921—now under Ufa—Dupont made the first film version of Wilhelmine von Hillern's novel *Die Geier-Wally*, with staging by Paul Leni and with Henny Porten, Albert Steinrück,

Wilhelm Dieterle, and Eugen Klöpfer in the lead roles. In 1922, Grossmann had nothing but praise for the first part of Dupont's melodrama *Kinder der Finsternis* (*Children of Darkness*), though he had nothing but scorn for the second part:

> This sequel to a powerful social drama is a pathetic story of jealousy in which the insipid daughter of a millionaire struggles in vain against a victorious daughter of the proletariat. In an insufferably fraudulent scene, both women collapse at the bier of the man they both loved, and a dance coda—"Life dances on"—is tacked onto the end.[18]

The "quick-thinking newspaperman" Dupont set no store by intellectual distinctions between kitsch and art; for him the trivial tale of jealousy was just as redolent of the world, just as "authentic," as the social drama. Curiosity about everything going on in the world nourished his urbane virtuosity. And curiosity was a motivating force of Weimar's middle-class public, of Berlin's post-revolutionary culture, keen for news and diversion. Ufa's democratic tendencies were nourished by that same curiosity, a concern with the superficial appeal of subject matter and a disregard of any and all dictates as to what was artistically or philosophically acceptable.

Ufa's major artists did not compete with bourgeois high culture and did not get involved in the political battles of the day either. "The differences between republicans and monarchists can't be shown in film," Herbert Jhering said in his critique of Paul Leni's *Verschwörung zu Genua* (*Conspiracy in Genoa*, 1921), also a Gloria film. "This film is effective only when it functions as a pictorial composition set apart from its theme. And the pictorial composition is most successful when it focuses on presenting the intrigue separated from all content."[19]

The flip side of this democratic urbanity—which appeared early on—was a peculiar indifference toward the heart of the social and historical material that film, no less than theater or literature, must take as its subject. That indifference would have heavy costs, for the more attention the Ufa virtuosos gave to "pictorial composition set apart from its theme," the more they lost sight of Weimar's major theme: the viability of democracy.

In this respect, the cinema of the early Weimar Republic shows some parallels to, but also major differences from, the theatrical life of the era. The theater of the 1920s is regarded as an art "on which the revolution of 1918 left a real and indeed a significant mark"; during often dramatic conflicts over the content of plays and styles of direction, "the political responsibility of the theater" was "constantly discussed," and under Leopold Jessner at the Prussian State Theater in Berlin, the stage became "a forum in the battle against despotism and the bourgeoisie and for the invigoration of our newly acquired freedom."[20] There is clearly nothing comparable in the film industry. (The debates occasioned by *Fridericus Rex* in 1922 are a striking exception to which we shall return.) Brawls like the one over Jessner's production of *Wilhelm Tell* in 1919 did not occur in cinemas until the National Socialists began instigating them in the early 1930s.

Politically engaged stage actors, companies, political collectives, and other theater groups outside the establishment had considerable influence on the theatrical culture of Weimar, and they participated in efforts to create "from the political experience of the present a new foundation for theater."[21] But the first comparable development in cinema was the founding of the leftist "people's film" movement after 1928—much later, when the overall social situation had changed significantly. Ufa itself, for example, had by then been taken over by Hugenberg and had veered sharply to the right.

On the stage the interest in new aesthetics resulted from the disintegration of theatrical conventions. But in cinematography it grew from a developing technology that was inspiring new discoveries every day, from a fascinating new language of light and shadow that had produced a vocabulary with no apparent limits but still no mature grammar.

In Ufa's golden age, directors like Murnau and Dupont and cameramen like Karl Freund and Carl Hoffmann could devote themselves with radical single-mindedness to developing cinematographic means of expression and to discovering the secrets of pictorial language. Some of the films they created are counted among the masterpieces of film history. At the same time, however, the destiny of Ufa was changing. It had been democratically open to social trends during the years of its expansion and had refused to put itself in the service of any political agenda, but it evolved into the keystone of a conservative, nationalistic, and centrally controlled media empire during the very years when Murnau and Lang were creating their masterpieces. Those master directors could not yet suspect that their work, as in *The Nibelungs* and *Faust*, would very soon, explicitly or implicitly, have "political consequences."

Historical dramas on the stage and historical spectacles on the screen in the early 1920s reflected the mood of a society in motion but with no direction—and a movie and theater audience not so much politicized as stirred up. It was sheer excitement rather than a shared political idea that at a Reinhardt production of Romain Rolland's *Danton* at the Grosses Schauspielhaus in 1920 "lifted [the audience] out of their seats and created a momentary unity between the actors and the spectators."[22]

A year later the Russian director Dimitri Buchowetzki, who was working in Germany at the time, filmed for Hilde Wörner's little production company his *Danton* based on Georg Büchner's play. Emil Jannings played the title role; Werner Krauss played Robespierre, as he had in the Reinhardt production. The premiere was in the Ufa-Palast in June 1921. Buchowetzki, guided by the great theatrical model, tried to transpose Reinhardt's style onto the screen, as in the seething crowd scenes and in the scene of the revolutionary tribunal "where the figures stand out so powerfully before the dark backdrop and display that carefully structured grouping that is a hallmark of Reinhardt productions."23 But this adaptation of a style, this experimentation with an already available aesthetic solution in a new medium, took the place of a genuine engagement with the historical material. (This was not the case with Lubitsch, who subjected the material of history to sarcastic revision with a technique of unmasking.) On the basis of his *Sappho*, produced for Union in 1921, Buchowetzki joined the ranks of Ufa's directors. His Wörner film *Othello* (1922, also with Jannings and Krauss) was distributed by Ufa.

In its growth years, Ufa produced or distributed just about anything that promised financial success or praise from the critics, or both—historical dramas (like Ellen Richter's production *Lola Montez, die Tänzerin des Konigs* [*Lola Montez, the King's Dancer*, directed by Willi Wolff, 1922]); movies based on modern literature (Felix Basch's *Der Strom* [*The Stream*, 1922] from Max Halbe's play of that name); contemporary social issues (*Der schwarze Gott* [*The Black God*], a 1921 Messter production directed by Alfred Halm); and a string of comedies produced by Bolten-Baeckers (*Leo und seine zwei Bräute* [*Leo and His Two Brides*, 1921, directed by Leo Peuckert], *Der Herr Papa* [*Mr. Papa*], *Es bleibt in der Familie* [*It Stays in the Family*], and *Knoppchen und seine Schwiegermutter* [*Knoppchen and His Mother-in-Law*], all made in 1922 and directed by Heinrich Bolten-Baeckers).

Karl Grune made his early films for Gloria, among them *Die Nacht ohne Morgen* (*The Night without Morning*, 1921), *Mann über Bord* (*Man Overboard*, 1921), and the Henny Porten film *Frauenopfer* (*Women Victims*, 1922) with Wilhelm Dieterle and Albert Bassermann. Hans Steinhoff, later one of Ufa's most reliable directors under the Nazi regime, began his career with Gloria, too, with *Der falsche Dimitry* (*False Dimitry*, 1922). In 1921–22, Ufa's cultural division produced Wilhelm Prager's fairy-tale films *Der kleine Muck* (*Little Muck*), *Tischlein deck dich* (*Table, Set Yourself*), and *Der falsche Prinz* (*The False Prince*); also—citing the collaboration of a number of medical sex experts—the educational film *Steinachs Forschungen* (*Steinach's Researches*). The "popular" version of this film, which according to the censor's list was approved only for "certain audiences," premiered in the Ufa-Palast am Zoo in January 1923.

During the young Weimar Republic, Ufa functioned like a media department store that was quick to capitalize on trends of the times and to provide an image for the uprooted, novelty-hungry city dweller to emulate. "The middle-management employee was the type from which this image was developed, for this social level was regarded as the crucial sphere where the democratization and homogenization of the entire society was gradually taking place."24

The middle-management type wanted social integration, and this was the great liberal experiment and the great democratic illusion of the Weimar Republic. Ufa took part in the experiment, and the illusions associated with that experiment were the materials from which Ufa made its films.

Experiment and illusion, democracy, liberality and libertinage, addiction to pleasure and demimondaine villainy, a love for the kinky and a readiness to sin—no one in the industry better embodied these qualities than the actor and director Reinhold Schünzel, with his intelligent, slightly caddish sensuality. While Carl Mayer was preparing the way for the "German chamber film" in his work with Lupu Pick (*Shattered*, 1921, produced by Rex-Film) and Leopold Jessner (*Hintertreppe* [*Back Stairs*], 1921, with Henny Porten), Schünzel was testing his talent in three ways at once: classical drama, "morals films," and historical spectaculars. He used the dizzying quality of the *Zeitgeist* and Ufa's deliberate lack of commitment to any single approach for his own purposes and—working independently and on the periphery of Ufa, as it were—made films that were distinctly his own.

Since 1916 Schünzel had been cultivating his image on the stage, in innumerable film comedies, and in collaboration with Richard Oswald (*Anders als die Andern* [*Different than the Others*], *Unheimliche Geschichten* [*Weird Tales*], both 1919).

> There is no other actor of whom one is so ready to believe the worst when he glides onto the scene from the shadiest quarters of the big city. He brings a terrifyingly convincing realism to a milieu that does not really come alive until his entrance. So powerful is his presence that he seems to us to be sin incarnate, without equal in his cynical brutality, his devious eroticism, and his demonic cunning.[25]

With his filming of Hebbel's *Maria Magdalene* (1919), his milieu film *Das Mädchen aus der Ackerstrasse* (*The Girl from Acker Street*, 1920), and his monumental epic *Katharina die Grosse* (*Catherine the Great*, 1920), complete with 4,000 extras and 500 horses, Schünzel launched his career as a sorcerer of film direction, a career to which Propaganda Minister Goebbels put an abrupt end in 1937.

Maria Magdalene and *Catherine the Great* were produced by Cserépy-Film, which was controlled by Ufa after 1922 and which (becoming Film-Gesellschaft am Dönhoffplatz) was completely absorbed by it in 1924. In Reinhold Schünzel, the Hungarian-born producer and director Arzen von Cserépy was employing a complete nonconformist, a "shady type"; and in 1922–23 he outraged the entire left with his four-part *Fridericus Rex*, distributed by Ufa. This gave the Weimar Republic its first major political film scandal. The film has often been cited to prove that from its beginnings Ufa was an instrument of the nationalistic right, designed "to manipulate the consciousness of the masses to suit its purposes."[26] Other writers have seen *Fridericus Rex* as the first unmistakable sign of what rapidly became Ufa's unswerving drift to the right. The first thesis is hardly tenable; the second requires elaboration.

The first two parts of the film—*Sturm und Drang* (*Storm and Stress*) and *Vater und Sohn* (*Father and Son*)—premiered on January 31, 1922, in the Ufa-Palast am Zoo. They were followed in March 1923 by the third and fourth parts, *Sanssouci* and *Schicksalswende* (*Turn of Fate*). In Guido Seeber, Cserépy had a superb cameraman and in Otto Gebühr an actor who had begun a long-standing career as Frederick's double in Carl Boese's 1919 film *Die Tänzerin Barberina* (*The Dancer Barberina*).

Walter von Molo, the screenwriter for the fourth part, was clearly not a republican. His historical novels were gobbled up by German nationalists; their crass, pulpy effects accounted for their "good fortune in being grossly overvalued by the press as well as by the book-buying public."[27] Later movies about Frederick II, like *Der Choral von Leuthen* (*The Anthem of Leuthen*, 1933, directed by Carl Froelich) and *Fridericus* (1936, directed by Johannes Meyer), were also inspired by Molo's novel. (But in 1924, the Social Democratic *Vorwärts* printed a quote from this very author forcefully objecting to a portrayal of the King of Prussia as a patriotic taskmaster: "It is a crime . . . to make him a vapid patriot, a tendentious film hero, a character in an operetta, an idol to worship. Instead, we should seek out the Fridericus hidden within us and probe there for his truly human qualities."[28])

Franz Porten had made "Prussian films" as early as 1912 and 1913. But now cinema indulged in a downright inflationary exploitation of the Prussian theme: according to Eberhard Mertens[29] no less than forty-four productions utilized it before the end of World War II, twenty-seven of them during Weimar. The politics of the postwar years and the young democracy's ideological and psychological volatility were favorable to "Frederick II of Prussia, still called 'the Great,' who with a display of self-discipline notorious in history transformed himself from a pampered flute player into Old Fritz—tough, shrewd, industrious, in short, splendid, worn down by lifelong exhausting work, the first servant of his state."[30] He was one of those historical symbols around which, in the minds of many Germans (even in the younger generation), a mythology resistant to republicanism formed.

The father-son conflict in the first two parts of the Frederick movie both hid and symbolized a central conflict in the Weimar Republic—the struggle of one Germany against the other. In 1925, after the sudden death of the Social Democratic President Friedrich Ebert, "the father-son conflict was transposed into reality on a wider stage," as Peter Gay has written.[31] The subsequent election of Paul von Hindenburg was a defeat for one Germany—the "people's bloc," made up of the SPD and the Democratic Party—but not for the "Reich bloc," the other Germany, which published campaign appeals like this: "Hindenburg was your leader in a great and difficult time. You followed him. You loved him! He never abandoned you. Fight for him again now. Loyal leader that he is, he wants to march at the head of your columns and serve his fatherland in building a peaceful society!"[32]

Hindenburg and Ludendorff, bankrupt political and military leaders, had the sympathy of all those Germans who believed that their country had been treacherously led into war and who dreamed of revitalizing Germany as a world power. Ufa adapted to these nationalistic trends, conformed to them, helped develop appealing images that expressed them. But the leftist, democratic, and revolutionary "outsiders" in Weimar had not been driven from the field, and this nationalistic movement was only one element, though clearly a strong one. Most of Ufa's artists sympathized with the "people's bloc," while its conservative investors and their political allies had long since decided in favor of the "Reich bloc" and Hindenburg. There was controversy and confrontation, and they were first acted out, with great vehemence, in Ufa's cinemas.

"The distributors' advertising campaign [for *Fridericus Rex*] alone was enough to rouse the forces pro and con."[33] German Nationals organized parades in support of the movies; Social Democrats and Communists called for protests against them. All over Germany there were leaflet wars, and the films could often be shown only under police protection. Leftists were outraged by the obsequiousness of the Prussian ministers who had allowed filming in Charlottenburg Palace, and they protested against the "reactionary" theaters that showed this nationalistic "filth and trash" on their screens. *Vorwärts* called for a boycott, ran detailed reports about striking theater owners who were joining in the protest, and recommended that a regional ban on the film be made national. The left protests were highly visible, but the other side was stronger, it seems, promoting a mass hysteria against which dialectical cunning was the only effective weapon. Decades later the film critic Hans Feld had this recollection:

> It was hardly possible to counter that mass hysteria head on. The only chance the opposition minority had was to confuse audiences who had no historical knowledge, and it used this tactic at premieres in the big cities, especially Berlin. All it needed was recognition of the [eighteenth-century] uniforms and a quick reaction time: the rest was easy. Whenever Austrian, Russian, or French soldiers appeared on the screen, the protesters applauded wildly, inspiring their less well informed fellow viewers to join in enthusiastically. It took a few minutes before the dupes realized, with the aid of subtitles, that they had been cheering the enemy on and that the Prussians were on the retreat.

But even Feld could not free himself of the mythic spell cast by the Prussian King, for he added: "This subterfuge of war was in a sense an adaptation of a tactic Frederick employed. Old Fritz used to throw his often much stronger but unprepared opponents into panic by launching swift attacks on their flanks."[34]

This was the very public, with all its moods, desires, and ideological preferences, that Ufa had to win over if the company was to ensure and increase its financial success, and so it reacted according to the basic capitalistic principles, not those of a political propaganda agency. In the interest of business, the directors and writers saw no reason to discourage the anti-democratic emotions and authoritarian dreams of so much of their audience.

Toeplitz has noted that even in this film, with its sharp protest against resignation (supposedly encouraged by the left), a "trace of the expressionistic filmmaker" can still be seen: The "soldier king," Frederick's father, is portrayed in exactly the same way as the demonic tyrants of the Caligari-type films, "as a lonely human being whose loneliness drives him to autocracy and tyranny."[35] Even *Vorwärts* dared suggest in 1922 that the film's first part, which "cast light on Frederick William's sadistic cruelty," could be regarded "as a film serving republican enlightenment."[36] Writing in the *Weltbühne* in 1923, Roland Schacht disagreed with the incensed spirits in both camps. This film, he said, was an entertainment for minors and had little political content. "We have to have our picture books. The politicians can calm down. There is no political ax grinding here."[37] And in *Die Glocke* Robert Breuer asked, "The Ufa-Palast holds two thousand people and is filled two or three times every day. This has been so for a whole month or longer. Are all those people fools, enemies of the republic, monarchists?"[38]

"We have to have our picture books." The Ufa of the early 1920s was an expanding picture factory, a media department store, whose management developed a talent for supplying multitudes of images for its public's multitude of dreams. Whether Ufa was serving up adventures in distant India, chase scenes in labyrinthian castles, mysterious happenings in a small German city, horrors of the Berlin underworld, love of a millionaire's daughter for a worker or of a crown prince for a music teacher's daughter—the Ufa picture books were always aiming—in an uncomplicated, varied, still uncertain language—for something that would enrich people's everyday lives and compensate them for the repression of their radical desires. "Frederick has taken his place among the stars," Friedrich Siebert wrote, "and yet still lives on uneradicably in our little lives. He is part of our everyday existence, even if we know nothing of him. His glory is a presence in our impoverished world."[39]

There may have been "reactionary" and "revolutionary" films. The Frederick films polarized those two camps and made visible the line between them. But in the experience of cinema itself, as in the emotions and dreams of human beings, "progressive" and "regressive" elements coexist and can amalgamate in unlikely forms. Ufa in 1922–23 was synonymous with the universality of cinema. It was vulnerable to political reaction, but not yet in its grip.

9.

The Builders' Guild
in Ufa's Studios

A N instinct for business and art, love of one's trade, and a feel for what
the public wants—the ideal conditions for holding these very different
factors in a productive balance prevailed in Ufa's studios for several years.
The company's best minds thought about this new medium of film, articulated their dreams and artistic ambitions for it:

> If by interesting lighting or focusing on the stairs or populating the scene
> with the right faces one can lend a touch of high style to a crummy bar
> patronized by thieves and whores, as, for instance, the old Dutch paintings
> do, then this crummy bar can emanate as much art as a Gothic cathedral
> can. It is immaterial what subject one chooses for making an artistic film.
> The only essential condition is that it be made by artists who know what
> the public wants but also know what they themselves want.[1]

Erich Pommer wrote this at the end of 1922, as the top executive of Decla-
Bioscop and chief of all Ufa's production studios.

In the culture of the Weimar Republic, where mysticism struggled
against rationalism, the Middle Ages against the Enlightenment, a call for
"synthesis" and "cohesion" often replaced the analytical impulse, the sense
of complicated interplays of divergent forces. But, as Peter Gay has written,
"not everyone who sought connections and unity in the 1920s was a victim
of regression. A few . . . tried to satisfy their need not by flight from the
world but by mastering their world; not by cursing technology but by using
it; not by irrationalism but by reason; not by being nihilistic but by being
constructive—and that in a completely literal sense."[2] Like other media of
modern industrial society—photography, the illustrated press, and, soon,
radio—film was based on applied science and technical rationality.

Gay notes the contribution that progressive architects and their "constructive" thinking made to the democratic potential of Weimar. Erich

Mendelsohn, for example, who built Berlin's Universum Film Theater in 1927, stressed that "the architect has to combine analysis with dynamics, reason with irrationality." In his Bauhaus program of 1919 Walter Gropius had called for an end to the traditional division between arts and crafts: "Pretentiousness that divides the classes" is inappropriate to the times, he said. "Architects, sculptors, painters, we all have to return to craft!"[3] Erich Pommer advocated this concept of craft, too. Like Gropius, he was working on a "new structure of the future that will comprise everything in one form."

The film industry, child of a scientific age, required technical innovation and helped to promote it. Indeed, some observers felt that "nowhere was technical progress as strikingly evident" as in the film studio.[4] Cinematography had collaborated with the technology of modern warfare; after 1918 it profited in Germany from the estate of the now discontinued aircraft industry. In Berlin-Johannisthal, for example, the largest film-production studio in Europe took shape on the grounds of the former Albatros-Werke. Johannisthaler Film-Anstalten (Jofa), consisting of a double hall with a total floor space of almost 3,500 square meters and an outdoor area of more than 20,000 square meters, started operating in May 1920. "On the east side, which is the airport side, the studios can be completely opened up to the outside by means of big sliding doors, thus doubling the usable space of each studio."[5] Or the hangar's large interior could be divided into several smaller studio units and rented out simultaneously to different production companies. Once floodlights were available, the studios did not have to rely on daylight and on uncertain weather, so outdoor filming ceased to be a concern; even large outdoor structures were now built mostly in studios. Before 1930, nearly 400 films were made at the Johannisthal studios, among them Buchowetzki's *Danton* and the four *Fridericus Rex* films. Prometheus-Film rented space in Johannisthal for its productions *Schinderhannes* (1927–28, directed by Kurt Bernhardt) and *Mutter Krausens Fahrt ins Glück* (*Mother Krause's Happy Journey*, 1929, directed by Phil Jutzi).

It took still another aviation establishment to surpass the dimensions of the Johannisthal studios. In July 1923, with the founding of Filmwerke Staaken, the huge hangar at the Staaken Airport near Berlin became the largest film studio in the world, with a floor area of almost 18,000 square meters and a ceiling height particularly advantageous for big productions:

> The space available for filming is eight times larger than the floor area of all the Berlin studios together. Until now, the highest structure possible in Berlin studios was 11 meters. Staaken will permit structures up to 28 meters. . . . It offers new options for bringing into the studio constructs that were once possible only outdoors and that will now be totally accessible to the refinements of artificial lighting.[6]

A special achievement of the Staaken studio was a 60-by-25-meter backdrop-cum-ceiling that offered a good surface for sophisticated lighting techniques first tried out in the war. It "was a wall built of wood and plaster, but because of its slight curvature and consistently bright and shadowless illumination, it created a convincing illusion for the camera, and then for the human eye in the theater, of sky overhead and an unbounded hori-zon."[7] The producer and director Hans Neumann, who became head of Ufa's theater branch in 1926, presided over Staaken; the first director he let sample the qualities of the studio was Robert Wiene, with his monu-mental epic *I.N.R.I.*, which took ninety days to film in the summer of 1923.

But it was the studio of Neubabelsberg, in southwestern Berlin, that became the embodiment of and synonym for Germany's film industry.[8] Located at Stahnsdorfer Strasse 99–101, it was rechristened with the mag-ical name of Ufa-Stadt-Babelsberg, Ufa-Strasse 99–103, in the mid-1930s. Under the supervision of its technical director and cameraman Guido See-ber, Deutsche Bioscop had built the first glass studio here in 1912; a second, larger glass atelier was built in 1913; and after the war film and prop storage were added to the property, which was taken over in 1922 by Decla-Bioscop and by Ufa in the fall of 1924. Ufa immediately set about expanding the facilities and in 1926 completed a new film studio designed by Carl Stahl-Urach that made it Europe's largest:

> The new filming hall with its steel framework and massive walls measures 123.5 meters long by 56 wide and 14 high at the catwalks. With all aux-iliary space included, the total floor area is about 8,000 square meters and the total enclosed space 20,000 cubic meters. The facility has all necessary technical equipment and options. The large hall can be divided by mov-able masonry walls so that several major films and a number of smaller films can be shot at the same time.[9]

If one includes the Neubabelsberg grounds with their area of 40,000 square meters as well as the Tempelhof facilities the company had acquired earlier, then even before the introduction of sound film Ufa had production ca-pacities rivaled only by American ones.

The studios and outdoor sets of the Ufa city became the scene of a much admired adventure in montage that was often written about. Siegfried Kra-cauer called it a "calico world" that offered amazing, seemingly surrealistic perceptions. Anyone who visited Neubabelsberg (Hugenberg regulated the stream of visitors, and admitted to his realm only politically acceptable guests or people important to the company) was immersed in a chaos of forms; human history was fragmented here into thousands of *objets trouvés* in a maze full of mysterious connections and befuddling absurdities. It was the world, but without coherence, and constructed of insubstantial mate-rials, good only for fleeting illusions. This was a fragmented universe of papier-mâché, canvas, plywood, and colored paper.

A reporter who visited Neubabelsberg in 1924 for *Film-Kurier* inspected both the gloomy buildings for *Der Turm des Schweigens* (*The Tower of Silence*, 1924, directed by Johannes Guter) and a castle "with breathtaking romantic atmosphere and an ominously glittering moat, a house overgrown with gorse on the moor, and a village church with its run-down cemetery" from *Zur Chronik von Grieshuus* (*Concerning the Chronicles of Grieshuus,* 1924–25, Arthur von Gerlach). In the distance he could see the wall stormed by the Huns in Fritz Lang's *Nibelungs,* and "from behind some bushes the dragon (now dead) was peering out." A few steps farther on rose "a gigantic apartment-house wall, sixty meters high, that with its innumerable windows and unending monotony of form represented the city in Murnau's *The Last Laugh.*" In addition, there was an entire "city square with a huge hotel, which in reality had only four stories but would appear in the film to be a skyscraper." Sixty automobiles, "real ones and models, appear at the intersection, and the perspective achieved here is admirable."[10]

Siegfried Kracauer described the phatasmagoric quality of Neubabelsberg: The directors' "lack of piety" and refreshing "lack of historical sense" stopped at nothing. "They construct whole cultures and destroy them again." Natural laws were declared null and void. An "unsubstantial appearance of make-believe"[11] hung over Ufa's world in Neubabelsberg.

Filming in the huge new studio also produced marvelous montage effects, achieved with lights, props, and "spectral" movement. In 1923 *Der Kinematograph* observed the shooting of the Sermon on the Mount for Wiene's film *I.N.R.I.:*

> In front of the artificial horizon are sand dunes with about two thousand people arranged artfully on them. Movable dunes can be simply pushed aside in two or three hours and reduced to wood and sand again outdoors. . . . Hundreds of lights glow overhead; all of them, or selected ones, blaze up or dim at the command of the rheostat. Spotlights mounted at forty meters—almost sky-high—stab in from the sides. Truly a sea of light. And now the huge doors slowly slide open, as if manipulated by spectral hands. Daylight floods in and mixes with the thousand electric lights. The shooting begins.[12]

Under the hegemony of Ufa, a new type of film studio developed. The acceleration of capital accumulation and investment; the rapid development of technology (especially the more mobile camera and more sophisticated lighting techniques); the organizational talents of producers like Erich Pommer; and, finally, the inventiveness of directors, cameramen, stage managers, and technicians—all these came together on a scale unprecedented in cultural history. More than a few of those involved were convinced they were working on an all-inclusive artistic structure or, as Gropius put it, on a "new structure of the future that will comprise everything in one form."[13]

The search for meaning, for "synthesis," for salvation remained crucial. A film like *I.N.R.I.* was both spectacle and sermon, sensation and consolation for starving souls. The production technology and the chaos of montage in the studios showed how the artificial dreams were brought together on the screen as unified, organic messages, as complexes of meaning with strong structural principles. The contradiction between the mode of production and the end effect was huge, and only the initiated were fully aware of it.

The Ufa studio was a place of mixed motives; it could turn out films with high artistic ambitions as well as routine stuff, classics of German silent film as well as fodder for daily consumption and a quick return on investment. As Helmut Weihsmann has written, direction and acting, sets and props, lighting and camera were all working toward "a new symbiosis." (However, his conclusion "that almost all of Ufa's films . . . achieved significance for film history . . . and shaped our vision of cinema in essential ways"[14] is mistaken.)

Figures compiled by the *Film Yearbook* show 244 films produced in Germany in 1925. Forty-seven of these were either produced, commissioned, or distributed by Ufa.[15] Of the forty-seven, four have won a place in every important history of film: Murnau's *Tartüff* (*Tartuffe*), Dupont's *Variety*, Gerlach's *Concerning the Chronicles of Grieshuus*, and the cultural film *Wege zu Kraft und Schönheit* (*Ways to Strength and Beauty*) by Wilhelm Prager. Other films have been lost, but in many cases reviews or staff lists permit a fairly exact ranking of each.

In that year as in other years, Ufa comedy was a popular commodity but of extremely varied quality, ranging from the routine comedies of Max Mack (*Vater Voss* [*Father Voss*] and *Das Mädchen mit der Protektion* [*The Girl with a Patron*], with Ossi Oswalda and Willy Fritsch) to Alexander Korda's *Der Tänzer meiner Frau* (*My Wife's Dancer*); from Heinrich Bolten-Baecker's simple, popular comedies (*Der Herr ohne Wohnung* [*The Gentleman without a Residence*], *Die zweite Mutter* [*The Second Mother*]) to *Das Fräulein vom Amt* (*The Telephone Operator*) by Hanns Schwarz, a film on which Fritz Arno Wagner (camera), Erich Czerwonski (sets), Henrik Galeen (screenplay), and Giuseppe Becce (music) worked—among Ufa's best artists. With *Ein Walzertraum* (*Dream Waltz*), starring Mady Christians, Willy Fritsch, and Jacob Tiedtke, Ludwig Berger created "the perfectly executed pattern for all later Viennese operetta films done in the style that Willi Forst would develop to perfection."[16] And Hans Neumann produced—"in a parodistic, Offenbach style that is not suitable for films in the year 1925 but is nonetheless a style"[17]—his Shakespeare travesty *Ein Sommernachtstraum* (*A Midsummer Night's Dream*) with Werner Krauss, Valeska Gert, and Alexander Granach. Guido Seeber was the cameraman, Erno Metzner was in charge of sets, and Klabund wrote the subtitles.

Along with his melancholy *Tower of Silence* (some of which was filmed on Rügen with Günther Rittau as cameraman), Johannes Guter also worked in a lighter vein, directing in 1925 the comedies *Herrn Filip Collins Aben-*

teuer (*The Adventure of Mr. Philip Collins*) and *Blitzzug der Liebe* (*Express Train of Love*), both with Ossi Oswalda and screenplays by Robert Liebmann. Kracauer calls them potboilers "located nowhere and void of genuine life."[18] Karl Grune, who created a major film of urban life in the 1920s with *Die Strasse* (*The Street*) in 1923, based his film *Eifersucht* (*Jealousy*)—"a tragicomedy between man and woman"—on a book by Paul Czinner and cast Lya de Putti and Werner Krauss in the lead. Ellen Richter and Willi Wolff brought the globetrotter film to its pinnacle of achievement with *The Flight around the Earth*. Rochus Gliese put aside his "expressionistic" tendencies and turned to lighter material in *Die gefundene Braut* (*The Found Bride*). "It's no exaggeration," *Der Kinematograph* wrote, "to say that the public has not seen anything so hilarious since Lubitsch's *Puppe* (*The Doll*) and that Gliese has finally found his great talent—and love—for comedy."[19] (The credits for this film list Jenny Jugo by name for the first time in a film role; in the 1930s she developed a subversive intelligence in comedies by Erich Engel.)

Two successful historical films by Arthur Robison—*Pietro der Korsar* and *Manon Lescaut*—were also produced in 1925. Joe May based his *Der Farmer aus Texas* (*The Farmer from Texas*) on Georg Kaiser's comedy *Kolportage* and included some American actors in the cast. *Berliner Tageblatt* counted this film, along with *Tartuffe*, among Ufa products that had cost millions to make but had been "almost total flops" at the box office and contributed to Ufa's debt crisis.[20] Another expensive film of the year was *Die Prinzessin und der Geiger* (*The Princess and the Fiddler*), a German-British co-production undertaken by Ufa with Gainsborough Pictures of London. The director was the Englishman Graham Cutts. Jane Novak, Walter Rilla, Bernhard Goetzke, and Rosa Valetti played the leading roles. The book (based on Raymond Paton's novel *The Blackguard*) as well as the sets were by Alfred Hitchcock, who was working in Germany at the time. During a pause in the shooting, Hitchcock received an impromptu lecture from Murnau, who was filming *The Last Laugh* in the neighboring studio. How the decor looks on the set was of no importance, Murnau told him. "All that matters is what you see on the screen."[21]

The year 1925 was a normal production year for Ufa, with its normal miscalculations and its normal censorship battles. *Das Mädchen mit den Schwefelhölzern* (*The Match Girl*) was one of the first sound films made with the Tri-Ergon process (direction: Guido Bagier; screenplay: Hans Kyser). The technical quality was so bad that the premiere in the Mozart Hall on December 17 was a flop. A Union film with the title *Frauen, hütet Eure Mutterschaft!* (*Women, Guard Your Motherhood!*) had a more complex background: it was the end result of a seven-year censorship struggle, seven years of an unsuccessful battle against Germany's controversial antiabortion law. In 1918, Georg Jacoby had directed *Keimendes Leben* (*Budding Life*) for Union with Emil Jannings and Hanna Ralph in the leads. The two-part movie premiered in October, still in wartime, in the Ufa theater on Kurfürstendamm. A third part, with the sensational title *Moral und Sinnlichkeit* (*Morality and Sensuality*), appeared the next year during the brief censorship-free interlude before the new motion picture law went into effect. In 1924, Jacoby's complete film was revised and presented to the censors under the title *Muss die Frau Mutter werden?* (*Does a Woman Have to Become a Mother?*); in April 1925 it was banned after an appeal. *Women, Guard Your Motherhood!* was the third version; presumably[22] it had initially pleaded against the antiabortion law, but the Weimar censors not only stripped it of its intent but so distorted it that it yielded a message diametrically opposed to its original one.

In 1925 Ufa's leadership position was uncontested, though the first signs of a major financial crisis were multiplying. In Neubabelsberg the best actors of their time, a legion of extremely competent film artisans, and an elite of directors, cameramen, set designers, screenplay writers, and musicians worked on a wide range of themes, subjects, and artistic styles. They put their talents in the service of the bold experiment, the reliable market product, and the pathetically mediocre potboiler alike. Ufa was a melting pot of all the virtues and vices of contemporary cinematography. It dominated the field but could not entirely eliminate its competition. E. A. Dupont, for example, director of *Variety*, also worked for Terra-Film in Berlin in 1925, making *Der Demütige und die Sängerin* (*The Humble Man and the Chanteuse*) based on a novel by Felix Hollaender. Founded in 1920 with a capital of 10 million marks, Terra-Film took over Eiko-Film and its studios in Marienfelde in 1922. And other, much smaller firms produced some of the silent-film classics of the Weimar years. Georg Wilhelm Pabst, for example, was working for Sofar-Film-Produktion in Berlin when he made *Die freudlose Gasse* (*The Joyless Street*) in 1925 with Willy Haas as writer and starring Asta Nielsen, Greta Garbo, and Werner Krauss; Guido Seeber was chief cameraman.

Only when we appreciate this compartmentalized yet cooperative industrial enterprise in the service of fantasy, this daily investment of creative energy in products for mass consumption, and the goal of fast, efficient amortization—only then can we appreciate that "messianic" spirit of the "medieval builders' guild" which, the film architect Robert Herlth thought, should inform everyone involved in film production. Just as cathedrals used to be built, so now, under the wing of Ufa, images valid for all time should be created for the screen. "From the director to the lighting foreman and the editor, film is a collective work of art."[23] The set supervisor, the film architect, Herlth felt, should be the *spiritus rector*, the intellectual and artistic model for his colleagues.

The role of architects in the "total artwork" of the classic German silent film indeed cannot be ignored, and Ufa developed a concept of collective work that gave the architectonic imagination latitude and influence such as it never had again. Henri Langlois claimed that "the metaphysics of decor" was the secret of German film; the film architect was "the alchemist of a world that the magic of his skills let him conjure up."[24] Kracauer notes that Paul Rotha coined the term "studio constructivism" to characterize that " 'curious air of completeness, of finality, that surrounds each product of the German studios.' "[25] Kracauer himself was of the opinion, however, that in its sympathy for the avant-garde and abstractionists Ufa had "been guided as ever by the maxim that art is good business or, at least, good propaganda."[26]

Erich Pommer's famous challenge to the production team of *The Last Laugh*—"Please invent something new, even if it's crazy!"[27]—has more than anecdotal value. The "something new" that Pommer wanted was a stunning aesthetic innovation, born of a passion for tinkering and a love for the medium, that by virtue of its own dynamic would bring commercial success and the export profits that Ufa desperately needed. Things did not always work out that way, but when they did, the success confirmed the validity of his plea. Robert Herlth and Walter Röhrig collaborated on the sets for *The Last Laugh*, and Herlth reports that after the film was shown in the United States, a number of telegrams came in from Hollywood. "Where and with what cameras did you shoot this film? As far as we know, neither a camera of this capability nor a city of this kind exists in America." Herlth's comment: "The Americans, accustomed to working with precise technology, couldn't imagine that we had opened up new territory using the most primitive means."[28]

The emphasis in Ufa's magical kitchen was not on technical perfection of the machinery but always on the collaboration of technology and imagination, a "truly cooperative effort . . . whose boldness would spellbind the viewers," as Fritz Lang euphorically put it.[29] More important than technology was a spirit of invention, the alchemist's passion for the self-appointed task of creating new, unprecedented compounds. Herlth was probably not exaggerating when he said of Murnau: "The work was a kind of intoxication for him, an enchantment with a process that is familiar only to the research scientist or the surgeon during an operation."[30]

The Ufa studio could become a "builders' guild" because its architects claimed the right to create worlds anew in the studio, not reconstructions but models projected by a bizarre, romantic imagination free to wander where it would, sometimes even into nightmare. The outside world and its standards did not apply here. The studio's dimensions and perspectives defined the shape life would take. Its walls formed the cosmos for miniature worlds of plaster, wire, cardboard, "calico," and color. Constructed by the architects, textured by infinite modulations of the floodlights, and created once again by the camera, these worlds then appeared on the screen as autonomous, "integrated" constructs. The sets had no value in themselves. The final arbiter was the camera's eye, or, rather, the image on the screen, for that image ultimately dictated the tectonics of buildings, the perspectives, the distortions of perspective, the lighting, and the atmosphere.

In 1920, for Paul Wegener's Union film *Golem, How He Came into the World*, Hans Poelzig had constructed a medieval Prague of the imagination on a hermetically closed set consisting of fifty-four buildings, some of them life-sized, others in miniature. Tied in as they were with the city walls and the synagogue and woven together with steps, fountains, and arches, they seemed parts of an organic whole. Poelzig, Paul Westheim wrote, had not intended to reconstruct old Prague. "He created a mood, evoked a mood from an architecture that was all the more spellbinding for the quiet power it drew entirely from its structural elements."[31]

The quiet power of structures—adherence to that idea amounted to a campaign against "reality" and a renunciation of realism. But this ideal was fully achieved in only ten or fifteen works at the most. In its search for a new artistic language, the bourgeoisie reclaimed its old culture in the Ufa cosmos. The bourgeois era had produced an inexhaustible repertoire of aesthetic material, but deep cracks marred the tableaus of the nineteenth century. New montages were needed to produce new syntheses. Things were not left to chance, nor were they made to conform to the "verisimilitude" of "naturalism." Siegfried's ride through the "petrified forest" in *The Nibelungs* was filmed entirely in the studio. "The straight, plaster tree trunks of the magic forest and wagonloads of salt scattered on the studio floor created the illusion of a snow-covered, frozen forest. The similarity of the tree trunks to cathedral pillars meant to suggest a sacred space," Weihsmann wrote.[32] Erich Kettelhut, who worked with Otto Hunte and Karl Vollbrecht on the sets, recalled that these "trees" measured more than two meters in diameter. Invididual beams of light suggesting sunlight filtering through foliage made realistic details unnecessary. The precisely calculated interplay of light and dark, "structured light," replaced the variety of nature. "We had long discussions about this forest," Kettelhut recalled, "but we agreed from the start that it would have to be a stylized forest if we were going to preserve the unity of the picture sequence. I consider it one of the most supreme rules . . . never to agree to a breach of style."[33]

When Fritz Lang directed *Das Testament des Dr. Mabuse* for Nero-Film in 1932 and shot some scenes outdoors, he forced onto the unpredictability of nature the artificiality of the studio, this time, however, very differently. Here, modern technology made nature more "natural," made reality more "real." Once again a forest was needed, and with a great investment of effort and money, one was "rebuilt" for the shooting. With 140 floodlights and 30,000 meters of cable Lang and his cameraman, Fritz Arno Wagner, transformed the Spree forest so that they could conjure up their own Spree forest on the screen. Lotte Eisner, then a young reporter for *Film-Kurier*, witnessed this huge nocturnal montage:

A tangle of cut-off wires is hanging from a telephone pole. The lines had to be laid underground and rerouted because this whole area was transformed. . . . Felled trees are being hauled around . . . transported on wooden pallets and then replanted in the ground where their creator Lang determines they should stand. Lang himself joins in the work, fetching a few shrubs, which he plants where he wants them. Long-stemmed grass blades are stuck into the ground one by one. Lang surveys his work and, lo! he does not yet find it good. The living stuff of nature is shuffled around and restructured some more. . . . And then, on the wooden railway, he travels the whole stretch behind Wagner's mobile camera, keeping a sharp eye out, constantly calling for improvements, his eye becoming as one with the eye of the camera.[34]

Just as Lang destroyed nature only to re-create it as an image on the screen, so for this same film he spent a great deal of money to renovate an abandoned industrial area in Spandau so that he could then reduce it to rubble in an apocalyptic orgy of destruction recorded by sixteen cameras. Create and destroy, destroy and re-create. The logic of capitalism (and modern warfare as a form of capital investment) found methodological expression in Lang's mode of production.[35] Sometimes modern technology transformed the Ufa studio into a cross between a factory and a medieval alchemist's laboratory. "Fire extinguishers in action, steam rising up from dozens of pipes, on top of that the vapors from all kinds of acids, and the whole business stirred into chaos by airplane engines"—such was cameraman Carl Hoffmann's description of the scene in Murnau's *Faust* in which the Devil is invoked.[36]

In the golden age of the German silent film, technology was regarded by everyone in production as a means to an end. The "end" was a vision that was either called for by the screenplay or developed in the director's head. By means of innumerable sketches and in endless conferences, the set designer, the cameraman, the technical staff, or all of them together would modify the idea, sharpen it, and expand upon it until all the variables had been defined down to the last detail.

Long before shooting began, the film architect and cameraman had intensive discussions in which the set designer presented sketches and plans, which also established camera angles, perspectives, lens settings, and lighting suggestions the cameraman could use. These conferences drew the various film métiers together, not only making people more familiar with each other but also helping them develop a better understanding of the film's intentions and its design.[37]

This "drawing together," this mysterious communication among talents, this "alchemy" of minds, makes it difficult for us today to determine what the key factor in any given film was. Was it the director's planning, the practicability of the set, the lighting design, the mobility of the camera, or (more rarely) the ability of certain performers to incorporate their body language into the filmic reality? The same impulse that suggested the medieval builders' guild (*Baühutte*) to Robert Herlth inspired Karl Freund, probably Ufa's most gifted cameraman in the 1920s, to think in terms of "intellectual firms" that should be formed within and outside the studios. "Their inner nature is determined by a completely organic cooperation among their individual divisions. They have to come together on both human and artistic grounds. They have to learn their technology from each other and teach it to each other."[38]

The excerpts that Lotte Eisner has published from Robert Herlth's papers give wonderful insight into the *modus operandi* of Murnau's team. Herlth describes how Freund's fully automatic camera became mobile, liberated from its tripod, how it was used at different heights with the help of an extension ladder, and how, mounted on a bicycle, it could cross a hotel lobby. "Now there was no stopping him. At one moment Freund would have his camera strapped on his belly; at the next it would be gliding through the air on a ramp; at still another it rode around with him on a wagon I had built and equipped with rubber wheels."[39] In a famous scene in *The Last Laugh* Emil Jannings in the role of a doorman is wakened from his dreams early in the morning by a trumpet. The challenge was to make the viewer visualize a "flying tone":

> On the grounds in Babelsberg where the courtyard had been built, a special basket-like construction was hung between the second-story window and the ground-floor window. The camera was mounted in a gondola hung on tracks that could travel across the entire courtyard on a downward slant for about twenty meters—from the ear of the sleeping Jannings to the mouth of the trumpet.[40]

As it turned out, the block-and-tackle specially designed to control the gondola was inadequate for the task, and the shot was made by placing the camera upside down and pulling it upward. Karl Freund himself recalls how he achieved another effect: "In a scene where Jannings was supposed to act drunk, I strapped the camera to my chest (with batteries on my back for balance) and then staggered around like a drunk."[41] The historians' quarrel over who should be credited with the invention of the "liberated camera"—Murnau, Freund, or the screenplay writer Carl Mayer—is the most convincing proof we have for how successfully the artists in Ufa's magic kitchen complemented each other and spurred each other on.

Herlth describes his cooperative efforts with the cameraman Carl Hoffmann in Murnau's *Faust*:

> There was still no crane at that time, so when we had to film the flight on Mephisto's cloak, our solution used Hoffmann's idea of building a narrow plaster ramp on which a carriage with large rubber-tired wheels

and the camera mounted on it could be rolled. The plaster ramp went up and down like a roller coaster. That was supposed to convey the up-and-down movement of the flight. The landscape consisted of models, for aerial shots would have been limited and, being real, would not have conveyed a medieval, romantic atmosphere.[42]

Even though the ramp was carefully constructed, slight irregularities in it produced bumps and jerks in the trial shots. The sight of a flatbed truck suggested another solution to Herlth and Röhrig, and they built a filming dolly with a low platform and heavy wheels that enabled them to shoot "flowing sequences" and transitions. The flight on Mephisto's cloak, the dynamic up-and-down motion of the camera, the plastic effects created by lighting—all that produced in *Faust* a new visual quality that was called "abstract" film architecture.[43] Indeed, large segments of this film still strike a viewer today as coming from an experimental film by a post-Expressionist abstract artist, incorporating all the sophisticated techniques developed in Neubabelsberg.

When Herlth remarked that aerial shots "would have been limited and, being real, would not have conveyed a medieval, romantic atmosphere" he revealed a tendency that was anything but modernist and seemed to run counter to the technological consciousness and realistic aesthetics of Ufa's best people. The miniature landscapes that Herlth and Röhrig created in a huge shed at Neubabelsberg—"larches and pines made from bundles of reeds, clouds of fiberglass, waterfalls, wheatfields of grass stalks (which were laboriously stuck into soft plaster)"[44]—were modeled on paintings by Albrecht Altdorfer. The decision to use this painter as a model was not a chance one. Altdorfer (about 1480–1538) created the first "pure" landscapes in German painting, and according to a history of art published in the 1920s, he ranked, "precisely because of his German qualities, among the most appealing German artists of his time."[45] What was so appealing was his poetic, evocative view of nature and his romantic, idyllic interpretation of his subjects.

Romantic echoes from the German Middle Ages thus became, in the ultra-modern film factory of Neubabelsberg, the material of a vision that once again romanticized and glorified history and reality. As if through colored glass, the architects studied the art of past centuries in search of a home for their vague yearnings, and they called that home "the Middle Ages." The flip side of their technological sophistication and highly developed modernity was a flight from the modern, an escapism. And this was deeply rooted in the ideological undercurrents of the Weimar Republic. In the widespread "hunger for wholeness," Peter Gay writes, unarticulated phobias and hatreds were gathered. "On closer inspection, they revealed themselves as symptomatic of massive regression arising from great fear: the fear of modernity."[46]

The philosophy of the Enlightenment, Marx and Darwin, psychoanalysis and sociology, trends in modern art, and new technologies of communication evoked tirades of hatred from many reactionary demagogues in the 1920s. A "conglomerate of hostility presented itself as philosophy" and prompted the historian Ernst Troeltsch in 1922 to warn of the German's characteristic "mixture of mysticism and brutality."[47] It is characteristic, too, of the internal contradictions within the German film industry and especially of Ufa that the era's most modern medium, which aggressive reactionaries declared an archenemy, generated powerful mixtures of brutality and mysticism and even lent them the aura (as in Lang's *The Nibelungs*) of a specifically German "high culture" transcending the limits of bourgeois culture. "My goal in *The Nibelungs*," Lang wrote, "had to be to create a film that did not trivialize the sacred and spiritual yet still belonged to the people and not . . . to a small number of privileged and cultivated minds."[48]

Murnau was especially fond of "old-German material. Little cities with timber-framed houses and narrow, winding streets"[49] lend atmosphere in films like *Nosferatu* (Prana-Film, 1921), *Phantom*, and *Faust* (Ufa, 1925–26). In the 1920s, this romantic idyll was still a reality in not only the German psychic landscape but also the physical one. Village life in the German provinces and the medieval character of Germany's small cities were still intact, which was not the case after 1945. The "little German city" into which Hitler's regiments soon marched was still very real, a holdover from the nineteenth century, with its Gothic gates, ivy-covered walls, and steep, tiled roofs. Carl Spitzweg's paintings were still popular, and the big world with its noisy highways was still far off.

In the "gothicizing" films of the Weimar Republic the German small-city idyll became the scene of unspeakable horrors and bloody, irrational crimes. But even when, as in *Nosferatu*, a vampire descends or, as in Lang's *Destiny*, Friend Hein takes up residence by the city wall, the romantic ambience remains undisturbed and "timelessly" invulnerable. With loving attention to detail, the directors and their architects built their images of intact German provincial life. "View over the roofs of a small, old-fashioned city in the style of the 1840s. Sun shining cheerfully on the peaked roofs and green city squares" is how Henrik Galeen's lyrical screenplay prose pictured the opening scene for *Nosferatu—Eine Symphonie des Grauens* (*Nosferatu—A Symphony of Horror*).[50]

Murnau's penchant for old German material was obviously not "fear of modernity." His use of technology and the geometrical awareness evident in his films identify him as decidedly modern, like Lang. But the contradiction already present in Paul Wegener's films—between the technical capability and the organizational form of the medium on the one hand and the "images of a pre-industrial age" evoked on the other—becomes particularly striking in the "classic" works of German silent film. Mysticism and modernity, the trust in the values of a pre-revolutionary "intact world" and the inklings of horror lurking beneath the roofs of the stolid little city, enter into an ambiguous symbiosis.

Ufa's studios were the scene of a unique and politically explosive controversy, an antagonism that was reflected in film subjects, in the "technology" of the medium, and in the production process. It was the same dilemma that had faced the Expressionist avant-garde of 1918–19, the same dilemma that had plagued the "November group" of revolutionary artists, the Working Council for Art and the Weimar Bauhaus. German geniuses had come together, "inspired by a half-religious zeal to make everything new."[51] This spirit—which was not immune to pseudo-religious autosuggestion, and which was especially tailored for what Fritz Stern has called the "vulgar idealism" of the sentimental and gullible German petit bourgeoisie[52]—appears in the prose of Thea von Harbou and in some of Ufa's press propaganda. In 1926–27 it brought about, in Fritz Lang's *Metropolis*, a catastrophe of monumental proportions (as well as the company's greatest financial disaster). The paradoxical contradiction between the "old German," regressive subject matter of many films and the freedom of artistic and technical organization was indicative of the ever-widening gap between the dangerous fantasies of the era and the efforts of enlightened progressives to understand the times.[53] Ufa's studios were, in the words of Ernst Bloch, a "melting pot" for Weimar and for both its progressive and regressive elements. They were defenseless against a violent takeover by forces that stood ready to inject new meaning into them and to fill the emptiness in them with a false religion.

10.

The Aesthetics of the Grandiose
in Ufa's Theaters

"I HAD long since given up the habit of regarding every Berlin mosque as a Muslim house of worship," Joseph Roth noted in 1925. "I knew that mosques were movie theaters here, and the Orient was a film. Once, many years ago when I was still religious, I wanted to go to early Mass. I went into a church, but it was a railroad station. I learned later that architectural style is meaningless and that red-brick warehouses with lightning rods on them are where the altars stand and where the word of God is heard."[1]

The productive and at the same time dangerous disarray in which German society found itself was perceived by the alert observer as a chaos loaded with tension, incoherent, a chaos waiting for "a necessary reversal." "In the streets of Berlin one is often struck by the realization that everything will suddenly break apart here one day."[2] Movie-theater façades ablaze with advertising reinforced the impression of a world with no clear limits and no solid ground underfoot. In the midst of the harsh realities of everyday life, they were peddling anti-realities visible from far off in the very architecture of the theaters themselves, even though they never achieved, or aspired to, the extreme montages that Fernand Léger found in 1931 in America: "incredible combinations of every European and Asiatic style; each one a colossal chaos designed to be irresistibly attractive and even more bombastic than the competition next door; incredible structures born of the principle: The more opulent, the better!"[3]

In Germany, the spectrum of movie-house architecture in the 1920s ranged from massive, pseudo-classicism to lean "functionalism" and, in the interiors, "from dramatized court theater to spatial experiments of the New Architecture."[4] Ufa developed in this field, too, an energy that formed the style and tastes of the times. Its theaters displayed fresh new lines, a new "façade culture,"[5] and added their own special accents to the face of the city.

Berlin—the industrial and commercial metropolis, the capital city, the El Dorado of the fine arts, and the center of democratic mass culture— offered an ideal field for experimentation. The provinces followed Berlin's example, usually on a smaller scale; at the beginning of the sound-film era Ufa would build Europe's largest movie house, with a capacity of 2,750, in Hamburg. Ufa also planned a "prototypical movie theater," "an architectural pattern to be followed in all German cities, much as a mother convent prescribed the architecture of its subsidiaries."[6] But this plan was never carried out; film does not lend itself to being marketed in uniform packaging. The economic need to "walk a fine line between extremism and conformity, between spectacular innovation and commitment to tradition" did not encourage an architectural monoculture but, rather, stimulated the imagination. "In the midst of social and architectural gloom the movie theaters were islands of light. Especially in the first years after the war, they linked the traditional, solemn buildings with the élan of the New Architecture."[7]

Between 1920 and 1929, the number of German movie theaters grew from about 3,700 to about 5,000. In 1927, 337,342,000 movie admissions were tallied in all of Germany. In 1925, Berlin alone accounted for more than 44 million. The number of small theaters fell steadily while the number of large ones (over 1,000 seats) grew. In Berlin in 1925 there were 342 theaters with a total capacity of 147,612 seats. Of those, 180 were small houses (fewer than 300 seats), 48 medium-sized (between 600 and 1,000 seats), and 22 were "film palaces" with more than 1,000 seats. In 1925, Ufa owned 91 theaters throughout Germany.[8]

Of the large theaters built before the First World War, the one of greatest significance was the Marmorhaus (Marble House), designed by Hug Pal. Its solemn monumentality and the imperial geometry of its façade, divided as it is into large surfaces, still sets the tone of the Kurfürstendamm near the Kaiser-Wilhelm Church today. Pal sought to link old Egyptian and Greek elements with "Germanic" weight. Part royal palace and part cult temple, the Marmorhaus was in the same class as the museums and theaters of the Wilhelmine era, evoking "the sublime and the sacred, as if it contained images that would endure forever."[9] But the films shown here reflected instead decaying realities and shattered certainties—*The Cabinet of Dr. Caligari* (1919–20), Dupont's Ufa film *Variety*, and *Giftgas* (*Poison Gas*, 1929, based on the play *Giftgas über Berlin* [*Poison Gas over Berlin*] by Peter Martin Lampel and directed by Michael Dubson).

The Gloria-Palast, located directly across from the Marmorhaus, gives Kracauer a prize example to support his thesis that a "cultivated ostentatiousness of surface"[10] was the key feature of the new movie palaces. In its interiors, the critic Dieter Bartetzko found "cleverly simplified renderings of the spatial extravagance of Baroque palaces and theaters."[11] Commissioned by the Gloria-Gesellschaft and funded in part by Ufa, it was built in 1925–26 by Max Bremer and Ernst Lessing. The theater (with 1,200 seats) opened its doors with Murnau's *Tartuffe* on January 25, 1926, and its advertising emphasized the fancy tone that the Gloria-Palast hoped would win the public's favor: "Germany's most elegant premiere theater located in the heart of west Berlin. The motion-picture theater of good society will premiere the best films in the most distinguished of settings."[12]

Ironically enough, another premiere—G. W. Pabst's psychoanalytical case study *Geheimnisse einer Seele* (*Secrets of a Soul*, 1925–26), with Werner Krauss and Ruth Weyer and produced for Ufa by Hans Neumann—brought the respectable society of west Berlin face-to-face with its own repressed drives, its anxieties, and its hidden murderous impulses, although the film undercut the incisiveness of its analysis and the subtle, ingenious camerawork of Guido Seeber, Curt Oertel, and Robert Lach with an utterly banal happy ending. Other major Ufa premieres in the Gloria-Palast were *Der Geiger von Florenz* (*The Fiddler of Florence*, 1925–26, with Elisabeth Bergner and directed by Paul Czinner) and Karl Grune's pacifist film *Am Rande der Welt* (*At the Edge of the World*, 1927). This film struck Ufa's management—immediately after Alfred Hugenberg's takeover—as so radical that, over the director's protests, they mutilated it beyond recognition. Another Gloria-Palast premiere was Johannes Guter's film *Ihr wunder Punkt* (*Her Sore Point*, 1929, with Lilian Harvey and Willy Fritsch). Robert Liebmann based the screenplay on a novella by Frank Maraun. Pabst's film of Wedekind's *Die Büchse der Pandora* (*Pandora's Box*), produced for Nero-Film and starring Louise Brooks and Fritz Kortner, premiered in the Gloria-Palast in February 1929—again hardly flattering the conservative camp.

If the Gloria-Palast was the springboard for many "major society films" in which upper-class people could inspect not only their emotions but also the cultural inventory of their own world, the smaller Ufa-Theater am Kurfürstendamm, which opened in 1913 and which Ufa took over when it acquired Projektions Union's entire chain of theaters, served as an experimental venue for artistically ambitious films. Among these were Rex-Film's "chamber films" *Shattered* (1921) and *New Year's Eve* (1923), directed by Lupu Pick. Joe Hembus regards *Die Abenteuer eines Zehnmarkscheins* (*The Adventures of a Ten-Mark Bill*), written by Béla Balázs and directed by Berthold Viertel for Karl Freund's Fox-Europa Film in 1926, as a "pioneering work of the New Objectivity";[13] and in *Menschen am Sonntag* (*People on Sunday*, 1929–30), another avant-garde film of the late 1920s, Robert Siodmak, Edgar G. Ulmer, Billy Wilder, and Fred Zinnemann achieved unprecedented realistic effects of documentary quality. The makers of this film were later successful in Hollywood, but in 1929 they were still unknown in Berlin and Ufa had no confidence in them. The firm did not expect to make money from the movie, even though Eugen Schüfftan, much in demand as a special-effects man after *Metropolis*, had been the cameraman. According to Curt Riess's account, it was thanks to Hanns Brodnitz, chief executive of Ufa's theaters in Berlin and a man with an eye for quality, that *People on Sunday* premiered in the Ufa-Theater am Kurfürstendamm.[14]

Ever since its opening in September 1919 with Lubitsch's *Passion*, the Ufa-Palast am Zoo had been the uncontested flagship of Ufa's theaters. After remodeling by Carl Stahl-Urach in 1925, it contained 2,165 seats. On the outside it resembled a massive Romanesque citadel whose rough-hewn stonework and square tower were evocative of "Germanic heritage." The interior shone

> all red and gold with soft, heavy purple on the floors and walls. In spite of the hugeness of the auditorium, it is more inviting than many a chamber theater. Among its special offerings are an orchestra of seventy-five and high, pleated gold curtains that, illuminated by dozens of spotlights, provide an uninterrupted play of fantastic color.[15]

Ventilation was supplied by "an electric zeppelin that swept through the house during intermissions and sprayed eau de Cologne about with an atomizer." The orchestra was directed by Ernö Rapée, who had been musical director in New York's Capitol Theater, and Alexander Oumanski directed the house's ballet company. Rudi Feld was in charge of advertising on the theater's façade and for the opulent "stage shows" that preceded the films.

Joseph Roth found the Ufa-Palast a phantasmagoria of vapid opulence and bombast:

> I sat in the third row back from the curtain of green velvet. Suddenly the hall went dark; the curtain opened slowly; and a mysterious light that God could never have created and that nature will never manage to produce in a thousand years poured over the front of the stage in soft cascades. It was as if someone had taken years to tame and train waterfalls for domestic use and had brought them to the walls of this palace where they poured down circumspectly, altogether civilized and bent to the service of human needs. Elemental energies with good manners, natural forces that had learned their lessons well. The illumination presented at one stroke the first glimmer of dawn and the red glow of sunset, heavenly clarity and hellish vapors, city glare and forest green, moonlight and midnight sun. What nature produces in boring sequence and in regions separated by vast distances was now compressed into one room in one minute. It thus became clear that an unknown and powerful divinity was at play, or at serious work, here. There wasn't room enough for us to sink down on our knees, for we sat too close together. But if this image is possible: Our knees sank down, so to speak, by themselves.[16]

The sacred atmosphere fraudulently evoked, extravagant imitations that outnatured nature, theatrical exploitation of light, an overwhelming of the senses—such were the elements of mood manipulation that predestined the Ufa-Palast for a special role when the National Socialists enlisted the arts in the service of politics. The transformation of a republic into a dictatorship was to be reflected in the metamorphosis of this theater "from a neo-Romantic palace to a structure embodying the dignity of the new state."[17]

But into the late 1920s the Ufa-Palast retained a double function as Ufa's showpiece and as a forum for a democratic and pluralistic film culture, a cult temple of the senses and—as the showings of Cserépy's *Fridericus Rex* films demonstrated—an arena for political debate. Both Buchowetzki's *Danton* and Joe May's *The Indian Tomb* were first shown here, also Murnau's *The Last Laugh* and *Faust*; Fritz Lang's *Metropolis*; Arthur Robison's *Manon Lescaut*, with Lya de Putti, Wladimir Gaidarow, Siegfried Arno, and Marlene Dietrich; Karl Grune's *Die Brüder Schellenberg* (*The Schellenberg Brothers*, 1925–26); and Richard Eichberg's smash hit *Die keusche Susanne* (*Chaste Susanne*, 1926), with Lilian Harvey and Willy Fritsch.

The nearby Capitol am Zoo on Budapester Strasse, designed by Hans Poelzig and opened in December 1925, was Ufa-Palast's counterweight. Poelzig, who, like Gropius, belonged to the reform wing of the German Workers League, had been regarded as an able theater architect ever since he had converted the Schumann Circus into the Grosses Schauspielhaus. Two years after the Capitol he built the Deli-Kino in Breslau, and in 1929 he was the architect for the Berlin Babylon. His original draft for the Capitol called for a design somewhere "between a functionalistic office building and a pathos-laden, neoclassical embassy."[18] Despite major changes, the façade retained the classical clarity of its horizontal lines, and it offered impressive possibilities for neon lighting. As in the Grosses Schauspielhaus, Poelzig showed himself an expert with interior lighting—where light rays spread out from the center of the dome, adding an especially appropriate touch for a movie house. Functional but not boring, the Capitol represented a counterpoint for the overworked eclecticism of the neighboring Ufa cathedrals.

The Capitol, which had about 1,300 seats, steered a different course with its premieres, too. February 1926 saw the German premiere of Charlie Chaplin's *The Gold Rush*, with a prologue spoken by Curt Bois. Chaplin's *Circus* followed in 1928. The Capitol also showed Gerhard Lamprecht's socially concerned films *Die Unehelichen* (*The Illegitimate Children*, 1926) and *Der Katzensteg* (*The Catwalk*, 1927), based on the novel of the same title by Hermann Sudermann. In 1926 it screened Henrik Galeen's remake of *The Student of Prague* with sets by Hermann Warm and Conrad Veidt in the starring role that Paul Wegener had played in 1913. And with tearjerkers like Wilhelm Dieterle's *Die Heilige und ihr Narr* (*The Saint and Her Fool*, 1928), based on the pulp novel by Agnes Günther, the Capitol made its concessions to the taste of "little shopgirls," who found "unimagined insights into the wretchedness of humanity and the goodness dispensed from above."[19]

With the construction of the Mercedes palaces on Utrechter Strasse and in Neukölln, of the Lichtburg at the S-Bahn station Gesundbrunnen in 1930, and the Titania-Palast in Steglitz, movie-theater architecture moved into a new phase dominated by monumental "objectivity" and an oppressively massive scale that anticipated National Socialist architecture. A "block concept"[20] prevailed that was later adopted as "progressive." A truly progressive building, however, was the Universum am Kurfürstendamm (now the Berliner Schaubühne on Lehniner Platz), which opened in 1928 and seated 1,800 people. This Ufa movie house, with its massive elegance and streamlined façade, seems to loom onto the boulevard like an ocean liner. Its designer, Erich Mendelsohn, had no intention of building a "rococo palace for Buster Keaton"[21] but wanted instead a new synthesis of "space, color, and light."

If the designs of movie theaters were risky, that judgment applies even more to the "stage shows" that accompanied film showings before World War I and were developed further in the 1920s. Vocal and instrumental music, ballet, pantomime, variety, acrobatics, and all kinds of other acts served as a setting for the main cinematic feature. "The theater manager has to understand, of course, how to put together a mixed program of this kind with tact and good taste," wrote *Reichsfilmblatt* in 1926.[22] "A stage show can become an *enfant terrible* if it is thrust indiscriminately into the film program."

That happened all too often. But where tact and good taste were at work, "a stunning, revue-like form emerged from cinema, an all-inclusive art work," Kracauer wrote, though he detected in it regressive yearnings for the stage and reactionary tendencies. The stage diversions were "framed in draperies and drawn back into a unity that no longer exists."[23]

Here, too, Ufa was a leader. "Without resorting to the tasteless American device of overwhelming the audience with masses of performers and excessive sets," Franz Heilburg, manager of the Ufa-Palast am Turmstrasse, developed a stage show for Dupont's *Variety* in 1926 that blended two- and three-dimensional stage reality and won praise for its fluid transitions and impressionistic *trompe l'oeil*:

As the curtain went up we saw faintly glowing lamps in the dusky light and heard carnival music played by hand organs. The lighting brightened gradually, and we saw carnival booths, the largest of which bore the film title *Variety*. Artistes appeared with their various tricks, girls danced, a juggler performed, and the lights dimmed again until all we could see were the shadowy forms of performers doing their routines. The only light came from the juggler's torches, the word "Variety," and the decorative bulbs on the booths. A scrim was then lowered, and the movie's carnival scene was immediately projected onto it, its action blending with that on the fading stage until the film screen was lowered. This and the other preliminaries lasted fifteen or twenty minutes, just long enough to prepare the audience.[24]

The bizarre theater interiors and stage shows were meant to put spectators in a festive mood, to steer their attention tactfully toward the feature, and to make them receptive to its message. And in their outdoor ads, with full-color pictures of the stars, gigantic letters, and neon figures, film overwhelmed architecture. The sensations of the screen leaped out onto the street, scattering their tidings about in the hectic life of the city. With his ingenious manipulation of light and movement, Rudi Feld, Ufa's advertising chief, transformed theater façades into huge screens and showplaces for spectacular mechanical effects. For the premiere of Fritz Lang's *Woman in the Moon* (1929) he draped the Ufa-Palast am Zoo in a tapestry of lights, converting it into an image of the cosmos. Above the three entrances a model rocketship was regularly shot out of a globe and then disappeared in the artificial night sky. And for the premiere of Lang's *Spione* (*Spies*) in 1928, the main façade was decorated with a huge, stylized, and harshly illuminated eye. The letters of the film title extended the entire width of the central façade and changed form, becoming oversized pupils from which spotlights shot out over the sidewalk crowds.

The urban environment was part of this advertising art. For the premiere of Joe May's *Asphalt* (1929),

> a huge transparency, showing a section of a city street, is mounted on the façade of the Ufa-Palast am Zoo and is alternately illuminated and darkened. In the foreground automobiles are pictured in constant motion. The most surprising and powerful effect is achieved by the movement of two wooden gates that close over the transparency and then part again. In gigantic letters mounted on the gates is the word "Asphalt," which blazes up in thousands of lights once the gates have covered the transparency and then dominates the otherwise darkened façade of the theater.[25]

The city street portrayed in the advertising transparency then appeared again during the credits for the film.

The façades changed from day to day and week to week; they were advertising as the cinema's "second skin," illumination as a form of "nocturnal architecture."[26] But all this glitter also helped to disguise the fact that the cinema's economic situation was anything but rosy, not to mention that most of the people in the audiences were living under difficult conditions and some were barely making a living at all. The contrast between these oppressive economic problems and the glowing image presented to the world, a contrast Harry Kessler had noted as early as 1920, had by the mid-1920s become a key feature of Weimar democracy.

Ufa's ingenious but ultimately vapid advertising spectaculars reflected the atmosphere of Berlin's Luna Park, which, as he observed to his surprise on a Sunday in May 1920, had taken on a "Babylonian appearance" with its "hanging terraces and pyramids of light reaching up into the night sky." People had come by the thousands to see a fireworks display. "There is a feeling of something unnatural and feverish here in this opulence and this apparent unconcern for wasteful extravagance in the midst of a blood-stained Berlin teetering on the edge of an abyss."[27]

The fireworks were for the masses. The solemn film premieres in the West Berlin film palaces, however, were for the well-to-do who thought themselves cultured, for an elite that in fact was largely made up of par-venus, war profiteers, and upstart politicians. One basked in the deceptive glow of a sham culture among friends who pretended they had created a new whole, a new synthesis. Everything was "precious"—the ladies' clothes and jewelry, the chandeliers in the foyers, the artists whom the manage-ment hired for the stage shows.

It was in this kind of atmosphere that the opening of the Gloria-Palast was celebrated on January 25, 1926, with the premiere of Murnau's *Tartuffe*. The new theater under the direction of "General Intendant" Otto Wilhelm Lange gave its guests a fancily designed program about not only the film but also the stage show. The program began with the overture to Luigi Cherubini's opera *Ali Baba*, with Ignatz Waghalter conducting. The theater directors doubtless thought its tone in keeping with the "Baroque" style of the building and the classical theme of the film. After the musical prelude came a ceremonial poem, written by Herbert Eulenberg and spoken by Camilla Spira. Eulenberg, who was celebrating his fiftieth birthday that day, was a very popular dramatist and novelist of the Neo-Romantic school. By 1926, the height of his fame was past, but he was still regarded as a noble spirit of an "idealistic" nature, a writer who had put naturalism to rout. Also, his famous play *Schattenbilder* (*Shadow Images*) in Düsseldorf had shown that he considered it his mission to educate the masses in bourgeois culture. His poem for the opening of the Gloria-Palast began on a light note and ended with a plea in which ominous undertones were audible: "Fill your gaze with light and glory / Before the curtain falls and buries us! / We are flowering still, surrounded by the blossom's perfume. / Know then this as your greatest bliss: You live!"[28]

The next item on the agenda was an Ufa cultural film titled *Zeitlupen-revue aus der gefiederten Welt* (*A Slow-Motion Revue from the World of Birds*). It formed a transition to the high point of the stage show—impro-visations based on Frank Wedekind's pantomime *Die Flöhe* (*The Fleas*), which was meant to introduce in person Lil Dagover, who played Elmire in *Tartuffe*. The printed program closes with a hymn of praise for "cock-eyed" urban culture: "The jazz band, the railroad, the machine, the auto-mobile, sports, boxing—it is all animated by rhythm, and what provides the vital spark, the artistic and astonishing element? Syncopation!"[29]

Ufa's grandiose posing and self-aggrandizement were dutifully reported in the daily reviews and even in the film-industry press. Because the leading trade publications like *Der Kinematograph* and the *Lichtbild-Bühne* had sold out to economic and political interests, they were incapable of unbiased criticism or judgments based on sound analysis. *Der Kinematograph* in particular, which had been been taken over by Scherl in 1923 and was therefore part of Hugenberg's concern, had nothing but vapid praise to offer whenever it reviewed an Ufa premiere; when Hugenberg took Ufa over in 1927, the Association of Berlin Film Critics no longer accepted editors and writers for that or any other Scherl publication as members.

It is therefore not surprising that *Der Kinematograph* gave the premiere of the Murnau film a panegyric that was truly outstanding for its lack of imagination and its hackneyed language. There was nothing about the film that did not come in for praise: "the superb photography" by Karl Freund, the "excellent architecture" by Robert Herlth and Walter Röhrig, the "truly brilliant casting" of Emil Jannings in the title role, the dramatic art of Lil Dagover, "a sophisticated, worldly actress who, in this role, played a classical part in a classical style." Even the observation that Giuseppe Becce's music was nothing but "reworkings of well-known popular themes" somehow managed to be praise, suggesting that this was perhaps the right approach for good film music.[30] This was the mode in which Ufa and the other major German film companies trained its apologists and encouraged sycophancy among writers.

The premiere of Murnau's *Faust* on October 14, 1926, was turned into a neo-baroque event of the first order. The company's propaganda machine had worked overtime to keep the filming of Germany's national poem by a master director very much in the news. Now it promoted the premiere as a world-class event in which the political and cultural *crème de la crème* of Germany's capital city were more or less obliged to participate. The tone of the report that appeared in the *Lichtbild-Bühne* the next day did full justice to the exalted status of the premiere's audience. It concluded as follows:

> In spite of the many honored guests representing Berlin's political elite at the Ufa-Palast, the public's interest before the show was concentrated mainly on a young blond girl who was appearing for the first time in the flower-bedecked actors' box: Camilla Horn, who plays Gretchen in the film. After the young actress appeared before the audience again, this time on stage after the film, Ignaz Wilhelm, the director of the evening's program, read two telegrams, one from Murnau in Hollywood and the other from aboard the *Albert Ballin*, on which Jannings was traveling to America. Both men sent best wishes for the German premiere.[31]

The splendor of the event easily concealed the fact that Ufa, indeed the entire German film industry, had been in serious financial straits for over a year. During debates over the causes of this crisis, the production chief, Erich Pommer, left Ufa in January 1926, three days before the opening of the Gloria-Palast with his *Tartuffe*. In April he departed for the United States, as had Leni, Dupont, and Berger before him, as well as Pola Negri,

Lya de Putti, and Conrad Veidt. The first Ufa exodus to Hollywood had long since begun. And now Murnau, already at work in the United States on preparations for his Fox film *Sunrise*, was conspicuous by his absence from the premiere of his own masterpiece, as was his lead actor, Emil Jannings. Murnau's telegram with best wishes was also his letter of farewell to Ufa and the German film public.

11.

The Balance after Liquidation:
The Cathedral in Crisis

MURNAU'S and Jannings's move to Hollywood was a major loss of artistic talent, but Ufa's most serious loss was the departure of Erich Pommer, who left the company nine months before the *Faust* premiere to join the Famous Players–Lasky Company and produce *Hotel Imperial*, starring Pola Negri and directed by Mauritz Stiller.

Pommer had been Ufa's production chief ever since the merger of Ufa and Decla-Bioscop. He had kept in touch with every aspect of the industry—business policy and artistic ideas, technical challenges and organizational duties, the tastes of both the masses and the avant-garde—and thanks to his great versatility he had amassed considerable power. In the German context, he was the first modern film producer. Like no one else of his time, he understood the new medium's special qualities and knew how to coordinate its commercial and artistic aspects. If the success of German film in the 1920s was due to a "perfect coordination of its various technical divisions," as the film historian Wolfgang Jacobsen has written,[1] and if its best products displayed a harmonic tension among the elements essential to Ufa's vitally important export business—filmscript, camera, lighting, sets, direction, and acting—then most of the credit must go to Erich Pommer. He was the great pioneer.

In February 1923 Pommer had taken over management of Ufa's three big production companies: Messter, Union, and Decla-Bioscop. (The designations "Decla-Film of Ufa" and "Union-Film of Ufa" were briefly used but then dropped after 1925.) Every one of his major productions in 1923–25 has a permanent place in film history: *Driven from Home* (F. W. Murnau, 1923), *Der verlorene Schuh* (*The Lost Shoe*, Ludwig Berger, 1923), *Die Finanzen des Grossherzogs* (*The Finances of the Archduke*, F. W. Murnau, 1923), *Concerning the Chronicles of Grieshuus, Michael* (Carl Theodor Dreyer, 1923–24), *Komödie des Herzens* (*Comedy of the Heart*, Rochus

Gliese, 1924; Murnau and Gliese wrote the book together under the pseudonym "Murglie"), *The Last Laugh, Pietro the Corsair, The Princess and the Fiddler* (Graham Cutts, 1924–25), *Tartuffe, Variety, Metropolis* (Fritz Lang, 1926–27), *Manon Lescaut* (Arthur Robison), *Dream Waltz* (Ludwig Berger, 1925), *The Fiddler of Florence, The Schellenberg Brothers. Metropolis,* like *Faust,* was still in production when Pommer left Ufa.

When Pommer resigned at the end of January 1926, *Das Tage-Buch* ran a long article by Stefan Grossmann that clearly laid out the achievements of this producer now fallen into disfavor and alluded to some of the disagreements that had led to his resignation:

> Pommer rid the film world of its founders' dilettantism. Systematically and tenaciously he elevated German film to the level of a serious artistic medium, and he was able to win German writers of stature over to film. . . . In his search for directors, Pommer displayed his keenest instincts. As we all know, a good nose is sometimes worth more than a good head for figures. From the swarm of flashy experimenters Pommer selected the four or five genuine talents and then knew how to keep them. It may be that the accountants can say now with hindsight that Pommer didn't keep a tight enough hold on the purse strings, but no mere accountant could ever have enlisted, inspired, and retained Ludwig Berger, Fritz Lang, Murnau, and Dupont.[2]

Pommer's successor was the chief of Ufa's cultural division, Major Alexander Grau, whom the Royal Prussian Ministry of War had charged in 1917 with managerial duties on its behalf. Grau was, as Grossmann wrote, "a cultivated officer, as likable as he is a man of goodwill." He was expected to be conscientious and well-ordered, but beyond that no one could guess. "Ufa can no longer draw on unlimited resources," Grossmann rightly observed, "and what it is lacking in money it will have to make up for with good ideas. Competition with the expansion-hungry Americans has never been so demanding. It's to Major Grau's credit that, ordered to an imperiled post, he has taken on his assignment without complaint or hesitation. But cinema campaigns are usually won in a less military manner."

Ufa was founded in a military manner, of course, and under the wing of the armed forces it had successfully fought its first campaigns. But by 1925–26, the political and economic fronts were completely different. Industrial offensives were driven by new inventions and new technologies, but most importantly by dollars. The competitive battles of the monopolies were carried out by peaceful means, but no less aggressively for that. Hard-pressed by the American production giants, not only Ufa but the entire German film industry was in an extremely dangerous situation.

Germany's economic improvement, which set in after the replacement of the Rentenmark with the Reichsmark and was at least superficially evident from 1925 on, was largely due to injections of foreign capital. The

Dawes Plan—along with the end of the occupation of the Ruhr, the lowering of reparation payments, and significant loans to Germany—had opened the way for foreign, especially American, investors. A period of false prosperity ensued. German industry formed concerns and cartels, wages increased, the number of the unemployed dropped (in 1928, down to far less than a million). The image the Weimar Republic presented between 1924 and 1928 was of a stable economy under essentially conservative administrations. "Social Democratic votes frequently saved the government's skin, but the Social Democrats had no place in that government for almost five years."[3] But the horrors of inflation had not been forgotten, and the extreme voices of 1918–19 could still be heard, though they sounded subdued. The Weimar Republic around 1925 was "a handsome façade behind which an unpleasant reality was hidden."[4]

Things were not pleasant behind the handsome façade of the film industry, either. The economic situation had dramatically worsened. During inflation the devaluation of the currency had held off foreign competitors who saw no chance for profit in the German market, which gave at least the big companies the chance to sell their films abroad at low prices, but after the currency reform the situation changed from one day to the next. "Once the mark was stabilized, sales abroad dropped off sharply, and the German market was flooded with foreign films, American ones especially. After a short boom in German film, production noticeably fell off."[5] This risky product with unpredictable sales potential, which even on the domestic market made life hard for producers wanting quick returns, was now pulled into the maelstrom of crisis-prone international finance. In international competition, what made the difference was the amount of capital and the speed with which the return on capital was realized. The film economist Bächlin has calculated that in the United States' approximately 22,500 movie theaters, a single film might be seen by about 18 to 20 million people. In Germany, however, with its 5,000 theaters, a film would be seen on average by only 4 to 5 million. Given rising production costs, the amortization of a film became harder and harder.[6] "If production costs for a feature film averaged 8,000 to 10,000 marks in 1910 and about 12,000 in 1920, they climbed rapidly and constantly in the following years until, in 1928, the last year of silent films, they reached 175,000 marks."[7] Production costs for Ufa's major productions had long since exceeded a million marks.

By establishing quotas, the office for foreign trade kept the domestic market from being flooded with foreign films and stabilized the market share of German films at about 40 percent. The few firms with enough capital behind them to offer a widely varying program—Ufa, Deulig-Film, the Emelka concern, Terra-Film, and National-Film—fought among themselves over how that 40 percent would be divided up. If one of their films lost money, they could make up the loss with profits from more successful productions. Then, too, with their studios, real estate, and chains of theaters, they could offer collateral for big loans if they needed them, a privilege not shared by the many smaller companies that survived primarily by producing films on commissions from the market-controlling firms. Financing ongoing film production on the basis of a company's proprietary capital became harder and, eventually, impossible.

Because the vertically structured concerns were attractive to the banks and to industrialists with an interest in film, consolidation in the film industry rapidly progressed. In 1926–28, eighty-two German production companies had at their disposal nominal capital of 61.5 million marks, of which the sixteen leading stock companies controlled 60 million.[8] Similarly, a small minority of the distributors controlled 70 percent of the available films. The producers were also taking distribution more and more into their own hands. "The big production companies were eager to take distribution away from independent companies and to retain distribution profits as subsidiary income that they could use to offset production losses."[9] And the American competitors accelerated the concentration process, too. By means of their own distribution companies set up in the principal European cities, they were trying to gain influence over the European market, and they soon founded production subsidiaries in addition to their distribution companies.

Thanks to increased income from the profitable distribution business, Germany's big firms were able to compensate more easily for their production losses. Ufa and Emelka were especially aggressive about expanding activity in the mid-1920s. Counting as "Ufa films" only those actually produced by the company, Ufa's share of total German production in 1927–29 averages 7 percent; but the films that its subsidiaries Ufa-Leih (Ufa Distribution), Hansa-Leih, and Decla-Leih put into circulation together amounted to an average of 17 percent of the total volume of films distributed.[10] This dominant market position ensured Ufa's influence over the programs of the production companies dependent on it. In many cases, Ufa assumed the complete financing of a film planned by a smaller company, and "reserved the right to decide all major questions, from the direction of the film to the sharing of the profits. By far the great majority of German films were produced on this commission system."[11]

As *Das Tage-Buch* saw the situation in December 1924, the German film industry had succumbed to a "stabilization crisis" precipitated by the introduction of the Reichsmark, and this condemned to insignificance the small and middle-sized companies that refused to just quit. With a turnover period roughly equivalent to that in agriculture, the film industry's distress was obvious, and it began to concern Germany's big business. As in the United States under the auspices of William Randolph Hearst, so in Germany a "natural" liaison had developed between newspaper empires and the film business, but in Germany the most powerful newspapers were in the hands of heavy industry, and "characteristically these same industrialists . . . expanded into film production once they acquired press organizations."[12] This was true of Alfred Hugenberg, who controlled Scherl Publications and Deulig-Film (with its influential newsreel the *Deulig-Woche*), and Hugo Stinnes, whose industrial conglomerate included the *Deutsche Allgemeine Zeitung* and Westi-Film.

In the United States, where according to the *Film Yearbook* $1.5 billion had been invested in movies in 1927,[13] observers of the crisis in European film were fascinated and puzzled. Benjamin Hampton, in his 1931 *History of the Movies*, is a good example of the American take on the situation. Hampton duly noted that bankers, industrialists, and newspaper magnates had given financial support to German film production and had helped to accelerate concentration within the industry, but he went on to note that only a few German films—*Passion*, *Variety*, and *The Last Laugh*—had had the good fortune to be accepted by American audiences. (The later agreement of December 1925 that proved so favorable for American concerns he represented as a personal financial favor that Adolph Zukor and Marcus Loew granted to a hard-pressed Ufa, an experiment that unfortunately turned out badly and had to be terminated.) Full of sympathy, Hampton enumerated the hardships faced by German film actresses who, even if they were stars, couldn't expect to earn more than 20,000 marks a year, and on top of that had to buy their own expensive costumes for society films. But the reasons for the depressing situation in Europe were obvious, Hampton thought. From the beginning, European film production was out to satisfy the tastes not of the mass audience but, rather, of the educated classes. Instead of giving entertainment to the broad public, German producers had competed with the theater and aimed for the applause of those who by virtue of background and education preferred the stage to the screen. The inevitable result was that American films in Europe had enjoyed a tremendous success with the very classes that European filmmakers had ignored. This, he concluded, was the whole secret of Hollywood's success.[14]

It has to be said to the credit of the German film industry and Ufa in particular that they were willing to learn from the Americans. In October 1924 Ufa's head office sent Erich Pommer and Fritz Lang to the United States, preceded by the executive Felix Kallmann. They visited Ufa's office in New York and its chief, Fredrick Wynne-Jones; they attended the New York premiere of Lang's *The Nibelungs* (certainly one of Pommer's top priorities was to improve the sale of German films in the States). But the Germans made no secret of the fact that they had also come to learn from Hollywood. Meetings were arranged with Douglas Fairbanks, Charlie Chaplin, Mary Pickford, Samuel Goldwyn, Joseph Schenck, Marcus Loew, Thomas Ince, and Ufa's first emigrant, Ernst Lubitsch.[15] In Universal City they watched filming for *The Phantom of the Opera*, and Lang expressed his admiration for the technical capacities of American studios. One result of this visit was Lang's film *Metropolis*, and I shall have more to say about the conclusions that he and his company drew from their American experience. For critical observers of Ufa, it was Ufa's major productions on the "American" scale, designed specifically to compete with similar products from the other side of the Atlantic, that brought the company to its knees.

Ufa's aggressive strategy of expansion that had brought it dominance during the inflationary period gradually led to its undoing after the stabilization of the Reichsmark. The crisis evolved slowly, and Ufa's business managers apparently did not take it seriously at first and continued their old expansionist policies. In 1925 Ufa acquired Martin Dentler Film Braunschweig and also the majority of stock in Afifa (the largest copying establishment in Germany) and in a real-estate company that owned the grounds of the Gloria-Palast. In April 1927, after Hugenberg took over the company, Ufa absorbed the AG für Kinematographie und Filmverleih (based in Worms and Mannheim). These new acquisitions depleted Ufa's capital but suggested to the outside world that its business policies were basically sound. In reality, it was overinvesting in production: the monumental films of 1924–26, of which Lang's *The Nibelungs* and *Metropolis* are the leading examples (*Metropolis* was the first film that cost more than 5 million marks to make), were financial miscalculations attributable in large part to this management megalomania.

With these large-scale productions Ufa planned to challenge Hollywood at its own game and to move seriously into the American film market. But was this the right course? In any event, the German market was too small to earn back the production costs of *Metropolis*, foreign sales were uncertain, and the hoped-for success in the United States did not come to pass. American moviegoers were not interested in a Pan-Germanic epic like *The Nibelungs*. In early 1925, even before work on *Metropolis* had begun, Ufa's management had to admit that it could not get out of financial trouble without outside help. The annual report put an optimistic face on things, but according to Traub's figures, the company's losses stood at more than 36 million marks and its liquid assets at only half a million.[16]

Ufa took out a loan for 15 million marks, for which bonds at 10 percent and "under certain circumstances exchangeable for stock" were issued.[17] The value of the capital stock, raised in the meantime to 45 million marks, was now offset by debts amounting to more than 50 million. According to figures researched by Lipschütz, Ufa still had open reserves of 15 million marks. But management, the directors, and anyone who knew the facts could no longer ignore this now-full-blown crisis. The moment for intervention by the big American companies had come, a historic moment that moved Jean-Luc Godard to remark more than fifty years later that a "true history of cinema" would have to contain a "history devoted to contracts alone," a "history of film history." "The Americans made contracts with the German film industry toward the end of the silent-film era, when the German companies were down and out and couldn't get back on their feet.

Contracts between Paramount and Ufa allowed the industry to recover before the Hitler period began."[18]

Hollywood's moguls had literally raced each other to Berlin in December 1925. They all wanted to be the first to stake a claim on Ufa's territory. "MGM and Paramount's top executives embarked secretly in mid-December on the *Majestic* from New York at the same time that the president of Universal left on the *Leviathan*," the *Chicago Tribune* reported. "The *Majestic* passengers arrived in Cherbourg two hours earlier than the chief of Universal, and to gain time they hurried to London and flew from there to Berlin, arriving ten minutes ahead of Universal's president. After two weeks of intense negotiations, however, the race ended with a compromise agreeable to all sides."[19]

What the *Chicago Tribune* tactfully called a compromise was no more or less than Ufa's capitulation to the Americans. Paramount, as distributor for Famous Players–Lasky and MGM, deigned to enter into a joint contract that granted the crippled German firm credit in the amount of $4 million (a little under 17 million marks). All partners to the contract agreed to found a joint distribution organization, Parufamet, fifty-fifty German and American. In return, Ufa committed itself to take twenty films annually from each American partner and to reserve 75 percent of showing time (later reduced to 50 percent) for them in Ufa-affiliated theaters. Paramount and MGM would each take ten Ufa films a year for distribution to American theaters—with the onerous proviso that they "suit the tastes of American moviegoers."

Universal's representative arrived late in Berlin, but he did not come in vain. He, too, offered Ufa a loan—$275,000—and got in return Ufa's commitment to place fifty Universal films in German movie theaters.

> These two contracts enabled the Americans to collect through Ufa's theaters alone about one half of all the rental fees available in Germany. The purpose of their agreements with the German film firms . . . was, through liberal injections of capital, to make the German film industry increasingly dependent on them and thus to weaken significantly their major foreign competitor.[20]

The draft of Ufa's annual report for 1925–26 suggests that management regarded these American contracts as defensive maneuvers in a battle for the survival of Germany. Yet Ufa had submitted to a contract that in reality cleared the way for a frontal American attack on the German market but left the distribution of German films in the States dependent on American decisions. The report revealed other interesting details: an interest rate of 7.5 percent was set for the $4 million loan, and a "mortgage on the real estate at Potsdamer Platz" was put up as collateral.[21] Ufa had thus pawned its own office building to avoid a disaster that its top management seemed to feel would have been no less than a catastrophe for the fatherland.

The Parufamet contracts did not improve Ufa's situation in the least.

When the board met in the Cedar Room of the German Bank on Mauer-strasse in Berlin on December 10, 1926, it read the draft of a sobering annual report which began: "The fiscal year 1925–26 did not live up to the expectations we had for it."[22] A great deal was glossed over at this meeting and much more pushed aside as unimportant, but anyone willing to read between the lines of the minutes will see that the situation was horrendous. Stauss opened the meeting by suggesting why the hopes for the year had not been met, but he mentioned only secondary points: "excessive unem-ployment" in Germany and therefore reduced purchasing power, also the German entertainment tax, which did in fact impose a very heavy burden on the entire movie industry.[23] But he circumvented the main problem, the Parufamet deal.

Ferdinand Bausback, who had succeeded Felix Kallmann as chief exec-utive and had been in office for a year, also began with diversionary tactics. Improved management had produced "tangible results," he said. The num-ber of employees, 6,000 at the end of 1925, had been reduced by 1,100 by October 1926; the payroll of 16 million marks had been cut by half a million. The minutes then contain, in no particular context, this rather odd sentence: "Business abroad appears capable of considerable expansion pro-vided that the quality of available films is good."

But just how precarious the situation was became clear in Bausback's income projections. From Ufa's distribution companies he expected to re-alize about 8 million marks and from the Parufamet agreements 4 million. The jewel of Ufa's production, Fritz Lang's *Metropolis*, which had just been completed, was listed as a separate entry with an expected profit of one million. Bausback added, however, that all these estimates were "quite op-timistic." Liquidation of the company's bank debt was essential for an up-swing. Unfortunately, the expected profit of 3.1 million marks for the coming year made "only a relatively modest dividend" possible. Of greatest importance was that Ufa needed 12 million marks to produce thirty to thirty-five films in the coming year. Bausback's summation revealed at what a loss he really was: "The film industry is still so much in a developmental stage and still dependent on so many unpredictable factors that we have to expect on the one hand reduced returns, and on the other hand not insignificant opportunities for greater profits."

Some board members seem to have regarded all this talk as so much eyewash; Siegmund Bodenheimer, vice president of the board and chief executive of the Darmstadt and National Bank, did not mince words. In his view, the American contracts had done Ufa "a great disservice" in its artistic program. Since the American films had been flops in Germany's theaters, "the public has developed a hostile attitude toward Ufa." In a vaguely worded attempt at mollification, Bausback and Siegmund Jacob responded that "the two American companies would no doubt make better films in the future and, more important, ones better adapted to European tastes." But even they had to concede that German moviegoers had been "irritated by the Americans' decision, which did not have our approval, to show the film *The Four Horsemen of the Apocalypse.*"

With this film, directed in 1921 by Rex Ingram and starring Rudolph Valentino, the Americans had returned to the lucrative business of war films, that "iron repertoire"[24] that had never had much regard for the political sensitivity of other nations. According to Hampton, this film was extraordinarily successful in the States and earned back many times over what Marcus Loew had invested in it. In 1926, the Reich Association of Motion Picture Theater Owners asked cinema operators throughout the world to eliminate it from their programs "to further the cause of genuine world peace." (Zglinicki claims that in 1926 MGM was "forced to destroy" all its copies of this and two other war films.[25]) But Hollywood, with its reckless film imperialism, could peddle its wares without worrying about political or cultural consequences. In 1912, 90 percent of all the films shown worldwide had come from France, but by the late 1920s the United States controlled 97 percent of the world market. Of the remaining 3 percent, Germany accounted for the lion's share, and not only Ufa felt the impact of American competition. In 1928, Warner Brothers acquired the National-Film-Verleih- und Vertriebs; the film company Bruckmann worked together with Universal; Rex-Film and Phoebus-Film became dependent on United Artists and MGM, respectively. It was only a matter of time before a "national front" much given to chauvinistic rhetoric would form in Germany to do battle against the omnipotence of the dollar. The spokesman and influential promoter of this "new direction" was the nationalistic industrialist Alfred Hugenberg.

Things came to a head at Ufa in late March 1927. The voices of finance and industry had all the decision-making power on Ufa's board. Erich Pommer had by this time been in the United States for a year,[26] and the bankers, led by Stauss, were in control. *Berliner Tageblatt*, which had drawn up a "Liquidation Balance Sheet of the Stauss–Pommer Era" for its readers, now published a series of articles about the "Fate of Ufa," the "Film Industry's Struggle for Survival," the "Ufa Dictatorship," and the "Last General Assembly of the Old Ufa." On April 2, 1927, *Das Tage-Buch* put on display "The Wreckage of Ufa."[27]

On March 24 the executive committee of the board had met to deal with only one item of business: the sale of Ufa's offices on Potsdamer Platz (including responsibility for the mortgage held by the Americans) to a consortium formed by the Hardy banking house. At the beginning of the meeting, however, Stauss announced that "negotiations were in progress with a number of persons and firms interested in Ufa," among them an American group that wanted to establish a theater chain; the tentative plan was to incorporate Ufa's theaters into this enterprise for 30 million marks. All these negotiations, Stauss said, were "incredibly time-consuming" and very much up in the air. The executive committee would convene again "as soon as the negotiations arrive at some firm results."

That point was reached four days later, as the minutes of a meeting on March 28 indicate: "Stauss reported that the negotiations in progress with the Hugenberg group and Otto Wolf were on the verge of completion." There was no further mention of American participants. A day later the chairman said that "late last evening the negotiations with the Scherl group [owned by Hugenberg] had finally been brought to a satisfactory conclusion."[28]

Universum-Film AG—with its 140 subsidiaries, its branches in Amsterdam, Budapest, Helsingfors, London, Prague, Rome, Stockholm, Vienna, Zurich, New York, and twenty-seven other cities, with its 134 theaters all over the world, with its total of 390,000 square meters of studio space in Tempelhof and Neubabelsberg—this now crippled giant called out for a savior, and it found him in the form of an industrial magnate, a "conservative revolutionary" determined to use politics to increase his economic power, to use his economic power to increase his political influence, and to use his power over the media to serve both his economic and his political ends.

We shall examine in more detail the terms and consequences of this transaction, but we should note here that an early consequence was the return to the film industry of a man who before World War I had advocated the use of cinema to serve Germany's interests abroad, who later had founded the Deutsche Lichtbild-Gesellschaft, and who after 1918 took over direction of Scherl Publications for Hugenberg. On March 19, 1927, Ufa's board learned that the Hugenberg group requested "that Herr Generaldirektor Klitzsch be authorized to conduct the business of the company."[29] Hugenberg's wish was the Ufa directors' command, and the next day they unanimously authorized "Herr Generaldirektor Klitzsch in his capacity as expert consultant, to supervise the business conduct of Ufa and to reorganize the company to the degree he deems necessary. The management of the company is hereby instructed to follow Herr Klitzsch's directives."[30]

With flags flying, Ufa yielded to this new strong man. Ludwig Klitzsch, who at one time had labeled the founding of Ufa as an attack on DLG and had deliberated about countermeasures to serve the interests of German heavy industry, that same Ludwig Klitzsch now stood on the bridge of the giant vessel Ufa. Alfred Hugenberg's victory was complete.

12.

Mind and Power:
Ufa and the Intellectuals

Tʜᴇ crisis at Ufa alarmed Germany's intellectuals and drew their attention to the "dependency of film production on capitalistic stock
companies."[1] In the early 1920s alert observers had kept their eye on the
interrelationship of politics and economics in the film sector, on heavy
industry's lust for power in it, and especially on Hugenberg's activities; in
articles for *Die Weltbühne, Das Tage-Buch,* and *Berliner Tageblatt* they had
analyzed these factors for their readers. Now, *Die Weltbühne* described the
situation with biting sarcasm:

> In the last row of the Exalted Assembly [of the new Ufa] sit the new
> matadors: Hugenberg, a general in civilian clothes, with his crew cut and
> waxed mustache, only slightly gray despite his sixty years, grinning jovially
> but at the same time duly serious, as is only right and meet in these difficult
> times. Next to him, flaxen-haired, coarse and red as a master sergeant, his
> general director, Klitzsch, who up to now has commanded the Printed Paper
> Division [i.e., Scherl] but is now expected to lead the Army Group Silver
> Screen to victory. They wait modestly in the background until, at Item 5 on
> the agenda, Privy Councillor Alfred Hugenberg—surrounded by eighteen
> paladins, manorial lords, captains and lessees of crown lands, first lieuten-
> ants, and experts on agricultural economy—is elected to the board with-
> out a single vote cast against him and an hour later is elevated to the
> chairmanship.[2]

Axel Eggebrecht thought Hugenberg's victory was a triumph of German
provincialism: "Inferiority has been institutionalized. From here on, it will
be difficult to deal seriously and critically with the film frippery of this
country."[3]

This was a radical, and premature, prediction. We shall see that Ufa was
not transformed overnight into a press office for the Pan-German Union.

Hugenberg was a superb tactician, and he had no interest in using his rise to power to politicize film production either too quickly or too prominently. The first thing he did was ascertain what the potential was, and it was precisely Ufa's artistic, literary, and technical potential, unmatched anywhere else in Germany that resisted both provincialization and any efforts to make it conform to narrow political ends.

An ambiguity typical of the German intelligentsia arose here and led to a paradox. On the one hand, the critics who found their worst fears confirmed were in a minority among Ufa's artists. Many talented and successful directors, actors, authors, set designers, and cameramen—if they had not gone abroad to learn more or to earn more money—set their hopes on a resurgence and a new artistic blossoming of Ufa. They stayed with Ufa, just as many of them would stay after 1933, either with mixed feelings or unconcerned about the political changes. On the other hand, the persistence of these politically indifferent but artistically competent people was the very factor that prevented a rapid decline to the level of "cheap trash films" that Eggebrecht and others with him thought was inevitable. Solid professionalism, pride in craft, and delight in technical experimentation—the very qualities that are often and usually correctly regarded as "secondary virtues" of the "unpolitical" German specialist—prevented a dictatorship of mediocrity. This ambiguity and inner contradiction continued to define the internal situation of the film industry under National Socialist rule.

Ufa's history is part of the history of German intellectuals in this century. Politically alert and artistically ambitious intellectuals were in no small measure linked with the path Ufa took, though this is usually glossed over in the cheap rituals of denial that leftist cultural critics indulged in after the end of Fascist rule and that are still with us today. Germany's artists and intellectuals with their divided consciences helped to form a chameleonlike image of Ufa in the 1920s, and they bear responsibility, too, for the development of the firm in the 1930s.

Jerzy Toeplitz describes only one aspect of this when he stresses that the expressionists of the 1920s retired into inner worlds and tore down their bridges to the outer world. They focused on the individual human being and his experience, he says, and at the same time rejected the possibility of bringing the individual into "harmony with society." Was their work indeed "cut off as if under a bell jar"? Was "all their attention and their zeal for understanding" devoted to maintaining their own equilibrium, to healing their own "sick souls"?[4]

Clearly, to the extent German intellectuals took an interest in cinematography, their gaze moved from the interior life toward the exterior one; their eye responded to the surface sensations of a hectic civilization and to the shrill dissonances of a fragmented society. H.-B. Heller correctly points out that even the early theoretical and programmatic writings of German film artists like Max Mack and E. A. Dupont explicitly rejected the inwardness and refinement of bourgeois high culture.[5] Even Hugo von Hof-mannsthal, who was if anything the opposite of the nervous, modern literatus who sucks up everything new by osmosis, was fascinated with cinema. In his 1921 essay "Der Ersatz für die Träume" ("The Substitute for Dreams"), he wrote rapturously of that "half-dark room crammed with people and animated with fleeting pictures," in which the eye "finds the thousandfold image of life," that atmosphere in which people "enter into an utterly direct, uninhibited relationship with an extraordinary if oddly presented intellectual heritage." He found all this "almost worthy of reverence."[6] And Iwan Goll celebrated film as a "wonderful thing for writers" because, based on motion as it was, with its "rapid piling up of totally unrelated situations," it made possible "a new, active art for the many," an art comparable to the "cathedrals of the Middle Ages and the temples of Asia."[7]

These are by no means extreme voices. We hear in statements from authors of the most varied literary and political camps an affinity for the age of "fragmentation" and montage, an age that expressed itself in shattered, incoherent urban realities and at the same time seemed mysterious.

The general debate about the new medium, in which many well-known writers participated, epitomized the tragic, sometimes tragicomic, polarity so familiar in German intellectual history between Classicism and Romanticism, order and chaos, solipsism and the brotherhood of man, expressionist ecstasy and "New Objectivity." This antinomy defined the relationship of the German intelligentsia to the new medium of film, and it nourished their interest in Ufa, misleading them into projecting their visions of hell onto it—but also all their desires for an El Dorado.

An important element in this web of contradictions—as in all other aspects of cultural life in the Weimar Republic—was the Jewish intelligentsia. About 1930, when the "folkish," nationalistic right was encouraging blind anti-Semitism, the influence of Jewish intellectuals in Germany's cultural life, particularly in Berlin was at a peak. "The culmination of Jewish emancipation coincided tragically . . . with the nadir of the liberal spirit in the Weimar era."[8]

Only six months after the "tactical" rather than ideologically committed anti-Semite Alfred Hugenberg assumed power in Ufa, Erich Pommer, a Jew, was called back to Neubabelsberg. Pommer's abilities helped to further developments that ultimately deprived him of his citizenship and civil rights and drove him into emigration, and that led to the physical destruction of millions of his fellows.

As Pommer was returning, Siegmund Jacob (who was to die in Auschwitz) was fired, not, apparently, for "racist" reasons but because Hugenberg considered that he had inadequately controlled the company's financial operations and condoned incorrect business practices.[9] Then Paul Davidson, in a state of depression and extreme isolation, committed suicide in

June 1927. It must have struck many of his friends, especially his closest colleagues from the past, like Lubitsch and Jannings, as an ominous sign.

The representation of Jewish bankers on Ufa's board and of Jewish specialists and artists in its administration and production was comparable with the influence of Jewish publishers and journalists in Germany's daily press and with the prominent position that Jewish directors and actors held in Berlin's theaters. At the opposite end of the spectrum from the nationalistic Scherl publishing house were two major houses in Jewish hands of liberal, democratic convictions: Mosse, which published the *Berliner Tageblatt* and the *Berliner Volkszeitung*, and Ullstein, with its *Vossische Zeitung*, *Berliner Illustrierte Zeitung*, and popular magazines like *Die Dame*, *Uhu* (*The Owl*, Ullstein's logo), and *Modenwelt* (*Fashion World*).

Among the leading Jewish editors and writers were Theodor Wolff, Alfred Kerr, and Hermann Sinsheimer with Mosse; Monty Jacobs, Arthur Eloesser, Max Osborn, and Egon Jacobsohn with Ullstein; Kurt Pinthus with the *8-Uhr Abendblatt* (*Eight O'Clock Evening News*); and Bernhard Diebold, Ernst Heilborn, Otto Hirschfeld, Siegfried Kracauer, and Max Nürnberg with the democratic, cosmopolitan *Frankfurter Zeitung*. Right up until the last days of the Weimar Republic they all took part in the great democratic enterprise of open debate and political culture that had begun in November 1918, though from the very first days they had suffered heavy attacks from the conservative camp. In these years, S. Fischer alone published Jewish authors like Alice Berend, Alfred Döblin, Stefan Grossmann, Bernhard Guttmann, Arthur Holitscher, Felix Hollaender, Alfred Kerr, Richard Lewinsohn-Morus, Walter Mehring, Arthur Schnitzler, Siegfrid Trebitsch, and Jakob Wassermann.[10] Prominent Jewish actors went from Max Reinhardt's theaters to film, some to Ufa: Elisabeth Bergner, Ernst Deutsch, Alexander Granach, Fritz Kortner, and Maria Fein. From Viktor Barnowsky's stage came Felix Bressart and the director Leo Mittler, who in 1929 made his proletarian, realistic film *Jenseits der Strasse—Eine Tragödie des Alltags* (*Harbor Drift—A Tragedy of Everyday Life*) for the Communist company Prometheus.

E. G. Lowenthal notes that listings like this might seem, especially to readers outside Germany, "pedantic or parochial." But the justification, indeed necessity, for such a list is that all the individuals named above "were persecuted, without exception and without mercy, by the National Socialist regime and, beyond that, were often and publicly attacked by the German radical right long before 1933 simply because they were Jews."[11]

The number of prominent directors of Jewish background who worked for Ufa or were affiliated with it was roughly proportional to the Jewish presence in all of German cultural life. To name only a few: Kurt Bernhardt, Paul Czinner, Ewald André Dupont, Fritz Lang (his mother was of Jewish background), Ernst Lubitsch, Joe May, Max Ophüls, Lupu Pick, Leontine Sagan, Reinhold Schünzel, and Robert Siodmak. Among the outstanding

Jewish screenplay writers were Norbert Falk, Carl Mayer, and Robert Liebmann. Paul Dessau, Werner Richard Heymann, and Edmund Meisel made names for themselves as film composers. And finally, along with those I have already named, successful Jewish actresses and actors included Grete Mosheim and Ellen Richter, Siegfried Arno, Curt Bois, Julius Falkenstein, Max Landa, Peter Lorre, Max Pallenberg, Hermann Vallentin, and many others. What Lowenthal said in general about Jews in the public life of the Weimar Republic applies to them as well: "There were of course here as anywhere greater and lesser talents. But the reality is that Jewish scholars, writers, musicians, and theater people as well as non-Jewish ones had done their part to spread the fame of Berlin and Germany throughout the world."[12] And the fame of Ufa as well.

Of all the prominent authors of the 1920s, none articulated stronger objections not only to Ufa but to the (silent) film per se than Alfred Döblin. "The writer's instrument is language. Film doesn't speak. What business does a writer have with film?" he asked.[13] Film, he thought, "cripples, stunts, perverts the imagination by forcing it into a single dimension: the optical." It was an accidental by-product of modern technology, working like a sieve or a dreadful funnel: "No art can come through intact." Döblin's criticism was hostile to technology—like that of many of his colleagues— blind to the aesthetics of film's pictorial language, and profoundly skeptical of the mass audience's "lack of discrimination." He was disgusted by "the frightful commodity character of film." The people in charge of the industry were businessmen guided by business principles: "profit versus art." However, Döblin did not conceal that he had tried his hand at film scenarios, and when Phil Jutzi filmed *Berlin Alexanderplatz* for Allianz-Film in 1931, with Heinrich George in the role of Franz Biberkopf, he agreed to work together with Hans Wilhelm and Karl Heinz Martin on the screenplay.

Not all writers who tried their luck with screenplays gave up as quickly as the poet Oskar Loerke, who met with his friend Hans Kyser on a May morning in 1924 to adapt his "Fischdampfergeschichte" ("Fishing Boat Story") for the screen and noted in his journal that evening: "The kitsch, the tawdriness is a torment for me. I decided to give it up because there was no guaranteed income from it, which was the only thing of interest to me. Floundering around like that wears you out quickly."[14] Carl Zuckmayer also had strong reservations—"The system is false, industrial, mechanistic, like the word 'filming' "[15]—but he did not stop the adaptations of his work for the films *Qualen der Nacht* (*Anguish in the Night*, directed by Kurt Bernhardt, Ikarus-Film, 1925–26), *Der fröhliche Weinberg* (*The Merry Vineyard*, directed by Jakob and Luise Fleck, Film Produktions, produced in Ufa's studios, 1927), and *Schinderhannes*. He had no part in the film version of his play *Katharina Knie* (directed and produced by Karl Grune and made in Neubabelsberg in 1929; Franz Höllering wrote the script), but he claims in his autobiography that the scenario that he, Robert Liebmann, and Karl Vollmoeller wrote for Josef von Sternberg's Ufa film *The Blue Angel* was all his own work.[16]

The contradiction between verbal rejection and often shamefaced collaboration characterized the relationship of many writers to the German film industry and its largest company. Only a few declared themselves for film as early and as openly as Bernhard Kellermann, who wrote this response to a 1913 questionnaire circulated by the *Börsenblatt für den Deutschen Buchhandel*:

> I am by no means unaware of the risks a novel runs if it is made into a film, but I see no reason to exaggerate them. The knowledgeable viewer can in most cases easily reconstruct the original work quite well from a film, and the unsophisticated one will benefit from the film as much as, if not more than, he would have from reading the book. As for the economic aspect, movies are such a powerful advertising instrument that the filming of a novel can only work to the benefit of author and publisher.[17]

Kellermann's famous novel *Der Tunnel* was published in 1913 and was filmed for the first time in 1914–15 for Union, with William Wauer directing, Friedrich Kayssler and Fritzi Massary in the lead roles, and sets by Hermann Warm.

In 1925–26, the film version of Kellermann's novel *The Schellenberg Brothers*, which had already appeared in the *Berliner Illustrierte* and was directed for the screen by Karl Grune, became one of Ufa's great successes of the season. Grune had collaborated with Willy Haas on the screenplay, the film was produced in the Johannisthal and Tempelhof studios, and Conrad Veidt played the double role of the two dissimilar brothers. (Werner Richard Heymann composed the music, conducted at the premiere in the Ufa-Palast am Zoo by Erno Rapee, Ufa's senior music director.) The plot summary in the program exemplifies the kind of prose that Ufa's advertising department regularly ground out:

> Factories spring up out of the ground; the stock exchange thrashes about in golden convulsions; oceangoing freighters pass from one owner to the next—and in the bar, laughing cynically, sits an elegant gentleman who can control this whole inflationary world with a wave of his hand. Yes, Wenzel Schellenberg is the hero, and *The Schellenberg Brothers* [is] the portrait of those uncertain times when all the clocks seemed to run faster and the work of years could be squeezed together in an hour.[18]

Ufa let itself in for no end of trouble with the subtitles for Murnau's *Faust*, destined to become Germany's cinematic national monument. Hans Kyser, a playwright and novelist, had come over to film after much hesitation and in 1924 had written several screenplays; now he was commissioned to write the one for *Faust*. Kyser decided on a melding of elements from Goethe, Christopher Marlowe, and the old folk legend. He was also so bold as to write lines of his own, which, however, did not find favor with the Ufa team responsible for the film. Director Neumann, determined to fire Kyser, traveled to Hiddensee himself to engage Gerhart Hauptmann for the job: for the most important drama by Germany's greatest writer and thinker, filmed by Germany's most powerful film company, no less than Germany's most famous living author would do. Such must have been the line of thinking.

The failure of the collaboration with Hauptmann is a sore point in Ufa's history, and a foreshadowing of worse disasters to come. Hauptmann insisted on writing his own completely new text, and he asked for double the fee of 20,000 marks that Ufa had offered. In mid-August Neumann sent him a telegram conveying his "great pleasure" over Hauptmann's decision "to provide completely new subtitles for our *Faust* film. We will be happy to pay the requested honorarium of 40,000 marks and to grant you publication rights."[19] In the meantime, the film had already been edited, and the advertising campaign was under way. Hans Kyser, who had gotten wind of the negotiations with Hauptmann, sounded an alarm in an open letter to the *Berliner Zeitung*: Anyone who dared add new verses to this film ("even if they were by Goethe himself") "belongs in a kindergarten for film dramaturges." Hauptmann responded (in a letter that has been preserved only in draft form) that the subtitles written by his "esteemed friend" Kyser were "so sublimely vapid and inane that no amount of editorial improvement could breathe life into this sorry, trivial stuff."

Hauptmann's couplets, however, were no great improvement; indeed, Ufa's directors found them horrible. In desperation, Neumann turned to Hauptmann's wife, Margarete, asking her to urge her husband "to revise some of the verses once more and—if I may put it this way—popularize them." But this rescue attempt failed. On October 7, only one week before the premiere, Ufa informed the author that "unexpected difficulties" had cropped up. The film ran with Kyser's text. Ufa had Hauptmann's verses printed up in a brochure offered for sale in its theaters.

Gerhart Hauptmann's contact with Ufa was not limited to his disappointing experience with *Faust*. In 1922, on his sixtieth birthday, Murnau's film version of Hauptmann's novel *Phantom* had premiered in the Ufa-Palast. An Uco production of Decla-Bioscop, the film had a second gala premiere a week later on November 20, in a "special showing to benefit needy writers." The program opened with Bruno Schulz conducting Nicolai's overture to *The Merry Wives of Windsor*. Hauptmann himself contributed an homage to cinema in the printed program:

The demand for films is so great that we can justifiably call this intellectual nourishment a kind of foodstuff for the people, like bread and potatoes. The almost unlimited demand calls for correspondingly large production. And because we are dealing with intellectual foodstuff for the nation here, the producers carry a heavy responsibility, for if the nation is nourished with inferior, dilute, or in any way spoiled foodstuffs, the effect is devastating.[20]

Also in 1922, Hanns Kobe directed *Die Ratten* (*The Rats*) for Grete-Ly-Film, distributed by Terra-Film. With Emil Jannings, Lucie Höflich, Eugen Klöpfer, and Hermann Vallentin, *The Rats* had a star-studded cast and, in Karl Freund, a superb cameraman. Julius Sternheim (a brother of the playwright Carl Sternheim), wrote the screenplay: he was Ufa's press chief at the time, and in an article in *Das Tage-Buch*, he had tried to woo writers to cinematography: "An author betrays his total ignorance of the situation if he assumes that the director is his natural enemy. The idea seems downright ludicrous if one is aware of the great demand for good manuscripts at this very moment and of how highly they are valued."[21]

Gerhart Hauptmann's older brother, Carl, who died in 1921, had interpreted the characteristics of film with greater self-awareness than most writers: "Film admonishes the writer to bring back into the primal realm of gesture an overly refined and intellectualized language too far removed from physical expression. It admonishes him to recover the physical, palpable, living, breathtaking power of primal communication, admonishes him to breathe, not speak."[22] Two years later his play *Driven from Home* provided the basis for Murnau's Ufa film of the same title. The reviews were not favorable. For a subject like this, a tragedy involving jealousy among peasants leading isolated lives, the epic and the theater were more appropriate media, it was thought. "Film requires a rapid sequence of powerful images driven by plot. As films, psychological tragedies in a restrictive milieu are slow paced and wearying."[23]

Ufa contributed nothing but the newsreel to the 1927 premiere of *Die Hose* (*The Trousers*), based on Carl Sternheim's stage comedy. Hans Behrendt had made the film for Phoebus-Film with Werner Krauss, Jenny Jugo, and Rudolf Forster in the lead. (The supporting role of the Jewish barber Mandelstam was played by Veit Harlan, later a favorite of Goebbels and a director of National Socialist propaganda films like *Jud Süss* [*Jew Süss*] and *Kolberg*.)

> Krauss in the role of Theobald Maske . . . is a scientific monstrosity, a tadpole, a formidable beast that crows and spits and screeches and stalks about in his domestic henhouse with his comb swollen up, as if the specter of the petit bourgeois had suddenly emerged full-blown from a beery cloud, a Saturday-night poker game, the stuffy warmth of the marriage bed.[24]

But in the crisis year of 1927 the laughter that greeted this performance was a laughter of despair and impotence, of revulsion from a monster that would soon take on political form.

Ufa had no scruples about exploiting the works of contemporary writers, very often only a few weeks after publication, if it sensed that a trail, however faint, led from those works to the fears, hopes, and yearnings of the masses. And with equal zeal, innumerable famous and unknown writers offered their services to the new medium, eager for fame, drawn by the good pay, and also full of hope that they had at last found a connection with the masses. Intellect was drawn to economic power, and economic power to intellect. Socialism, the salvation of the world, a radical change of existing conditions? Ufa found a way to translate such concerns into powerful pictorial language. Pacifism, reconciliation among nations, human love as a force to change the world? Help yourself, Mr. Author. If you accept our terms, Ufa's studios, professional staff, and props are at your disposal.

So it was in 1928 that the novella *Karl und Anna* by the pacifist author Leonhard Frank was made, at great cost, into *Heimkehr* (*Homecoming*), a "Joe May film produced for Ufa by Erich Pommer." May filmed in Neubabelsberg and on location in the Hamburg harbor, with Lars Hanson, Dita Parlo, Gustav Fröhlich, and Theodor Loos. His cameraman was Günther Rittau. As an Ufa press release explained, sets of "a large Siberian mine, genuine in every detail," and of "a Russian provincial railroad station with all the life and activity of those eventful days and nights" were built for this story of a love triangle set in the chaos of the postwar period. "A rotating steel structure fifteen meters high, employed for the first time in Germany, has enabled Rittau to shoot from entirely new and surprising angles."[25] This was the camera crane that Pommer (who had returned to Ufa only a few months before) had developed in Hollywood for his Paramount production *Hotel Imperial*, a device that enabled the camera to move both horizontally and vertically and anticipated the freely swiveling camera dolly that Pommer built for Joe May's *Asphalt* in 1929.[26]

In the tension between Ufa and the intellectuals some remarkable liaisons were formed. Personal vanity, business connections, and the temptations of nepotism were often decisive. Any writer who made a mark, whether with a cultivated, bourgeois publisher or as a pulp novelist, found himself, willy-nilly, working for the movies. One unexpected collaboration was that of the successful Austrian travel writer Colin Ross with Hans Neumann on a screenplay for a psychoanalytical film, *Secrets of a Soul*, directed by G. W. Pabst and distributed by Ufa's cultural division. After the playwrights Arnolt Bronnen and Bertolt Brecht had jointly won a prize of 50,000 marks in a screenplay contest put on by Richard Oswald Film, Bronnen wrote an obituary for himself as a playwright: "Now he'll sit in hell and write films. He'll fry there, but film, thank God, has no literary ambitions."[27]

"At home in contradiction" is how H.-B. Heller characterized the position of many writers who vacillated between traditional literary work and the film industry.

No matter how vigorously theoreticians propounded the aesthetic autonomy of the new medium . . . writers . . . preferred developing film scenarios
from literary sources rather than from originally "filmic" material. The
aura of the tradition-laden literary genre—no matter how questionable
the quality of the specific work chosen remained essential (and perhaps
profitable as well).[28]

For two of Ufa's outstanding screenwriters, an opposition between traditional literary forms and the new medium did not exist. Thea von Harbou
and Carl Mayer may have had different conceptions of what a filmscript
should be, but they agreed that writing for the cinema was an independent
aesthetic activity and that it required both passionate dedication and inspiration specific to the medium of film. Harbou continued as a novelist
after she had discovered, through her collaborations with Fritz Lang at
Decla-Bioscop, her gift for film, but *Das Nibelungenbuch* (*The Book of the
Nibelungs*), published by the Munich house Drei Masken in 1923 and illustrated with photos from the film, as well as her novels *Metropolis* (1926)
and *Spies* (1928), both published by Scherl, were all written at the same
time as the films of the same title. In other words, the novels and the films
were products of an integrated effort. (An exception was her novel *Woman
in the Moon*, published by Scherl in 1928 before she began work on the
screenplay.)

This integrated method of work was not just a new form of literary production; rather, writing for Harbou came to mean writing for film in the
strictest sense. Even when working in traditional prose forms, she was
guided, if not by a specifically filmic perspective, then at least by an eye
for the potential of her work for movies. In ten years of collaboration with
Fritz Lang she realized for the first time the idea of modern media linkage,
an accomplishment that was possible partly because of her unprejudiced
view of the literary métier but also of course because of the excellent working arrangements between Ufa and Scherl.

With this most diligent of Ufa's authors, we cannot but be surprised by
a phenomenon typical of the German film industry and of Ufa in particular,
namely a coexistence in one person of on the one hand technical competence, an interest in modern production methods, and an "operative" relationship with the complex structure of the entertainment business and,
on the other, conservative inwardness and a reactionary political orientation. Thea von Harbou came from an impoverished family of the landed
aristocracy, last resident in Saxony; despite limited financial means they
had been able to educate her with governesses and tutors, and she had
absorbed a governess's limited view of the world and of human nature—
as so often occurred with daughters of the aristocracy and haute bourgeoisie
in the nineteenth and early twentieth centuries. "Her outlook, like that of
most members of her class, was 'Pan-German,' a mixture of extreme right-

wing nationalism and a muddled brew of racist, Pan-Germanic, and expansionist ideologies."[29]

Harbou also absorbed in her childhood German emotional traits such as affection for animals and a pious love of nature, and at the same time an enthusiasm for Karl May (which she would later share with Fritz Lang) and an openness to modern technology. This latter affinity, as is so often the case in the German psychic makeup, tended both to glorify and to demonize technology; she later observed that she had always been attracted by "the soul of the machine, the living, the vital element in the works of technology."[30] Her fascination with exotic locales blended seamlessly with a militant colonial ideology. (In 1921 she complained publicly that the German people had failed to recognize the moment "when the door to a great future stood open for them."[31])

During World War I, she had written evocations of passionately loving and long-suffering German women and appeals to Siegfried-like, German youth, books with titles like *Deutsche Frauen: Bilder stillen Heldentums* (*German Women: Portraits of Quiet Heroism*), short stories, 1914; *Du junge Wacht am Rhein! Ein Kriegsbuch für die deutsche Jugend* (*You Young Guardians on the Rhine! A War Book for German Youth*), 1915; and *Die deutsche Frau im Weltkrieg* (*The German Woman in the World War*), essays, 1916.[32] These texts, like the Nibelungs novel later on, mix in both their motifs and their images her special blend of maudlin sentimentality and bloodthirsty inhumanity.

From a superficial viewpoint, Thea von Harbou fulfilled all the requirements of Ufa, if one sees it, as the firm's leftist critics have, as a nationalistic witches' kitchen in which all the evil spirits of Prusso-German reaction found a home. But until Hugenberg's takeover, she in fact represented only one element in the company's ideological spectrum, and republican and liberal elements competed against this.

Harbou's relationship with Lang was a harmonious one in the early years. According to her biographer, Reinhold Keiner, an "initially strong emotional attraction, shared nationalistic convictions, and artistic harmony in their films" formed the basis of their marriage and their working relationship.[33] Both are equally responsible for the stylistic and ideological confusion in their joint films. They shared, in particular, a sometimes strained "will to art," which led them to overemphasize, as in *Destiny*, the artistic merit of their medium. (This insistence on "art" had its parallels in the "Stefan George cult" and "Rilke fever" infecting Weimar's literary life.) Lang's break with Ufa and his falling out with Thea von Harbou occurred simultaneously, but political differences were not involved: these became evident only after Lang had emigrated and made anti-Fascist films in America, while Harbou, a member of the National Socialist Party from 1932 on, maintained her Nibelungs loyalty to Ufa until 1945. (Reliable sources indicate, however, that she was never a convinced Nazi or an anti-Semite.[34])

In every intellectual position, Thomas Mann said, a political element is latent. It is certainly true of Thea von Harbou that her politics were hidden in her inward-looking, pathos-laden, "vulgar idealism," but if anything, that made it all the easier for the German petit bourgeois to resonate to them. Murnau had her write for some of his films, too: *Der brennende Acker* (*Burning Soil*, produced in 1921–22 by Goron Films; Willy Haas and Arthur Rosen collaborated with Harbou on the book), the film version of Hauptmann's *Phantom*, and Lang's Ufa films *Driven from Home* and *The Finances of the Archduke* (based on a novel with that title by Frank Heller). Other important films she wrote for Decla-Bioscop or Ufa during the 1920s were *Der steinerne Reiter* (*The Stone Horseman*, directed by Fritz Wendhausen, 1923), *Die Prinzessin Suwarin* (directed by Johannes Gunter, 1923), *Michael* (directed by Dreyer, who was already famous by then and who radically reworked her script), and Arthur von Gerlach's *Concerning the Chronicles of Grieshuus*, based on a novella by Theodor Storm. The protagonists, fit for ballads all, were cruel manorial lords and self-sacrificing peasant girls, exiled princesses, debt-ridden artists, and feuding brothers.

In 1928 Ufa issued a publicity release that was a tribute to its most productive writer; the text, portraying her as a lonely Norn of Neubabelsberg, has echoes of Thea von Harbou's own excessive language:

> Here the endless rolls of film glide through her indefatigable hands as she edits the negatives and the positives. Here in the little viewing room No. 5 strips from movies-in-the-making flicker past her attentive eyes. And here among innumerable rolls of film and surrounded by the brooding buildings of the film city her novels and scripts take shape. Not a minute of the day goes by unused.[35]

In every intellectual position a political attitude is latent. True as that is of Thea von Harbou, it is even truer of Carl Mayer, though in a completely different sense. Mayer was the most important German film writer of the 1920s and a stroke of extreme good fortune for the directors who worked with him. Along with Lang and Murnau, the cameramen Karl Freund, Carl Hoffmann, and Fritz Arno Wagner, and the architects Robert Herlth, Walter Röhrig, Hermann Warm, Otto Hunte, and Erich Kettelhut, he belonged to that core group of devoted pioneers who for a short time around 1925 transformed Ufa into a "builders' guild" possessed by bold dreams and visions of aesthetic utopias.

"In all the many hours and days I talked with Mayer," Paul Rotha reported, "I can't remember his ever saying anything political. He was an artist through and through, if such a thing as an apolitical artist is possible. He never talked with me about politics, only about people."[36] But in his relationship to people, in the use of his linguistic and dramaturgical skills to illuminate human relationships, Mayer was a politically thoughtful and socially conscious artist par excellence. He was an observer who understood how to think with his eyes. He could transpose what he saw and thought into "speaking" film images, because the camera was not just a helpful optical device for him but an extension of his senses and his mind. Mayer produced no independent literary texts. He wrote only for film, and writing was for him only a preliminary step in the filmic process. His screenplays, despite the clear expressionistic echoes in them, were an original literary genre with their own style.

The films that Mayer wrote for Ufa or companies affiliated with it were few—from the early Rex film *Der Dummkopf* (*The Dimwit*, 1920) to Murnau's *Tartuffe* (1925), the high points being Lupu Pick's *Shattered* and *New Year's Eve*, for which the concept "chamber film" was developed (a misleading idea because borrowed from, and suggestive of, the theater), and Murnau's *The Last Laugh*. Mayer had become famous with *The Cabinet of Dr. Caligari* in 1919–20. Among his other "chamber films" is *Back Stairs* directed by Leopold Jessner and Paul Leni for Henny Porten Film.

Of *The Dimwit*, *Lichtbild-Bühne* wrote that its strong point was Mayer's "script, which achieved psychological impact and presented a unified whole."[37] *Shattered*, a family tragedy played by a cast of four crowded together in a railroad flagman's shack, surprised the public and the reviewers because it was a "textless film play,"[38] one of the first silent movies that had no need of extensive subtitles explaining and paraphrasing the action. Mayer used details in the set and props and mimetic gestures to render states of mind as well as their social context with great precision, introducing, Rotha felt, "a new, sociological use of cinema."[39] His next film, *Grausige Nächte* (*Nights of Terror*, 1921), also directed by Lupu Pick, was based on a mystery story involving the illegitimate child of a consul's wife. The story was conventional and crass, but with a keen eye that could see beyond the limited subject matter, *Film-Kurier* picked up on what was truly innovative: Mayer's ability to think and write in visual terms; film was Mayer's "mode of thought," it noted. He was "an original talent who had something to say." For him, film was not a surrogate medium but an independent one "that could hold its own with any other form of expression."[40]

Many of Mayer's contemporaries, including some from abroad, made similar assessments. René Clair, for example, said of Arthur von Gerlach's Union film *Vanina—The Gallows Wedding* that its originator, Carl Mayer, had grasped the essence of film.[41] The films Mayer wrote and worked on prompted critics and colleagues to view film with greater precision, which in turn greatly benefited the development of film criticism. Indeed, the effect was felt throughout the film culture whose growth Ufa was helping make possible: a new awareness of the unique qualities of the medium, its sensory and visual intensity, which drew literary intellectuals to movies. They perceived, or at least sensed, the limits of familiar forms of verbal communication, because in films like Mayer's they could see how they "were overcome by the power of [their] images."[42] Here, under the auspices of Ufa and its crassly capitalistic production and distribution arrangements, a new aesthetics of communication was beginning to take form, a new culture of perception, and it contained the promise of emancipation. The artists working in Ufa's studio around 1925 can hardly be blamed for the company's later betrayal of these hopes and, under National Socialist rule, its liquidation of its own past.

The hour-long film *New Year's Eve*, which renders the final hour of a year as reflected in the events and moods in three different social milieus, premiered on January 3, 1924, in the Ufa-Theater am Kurfürstendamm. The self-contained quality of the script was evident even then; in the same year it was published by Gustav Kiepenheuer in Potsdam.[43] Herbert Jhering wrote later that this film, totally dependent on the elements of light and movement for its effects, "has to be judged in a fundamentally different way." German film had never, he felt, come so near as this film had to attaining "absolute film art." Parallel montage was used not just for banal contrast but "as a motif of motion, as a rhythmic counterpoint," yet Mayer always began with people and returned to them.[44]

It is not surprising that the impulse for *The Last Laugh*, Murnau's major work and one of the most famous Ufa films of the Weimar Republic, came from Carl Mayer. According to Paul Rotha, a newspaper report about a toilet attendant whose poverty drove him to suicide prompted Mayer to write this story.[45] A hotel doorman, demoted to the men's-room detail by his boss, tries to sustain his dignity by keeping his doorman's uniform, but he is destroyed psychologically by the emotional coldness of the world around him—another of the innumerable victims in the struggle for survival that the crisis of capitalism has forced on the have-nots. Lotte Eisner relates that Lupu Pick was to have directed this film and wanted to group it together with the earlier *Shattered* and *New Year's Eve* in a trilogy, but differences of opinion between him and Mayer ended that plan.[46]

The unresolved debate about a "second ending" to the film, a "tacked-on" happy ending, still goes on today. "Do we owe this crude epilogue to Mayer or to Murnau?" Eisner asked, and the cinematically brilliant sequences in the hotel, in the rear courtyard of the apartment house, and in the dream scenes made her regret "all the more the banality of the trivial happy ending . . . about the millionaire who dies in the men's room and leaves all his money to the attendant. Murnau is as dull here as his Berlin audiences. And the effect of this ending, like that of the so-called Ufa style, is embarrassing."[47]

Probably neither Mayer nor Murnau was responsible for this ending à la Dawes Plan and the "new prosperity" of 1924, nor was Emil Jannings, who played the doorman and who claimed in his memoirs that for reasons of a "purely artistic nature" he had pushed this change through "despite the hubbub of the literati" against it. He was never satisfied to present only the negative side of things, he said. The doorman and his bitter fate "represented defeat without any outlook beyond it, and it was just such an outlook I needed, for I have to have faith in the world!"[48] Jannings's account no doubt is one of those self-idealizations that sometimes deviate significantly from historical truth. According to information Rolf Hempel received from Otto Mayer, Carl's brother, Mayer opposed this fairy-tale ending, but "Ufa made production of the film conditional on it." Hempel also cites a 1962 report of Erich Pommer's, according to which "it took ten meetings to convince the writer Carl Mayer to write this happy ending. 'We added the happy ending because the film would otherwise have been like real life and would have been a failure commercially.' "[49] No company documents can either confirm or refute this report. The economic misery of the man in the street was not taboo for Ufa at that time, but the relentlessness with which Murnau and Mayer depicted the doorman's decline into total isolation did cause consternation.

With the help of the only subtitle in the film, Mayer provided an ironic transition to this second ending. But the irony did not go unnoticed. After the premiere on December 23, 1924, in the Ufa-Palast am Zoo, Jhering wrote in the *Berliner Börsen-Courier* that the film had made an "extraordinary virtue" out of the "ordinary necessity" of having a happy ending. "The epilogue is introduced with such wit and perfect pacing that this sudden turn of events is not disconcerting."[50] Kurt Pinthus even thought the unexpected happy ending was a "stroke of film art admirably integrated" into the whole.[51]

In spite of its sorties into social criticism, *The Last Laugh* won acclaim from institutions of the Weimar bourgeoisie, too. According to a report in the *Lichtbild-Bühne*, a Cologne festival showing, attended by Chamber of Commerce leaders, was a first-class social event.[52] The film was also one of Ufa's few great successes abroad. It ran in London and New York for weeks to sellout crowds, and the consensus in the Anglo-American press was that German cinema was well on the way to winning back for Germany the respect it had lost in the world.

13.

Was There an Ufa Style?
The Limits of Illusion

O N April 22, 1927, in a routine daily meeting, Ufa's senior managers decided to make the advertising for Ufa's theaters uniform throughout Germany. Posters and advertising texts would in future be sent out to the provinces "en masse from Berlin." A few days later, on May 5, another decree came down:

> Ufa will develop specific regulations governing the uniforms that different categories of personnel will wear. These regulations will apply to personnel in both Berlin and the provinces, and a table including illustrations of the different uniforms, like that of Scherl, will be maintained.[1]

On May 14, Ufa's management found cause to register displeasure on another front: "Liane Haid has appeared in a film made by the firm of Lothar Stark in costumes she wore in the Ufa film *Der letzte Walzer (The Last Waltz)* and that she illegally took with her. An injunction against Mr. Stark will be obtained." Arthur Robison had just completed directing *The Last Waltz*, the first co-production of Ufa and Paramount, an operetta film based on music by Oskar Straus with a cast that included Willy Fritsch, Ida Wüst, and Hans Adalbert von Schlettow. Liane Haid, a charming Viennese type with a come-on look and an early star of Austrian silent film, was much in demand after her success in Richard Oswald's *Lady Hamilton* (1921).

But Ufa's management applied different standards to her partner, Willy Fritsch, recording in its minutes from June 3 that he would "receive as part of the terms of his contract a monthly clothing allowance of 500 marks. Special provision will be made for each individual film as well, this amount not to exceed, however, an additional 500 marks per month."

Ufa was renovating its public image completely. Senior managers had come to think that the whole organization needed to develop a recognizable aesthetic profile that would set it apart from the entertainment industry's chaos and affirm its special market value. If it is possible for a firm—a faceless, economic power structure with complex inner workings difficult to oversee—to have an aesthetic "emanation," then Ufa did its best to project just such an aura. The company realized that the sum total of details, seemingly insignificant in themselves, would make its image, so those details had to have visual symbolic value and stand out from the flood of other trademarks. Examples were the famous Ufa rhombus, the large-format film poster, the uniform layouts of newspaper ads, and the uniformed elevator boy in the Gloria-Palast. No less important than a star's costume was what he wore when he frequented cafés on Kurfürstendamm. Ufa dressed up, and its costumes unexpectedly turned out to be uniforms.

Subtle differences in treatment took into account the hierarchy of the stars and their different market values. Ever since his role in Joe May's *The Farmer from Texas* (1925), Willy Fritsch, as a likable, nervy go-getter type, had been an undisputed star whom the public identified with. Fritsch was as much a part of Ufa's animate inventory as he was of its "façade." Like the magic rhombus, his face on posters, in showcases, and above theater portals advertised the uniqueness and omnipresence of Ufa's dream factory. The clothing allowance was a concession to this commanding image, which lent additional splendor to the company's name. But Ufa's managers did not accord Liane Haid comparable rank. She had sinned against the company and its aura by "illegally" using her Ufa costumes in another company's production. The legal grounds for the injunction Ufa's attorneys obtained was misappropriation of property, but psychologically the issue was theft of aura, misuse of the immaterial, though visible, values that made up Ufa's luster. Ufa's legal action was therefore not against her but against the competing firm.

The world of Ufa's symbols was part of cinematic reality; it enlarged and enriched "the fascinating second reality of cinema and the consumer culture depicted within it."[2] In the Weimar Republic, consumerism was a kind of asylum for the socially disintegrated petit-bourgeois ego. "The public visibility of the entertainment culture almost completely hid the dependence, insecurity, and poverty of the average white-collar employee's existence." Cinematic reality functioned as a substitute reality. Just like an automobile or elegantly furnished apartment shown in magazine ads, the stars' wealth and supposedly libertine lifestyle were objects of desire. And the period's universally proclaimed sexual liberation was in fact "realized only voyeuristically in the movie theaters."

In both movies and ads human beings were reduced to objects. Stripped of personality, they became stereotypes of "white-collar culture" and its dreams. Fashions, haircuts, facial shapes, and "physical sensuality" conformed, in the male stars, to the pattern of the charming young man who overcomes all obstacles to get ahead. Women were sex objects, most crassly perhaps in the image of the chorus girl, lacking all individuality and seen only as part of a line, a "dance machine," a dancing body "trained and drilled according to certain simple techniques," a movement machine, as the critic Fritz Gliese put it.[3]

It is no doubt true that this "physical-sensuality cult" arose directly "from the new demands of the production system"—of large-scale industry organized according to the famous scientific-management principles of F. W. Taylor, although it is perhaps stretching it to argue, as Gert Selle has done, that the movie executives "were also attempting by aesthetic means and psychic violence to achieve certain goals of socialization," that "whoever controlled the production and distribution systems—and for all practical purposes that was Ufa—also controlled to a great extent the malleable sensory world and the mentality of great masses of people."[4] This thesis assumes a level of sophistication in social policy and cultural theory that was simply not present among Ufa's directors and senior managers. It assumes a conscious exercise of "power on the part of the manipulators." In those complicated interactions between economic and aesthetic factors, the manipulators were probably being manipulated themselves and were instruments of more profound structural changes. Both in its regulation of uniforms for its personnel and in its clothing allowance for Willy Fritsch, Ufa was attuned to a trend of the times, the trend to create uniformity and to reduce human beings to objects. And this certainly touched "on the motivational makeup of the déclassé population, on their muddled memories, their fears of powers they could not comprehend, their petit-bourgeois hopes of happiness."[5]

Was there an Ufa style, a specific Ufa aesthetic, a set of guidelines for producing and reproducing "lovely perceptions" and "pleasant feelings"? Anyone trying to answer this question should keep in mind the world of symbols of which Ufa was a part.

"Though it is a good thing that a play is created in order to make the world clearer, there is nonetheless a guilty duplicity involved if we confuse the sign with what it points to," Roland Barthes wrote in "Everyday Myths." And using the example of those "odd" haircuts in movies about ancient Rome, he makes clear what a sign is: "The fringed haircut provides incontrovertible evidence that we are in ancient Rome," where "the Romans are Roman by virtue of an eminently visible sign: the fringes of hair on their foreheads."[6]

In the world of illusion, "ritual signs need only be introduced to suggest the idea of sex and to evoke it," Barthes says of the striptease. The ritual signs contradict nakedness; they belong to the category of coverings, decor, accessories, and stereotypical movements—and they put the object of our desire beyond our reach. Just like the unveiled body of a woman in a striptease, so in a movie, thanks to the figure of the star, the person as a social being is pressed "into the enveloping comfort of a familiar rite," becomes "unreal, smooth, and self-contained, like a beautiful, shiny object that precisely because of its extravagance is beyond human reach."[7] As Barthes notes in his essay on "Garbo's Face," this is especially true when the star's "makeup takes on the snowy impenetrability of a mask." "It is not a painted face; it is a plasterlike face, closed off at its surface by its color and not by its lines."[8]

The "snowy" reserve of the silent-film masks—especially of the actresses whose beauty was celebrated as eternal—makes access to the "physical sensuality" of the early stars difficult for today's viewer. Well into the late 1920s, movies paid homage to that kind of hermetic beauty, and Ufa's films were no exception. Lya de Putti as *Manon Lescaut* in Arthur Robison's film defended herself, in her role as an eighteenth-century woman, against the masculine terrorism of a feudal, absolutist society; as a physical being in front of Theodor Sparkuhl's merciless camera, she fought against a heavy layer of chalk-white makeup that would have robbed her face of individuality had it not been for her dark eyes, sometimes wandering dreamily, sometimes flaring with passion.

The attempt to define an Ufa aesthetic on the basis of its stars and their erotic charisma runs up against a historical problem. The Ufa stars—Henny Porten, Lil Dagover, Brigitte Helm, and Lilian Harvey; Emil Jannings, Werner Krauss, Gustav Fröhlich, and Willy Fritsch, to name only a few—developed at a time when German film, in the grip of big business but also under the influence of the educated haute bourgeoisie, had gone beyond the anarchistic excesses, the uninhibited celebrations of kitsch, and the explosive sensuality of its early years and was orienting itself to middle-class "taste." That shift had an interesting negative effect on the quality of film eroticism and on the erotic expectations that accompany every visit to a cinema. If Barthes thought the striptease numbers at the Moulin Rouge were a "typically French form of exorcism that was far less intent on destroying the erotic than in domesticizing it," reducing it to petit-bourgeois "domestic furnishing,"[9] then it can be said even more of the European, especially German, film stars of the late 1920s that they lent their charisma to an inhibited middle-class eroticism that stripped the erotic of its magical qualities.

As early as 1920 Carlo Mierendorff furiously attacked the "philistinization" of film and the replacement of the truly erotic with the perfumed mediocrity of that new genre the "society film." "Instead of the whorehouse, we get the bar; instead of the wedding night, the wedding; instead of lingerie, décolletage; instead of rape, perhaps an embrace." Ufa rapidly became the most important producer and distributor of these "society films," which, he thought, promoted a "romanticism of capitalism," as devoid of soul as it was antagonistic to the body. "All we get now is salons, banquets, boudoirs, bows, smiles. Always the same stuffed shirts, dreary, boring." "The philistine has triumphed. Too timid and bloodless to indulge in excess himself, he will tolerate nothing but platitudes."[10]

Ufa's increasing emphasis on external splendor—the opulence of its theaters with their glittering façades, its gala premieres and "stage shows," its advertising campaigns and uniform regulations—went along with a stunting of sensuality in its films, a trend to middle-class conformity in its stars, and what one might call a secularization of the star and diva cults that in other countries, notably the United States, were almost pseudo-religious. The film historian Enno Patalas points out that the European film actor was generally perceived as the "medium for an idea," not as an "autonomous idol" who could revel in his own perfection as long as he held the hearts of the public in his hand.[11] This was especially the case in Germany, where the film star was "more a representative of the dominant ideology than of the unconscious yearnings of the collective soul," though when ideology and the impulses of the collective soul coincided, as they did in the case of the "war heroine" Henny Porten in her films of 1914–18, a star of a type found only in Germany was created.

Stars with international appeal, the kind of stars Hollywood produced, found no place in Ufa's studios. In the early years, Lubitsch succeeded in promoting Pola Negri into such a figure. As Willy Haas put it: "She is the vamp par excellence. If there ever was a vamp—either in Chemnitz or on the Missouri River—then she is it."[12] But then Pola Negri was the first European actress to be offered a long-term contract in Hollywood, and as a rival to Gloria Swanson, she was the first of Hollywood's foreign "exotic beauties that would later include Greta Garbo, Marlene Dietrich, and many others."[13] Sophistication and a touch of the exotic—the two main ingredients in the mystery and erotic appeal of stars—were essentially alien to the middle-class outlook of German film performers trained on the stage.

Marlene Dietrich, the only authentic *femme fatale* that German film produced, quickly became an international idol after her success in Josef von Sternberg's Ufa film *The Blue Angel*. Different movies are cited for her debut, depending on whether censorship records or premiere dates are consulted. Her first film appearance was most likely in Joe May's *Tragödie der Liebe* (*Tragedy of Love*, produced in 1922 and premiered on November 6, 1923).[14] In this potboiler of a mystery story involving a murdered count, a boxer, and a cheerful coquette, Dietrich had a supporting role in the shadow of famous colleagues like Mia May, Ida Wüst, Emil Jannings, Wladimir Gaidarow, Paul Biensfeldt, Rudolf Forster, and Paul Graetz. In Kurt Bernhardt's Terra-Film *Die Frau, nach der man sich sehnt* (*The Woman Men Yearn For*, 1929), a love triangle that ends with a death, she showed for the first time, as Fritz Kortner's partner, a hint of that remote lasciviousness, at once sensual and beyond sensuality, that would make her famous. Then, as Lola-Lola in *The Blue Angel*, based on Heinrich Mann's novel *Professor Unrat*, Marlene Dietrich became a star: "more a symbol of eros than a lover or beloved,"[15] aloof and worldly, with her androgynous elegance and provocative independence. A unique phenomenon in film and cultural history, she had, by 1930, already left the Germans behind and was several sizes too large for Hugenberg's Ufa. Under the wing of Sternberg and Paramount, she was well on her way to becoming "an erotic figure of international appeal."[16]

In Germany the public was looking for more "respectable" models. Wild stories invented about the stars—most of them outlandish, trumped-up fairy tales designed to suggest that they inhabited the dreamworld of their films—drew less and less interest in the crisis seasons after the crash of 1929. Theda Bara, the first vamp in film history and the daughter of a Danish tailor in Cincinnati, perpetuated the legend that she first saw the light of day in the Sahara Desert as the child of a French artist and an Arab mother. Fern Andra, a German-American demimondaine of Ufa's early years, published a brochure in which she claimed she retired to an Italian cloister every year for several months to meditate and gather strength for her next film. But Ufa dispensed with these farfetched yarns. They were no longer appropriate in a period of economic rationality and industrial constraints.

As early as 1923 Friedrich Sieburg had written that the star was the hero that "a population organized for purely economic purposes and therefore incapable of heroism fantasized themselves as being."[17] But in 1932, Rudolf Arnheim detected that the star myth had been drastically diminished within two years. Jannings, Arnheim said, had been stripped of the great passions he had embodied in *The Blue Angel* and was now nothing more than a "well-groomed, amiable robber chief, a matinee idol in his best years." A movie like Robert Siodmak's Ufa sound film *Stürme der Leidenschaft* (*Storms of Passion*, 1931) "passes for high tragedy these days!"[18] A calculating spirit and a land of Prussian Protestant narrow-mindedness—the flip side of Ufa's glory from the beginning—rubbed off on the movie plots and the psychic constitution of many film heroes. Ten years earlier Kurt Pinthus had made the sarcastic "practical" suggestion that Henny Porten be made Germany's President, that her salary be reduced accordingly, that the highest possible prices be demanded for export sales of her films, and that the profits be used to wipe out Germany's reparation debts.[19] After the catastrophic failure of Lang's *Metropolis* and the disappointing results of the Parufamet deal, Ufa's business managers were probably thinking along similar pragmatic lines, though nowhere near so boldly and imaginatively.

If there was an "Ufa aesthetic"—an aesthetic that involved its "philosophy," marketing strategy, relationship to mass consciousness and to the real political power structure—then it was most clearly embodied in Fritz Lang's *Metropolis*, a film that could have been made only in Germany, only at the zenith of the Weimar Republic, and only in Neubabelsberg. In this film we find all the elements that had made possible Ufa's dominance of the industry since 1917, that had contributed to its triumphs and brought it to the brink of disaster, and that would finally precipitate its subjection to dictatorship: a strong capital base, squandered carelessly, a talent for large-scale organization and a tendency to go astray in microscopic detail; devotion to artistic excellence and to its perversion, which was empty perfectionism; a delight in the imaginative use of technology and in its reverse, which was mere technical slickness; a quest for philosophical power, but pursued in an intellectual vacuum; a "will to form" that produced an amorphous ruin; craftsmanship, imagination, and diligence, and the waste of all those virtues through intellectual arrogance and the lack of a governing concept. In many respects, the fate of *Metropolis* symbolized the fate of Germany's first republic.

After seeing *Metropolis*, H. G. Wells wrote that his faith in the enterprising spirit of the Germans had suffered a major setback:

> In the worst traditions of the cinema, absurdly overconfident and self-satisfied, convinced of the power of loud advertising to bring in the public, without fear of serious criticism, without the faintest awareness of science or of perspectives outside their own immediate circle, they went to work in their gigantic studio producing yard upon yard of this ignorant, old-fashioned drivel and destroying the market for every better film.[20]

But Wells did not see, and perhaps did not want to see, the high level of cinematic virtuosity and the German desire for perfection crystallized in this film. *Metropolis* was and remains a German problem.

Lang took seventeen months—from the end of May 1925 until the end of October 1926—to translate into wholly original film images his vision of class warfare in a utopian city of the twenty-first century. During those seventeen months, Ufa organized a publicity campaign: it gave first the Berlin papers, then the smallest provincial papers figures on the investment in personnel and materials required to produce *Metropolis*, representing it as some kind of cultural achievement: 36,000 extras including 750 children, 100 blacks, and 1,100 "skinheads"; more than 500 skyscrapers; 1.3 million meters of film; 1.6 million marks for wages alone.

During the war, the Army Supreme Command had demonstrated how millions of marks and millions of soldiers could be set in motion, moved about, squandered, and ultimately destroyed. During inflation, the Germans had learned to deal in billions when they shopped for basic foodstuffs. Almost every day the press tossed about the figures on the war debt Germany would be paying off until the end of the century. The Dawes Plan of April 1924, which had reorganized the Reichsbank under Allied supervision and provided a schedule for reparation payments and a loan to Germany of 800 million gold marks, and which had ushered in a phase of relative prosperity, was understood by most Germans primarily in terms of numbers. Now Ufa was applying the mathematics of war and economic competition to entertainment and, as Theodor Heuss noted in his *Metropolis* review in 1927, was cultivating "a number snobbism"[21] to which the

Oskar Messter (on horseback), 1914

Messter's studio

In Messter's studio, 1911, with Henny Porten being directed by Adolf Gärtner

Paul Davidson

Asta Nielsen, in *Rausch* (*Intoxication*)

Max Skladonowsky with his bioscope
projector, about 1920

Henny Porten, about 1920

Ernst Lubitsch, about 1920

Joe May

Reinhold Schünzel

Carl Mayer

Erich Pommer, 1923

Sumurun (*One Arabian Night*), with sets by Kurt Richter and Ernö Metzner

Der Student von Prague (*The Student of Prague*), with Paul Wegner (right)

Filming *Der Totentanz* (*The Dance of Death*), Urban Gad (left), Fritz Weidmann, and Asta Nielsen on the set, Guido Seeber at the camera

Two views of Messter's glass studio on Friedrichstrasse in Berlin

The Deutsche Bioscop studio

Carmen (*Gypsy Blood*), with Pola Negri and Harry Liedtke (left)

Die Herrin der Welt (*Mistress of the World*), with Mia May

Madame Dubarry (Passion)

Filming *Das Weib des Pharao* (*The Loves of Pharaoh*)

Germany's President Ebert (left) at the filming of *Anna Boleyn* (*Deception*), with Paul Davidson (middle); Henny Porten and Emil Jannings in costume; Ernst Lubitsch (above); and Hanns Kräly (between Porten and Jannings)

The coronation procession in *Deception*

Veritas vincit, with sets by Paul Leni and Siegfried Wroblesky

Das Indische Grabmal (*The Indian Tomb*), with Mia May and Conrad Veidt

Bernhard Goetzke and Lil Dagover in *Der müde Tod* (*Destiny*)

Destiny, with sets by Robert Herlth, Walter Röhrig, and Hermann Warm

Fridericus Rex, with Otto Gebühr

Dr. Mabuse, with Rudolf Klein-Rogge

Der Golem, wie er in die Welt kam (*Golem, How He Came into the World*), with sets by Hans Poelzig and Kurt Richter

Der Flug um den Erdball (*The Flight around the Earth*)

Preparing the set for *I.N.R.I.* in Staaken

Two views of the Great Hall in Neubabelsberg

Die Nibelungen (*The Nibelungs*), directed by Paul Richter; sets by Otto Hunte, Erich Kettlehut, and Karl Vollbrecht

A still photo being taken during the filming of Siegfried's battle with the dragon in *The Nibelungs*

Neubabelsberg: (clockwise from upper left) the Ufa administration building, costume storage, a workshop, and a makeup room

Faust, with Emil Jannings and Gösta Ekman flying on Mephistopheles's cloak

Work on the sets for *Faust*, designed by Robert Herlth and Walter Röhrig

The Gloria-Palast, Berlin

The front of the Ufa-Palast am Zoo, Berlin, advertising an Al Jolson film

The Ufa-Palast am Zoo, with a display for *Frau im Mond* (*Woman in the Moon*)

The Ufa-Palast am Zoo, with a display for *Asphalt*

The Ufa-Palast am Zoo at the premiere of *Der Kongress tanzt* (*The Congress Dances*)

Alfred Hugenberg, 1928

Ludwig Klitzsch, 1941

The staff of the Afifa copying facility in 1926

Thea von Harbou listening to Fritz Lang, on a set

Thea von Harbou in 1927

Hans Albers

Emil Jannings in *Der letzte Mann* (*The Last Laugh*)

Filming *Der letzte Mann* at night

Der Liebe der Jeanne Ney (The Love of Jeanne Ney)

Die Drei von der Tankstelle (The Three from the Filling Station): (from left to right) Olga Tschechowa, Fritz Kampers, Heinz Rühmann, Oskar Karlweis, Lilian Harvey, and Willy Fritsch

Building the models for *Metropolis*

Metropolis sets by Otto Hunte, Erich Kettelhut, and Karl Vollbrecht

Metropolis

Die Wege zu Kraft und Schönheit (Ways to Strength and Beauty)

(left to right) Erich Pommer, Lilian Harvey, and Willy Fritsch arrive in Vienna for the premiere of *Liebeswalzer* (*Waltz of Love*)

The inventors of the light-sound process: Joe Engl, Joseph Massolle, and Hans Vogt with their loudspeakers

Entrance to the "sound cross" at
Neubabelsberg

Asphalt, with Betty Amann and Gustav Fröhlich

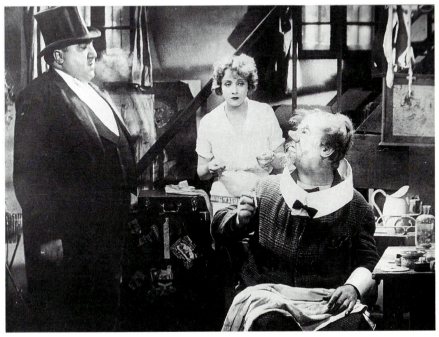

Der blaue Engel (*The Blue Angel*): (left to right) Kurt Gerron, Marlene Dietrich, and Emil Jannings

Marlene Dietrich in *The Blue Angel*

public did not fall victim so much as the company itself. Production costs had initially been estimated at 1.5 million marks, but by the time the film was done, Ufa had spent 5.3 million. The prospects for earning that back, even if the earnings were above average, were slim. Ufa management made Erich Pommer the scapegoat—Pommer, of all people, who had always argued not for quantity but for artistic quality.

The film started to take shape, Lang said later, with his first look at the skyscrapers of New York City. That was in October 1924, when Ufa had sent him and Pommer to the States to study American filmmaking methods. "I roamed the streets all day. The buildings struck me as a vertical curtain, glistening and very light, an opulent stage backdrop hung against a gloomy sky to dazzle, to distract, and to hypnotize."[22] Making sophisticated use of the Schüfftan process to shoot his panoramic skylines, Lang and his cameramen, Karl Freund and Günther Rittau, gave a magical, glassy quality to the glistening transparency of their imagined skyline, making it both dreamy and nightmarish. Lang shared with the Weimar bourgeoisie an ambivalent attitude toward America, a mixture of fear and fascination, scorn and inferiority complex; and he projected this ambivalence onto his vision of capitalism *per se*. This very mixture of fascination and terror is why *Metropolis* so precisely reflects society's lack of structural clarity in its psychic and ideological makeup. Much was possible, and just about anything seemed possible: liberation or catastrophe, destruction or salvation, totalitarian order or total anarchy. It is hardly the fault of Thea von Harbou's unspeakably simpleminded script alone that in trying to solve the problem of class for all time, *Metropolis* culminates in a platitude straight from a German verse anthology: The heart is the link between hand and head (which is to say, between wage work and capital). As Kracauer says, this formulation could "well have been formulated by Goebbels";[23] and the film's final sequence, in which the working masses in front of the rulers' cathedral go down on their knees before the cross he convincingly interprets as a symbolic anticipation of Fascist rule to come.

If *Metropolis* anticipated what lay in the near future, it also reflected contemporary experience intertwined with mysticism, "old German" material, and pseudo-religious philosophies of salvation—all the regressive dream material of the Weimar Republic, all the temporarily stalled projects of Germany's extremist reactionary forces. In the fall of 1923, Hugo Stinnes, the most powerful "business leader" of the time, in secret talks and confidential communications with the American ambassador, had developed a socially catastrophic strategy for crushing organized labor: reinstitution of the ten-hour workday, disbanding of the legislature, installation of a dictator or triumvirate with military command powers, suppression of the Communist wing of the workers' movement. "The expectation is," Ambassador Houghton reported to the State Department, "that socialism would be permanently eliminated as a political mode of existence in Germany and that laws and regulations that hinder production and serve no useful purpose would be immediately rescinded."[24] Stinnes was worried about the possibility of right-wing parties beating him to the punch by staging a coup, which would mobilize the Western democracies against Germany. In his view, the ideal situation was to have a Communist revolt initiate this process.

Fantasies of this kind preoccupied innumerable conservatives, and these same fantasies reappear in *Metropolis*, some as visions of horror, some as elements of plot—as in the images of oppressed proletarians herded like animals into endless marching columns, and in the figure of the robot Maria, who stirs up rebellion and thus creates the impetus that sets the drama's involved pacification process in motion or, as Kracauer put it, furnishes the "pretext to crush the workers' rebellious spirit."[25] Lang, who called himself a "sleepwalker," worked as a dreamer reworks the material of the day in nocturnal images, reshaping it, placing it in new contexts, altering its logic. Why all this fuss? Willy Haas asked. The result was "a profound, inner absence of style," in turn "a symptom of something much more troubling, a belletristic lack of engagement that desperately needs tomorrow and yesterday so that it can avoid today."[26]

This lack of style, however, was in no small measure the result of an obsession with artistic and technical perfection. Once again—with the American film magnates at Ufa's doorstep and Hugenberg ready to pounce—the Neubabelsberg and Staaken studios became laboratories for cinematic innovation. Aenne Willkomm, the costume chief, racked her brains developing a "color theory"[27] for black-and-white film. The architect Otto Hunte worked for months on model skyscrapers, futuristic automobiles and airplanes, and a new Tower of Babel that would seem 500 meters high. Hunte and his fellow architect Kettelhut disagreed about the design of this tower. Lang favored Hunte's design, based on Old Master paintings. "The discussion digressed into fine points of psychology, strayed from the matter at hand, became downright aggressive. Thea von Harbou and Fritz Lang finally decided the issue as they saw fit. Every scene, every image, often even every camera setting was discussed and predetermined in this way."[28]

Karl Freund and Günther Rittau worked for almost a week on a single shot that used the Schüfftan process to blend the film models into a real scene. The result of their labors: 40 meters of film comprising 2,100 individual images whose running time on the screen was ten seconds. The construction of the models used in the factory explosion took four weeks; filming the explosion itself, which obviously could not be reshot, took a minute and a half. "The slightest error would have rendered the work of four weeks useless. About 300 model automobiles were used in the shots of traffic moving on Metropolis's major road, and after each frame was shot, every single car had to be moved ahead a few millimeters to create the impression of movement."[29] For the long-distance call between the industrial chief Fredersen and his machinists, Freund invented the first "television telephone," at least the first one in film.

However detailed the reports in Ufa press releases and in their own memoirs, Freund and Rittau, Hunte and Kettelhut all display an odd reticence on key points. "It would take us too far afield to explain all these things in detail,"[30] said Rittau. Never at a loss for words in describing the *effects* they wanted to achieve, Hunte and Rittau invoked this excuse to avoid describing exactly how they achieved them. Understandably, they did not want to reveal all the tricks of their trade, but the mystification of the production process, like keeping secrets despite a show of openness, was an element of Ufa's propaganda strategy.

Quite apart from that, though, Ufa's film specialists displayed a curious mix of eagerness to achieve and unwillingness to reflect, of technomania and aphasia. They were "doers" (a concept that came into currency with the "New Objectivity" of the 1920s) and did not go in for analysis or self-analysis. They gave little thought to the context in which their work and achievements belonged. And when they spoke of "the big picture"—the history of *Metropolis* and its "morality"—they mumbled the same kind of murky, lyrical platitudes that came from Fritz Lang and Thea von Harbou. In Ufa's advertising for *Metropolis*, we find insipid philosophical reflections coming from people who put the highest possible demands on themselves as architects, cameramen, film technicians. This interplay between perfectionism and inarticulateness, like that between mysticism and intellectual vapidity in the plot of *Metropolis*, was part of the "Ufa aesthetic," and also of Ufa's culture and politics in the Weimar years.

"What is this?" a horrified Hans Siemsen asked in the pages of *Die Weltbühne* after he had seen *Metropolis*. "This is not just *Metropolis*; it is not just German film. It is . . . all of official Germany as we know it and experience it every day on our own hides."[31] Siemsen gleefully picked up H. G. Wells's devastating critique and reprinted excerpts from it, as did the *Frankfurter Zeitung*. With one key point Wells hit a German nerve. The "crowning idiocy" in the film, he said, comes in the transformation of the robot into the figure of Maria. Here, "antiquated German novels" were the root of all evil.

> For a short while one senses a faint hint of Mephistopheles. Even with Ufa, Germany can still be that good, old, magic-loving Germany. The Germans will probably never be able to rid themselves of the Brocken. Walpurgis Night is the name day of the German poetic imagination, and German fancy will no doubt always have to cut its awkward airy capers with a witch's broom between its legs.[32]

That enlightened criticism ridiculed but failed to analyze "magic-loving Germany" would, of course, be avenged all too soon. "Without a strug-

gle, Germany delivered heaven as well as hell, theologians as well as luna-
tics, into the hands of reaction."[33]

(Where *Metropolis* is concerned, German fancy has continued cutting
awkward airy capers. In the 1980s Joe Hembus composed a panegyric ode
to Lang's film; after quoting approvingly the comment of the "positive"
critic Gérard Legrand that the epoch-making uniqueness of *Metropolis* and
its creator consisted in the embodiment of absolute nothingness, Hembus
surprisingly swung over into the other camp and celebrated *Metropolis* as
"a retrospective and speculative fantasy on the great myths of humanity,"
as the creator of a "primal and all-overarching myth."[34])

In November 1926, the censors designated *Metropolis* "educational" and
"artistic." The premiere on January 10, 1927, in the Ufa-Palast am Zoo was
a gala affair. The reviews were not chary with praise, but there were negative
and undecided voices as well, which—disregarding the pans from the leftist
intellectual press that Ufa regarded as marginal anyhow—seem to have
occasioned panic in the firm. Soon after the premiere Ufa issued a pamphlet for cinemas throughout Germany giving not only a detailed plot summary, possible headlines for local papers, and suggestions for pictures and
texts contributed by artists involved with the film, but also a notice that
the façade of the Ufa-Pavilion on Nollendorf Platz would, for the duration
of the *Metropolis* run, be "silvered by a new process" and equipped with
an immense bronzed replica of the alarm system in the movie. (The press
office took the precaution of perforating the pages meant for local papers,
and it urged theater owners "to tear out these pages and give that section
only, not the entire press booklet, to editorial offices"[35]—a precautionary
measure meant to thwart journalists hostile to Ufa who might be waiting
for a chance to catch the company redhanded at its PR tricks.)

But despite these efforts, distribution slowed down as early as the spring
of 1927. Ufa's management, now under Alfred Hugenberg and Ludwig
Klitzsch, decided on April 7 to try to influence Parufamet Distribution "to
let *Metropolis* continue showing for the present in about ten to twelve large
provincial cities—in the American version and if possible with the Com-
munistically tinged subtitles removed—and to bring it back to Berlin in
the fall or, in case of bad weather, in the late summer." A day later, management considered the subtitles once again: "The pietistic passages introduced into the film in America should perhaps be excised." For the rest,
in hopes of making an added several hundred thousand marks, management
accepted Parufamet's suggestion of taking the film off the current program
entirely and bringing it back in August.[36]

When *Metropolis* was submitted to the censors again on August 5, its
original length of 4,189 meters had been trimmed down to 3,241. Enno
Patalas, who in many years of work for the Munich Film Museum has put
together a version that follows the scene sequence of the original but
is not complete, has reconstructed in what questionable ways the film was

"rigorously and systematically mutilated."[37] Only the audience at the Berlin premiere, and possibly the audiences at the Ufa-Pavilion, saw the complete two-and-a-half-hour version. In the spring of 1927 the negative of the Paramount version was cut, and this was the version that was distributed throughout the world. Ufa's management declared this same version suitable for theaters in the German provinces—with, however, its subtitles excised.

On June 3 production chief Major Alexander Grau was told to initiate "as soon as possible a discussion with Mr. Lang about his next film. All production details should be spelled out as precisely as possible and recorded in the files so that constant supervision of Mr. Lang's production is possible and cost overruns can be prevented."[38] *Metropolis*, the "world's greatest film," which was going to beat the Americans at their own game, had been a disaster for Ufa. A second disaster of comparable proportions had to be avoided at all costs. But Fritz Lang had learned some lessons, too. His next two films, *Spies* and *Woman in the Moon*, were under the aegis of Ufa but his own productions.

14.

The General in Civvies:
Ufa under Hugenberg

PRIVY Councillor Dr. Alfred Hugenberg, who became Ufa's master in March 1927, had developed early in his career a lively interest in ideological questions and also a high degree of tactical skill in initiating political and economic undertakings that bore his ideological stamp. In 1890, just turned twenty-five, the still unknown young attorney had founded the Allgemeine Deutsche Verband (Universal German Union), which in 1894 changed its name to the Alldeutsche Verband (Pan-German Union) and in the next four decades pursued policies that considerably eased Adolf Hitler's rise to power. In 1893 Hugenberg became chief adviser to the colonization commission for West Prussia and Poznan, founded by Bismarck, which promoted the sale of large Polish and German estates to German farmers to increase the German influence there.

In October 1909 he made his first big step up in the world, becoming chief executive officer of Friedrich Krupp in Essen: "in the service of industry, of the fatherland, and of war," as his biographer Otto Kriegk noted with great satisfaction.[1] "From his office in the so-called hunger tower in Essen," the historian Willi A. Boelcke has written, "emanated important decisions in German history. Under him the Krupp works moved toward world war on a broad, secure road."[2]

By 1916 Hugenberg, in the meantime a privy financial councillor, had acquired Scherl publishing with help from nationalistic finance companies—Ausland and the Wirtschaftliche Gesellschaft, which had funds from Krupp, Stinnes, and others at their disposal. With that purchase Hugenberg acquired a nerve center of modern mass communications, for August Scherl had created in the *Berliner Lokal-Anzeiger* a newspaper

that offered something for everybody and everything for most everybody, that reported quickly, comprehensively, and indiscriminately, that had no opinion, no character, no profile, that took up no one's cause but its own, that had no other goal than to print as many ads as possible and increase circulation as much as possible.[3]

After the war, Hugenberg focused his energies on pulling together again the defeated regiments of reaction. In 1919 the Economic Association for the Promotion of Intellectual Reconstruction in Germany was formed with the industrialists Kirdorf, Vögler, and Hugenberg at its head. In 1920, Hugenberg was elected to the Reichstag as a member of the German National People's Party (Deutschnationale Volkspartei [DNVP], of which he would become chair in 1928), and in the same year that he took control of Ufa he explained his media policy at a gathering of this party. His goal was to "bring back to the national cause" those national elements that were showing signs of wavering "or to hold them to the national track." It was most important not to let them fall to the leading democratic newspaper houses, that is, to Ullstein, Mosse, and the *Frankfurter Zeitung*.[4]

"A small man, slim, with white hair that is cut very short and sticks up like a brush, glasses, a funny mustache . . . This odd little man who is dressed as if he had to feed a family of five on the salary of a junior bookkeeper has probably twenty souls residing in his breast."[5] Such is Curt Riess's description of the man who owed his success to a mix of profound conservatism and a modern, technocratic instinct for power, of basically anti-democratic convictions and a good nose for the phenomena of mass civilization. For Hugenberg, running big businesses and engineering successful political intrigues were both organizational jobs, and like the Army Supreme Command in the last years of the war but with vastly greater talent, he applied his skills to the complicated fields of political propaganda and the psychological manipulation of conflicting mass emotions.

His lieutenant, Ludwig Klitzsch—"a somewhat roundish man of middle height with dark horn-rimmed glasses and blond, carefully parted hair that is already rather thin, a man who looks very reliable and perhaps a bit philistine"[6]—thought along the same lines. As the founder of DLG and manager of Scherl, he had become an experienced nationalistic media expert, and as the Scherl delegate on Ufa's board he had the administrative know-how to clean house effectively.

Klitzsch had noted the dangers of taking over Ufa's heavy debts, but for Hugenberg—or so it was represented in the Scherl papers—the "national interest" was more important than economic considerations. When Hugenberg decided to restructure Ufa, his media empire included, apart from Scherl, the Allgemeine Anzeigen (General Advertising), the Telegraphen-Union (one of the most important German news agencies), and Deulig-Film and its newsreels, as well as a number of firms that sold newsprint to provincial newspapers. Quite apart from the "national interest," Hugenberg saw possibilities for economic expansion.

The Ufa restructuring took the form of a large-scale financial maneuver that put all the trumps in Hugenberg's hand and left the German Bank, which up until then had held most of the stock, with major losses. According to the bank's calculations, Ufa was worth 74.5 million marks, a price Hugenberg found unacceptable. So a reorganization based on the higher mathematics of capital transactions was arranged. First, the existing joint stock worth 45 million marks was reduced to a value of 15 million by consolidating it at a ratio of 3 to 1, then boosting it back up to 45 million with an additional payment. For the relatively modest sum of 13.5 million Hugenberg's concern bought into Ufa, and then secured an absolute majority by acquiring for 3 million marks all the stock that carried twelve votes, thus gaining control over the administration and board of directors. The German Bank withdrew its demand for 21.7 million marks due it in interest and commissions and took over bonds in the amount of 11.25 million. Others, apart from Hugenberg, who acquired large blocks of stock were the Otto Wolff concern and I. G. Farben, with its subsidiary film factories Agfa, Lignose, and Glanzfilm, which saw a major market in Ufa and wanted to do business with it. Then the real estate on Potsdamer Platz, with the Ufa office building and the Romanische Haus containing the Gloria-Palast, was sold for 9 million. Under its new masters Ufa came out of the restructuring with a profit of about 50 million marks and was able to cover its bank debts and other obligations completely.[7] Germany's largest film company, which critical observers had written off as a "wreck," had recovered almost overnight, and it was again under firm leadership, which from here on had the final word on appointments to the board and on matters of internal governance. Scherl Publishing noted with satisfaction in an internal memo "that we control an unquestioned voting majority. It follows from this that the business conduct of this firm is completely in our hands, a state of affairs that the presence of our people in the firm's top management positions permanently guarantees."[8]

Only five directors from the founding board of 1917 remained on the new board under Hugenberg's chairmanship: Consul Salomon Marx and Commercial Councillor Paul Mamroth of the AEG and bankers Emil Georg von Stauss, Herbert M. Gutmann, and Max von Wassermann. Joining these veterans were, along with other financiers like Siegmund Bodenheimer and Fritz Andreae and industrialists like Otto Wolff and Fritz Thyssen, representatives of the Prussian landed aristocracy and German colonial interests such as Hans von Goldacker, crown-land lessee Egbert Hayessen, and the retired sea captain Wilhelm Widenmann, CEO of the Deutsche Überseedienst (German Overseas Service).

Ludwig Klitzsch, who also continued as chief of Scherl, soon had the reins firmly in hand. As chief executive he was empowered to act on behalf of the board and for all practical purposes to function as a CEO (which title he held from 1931). At the first meeting of the new senior management team on April 5, 1927, he recorded in the minutes that far-reaching personnel measures would "reestablish . . . the unity of management that may to some degree have been lost through the reorganization negotiations and at the same time make clear . . . the tactical procedures as to the financial restructuring and general reorganization of the firm." The most important decision from this meeting concerned Klitzsch himself: he would personally take charge of "the further execution and supervision of the financial restructuring now in progress."[9]

The organization of Ufa's finances and "relations with America" was entrusted to Consul Marx. The general conduct of business and responsibility for overseas enterprise remained with Bausback; Major Grau stayed chief of production for the time being, and a little later, in connection with the community of interests formed with Deulig-Film, he was named chief of the technical division alongside Hermann Grieving.

The detailed minutes of daily management meetings offer great insight into the routine work of this group.*[10] Klitzsch and his managers attended to every minute detail that affected Ufa's financial restructuring and the rationalizing of its internal operations, from the establishment of a uniform half-hour lunch break to moving the administration from Potsdamer Platz to Kochstrasse (where Scherl was located and where Springer would set up its central offices after World War II), from the elimination of two weeks' pay granted to blue-collar employees in case of illness to the suppression of a strike by the technical personnel in the Neubabelsberg and Tempelhof studios. ("All strikers will be fired immediately. Whether they are rehired again after the strike will be determined on the basis of their competence and their role in the strike."[11]) Comparatively exotic matters were also found worthy of discussion—a request from the Queen of Romania, for

---

* It is striking that at the same time that a policy was initiated of "strict sifting and reduction of personnel," key Ufa positions were filled with experts from Scherl. A report to Klitzsch by the head of the newly established organization department describes the criteria for the restructuring. The goal was an "intellectual and spiritual redirection" of all Ufa personnel toward values such as "punctuality, order, and honesty." Departments like Records and Purchasing, which were "in a totally chaotic and disorganized state," would have to be tightened up, "sifted," and reorganized. Above all, a film control department would have to be created, mostly from "the distribution sector."

> It has a supervisory, mediating, and administrative role, stepping in and providing information as early as the drafting stage of filmscripts, and then representing and keeping informed all interested parties until the finished film is delivered. It is the sole point of delivery for sample copies; it participates in drawing up contracts with producers; it organizes internal screenings of new films for the purpose of criticism; it is in charge of censoring and of any dealings with government censors and other important authorities. . . . Setting up a film control department underlines the principle that the commercial agents of film distribution, because of their experience in and knowledge of domestic as well as foreign markets, have to have (while upholding the artistic interest of production) the decisive voice in setting up and executing the production program.

With these regulations, the precedence of distribution over production formally became law within Ufa. And in terms of politics, the stage was set for conflicts between state censors and Ufa's production department.

example, to make a film with Ufa at her own expense concerned "primarily with her person," or a request from Prince Rangsit of Siam to visit the Neubabelsberg studios incognito.[12] Permission was granted in both cases.

The main focus, however, was on stabilizing the financial situation. Management prescribed reduction in three ways: "clarification" of the production program, rental of studios not required for production, and sale of all theaters "that we would like to be rid of." The hoped-for result was to get Ufa "to a point at which its financial operations will be completely surveyable. At that point we can set about acquiring additional capital."[13]

At the same time, however, the absorption of Deulig-Film was discussed; it was resolved that "all members of Ufa's senior management . . . will be appointed to the senior management of Deulig-Film."[14] At the end of July 1927 it was decided to purchase Deulig's entire business for 618,700 marks and to incorporate it into Ufa.

The "new" Ufa also took the lead in the battle against the Weimar government's entertainment tax, which absorbed about 12 percent of income at that time. It had employed a two-pronged strategy: it negotiated tenaciously with the relevant Ministries and at the same time tried to stir up moviegoers against the tax with film strips entitled "Of Concern to All!"

Ufa's top executives gave special attention to lowering production costs and liberally dispensed reprimands and instructions on this score. When they learned that G. W. Pabst would exceed costs by 102,000 marks for *Die Liebe der Jeanne Ney (The Love of Jeanne Ney)*, they warned him that an overrun was out of the question and threatened to break off production "if necessary." But management was not always consistent. In the case of Arnold Fanck, a patriotic director of nature and sport films, they authorized an overrun of 60,000 marks for *Zurück zur Natur (Back to Nature)*. But then again concerning Fritz Wendhausen, who used up 52,858 meters of film for *Donald Westhof*, Ufa's management concluded briskly: "Such people may not be employed again."[15]

With artists' salaries Klitzsch's decisions were remarkably generous, if carefully tailored to each individual case. The cameraman Kurt Courant, for example, received 3,000 marks per month plus a 500-mark "equipment allowance." Courant had been cameraman for Sven Gade's *Hamlet* (with Asta Nielsen) in 1921 and worked on Fritz Lang's *Woman in the Moon* and Kurt Bernhardt's *The Woman Men Yearn For* in 1929. Willy Fritsch earned 3,500 marks per month, too. Oskar Kalbus, later a well-known film historian under the Nazi regime, assumed management of Ufa-Leih (Ufa-Distribution) for a salary of 1,800 marks. A secretary earned between 200 and 250 marks a month in 1927; mid- and upper-level employees received 800 to 1,200. For Ludwig Klitzsch, special rules applied: the as yet uncrowned chief drew a monthly salary of 7,500 marks and an annual allowance of 30,000 marks for official expenses. He also had at his disposal another 30,000 marks per year for "educational travel." He was not expected to submit detailed records of expenses. In addition, Klitzsch took in 3 percent of the net profit distributed to stockholders.[16]

Differences with Parufamet were of great concern. This German-American construct, originally conceived of as Ufa's salvation, was an endless source of grief. There were constant problems with "anti-German" films that made their way from American studios to German theaters, so Ufa's management decided, for example, to "Germanify" for worldwide distribution King Vidor's MGM production *The Big Parade*, one of the outstanding antiwar films in Hollywood's history.[17] Parufamet was to be convinced "to alter all the copies of *The Big Parade* everywhere in the world to conform to the version intended for Germany and to show only such copies. Only on this condition will we bring the film out in Germany."[18] Klitzsch personally undertook the negotiations, and in early May 1927 he opened discussions with Adolph Zukor to alter the Parufamet contract. His goal was to change to Ufa's advantage the way films were selected, the length of the runs, and the rental fees. In August, Ufa succeeded in mobilizing the National Association of German Motion Picture Theater Owners against Hollywood's allegedly "anti-German" films—in reality antimilitaristic films.

In its battle against the leftist and democratic press and in decisions affecting the public image of the company, Hugenberg's management showed a clear political profile right from the start and, quite literally, showed its colors, getting involved in the controversy over whether the black, white, and red flag of the German monarchy or the black, red, and gold flag established by Weimar's constitution as Germany's national colors should prevail. "All in all, probably more flags than in previous years," remarked Harry Kessler on Constitution Day in August 1927, for, as he knew well, "the vast majority of captains of industry, powerful financiers, the civil service, the armed forces, the judiciary, the large and medium-sized landowners (Junkers), the university professors, and students all remain, now as before, hostile to the republic."[19] In this context, Ufa's decision to continue using black, white, and red margins on its program posters even though the colors "had in a very few isolated cases given political offense"[20] has to be seen as a clear statement of political allegiance.

The reporting in the democratic and leftist-liberal papers repeatedly provoked Ufa's management to take a militant stance. The Ullstein papers, for example, had "repeatedly printed reports about Ufa that cannot be regarded as objective." For a while no action was taken, but Klitzsch asked that articles about Ufa coming from the Ullstein papers be separated out from other press notices. He obviously was giving special attention to surveillance of the enemy, and soon Ufa initiated reprisals. "In view of the continuing biased attacks" in the *Lichtbild-Bühne* and *Berliner Tageblatt*, it was decided not to advertise anymore in the former, a respected film magazine. Because Rudolf Mosse, the publishing company against which this policy was directed, also controlled a majority interest in 8-*Uhr Abendblatt*, Ufa's ads were pulled from that, too.[21]

The minutes of 1927 contain frequent mention of a two-part compilation titled *Der Weltkrieg* (*The World War*, directed by Leo Lasko), referred to first as an "army film," then as a "world-war film." It consisted of film material from the Reich war archives and numerous scenes filmed "in the documentary mode." Kurt Tucholsky in his published comments repeatedly attacked this "unspeakable Hugenberg film, which incites people to new wars yet continues to go unpunished in Germany,"[22] yet Ufa treated it as if it were a work of great national and political interest. It told Parufamet, which wanted to handle the film, that distribution by this German-American organization would discredit the movie. (Parufamet ultimately received a copy for distribution in the United States, but only on condition of a solid guarantee that it would be shown and on the understanding that "no biases would be introduced."[23]) And Ufa was notably pleased that Foreign Minister Gustav Stresemann declared himself "satisfied" after a private showing. In an obviously politically motivated move, Klitzsch and his colleagues decided to show the movie three times a day in the Ufa-Palast during the national convention of the Stahlhelm,[24] a paramilitary organization supported by Hugenberg and made up of World War I veterans (in 1933 it was incorporated into the SA). But the Stahlhelm convention was a failure. As Tucholsky noted in *Die Weltbühne* on May 17, 1927, "The Stahlhelm has withdrawn from Berlin, and if the newspapers on both the right and left hadn't made such an ungodly fuss about their pathetic little parade, most Berliners would never have known that a few superannuated officers had ever wanted to take the city."[25]

Ufa's management was vexed when the Foreign Office intervened and had the film *Blutbrüderschaft* (*Blood Brotherhood*) removed from Leipzig theaters for the duration of the spring fair in 1927. The government was apparently reluctant to impose the film's nationalistic tendencies on the city's international guests, and Ufa's request for 10,000 marks in damages "for advertising losses and forfeited income" fell on deaf ears.[26]

Both political and economic motives were involved in the new management's radical revision of Ufa's contract terms. The new regime made clear that once-acceptable corruption would no longer be tolerated. When the director and producer Richard Eichberg signed with Ufa, he had to confirm in writing "that neither in the past nor in the future had he granted or would he grant, directly or indirectly, financial favors to any Ufa employee or any individual in any way affiliated with Ufa." This passage was incorporated in all future production contracts.[27]

Eichberg's colleague Reinhold Schünzel stirred up trouble when he began shooting *Gustav Mond, Du gehst so stille* (*Gustav Moon, You Move So Quietly*) without having submitted a script in advance. What happened next is a classic example of how German nationalistic bureaucrats dealt with an independent-minded nonconformist. "We decided to check whether he is obliged by contract to present his script beforehand. If that is indeed the case, he will be notified in writing that we will have to hold him responsible for any losses we may incur as a result of this omission on his part."[28]

The company Fritz Lang founded after the disagreements over *Metropolis* received a reprimand from Ufa for publishing an ad for Lang's next film in *Der Kinematograph*, for "by the terms of our contract advertising remains Ufa's prerogative."[29] Another dictate called for a clause in all future production and direction contracts "that allows us to edit or alter the completed film as we see fit."[30] In one case the new Ufa managers even made retroactive use of this unilaterally declared right. Karl Grune's *At the Edge of the World* (1927, with Brigitte Helm, Camilla von Hollay, Albert Steinrück, and Wilhelm Dieterle; camera: Fritz Arno Wagner; music: Giuseppe Becce) had been completed before Hugenberg's takeover and, with a few insignificant reservations, approved by management. Nine months later, the new Ufa managers made such drastic cuts and revisions that Grune sued to have his name removed from the film credits and the company's ads. *At the Edge of the World*—an idealistic, pacifist film full of love for humankind, and with many concessions to the sentimental tastes of the moviegoing public—told the story of a miller and his family caught up in the chaos of war: espionage, betrayal, and horror cannot prevent two human beings from loving each other—or a new generation arriving that will not kill but will build new mills and bake bread for hungering humanity. This political perspective did not sit well with Hugenberg's watchdogs, and Grune complained about their censorship in an open letter to *Die Weltbühne*:

> Major cuts and changes in subtitles, reorganization of material, and the omission of certain ideas were suggested to me, first in dictatorial tones, then later in somewhat milder form; I was obliged to reject these changes. Now, without my consent, Ufa has made changes it deemed good and has released the film in an abridged version that distorts its intent. Ufa rejected my repeated demands to see the film first.

The most drastic distortion of meaning came at the end of the film, with its call for peace set against a vision of Golgotha in the background. "All these alterations of philosophical and artistic intent still did not satisfy Ufa, and their final suggestion was to add the subtitle 'A Film for Tomorrow.' In view of all this, I am forced to decline responsibility for this film." The furor showed, *Die Weltbühne* thought, "the real face" of the new Ufa, "and we hope it will prompt the public, which in Berlin is made up predominantly of democrats, socialists, and pacifists, to keep a sharp eye on what goes on in the temples of the newly minted art entrepreneur Hugenberg."[31]

(Karl Grune went on to direct historical dramas, such as the two-part

Prussian film *Königin Luise* [*Queen Luise*]for Terra-Film. For *Waterloo*, he used Abel Gance's techniques in *Napoleon*. In 1929, he founded his own production company and made *Katherina Knie*, based on Zuckmayer's play. In 1933 he emigrated to England.)

The transformation of Ufa into an archconservative company under strictly nationalistic leadership was not yet felt in the production program, but it was certainly noted in Ufa's political profile and the image it sought to project, and the liberal and democratic press did indeed follow the transformation closely, commenting on it usually with biting irony. The most outspoken opposition came from the magazine *Film und Volk*, the organ of the Volksfilmverband (People's Film Association), founded in early 1928. Well-known intellectuals with democratic sympathies, such as Heinrich Mann, Erwin Piscator, and Béla Balázs, had helped organize this group; and many others—among them Leonhard Frank, Heinrich George, John Heartfield, Herbert Jhering, Alfred Kerr, Käthe Kollwitz, Leopold Jessner, Asta Nielsen, and Kurt Pinthus—supported it in strengthening the "potential alliance" between the revolutionary workers' movement and the democratic middle class. In the first issue of *Film und Volk* Rudolf Schwarzkopf, executive director of the association, launched an offensive against Ufa and the entire capitalist film industry with the slogan: "The enemy stands to the right, and so does the enemy of film. We will defeat them if we stand united!"[32] Is cinema the theater of the people in our time? *Film und Volk* asked. The proliferation of trusts in the movie industry, the market dominance of large firms like Ufa, Terra, Phoebus, and Emelka, and their affiliation with the mass press worked against that. And, the magazine pointed out, the entertainment tax the industry was fighting was passed on to the public by the theater owners anyhow. (The disunity of the German left and the deadly ideological enmity of the Socialists and Communists could not but divide this "alliance" against itself, but despite that, *Film und Volk* remains an important source for film history.)

Willi Münzenberg, organizer of Internationale Arbeiterhilfe (International Workers' Aid) and founder of Prometheus-Film, led the ideological battle against Ufa. The revolutionary workers' movement, he said, was wasting its energies fighting the bourgeois press. "Hugenberg's film activity is a hundred times more dangerous than his newspapers. Very few workers read the Hugenberg papers, but millions of workers see the nationalistic and counterrevolutionary films from Hugenberg's poison laboratory."[33] And he said, the "Lohmann scandal" demonstrated how closely government ministries and agencies worked together with this "nationalistic film factory."

Münzenberg was mistaken about one detail—it was not Ufa but Phoebus that had received through the agency of a Captain Walter Lohmann in the Navy Department 10 million marks from a secret fund for rearmament and military propaganda—but news of this scandal, which broke in 1927, initiated a debate in the Reichstag that ultimately led to the resignation of Defense Minister Otto Gessler. Where the money actually came to rest could never be clarified, but despite this generous subsidy Phoebus was on the brink of ruin and had to sell its theaters to Emelka. The government supported this financial restructuring by secretly guaranteeing a loan of more than 3 million marks.

Understandably, neither Ufa's films nor those of other big companies found much favor in the eyes of *Film und Volk*'s critics. In its regular short reviews, the magazine offered nearly complete coverage of current films— these remain today an invaluable overview of movies in the years 1928– 30—and the anti-Ufa tone is clear. In the months of March, April, and May 1928, the Ufa film *Der geheimnisvolle Spiegel* (*The Mysterious Mirror*, direction and camerawork by Curt Hoffmann) stood out as "about the limit of what an audience could be expected to tolerate in the way of stale gothic romance and unlikely psychology." In Carl Froelich's *Lotte*, "our beloved Henny Porten with the eyes of a faithful dog" masquerades as a girl of the proletariat so that she may appear all the more magnificent when she winds up as a count's bride; and in Ring Film's *Mann gegen Mann* (*Man against Man*), distributed by Ufa, Harry Piel is not funny—as Americans were in their best detective films—but a serious model of German thoroughness. Of *Die Sache mit Schorrsiegel* (*The Schorrsiegel Affair*, directed by Jaap Speyer and produced by Terra), *Film und Volk*'s reviewer noted that Ufa seemed to feel obliged to make a film of every bad novel available (in this case, one by Fred Andreas).[34]

Weimar's left wing did not spare Fritz Lang either. His film *Spies* was "an overblown nothing . . . deadly boring despite the most gaudy and expensive of special effects." *Woman in the Moon*, which cost 2 million marks to make, offered "additional evidence of intellectual bankruptcy." Max Brenner said of it: "It was hardly necessary to travel to the outer reaches of the cosmos to assemble this overdose of murder and violence, of theft and deception." Brenner correctly perceived that Lang's direction had made it impossible for his leading lady, Gerda Maurus, to realize her talents, while in Johannes Meyer's Ufa film *Hochverrat* (*High Treason*), "a dime-a-dozen story from the conspiratorial atmosphere of prewar, imperial Russia," she seemed "suddenly liberated and at ease."[35]

Tsarist Russia became a favorite subject for Ufa toward the end of the 1920s. This was to some extent no doubt a reaction to the films by Eisenstein, Pudovkin, and other directors of the Soviet avant-garde, the importation of which the left had fought hard to achieve. *Film und Volk* railed against the "tasteless, mindless, and even counterrevolutionary Russian émigré films that have recently flooded Berlin's film theaters." A classic example was the Ufa film *Der weisse Teufel* (*The White Devil*, 1929–30), based on Tolstoy's novella *Hadji Murad* and directed by Alexander Wolkoff. A number of Russian emigrants were involved in it, among them the assistant director Anatole Litvak, who later became a success in the United States.

Unlike the bourgeois film critics, *Film und Volk*'s reviewers also followed Ufa newsreels. In November 1929, the magazine presented its readers with some interesting figures. Ufa's production budget for the year had been 9.5 million, a slight increase over the 9.1 million of the previous year, and while the number of feature films fell from 33 to 21, the number of newsreels rose significantly from 100 to 160.

> If the politicization of Ufa is obvious anywhere, then it is in the newsreels. That the production of newsreels involves much less risk and expense only adds to the attractiveness of this politically important branch of the business. A further advantage is that newsreels receive hardly any attention from the literarily inept film critics of all political persuasions.[36]

The newsreel as a propaganda weapon in the day-by-day political struggle —here, too, then, Hugenberg's Ufa developed techniques that Joseph Goebbels would energetically cultivate and systematize a few years later.

Where the Weimar left saw a cunningly concealed counterrevolutionary strategy lurking in every pulp novel and Ufa potboiler, Hugenberg's nationalistic lieutenants kept a weather eye out for Bolshevist snares. Even before Pabst was reprimanded for cost overruns on *The Love of Jeanne Ney*, the material of the film itself, taken from a novel by the Soviet Russian Ilya Ehrenburg, had already provoked their extreme displeasure. This love story of a Frenchwoman and a Russian revolutionary begins in the Crimea during the October Revolution and comes to a "tragic" end, well larded with pathos and sentimentality, in Paris. Pabst's film (camera: Fritz Arno Wagner; sets: Otto Hunte; lead roles: Edith Jehanne, Uno Henning, Brigitte Helm, and Fritz Rasp) surprised viewers with its frenetic revolutionary scenes (influenced by Soviet film) and disappointed them with the conventionality of the Paris sequences. But at its best it was a successful "report on the diseases of European society" in 1918, with subtle camera movements and sharp montage.[37]

After the signing of the German-Soviet neutrality agreement of 1926, even the nationalistic right was not disinclined to do business with the Soviet Union, as long as it was profitable. And even Ufa was impressed by Eisenstein and Pudovkin and eager to imitate their advanced camera and montage techniques. Still, Ufa's initial reaction to Ehrenburg's novel and its positive rendering of the Bolshevik Revolution was panic; it exercised strict control over the script (by Ladislaus Vajda and Rudolf Leonhard) and prescribed a happy ending to the otherwise rather morbid depiction of Western European society. This deviation from the novel drew a massive public protest from Ehrenburg, who complained that Ufa's changes had "crushed" the soul of his work.[38]

In his memoirs *Menschen—Jahre—Leben (People, Years, Life)* Ilya Ehrenburg describes the unsettled atmosphere in Ufa's studios right after Hugenberg's takeover and the mood of the Russian emigrants who took part in the production.

> Even though they knew that the script, which had been hastily hammered together, was shot through with inconsistencies, the Germans, with that pedantry native to them, struggled manfully for authenticity of detail. They asked the Soviet ambassador for advice and engaged General Schkuro, who was touring Germany . . . at the time, as a consultant. [At the studio] I saw the arcaded streets of Feodossya, a filthy Russian hotel, a Montmartre bistro, the study of a stylish French lawyer, the armchair of a grand duke, several vodka bottles, a statue of the Virgin Mary, cots in a flophouse, and many other props. Moscow was fifty paces away from Paris, and a Crimean hill rose up between them. A French railroad car separated the White Guard's bar from the Soviet tribunal.

For a drinking scene, Pabst engaged former officers who had served under the White Russian General Denikin.

> They had saved their uniforms, whether in hopes of a restoration or a film engagement, it's hard to say. Epaulettes sparkled on their shoulders; fur hats sat rakishly on their heads; the skull emblem of the Death Battalions stood out on their sleeves. I recalled the Crimea in 1920 and felt distinctly uneasy.[39]

In the case of Joe May's film *Homecoming* (1928)—which also added a happy ending to the story of two German soldiers during and after the war and falsified the novella on which it was based, Leonhard Frank's *Karl und Anna*—Ufa's managers had to issue a public clarification: A plot summary that had appeared in *Ufa-Dienst* might leave the impression that the film had "Bolshevist tendencies. We have determined that such a view is not objectively correct"—such was management's dictum of March 30, 1928.[40]

Homecoming was the first film made by Erich Pommer–Produktion under Hugenberg's Ufa. Germany's most successful producer had been back from Hollywood and in Neubabelsberg since November 1927. Klitzsch had gone to the United States that summer to convince Paramount and MGM to change the Parufamet contract and at the same time to negotiate Pommer and Lubitsch's return to Germany. Not long after, Lubitsch signed a contract with Paramount and remained in the United States, but Klitsch was more successful with Pommer. A contract concluded in November guaranteed Pommer a certain measure of independence by having the American Producer Service Corporation represent him and collect royalties from Ufa for the films he produced. The contract stipulated that for three or four films per year Pommer would receive a salary of 300,000 marks and royalties on the foreign-distribution income.[41]

Although Klitzsch did not understand complex artistic questions or the genuine aesthetic qualities of film, he did have a talent for finding and keeping Ufa people who had that understanding and who—he was clear on this point—were indispensable for the firm's business success. His commercial ambitions and organizational ability went hand in hand with a pragmatic instinct for competence in fields beyond his own competence, even in cases like Pommer's, where there was little personal affinity.

For example, it was his instinct for quality that led to Ernst Hugo Correll, formerly sole executive of the now politically and economically destroyed Phoebus, being named production chief at Ufa in January 1928. Correll had been a state's attorney in Lorraine before the war and had wound up in the film business more or less by chance. He brought to Ufa management several qualities in short supply there: artistic interests, wide reading, an engaging manner, and a readiness to compromise—all good, upper-middle-class virtues—but he also identified totally with the nationalistic principles of Ufa's senior executives and cooperated with the National Socialists after 1933.

Another example of Klitzsch's perspicacity about personnel was his commissioning of Günther Stapenhorst, a former exporter who had moved into the film industry in 1924, to form a production group similar to Erich Pommer's. Before emigrating in 1935, Stapenhorst produced a number of successful comedies for Ufa, also some notorious propaganda films like Gustav Ucicky's *Morgenrot* (*Dawn*, 1932–33). After World War II Pommer reported to the American occupation authorities that Stapenhorst was "creative, tactful, energetic" and "always very open about his anti-Nazi position."[42]

"The character of a production director is . . . very complicated. Two souls have to live in his breast, but they have to form a peaceful and harmonious family. Instinct and hard-nosed calculation must be united in him." That is how the directors Joe May and Hanns Schwarz characterized the function of a new creative type just invented by Ufa: the "production director."[43] In a memo to Klitzsch the technical business manager, Hermann Grieving, wrote on July 11, 1927:

> Up to now Ufa has functioned under a system that left the execution of films in the hands of the director, and a so-called manager was assigned to the director to supervise business matters. These managers—generally retired army officers—receive a salary of 500–750 marks. Actual production managers were not employed—if we disregard the top production management. This system has had serious disadvantages. Because handling a large number of films is beyond the capacities of a single production manager . . . I propose that we abandon the old system and hire production managers who not only are experts in film production but also, and above all, have enough influence on the directors that the latter are not completely free to do as they like without consulting anybody.

May and Schwarz were the directors of the last silent films Pommer produced for Ufa, and May directed two important urban films: *Homecoming*

(1928) and *Asphalt*. Schwarz soon became a master of the film operetta (*Ungarische Rhapsodie [Hungarian Rhapsody]*, 1928) and tsarist émigré subjects (*Die wunderbare Lüge der Nina Petrowna [Nina Petrovna's Wonderful Lie]*, 1928–29); Willy Schmidt-Gentner wrote the music for both these films. Willy Fritsch and Dita Parlo played eternal lovers in *Hungarian Rhapsody* (backed up at the premiere in the Ufa-Palast by sixty house musicians and a Gypsy ensemble), while in *Nina Petrovna's Wonderful Lie* Brigitte Helm and Franz (later Francis) Lederer played a variation on the theme of *Manon Lescaut*. (Ufa had originally planned to have Arthur Robison, the director of *Manon Lescaut*, direct this film, too.) For these films Ufa again supplied Carl Hoffmann, one of its best cameramen, and Robert Herlth and Walter Röhrig, its star architects. Sound effects and music were synchronized for both films, which is to say that Ufa considered them worthy vehicles for launching the company into the new world of sound film.

Schmidt-Gentner composed the music for the Joe May films, too. Günther Rittau, who had worked so successfully with Fritz Lang, was the cameraman. In *Asphalt*, a policeman played by Gustav Fröhlich succumbs to the evil yet charming wiles of a classy demimondaine played by Betty Amann. This Pommer–May film displayed once again, before the transition to sound, all the virtues and vices of Ufa's experimental workshop and of its infatuation with its own monumentality. The critic Hans Feld recorded details of the shooting:

> The studio doors open, and then behind them, to the right and left, the big sliding doors open. The street leads onto the outside grounds, and in the distance is the façade of an office skyscraper with an exact replica of the Ufa office building's entryway. Posters advertise *Asphalt*. A film within a film, an amusing visual gag.[44]

The play of technical possibilities, of *trompe l'oeil* and film-within-a-film techniques, is an intoxicating game for the viewer, who can yield to the momentum of the images and the enchantment induced by the play of illusion. Transparencies, labyrinths, the ground slipping out from under one's feet—film and the complicated machinery that made it possible was an expression of the times.

Homecoming premiered in the Gloria-Palast in late August 1928. At that moment, Harry Kessler was traveling via Luxembourg and Longwy to Verdun and from there on to Reims:

> The little white crosses crowded together in the military cemeteries, thousands upon thousands of them, seem tiny and almost shabby in the vast landscape. The souls of the dead live on in this landscape, not in the crosses, and they are calling not just for eternal peace but also for vengeance on those guilty of this crime.[45]

And also at that moment, Privy Councillor Alfred Hugenberg, master of Ufa and of Scherl,* articulated the new party line of the German National People's Party:

> We shall form a united front if we can only let the iron clasp of our philosophy pull us together and in its embrace melt down everything that is soft and fluid in us and recast it as stone. Anyone who would stand in our way will have to step aside or be melted down, too.[46]

---

* Dissatisfaction with Hugenberg and his politics was expressed repeatedly within Ufa. On February 22, 1928, management had decided, "in view of several incidents . . . to stop hiring and to discontinue employment of persons—especially in the area of artistic production—who have made malicious public attacks on Privy Councillor Hugenberg or who are likely to do so [!] or have taken part in or will take part in such attacks."

15.

German Musicality and
the Arrival of Sound Film

1927–28: In the intellectual marketplace and in many a reader's mind Oswald Spengler's *Preussentum und Sozialismus* (*The Prussian Character and
Socialism*) had been stirring up confusion for eight years and his *Untergang
des Abendlandes* (*Decline of the West*) for six. They were clear attacks on
the Weimar Republic and the Western democracies, propaganda tracts for
an "authoritative socialism" of Prusso-monarchistic provenance. Soon after
1918 Hugo Stinnes and his friends had been dreaming of an "authoritative
socialism" under the command of heavy industry as a salvation from the
chaos of democratic parliamentarianism. And in *Metropolis* Fritz Lang had
created images, as naïve as they were bold, to accompany those desires.

1927–28: Adolf Hitler, whose access to the aristocrats of wealth had up
to now been limited to successes as a speaker in the salons of the piano
manufacturer Bechstein, the Munich publisher Hugo Bruckmann, and the
Wagner House in Bayreuth, now started promoting his cause with Ruhr
industrialists. Otto Dietrich, a young editor of the nationalistic *München–
Augsburger Abendzeitung*, put him in touch with the Pan-German movement and so with Emil Kirdorf, the "Wotan of German heavy industry,"[1]
founder of the German coal cartel and for many years CEO of the Gelsen-
kirchener Mining Company. Economic power and political adventurism
were sending out their first, tentative feelers toward each other. In that
same year Ludendorff published two polemics in which he tried to revive the "stab-in-the-back" theory to explain Germany's defeat in World
War I. The German National People's Party lost the elections of May 1928
and Hugenberg became party leader. During the campaign, he had been
the first to use a phonograph as a means of political agitation.

While Hugenberg was summoning the German Nationals to battle
against the "system of committees, commissions, the waste of all our energies in argument and counterargument,"[2] other advance troops of the

"conservative revolution"—from the Free Corps to the Black Army of the Reich, from the League of the Stahlhelm to the "national Bolshevists" gathered around Hans Zehrer's magazine *Die Tat*—had long been prepared to march on into a Führer's state, a "national community led from above." Their propaganda berated Weimar democracy for being a monster born of the "golden international" of Wall Street and the "Red international" of Soviet collectivism. It scorned the "Jewish financial aristocracy" as well as "Jewified" urban culture and the "Jewish Bolshevist"–led workers' movement, and it was especially successful in mobilizing the petit bourgeoisie against an incomprehensible, dangerous, "modern" world in which anonymous forces of money and industry seemed to conspire against human beings.

"Alienated" industrial work and its nearly impenetrable complexity encouraged these regressive modes and a yearning for escape. The abyss between work and nonwork, between material necessity and emotional needs, seemed more and more unbridgeable. "To ward off psychic catastrophe, modern man has to separate the hours given to the inner life from those spent satisfying his daily wants. Just one moment of real clarity and insight, and he either must commit suicide or seek refuge in a double life," Ehrenburg wrote in *Die Traumfabrik* (*The Dream Factory*).[3] The substitute world of illusion which the modern worker could find in the manufactured products of the culture industry offered a means of survival, and the counter-reality of the movies functioned like a drug that restored emotional balance and self-confidence. The melodramatic construct of the "society film," for example, seemed a worthy substitute for life not lived and for absent self-esteem. The avant-garde film theoretician Hans Richter thought that the collective soul of déclassé consumers yearned to absorb "moral quality" from the contemplation of wealth and a superior lifestyle, a moral quality attributed to the better classes and equated with the absence of everyday cares and worries.[4] (Horkheimer and Adorno later called this the "evil love" of the governed for those who govern.)

These films did not ever even try to portray the reality of upper-class life. Melodramatic cinema was a more powerful, or in any case a more suggestive, elixir than any realistic presentation could have been. In film, melodrama *is* "reality." The movies of Ufa and other big companies in the late 1920s show the German middle-class film coming into its own.

The lack of "a sense for facts tested over time and of an established artistic tradition of realism"[5] had created among artists and writers of the New Objectivity an urge for authenticity, indeed, a fetish for empirical and documentary facts. But in the German film industry (in contrast to the British and American ones) the result was the opposite: a widespread atrophy of the realistic impulse in favor of a murky "world of muddled mind and emotion dripping with fog and enchantment."[6] There was no German film in the late 1920s that measured up to the standards of radical realism, not even, despite many claims to the contrary, Walter Ruttmann's slice-of-life film *Berlin—Die Sinfonie der Grossstadt* (*Berlin—The Symphony of the City*, Deutsche Vereins-Film, 1927). Its kaleidoscopic structure reflected not realism but rather the New Objectivity's vapid model of democracy, of a "smoothly functioning, pluralistic distribution system."[7] But a truly unique event in the cinema of the late Weimar Republic was Erno Metzner's *Polizeibericht Überfall* (*Police Report: Hold-Up*, Deutscher Werkfilm, 1928), which was banned by the censors. This short film recorded an everyday street crime with a realism neither achieved nor even attempted by any other film. Avoiding illusion here did not lead to a loss of sensory impact (as it did in so many novels of the New Objectivity) but, on the contrary, exploited the expressiveness of facts.

In *Metropolis* (1926–27) and *Spies* (1927) the New Objectivity left its mark on Fritz Lang's work, foreshadowing a terrifying future. The rationality of the technical age and its machine rhythms celebrated in the grandiose introductory sequence of *Metropolis* is ambiguous and amounts ultimately, as in Ruttmann's Berlin film, to "soulless" abstraction, dismantling time and space, separate from, and apparently independent of, human energy. A. Kraszna-Krausz summed up this point well at the time:

> As in an ultramodern factory, the conveyor belt of the plot rolls on at a rapid pace, and all along the belt stand individual sequences like mechanized workers who quickly perform their one-minute operation—quickly, without worrying about the entire process, without wanting or being able to think about the purpose or practicality of the whole.[8]

As an informing principle for film montage, the New Objectivity picked up the rhythm of industrial production and wove it into the structure of film narration.

Ufa's cultural hegemony and the effect its vapid melodramas and ambiguous visions had on Germany's everyday culture and consciousness in the final years of the Weimar Republic resulted as well from a basic failure on the part of the left, of progressives, and of all those who thought themselves in league with the forces of enlightenment. In the name of enlightenment they ignored the human need for "food for dreams," yielding that territory to the film companies "without a struggle," as Ernst Bloch pointed out. Both advocates of enlightened progress and the cultural branch of the workers' movement believed that the struggle for the dark side of consciousness, for its unspoken desires and repressed lusts, its eagerness for intoxication, and its yearning for sensual joy was not worth the trouble. Indeed, these factors were often, openly or silently, dismissed as bourgeois relics left over in the proletarian soul and doomed to extinction.

And so a vacuum developed, for neither the "authentic" films appealing to morality and reason, like *Westfront 1918* or *Kameradschaft* (*Western*

Front 1918 and *Comradeship*, 1930–31, both directed by Pabst for Nero-Film), nor the leftist productions supported by Willi Münzenberg's International Workers' Aid, like Phil Jutzi's *Mother Krause's Happy Journey* or Bertolt Brecht's *Kuhle Wampe* (Prometheus und Praesens-Filmverleih, 1932), captured the imagination of the people. The films that did were Ufa's melodramas, comedies, Prussian films, waltz dreams, and barracks comedies. One cannot ascribe this success solely to the concentrated economic power of Hugenberg's company. In the left's indifference to the psychic and emotional life of the working class, "tightly interwoven with that of the bourgeoisie," critics have seen a grave sin on the part of the Marxist parties and a premise for the victory of Fascism in Germany.[9] Ufa was by no means at one with reactionary forces—not, at any rate, before Hugenberg's takeover. But it did help the reactionary forces in Weimar to gain and keep a monopoly over the imagination of the masses, and it was able to do this all the more easily because no one else seriously contested its claim.

From the beginning, Ufa meant to dominate not only the entertainment market but also the less well developed field of instructional films devoted to culture and science. Ufa's cultural division, founded in 1918 under the direction of Ernst Krieger, was in tune with the consolidating processes under way in industry, and with the changing dynamic of international natural sciences, evident since the 1870s. The instructional film, Ufa declared in a manifesto of 1919, was "a political pioneer." Movies could, with greater ease and in more diverse fields than the printed word, "win recognition for German accomplishments in science and commerce among peoples beyond our borders and beyond the oceans."[10]

Ufa's cultural division, at a sample showing of its wares in Hamburg in December 1919, emphasized the high quality of its instructional films in all fields of science and scholarship, of adult education and public welfare, of arts, crafts, and technology,"[11] and from the outset it sought to cooperate with cities, universities, schools, technical schools, and institutions for continuing education. In a series of publications it informed the interested public about its offerings and about details of their distribution and presentation. By 1919 and with the help of numerous expert advisers, Ufa had made more than a hundred instructional films on subjects in medicine, science, technology, ethnology, and agriculture.

Just one year after Germany's military defeat, and in view of the prohibition against German rearmament, the instructional film as "political pioneer" had, in the minds of Ufa's management, a very specific ideological mission to fulfill. Many of these films were devoted to the "physical development" of German youth and also, as was clearly stated, to "military service." The most important was *Ways to Strength and Beauty*, directed by Wilhelm Prager (1925), dedicated to the "invaluable strengthening of youth," a "film about modern physical fitness" blessed by the censors with the designation "educational." This film made not the slightest attempt to conceal its advocacy for restoring Germany's military capability. *Die Welt-bühne* said of its musical collages, arranged by Giuseppe Becce:

> The old military melodies sound as wonderful now as on the day they were first played as we watch how, in the glorious past, the Prussian sergeant made men of strength and beauty out of common peasants. And in the presence of this union of music and film image in which one form of pure beauty is accompanied by another, even the most shortsighted of us cannot doubt that if we travel these ways to strength and beauty the destination we will inevitably arrive at is our Hindenburg and the reestablishment of conscription and compulsory military service.[12]

Ufa also understood the work of its newsreel division in a comparably pioneering way. "Our newsreels are valuable allies in the battle against Versailles"[13] was the unequivocal statement of a special Ufa publication issued in 1939 to celebrate the twenty-fifth year of newsreel production. Directly descended from the Messter and Deulig newsreels, Ufa's first newsreel, shown on September 17, 1925, opened with a clip of Paul von Hindenburg, who had been elected Germany's President in April. Ufa newsreels were soon being shown in Finland, Holland, Austria, Switzerland, Czechoslovakia, and Hungary, and, later, in Bulgaria, Greece, the Balkan states, Norway, Portugal, Spain, and even in Brazil, Southwest Africa, and the United States. Until March 1933, Ufa continued to distribute silent-film newsreels, but on September 10, 1930, it released the first Ufa newsreel with sound, just one day before the first sound newsreel issued by Fox-Film. (Emelka followed a little later.) Ufa had recruited Emil Jannings for the debut. In an upbeat "talking-picture speech," Jannings told the public:

> Nothing will ever happen again anywhere in the world without your being an eye and ear witness to it. If a volcano erupts, our cameraman will be there. If a tiger roars, our cameraman will be on the watch for him. Our sound camera won't miss a thing. It will bring you the crowning of the beauty queen and the heavyweight champion of the world's greetings to his country.[14]

The introduction of sound encountered formidable obstacles and resistance in the German film industry. Ufa had watched with great mistrust as the Americans pressed ahead with the technology—as late as April 1927, management decided "for the present not to devote further attention to talking film"[15]—but finally, wanting to maintain its primacy in a rapidly changing market, it took the plunge. Hypnotized to the point of paralysis, Ufa's managers were confronting a technical process that involved considerable financial risk and left some of them feeling at the mercy of technological progress and its inherent dynamic. As Hans Richter saw the situation, technical progress and profitability were at odds: "In its present situation the industry is suffering from overproduction and does not want discoveries, inventions, and progress so much as to prevent any movement that might make things still more difficult."[16]

Even before 1919, three German inventors—Hans Vogt, Jo Engl, and the ingenious tinkerer and autodidact Joseph Massolle—had developed the equipment essential for light-sound recording. The process, which required highly sensitive photoelectric cells as well as improved microphones and amplifiers, involves the transformation of sound waves into light oscillations that can be translated in turn into electrical impulses and thus made audible again as sound waves. The first public showing of a sound film employing this "Tri-Ergon" process took place on September 17, 1922, in the Alhambra theater on Kurfürstendamm. The audience was enthusiastic, but the press and the film industry were not. Forced to sell their patent to Swiss financial supporters, the three inventors, now working as technical advisers to Tri-Ergon St. Gallen, continued perfecting their process. With improved pickup and reproduction equipment, Massolle eventually got Ufa interested. In January 1925 he signed a contract with Ufa and became, though only for a few months, technical director of Ufa's first sound-film division. But Ufa's first sound film, *The Match Girl*, which premiered in December 1925, was a total disaster in terms of sound quality, and given the developing economic crisis, Ufa's management decided to abandon further experimentation for the time being. After Hugenberg's takeover, Klitzsch's tight-fisted regimen steered away from the "talking film" with its incalculable technical, financial, and legal problems.

In the meantime, the development of sound had advanced rapidly in America; the advent of sound moved the competitive film industry into the new territory of patent law and drew another player, the electrical industry, into the fray. In 1925 Western Electric introduced a needle-pickup process that Warner Brothers snatched up in the hope that talking movies would rescue them from bankruptcy. Their film *The Jazz Singer*, with its vocal numbers and spoken dialogue, was a worldwide success and brought about a major breakthrough in Europe, too. The counteroffensive in the United States came from the William Fox company, which had bought from Tri-Ergon the American rights for the German light-sound process and had further refined it in their Movietone system. The first Movietone film, *What Price Glory*, premiered in January 1927. To acquire the necessary amplifiers, Fox had to work out a deal with Western Electric, which, for its part, was worrying about competition from General Electric, America's largest electronics trust. The Radio Corporation of America, a subsidiary of General Electric controlled by the Rockefellers after 1930, had developed Photophone, a system similar to the German light-sound system, and the two American giants soon shifted their competitive battle onto the European market and tried to extend their markets by selling rights to their sound systems.

In Europe, fifteen different systems involving three thousand patents were competing with each other. In 1925, Deutsche Tonfilm, affiliated with I. G. Farben, acquired a Danish license for the German-speaking countries and signed a monopoly contract with Phoebus-Film for the production of sound films. A little later, a company was founded in Holland, Küchenmeister, that began producing light-sound films with a system it had developed independently. "Given this muddled state of affairs in which any practical work was impossible and the danger existed that German sound film would never get off the ground,"[17] General Consul Brückmann, representing Deutsche Tonfilm, invited the most important European patent holders and spokesmen for the electronics industry to a meeting in Berlin's Kaiserhof Hotel in 1928 to consolidate efforts and bring together under one roof all the patents with promise for the future. The result was the formation of the Tonbild Syndikat (Tobis), a merger of Tri-Ergon-Musik, Küchenmeister, Deutsche Tonfilm, and Messter-Ton. The capital stock was 12 million marks. "German inventiveness" was the great technical asset of Tobis, Traub asserted, but the company's financing was predominantly in non-German hands.[18] (Küchenmeister and other Dutch parties soon controlled 75 percent of the capital in Tobis.)

Ufa still maintained a wait-and-see position. It had no more part in the founding of Tobis than did AEG or Siemens and Halske; in a countermove to the Tobis initiative, they founded Klangfilm two months later, in October 1928, with capital stock of 3 million marks. Faced with the threat of a Central European patent war that would cripple everyone in the long run, Tobis and Klangfilm concluded a "friendship contract" in March 1929. By its terms,

> Tobis would be responsible for the manufacture of sound film and the marketing of sound-recording equipment; Klangfilm for the manufacture of sound-recording and sound-reproduction equipment. The filming and recording process was called System Tobis-Klangfilm, the projection and reproduction process System Klangfilm-Tobis. The purpose of the contract was monopolistic control of the sound-film market, from which all outsiders were soon excluded.[19]

This new sound-film cartel in Europe was determined to assume control of the Continental market and to fight with the Americans for it. But they were on the defensive, because the American companies already held the lead both with more sound films and technically more sophisticated projectors, and they continued their tried-and-true investment policy in Europe: Warner Brothers, for example, acquired a majority of the capital in National-Film and at the same time supplied the theaters with projectors suitable for their films on condition that Warner films be shown only with these projectors.

The Warner sound film *The Singing Fool* premiered in Germany in the

Gloria-Palast on June 3, 1929, and took the Berlin public by storm. However, it also unleashed a new patent war that threatened to cripple the entire sound-film market. Neither the film companies, which had already invested a lot of money in the new technology, nor the electronics industry, which wanted to see their patents generating income internationally, wanted to be stalled over legal quibbles. In June 1930, all the warring parties buried the hatchet with the "Paris sound-film peace treaty," which assured regulated competition for the next fifteen years. The agreement contained two crucial decisions. "Interchangeability" was guaranteed, so that any sound film from a participant could be recorded and shown with any patented equipment; it was also agreed, as is customary in peace accords, to divide the world up anew into exclusive market areas. Germany, Austria, Switzerland, Holland (and its East Indian colonies), the Balkan states, and Scandinavia fell to the Tobis-Klangfilm group. The American companies took over, in addition to the United States and Canada, India, Australia, and the Soviet Union. The rest of the world was declared an open market. "The danger of an American patent monopoly in Europe was thus precluded."[20]

By 1928 Klitzsch had appointed a committee to study sound film, and on its recommendation sound-film projectors from different systems were installed in Ufa theaters. Well before the Tobis-Klangfilm agreement, Ufa had Klangfilm projectors, which made it independent of the Tobis monopoly. In August, the Gloria-Palast showed some experimental sound films made by Küchenmeister in Ufa's Tempelhof studios. Then Klitzsch went to see for himself what the powerful American competition was doing. The Germans, in New York,

> found that sound film dominated the scene almost completely, and they had to conclude that the future belonged to this innovation. . . . This raised great concern about how Germany would meet this challenge. Then a little incident occurred that made the difficult decisions to come seem less daunting. The German visitors came upon the program the band was playing in the lobby of their hotel; of thirteen pieces listed, nine were German or Austrian, and suddenly a picture of the future emerged in which German music in consort with sound film would conquer the world. After a stop in London to study the film situation there, Ufa's management decided back in Berlin to make the change to sound film. With this decision, Ufa became the first German firm in the sound-film market and gained an invaluable lead.[21]

It was obviously in the interest of German industry to deal only with Klangfilm, founded by AEG and Siemens. Hopes for exclusive rights to sound-film production with the Klangfilm system may have been dashed by the Tobis-Klangfilm agreement, but Ufa still managed to secure preferred status for procuring equipment and was the only German firm with its own sound-recording equipment. Everyone else had to rent equipment either from Ufa or from Tobis. But Ufa could not realize its project for a "European community of interests" under German hegemony, an ambitious plan "to protect Germany from the new American threat."[22]

Production Chief Correll was charged with bringing his company into the era of sound-film production, and under his direction suitable studios were constructed in Neubabelsberg beginning in February 1929; in seven months "this extraordinary achievement was complete."[23] On September 29, the company presented the "sound cross" in Neubabelsberg to the press: a complex of four bunkerlike studios,

> laid out in the form of a cross and surrounding an interior courtyard to which the rooms for the sound cameras are attached. . . . Light-sound and needle-sound equipment are available, and both kinds of systems can be used simultaneously. The needle pickup or record system is used primarily for checking quality, because it lets the director have an immediate replay of the "sound track" and thus permits immediate corrections of flaws in the recording.[24]

The following year, the big "silent-film building" with its three studios and glass studio was renovated for sound-film production and turned into massive, soundproof structures. In 1931, the two glass studios in Tempelhof were converted to sound.

Architecturally, Ufa was transformed into a fort. When the glass studio went, so did the transparency. Daylight and extraneous sound were banned from the film factory. Europe's largest film company walled itself in; when filming was in progress, silence was the highest commandment. New building complexes soon arose around the "sound cross"—special workshops and editing rooms for sound-film editing, new viewing rooms, a special-effects studio equipped for reverse projections, a copying plant for sound films. A month before the crash on Wall Street and the onset of the Great Depression, the old film city had been transformed into a modern media center.

Gläserne Wundertiere (*Mythological Glass Animals*), Ufa's first sound film to be shown to the public, was produced by the cultural division and premiered on August 2, 1929, in Berlin's Universum-Theater. On December 16 the Ufa-Palast am Zoo hosted the premiere of Ufa's first full-length feature made with Klangfilm's light-sound process: *Melodie des Herzens* (*Melody of the Heart*), a tragic love story of a peasant girl and an army corporal in Hungary; Hanns Schwarz directed Dita Parlo and Willy Fritsch in the leads. Werner Richard Heymann, assisted by Paul Abraham and Viktor Gertler, drew on Hungarian folk songs in writing the score; Erich Kettelhut did the sets; Günther Rittau and Hans Schneeberg managed the cameras. Ufa made a silent version as well as a sound one, and for foreign-language versions the actors had to deliver their dialogue and song lyrics in English, French, and Hungarian. Erich Pommer's production team, which made *Melody of the Heart*, became the core group in Ufa's sound-film production. The four other production teams—under Fritz Lang, Gregor Rabinovitsch, Gunther Stapenhorst, and Alfred Zeisler—continued to concentrate on silent films until the early 1930s.

Melody of the Heart signaled the beginning of the sound-film era in Germany, but other productions in 1929 had prepared the way for it. Of the 224 German films made that year 14 were partially or wholly sound films.[25] In January, *Ramona* and *Das letzte Lied* (*The Last Song*), the first two sound-film shorts using the Tobis system, were shown in the Tauentzien-Palast. The film that followed, *Ich küsse Ihre Hand, Madame* (*I Kiss Your Hand, Madame*, directed by Robert Land for Super-Film and Deutsches Lichtspiel-Syndikat), was a silent film with one sound scene in which Harry Liedtke "sang" the hit song of the title to Marlene Dietrich, with the voice of Richard Tauber dubbed in. In March came the premiere of the first full-length German sound film, Walter Ruttmann's documentary *Melodie der Welt* (*Melody of the World*), produced by Tobis in cooperation with the Hamburg-America shipping line, with music by Wolfgang Zeller. In October and November came the German-language versions of E. A. Dupont's *Atlantic*, produced in England, and Bryan Foy's Warner production *Die Königsloge* (*The Royal Loge*), with Alexander Moissi and Camilla Horn. The first "hundred-percent" sound film produced in Germany was *Dich hab' ich geliebt* (*It's You I Have Loved*), made by Aafa-Film and directed by Rudolf Walther-Fein. A week after the Ufa premiere of *Melody of the Heart* Carl Froelich released *Die Nacht gehört uns* (*The Night Belongs to Us*), a sound film of his own production.

Through its alliance with Klangfilm, Ufa enjoyed privileges that allowed the company to convert its approximately one hundred theaters to sound-film projection in a short time. The nearly five thousand other theaters without big-company affiliation and their own capital resources, had to pay the high rental fees imposed by Klangfilm. In 1929, only 223 theaters were able to convert to sound; by the end of 1930, 1,864 had made the change; two years later, 3,820; but it wasn't until 1935 that conversion was complete. This major economic and technical retooling absorbed more than 50 million marks and precipitated the demise of many companies. Ufa alone invested 20 million marks in the conversion of its studios and theaters, in sound-film experiments, and in the first year of production.[26]

The victory parade of sound film accompanied the final phase of the Weimar Republic and outshone a series of political crises that led ultimately to the collapse of German democracy. While Ludwig Klitzsch was dreaming in a New York hotel of how the new medium of sound film would enable German music to conquer the world, Alfred Hugenberg was agitating for "consolidation of the right" against the "trash" of parliamentary democracy, for "the total amalgamation" of the social question with the "national idea," for the German National People's Party as the "party of vision," the only party destined to save "the soul and the economy of the German nation."[27] And in those very September days of 1929 when Ufa was showing off its new sound-film center in Neubabelsberg, Hugenberg was stirring up reactionary feeling in the Reich Committee for German National Aspirations against the Young Plan, which joined debts and reparations together; propagandizing with the Pan-Germans, with Franz Seldte, the leader of the Stahlhelm, and with Adolf Hitler against the "lie of German war guilt"; and threatening any member of the government who signed the Young Plan agreement with a prison term for treason.

Foreign Minister Stresemann, the main target of Hugenberg's attacks, after lengthy negotiations had won agreement from France's Aristide Briand to end the occupation of the Rhineland; in early October 1929 after a period of obvious ill health he died of a stroke. "In the long run he probably would not have been able to hold out against the forces opposing him, but if he had lived, perhaps the Weimar state would not have ended quite so ignominiously."[28] Kessler's account of Stresemann's funeral conveys the ceremony's gloomy, oppressive atmosphere. It was an ostentatious display of mourning, a foreshadowing of the farewell to the republic, and it had all the trappings of Prussian film tragedy:

A gloriously warm and sunny day from which one entered the somewhat darkened and crepe-bedecked plenary hall of the Reichstag as if coming into a mausoleum. . . . The coffin was draped with a golden banner decorated with a black eagle. Because the eagle had red talons, the banner was officially but *timidly* black, red, and gold, not *boldly* black, red, and gold, as it had been for Walter Rathenau [a Jewish industrialist and cabinet minister, murdered by reactionary nationalists in 1922]. And several of the ribbons on the floral wreaths were black, white, and red. Frau Stresemann, heavily veiled, sat next to Hindenburg in the former royal loge. Next to it, in the diplomats' loge, were all the ambassadors in full dress with medals. Hermann Müller gave the funeral oration: good, but uninspired. He looked on the verge of death himself, yellow and emaciated.[29]

While the Weimar Republic became moribund, its largest film company was enjoying a new lease on life. It was even, as Traub put it, "on the road to freedom," the advance guard of the German film industry's emancipation from "excessive American influence."[30] On his first American trip in the summer of 1927 Klitzsch had, in fact, renegotiated the Parufamet contract, and because the American parties made any modification dependent on the repayment of the $4 million loan, the German Bank had to come to the rescue. A firm schedule of repayments was set up, and Klitzsch came away with looser Parufamet terms: the duration of the contract was shortened by four years; Ufa's obligation to supply films was cut in half, from forty to twenty; and the percentage of American films it had to show in its theaters was reduced from 75 to 33⅓ percent. Parufamet continued to distribute only American films and gradually lost importance. It was disbanded in 1932.

The improvement in Ufa's fortunes obscured the actual situation for German film as a whole, however. In the battle over sound-film patents, a few monopolies had had their way at the expense of the mid-sized and small firms. In the production sector, Tobis controlled sound-equipment distribution, and the poverty of the smaller production companies worked to its advantage, either guaranteeing it a share in their production or making them dependent on its studios. In 1932, no less than 32 percent of Germany's total production came out of Tobis's Jofa studios in Johannisthal. The rapid rise in production costs left the smaller companies in severe financial straits, and the number of German movies produced fell from 224 silent films in 1928 to 132 (all sound films by now) in 1932. At the same time, the language barrier reduced the number of available foreign films: box-office receipts dropped and so did market demand. Despite the impressive balance sheets that Ufa, Tobis, and Terra could show, the German film industry as a whole was in trouble. The Depression had a disastrous impact on German buying power; between 1928 and 1932, national income dropped by 42 percent, the number of movie tickets sold by 32 percent, and the gross income of theater owners by 36 percent.[31]

Now Ufa's power politics bore fruit. Its economic advantage allowed it not only to come through the crisis years before 1933 unscathed but in many instances to give greater weight to political concerns than to economic ones. Politics became increasingly important in the conduct of the business, and "the nationalistic outlook of the new management made itself felt in every aspect of the firm's activity."[32] Ufa's managers decided, for instance, not to let its theaters accept advertising from leftist newspapers, and they refused to provide a synchronization studio for Lewis Milestone's film version of Erich Maria Remarque's novel *Im Westen nichts Neues* (*All Quiet on the Western Front*) or even to allow the film to be shown in Ufa theaters. They also decided not to rent any more Soviet films and began refusing orders from the Soviet Union for copying work. As Ufa's house writer, Hans Traub, put it, the company wanted to exercise caution "where foreign activities might adversely affect German prestige or were guided by philosophically incompatible positions."[33] When Ufa was accepted for membership in the Kaiser-Wilhelm-Gesellschaft zur Förderung der Wissenschaften (Kaiser Wilhelm Society for the Advancement of the Sciences and Humanities), Traub regarded the invitation—no doubt quite correctly—not only as an honoring and recognition of film itself but as a by-product of the firm's financial restructuring by the nationalistic Hugenberg.

Ludwig Klitzsch, since May 1927 president of the Spitzenorganisation der Deutschen Filmwirtschaft (Spio, Council of the German Film Industry), streamlined this umbrella organization's internal structure and saw to it that Spio vigorously addressed political issues affecting the industry: government quotas on the import of foreign films, a reform of the motion-picture law, questions of censorship, and, as in earlier years, the all-important matter of the entertainment tax. Spio's new argument was that film shows should be tax free because they served the goals of "national education" and "national recreation," two concepts that would soon become staples in the ideological jargon of National Socialist film policy.

By 1929 Ufa's internal reorganization was largely completed. The long-established practice of commissioning films to smaller firms was cut back, and where more than half of Ufa's films in 1927–28 had been produced in other companies' studios, by 1929–30 all production was under Ufa's own direction. Erich Pommer was largely responsible for the increased importance of the "production directors," and it was decided to include their names in the credit rolls.

In every respect, Ufa saw itself as a model for an industry in search of "inner consistency" and uniform guidelines. In Hugenberg's film factory everything—from the packing of film reels for shipment to equipping them with uniform leaders, from the care of film copies to the training of projector operators—was done according to prescribed rules. Because some elements of the film-trade press were not friendly to Ufa, the firm's management transformed its internal house organ *Ufa-Magazin* into the PR publication *Filmmagazin*. At Neubabelsberg the venerable cobblestone street gave way to pavement, and the tracks of the old transportation system yielded to modern electric trucks. A "wildcat film strike" in the summer of 1928 passed, as Traub noted with relief, "without any damaging effects."[34] Law and order became the guiding principles in Germany's leading film company.

16.

Revue and Decline:
The Last Years of the Republic

IN their own way Ufa's revue and operetta films orchestrated and illuminated an unprecedented contemporary tragedy: the death throes and demise of Germany's first democracy. Economic crisis and self-inflicted political impotence on the one hand, and *Liebeswalzer* (*Waltz of Love*), *Die Drei von der Tankstelle* (*The Three from the Filling Station*), *Bomben auf Monte Carlo* (*Monte Carlo Madness*), and *Der Kongress tanzt* (*The Congress Dances*) on the other. It seemed as if the Weimar Republic was dancing its way toward the abyss with reckless musical abandon.

Just five days before the world premiere of Sternberg's film *The Blue Angel* in the Gloria-Palast, a long illness reached its critical stage: the resignation of Hermann Müller's cabinet on March 27, 1930, the last coalition between the Social Democrats and the middle-class center, marked the end of a risky democratic experiment that had for a while been viable. The "Bloody May" of 1929, when the Social Democratic police chief Zörgiebel had ordered troops to fire on Communist demonstrators, had made it clear that the united anti-Fascist front of proletarian parties was nothing more than a delusion in the minds of the workers and a demagogic catchword in the speeches of their leaders. The results of the December 1929 elections in Thuringia, and the entry of National Socialists into a German cabinet for the first time, anticipated developments in the country as a whole.

With the dissolving of the Reichstag on July 30, 1930—an event applauded by the German National People's Party, the National Socialists, Communists, and even many Social Democrats—the Weimar Republic openly celebrated its fatal crisis. New elections on September 14 gave the NSDAP 6.4 million votes and 107 seats in the Reichstag; this merely "ratified the death the republic had already died in the spring."[1]

The next day Ufa celebrated the premiere of its musical *The Three from the Filling Station*, directed by Wilhelm Thiele. This was Ufa's first operetta film inspired entirely by music and at the same time a parody, a lively, lighthearted movie about three men out of work, a mortgaged house, and a failed banker. Lilian Harvey, Willy Fritsch, Oskar Karlweis, Fritz Kampers, and Heinz Rühmann played the leads; Werner Richard Heymann composed the music; and Robert Gilbert wrote the lyrics, some of which attained no little fame ("A Friend, a Good Friend," "Now Comes the Big Question Mark"). A simultaneously produced French version with the title *Le Chemin du paradis* was a smash hit in Paris in November.

Government by emergency measures invoked under Article 48 of the Weimar constitution by Chancellor Heinrich Brüning went into effect, not only making the Reichstag itself superfluous but also subjecting parliamentarianism as the basis of democracy to public scorn. Conservative elements in the middle class and some government leaders as well, weary of parties and the legislature, called for a "rational"—by which they meant authoritarian—solution. Corruption, bombastic displays by speakers and their factions in the nearly powerless Reichstag, and street warfare between Communists and Fascists were daily accompaniments to the self-destruction of the republic.

As under Kaiser Wilhelm in the years before the war, a theatrical and movie atmosphere again bathed everyday political life in a spectral light and lent fuel to the cynics' fires. In September 1929, news broke that the Sklarek brothers, who owned a Berlin textile factory, had embezzled millions of marks, and when it was learned that their firm had bribed Social Democratic politicians in the municipal government, the scandal, "lovingly tended by the right-wing press, spread a foul smell throughout German politics."[2] A little later, newspapers were complaining about the actress Lilian Harvey, who, born in the slums of London, had her relatives driven away from the door of her palatial villa, "where she gave orgiastic parties in the company of the Sklarek brothers." She took a bath "in German champagne" every day and had her fingernails painted with melted pearls.[3] The number of unemployed hovered between 4 and 5 million—it reached an all-time high of 6 million in 1932—and reactionary forces found new proof every day of the "degeneracy" of the "democratic system."

The rapid drop in value of German securities on the international exchanges after the September 1930 elections, the flight of foreign capital, and the failure of the Darmstädter und Nationalbank, one of Germany's four largest credit institutions, no doubt reminded many people of the inflation years, and of the way a stock-market crash had been equated with the end of the world by Norbert Jacques and Fritz Lang in their Mabuse films. The aged Reich President Hindenburg had to sign emergency measures; he of all people, "who in those realms of feeling that lay beyond his oath of office saw himself as a regent of the Hohenzollern dynasty, formed the last barrier before the deluge of National Socialism."[4] In two ballots held in March and April 1932, the votes of Hindenburg's Social Democratic backers reelected him President. With a lead of 6 million votes, he emerged clearly victorious over his only serious opponent: Adolf Hitler.

But Hans Albers was the real winner that spring. In the Ufa film *Der Sieger (The Victor)* by Hans Hinrich and Paul Martin, Albers played a postal clerk who loses all his money on the horses but wins the heart of a billionaire's daughter. At the Gloria-Palast three orchestras at once—the Comedian Harmonists, Hans Bund's Jazz Orchestra, and Ufa's symphony orchestra—played the bouncy accompaniment for this ode to a con artist.

"It has often been noted with dismay that we have to take refuge in vapidity if we want to enjoy ourselves," wrote Rudolf Arnheim[5] in his 1931 review of the premiere of *Monte Carlo Madness*, directed by Hanns Schwarz. The film's feeble plot revolves around the captain of a warship who loses his Queen's money in Monte Carlo and then threatens to bombard the casino. The vapidity of this gunboat operetta, with its mix of Mediterranean elegance and Teutonic brutality, created an escapist realm where aggressive fantasies and German revenge dreams vented themselves. And in Hans Albers, a muscular type with almost supernatural sex appeal, the public had an athletically gifted alter ego who could enact those dreams and fantasies for them.

> His face was modeled in late Hellenistic style by a French pastry cook, but it is rescued from blandness by predatory eyes that burn with such white heat that it's surprising the fire inspector allows his films in movie theaters. Granted, the fire is not delivered by Prometheus but has its origins in glandular secretions, but despite that, it warms the souls of both culturally modest and culturally demanding patrons. . . . At the same time there is in his blindingly keen gaze a kind of hidden fear of his own temperament, a kind of weakness in the face of his own strength, that is a counterweight to all those muscles.[6]

Monte Carlo Madness premiered in the Ufa-Palast am Zoo on August 31, 1931. A few weeks later, Hugenberg invited the "national opposition" to a military review in Bad Harzburg. In the spa hall draped in black, white, and red, Pan-Germans, German Nationals, and National Socialists gathered with Hugenberg and Hitler at their head. Other prominent dignitaries were leaders of the Stahlhelm and the Reichsland League; of the German People's Party (which after Stresemann's death had moved far to the right) and the Economic Party; retired generals and admirals, including Hans von Seeckt, until 1926 army chief of staff; the Hohenzollern princes Eitel Friedrich and August Wilhelm; and several conservative university professors. Among the "business leaders" were two Ufa board members, Emil Georg von Stauss and Fritz Thyssen. In his opening remarks, Hugenberg asserted:

> The majority of the German people are here with us. They are calling out to the holders of sinecures and overpaid public offices, to the power prof-

iteers and the political bosses, to the owners and exploiters of dying organizations, they are calling out to the parties in power: A new day is dawning. We don't want you anymore![7]

Hitler showed a rather moderate face in Harzburg, but the resolution Hugenberg presented to the assembly was indistinguishable from an NSDAP document in intent and language: "Only a strong national state" could "realize our potential in every area and implement the social measures necessary for the formation of a true national community. We ask sacrifice and fulfillment of duty from all fellow patriots."[8]

Given the perspective of the intervening decades, the demise of the Weimar Republic ultimately appears to have been a cultural and psychic tragedy for the Germans, burdened with a psychic legacy of feudalism "that lies slumbering deep in the German temperament," as George W.F. Hallgarten has written.[9]

The Nibelungs atmosphere must have affected many a republican, for why else did so many observers think Fritz Lang's Germanic epic was "modern" and understand it as a commentary on Germany's present situation? The excess of malice and betrayal, of political deviousness and demagogic nastiness in the last years of Weimar encouraged among many Germans "an unconditional commitment to the service of one's lord" which is the quintessence of this degenerate feudalism, and when Joseph Goebbels praised Fritz Lang's work in 1929, calling it the "film of German loyalty," he expressed not so much what the masses thought as what they felt. Perceptions of the past as well as of the present were disastrously out of line, and the misalignment, deeply rooted in Germany's psychic economy, served the cause of reaction.

On April 1, 1930, the Ufa-Palast had hosted the gala premiere of a very different "film of German loyalty," one that illuminated the masochistic nature of the subjugated soul and the sadistic one of the oppressor. The evening ended with prolonged ovations from the illustrious audience and innumerable curtain calls for the lead performers, Emil Jannings and Marlene Dietrich. With Josef von Sternberg's *The Blue Angel*, Ufa confirmed its claim to leadership and demonstrated its determination to synthesize art and commercial success in "prestige films"; it also displayed, as Jerzy Toeplitz has noted, its still considerable "political elasticity."[10]

Heinrich Mann's 1905 novel *Professor Unrat*, on which the film was based, was the work of a prominent radical democrat who was also a patron of the leftist People's Film Association and openly hostile to Ufa. Yet the idea that the film was made "behind the backs of Ufa's top managers, so to speak,"[11] is mistaken. Ufa's smoothly functioning chain of command made "subversive" productions impossible, especially ones of this magnitude. Ludwig Klitzsch gave priority to business considerations in his decision to work with Heinrich Mann, and put aside his political reservations "for the good of the firm."[12]

Once again Ufa showed that commercial energy has the power to achieve quality, and that capitalistic calculations can give rise to an unintended and unwanted dialectic. In this case the dialectic later exploded in a violent controversy that recalled the golden days of Ufa's early pluralism. Though long since in nationalistic hands, Ufa was still sensitive to impulses generated by the political and psychological chaos of the times, and moreover, it still insisted on quality, which was guaranteed given the people assembled for this production: the Hollywood director Sternberg, the scriptwriters Carl Zuckmayer, Karl Vollmoeller, and Robert Liebmann; the composer Friedrich Holländer, and a cast of stars like Kurt Gerron, Rosa Valetti, and Hans Albers even in supporting roles. With that kind of talent, Ufa was aiming for international success, and if for no other reason could not wear reactionary blinders.

Pommer and Jannings had agreed on Sternberg as the director for a major Ufa film. Jannings had maintained ties with Sternberg since their time together in Hollywood, when they made *The Last Command* for Paramount in 1928. When Sternberg arrived in Berlin in August 1929, the first idea suggested to him was one Jannings had for a film about Rasputin, but Sternberg did not take to it. He said to the press only a day after his arrival that plans called for "a world-class film, by virtue of the production resources available,"[13] but what would it be? Jannings, indefatigable in his search for roles that suited him well, suggested Mann's *Professor Unrat*, and this met with approval all around.

The agreements Ufa's contract department drew up document the firm's readiness to reward above-average ambitions. Heinrich Mann received 25,000 marks for the rights to his novel, as well as a guarantee of 10,000 more if the film was sold in the United States. Karl Vollmoeller and Carl Zuckmayer were paid 23,000 and 16,000, respectively. Sternberg was assured of $40,000, and Jannings could celebrate the record sum of 200,000 marks. Marlene Dietrich, who was still almost unknown, received the comparatively modest fee of 20,000 marks. (Wolfgang Jacobsen reports that Pommer's wife, Gertrud, had called his attention to Dietrich.) The dancer La Jana, Hertha von Walther, and Trude Hesterberg had all been considered for the female lead.[14]

Among Pommer's many duties was the one of selecting the technical team, which in the early days of sound film was especially important. With his choices of the cameramen Günther Rittau and Hans Schneeberger, the architects Otto Hunte and Emil Hasler, "the first sound technician of genius, Fritz Thiery,"[15] and the American editor Sam Winston, Pommer assembled a team of unquestionable quality. Once again production costs far exceeded budget, climbing to almost 2 million marks, but the investment was fully justified.

With this film, in its second year of work with sound, Ufa produced an achievement which Kurt Pinthus called "a rapid advance in German recording methods." "How subtly sound can be shaded; how artfully it can be layered or used to establish a mood, coming on just a few seconds ahead of the picture; how powerfully silent moments or glances and spoken sentences or noises can accentuate each other."[16] And in this same year that saw the onset of the Weimar Republic's mortal crisis, Ufa produced a film with a penetrating insight into the psychological premises for the Fascist rise to power. One reason for the success of this film, Kracauer has said, was "its outright sadism."

> *The Blue Angel* poses anew the problem of German immaturity and moreover elaborates its consequences as manifested in the conduct of the boys and of the artists, who like the professor are middle-class offspring. Their sadistic cruelty results from the very immaturity which forces their victim into submission. It is as if the film implied a warning, for these screen figures anticipate what will happen in real life a few years later. The boys are born Hitler youths.[17]

In their script, the writers had stressed Unrat's personal tragedy, playing down the social criticism in the novel and almost entirely omitting the sarcastic portrayal of small-city life in the Wilhelmine era. These were clearly concessions to the political leanings of Ufa's board and senior managers, but they were compensated for by another, much more acute and timely probing. This one, even if most viewers at the time were unaware of it, plumbed the psychic depths of a national community that in its political immaturity had already virtually chosen catastrophe. Heinrich Mann probably picked up this subliminal message, for he publicly expressed approval and praise for the movie—to the surprise of some of his friends and also of Ufa's directors, who would have welcomed a rejection of the film from this politically unacceptable author.

But Ufa's managers, understandably, were not interested in a public battle with an author they had hired. Instead, Hugenberg put out the word in the Scherl newspaper *Nachtausgabe* that Ufa had succeeded "in making a work of art out of Heinrich Mann's vile book."[18] Pommer took management's criticism as an attack on his concept of the film, as well as a disparagement of Mann, and responded dramatically. On the day of the premiere, in Mosse's *Berliner Tageblatt* he declared in no uncertain terms his solidarity with the writer:

> Not only the preparation of the script but also the production of the film were carried out in constant consultation with Heinrich Mann. At a private showing I arranged for him in Nice several days ago, he expressed total satisfaction with the final version of *The Blue Angel*. From these facts it is perfectly clear that *The Blue Angel* was made not against but with Heinrich Mann, for whom I have the highest admiration.[19]

Sternberg's exacting portrait of the authoritarian philistine rubbed the National Socialists the wrong way, and the Bavarian edition of the *Völkische Beobachter* venomously struck back in 1931, when the film was reshown in

Munich. "We see at work here a deliberate Jewish detraction and vilifica-
tion of the German character and German educational values. Even Jewish
cynicism rarely sinks this low. One need only glance through the names of
this film's makers: nothing but Jews with Galician faces that are enough to
make one vomit."[20]

The years 1930–31 were years of brawls in cinemas, of increased censorship, and of resistance to a "regime of billy-club complacency and political
film deals," as Hans Taussig, in his magazine *Kino*, described the dominance of Ufa and its friends in business and government. In the Ufa-Palast
am Zoo there was loud protest against Gustav Ucicky's *Das Flötenkonzert
von Sanssouci* (*The Flute Concert at Sanssouci*, 1930), one of the most
aggressive and commercially successful of the *Fridericus Rex* series; in Dresden students at the technical university demonstrated against the hypocrisy
of one of Ufa's innumerable sentimental films. "In both cases," Taussig
noted, "pained and insulted members of the audience were driven from
the theater with billy clubs." In December 1930, a horde of National Socialists led by Goebbels broke up the premiere in the Mozart Hall of Lewis
Milestone's antimilitaristic film *All Quiet on the Western Front* (1930), and
the film was banned by the censors.

Nonetheless, the nationalistic right, not to mention the National Socialists, still complained about the censors' laxity. As late as 1943, the official
Ufa historian, Hans Traub, complained of the Weimar "disorderliness,"
recalling that *Revolte im Erziehungshaus* (*Revolt in the Reformatory*, directed by Georg Asagaroff for Grohnert-Film-Produktion, 1929), based on
Peter Martin Lampel's play, had been banned four times before being released. *Ins dritte Reich* (*Toward the Third Reich*), an SPD propaganda film
against the National Socialists, was also banned, he reported, though, for
reasons he could not understand, the censors had initially passed Milestone's *All Quiet on the Western Front*. Traub makes perfectly clear to which
political camp the censors under Brüning bowed.

> If, despite these aberrations, the German film censors for the most part
> faithfully carried out their national duty, that is in large part due to the
> influence of Ministerial Councillor Dr. Seeger, for many years chief of the
> censorship office. Public recognition of his efforts came with his appoint-
> ment after 1933 as head of the film division in the Reich Ministry for
> National Education and Propaganda.[21]

Traub notes with satisfaction that by 1931 the first NSDAP cells had begun
agitation in cinema and theater organizations.

A dramatic change in mood had taken place. In 1926 theater owners had
successfully warded off a storm of reactionary protest against Eisenstein's
Potemkin, and in 1927, the Foreign Office under Stresemann had put a
damper on Ufa's nationalistic plans for the Leipzig Fair. But now Spio
raised no protest against Fascist terror and readily acquiesced to the dicta

of censors aligned with Hugenberg. "This silence," the critic Taussig wrote, "speaks a clear language. It shows that these men have lost every last iota of regard for the ravaged dignity of an industry that would like to be counted among Germany's leaders."[22]

What leftist and liberal moralists decried as a political loss of face had, of course, its palpable, practical causes. The film business was once again in grave difficulties, occasioned this time by the Depression and the costly conversion to sound. Reduced production in 1928–32 was the effect of a genuine structural crisis; small firms without adequate capital resources collapsed; then in 1932 the bell tolled for the larger firms as well. Within a few months, seven out of ten stock companies with more than a million marks in nominal capital collapsed. Only Ufa and Tobis survived on their own resources. Terra had to be bailed out by a Swiss financial group. Emelka's assets after liquidation were absorbed by Bavaria Film. National-Film, Deutsche Lichtspiel-Syndikat, Südfilm, and other mid-sized and small companies failed at the same time. Support from the banks, on the verge of collapse themselves, was no more likely than financing or outright subventions from the state. Like the governments before it, Brüning's cabinet was not even willing to make a significant cut in the entertainment tax, which as late as 1932 still amounted to 10.5 percent on the retail price of a movie ticket. With 18.5 million marks, movie theaters were contributing almost half of all municipal entertainment-tax revenues.[23]

At this point, the Council of the German Film Industry, led by Ufa, developed its Spio Plan: the film historian Jürgen Spiker has correctly said of it that it accelerated "the seamless transition from a media industry based on private capital to an essentially state-owned one that remained committed to the profit principle."[24] Thanks to its export business, its lucrative production of cultural and advertising films, and its income from Afifa's copying work, Ufa had come through the crisis unscathed, though it could not pay any dividends in 1932–33 (in previous years dividends had been between 4 and 6 percent); the fact that it had succeeded in reducing the average production costs for a sound film from 579,000 to 450,000 marks between 1930 and 1932[25] shows that unlike most other firms, it had survived the structural crisis by containing costs. Ufa consequently thought it must seize the initiative for economic reform on behalf of the entire German film industry, and because it dominated Spio, and Klitzsch (now officially Ufa's CEO) was its president (his production chief Correll and his distribution director Wilhelm Meydam were on the board), it seemed the appropriate vehicle.

Klitzsch, who had been received in the United States by Will Hays, president of the Motion Picture Producers and Distributors of America,

> put himself forward more and more as the representative of the German film industry who explained both at home and abroad the accomplish-

ments and the problems of his business, who solicited trust and support, and who at the same time stressed the crucial role that Ufa had played in the quantitative and qualitative development of the German cinema. He knew how important it was for the medium to present its case publicly, especially at home, if it was to garner support from the state.[26]

Klitzsch's programmatic statements, which drew increasing interest in the early 1930s, made clever use of a whole range of arguments that impressed on the public the economic importance of movies in Germany's export trade, their entertainment value and the diversion from everyday cares they offered, the pedagogical function of cultural films, and the national obligation of filmmakers "to appeal to the entrepreneurial energies and self-confidence of our people."[27] He believed he was acting on behalf of the greater good, yet everything he said and did served the well-being of Ufa, its commercial success, its public image, its political future. And indeed, it was clear that Ufa's policies would point the way for Germany's entire film industry. In 1931–32, the weakness of the competition made for the "obvious conclusion that solidarity with the largest, purely German enterprise was essential."[28] Ufa's "purely German" substance had a special radiance: competing companies could stay alive only with the help of foreign investment, but some (like National-Film) found that the investment of foreign capital led to their downfall.

The Spio Plan, drafted primarily by Salomon Marx, centralized the film industry still more, asserted the priority of production over distribution, and argued for a state-controlled economy that would work against the forces of free competition. The plan favored large premiere theaters owned by the big companies to the detriment of small theaters obliged to book films "blind" for specific times, that is, without having seen them in advance and often even before production was completed. Spio recommended doing away with internal democracy in the different interest associations and replacing it with a strong guiding hand; the idea of a film ministry was bruited, and this greatly accelerated the subjugation of movies to a Reich ministry with dictatorial powers.

Spio's first step was to appropriate to itself—in the interest of the few remaining big companies—exclusive control over the disposition of available means of production as well as over the distribution and rental of films according to centrally dictated guidelines. The functions of traditional industry associations would be limited to monitoring their members for compliance with the Spio guidelines and to eliminating insubordinate producers, distributors, and theater owners.

Even before January 30, 1933, the plan turned the earlier missions of the associations around 180 degrees. Instead of being democratically legitimized organizations representing the interests of their members . . . they were now supposed to act as disciplinarians and, if their members misbehaved, to put them out of business.[29]

While Hugenberg's lieutenants at Ufa, disguised as Spio functionaries, promoted the development of state centralism, which in their own view could be accomplished only by a "strong national state," Ufa itself approached the high point of its commercial power and cultural influence. In 1931 it had seventy-one subsidiaries, among them six production companies, five distributors, and thirty-seven theater companies. Nineteen firms abroad operated under the Ufa trademark.[30] These were joined by Bohème Verlag in Vienna and, a little later, by Ufaton Verlag, which, with its flourishing sheet-music and record business, sold music from Ufa operettas. "The playing of film music in cafés, at public events of all kinds, in house concerts, and, most important, on the radio," Hans Traub opined, "sparked a strong interest in sound film."[31] In 1932 no less than 115 cinemas were Ufa theaters, all of them equipped by now with expensive sound systems; Ufa's distribution organizations supplied films to nearly two thousand theaters throughout Germany.

According to figures supplied by the Deutscher Städtetag (Council of German Cities)—which was interested in having the film industry, especially film theaters, flourish because of the tax revenues they would generate—1.5 million more moviegoers visited Ufa theaters in 1931–32 than in the previous year. Lower ticket prices in response to unemployment and the Depression brought a 10 percent drop in income, however. "Despite difficulties with currency exchange," foreign profits rose by 45 percent over the previous year.[32] In 1930–31, the balance sheets showed a profit of more than 3 million marks,[33] a figure that bore witness, for the first time since the crisis of 1925, to sound business policies throughout Ufa.

The rapid rise in foreign business was especially significant. In 1930, a foreign division was added to Ufa's domestic distribution organization (Ufa-Leih), and its mission was to revive the old goals of the Deutsche Lichtbild-Gesellschaft and Ludendorff's vision of 1917. "Its task," Traub wrote, "is to propagate German culture, a clearly formulated goal when Ufa was founded, which has come to the fore again since 1927. . . . We have even observed that many people in the Balkan states have learned German simply to follow German sound films."[34] There were Ufa premiere theaters in Budapest and New York. Ufa dealt with obstacles to realizing its ambitions in England and the United States by establishing press offices and subsidiaries with affiliated press and propaganda offices around the world.

From the beginning of the sound-film era, Ufa produced its most important films in foreign-language versions as well as German ones. The films were not dubbed yet; rather, expensive foreign-language versions were made, often employing foreign actors. Audiences in London and Paris—audiences that Hugenberg and his friends counted among their archenemies—were treated to English and French versions not only of gold-plated entertainment fare like *The Waltz of Love* and *The Three from the Filling Station* but also of nationalistic German films like Gustav Ucicky's *Yorck* (1931). Of the 137 German sound films of the 1930–31 season, more than a third, most of them Ufa products, were released in several languages. The "pre-Fascist" Ufa was a polyglot operation remarkably open to the world. (With the imposition of the National Socialists' autarkical policies, the 30 million marks that German films earned abroad in 1931 sank in 1933 almost overnight to 3 to 4 million, just barely 5 percent of the production costs.[35])

In artistic terms, Ufa's production in the early 1930s remained at a high level. The company was still a workshop for the best Germans working in movies. Ufa's employees in the studios, editing rooms, script offices, and advertising department were still fired with the ambition that had driven them a decade before in the era of Murnau and Fritz Lang.

Erich Pommer's guiding principle that the "commercial film" and the "artistic film" had to form a synthesis had taken hold in the production teams and had become the standard for Ufa's regular actors, authors, directors, cameramen, and sound technicians, even though the company's managers were more interested in limiting political and artistic freedom in ways dictated by the struggles for power in the last years of the Weimar Republic. Ufa under Hugenberg, like Ufa before Hugenberg, had obviously stamped out patterns of moral and aesthetic conformity that became characteristic of its productions; it remained for the National Socialists to invest conformity with the force of law and to subdue cinema's erratic, quirky, "subversive" qualities, which appeared even in Ufa films made purely for the mass entertainment market.

Until the end of 1932, the presence of Erich Pommer, chief of Ufa's most important production team and an energetic opponent of vapid popular taste, guaranteed the production of films that were commercially successful and also drew critical acclaim at home and abroad. In these years Pommer supervised the production of outstanding films in all genres (with the exception of "national" films): musicals like *Melody of the Heart, Waltz of Love* (Wilhelm Thiele, 1929–30), and *Liebling der Götter* (*Darling of the Gods*, directed by Hanns Schwarz, 1930); comedies like *Einbrecher* (*Burglar*, directed by Hanns Schwarz, 1930), *The Victor, Ein blonder Traum* (*A Blond Dream*, directed by Paul Martin, 1932), and *Ich bei Tag und du bei Nacht* (*I by Day and You by Night*, directed by Ludwig Berger, 1932); Sternberg's *The Blue Angel*; and the three original Ufa operettas *The Three from the Filling Station, Monte Carlo Madness*, and *The Congress Dances* (Erik Charell, 1931); a courtly melodrama like *Ich und die Kaiserin* (*The Empress and I*, directed by Friedrich Holländer, 1932–33) and the adventure *FP 1 antwortet nicht* (*FP 1 Does Not Answer*, directed by Karl Hartl, 1932).

Outstanding quality was also the hallmark of Robert Siodmak's early films, with their ambiguous plots and problematic characters.

Siodmak's Ufa debut, which he recorded himself in great detail in his memoirs,[36] illustrates the firm's elasticity and capacity for integration. In 1929, working essentially alone with almost no money and under trying technical and organizational conditions, Siodmak made an extraordinarily realistic milieu film, *People on Sunday*, which has an almost documentary quality. At first, no theater owner was willing to risk showing it, but Hanns Brodnitz, senior manager for Ufa's Berlin theaters, had faith in the originality of this experimental film, and he arranged for a premiere in the Ufa Theater am Kurfürstendamm on February 4, 1930. The very next day Ufa hired Siodmak as a writer and soon promoted him to director. His first film, *Abschied* (*Farewell*, 1930), a sensitive presentation of human tragicomedy in a small boardinghouse, revealed in its poetic images and acoustic subtleties all the marks of a carefully structured film composition. With this film, in which Brigitte Horney made her debut and Eugen Schüfftan did the camerawork, Ufa—fully realizing that the returns would probably be modest—took its chances with an experiment in poetic realism.

Bruno Duday produced *Farewell*, but Pommer took over production for Siodmak's next movies, which starred performers with box-office appeal: *Der Mann, der seinen Mörder sucht* (*The Man in Search of His Murderer*, with Heinz Rühmann in the lead role, 1930); *Voruntersuchung* (*Preliminary Interrogation*, with Albert Bassermann, Hans Brausewetter, and Gustav Fröhlich, 1931); *Storms of Passion* (with Emil Jannings, Anna Sten, and Trude Hesterberg, 1931); and *Quick* (with Lilian Harvey and Hans Albers, 1932). In Toeplitz's view, Siodmak's career proceeded "from the brilliant, avant-garde experiment to the sure box-office hit"; He gradually gave in to "the pressure of the banal scenario, the star performers, the money-making attraction."[37] But avant-garde experiment and commercialism were not yet diametrically opposed at Ufa. Pommer struggled to reconcile those two extremes, and what he was able to teach Siodmak in these years was of great use in Siodmak's later directing career in Hollywood.

In the summer of 1931, when Erik Charell, the revue specialist of Berlin's Grosses Schauspielhaus, was making *The Congress Dances*, the most opulent of all Ufa's revue and operetta films, the Weimar Republic was on the verge of bankruptcy. While in front of Carl Hoffmann's camera the Congress of Vienna and Europe under Metternich was coming alive again as salon intrigue, high-society comedy, and fairy tale, the collapse of several major banks sparked a run on credit institutions, and emergency "bank holidays" had to be declared. And while Lilian Harvey, ensconced in an open coach and trailed by a camera dolly, rode several hundred meters through an opulently reconstructed Austrian studio landscape on her way to a rendezvous with Tsar Alexander (Willy Fritsch) in his summerhouse, and while the cheering "common people" along the wayside chimed in on her song "Das gibt's nur einmal, das kommt nie wieder" ("This Happens Only Once and Never Again"), and while the Ufa orchestra melted the sequences of image and motion together into a screen enchantment that still inspires admiration today—while, in other words, Ufa was doing its all "to ignite a fireworks display ablaze with dazzling uniforms, luxury, entertainments, and balls,"[38] the government introduced foreign-currency restrictions and issued its Second Order for the Stabilization of Business and Finance, which included tax hikes and cuts in government spending that far exceeded previous measures in their severity. "The limits of what we can impose on our people in the way of deprivation have been reached!" the Brüning cabinet confessed.[39]

Otto Wallburg, Conrad Veidt, Carl Heinz Schroth, Lil Dagover, Alfred Abel, Adele Sandrock, Margarete Kupfer, Julius Falkenstein, and Paul Hörbiger, playing the roles of kings, counts, princes, and other assorted nobility as prescribed in a screenplay by Norbert Falk and Robert Liebmann, celebrated Napoleon's defeat, while in London a quickly convened Seven Powers conference deliberated on Germany's financial crisis. When Charell's film premiered on September 29, 1931, in Vienna's Scala, the economic situation in Germany had taken still another turn for the worse. The Reichsverband der Deutschen Industrie (National Association of German Industry) demanded a reduction of public expenditures and a lowering of wages and salaries. Leading spokesmen for heavy industry were putting their hopes—more or less openly—on Hitler. Fritz Thyssen was willing to finance lavishly not only the building of the Brown House as a National Socialist headquarters in Munich but also the "lifestyle of a modern superNero" for Göring.[40] In late January 1932 he organized a meeting of the Dusseldorf Industry Club that gave Hitler access to Germany's industrial leaders, a step that was to prove crucial to his success.

In the meantime, the campaign for the presidential election of March 1932 was in full swing. Goebbels had 50,000 small-format recordings with propaganda texts on them sent out through the mail, and for the first time he made a ten-minute speech on sound film, a strip meant to be shown after dark on central squares in major cities. In this campaign, the NSDAP intensified its rivalry with Hugenberg and his German National People's Party. The high point of this effort came in October, when Goebbels, with the help of 10,000 SA members, turned a DNVP gathering in Berlin's Neue Welt into a National Socialist propaganda rally. In early November, Berlin was rocked by a strike of trolley-car workers led jointly by the NSDAP and the Communist Party. From Goebbels's point of view, this was a crucial battle in the National Socialists' campaign to win over the Communists in Berlin and to attract workers throughout the country to the NSDAP cause.

German workers, provided they were not in the direst poverty and totally demoralized or had not been pulled into the maelstrom of politics as pickets or strikebreakers or foot soldiers of the SA or "Iron Front," poured into the movie theaters in droves. Ufa films in 1932 looked to divert their audiences and dazzle them with images of a carefree everyday life or with sensually appealing fantasy worlds. *Das Lied einer Nacht* (*The Song of a Night*, directed by Anatole Litvak, with Magda Schneider and the singer Jan Kiepura), *Das schöne Abenteuer* (*The Beautiful Adventure*, directed by Reinhold Schünzel), *Der weisse Dämon* (*The White Demon*, directed by

Kurt Gerron, with Hans Albers and Gerda Maurus), and *Wenn die Liebe Mode macht* (*When Love Sets the Style*, directed by Franz Wenlzer, with Renate Müller and Georg Alexander)—these films were either musical comedies about love, marriage, and "frivolous" goings-on in "society," or inane, cliché-ridden tales of a big wide world that yielded its secrets only to the diligent and deserving. Meanwhile, *The Congress Dances* had inspired a new cult of beauty even in the cultural pages of the bourgeois press. Oscar Bie, music critic for the *Berliner-Börsen-Courier*, praised the "photographed music" of Ufa's most expensive operetta: "The law of cause and effect is annulled; the limits of space fall away; only time runs on and on. In exquisite images, this film evokes the vital rhythms of the world, of history, of being."[41]

Ernst Bloch realized in 1932 how skilled the forces of reaction were in the use of "noncontemporaneity." The Depression in Germany, he observed, was taking place in a country burdened "with a great residue of precapitalistic material." Seven-league boots of misery could carry one into the past just like the seven-league boots of happiness in the fairy tale.

> As the failure of measures to repress genuine socialism becomes more obvious, and as big capital's need for Fascist dictatorship—and the necessary accompanying narcotics, which are dictatorship in another form—becomes more urgent, the more often it offers up the ceremonies and masquerade balls of the previous century, the more adept it becomes at decorative painting.[42]

Ufa operetta linked the narcotic effect of "decorative painting" with the "national" Prussian film. In that close union of "noncontemporaneity and intoxication," Bloch said, both genres found their mysterious, modern meaning. In Toeplitz's view, a "visible change in the repertory policy of Ufa" did not set in until 1931–32;[43] and only in May 1932, after Brüning was replaced by Hugenberg's lieutenant Franz von Papen, did the company, at the request of the National Association of German Industry, make the production of "national" films the order of the day. In reality, the transition was more gradual; politics and business had been closely linked as early as 1927.

There is no doubt that the board and management put increased political pressure on the production groups throughout 1932, and Hugenberg, whose primary interest was propaganda useful in day-to-day political battle, presumably found Otto Gebühr as Frederick the Great more to his taste than Willy Fritsch playing Tsar Alexander in a Vienna heady with wine. Ufa's annual meeting in July 1932 responded positively to the right-wing industrial faction's campaigns on behalf of the authoritarian state. At this meeting, Correll declared the "mere screenplay technicians" obsolete and called for "poetic temperaments with German sensibilities."[44] Correll announced that future films would attend less to "satisfying the need for diversion" and turn more to the "idea of national improvement." They would ask questions "we shall have to answer." "In the future, we want to see people in movies who are pursuing clear and positive goals, whose character moves them to do battle with the world, and who on a national or purely human level struggle inwardly for worthy causes."[45]

Nonetheless, in the *Frankfurter Zeitung* in late July, Kracauer correctly noted an interesting contradiction: another programmatic statement, based on company information and published in the *Film-Kurier*, differed by 180 degrees from Correll's statement and declared Ufa's intent to stand by "film as entertainment."

> In its program planning, Ufa will take into account the psychic state of the contemporary world. The Depression, personal economic privation, and political dissension are factors that weigh heavily on people today. What need could be more pressing than a program of films designed to ease their psychic distress, films that offer a combination of edification, diversion, and entertainment?[46]

This contradiction anticipated the debate between "philosophy" and "entertainment" that would be conducted very soon within the National Socialist camp. A complicated enterprise like Ufa could not be instantly converted into a conduit for the resolutions of the National Association of German Industry. The influence of Fritz Thyssen on the board, Hugenberg's ongoing agitation, and Klitzsch's managerial powers doubtless helped to determine Ufa's repertoire, but they could in no way effect a total shift in production from one day to the next. The year 1932 therefore saw at most only an intensification of trends at work since 1927.

Moreover, Ufa did not yet abandon the light genre for "national" films. It had launched the long series of Prussian films in 1922 with Cserépy's *Fridericus Rex*. In the intervening years, primarily smaller firms had continued to work with this material, either on commission from Ufa or on their own, and these smaller companies—those that survived—shaped the Prussian-film boom of the early 1930s, too. Of eight "fatherland" films premiered in 1931–32, Ufa produced and brought out through its own distributors only two—*Yorck* and *Der schwarze Husar* (*The Black Hussar*, directed by Gerhard Lamprecht, 1932). The others were made by smaller companies like Zelnik, Aafa, Phoebus-Tonfilm, or Biograph. The Frederick theme and similar "national" subjects amounted to a syndrome that almost the entire film industry in Germany had a part in developing. But Ufa in particular established cultural, social, and psychological directions that other companies soon followed.

For the rest, light entertainment of all kinds—musical comedies, social comedies, romances, and "folk" humor—dominated the offerings of Ufa's distribution organizations in the last weeks and months of Germany's democracy. *Der Frechdachs* (*The Wise Guy*) by Carl Boese and Heinz Hille; *Die Gräfin von Monte Christo* (*The Countess of Monte Cristo*) by Karl Hartl (with Brigitte Helm, Rudolf Forster, and Gustaf Gründgens); *Ein toller Einfall* (*A Brilliant Idea*) and *Es wird schon wieder besser* (*There'll Be a Turn for the Better*) by Kurt Gerron; *Strich durch die Rechnung* (*The Best of Plans Can Go Astray*) by Alfred Zeisler; *Wie sag ich's meinem Mann* (*How Will I Tell My Husband*) by Reinhold Schünzel; and *Zwei Herzen und ein Schlag* (*Two Hearts and One Beat*) by Wilhelm Thiele. To commemorate the hundredth anniversary of Goethe's death, Ufa offered two celebratory shorts featuring "Goethe's writings in pithy excerpts":[47] *Der Werdegang* (*The Apprenticeship*) and *Die Vollendung* (*The Mature Years*). Fritz Wendhausen directed; Theodor Loos and Luise Ullrich played the leads.

The premiere of the Goethe films on March 18 came during the "Easter peace" that Chancellor Brüning had imposed on the rival parties during the campaign, evoking rage and scorn from Goebbels, the Nazi propaganda chief and Gauleiter for Berlin. "That's a typical bourgeois trick if there ever was one. You're at war, but shooting is forbidden for three weeks!"[48] Rumors of an imminent Hitler putsch, of large-scale preparations for civil war, and of plans for a workers' armed rebellion led by the Iron Front circulated throughout Germany.

Ten months later, on January 28, 1933, Harry Kessler noted in his journal:

Schleicher toppled, Papen entrusted with negotiations for forming a new government. . . . The whole business is a mixture of corruption, underhanded deals, and favoritism worthy of the worst periods of absolute monarchy. The only new element this time is how quickly all these poisonous toadstools have sprung up in the shadow of dictatorship.[49]

The meetings of Ufa's managers in January 1933 were, as usual, taken up with routine chores. On January 6, they approved the purchase for 12,550 marks of an airplane from the Klemm-Werke for an "aviation film." A few weeks later, however, the film was struck from the production plan. A week later, management approved a new director's contract for Reinhold Schünzel, who would receive 30,000 marks for two films; the architects Herlth and Röhrig were engaged for another year at a monthly salary of 2,000 marks each. On January 25, management considered Willy Fritsch's request to raise his monthly salary from 16,000 to 18,000 marks.[50]

On the evening of January 30, 1933, in Berlin's Kaiserhof Hotel, Kessler happened to run into Emil Georg von Stauss, head of the German Bank and Ufa board member, and Kessler allowed himself to take "a nasty little dig." He was pleased to hear, he told Stauss, that Otto Wolff (after Hugenberg Ufa's largest shareholder) had paid off Hitler's debts. "Stauss bristled and, red in the face, denied the remark with angry mutterings." On this evening, Kessler reports, Berlin was in a festive mood.

SA and SS groups and uniformed Stahlhelm members are roaming the streets. Spectators pack the sidewalks. In and around the Kaiserhof an outright carnival is under way. Uniformed SS troops formed lanes in front of the main entrance and in the lobby. The SA and SS were patrolling the corridors.[51]

On this January 30, Ufa's management formally delivered to the Council of the German Film Industry a document that called for a rule of power in film politics (up to then management had treated this as a secret, company-internal document with the working title "Spio Plan").

The next day Ludwig Klitzsch read aloud in the management meeting "a letter addressed to Privy Councillor Dr. Hugenberg, in which Ufa's management expressed its congratulations on the occasion of his appointment [by Hitler] as Minister of Food and Commerce. . . . Management gave its unanimous approval to the content and form of the letter."[52]

Routine decisions followed. Those days, the most dramatic and fateful in recent German history, were workdays like any others for Ufa's exalted senior managers. These gentlemen had done their part to pave the way for these events, and now, content with how things were going, they could get on with the order of the day.

Part
Two

17.

Rituals of Death: The Year 1933

UFA'S first gift to the new regime was *Dawn*, and the "Führer" and Chancellor received it in person three days after he assumed power. For the premiere of this film by Gustav Ucicky on February 2, 1933, Adolf Hitler and his closest colleagues reserved the first balcony of the Ufa-Palast am Zoo; Hitler saw to it that he was flanked there by two bourgeois, conservative members of his cabinet, Franz von Papen and Alfred Hugenberg. Two days later, Goebbels noted in his diary that the film's central message was: "We Germans may not know how to live, but we have a real talent for dying."[1] *Dawn*, Ufa's calling card to the new regime, with its brooding, violent mysticism of death, sounded a German leitmotif and touched on a basic element in National Socialist psychology.

Gerhard Menzel, a playwright who had begun working with Ufa in 1932, in writing the screenplay turned a national trauma into a heroic experience. For conservatives, the lost U-boat war of 1917–18 still weighed heavily, and *Dawn* indulged their lust for revenge as well as that fatalism which stares at a death-ridden history, eyes dimmed with patriotic tears. "Once again they sail against England. The flag of war flutters proudly in the wind, for Germany will live, even if we must die!" Thus the *Illustrierte Film-Kurier* summed up the message.[2]

Ufa had made the film in 1932 with Günther Stapenhorst in charge of production and a cast of Rudolf Forster (as Lieutenant Commander Liers), Adele Sandrock, Fritz Genschow, and Camilla Spira. Herlth and Röhrig made the sets; Carl Hoffmann was cameraman. No one could have foreseen, when the film was in production, that its premiere would coincide with the political victory of the ideology it espoused. Ucicky, a clever but not very original director, had helped to build up Ufa's stock of "fatherland" films; with *Dawn* that repertoire achieved its high point at just the right moment. Ucicky and Menzel went on to make National Socialist propaganda films until the end of the war and continued their collaboration after 1945.

Dawn was dedicated to the memory of 6,000 sailors and 199 German U-boats that had gone down in action. "Maybe death is life's only event," Lieutenant Commander Liers remarks philosophically. The old folksong about dawn lighting the way to an early death was the musical backdrop for the destructive romanticism of this film. From the beginning the National Socialist movement had been adept at spectacular "propaganda with the aid of a corpse," as Kessler put it. And Ufa, from its first premiere after Hitler's seizure of power, gave the movement's sinister death cult its cues.

Goebbels himself staged numerous heroes' funerals in the weeks before January 30. "The Hitler youth Wagnitz was carried to his grave, with so many Berliners paying their last respects that he might have been a king," he wrote in his diary (later edited for propaganda purposes). An "infinitely long procession" wound its way to the cemetery through "endless walls of mourners" to lay the murdered lad to rest "in the maternal womb of the earth." "A fantastic picture in the gray evening mist of the city."[3]

The National Socialists soon expanded these memorial marches and services for the dead into "Good Friday spectaculars . . . in which, as has been said of Richard Wagner's music, the splendor is an advertisement for death," as Joachim Fest has written.[4] Advertising for death or propaganda with a corpse was not the only element in National Socialist mass gatherings, but it was a major one, and the modern mass media helped to transmit these events to a wider audience. What tens of thousands experienced in person was multiplied for the eyes and ears of millions of moviegoers and radio listeners.

Film premieres became rites for the dead. On September 12, 1933, Reich youth leader Baldur von Schirach stepped in front of the curtain in Munich's Ufa-Palast and addressed the party elite gathered in the loge. He wrote later:

> It was the time of the worst terror. At a general muster of the Berlin Hitler Youth, I stood before two thousand Hitler youths and spoke to them of sacrifice, the Führer, and heroism. An oppressive atmosphere hung over this gathering. We sensed that something dreadful would happen. . . . The next morning the Hitler youth Herbert Norkus died at the hands of a Marxist murderer.[5]

The hall lights went out; muffled drumbeats sounded; and the curtain went up on the film *Hitlerjunge Quex* (*Hitler Youth Quex*), Ufa's first official tribute to Fascist funereal pomp.

In a letter to Ernst Hugo Correll, Goebbels thanked everyone involved in the film—the director Hans Steinhoff and the performers Heinrich George, Berta Drews, Claus Clausen, and Rotraut Richter—noting that they "had distinguished themselves in the artistic presentation of National

Socialist ideas."[6] Once again, Germany's most important film company was indisputably avant-garde.

This event was preceded by months of uncertainty, and of tactical jockeying and maneuvering in the newly formed Ministry for National Education and Propaganda and in the film industry, where overly zealous opportunists made several embarrassing efforts to beat the Fascist martyrologists at their own game. A few weeks before Hitler's takeover of power Bavarian-Film paid its respects to the new regime with *SA-Mann Brand*, a glorification of the "unknown soldiers" who had fought for the Nazi cause. The direction was entrusted to Franz Seitz, an old hand at turning out Grade-B movies, and even the NS newspaper *Der Angriff* took an extremely dim view of the results; Oskar Kalbus said later that the movie "bordered on opportunistic kitsch," that goodwill had succeeded in producing only "sentimentality and fake art."[7] The Horst Wessel film *Hans Westmar* met with harsh rejection, too. Directed by Franz Wenzler, based on the Wessel book by Hanns Heinz Ewers, and produced by Volksdeutsche Film, a company formed just to make this movie, *Hans Westmar* was even banned by the censors on the grounds that it did justice "neither to the figure of Horst Wessel nor to the National Socialist movement as the embodiment of the state."[8] Goebbels was professionally sensitive to the damage that cultural "bandwagoneers" could do to his cause, and in early April he issued a statement "against the rapid spread of national kitsch. . . . The movement does not deserve to be trivialized at the greasy hands of low-down profiteers." Or as he put it on another occasion, National Socialism did not "by any means license artistic incompetence."[9]

On March 14, Goebbels, who up to this time had been Gauleiter for Berlin, was sworn in by President Hindenburg as Minister for National Education and Propaganda, and the very next day he noted the difficulties he was having in "defining the jurisdiction of my department in relation to other already existing ministries," though he added reassuringly that "we Nazis always work things out quickly because we bring sound common sense to questions like this."[10] In the coming years internal rivalries in the party and behind-the-scenes struggles for power obliged common sense to take a back seat time and again. The new Ministry was organized into departments for the press, film, radio, and theater. The director of the film department was Ministerial Councillor Ernst Seeger, who had been general counsel for the Office of Photography and Film at the end of World War I; in the Weimar Republic he had made a name for himself as the highest-ranking film censor in the Ministry of the Interior. Eberhard Fangauf, who had worked in Ufa's cultural-film division and been an NSDAP member since 1931, headed the office for film technology and reporting in Seeger's department. In the summer of 1933, he oversaw the technical organization for Leni Riefenstahl's party-convention film *Der Sieg des Glaubens* (*The Victory of Faith*).

Even before he took office, Goebbels had made it clear that the new government would brook no resistance in its usurpation of the mass media. When an act of Communist sabotage kept the radio station in Stuttgart from broadcasting one of Hitler's speeches, Goebbels left no one in doubt.

> Because we could not fly back that night, I had the responsible people from the radio station come to the hotel, and I read them a riot act the likes of which they had never dreamed of in their worst nightmares. The next day a telegram relieved two of them of their offices. The third will presumably have learned not to sabotage us again. Word that a revolution is in progress does not seem to have gotten around yet in Germany.[11]

Goebbels adopted somewhat more cautious tactics when on March 28 he invited prominent people in the film business to a first meeting in the banquet hall of Berlin's Kaiserhof Hotel. (The Kaiserhof had hosted the preparatory meetings for Ludwig Klitzsch's Deutsche Lichtbild-Gesellschaft in 1916, as well as those for Tobis during the sound-film wars of 1928. In the election campaign of 1932, it had served as a kind of Führer head-quarters.) According to Curt Riess's imaginatively embellished description of the event,[12] the banquet hall was full to overflowing a half hour before Goebbels appeared, many of the invited guests in SA or SS uniforms. The most eminent actors—Hans Albers, Willy Fritsch, Conrad Veidt, and Emil Jannings—put in an appearance. A group of particularly zealous boosters of the new regime expressed outrage at the presence of Jewish actresses like Grete Mosheim and Lucie Mannheim. Goebbels arrived punctually, accompanied by Prince Wilhelm August of Prussia and the infamous SA leader and later police chief of Berlin Count Wolf Heinrich Helldorf. The producer and director Carl Froelich gave a little speech, noteworthy for its lack of political clarity, and then Ludwig Klitzsch spoke with what Riess found to be good sense, seriousness, and even a certain courage. He spoke of "rumormongering," obviously meaning the government's campaign then being initiated against Jews living in Germany, and he criticized political "bandwagoneers" (which only proved how empathic he was, for a few days later Goebbels adopted the term for zealous opportunists in the cultural sector).

Goebbels was conciliatory and seemed on the whole to confirm those who did not fear the new government would restrict artistic freedom. The National Socialist state, he said, had no intention "of forcing artistic and intellectual activity into uniform or into any pattern." On the contrary, "Art is free, and art should remain free." It must, of course, regard itself as subject to norms of morality and political philosophy "without which a national community is impossible," and the state would take a regulatory hand if those norms were overstepped. Goebbels obviously saw no contra-diction in an art that was both free and subject to regulation dictated by norms of morality and political philosophy, for he went on to say: "Do not think we consider it our task to make your lives miserable. The young men now in the government are extremely well disposed toward Germany's film artists." But he also made one thing perfectly clear: "We have arrived. . . . What is will remain. We shall not leave."[13]

Goebbels did not permit himself any anti-Semitic invective in this speech. No doubt he realized that this issue was the touchstone by which Ufa's politically undecided or disinterested artists would test the regime's moral trustworthiness. Indeed, he astonished everyone when, in a digression, he cited several early film masterpieces that were shaped or produced by Jewish artists and were anything but models of National Socialist thinking. Eisenstein's *Potemkin*, for example, was "so well made that it could make a Bolshevist of anyone without a firm philosophical footing." He also named Irving Thalberg's production of *Anna Karenina*, with Greta Garbo (directed by Edmund Goulding, 1927); Fritz Lang's *The Nibelungs*; and *Der Rebell* (*The Rebel*, directed by Luis Trenker and Kurt Bernhardt and produced for Deutsche Universal-Film by Paul Kohner, 1932). This was connoisseurship and sound aesthetic judgment; he showed enthusiasm for the medium; he proclaimed that tendentious art could also be great art.

The anti-Semitic indoctrination of film managers was done privately and in conversations. Ludwig Klitzsch probably thought, as Hugenberg and the German National leadership did, that Hitler would be in power for only a few months at most and would make way for traditional conservatives. In any case, there was no returning to democracy for either Klitzsch or Hugenberg: "On the one wing, the National Socialist Party and, on the other, the genuine right, the Black-White-Red front. Separate marching routes, but an agreed-upon common goal"[14]—this was Hugenberg's watchword before the elections of March 5, which brought the governing coalition 51.9 percent of the vote only through the use of widespread government terror. In April, after passage of the Enabling Act that gave the government dictatorial powers and the Civil Service Law that required the retirement of "non-Aryans," Hugenberg went about "cleansing" his departments. Jewish and Social Democratic officials were the major victims.

Whether or not Klitzsch had any personal scruples concerning his Jewish colleagues, he was fully aware that a significant portion of Ufa's artistic potential and several of its key supporters were in jeopardy. A day before the meeting in the Kaiserhof, Goebbels had drafted an appeal calling for the boycott of all Jewish businesses in Germany. "The Jewish press whined with fear and dismay," he noted in his diary.[15] On March 28 the appeal was published, and by that evening at the latest, Klitzsch must have understood that the National Socialists were determined to let actions follow on their words. Hans Barkhausen (who was employed in Ufa's theater management at the time) reports that Goebbels and Ufa chief Klitzsch met after the Kaiserhof meeting, and that Klitzsch "derived no pleasure" from the conversation.[16] Notwithstanding, the guillotine-like precision with which Ufa's management set about the anti-Semitic "cleansing" of the company the very next day is staggering. The blacklists must have been prepared in advance.

The only item of business on the agenda for Ufa's management on February 3 had been this decree:

> Contact with the government will be Mr. Klitzsch's exclusive province. If individual members of management have the need or desire to be in touch with the government, they will notify Mr. Klitzsch in advance. Mr. Klitzsch also requests notification of any ties or obligations of a social nature for whatever reason with members of the national government or the Prussian government.[17]

In these days of uncertainty, the chief was determined not to lose control of communications with the new regime. And on March 7 management gave detailed attention to the question of the "national film" and to related production proposals for 1933–34. They rejected Bismarck as a subject "because of too great a historical proximity to that era." In a proposal about Prince Louis Ferdinand and the Wars of Liberation against Napoleon, they saw a tie to "Germany's current awakening" but feared that a Prussian theme might be regarded as outdated. A film about Prince Eugene of Savoy, they thought, might stir interest in the Führer principle and the "warding off of the Bolshevist threat." An idea for a movie about colonialism was discussed at length, something showing "how enterprising German youth, backed up by a mighty nation with 500,000 bayonets and a powerful fleet, opened up *Lebensraum* and new possibilities of life in the larger world." The subject carried with it advocacy of an idea "that is innovative and farsighted."[18] (If one recalls that it was the colonial issue that prompted the National Socialists to force Hugenberg out of Hitler's cabinet a few months later, this discussion has a special irony.)

The minutes of March 29, the day after the Kaiserhof meeting, begin with a management decision to make a cultural movie about Germany, "because the theatergoing public will soon be especially eager for films of a purely German character." The next resolutions were recorded on separate pages marked "Confidential." This key passage appeared under point 5 on the agenda:

> As a result of the national revolution taking place in Germany, the question of continuing the employment of Jewish staff members in Ufa has become pressing. It will henceforth be our policy, where possible, to terminate contracts with Jewish employees. Further, we shall take immediate steps to terminate the contracts of individuals affected by this policy. Every vice president will decide which employees in his department are to be discharged immediately and which are to be separated from service in Ufa by means of a gradual reduction in force. Cases in which hardship can be demonstrated are to be handled with consideration. Salary

payments after notice of termination are to be discussed with Mr. Klitzsch.[19]

Then, in a military manner and in inimitable bureaucratese, twenty-seven individual cases were taken care of. Within an hour and recording the actions on only a few sheets of paper, Ufa's managers divested the company of many of its best directors, actors, producers, composers, authors, and technical specialists. And they did not stop there: in light of the "national revolution," personnel changes would be unavoidable in its offices and reception rooms, too.

Erik Charell, director of the hit *The Congress Dances*, was at the top of the list. A contract already signed with him for a film about Odysseus had to be "immediately brought to termination . . . not only because Charell's personality would impede the production of the film but also and primarily because marketing the film would meet with considerable resistance from the national German public." The company attorneys, Donner and Boehmer, were told to terminate the contracts.

The contracts with Charell's screenplay collaborators, Franz Schulz and Robert Adolf Stemmle, were broken, too, "in view of the altered circumstances." Schulz had worked on the scripts of many successes like *The Three from the Filling Station* and *Monte Carlo Madness*. Stemmle, who had begun as an assistant director under Charell and Ludwig Berger, was regarded after his work on Trenker's *The Rebel* as an up-and-coming writer, though he had called attention to himself back in 1929 with texts smacking of social criticism. Yet despite these issues, Stemmle was to work for Ufa again as a director starting in 1936; and in *Mann für Mann* (*Man for Man*, 1939) and *Jungens* (*Boys*, 1941) he made National Socialist propaganda films that offered, along with the officially required party line, some keen observations of the working-class milieu in the Nazi state.

The Ufa chiefs' next decision affected Germany's most important film producer and the mastermind of almost all the company's great successes: Erich Pommer. His contract was "to be terminated in view of the impossibility of realizing his productions under present circumstances." Ludwig Berger's *Walzerkrieg* (*War of the Waltzes*), for which the screenplay was already complete, would still be produced, but *Ljubas Zobel* (*Ljuba's Sable*) would be dropped. "Mr. Correll has been requested to take care of this matter in personal conversation with Mr. Pommer."

Erich Engel, the successful director of spirited comedies for Terra and Deutsche Universal-Film, was accused of having spoken "against employing Christians" at the Deutsches Theater; this made him "a crass Communist." The director Fritz Wendhausen had reported the alleged incident to Ufa; he was to be asked about it once again, the minutes read, and if the report was accurate, Engel's contract (for a film starring Brigitte Helm) would be canceled. The matter seems to have come to naught, for in that same year

Engel made *Inge und die Millionen* (*Inge and the Millions*), a hit movie with timely attacks on currency manipulators in the Weimar Republic.

A special arrangement was offered to Werner Richard Heymann, director of the Ufa orchestra and composer of many popular sound-film hits. The wording of this proposal is a stellar example of the perverted morality prevailing in Ufa's executive suites and in others as well:

> In view of Werner Richard Heymann's excellent character and the fact that he fought in the front lines during the war, the management of this company has decided to petition the government for his continuing employment with Ufa, considering that he has been baptized and is a member of the Protestant Church.

Heymann's reaction to this insult was to emigrate immediately.

Ufa's management made no such exceptions for the screenplay writer and dramaturge Robert Liebmann and his colleague Hans Müller, or for the sound technician Dr. Goldbaum or for the production assistant Viktor Gertler, who was discharged as a Hungarian and a Jew, or for Heymann's assistant Gerard Jacobson ("Objections to collaboration with Werner Richard Heymann in his private employ will not be raised"). Ufa's management also decided not to renew Ludwig Berger's contract once production of *War of the Waltzes* was complete. Regarding the actors Julius Falkenstein and Otto Wallburg, the minutes have this to say: "Because the government parties harbor no reservations about their personalities, nothing stands in the way of continuing their employment. However, giving them leads should be avoided."

Ufa's managers decided that Rudi Feld, for many years Ufa's press and public-relations chief, could not "be kept in the long run." It was conveyed to him that he should set himself up as an independent. Ufa was willing to guarantee him assignments for six months. Ufa's executives were less considerate with several middle- and lower-echelon employees. The studio secretary Hartmann was to be let go at the next possible opportunity. The office workers Lilienthal, Mikolajewicz, Grunewald, and Breslauer would not be fired right away, but "their gradual reduction was contemplated."[20]

Two months after the Nazis seized power, Germany's most powerful film company hastened to do the will of the new masters and with these personnel decisions precipitated Germany's second great exodus of film artists—or at least hastened it, for the exodus had already begun. Elisabeth Bergner, Conrad Veidt, Fritz Kortner, and Peter Lorre were already abroad or were preparing to go. On their heels followed the directors Hanns Schwarz, Wilhelm Thiele, and Erik Charell.

The cancellation of Charell's Odysseus project resulted in an interesting 1936 lawsuit that Ufa filed against the Zurich Theater- und Verlag Company for repayment of royalties. The German court justified its finding in favor of Ufa with this argument:

[Ufa] pointed out that as a result of a total change in the thinking and taste of the German people a film in which a non-Aryan had been involved could no longer be shown in Germany. It had been explicitly agreed that if Charell were prevented by illness, death, or similar causes from carrying out his directorial work, the film company would have the right to terminate the agreement and the Zurich Theater- und Verlag would be obliged to pay back any sums previously received. Charell's race was a sufficient cause for cancellation as defined by the terms of the agreement.[21]

Werner Richard Heymann—a convinced pacifist, a member of the revolutionary Council of Intellectual Workers since 1918, and a colleague of Johannes Becher and Walter Mehring in his earliest work as a songwriter —emigrated to Paris by way of the Saar. By 1936 he was in Hollywood, where he worked for Ernst Lubitsch, among others.[22]

Robert Liebmann and Hans Müller were not mentioned in the credits for their last Ufa film, *War of the Waltzes*. Liebmann went to Paris and for Fritz Lang and Erich Pommer wrote the screenplay for *Liliom*, based on Ferenc Molnár's play. In 1938 he collaborated with Kurt Bernhardt on two further movies; of the career and fate of this Ufa chief dramaturge and versatile screenplay writer, *Cinegraph* has only this to say: "No information on the rest of his life is available; he may have died in the 1940s."[23]

Ludwig Berger's name was omitted from the credits of *War of the Waltzes*, too. After three years of unemployment, he got a contract in Holland; he directed films later in France and England; and returned from exile in 1947. Julius Falkenstein died in Berlin in 1933. Otto Wallburg emigrated to Austria in 1934 after the arrest of his son Reinhard, then went to Paris. In 1944 he was captured by the SS in Holland and died in the gas chamber a few days after his arrival in Auschwitz.

Ufa had been too precipitous in dispensing with Erich Pommer's services. Higher powers had a lively interest in retaining Pommer's talents for the German film industry. According to Pommer's son John, the Foreign Office wooed him, but he refused to work for the new regime. Only the year before, he had been in contact with Fox, and in January 1933 he signed a contract as chief of Fox-Europa. Curt Riess claims that Klitzsch personally interceded on Pommer's behalf and even communicated with Goebbels about him; Goebbels then tried to convince Fox to locate its European branch in Berlin (as it had originally intended).[24] When this plan failed, Pommer was issued a passport with a special visa from the Ministry of Propaganda and explicit permission for him to return to Germany at any time. At the end of May officials from the Ministry personally accompanied him to the train for Paris.[25] The government's solicitousness toward Pommer wakened his suspicions, though: when he left Berlin, he sent his chauffeur ahead to Hannover with his car; he left the train there and continued to France by car.[26]

Fritz Lang's departure from Germany, too, was dramatic. His two last films in Germany, which were also his first sound films—*M—Eine Stadt sucht einen Mörder* (*M—A City Hunts a Murderer*, 1931) and *The Testament of Dr. Mabuse* (1932)—had been made not for Ufa but for Nero-Film. On March 28 he had gone to the Kaiserhof, but the next day he learned that the censors had banned his *Mabuse* film, since Goebbels reportedly thought it demonstrated "that a group of men who are determined to go to any lengths and are serious in their intentions are clearly capable of overturning any state by force."[27] A few days later Goebbels asked to see Lang, a meeting Lang later described, always with new embellishments. The minister summoned him, Lang reported, to offer on Hitler's behalf the "leading position in the German film industry." "The Führer saw your film *Metropolis* and said, 'That is the man who will give us the National Socialist film!' " For Fritz Lang, this offer was reason enough to leave Germany as quickly as possible. "The meeting with Goebbels lasted until 2:30. The banks had already closed, and I couldn't get any money. I had just enough at home to buy a ticket to Paris, and I arrived at the Gare du Nord practically penniless."[28] Lang's passport, however, shows that he visited Germany twice in the summer of 1933.

Lang feared that if he openly rejected the offer, the vengeance of the propaganda minister would catch up with him, and even in the sleeping car on the way to Paris he did not feel safe. Lotte Eisner commented later that Lang had "slightly exaggerated" the danger he felt himself to be in and had retrospectively made himself out to be "politically persecuted and a martyr of Nazism."[29] Lang left Hitler's Germany unmolested, but he immediately became *persona non grata*. Goebbels's hacks were now obliged to explain how a "half Jew" and deserter had created films like *The Niebelungs* and *Metropolis*, which Germany's highest authority had declared models for a national film culture.

March 1933 was a month of resounding parades, rallies, and mass demonstrations held under a sea of swastika-bedecked flags. The National Socialists were celebrating. Their victory celebrations after the elections of March 5 alone lasted for a full week. The high point was "Potsdam Day" on March 21, a high point, too, for the Fascist death cult in the service of demagogy. The laying of wreaths on the graves of Frederick the Great and Frederick William I demonstrated to the German people and the rest of the world that the Hitler regime adhered to the values of the Prussian tradition. Children in school followed the events on the radio, businesses closed early, and once darkness fell, torchlight parades again filled the streets. Local gymnastics clubs and rifle clubs joined with the brown-shirted SA regiments and drew their undecided or politically indifferent contemporaries into the general tumult. Two days later, when the Reichstag passed the Enabling Act, dictatorship was legally established by parliamentary vote.

"Irretrievably sunk into retrogression, the bulk of the German people could not help submitting to Hitler. Since Germany thus carried out what had been anticipated by her cinema from its very beginning, conspicuous screen characters now came true in life itself," Siegfried Kracauer has written.[30] This same majority that brought the National Socialists to power did not of course perceive or admit that a "homunculus . . . in the flesh" was at loose in Germany and "raving Mabuses" were planning unimaginable crimes, nor was it ready to encounter in political reality the monstrous criminals from Fritz Lang's films or the nightmare figures of expressionist cinema. Bruised by the Depression, worn down and stupefied by the political intrigues and violent conflicts in Weimar's final years, most Germans wanted a secure economic life, a routine, everyday existence with its safety and its predictability. Normality.

The National Socialists therefore had a dual task: on the one hand, they had to invest their measures with the aura of a unique "national revolution" and present themselves as demigods selected by Destiny and enveloped in the tragic clouds of battle; on the other, they had to assure everyone that they were the only path out of daily distress, the only guarantee of economic stability and petit-bourgeois happiness within the privacy of one's own four walls. From the outset, the new rulers pursued this double strategy; their pomp-laden mass rituals, in which they portrayed themselves as heralds of fate and death, had a place and function in that strategy, and so did "unpolitical" entertainment movies. Propaganda with a corpse and ads for contentment and a full belly were allied.

"The state is to be a comfortable stall in which all obedient domestic animals are happy with their lot and will, upon demand, go docilely to the slaughter," wrote Harry Kessler when he left Germany on March 8, 1933 —a few days after the fire that demolished the Reichstag and the mass arrests that followed it all over Germany.[31] With unemployment figures in excess of 6 million, the state was far from comfortable, but the noisy propaganda created the impression it could move mountains. Also, there was statistical success to back up its claims: by the end of the year, unemployment was down by a third.

For many years to come, the daily routine, leisure activities, and private life of most Germans remained unchanged. The vast majority never had the anxiety of the persecuted minorities, the "constant fear of the knock on the door in the wee hours of the morning," but they also enjoyed within their homes a harmony with themselves and the world that was oddly out of joint with the times. Many films of the 1930s and even 1940s set their harmless plots in either an undefined "Now" or a timeless "Then," all proclaiming the value of small joys and contentment with one's modest lot.

The world outside—the SA and SS rallies, the speeches of the "Führer" and his flunkies—reached these Germans by radio, and anyone who didn't have a radio was encouraged to get one with slogans like "Germany will march in Nuremberg! Be there yourself! Be a radio listener!" What is often described as "propaganda saturation" was actually more like a propaganda siege. Even the most private citizen was surrounded by politics, and if he realized something new was invading his life, it was the experience—the first in the history of modern civilization—that politics was reaching him through the "virtual reality" of the mass media.

The rallies were like gigantic séances, inducing hypnosis among the people mustered there in military ranks. On the evening of May 1, Hitler celebrated his triumph over Marxism and the class identity of the German workers with a million and a half people gathering at Tempelhof for "National Labor Day," in the very place that had witnessed the "atavistic strategic planning" of Wilhelmine Germany and, in the second year of the republic, that spontaneous outburst of anger from the unfed extras in Lubitsch's film. The French ambassador, André François-Poncet, who was present, thought it was like a proletarian, militaristic High Mass in honor of a demigod.

All the spotlights went out, with the exception of the ones that bathed the Führer in a brilliant circle of light, making it seem as if he were floating over the waves in a magical skiff. . . . His aura . . . is much more physical than intellectual, and it is heightened by the surroundings, the theatrical setting, the contrast of light and shadow, the whole romantic production, the flags and uniforms, the glittering helmets and bayonets. . . . In this rapt crowd there are no doubt many people who hate and mistrust this man, but even they are shaken to the core and swept along like the boatman bewitched by the Lorelei.[32]

What this foreigner's eye grasped with such precision was the romantic staging of The Nibelungs, complete with its sets and light-dark contrasts, translated into "reality." As it had in Ufa's studios in the 1920s, so here that German synthesis of technical perfection and mysticism, of romantic pathos and theatrical sophistication, of modernity and the Middle Ages celebrated a triumph. A few films in the Nazi period with the help of montage would try to equal and surpass the propaganda impact of these events, and Ufa's newsreels were brilliant. But most of the films produced in Hitler's state offered vicarious experience, an antidote against propaganda and politics, relief from intense emotion, the enjoyment of small everyday pleasures outside this real-life drama of struggle and death.

In early 1933, radio orchestras and coffeehouse bands were still playing the hits from Ufa's sound films of 1932—the march from Alfred Zeisler's comedy about bicycle racing, The Best of Plans Can Go Astray, with Heinz Rühmann: "Rolling along, rolling along / Always in time, singing life's song; / Always be happy, never be sad; / Never be grumpy and never be mad!" Or Werner Richard Heymann's music that Lilian Harvey and Willy Fritsch had sung in A *Blond Dream*, with lyrics by Walter Reisch and Billy Wilder: "Everyone can make it! / Everyone has a turn! It's all up to you / what you go out and earn!"

Of the 135 full-length German films that passed the censors in 1933, 22 were Ufa's; Ufa's distributors also handled three foreign productions.[33] As in earlier years, German landscapes attracted the loving attention of many writers and directors. Following Manfred Hausmann's novel, Erich Waschneck set *Abel mit der Mundharmonika* (*Abel with the Harmonica*) in the north German lowlands. This was the setting, too, for the first filming of Felicitas Rose's *Heideschulmeister Uwe Karsten* (*Heath Schoolmaster Uwe Karsten*, directed by Carl Heinz Wolff), in which Marianne Hoppe debuted. This movie marked the beginning of a series of classic regional films that continued unbroken until 1960.

The milieu of the operetta and of high society, of carefree artists and leisured vagabonds, continued to be a box-office draw in films like Victor Janson's *Der Zarewitsch* (*The Czarevich*, with Marta Eggerth and Hans Söhnker), Joe May's *Ein Lied für Dich* (*A Song for You*, with Jenny Jugo and the celebrated singer Jan Kiepura), and Reinhold Schünzel's *Saison in Kairo* (with Renate Müller and Willy Fritsch). Shortly before he emigrated, the composer Friedrich Holländer made his debut as a director with the premiere on February 22 of Pommer's last production *The Empress and I*. His collaborator on the music for this "historical operetta" was Franz Wachsmann, who, like Holländer, emigrated to Hollywood by way of Paris. The end of June saw the premiere of the comedy *Kind, ich freu' mich auf dein Kommen* (*Child, I Look Forward to Your Coming*, with Magda Schneider, Otto Wallburg, and Julius Falkenstein)—the last Ufa film made by the Jewish and politically leftist actor and director Kurt Gerron, who died in Auschwitz shortly before the end of the war; in the middle of shooting Gerron had to relinquish the film's direction to Erich von Neusser and leave Germany.

The detective and con-man comedies of the late 1920s remained popular in 1933, too. In *Die schönen Tage von Aranjuez* (*Happy Days in Aranjuez*, with Brigitte Helm, Gustaf Gründgens, and Wolfgang Liebeneiner) Johannes Meyer filmed a story of love and jewelry robbery in international society. *Desire*, a Paramount remake of this film directed by Frank Borzage and produced by Ernst Lubitsch, starred Marlene Dietrich in the female lead and was a worldwide success. In *Ein gewisser Herr Gran* (*A Certain Mr. Gran*, with Hans Albers in the title role) Gerhard Lamprecht took up the theme of espionage. Alfred Zeisler's *Eine Tür geht auf* (*A Door Opens*) featured a series of suspenseful bank robberies. His *Stern von Valencia* (*Star of Valencia*, starring Liane Haid and Ossi Oswalda) pulled together all the motifs of the popular detective-story genre: sensational chases in exotic settings, unscrupulous international pimps, and painstaking police work. In the first year of Nazi dictatorship, the frivolous lifestyle and flirtation with crime featured in these films were like late-blooming "swamp flowers" of the Weimar Republic, going against the times and against the sensibilities of the law-and-order types.

Toeplitz has called most of the films made in 1933 typical products of a transitional period, in which it was hard to set out in a new direction and easy to mark time. "Everything was as it had been in the good old days, as if the apostles of the 'national revolution' had not sounded their battle cries."[34] And it remained true of Ufa right up to the end of Nazi rule that the flow of subjects from "the good old days" never dried up. Even in the very last days of the war, Ufa—by then a state company—was still making films that were hardly distinguishable from 1933 productions like *Des jungen Dessauers grosse Liebe* (*Young Dessauer's Great Love*, directed by Arthur Robison) or *Viktor und Viktoria* (directed by Reinhold Schünzel). They were all "mediocre," Toeplitz says, "devoid of élan and artistic ambition." Still, these mass-produced films drew on technical and stylistic skills developed to perfection in the early Ufa years, and one has to grant to Erich Engel, Reinhold Schünzel, and Max Ophüls (who in 1932–33 made his famous film *Liebelei* [*Dalliance*], based on Schnitzler's play, for Elite Ton-film Produktion and the Rhenish comedy *Lachende Erben* [*Laughing Heirs*] for Ufa) that they injected rhythmic composition, wit, and pace into even routine subject matter and insipid stories. Many of Ufa's artists in the years ahead sought refuge in these vapid, "unpolitical" entertainments whose only virtue was their craftsmanship. Working on them, they could try to escape the pressure and ideological demands of the state, the flood of regulations and decrees, the climate of anxiety and opportunism. The easiest thing was, in fact, to mark time, to settle in for a "transition." If one knew how to play one's cards right and not call attention to oneself, one wound up marking time for twelve years. The period of transition evolved into a permanent condition.

Ufa made only two tributary offerings to the propaganda machine of the new regime in 1933—Hans Steinhoff's *Hitler Youth Quex* and Gustav Ucicky's *Flüchtlinge* (*Refugees*)—but these two set the tone for the genre. Premature panegyrics to the SA and sentimental, hastily constructed compilation films like *Blutendes Deutschland* (*Bleeding Germany*, directed by Johannes Häusler; produced by Erich Wallis for Deutscher Film-Vertrieb) were left to second-class producers and directors. And overall, the repertoire of films dealing with "serious" or modern subjects was small, even including the Blood-and-Soil *Du sollst nicht begehren* (*Thou Shalt Not Covet*, directed by Richard Schneider-Edenkoben) and Gerhardt Lamprecht's *Was wissen denn Männer* (*What Do Men Know*), which dealt with "moral issues" and won the praise of the censors.

For Ucicky's *Refugees*, the producer, Günther Stapenhorst, assembled a first-rate team. Gerhard Menzel, author of *Dawn*, wrote the screenplay;

Fritz Arno Wagner was the cameraman; Robert Herlth and Walter Röhrig supplied the sets; Herbert Windt composed the music. The editing was done by Eduard von Borsody, whose camerawork had contributed to the expressive, shocking impact of Ernö Metzner's short film *Police Report: Hold-Up* and who in coming years directed important Ufa productions such as *Kautschuk* (*Caoutchouc*, 1938) and *Wunschkonzert* (*Wish Concert*, 1940). Hans Albers played the lead as a German officer who, "embittered and disgusted by the obsequiousness of the German Republic,"[35] goes to the Far East and in the chaos of war in Manchuria helps a group of Volga Germans flee to their homeland. "This film is inspired by the 'new spirit,' " Oskar Kalbus wrote, "because it embodies the high ethical principles of self-help and leadership."[36] Representatives of the "new spirit" were duly grateful: censors rated it "of particular artistic value," and on May 1, 1934, it was the first to receive the government's new state prize for film.

A half year earlier, Alfred Hugenberg had resigned from his post in Hitler's cabinet, and the German National People's Party had disbanded. This indefatigable champion of the "national movement," master of Scherl and board chairman of Universum-Film AG, had helped to bring Hitler to power, and now he was gone from the political stage. As late as March Hugenberg had been declaring war on democratic civilization in its entirety: "The Marxist school, the democratic literary clique, the internationally engineered subversion in theater and literature, in film and in the press—all these were the intellectual forerunners of the murder and terror flourishing today."[37] In the following months, the German Nationals became the target of attacks from the still influential "left" wing of the NSDAP, and Hugenberg himself became a scapegoat. The National Socialists branded him an "arch capitalist" and protector of large landholders, and in June the Nazi leadership forced him to resign: he had attended the world economic conference in London as Germany's delegate, demanding (in keeping with his nationalistic conservatism) a German colonial empire in Africa, which made it easy to pillory him as a spokesman for an obsolete imperialism and to portray National Socialism as modern and middle-of-the-road.[38]

There was also an attempt at a National Socialist putsch within Scherl. Fritz Lucke, editor-in-chief of the *Nachtausgabe* at the time, reports that his colleague Erich Schwarzer, wearing the uniform of an SS colonel, went into Ludwig Klitzsch's office and demanded that Klitzsch resign: the company had to be handed over to him, Schwarzer, representative of the new order.[39]

Hugenberg had clearly underestimated the political power of NSDAP adherents in his own empire, the extent to which the Propaganda Ministry would go to consolidate its power, and competition from the National Socialist press. Still, he remained until September 1944 the owner of a major newspaper concern completely under the control of the government, and until 1937 he retained the majority of stock in Ufa. But the political capital that the company had amassed before 1933 was lost. In 1931, Ufa dividends had played no small part in financing the election campaigns of the German National People's Party; about a million marks from the profits that Hans Albers, Willy Fritsch, and Lilian Harvey had brought in found their way into Hugenberg's campaign treasure chest.[40] Now he had to give up his political ambitions. Ufa remained in his control, but others were issuing the political orders in Neubabelsberg.

18.

Converting Ufa into a
State-Controlled Company

THE National Socialist government's first measures for subjugating and centralizing Germany's film industry were remarkably uncertain as to cultural policy and economic planning, and squabbles and struggles for power continued within the industry. The founding of the Film Credit Bank and of the Reichsfilmkammer (Reich Film Guild) in the summer of 1933 ended this phase; a new alliance of the state, bank capital, and the film business not only realized Ludendorff's original vision of Ufa in 1917 but also, with disastrous consequences, exceeded it.

What Goebbels called "alignment" with National Socialist goals wound up destroying the "aligned" systems. The extensive literature on this subject rightly describes the measures the Nazi state took as a strategy of total political and ideological control over the entire film business. But the question of how successful this strategy was has been neglected.

On February 18, 1933, Ufa's management announced its views on the economic and structural reorganization of Germany's film industry. Word of this impending Spio Plan had reached everyone, and fear of it was widespread, notably in the RdL (Reichsverband der deutschen Lichtspieltheaterbesitzer), the National Association of German Motion Picture Theater Owners, whose essentially middle-class members felt threatened by the big companies. However, the RdL's conservative but as yet "unaligned" leaders had a new opponent among their own ranks. A group of National Socialist theater owners in the RdL, led by party members Adolf Engl and Oswald Johnsen, were indulging in a radical, antimonopolistic rhetoric that had nothing good to say about Spio or Ufa. This moved the RdL leaders to side with Spio and its chairman, Klitzsch, who was still hoping to cooperate with Hugenberg's Ministry of Commerce.

Johnsen, meanwhile, was calling for the dissolution of Ufa and the other big companies. His argument blended pseudo-socialistic radicalism with crass anti-Semitism. In 1931 a study devoted to the "solution of the film problem from a National Socialist perspective" had claimed that cinemas, the great majority of which were supposedly under "German" management, were being "exploited" by Jewish producers and distributors; Spio, the major film companies, and even Ufa were "infiltrated by Jews," though in Ufa's case "at least management was in German hands," which did not help much, since "through its ties to foreign concerns" it was "heavily influenced by the Jewish element."[1]

The Third Reich's Ministry for National Education and Propaganda foiled the strategies on both sides. The companies' call for centralized government direction was heeded, but the reins were put in Goebbels's hands, not in those of the Ministry of Commerce controlled by the German National People's Party. And although Adolf Engl acquired control of the RdL only a few days after Goebbels was appointed to his Ministry, he never had a chance to put the "Führer principle" to work there. His anti-monopolistic rhetoric was already obsolete: Goebbels's Propaganda Ministry was on the verge of adopting a modified form of the Spio Plan.

In the National Socialist camp, Goebbels had won the upper hand against the National Socialist Workers' Cell Organization (Nationalsozialistische Betriebszellenorganisation [NSBO]) and Alfred Rosenberg's Front for German Culture, both of which wanted to force all "filmmakers" into their ranks, a prospect that filled almost everyone involved with horror. On the other hand, the new Propaganda Ministry had hardly won the confidence of film-industry leaders, though rivalry among the various National Socialist organizations sapped confidence in NSDAP film policy. On March 14, *Der Kinematograph*, the organ of Ufa and Spio published by Scherl, voiced reservations about a policy calling for state economic control and central control of production planning. By late April Goebbels felt obliged to set forth the basic principles himself during a visit to Neubabelsberg. "Reports of discouragement and pessimism" had reached his ears, he said, and there appeared to be a mood of uncertainty among filmmakers. He assured his listeners he was the "last person who wanted to let the German film die," for the art of film was dear to his heart, and he would do everything he could to promote its well-being. Still, the film industry would have to fulfill its primary task and be a "champion of national culture" instead of engaging in "menial chores" and pandering to pernicious trends of the times. "Alignment" with National Socialist goals, he made clear, was a non-negotiable requirement.[2]

Goebbels was even more forthright on May 19 at a meeting of the NSBO in Berlin-Wilmersdorf. In this "second film talk" he objected to the efforts in his own party to undermine his power, and he cast himself as the "protector" of film. "Interfering in the creative process with crude measures destroys not only the economic base but, more important, art itself, which is much more sensitive, spiritual, and sublime"; once again he attacked "social kitsch" and "bad art." But he left no doubt that his Ministry would exercise total control over the entire film industry, for which he held out the prospect of "an ambitiously conceived plan" for "revitalization."[3]

The establishment of the Film Credit Bank at the end of May produced what one historian has called a "new version of that alliance between the film industry, major banks, and representatives of the state"[4] that had put its stamp on Germany's film development with the founding of Ufa in 1917. As late as 1938, a student of the subject would claim that the Film Credit Bank was intended to strengthen mid-sized enterprises and was "particularly welcome among capital-poor producers."[5] But it was obvious in 1933 that the bank would promote the interests of the few powerful companies, accelerate concentration in the industry, and ultimately destroy the remaining smaller concerns. The Credit Bank's backing made it perfectly clear which interests were represented and how deeply they were involved: the German Bank, the Dresden Bank, and the Commercial and Private Bank together contributed 60,000 marks; the government's Reichskredit-Gesellschaft gave 20,000 marks; and the lion's share of 120,000 marks came via Klitzsch, ostensibly as a Spio representative but for all practical purposes on Ufa's behalf. The banks also pledged loans to the tune of 10 million marks. Their interests as well as those of Spio were soon conveyed to the new Reich Film Board.

The Film Credit Bank's board of directors expressed these shared interests of state, bank capital, and Ufa. The Propaganda Ministry was represented by undersecretary Walter Funk and the director of the film division, Arnold Raether. Among the bank directors was a holdover from 1917, a cofounder of Ludendorff's and Stauss's Ufa and still a member of its board: Johannes Kiehl of the German Bank. That the film business would send Klitzsch as its representative was a foregone conclusion. I. G. Farben, founded in 1925 and Germany's largest business enterprise, the one that would prove key to the "revitalization" of the arms industry, assured itself of influence at the Film Credit Bank through an Agfa representative. Thus, the old and the new guards of German capital were assembled under one National Socialist roof.

In exchange for promissory notes from production firms and acceptances from distributors, Goebbels's Film Bank provided up to 70 percent (later 50 percent) of any movie's production costs; to cover the loans, all the income from rentals had to go back to the bank. For 49 of the 121 films made in 1934, loans totaling more than 7.5 million marks were granted against total production costs of just under 15.3 million; in 1935, the loans climbed to 15.7 million and covered more than 60 percent of the total production costs.[6]

The numbers would suggest a sound financing system and a successful economic revitalization of Germany's film production. But they reveal nothing, of course, about the political and cultural costs. Credit was granted only to producers and distributors who belonged to the Council of the

German Film Industry and who were willing to submit to pre-production censorship. At first, a working committee of the Film Credit Bank made up, among others, of Klitzsch and the Propaganda Ministry representative, Arnold Raether, judged whether screenplays were politically acceptable and worthy of credit. Later, this task was taken over by a specially constituted Dramaturgical Office.

Preliminary political censorship did not conflict with the interests of Germany's essentially conservative film industry, which in part at least voluntarily aligned itself with the new regime. A production based on an approved screenplay and blessed with a loan was virtually insured against a censors' ban or demands for cuts and the financial loss that either would entail. The whole concept of the Film Credit Bank was in keeping with the ideas Ufa's management had proposed before 1933 in its Spio Plan, and when the Reich legislature reduced the entertainment tax from 10.5 to 8 percent in June 1933, the big film companies interpreted the move as further evidence that the National Socialists were serious about helping the business.

For Ufa and the entire film industry, the uncertain early months of 1933 had brought financial losses, though Ufa and Tobis managed to stay in the black. The report for fiscal year 1932–33 submitted to Ufa's executive committee in October[7] deviated only slightly from that of the previous year and showed a surplus of 28 million marks. But the net profit amounted to only 40,000 marks, and the board, once again chaired by Stauss, did not recommend a dividend distribution at the stockholders' meeting. "Economic and political developments at home and abroad as well as the total restructuring of the German film industry" had resulted in "unforeseen deficits."

These negative points were not discussed in detail at the stockholders' meeting, but the tenor with which they were recorded in internal working papers is noteworthy. Regarding the production balance sheet, management pointed out that early in 1933 two major projects of Pommer's, *Odysseus' Heimkehr* (*The Return of Odysseus*) and *Ljuba's Sable,* had to be canceled at a very late date. "The resistance against Erik Charell, Erich Pommer, and a number of actors and script writers forced us to drop both subjects from the production program." With other films, "the general uncertainty about the presentation of material" made major changes and postponements necessary, for which reasons Ufa had been unable to hold to its studio schedules, and the problem was compounded by the fact that many of the production companies Ufa had commissioned to make films "had relocated abroad"; management estimated the loss "from these unexpected interruptions in productivity" at at least 500,000 marks. Domestic distribution showed a loss of 400,000–600,000 marks. The theater business had suffered from a "lack of films with box-office appeal." And management also mentioned a much discussed disaster: Fritz Lang's "exceptionally profitable" film *The Testament of Dr. Mabuse* had been banned outright. A boycott of German films abroad had drastically reduced export business, too. Taken together, the losses had resulted in a balance that was 2.5 million marks below that anticipated. Management found one item in the loss column especially painful: "Settlements paid to discharged Jewish employees and the loss of productivity involved with those personnel changes alone accounted for expenses of 250,000 marks."

It would be wrong to conclude from this that Ufa's management or board was at odds with National Socialist film policy or with the measures taken by the Propaganda Ministry. On all fundamental matters government and film industry were in agreement. With the Film Credit Bank the government had shown that "national film art"—in other words, the well-being of the big companies—was close to its heart, and Ufa had quickly submitted to the regime. Nonetheless, this paper reveals Ufa's obvious dissatisfaction with the immediate consequences of the National Socialist measures. The loss of foreign business was especially disturbing. A few days before the stockholders' meeting on November 27, a letter from Ufa's managers to Stauss made this clear. The foreign boycott of German films had intensified after Germany's withdrawal from the League of Nations and was making itself felt everywhere in Europe except France, Germany's major export market.[8] So the mood in Ufa's executive offices was mixed. The dissatisfaction Ufa's managers felt derived, essentially, from a contradiction inherent in National Socialist film policy. On the one hand, all the regulations played into the hands of the big companies; on the other, a June order of Hitler's empowered him to assume centralized responsibility "for all aspects of intellectual activity affecting the nation,"[9] which took economic matters out of the companies' hands and placed them with the government.

> This raises the question whether the structure chosen by the National Socialists—keeping the individual firms' independence yet having a state-directed stabilization of the entire system—could produce results or whether it did not contain within itself the germ of another financial crisis such as the capitalistic lust for profit had brought about in the past.[10]

In addition to the foreign boycott, the policy of autarky that the Hitler regime adopted to demonstrate Germany's strength reduced the movies' export opportunities and threatened to sever a vital nerve. Moreover, foreign interest in the German market declined. Cut off from foreign impulses and ideas and prevented from submitting its products to international competition, German filmmakers had to retreat into an economic, intellectual, and aesthetic monoculture, which was of course destructive to their work. Cultural isolation brought with it a decline in quality, and Ufa's production teams, which had previously set industry standards, were acutely aware of this. In a report to management in mid-1934, the production department complained about the chronic lack of capable personnel that the mass firings and the isolation from foreign countries caused. "We lack writers and directors. There has not been enough time for younger writers to develop to the point where they can write usable screenplays. It will probably take several years. Talented directors have not emerged either." For 1934's total production of about 120 films, only nine good directors were available: Willi Forst, Karl Hartl, Gustav Ucicky, Reinhold Schünzel, Luis Trenker, Gerhard Lamprecht, Carl Froelich, Arthur Robison, and Erich Waschneck. "Each of these, working carefully, can make only two films a year. Trenker ordinarily makes only one." This meant that at best only twenty or twenty-five good films could be produced. "The rest are average and in most cases even worse."[11]

The exodus of well-known film artists led to a cutting back whose economic consequences showed in industry figures as early as 1935. Total production sank from 129 films in 1934 to 92, while production costs increased to about 400,000 marks per film.[12] The few remaining companies began fighting over the few good performers and directors left in Germany. Ufa and Tobis, Terra and Bavaria kept outbidding each other with offers of salaries, honoraria, and long-term contracts, even though the Spio Plan had called for drastic reductions in star salaries. Ufa, economically the most powerful company, led the way in driving personnel costs out of sight: by the end of March 1933, it renewed its contract with Willy Fritsch, meeting his request for 18,000 marks per month; a few days later, Hans Albers contracted to make three new films for a total of 210,000 marks.[13] In the coming years, actors' salaries of 200,000 marks and more per film became frequent.

After the exile of Jewish or politically undesirable colleagues, Germany's top artists now found themselves in an extremely privileged situation. A propaganda minister who was a movie fan and proclaimed his "great devotion" to art wooed them with generous offers and dangled promising prospects of large financial rewards and significant social privileges. Most of the people working in movies did not perceive the Reich Film Guild's system of forced organization as a political imposition at all. On the contrary, they felt ennobled, as it were, and flattered to be accepted into the artistic elite. Public honors and invitations gave many a star the sense of being not only an idol of the masses but also a member of a cultural legion of honor. When the government appealed to "creators of culture" for cooperation, most of them saw that as recognition of their achievements. Their privileges induced them "to go about their work with greater demands and reduced team spirit," one newspaper noted in 1936.[14] But then a close connection developed between adherence to the party line, amount of salary, and wasteful extravagance. Highly paid and pampered stars instigated "time-consuming and expensive debates over manuscripts and direction" or insisted on replacing directors, sometimes even in the midst of production. The extent of the corruption is evident in a contract that Ufa's management signed in the fall of 1934 for four films by Gustav Ucicky, guaranteeing him 50,000 marks a film and the following terms: "Within six weeks of the completion of each film, Ufa must commission the next film; if the Reich film dramaturge does not approve the subject matter or substitute subjects, the honorarium will nonetheless be paid within six months of the day on which Ucicky receives the commission."[15]

The salaries paid to actors and actresses also drove up the salaries for technical personnel; together with the increased fees for studio rental, extravagant sets, and expensive outdoor shots, this made for spiraling costs that industry observers noted with dismay. Ufa—after the fall of 1933 again under Hugenberg's leadership—had to defend itself against repeated attacks on its business practices, production costs, and salary policy. When Reich Film Guild president Fritz Scheuermann pressed this criticism too far and raised doubts about Goebbels's relations with the big companies, he was fired; his successor was the Württemberg minister Oswald Lehnich.

That Goebbels was well disposed toward Ufa helped the company weather some political scrapes. A particularly grotesque one began on October 21, 1933, when Richard Walther Darré, Hugenberg's successor in the Ministry of Food and a bitter enemy of Goebbels, put Ufa vice president Paul Lehmann into a panic with an early-morning telephone call. The enraged Darré "declared war [on Ufa] on behalf of the entire agrarian community."[16]

This was all about a film Ufa had just completed, the Blood-and-Soil drama *Thou Shalt Not Covet*, written and directed by the National Socialist writer Richard Schneider-Edenkoben. At the end of October, a day before its premiere, the *Deutsche Zeitung* published an article by one Alfred Mühr entitled "Background of a Film" that charged Ufa with "opportunism" on the grounds that the actor Walter Griep displayed physiognomic similarities to the Reichstag arsonist Marinus van der Lubbe standing trial in Leipzig at that very moment.

Ufa's managers understandably scoffed at the notion that in March they had hired an actor supposedly resembling a person who did not come into the public eye until October; to their relief, the leading National Socialist papers, *Der Angriff* and the *Völkischer Beobachter*, gave neutral reviews to the film. But despite this, the Agrarian-Political Office of the Greater Berlin District of the NSDAP forbade its members to see the movie, and Minister Darré continued his campaign in early November with a pugnacious article, "Marinus and the Soil," published in the *Nationalsozialistische Landpost*. Willi Krause jumped into the fray and in an article in *Der Angriff* launched a sharp attack on self-appointed defenders of "blood and soil." When the *Vossische Zeitung* sided with Darré and his farmers, Ufa instantly cut off its advertising with Ullstein.

The press campaign against Ufa continued until the end of November, and when Ufa's opponents even began attacking films from past years, Klitzsch himself wrote a personal letter to Goebbels calling attention to the increasing burdensomeness of this "Peasants' War." Darré's attacks, Klitzsch wrote, "have unfortunately shown us all too clearly that Ufa will have to reckon with significant interference in the future." Klitzsch gave Goebbels figures showing that Ufa spent 16 million marks a year making movies—two-thirds of Germany's total film-production capital. If Darré's campaign should continue, this capital would "in the foreseeable future suffer considerable reduction because of the losses that can surely be expected." Klitzsch estimated the losses already incurred in the "battle with Minister Darré" at 300,000 marks; he may have exaggerated. The company files contain no response from Goebbels, but Klitzsch's complaint probably sufficed to end the efforts of the "agrarian community" against Ufa.

Measured in terms of its declared goal of economic "revitalization," the National Socialist restructuring of the film industry failed. By the mid-1930s, mid-sized film companies had virtually disappeared, and in the big companies, rising costs, in large part self-inflicted, went on upsetting the balance sheets. Exports, a vital factor for the entire movie business before 1933, had shrunk to insignificance and contributed practically nothing to amortizing costs. In early 1937 a film newspaper spoke openly of rising costs as a "threat to the entire German film industry."[17] Movie attendance began to rise in 1933, however, and by 1936–37 it had again reached the high point of 1927–28. But in that same year production costs had grown out of all proportion and the latent financial crisis was now real and acute. At the first annual convention of the Reich Film Board in March 1937, Ludwig Klitzsch and Ferdinand Bausback, now board chairman of Tobis, estimated overall losses in the German film industry for the previous year at 10–15 million marks.[19]

In the meantime, Ufa was left as the only vertically organized concern continuing to operate in all facets of its business as at its founding. With 110 theaters, it dominated Germany's large urban market and premiere showings. By 1936 it had complete control of Berlin's cinema neighborhood near the Kaiser Wilhelm Memorial Church. Ufa, Tobis, and Terra shared the distribution business, and a few small organizations had a share in only a few regional markets. Sixty percent of film production was concentrated in Ufa and Tobis (Terra and Bavaria each accounted for 10 percent).

Only the capital resources of the big firms could meet the Propaganda Ministry's demands for "major national film," but their spiraling expenses were forcing them into difficulties beyond their powers to resolve. Between 1919, the first year of sound film, and 1937, average production costs for a feature film doubled from 275,000 to 537,000 marks. At the end of fiscal year 1936–37 Tobis booked losses of nearly 5 million marks and was on the verge of bankruptcy; only secretly arranged state loans saved it from collapse. Ever since 1935, the German government, through several front companies, had been buying up most of Tobis's stock from its Dutch owners, and now the company was ripe for government takeover, foreshadowing the path that Ufa and the others would take under National Socialist rule.

19.

The Censorship Machine:
Ufa and the Reich Film Guild

THE Reich Film Guild was the end result of a development originating with Hugenberg's planning staff before 1933, and it revealed the same lust for power on Ufa's part that was manifest in the Spio Plan. The Spio Commission, chaired by Ludwig Klitzsch, saw as its primary job the transformation of Spio into a compulsory organization: producers, distributors, or theater owners who refused to join would face the threat of not being allowed to work. The Act on the Establishment of a Temporary Film Guild of July 1933 helped to make Spio a guildlike state organization subject to government control. "Everyone in the industry—from the biggest entrepreneur and the top manager down to the lowliest technician, from the star actors and directors down to the last extra—was forced to join."[1]

The Film Guild Act suited Goebbels's totalitarian vision perfectly. It allowed for the rejection of an applicant or the suspension of a member if there was any evidence that the person lacked "the reliability necessary for employment in the film industry."[2] This vague formulation left the door wide open for arbitrary decisions, and notably did not define what the National Socialist government meant by "reliability."

The accumulation of offices by one person became the rule of the day. The first president of the Reich Film Guild, the lawyer and economic expert Fritz Scheuermann, was already chairman of the Film Credit Bank's board; Ludwig Klitzsch resigned once the transformation of the old Spio into the Film Guild was complete and all the major demands in the Spio Plan had been realized.

Like the other art guilds, the Reich Film Guild was charged with "Aryanizing" the National Socialist art and cultural sectors. However, the economic difficulties in the movie business and its losses due to the expulsion of Jewish artists forced Goebbels to put some limits on "Aryanization." The quota law established during the Weimar Republic was now adapted to suit the racial policies of the National Socialist state—everyone in the film industry had to be a German citizen and be able to prove his "German ancestry"—but Goebbels reserved the right to allow exceptions for foreign and "non-Aryan" artists if economic or even political exigencies made them advisable. In 1935 he charged State Commissioner and SS Colonel Hans Hinkel with "supervision of all non-Aryan artists," a necessary measure, the *12 Uhr Zeitung* reported on July 26, "because things had occurred recently that were contrary to National Socialist principles."

The amending of the old Motion Picture Law in February 1934 made pre-censorship a seamless process, following a film through every step of production from draft manuscript to the editing table. From now on, it was the Reich film dramaturge's job "to advise the film industry on all important questions of film production, to examine all manuscripts and screenplays presented to him, and to prevent the development of material contrary to the spirit of the times."[3] The first person to fill this office was the writer Willi Krause, a former editor of the Goebbels newspaper *Der Angriff* and without any experience whatsoever in film. That did not stop him, of course, from trying his hand at direction (under the pseudonym of Peter Hagen); in 1935 he made the Blood-and-Soil film *Friesennot* (*Hard Times in Friesland*) for Delta-Film. In 1936, he was replaced by Hans Nierentz, who had been chief of the Division for Art and Philosophy at the government radio station in Berlin.

This certifying of all film projects by the Reich film dramaturge, prior to examination by the actual censors, found little favor in the film industry, as one can imagine, and was often boycotted. In the summer of 1934, Ufa's production department complained to management that the Reich film dramaturge worked too slowly: "The Reich film dramaturge is supposed to process a scenario in forty-eight hours. A week is allowed for screenplays. As a rule, he takes longer."[4] Krause's "primarily negative" function seemed pointless: "It is not possible for one individual, after a necessarily hasty reading of a screenplay and without consultation with the authors, to pass sound judgment on a work on which four or five and sometimes more people of unquestionable National Socialist outlook have spent months." In one instance a group of authors (receiving honoraria of 25,000 marks) had worked for months on a script, only to have it come back with the determination that it could not be made into a film.

Reports like this alarmed Ufa's frugal managers, who entered the 520,000 marks that the pre-censorship process cost them for the first half of 1934 as "unproductive business costs." Goebbels's idea of comprehensive censorship both before and after production threatened the viability of the entire system. Then, too, because producers ignored many of Krause's objections and conditions, it often happened that films whose screenplays Krause had approved were banned by the censors anyhow. In innumerable conferences with Goebbels, with his undersecretary Funk, and with Krause,

Ufa's managers struggled to work out a compromise. At the end of 1934, a cabinet decision loosened the regulations. Scenarios and screenplays no longer had to be submitted beforehand for approval, but financing through the Film Credit Bank remained dependent on the Reich film dramaturge's approval. Goebbels finally wearied of his various agencies' daily quibbling with producers, and in June 1935, with passage of the Second Act to Amend the Motion Picture Law, he had himself appointed senior censor with unlimited powers to ban and alter films. Now he could bypass his own agencies and decide arbitrarily which films in which versions were suitable for the German people.

Mistrust grew both among the controllers and among those controlled, and the heavy barrage of ministerial guidelines, censorship requirements, decrees, and language prescriptions generated endless inconsistencies and confusion. Unexpected political complications arose. The best of Ufa's artists were of course unpredictable. The prominent "half-Jew" Reinhold Schünzel continued working in Neubabelsberg, turning out shocking slice-of-life films and comedies—sometimes roughhewn, sometimes elegant and ambiguous. His *Amphitryon* (based on Plautus' play), made in 1935, with Willy Fritsch, Käthe Gold, and Paul Kemp in the leads, was one of the most impudent and successful Ufa films of the 1930s. Then there was Detlef Sierck, a director specializing in melodrama, who was in constant demand. (In 1937 he and his Jewish wife, Hilde Jary, emigrated; in 1941 he started working in Hollywood under the name Douglas Sirk.)

Even after the loosening of preliminary censorship the government continued to make trouble for Ufa. As a management report of October 9, 1935, put it:

> The experience of 1933–34 taught us to be especially cautious and thorough in our planning. We faced particular difficulties in the fall of 1934, when, within a short period, production of four films was either forbidden outright or allowed to proceed only on conditions we simply could not meet.[5]

Two of these four projects were abandoned altogether for a loss of 73,500 marks, and production on the other two—*Frischer Wind aus Kanada* (*Fresh Wind from Canada*, directed by Heinz Kenter and Erich Older) and *Zigeunerbaron* (*Gypsy Baron*, directed by Karl Hartl and based on the Johann Strauss work)—was delayed. Though Ufa had succeeded "in negotiations with the Reich film dramaturge and other agencies over many months to arrive at a tolerable working relationship," delays in working out very complicated contracts with authors, directors, and actors had made for significant financial losses.

Goebbels's increased censorship powers magnified the uncertainty in his agencies and moved everyone to extreme caution. A complicated system developed of passing the buck and covering one's tracks. The far-flung net of political and ideological control in the Nazi state fostered the belief that film production was subject to a censorship system of implacable machine-like consistency. But the truth is that power on the defensive and without self-confidence developed an unwieldy system of discordant bureaucracies. From the point of view of the filmmakers, not everything was possible, but much was; and while what was possible was often risky, what was "impossible" was sometimes overlooked, silently tolerated, or even praised.

The puns and pointed remarks with which Schünzel larded *Amphitryon* were tolerated not only by Ufa's management but also by Goebbels as colorful trimmings on an expensive, prestigious production. In addition to a top cast, Ufa assigned its best technicians to this film: Fritz Arno Wagner as cameraman, Herlth and Röhrig as set designers, Werner Bohne for special effects, Rochus Gliese as costume designer, and Fritz Thiery as sound engineer. Franz Doelle wrote the music, and Günther Stapenhorst's production team was in charge. (*Amphitryon* was Stapenhorst's last Ufa production. When word spread that he had refused to join the NSDAP, he emigrated that same year, working first in London for Alexander Korda and later in Switzerland.) The result was a Pommer production without Pommer, a film alive with the spirit and élan of Ufa in its prime and infused with the "insolence of the Weimar Republic's culture," "a lonely exception" in National Socialist cinema, as one critic put it.[6]

Like other top Ufa productions of the late 1930s, *Amphitryon* was made simultaneously in French by Alliance Cinématographique Européenne; the French version was premiered in Paris in September 1935, two months after the German premiere in the Gloria-Palast. The system Ufa developed for these joint productions put at Schünzel's disposal, along with the French cast, artistic and technical specialists from Neubabelsberg who were used to working together.

While in preparation in late 1934 and early 1935, *Amphitryon* was frequently discussed among Ufa's managers. The novel and rather expensive optical tricks Schünzel and his team had come up with were one point of concern. But they were also worried about its satirical thrust. At a management meeting of December 11, 1934, to which Schünzel and Stapenhorst were invited, Ufa's managers approved the sets and then took up the title. Schünzel argued from the outset for *Amphitryon*, referring to the success that Ernst Lubitsch had had in 1919 with *Madame Dubarry* (*Passion*). Whether that was relevant or not, it is in any case interesting that he was recollecting an important Jewish colleague who had already emigrated to America and resisted all efforts to bring him back, and a film all but synonymous with the young Weimar Republic's revolutionary turbulence and rebellious culture.

Schünzel's boldness may have left Ufa's executives speechless; in any case, no one objected to the title. The distribution chief, Meydam, worried that the film might have "too little heart." Schünzel tried to dispel such objections by mentioning the movie's "hit tunes"—a born performer, he sang a few of them on the spot. Ufa had had great commercial successes with its musicals and operettas at the beginning of the sound-film era, and Schünzel knew well that the bosses liked this argument. "German musicality" was, as everyone knew, one of Ludwig Klitzsch's favorite ideas. Schünzel's concluding remark was that, "in accordance with the comment of the Reich film dramaturge, the film would not contain any persiflage."[7]

But the film's subtitle—*Happiness Comes Down from the Clouds*—was a touch of raillery as bold as it was unmistakable:

> The happiness that comes down out of the clouds was for Germans in 1935 an obvious reference to the divine Adolf Hitler, who had, in the famous first sequence of Leni Riefenstahl's *Triumph des Willens* [*Triumph of the Will*], swept down out of the clouds in his airplane to the party convention awaiting him in Nuremberg. Down below in Franconian Thebes the women parody the noble sentiments of the German warrior's wife:
>
> > Be courageous in this time of war
> > as our men do battle in blood and gore,
> > and whoever of them dies dismembered
> > will be by the fatherland eternally remembered.[8]

Amphitryon was lively cabaret, brilliant entertainment—and an insult to Hermann Göring. When, for example, Jupiter's wife, Juno (Adele Sandrock), has Mercury (Paul Kemp) address her as Highest Lady, the audience caught the allusion to the actress Emmy Sonnemann, whom the Reich Air Marshal had recently married. Schünzel and his team permitted themselves this national joke; Ufa's managers bet they would get away with it; the censors raised timid objections or looked the other way; and Goebbels was delighted to have his rival Göring exposed to public ridicule. Like all despotic agencies with power, the Nazi censorship offices functioned perfectly and irrationally at the same time, working feverishly yet also at cross purposes.

Contradictions of this sort accompanied the production of revue films throughout the 1930s and 1940s. Data that Helga Belach has assembled from the production histories of Ufa's revue films give us precise information about Ufa's expenditures, document management's tendency to degrade directors to mere subordinates, and illuminate the activities of the Propaganda Ministry and its chief, who rarely passed up an opportunity to have the last word in matters of casting, dramaturgy, and even direction.[9]

Reinhold Schünzel's spirited transvestite comedy *Viktor und Viktoria* (with Renate Müller, Hermann Thimig, and Adolf Wohlbrück; and sets by Benno von Arent, who later became Reich Set Designer) was made under the frugal regimen of the crisis years. Management rejected production chief Correll's suggestion that a dream scene be shot in animation, arguing that the estimated cost of 10,000 marks was out of all proportion to the movie's expected "return value." For *Mach' mich glücklich* (*Make Me Happy*) by Arthur Robison (1935), the final cost of 850,000 marks went well over the original estimate, and with *Und Du, mein Schatz, fährst mit* (*And You, My Darling, Will Go Along,* 1936–37), the director Georg Jacoby's expensive production numbers and sets created a 50 percent cost overrun. (An incident in the production history of *Make Me Happy* illustrates how stingy management could be in artistic matters—apart from its liberality with stars' salaries: to save 3,300 marks, the executives Correll, Grau, and Meydam decided among themselves how the movie should end, apparently without consulting Robison.)

With this last movie and the operetta *Gasparone* (1937), which followed, Jacoby promoted the career of Marika Rökk, who, under his direction in *Kora Terry* (1940), became the undisputed prima ballerina of National Socialist cinema. Even as early as *Hallo, Janine* (directed by Carl Boese, 1939), "Marika Rökk stole the show."[10] Ufa's managers had agreed on a lead role for her and a production budget of 700,000 marks long before disagreements about nearly everything else came up: director (Jacoby was suggested first, then Herbert Maisch), screenplay (Karl Georg Külb wrote it), production team (the job finally went to Max Pfeiffer), set design (Erich Kettelhut), and Rökk's co-star (Johannes Heesters). Production was delayed by several months, and it was a triumph of Ufa's frugality that the final bill came in 100,000 marks under budget.

At the command level of Ufa, Goebbels wielded ultimate authority and was a constant presence. He could be confident of unquestioning obedience from Ufa's senior managers; indeed, their willingness to submit to ministerial decisions often anticipated or obviated them. For example, Ufa managers had some reservations about the "background" of the popular comedian Max Hansen, who was being considered for the male lead in *Viktor und Viktoria*, but was ready to disregard them provided "they were not shared by the Propaganda Ministry, of which inquiry is to be made in this matter."[11] The inquiry sufficed: Goebbels did not accept Hansen, and the role went to Hermann Thimig. Shortly before this happened, the National Socialists had made Hansen the butt of a nasty demonstration: he had allegedly ridiculed Hitler in a hit song of 1932, implying that Hitler was a homosexual; and on September 8, 1933, at the premiere of his film *Das hässliche Madchen* (*The Ugly Girl*, with Dolly Haas and Otto Wallburg; directed by Hermann Kosterlitz for Avanti-Tonfilm), he was attacked, insulted, and pelted with tomatoes. He soon emigrated to Vienna and later to Scandinavia.

Casting for *Gasparone* proved no small chore, because the Propaganda Ministry had initially refused to approve Marika Rökk. We do not know what eventually moved Goebbels to drop his objections, but the pre-production changes in casting this and many other movies suggest the permanent influence the minister and his agencies exerted on Ufa. In her memoirs, Rökk voiced the suspicion that even in 1939, when she was on the road to stardom with *Hallo, Janine*, "the whole tenor of her films had not sat well with Goebbels."[12] And her companion and husband-to-be, Georg Jacoby, had not been allowed to direct this film because of his Jewish friendships. Reminiscences of stars who were successful under Hitler and Goebbels have to be read with caution, but they still convey the day-to-day atmosphere in National Socialist film production.

Ufa's first major color film, *Frauen sind doch bessere Diplomaten* (*Women Really Do Make Better Diplomats*, directed by Georg Jacoby, 1939–41), was from the outset entirely in the hands of top management, and thanks to ministerial interference, it became Ufa's most expensive enterprise of the late 1930s and early 1940s. Filming began in late July 1939; the film premiered in October 1941: this long production period was marked by crises, wasted motion, and technical and organizational breakdowns; in the end the film was a colossal failure. According to Rökk's recollections, the entire production team, which had disbanded when the film was finished, was then dragged back to Neubabelsberg, though the actor Karl Stepanek, who had an important supporting role, had in the meantime "gone to London and given a radio talk there."[13] Stepanek was well known for his portrayal of people of color. He had been in Ludwig Berger's *War of the Waltzes* (1932) and in the Tobis films *Fünf von der Jazzband* (*Five from the Jazz Band*, directed by Erich Engel, 1932) and *Es leuchten die Sterne* (*The Stars Shine*, directed by Hans Zerlett, 1938). The Propaganda Ministry instantly designated Stepanek *persona non grata*, and since a *persona non grata* did not exist for the state, he had to be removed from the screen—and the sight of the public—as well. Replacing Stepanek with Erich Fiedler required additional filming, which ate up almost 500,000 marks more.

20.

Bacchic Chaos: Consumerism, Eroticism, and Cinema in the Nazi State

F OR more than a third of the feature films that Ufa produced in the years 1935–36, we find "tasteful" entertainment in elegant or "folk" settings with an obligatory happy ending. The pattern of these films had been developed in the "society" and entertainment films of the 1920s, and of course they were not limited to German cinema. The characteristic feature was the tight link between erotic wish fulfillment (albeit monogamous) and the restoration of destroyed or threatened modes of life and production: "fulfillment in love" is realized only under the condition that at the same time damaged family relationships are repaired, conflicts within a business are resolved, or existing injustices are righted.

In *Fresh Wind from Canada*, an Ufa film by Heinz Kenter and Erich Holder, a North American capitalist puts a Berlin fashion salon on a sound financial footing and marries the owner's daughter. In *Die törichte Jungfrau* (*The Foolish Virgin*, directed by Richard Schneider-Edenkoben), the squabbling of local philistines threatens to torpedo a small town's annual theater festival. But all problems are resolved, and at the end the festival director embraces the lead actress. In *Liebeslied* (*Love Song*), by Fritz Peter Buch and Herbert B. Fredersdorf, Alessandro Ziliani, a singer from La Scala, plays a famous tenor who falls in love with a soprano from the provinces and with her help rescues a performance of *Madama Butterfly* at the Paris Opera. In Detlef Sierck's *Das Hofkonzert* (*The Court Concert*), not only is the obligatory music festival in a nineteenth-century provincial capital saved from disaster, but the royal family is enlarged by a love match between lovers of the appropriate class.

In *Weiberregiment* (*Women's Regiment*), directed by Karl Ritter, the battle between the sexes brings a Bavarian brewery to the edge of disaster, but at the end of the film's chaotic plot, orderly business structures are reestablished, and the misguided aggressions of man and woman have led

236

them to the safe harbor of marriage. In Schneider-Edenkoben's *Incognito*, the young chief of a big firm has to go through a capitalistic rite of initiation in the form of a mistaken-identity comedy before he grasps the laws of business administration and is allowed to marry the love of his life. In Paul Martin's *Glückskinder* (*Children of Happiness*), the lovers' happy ending assures a young reporter a career in a newspaper company and reestablishes order in an oil magnate's family. Oil and love are the key elements in Viktor Tourjansky's *Stadt Anatol* (*Anatol City*), too. A small Balkan city overcome by fever for liquid gold goes under in intrigues, crime, and a veritable firestorm, but the hero, with the help of a loving woman, builds the city up again and revitalizes the oil boom.

Der grüne Domino (*The Green Domino*), directed by Herbert Selpin, is about the correction of a miscarriage of justice: A young woman proves the innocence of her father, who has been in prison for twenty years, and finds her "life's partner" in a courageous young lawyer who helps her. In *Einer zuviel an Bord* (*One Too Many on Board*), directed by Gerhard Lamprecht, the case of a missing captain leads to a court investigation, to a just atonement, and to the happy reunion of a separated couple. In *Schlussakkord* (*Final Accord*), Detlef Sierck's first major melodrama, a court trial clears up the tragic family affairs of a musical conductor, clears a young woman of suspicion of murder, and brings the two together as a happy couple. The happy ending in Sierck's *Das Mädchen vom Moorhof* (*The Girl from Moorhof*) brings a similar reward to the just, in this case a young farmer who rejects the milieu of wealthy landowners to court a poor girl who has been made pregnant by her employer. And finally, there is Reinhold Schünzel's *Das Mädchen Irene* (*The Girl Irene*): the mother of a fatherless hautebourgeoise family is a "woman of the world" who falls in love with a man worthy of her; the adolescent daughter, in the battle for her mother, attempts murder and then wants to kill herself—but a happy ending calms all the waves, as the daughter sees the error of her ways, love gets its due, and family equilibrium is restored. Here the usual focus on masculine erotic desires are shifted, and instead of the usual conservative pattern the movie shows the struggle of a middle-aged woman for sexual fulfillment.

The traditional pattern of the successful entertainment film was maintained in most of the comedies, melodramas, and love films of the Nazi period, a viable conveyor of values in a virtually unchanged everyday world. There were also adventure films like *Unter heissem Himmel* (*Under Blazing Heavens*, directed by Gustav Ucicky, with Hans Albers and Aribert Wäscher) and musicals and operettas in the style of *Der Bettelstudent* (*The Beggar Student*), directed by Georg Jacoby (with Carola Höhn, Johannes Hessters, and Marika Rökk). After the war, the Allied military government classified as Nazi propaganda and banned only four of the thirty-four Ufa films made in 1935–36.

The "unpolitical" nature of these entertainments permitted their makers some harmless liberties that would have been unthinkable in "serious" films of a nationalistic, political bent. The loose morals that Willy Fritsch, Lilian Harvey, Oskar Sima, and Paul Kemp showed in Children of Happiness and Curt Goetz's lyrics celebrating idleness hardly fit in with German Fascism's heroic view of life, but on the other hand, the regime saw the value of allowing some relaxation, diversion, distraction, indeed, even occasional vacations from its daily siege of propaganda and indoctrination. Goebbels knew well that "unpolitical" entertainment helped to stabilize the "national body politic," to neutralize unfocused discontent, and to reconcile people to their fate as obedient consumers.

The gradual rise in real wages for workers and the increasing buying power of the middle classes in these years were primarily due to Germany's arms buildup, but they created the illusion of economic stability and strength. A kind of economic euphoria set in, and many Germans discovered the joys of consumerism with an intensity unknown during the Weimar Republic. Movies, especially "society movies," were like wish lists of desirable goods.

In 1933 Wilhelm Reich had caused a stir in the Communist workers' movement when he said that through this consumerist "chink in daily life" a petit-bourgeois mentality crept into the living quarters, heads, and hearts of the proletariat, that the acquisition of a bedroom suite or a stylish evening dress was evidence of proletarian susceptibility to reactionary propaganda.[1] Within a few years the increasing propensity of German workers to take on "middle-class" ways under the Nazi regime became a matter of concern to both Communists and Social Democrats. And the movies seemed prime evidence to support Reich's thesis. While the exotic luxury portrayed in many earlier films could be seen as dream material, drawing its allure from the unbridgeable gap between reality and unfulfilled wishes, some of the objects of longing presented on the screen now seemed as if they just might be within reach. Both the things and the people in the movies of the mid-1930s spoke to viewers as potential consumers, tempting them with the prospects of prosperity, however modest.

The "white-collar films" of the late Weimar Republic had been about everyday types with whom audiences could identify—"people like you and me"—waiting for a stroke of luck that would rescue them from banality and bring them happiness. "Happiness" was, by and large, synonymous with the accumulation of material goods. The small businessman buried in debt in Fresh Wind from Canada, the ambitious reporters in Children of Happiness, the factory owners and jewelers, artists and engineers, salesclerks, waitresses, and railroad conductors, the bank, post office, and hotel employees weighed down with everyday cares—all these 1930s movie characters carried on this tradition from the late Weimar period and formed with their audiences an imaginary "national community" that became all the more vivid as focus on, and expectations of, material well-being and private happiness intensified. Even the smart-set types, the artists and world travelers dressed in knickers and smoking briar pipes, seemed closer to everyday life.

The Nazi state's "symbolic rewards," which promised Strength through Joy to workers, and lower-echelon white-collar workers in particular,[2] promised the fulfillment of old dreams that film stimulated. The Strength through Joy programs offered cruises in the Mediterranean and North Atlantic, "cultural enrichment" in theaters and concert halls, courses in riding, tennis, and sailing—sports that had long been exclusively upper-class. The goals of these programs, national integration and support for the regime, were to no small degree attained. Advertising aimed at "normal citizens," whose daydreams had been stimulated by movies and magazines, urged them to buy their own homes and cars, radios and cameras, kitchens, fashionable clothes, and cosmetics—things that had been associated with the living standards known only in society films. Coca-Cola ads featuring movie stars promoted "the pause that refreshes." (A photograph of a movie theater in Essen taken about 1938 shows a huge banner across the entire façade on which a Coca-Cola girl smiles; above it, a poster advertises a movie starring Heinz Rühmann.[3])

The Führer's promise to motorize the German people with the People's Car, the Volkswagen; the automobile shows regularly featured in the annual cycle of National Socialist events; and the drastic reduction of prices for favorite Opel and DKW models—these suggested not only a "consumer-friendly" trend in the Nazi economy but that movie-inspired dreams of mobility and freedom were becoming a reality. In 1935 a racing car made by Adler set thirteen new records on the Berlin Avus raceway, and at the same time movies about racing drivers became popular: Richard Eichberg's joint German-French production *Die Katz' im Sack* (*Cat in the Bag*), which the censors banned in September 1939, as they did other films with French involvement, and Franz Wenzler's *Der stählerne Strahl* (*Streak of Steel*, Pallas Film). Two years later Germany's star racing drivers, Rudolf Caracciola, Bernd Rosemeyer, and Hans Stuck, opened the automobile show in Berlin and simultaneously saluted Hitler by driving "with screaming engines"[4] from the Chancellery to the exhibition hall. The Berlin public went wild with enthusiasm. "Like the heroes of the Nanga Parbat expeditions who brave the eternal ice, or like the pilots in the Sahara in whom heart, mind, and body are one, the racing drivers embody the spirit of adventure and the elemental life."[5]

Consumerism and the glorification of technology, enthusiasm for sports and a longing for self-realization, a desire for adventure and the cult of "dashing masculinity"—all these blended together under the sign of the swastika. The symbiosis was all too susceptible to the regime's aggressive propaganda. Documentary and newsreel films of the "aviation hero" Ernst Udet's aerobatics and of the Nanga Parbat expeditions of 1934 and 1937 made their way into many households by way of Ufa's home-film distribution. Cheap, easily operated home projectors had become extremely popular; ironically, home-movie technology thus became a way for Fascist ideology to penetrate the four walls behind which the "national comrade" had retired to escape the Nazi propaganda net and indulge in "private" romantic fantasies about the natural world and proving oneself in it. Since the early 1920s, Arnold Fanck's mountaineering films had been preparing the way for this mythology of struggle and "propaganda for a superior humanity."[6]

Revue films—produced primarily by Ufa but also by Terra, Tobis, and Bavaria—showed choreography (derived from the kinetics of the New Objectivity) that was readily adaptable to National Socialist mass manipulation. German dance had an affinity with marching, and the movie ballets shared a style with the human masses organized into blocks for backdrops at Nazi gatherings. The human body thus became subject to the shaping hand of a demagogy that was essentially hostile to the body and the senses. "The body was a medium used to deceive consciousness," as one critic has put it.[7]

Obscured as it may have been by sentimental plots, glittering sets, and carefree waltzes, the double nature of a repressive morality was being expressed: on the one hand, a renunciation of drives and a reification of the body, and on the other, aggression advancing remorselessly in the rhythms of production and war. "The revue films are the Propaganda Ministry's military parades, its prize examples of peak production capacity and peak receptivity; they are much stronger in these respects than the openly political 'films of the nation,'" wrote the film critic Karsten Witte.[8] In the girls' goose step, in their uniform height, in the "snappiness" of the music and montage, erotic substance was reduced to matter; the female body was reduced to a commodity. The dullness of Prussian marching columns and squads forced its way onto the stage and before the camera; no effort was made to conceal its similarity to military exercises. Drill and war were Germany's present and future.

Middle-class audiences in the Wintergarten or Admiralspalast had once associated dancing with "feminine grace" or "erotic charm," but the revue of the Nazi period reduced it at a stroke to an aesthetic of military "smartness." The military snap of the Hiller Ballet's performance at the fiftieth anniversary of the Wintergarten, a delighted reviewer noted, was surpassed only by the band of Hitler's SS bodyguards.[9] Aggressively masculine men and women who melted in their arms danced and sang their way along the brink of an abyss. Even the revue films featured men "with an under developed sense of self . . . who established their identity by turning against women."[10]

Karsten Witte notes about the revue films that it was in the everyday context of Hitler's Germany that the concept of the "inner Reich Party

Convention"[11] developed—a metaphor for the German people's collective internalization of Fascism's obsession with monumentality and its geometric, hierarchical aesthetic. The Führer assembled crowds in Nuremberg in rows and blocks, while Ufa's revue films, appealing to everyone's sense of order and obedience to authority, took possession of the very thing that constituted each individual's "private" self: the need to relax, the capacity for experience, and the joy in beauty for its own sake. Structurally, the "inner Reich Party Convention" followed the same pattern as the external one. In both cases, as Gert Selle put it, "a serious effort was made to transform a weak I into a strong We."[12]

The National Socialist effort to shape Germany by means of "social sensuality" and to align it with the new ideology of course still had to contend with elements of Weimar culture that were still very much alive, not to mention numerous foreign influences. Into the 1940s the regime silently tolerated, sometimes tried to discourage, but did not massively suppress the younger generation's preference for American movies, jazz, and swing. German moviegoers could compare their revue films with American musicals like Jack Conway's *Dancing Lady* (Fred Astaire's debut in film, with Joan Crawford and Clark Gable, produced by RKO in 1933) and Roy del Ruth's *Broadway Melody of 1936* (MGM, 1936); these movies drew full houses—indeed had to, because German distributors were to some degree bound by long-term contracts with American film companies. Not until early 1939 did Ufa, yielding to pressure from the Propaganda Ministry, stop staging premieres for American films.[13]

Stan Laurel and Oliver Hardy were a hit on the screen, but also as guests in Berlin's Scala in 1937, and Walt Disney's Mickey Mouse was popular in Nazi Germany via various media. Movie houses like the Kamera in Berlin and mass periodicals like *Die Koralle* and *Stern* promoted American stars: Clark Gable, Greta Garbo, Joan Crawford, Katharine Hepburn, Claudette Colbert, and others enjoyed great popularity in Germany in the 1930s. Marlene Dietrich was not forgotten either: *The Scarlet Empress* (Josef von Sternberg), shown in Germany under the title *Die grosse Zarin*, was one of the great successes in Berlin in 1934, and Lubitsch's Paramount production *Desire* (directed by Frank Borzage, with Marlene Dietrich and Gary Cooper) premiered in Berlin's Capitol in 1936, nine days before the New York premiere. In a number of articles, *Das Magazin* defended Dietrich—and the vamp—against National Socialist campaigns that tried to combat her "undisguised erotic appeal" by promoting German stars like Paula Wessely and Marianne Hoppe, whom the National Socialists considered "representative of the new age, healthy in body and soul." *Das Magazin* regularly published pictures and biographies of American movie stars and in 1936 openly ridiculed the "home-baked" pleasures promoted by the National Socialist leisure-time culture.[14]

American movies, especially musicals, appealed in Germany not only to audiences but also to open-minded critics, who were not at all reluctant to express their admiration for American self-irony, for Cole Porter's and Irving Berlin's stunning music, and for the easy grace of Hollywood showgirls, tap dancers, and jazz singers. Critics like Erich Pfeiffer-Belli and Hermann Christian Mettin explicitly praised the Americans' uninhibited humor and self-confidence. In reviewing the 1936 MGM film *San Francisco*, directed by W. S. van Dyke, Pfeiffer-Belli said that German film producers should study American movies if they wanted to make "equally accomplished" ones.[15] And in 1942, in the third year of the war, Goebbels astonishingly conceded victory to Hollywood when, on the occasion of a visit from many prominent figures in the film world ("All the production chiefs are here") and a viewing of the American film *Swanee River* (with Al Jolson), he offered these "remarks on the creation of a new German folk-song film":

> The Americans understand how to use modern methods of presentation to create, from their rather small cultural resources, something usable for the present moment. In comparison, we are too weighed down by piety and tradition. We are reluctant to wrap our cultural treasures in modern garb, and the results consequently have a historical quality that smacks of museum films and is well received only by party, Hitler Youth, or workforce audiences. . . . The Americans have only a few Negro songs, but they present them in such contemporary form that they conquer large segments of the modern world with them. . . . We have much richer cultural stores at our disposal, but we lack the art and energy to modernize them.[16]

Goebbels's assessment shows a surprising sensitivity to the components of international show business, but he failed to understand a key point: the problem with German film was not so much the contradiction between tradition and modernity as it was National Socialism's all-out effort to do away with eroticism. As George Mosse has said, the attitude of German Fascism to sensuality was deeply rooted in the "history of respectability and middle-class morality,"[17] but it far exceeded traditional bourgeois prudery. The nakedness of the "Aryan" body as portrayed in the official sculpture of an Arno Breker or Josef Thorak was characterized, despite its reveling in muscularity, by a cadaverous—in any case, lifeless—rigidity: "nakedness without sensuality," as Mosse called it. The driving force behind the Nazi hostility toward sexuality was, Mosse argued, the commander of the Fascist death squads, SS chief Heinrich Himmler. "Sensuality, passion, and to a certain extent individuality itself were sacrificed."[18]

Film is by nature an erotic medium given to sensual curiosity. And in the most interesting productions of the 1930s and 1940s this medium did not abandon its native shamelessness, its tendency to seduce and enchant the senses. In *Final Accord* (made by Bruno Duday's production team with Willy Birgel, Lil Dagover, Maria von Tasnady, and Theodor Loos in the leads), Detlef Sierck, with the help of his cameraman Robert Baberske and the orchestra of the Berlin State Opera, realized cinema's sensual potential in the best melodramatic tradition. Fadeouts, mirror shots, dream scenes, the ocean as a visual metaphor for love, the emotional music—these extravagant devices went against the movie's reactionary plot and middle-class morality, giving the lie to the subordinate role it gave women and the wickedness it assigned to sensual desire. Sierck's work held in intricate balance the contradiction between an arch-conservative sexual morality and film's enchanting beauty, and this explains the fascination that some of the great Ufa melodramas, even some from the Nazi period, still hold for us today.

Ufa's senior managers, essentially aligned with the regime as they were and preoccupied with applying throughout the organization the permanent political and ideological pressure the government was putting on them, administered the creative potential still available in the company, but they could no longer develop it effectively or keep it. Ufa had either condemned its most able talents to inactivity or driven them into exile. So they concentrated on maintaining financial equilibrium and tactically circumventing the obstacles which the Reich film dramaturge's constant reservations, inquiries, and objections or Goebbels's arbitrary decisions put in the way.

A film company that not only toed the line but strove to respond when the party and government appealed to Germany's "national spirit" could hardly be a bulwark of cinematic culture. In late 1934, Correll and Grieving suggested that Ufa make its facilities available to the Strength through Joy program and produce "work-play" films."[19] That kind of faithful service to the regime ran oddly counter to the effort to win international acclaim for German cinema and, as Goebbels had demanded, to raise Germany's film production to new levels of achievement.

As in the Weimar Republic, so under the conditions of dictatorship, Ufa was more than a film factory. It was a political and cultural production system that, responding to state pressure, reflected the broken spirits, the suicidal blindness, and the distorted emotions of Germany's body politic —an endangered body politic whose daily life was increasingly twisted by a seemingly all-powerful government machinery.

The cyclical rituals of the National Socialist Party and its mass organizations, the Strength through Joy activities, the "Reich street collection campaigns," the soup-kitchen Sundays, and the Winter Aid Program with its slogans ("No one will go hungry or freeze") simulated a caring, national community committed to the ideal of spontaneous generosity. That was, of course, a fiction, echoed a thousand times over in the psychological microcosms of innumerable melodramas, comedies, and small-town idylls. Every happy ending confirmed both the flight into private life and confidence in the established order.

Ufa's films, not unlike these programs, created the illusion of human contact and lively emotion in a collective that was in fact hardened in heart and that was already censoring its own perceptions. The sense of being captive to a machine racing ahead to annihilation found relief in the movies' consumerism and in their focus on an inner life conditioned by generations of subjection to authoritarianism. Like the advertising slogan "German champagne is no longer a luxury item!" they encouraged mild intoxication as a way to national *joie de vivre*. Alcohol consumption increased in the last years of peace, though, for people were subject to insecurity, apathy, and depression. According to official estimates, in 1939 a million Germans suffered from alcohol-related problems. A year earlier, in preparation for the "Year of Health," 1939, the Hitler Youth had advocated a war against alcohol and nicotine abuse throughout Germany, but secret reports of the SS Security Service (*Reports from the Reich*, an invaluable source of information on daily life in National Socialist Germany between 1938 and 1945) noted in the first quarter of 1939 a "large increase in alcohol-related incidents and in the number of people arrested for drunkenness," especially in Pomerania and East Prussia, and an increase in the number of "cases of overwork and nervous exhaustion in the working population throughout the country."[20] Concerned observers of "national health" detected a "nervous" addiction to pleasure-seeking, a swinging back and forth between stupefaction and excitability, a volatile mix of emotion that was seeking relief in consumption, in drugs, but also in a mechanically experienced sexual "libertinage." In Ufa's revues, too, emotions were reduced to mechanical responses and found release only in the drill of the kick line.

Even into the late 1930s, however, surprising cultural juxtapositions were still possible; in their way, they, too, blinded people to the real situation and the nature of the Fascist dictatorship. When Mussolini made a state visit in September 1937 and Berlin became the stage for large-scale National Socialist self-glorification, the capital's entertainment industry offered a counter-program for the refined tastes of a chic clientele that remained untouched by the painful contradictions of the times:

The Kurbel theater on Kurfürstendamm ran a Marlene Dietrich week from September 25 through 30, 1937. While Mussolini rode down the Via Triumphalis, you could lose yourself in the world of *Shanghai Express* and afterward, in the Femina Bar, applaud Teddy Stauffer, who . . . with "Swingin' for the King" and "Goody, Goody" denied in his own way the bellicose, nationalistic impulses of the Hitler state. On that same evening—and for two months—a 20th Century-Fox movie filled the Marmorhaus, and people stood in line at the State Opera for the premiere of Igor Stravinsky's ballet *The Fairy's Kiss*. Many people declared this world, which ran counter to Nazi ideology, to be the real world. They regarded the contradictions with which the actual world was riddled as nonexistent and closed themselves off from the truth.[21]

The passion for movies flourished as it had before only during World War I and in the crisis years of the Weimar Republic, and whoever could afford to sought and found relief in overindulgence of every kind. And, contrary to its own propaganda, the government cynically indulged its own appetite for crass luxury in full view of the people. Cases of blatant corruption were hushed up, but corruption itself was paraded in public and became, like Göring's pathological need for opulence, part of the public *mise-en-scène*. Notorious alcoholics like Robert Ley were targets of open ridicule. The sexual adventures of a Joseph Goebbels became common knowledge, and the minister himself, nicknamed "the goat of Babelsberg," an almost tragicomic figure. Dissipation and pleasure-seeking assumed epidemic proportions and blended with latent fears, mistrust of one's neighbor, and fear of war. These distortions, so evident in daily life, suggest that the population was already in a state of psychological shock, a condition that produced extreme reactions a few years later in cities under bombardment, a condition of "bacchanalian chaos" exemplified by a scene that Hans Georg Studnitz witnessed when, after an air raid, he saw the inhabitants of a destroyed house dancing in front of the blazing ruins.[22]

In 1936 Goebbels himself succumbed to "bacchanalian chaos" when he fell in love with Ufa's Czech actress Lida Baarova, a passion that pushed him to the brink of personal catastrophe and nearly ended his political career. His taste for beautiful women was no secret, and his affairs provided an unending source of material for gossip. His own undersecretary, Karl Hanke, a close friend of Goebbels's wife, Magda, kept detailed books on his chief and compiled a list of thirty-six names, "some of them of unknown young girls, most, however, of society ladies and actresses."[23] Goebbels's biographers claim that he did not make use of his political power in his amorous conquests; the ladies simply succumbed to his charms. In the case of Lida Baarova, Goebbels himself succumbed to his emotions and his obsession with the feminine sex, which the historian Helmut Heiber rightly sees as a surprisingly human feature in this otherwise fanatic politician.[24] Goebbels scorned the "German" female type promoted by the NSDAP and preferred women of the world, especially exotic beauties with a touch of mystery about them, women who had become rare in Germany thanks to his own success in Germanizing art and culture, and who could be found, if at all, only in movies and particularly at Ufa.

Lida Baarova was twenty years old when Ufa hired her in 1934. She was not a star, but she was popular as the exotic vamp or woman of luxury in films like *Barcarole* (Gerhard Lamprecht, 1934–35), *Leutnant Bobby, der Teufelskerl* (*Lieutenant Bobby, the Devil-May-Care Guy*, Georg Jacoby, 1935), and *Die Stunde der Versuchung* (*Hour of Temptation*, Paul Wegener, 1936). Her partner in these films was Gustav Fröhlich, with whom she had a private liaison, too. According to Goebbels's biographers, Lida Baarova and Goebbels met at an NSDAP convention event; just before he was supposed to give an important speech, he said he had to discuss her next film with her. Making light of his political duties, Goebbels behaved like an Ufa production chief, and while the filled auditorium waited, he calmly went on to discuss with the surprised young woman which director and which production team would be most helpful to her in her career.

The passionate love affair that ensued lasted two years and became a political scandal when Magda Goebbels forbid her husband to enter their house on the Wannsee island of Schwanenwerder and seriously contemplated divorce. The matter required attention at the highest level; Hitler called Goebbels onto the carpet. The minister resisted the request that he give up his mistress and even offered to resign (he is said to have suggested that he be sent to Japan as ambassador). Hitler then *ordered* him to give up Lida Baarova, and the actress was summoned to the Berlin Police Presidium, where Count Helldorf told her she had to leave Germany immediately. Goebbels made a dramatic farewell telephone call to his beloved. Lida Baarova returned to Prague in the fall of 1938 and worked in Italy from 1943 on.

One historian claims that at the premiere of the Baarova film *Preussische Liebesgeschichte* (*Prussian Love Story*, directed by Paul Martin, 1938) Goebbels's undersecretary, Hanke, organized a "booing and hissing demonstration."[25] But there was in fact no premiere. The film, which delicately recounted the story of a youthful love affair of Kaiser Wilhelm I's, was banned by the censors in December 1938 after repeated submissions, and Klitzsch had to book the production costs as "political losses." Not until March 1950, five years after the end of Hitler's Reich, did the Freiwillige Selbstkontrolle der (bundes) deutschen Filmwirtschaft (Voluntary Self-Censorship Board of the [West] German Film Industry) release the film for public viewing, under the title *Liebeslegende* (*Love Legend*). And Baarova's *Der Spieler* (*The Gambler*), based on the Dostoevsky novella of that title, suffered the same fate. Directed by Gerhard Lamprecht and produced by Euphono-Film for Tobis, this film disappeared from German movie theaters three days after its Berlin premiere in late October 1938, not to surface again until 1950 under the title *Roman eines Schwindlers* (*Novel of a Swindler*).

Another myth concerns the slap in the face that Baarova's humiliated lover Gustav Fröhlich is supposed to have given his rival Goebbels, but it is a myth that fed dreams of rebellion: for a long time Germans enjoyed the pun that the actor's name offered (*fröhlich* means "happy, cheerful") and joked over the prospect that they too might someday "be *fröhlich*."

21.

Architecture, Film, and Death

L E O N Blum's remark that socialism represents a morality, Communism a technology, and Fascism an aesthetic[1] raises the question whether there can be aesthetics beyond political morality and political methods of domination. German Fascism usurped the role of aesthetics, but did it not also project an aesthetic plan for politics, with the result that its politics, conceived of as a "work of art," degenerated into destruction and put the attainments of human civilization at risk?

An examination of the cinema under National Socialist rule cannot provide a final answer to this question, but we should try for an answer nonetheless, not only because there were films that developed an iconography specifically tailored to the government's assumption of totalitarian control but also because the forms that Fascism chose for its self-representation were "filmic" in origin and its oft-noted synthesis of architectural structure and masses of humans in motion was inspired by a cinematic mode of perception. Central to that synthesis was death. "[Fascist] choreography," Susan Sontag has written, "alternates between ceaseless motion and a congealed, static, 'virile' posing. Fascist art glorifies surrender, it exalts mindlessness, it glamorizes death."[2]

The importance of the modern mass media in the impact of Nazi propaganda has often been discussed, also the transition, aided by radio and cinema, from theatrically staged reality to media reality. Goebbels was describing a film scene or, more exactly, a filmic icon staged in reality when, at the end of his diary, he described the evening of May 1, 1933, with these words:

I'm sitting in the back seat of the Führer's car as his triumphal parade passes between the masses of workers lining the streets from the Chancellery to Tempelhof. It defies description. It is impossible to take in the huge sea of people. The spotlights flash and shine over them. One sees them standing shoulder to shoulder in gray masses.

The film image slides into an "audio-image" that uses radio strategy:

> I open the event with a brief talk and ask for a minute of silence in memory of the miners who died in Essen that day. Now the whole nation falls silent, and the loudspeakers carry this silence out into both city and countryside. A powerful moment of community and felt connection among all classes and estates.[3]

It was not just in Goebbels's imagination that the nation "fell silent." This silence, which the strategy of the mass demonstration made "audible," was a component, indeed a high point, of its "architecture." "Max Reinhardt can ring down his final curtain," said a newspaper commentator the next day. "The German people have staged the greatest play imaginable."[4] The reporter grasped intuitively that megalomaniacal and unscrupulous "artists" were transforming an entire nation into a malleable mass, not only subjugating it to their political will, but pressing it into an aesthetic tableau.

It was not just in their monumental architecture, their transformation of city squares into arenas for military reviews, their use of city centers for cultic purposes that the National Socialists were creating a new world. They were also stage designers and lighting experts. They mastered the technology of backdrops and the aesthetic laws of montage. Albert Speer, Joseph Goebbels, Benno von Arent, and their assistants took the real world and shaped it to their visions. At innumerable mass meetings and demonstrations they blended theater and film. Cityscapes became stages for phantasmagorias created from plaster of Paris, papier-mâché, and light shows.

In September 1937, a total blackout of downtown Berlin was ordered in connection with an air-raid drill. At this same time, the city was preparing for Mussolini's state visit.

> During the blackout . . . Benno von Arent secretly transformed downtown Berlin into a theater landscape. Four rows of snow-white columns topped with golden eagles were put up along Unter den Linden. On various city squares, flagpoles 42 meters high were installed as well as pedestals decorated with fasces and swastikas. Building façades were covered with banners. When Hitler and Mussolini's cavalcade approached the downtown area early on the evening of September 27, the spotlights went on and, after darkness, created a sense of miracle.[5]

The sea of flags, the press reported, created "an ethereal effect, like colored light" pouring down over the enchanted crowds. There is no doubt that Max Reinhardt's mass spectaculars were as much the godparents of such events as the patterns of light in Fritz Lang's Ufa films or the opulent "stage shows" of the Ufa premieres in the 1920s. But the epoch-making conversion to the visual medium that Hofmannsthal had proclaimed in

1920 and the "electrification" of perception that had previously served the ends of art and entertainment—from Reinhardt's lighting techniques to the German silent film to Ufa's operettas—was now in the service of a politics whose purpose was intoxication and the obfuscation of reality.

Fascism as an aesthetic strategy transformed reality into theatrical and film images. "Flags, masts, the beams of light from the spotlights were our primary building materials," Albert Speer wrote.[6] Threadbare, insubstantial materials and electric lights were used to build "dematerialized" structures like Speer's "light cathedral" in the night skies; these elements shaped the imaginative yet monotone productions of Fascist propaganda, which aimed to destroy the idea of normality and norms in the minds of a subjugated citizenry. "All the effort expended in the aestheticizing of politics has one purpose. That one purpose is war," wrote Walter Benjamin. The self-alienation of people under Nazi rule went so far that "they could experience their own destruction as an aesthetic pleasure."[7]

In Nazi lyrics "destruction as a national value" was repeatedly celebrated, and the swastika flag was associated, as in an SA song of 1937, with "blood and destruction and tears, with smoke and ruins, suffering and hate and curses." Joseph Peter Stern, who cites these examples in a study of the National Socialist spirit of sacrifice and hope of redemption, stresses the connection between Fascist sadomasochism and the pseudo-religious cult of the genius, a connection further illuminated by the concept of the Füh-rer as a political artist:

> *We are a people evolving, raw stone*
> *You, our Führer, will be our stone mason. . . .*
> *Strike again and again! We shall stand patiently*
> *as your disciplined hand shapes us.*[8]

The most primitive expression of physical violence ("Strike again and again!") is made to seem aesthetically controlled. There is an echo here of motifs from German lyric poetry and artistic philosophy of the nine-teenth—even the early twentieth—century: a celebration of the master builders, masons, and stoneworkers who built the medieval cathedrals and the mythology of their guilds as sacred and esoteric workshops. National Socialism seized on these projections of a capitalistic, rationalistic age and incorporated them into its destructive ideology.

National Socialist "cinema," its political and aesthetic iconography with new dimensions, took place outdoors—on the fields at Tempelhof, at Mu-nich's Königsplatz, at the party conventions in Nuremberg. Its creators were aware of its affinity to theatrical and film spectaculars. Hitler's architect and, later, Minister for Arms Production, Albert Speer, recalled the pleasure he took as a student in Erik Charell's revues, though he did not like De Mille's "bombastic pomp." Years later, however, when he again saw pho-tographs of the model of the Great Hall he had designed as the centerpiece of Berlin as a "world capital," he could see the similarities to the "satrap architecture" in De Mille's epic films. "I recognized . . . the component of cruelty in it, the clear expression of the tyrant." Belatedly, Speer had seen the link between Fascist architecture and destruction. If he looked at his building plans "long and hard," he could see that he had, as he put it, "to a certain degree anticipated Hitler's downfall in these drawings."[9]

The forms of altar and catafalque are unmistakable in Berlin's Olympic Stadium, in the Nuremberg Party Convention Center, and in the exhibition and administrative buildings on Reichskanzlerplatz and Fehrbelliner Platz in Berlin. According to Dieter Bartetzko, in his study of National Socialist architecture, the regime's official buildings repeatedly reflect the motifs of that catafalque-like monument that Hitler unveiled under the side arch of Munich's Field Marshal Hall—which had been the goal of his failed putsch attempt in 1923. For the annual memorial march on November 9, his "stage managers" used spectacular lighting effects borrowed from the light-and-dark contrasts of silent movies; the streets of downtown Munich were darkened, torches and flames atop pylons "produced the desired occult atmosphere," and the crypt became a "public space."[10]

National Socialist "reality" imitated cinema, and cinema retired into the nooks and crannies available to it in true reality. While the gloomy pomp of the Nazis' mass parades and memorial services for the dead prepared Germans for "eternity," which is to say for death, most of the country's feature films, right up until the end of the war, were escape routes into imaginary shelters of middle-class privacy and normalcy.

The film tastes of the party leaders and Hitler in particular were in crass contrast to the heroic, Neronic aesthetic of official National Socialist culture. Until the war began, Hitler let hardly an evening go by when he did not watch, after a newsreel, one or two feature films, whatever happened to be new. He and Goebbels made the choices. According to Speer, who enjoyed the dubious privilege of attending many of these "dreary evenings" with Hitler's closest associates in Berlin or Obersalzberg, Hitler was especially fond of mediocre entertainment, love and "society" films. The demand was high for movies with Jannings and Rühmann and the current female stars: Lil Dagover, Olga Tschechowa, Zarah Leander, Jenny Jugo, and—still—Henny Porten. Films with tragic plots found no favor, but Hitler immensely enjoyed epics and revues; the latter, with their displays of "many bare legs, were assured of his applause."[11] And he often watched foreign films, even those that were banned for the public.

The conversation afterward never went beyond what Speer called "trivialities." His memoirs convey a picture of dreary, mindless film evenings attended by played-out decision-makers who were intellectually sluggish to begin with. The level of Ufa productions in the 1930s perfectly satisfied them, those Ufa films that had created the inner, psychic furnishings of their petit-bourgeois world—partly aggressive and choleric, partly manic-depressive. If Fascism was an aesthetic and if at the core of that aesthetic was a death cult encompassing the souls of millions, the creators of that cult were obviously unable to live up to the poses they struck for the benefit of the public. After a day of heroic work, that is, politics, the cohesive core of power broke down and dissolved among exhausted men who in the interests of "relaxation" ordered up the same poor fare they set before the people.

Interestingly enough, the great achievements of film architecture in Ernst Lubitsch's and Fritz Lang's monumental films of the Weimar years were not equaled in the National Socialist productions at Ufa or at other German film companies. Otto Hunte, Erich Kettelhut, and Karl Vollbrecht's utopian structures created for the upper city in *Metropolis* became reality in the "regimented state architecture"[12] of the Reich Chancellery and the Olympia Stadium; Speer's artistry with lighting, based on the lighting techniques of *The Nibelungs*, made magically illuminated allegorical figures of the Führer and his vassals; Siegfried's tomb with its massive stone sarcophagus evolved into a "dream image of Fascist necrophilia"[13] and was imitated repeatedly in the tombs and memorial structures of the NSDAP. But Germany's film art of the 1930s and 1940s "forgot" its distinguished past and sank to an insipid, petty level.

Bartetzko, who has a wealth of convincing examples to document the influence of the *Nibelungs* sets on buildings actually constructed by the Nazi dictatorship, concludes that Weimar's films were a kind of visual school that paved the way for the reception of the National Socialist aesthetic.

> The image and significance of the cinematic buildings interposed themselves like a filter, as it were, between the real architecture and its recipients. [Thus] did architecture as a creator of mood become accessible and understandable to the man on the street and become the basis for the Third Reich's architecture.[14]

So the stylistic parallels between Fritz Lang's film architecture and the show buildings of German Fascism are more than superficial. An element common to both is the tableau-like nature of these outsized buildings. The magic of the skyscraper backdrops in *Metropolis* derives, despite their perspective, from their two-dimensionality. They are "constructed pictures." The viewer is not invited to step into the inner world of this utopian city and move around in it. He is supposed to sink down on his knees in awe before it. National Socialist architecture, too, involved the "presentation of carefully composed pictures, of pictorial architecture,"[15] of tableaus generated by a pseudo-sacral strategy of intimidation.

In Speer's memoirs one occasionally senses his dismay that the party's representative buildings were designed without consideration for human beings. Especially neglected was the need of city dwellers to inhabit their town, communicate within it, pursue their work and pleasures in it. The literally oppressive weight of the colossal buildings drove each person back into isolation and left the citizen feeling small and insignificant. "You are nothing; your country is everything." By contrast, Ufa's monumental sets from the Weimar years were the stuff of the imagination, miraculous creations of true fictive power. They were meant to astonish and to inspire awe in the viewer, but in the end one could triumph over their illusory splendor when their creators let them go up—like Etzel's castle in *The Nibelungs*—in an apocalyptic firestorm.

Leni Riefenstahl's party-convention films, *The Victory of Faith* and *Triumph of the Will* (1934–35), as well as her Olympic films, *Fest der Völker* (*Festival of Nations*) and *Fest der Schönheit* (*Festival of Beauty*, 1936–38), transposed pictorial architecture to the movie screen. The films were personally commissioned by Hitler. *The Victory of Faith* was produced by the NSDAP's Reich propaganda division (with Arnold Raether as production chief); for the others and for *Tag der Freiheit!—Unsere Wehrmacht* (*Day of Freedom!—Our Armed Forces*, 1935), she herself was producer as well as director. All these Riefenstahl films were distributed by Ufa and premiered in the Ufa-Palast am Zoo, but in no other capacity did Riefenstahl work for Ufa. Her contacts with the company had been limited to her work as an actress in the mid-1920s, when she appeared in a scene in Wilhelm Prager's *Ways to Strength and Beauty* (1924–25) and when she played leads in Arnold Fanck's mountaineering films *Der heilige Berg* (*The Holy Mountain*, 1925–26) and *Der grosse Sprung* (*The Great Leap*, 1927).

Leni Riefenstahl's propaganda films are still regarded as avant-garde achievements, but the argument supporting that view, namely, that her exclusive concerns were beauty and perfection of form, is as banal as it is dubious. Precisely because she refused to consider the political implications of her work, she and her films became political issues. Preoccupied with the dynamics of her métier and totally caught up in her aesthetic obsessions, Riefenstahl invented an imagistic language perfectly adapted to the staged events before her camera. She created film monuments to the National Socialists' "architectural megalomania," and in her montages the essence of Fascist pictorial architecture, the synthesis of "ornamentation and mass," of rigidity and movement, found supreme expression. In her films she evoked from the reality so carefully arranged for her camera an emotional impact it would be difficult to surpass. This was the service she performed for the National Socialist dictatorship, and that achievement constitutes her only claim to a place in film history.

An anecdote passed on by Speer illustrates, too, that the staging of party conventions could easily be reproduced on the same scale in a film studio. When Hitler learned that some of the shots from the 1934 party convention were technically flawed, he ordered the important scenes reshot in the studio. Speer rented what was still the biggest studio in Europe.

In one of the big studios in Berlin-Johannisthal I built replicas of the podium, the speaker's lectern, and a section of the convention hall. Spotlights were trained on the lectern; the film staff ran about busily; and in the background Streicher, Rosenberg, and Frank paced up and down with scripts in their hands, diligently memorizing their roles. Hess arrived and was asked to perform first. Just as he had done in front of 30,000 spectators at the Party Convention, he raised his hand solemnly. With genuine emotion he turned to where Hitler was, of course, conspicuously absent and, standing at rigid attention, called out, "My Führer, I welcome you in the name of this convention. The convention will now proceed. The Führer speaks!" His expression was so convincing that from that moment on I could never again believe in the genuineness of his emotions. The other three, too, played their parts effectively in the empty film studio, talented actors all. I was thoroughly annoyed. Frau Riefenstahl, however, found the staged shots better than those made at the actual event.[16]

Speer owed much not just to the *Nibelungs* film but also to the early Ufa and its master director Fritz Lang (whom he never once mentions in his memoirs). In his 1939 plans for reshaping Berlin as a "world capital" (the work was to be completed by 1950), Speer, spurred on by Göring, designed an Aeronautical Ministry for the edge of the Tiergarten, Berlin's central park. The Ministry's banquet rooms would be crowned by Göring's private quarters, an immense penthouse high above the city. Speer wanted to make the roof into a kitschy paradise for the party elite.

Under the pretense of air-raid protection, I wanted to cover the uppermost deck with topsoil deep enough to support even very large trees. Forty meters above the Tiergarten would have been a park . . . with a swimming pool and tennis courts, also fountains, garden pools, arcades, pergolas, restaurants, and, above the roofs of Berlin, a summer theater with 240 seats. Göring was delighted and raved about the roof-garden parties he would give there: "I'll illuminate the dome with Bengal lights," he said, "and set off fireworks for my guests."[17]

It sounds like a copy of the pleasure gardens in which the ruling dynasties in *Metropolis* pass their decadent leisure hours. Lang, with amazing foresight into the post-modern world, had combined the delicacy of rococo, the opulence of Empire, and the nervous energy of Art Nouveau with the functionalism of New Objectivity. Now this chaos of forms served the pleasure of a ruling caste whose response to the very word "culture" was to reach for a revolver.

The imaginative and varied design that had characterized movie theaters in the 1920s and helped to change the face of Germany's cities was now absorbed into the all-encompassing solemnity of National Socialist architecture. The first sound-film theaters had anticipated the official buildings to come, but after January 30, 1933, cinematic atmosphere and filmic light-

and-shadow play became elements of a new official aesthetic. The movie theater's "second skin," its portals and street fronts, once the place for ingenious displays developed by Ufa's advertising chief, Rudi Feld, now became part of an overall strategy of illusion, especially for important political occasions or the premieres of "nationally" important films.

The Ufa-Palast am Zoo, first refurbished in 1925 and given a new main entrance in 1931, took on a huge false front behind which the old Romanesque battlements and arcades were hidden. In 1937, the hewn-stone wall of the main building disappeared behind a temporary front, too.

> Two massive stone pylons rose up steeply on either side of an entrance, and between them was a broad wall set back in a series of graduated steps. Only the complete absence of windows and Ufa's neon signs and posters instead of government symbols distinguished this movie theater from the new Reich Chancellery a few kilometers away on the Wilhelmstrasse.[18]

For major occasions such as the premiere of *Triumph of the Will* in 1935, a forest of swastika flags illuminated by vertical spotlight beams decorated the façade, and a huge imperial eagle, its talons on a laurel wreath encircling a swastika, spread its wings across the entire main entrance.

The model for this kind of nighttime architecture was Speer's "light cathedral," constructed of light beams and flags for the party convention of 1934. Speer had borrowed from Göring 130 antiaircraft searchlights, "the major part of the strategic reserve," so that he could direct their beams straight up into the sky like gigantic pillars. Long after the war he still considered this idea his most successful shaping of space and the only one that had stood the test of time. "Both solemn and beautiful, as if one were in a cathedral of ice," such was the judgment of the British ambassador, Sir Neville Henderson.[19]

Vertical light beams were used more and more often to illuminate cinema façades, and the provinces followed Berlin's example. A 1935 photograph shows the façade of Osnabrück's biggest movie theater, the Capitol (the Ufa-Capitol as of 1934), with soaring buttresses sharply accentuated by beams of light playing on them.[20] Under the National Socialists, Bartetzko wrote, the movie theater became a government building, and vice versa. "Magic and manipulation, the elements that sparked creative architectural ideas for movie houses, left their proper places and invaded the entire society."[21] They became part of a campaign of illusion that overwhelmed Germany's entire culture.

The end of the Fascist "total work of art" was strikingly captured in a now famous photograph. It shows a scene amid the ruins of Berlin in April 1945. In front of the destroyed façade of the Ufa-Palast a person wearing a gas mask is pushing a baby carriage along the shattered pavement. Above the bullet-riddled entrance hangs the undamaged Ufa rhombus, a relic of past glory.

22.

Ufa under State Ownership

"**P**EAK performance is the way to success!" This old Ufa motto was the guiding principle for the company's production program for 1937–38. In introducing that program Ufa's managers observed two significant factors about the German film industry: a "concentration of economic resources" and a "situation conducive to the optimum realization of artistic talents." The former encouraged them to plan forty new feature films for the coming year, the most ever undertaken since the introduction of sound film. Propaganda Minister Goebbels's "creative suggestions," they went on to say, had made "orderly development of artistic ideas" possible; "artistic excellence and maximum appeal to the public must be and will be one and the same in 1937–38, too." Ufa's executives were still mouthing Erich Pommer's old credo, but now it was merely rhetorical, lending the appearance of legitimacy to a state-controlled film factory.[1]

Political pressure was increasing markedly. The "alignment" with the regime that had been accomplished in Ufa's external workings continued to meet with internal resistance, and from Goebbels's point of view there were still too many key people in Ufa who had their own views and went about their business according to principles at odds with state doctrine. Goebbels no longer merely gave speeches and interfered in day-to-day production. He wanted a thoroughgoing restructuring from the top down, and in a letter of late 1936 Klitzsch was informed in no uncertain terms that his production chief, Ernst Hugo Correll, was no longer in the minister's favor.

Differences between Goebbels and Correll had been developing for a long time. On the surface, they were not of a political nature. Correll was not a member of the NSDAP (nor was Klitzsch), unlike other senior Ufa executives. (Hermann Grieving, chief of the technical division, and Oskar Kalbus, since 1933 chief of Ufa's distribution company, both joined the party in 1940.) But Correll was regarded as a man of "national outlook," and nothing indicated that he opposed government policies. Riess cites unnamed "informed sources"—as he often does in his book—to support his thesis that Correll lost favor with Goebbels because he had opposed giving Lida Baarova a long-term contract.[2] But it is more likely that Goebbels saw this professionally competent and self-confident producer as the most determined opponent of his ongoing interference in Ufa's affairs. Correll balked at taking orders from politicians, not because he objected to their politics, but because they lacked professional competence and their agencies were ill-mannered. Resistance to pre-production censorship imposed by Reich film dramaturge Willi Krause had come primarily from the production department (where the disastrous effects of that censorship had been clearest), and it was Correll who had brought the objections of his directors and producers to the attention of senior management. And, finally, Correll had also resisted Goebbels's effort to place loyal retainers like Hans Weidemann and Willi Krause in the company.

At a meeting of the executive committee of the board on December 14, 1936, Klitzsch reported "that a high-ranking official had criticized Vice President Correll's performance as chief of production and had suggested replacing him."[3] Klitzsch quickly added that he did not think the criticism was justified and that it was based on incorrect information. More important, he could not think of "anyone equally well qualified or indeed anyone whom he could responsibly recommend" as a replacement. That was the key point: Correll was indispensable, particularly for the "prestige films" so crucial to foreign business.

The executive committee asked Klitzsch to explain the terms of Correll's contract, which guaranteed him his position until the end of the next year and, if notice was not given by year's end, was automatically renewed for two years. Thus, Klitzsch said, notice would have to be given immediately, i.e., in December 1936. The dodge worked: "In view of the extreme importance of a good, professional, and undisturbed execution of the production program in the coming year" the company could not comply with the Propaganda Minister's request. Correll kept his job. Alfred Hugenberg did not, however, pass up the chance to do a favor for the National Socialists, and suggested that the possibility of shortening the contract period to December 31, 1938, be investigated. The executive committee "accepted this proposal unanimously"—with the result that Correll in fact remained with Ufa only until the spring of 1939.

Political pressure took other—and many—forms. The banning of films increased, and even Ufa was not safe from this. In October 1937 the censorship office retroactively banned the most successful sound film of the 1932–32 season, Erik Charell's The Congress Dances, because too many Jewish, emigrated, and politically undesirable artists were listed in its credits. Film criticism worthy of the name no longer existed. In a decree of

November 1936, Goebbels had forbidden art criticism of any kind that did not hold to the ideological standards set by the Reich Chamber of Culture.

What the National Socialists called "positive censorship" was a complicated system of evaluating and rating films. The Berlin censorship office was responsible for the ratings. With this assignment Goebbels made it clear that state bans and state rewards, the carrot and the stick, were two sides of the same coin. As early as June 1933 the ratings "Particularly valuable" and "Nationally valuable" were added to the existing ones of "Artistic," "Nationally educational," and "Culturally valuable." The system was expanded in later years, and by 1939 there were no less than eight ratings that producers could apply for. Films that excelled in the "national political" arena could win special distinction as "Films of the Nation." Of a total of 1,094 German films shown between 1933 and 1945, 347—almost a third—were awarded ratings, some of them several.[4]

The rating system spread out over the movie business a kind of map that placed the works in easily identifiable categories; some of them, like "Nationally valuable," served as a warning to the public and kept them away. And of course the artists reacted with mixed feelings. When Veit Harlan glorified the "Führer principle" in his Tobis film *Der Herrscher* (*The Ruler*, a freewheeling version of Gerhart Hauptmann's *Vor Sonnenaufgang* [*Before Sunset*], 1937), he was awarded not only the highest ratings ("of special national and artistic value") but also the National Film Prize for 1937. But then, even though he was a convinced National Socialist, he turned to melodrama and pure entertainment for the next three years. Not until 1940 and *Jew Süss* would he again distinguish himself as a pillar of the regime.

But the rating system was quite to the film companies' liking. Movies with ratings were partially or completely exempted from the entertainment tax.

The industry was not deluded into thinking that Goebbels was satisfied with the results of its "revitalization." He went on railing against the low level of film production, against kitsch and commercialization, and demanding art—and by that he did not mean just art with a National Socialist outlook. He did not appreciate the insipid fare which Ufa and Tobis, Terra and Bavaria were offering, he distrusted businessmen, and he referred repeatedly to artistic "genius" and creativity—qualities he wanted made more central in the film business.

For carrying out his commands he had a team of officials and circumspect technocrats such as Max Winkler, a business and media specialist, whom he appointed Reich Commissioner for the Film Industry in 1937. It was Winkler's initiatives and maneuvers in the interest of state centralization that account in large part for the optimism of Ufa's production plans for fiscal 1937–38.

The first annual convention of the Reich Film Guild in March 1937 amounted essentially to a declaration of bankruptcy; the German film industry was cut off from foreign trade and had been run into the ground by the government. Guild president Oswald Lehnich noted the impossibility of bringing expenses into line with income, and Klitzsch hinted that a reorganization of the industry was inevitable. Max Winkler had been quietly at work for several months now. His still-secret mission was to clear the way for the state to buy up the film industry's entire production and distribution capabilities.

As a fiduciary of the government from 1920 on, Winkler had a reputation as a discreet and skillful financial expert. He had expertise in the media from government work he had done on behalf of the German-language press and for the "preservation of German culture" in neighboring countries. After 1933, Winkler offered his services to the Ministry of Propaganda and the Reich Press Officer of the NSDAP, Max Amann, to help do away with private ownership of newspapers and to bring print under state control. Prohibitions and political chicanery had pushed many newspaper publishers so close to the brink of financial ruin that they had no choice but to sell on terms dictated by the National Socialist "buyers."

This process became the model for the film business. With the first steps toward "nationalization" of Tobis in 1935, a chain of state usurpations began that ended in the early 1940s with the almost total nationalization of Germany's film companies. Working through the Cautio Trust Company, which he had formed in 1929, Winkler discreetly negotiated with senior executives to acquire the majority of stock in all the major companies. Without himself being a board member or company executive, he could then make them comply with his directives. His objective was what Ufa described in its publications as the "concentration of economic power," and he considered the political and ideological consequences as mere side effects. As Goebbels saw it, the measures Winkler took served primarily to maintain and expand the organizations that the capitalistic egotism of each individual company had brought to the verge of bankruptcy. The government's policy of autarky had made nothing easy, but now ways and means had to be found to ensure the continuing existence of the entire industry.

After studying the balance sheets, Winkler concluded that a successful "consolidation of political and economic interests" would primarily involve the two most important companies: Tobis, with its sound-film patent rights, which was in debt and already nationalized; and the comparatively "sound" Ufa, the "pivotal point for the planned revamping of the film industry."[5]

Ufa's capital stock still amounted to 45 million marks, a good 23 million of that held by Scherl Publishing; Scherl also held voting rights to, and control over, a block of stock worth 2 million that belonged to I. G. Farben. The German Bank, midwife to Ufa and majority stockholder before Hugenberg's takeover, still controlled stock worth about 13 million marks.

Ufa's board was still made up of that Hugenberg clique of former German National People's Party members: bank presidents, industrialists, landed gentry, state land lessees, and retired naval officers. Also on the board was Andrew Thorndike III, who could trace his ancestry back to the *Mayflower* and who was chief executive of Hugenberg's advertising firm, Ala-Anzeigen. Thorndike's son, Andrew Thorndike IV, was chief agent for Ufa's advertising-film division. After the war, he would start a new career as a director in the Soviet zone, where he built up the DEFA studio for news-reels and documentaries.

The vice presidents directly under Klitzsch in 1937 were Ernst Hugo Correll for production; Wilhelm Meydam for distribution; Hermann Grieving for cultural films, advertising films, and newsreels; Alexander Grau— the only executive remaining from 1917—for theater management; and Paul Lehmann, who went to Tobis in October in charge of technical management.

Thus arrayed, Ufa went into its last battle as a private company, only to surrender meekly and with hardly a whimper to the National Socialist state. Its demise took place as smoothly as had its capitulation ten years earlier, when Emil Georg von Stauss and Ferdinand Bausback had delivered the crippled firm into the hands of Hugenberg.

It was Ludwig Klitzsch who negotiated with Winkler. As Spiker has written, it must have been "sober economic considerations and intimate knowledge of the National Socialist power structure" that moved him and his old chief to sell Germany's major film company, twenty years after its founding, to the National Socialist state.[6] This transaction was a favorable one for Hugenberg. After the war, he tried unsuccessfully to present himself as a victim of Nazi persecution and applied for 30 million marks in reparations for the alleged loss of Ufa. Hans Werner Osthoff, attorney for the reparations commission, made the case against him in 1950.

> Both Klitzsch and Hugenberg as well as their family members enjoyed the special favor of the National Socialist state. They even in a certain sense prepared the way for National Socialism. . . . The company executives were not only left unmolested but regarded as so reliable that they were commissioned with semiofficial and official tasks.[7]

Privy Councillor Alfred Hugenberg, though in 1933 still the target of demagogic attacks by the SA and Goebbels, was nonetheless awarded the Shield of the German Eagle medal for his cooperation with the government, and he was also well situated to realize his plans in the arms industry. In 1943, at the twenty-fifth anniversary of Ufa's founding, Ludwig Klitzsch was awarded the Goethe medal.

So on March 18, 1937, the ownership of Ufa once again changed hands. Under the sign of the swastika, Ludendorff's dream of a film factory totally subordinate to the government was finally realized. On Winkler's advice, the government took over Hugenberg's stock at 100 percent of nominal value—a politically motivated gesture of generosity on the part of the purchaser, for the market price of Ufa stock was considerably below its nominal value. No objections to the sale were forthcoming from the company's governing bodies. Ufa's decision-makers had long since established ties with the government and supported National Socialist policies. They were certain of the Propaganda Minister's favor and not only were spared financial losses but looked forward to a secure future under the government's wing. The great majority of production managers agreed, as did the few ideologically reliable directors who now set the tone at Ufa and the many actors and artists who had been decorated by the state and were disinclined to think about politics anyway.

For Hugenberg's share of Ufa, the government paid 21,250,000 marks. Hugenberg (or Scherl) received 9 million in Reich treasury notes at 4.5 percent; an additional 9 million paid off a debt he owed to the Dresden Bank; the rest he raked in as cash. Winkler acquired the German Bank's stock for 8 million marks, and he convinced the small stockholders that it was to their advantage to trade their stock for bonds with a set interest rate. The upshot was that by March 1939 Cautio was managing almost a hundred percent of Ufa's capital stock on behalf of the government.[8]

On May 4, 1937, a completely new board of directors emerged from the stockholders' meeting. The only holdovers from the founding generation were Emil Georg von Stauss and Johannes Kiel of the German Bank. The new board included close allies of Goebbels, like Carl Froelich, who later became president of the Reich Film Guild; and Hans Weidemann from the film division of the Propaganda Ministry; National Socialist artists and "state actors" like Paul Hartmann (after 1942 president of the Reich Theater Guild); Eugen Klöpfer (among other things, intendant of the Volksbühne in Berlin and member of the Reich Cultural Senate); Mathias Wieman (he was to take part in "fight-to-the-death" rallies toward the end of the war); and Karl Ritter (the most adroit of the Nazi propaganda-film specialists). Stauss was elected chairman of the board and of the finance committee; the artistic committee went to Carl Froelich.

Winkler's efforts were rewarded in the following years by an upswing in Ufa's fortunes—not only from the "movie boom" promoted by National Socialist mass organizations but also from the war when, as in 1914–18, the population's appetite for movies increased as enthusiasm for the war shrank.

Winkler's state restructuring of the other film companies followed the same principles that had proved so worthwhile in the purchase of Ufa. The Tonbild Syndikat (Tobis) became Tobis Filmkunst, with capital stock of 5 million marks and Cautio as the sole partner. Terra-Film was newly established as Terra-Filmkunst, also with capital stock of 5 million marks, in which Ufa and Cautio were equal partners. A year later, Ufa's share was increased to 51 percent, and Terra was incorporated into Ufa as a subsidiary. The Bavaria, in Munich, deep in debt, was liquidated along with its distribution organization, Bavaria Filmverleih, but then reestablished in February 1938 as Bavaria Filmkunst, with Cautio as the sole partner, acting on behalf of the government. (Winkler had at first resisted this new life for Bavaria, but yielded to Hitler's express wish that the "capital of the movement" have a film company.)

The German film industry now consisted of nationalized organizations whose mission, as dictated by National Socialist ideology, was to serve the "national community" and which were subject to the "Führer principle," which a law of January 1937 extended to stockholding companies. What exactly was meant by the "Führer principle" Emil Jannings—in the role of company chief Clausen in Veit Harlan's *The Ruler* (Tobis)—made eminently clear to his administrative staff and his recalcitrant family: "To serve the national community—that has to be the goal of every business leader who takes his responsibilities seriously. That is the guiding principle for my work, and everything else must submit to it, without question, even if I run this business into the ground because of it." Clausen disinherits his family and leaves his company to the state, "the national community." Someone "called from the midst of the people," the script says, will carry on his work: "The genius of a born leader needs no teachers."

Filmscripts pressed Nazi propaganda into pre-formed didactic dialogues, and the emotional climax of them all was the invocation of death and destruction. Indeed—and this is the ultimate consequence of Fascist mythology—in death and destruction the principle of leader and vassal is confirmed and apotheosized. And in the subordinate mentality of those conservative bureaucrats now running the movie companies, there must have been latent self-destructive impulses interwoven with their acceptance of economic imperatives and political obsessions. In 1937, many Germans had an inkling (even if they instantly repressed it) that this "Third Reich" was heading for war and an unprecedented cataclysm. Even "business leaders" like Hugenberg, Klitzsch, Stauss, and Winkler could not have been completely blind to this. Perhaps they did not even need to repress that awareness. As highly paid agents of the power elite, they sat in the command centers of their "aligned" empires and did their best to maintain the political system to which they owed their privileges.

At the end of 1937 Hitler ordered a state funeral: Erich Ludendorff had died at the age of seventy-two on December 20, almost twenty years to the day after the founding of Ufa. Ludendorff and Hugenberg's mad idea that Germany's colonial empire should arise anew had been officially rehabilitated that year: in March, Foreign Minister Ribbentrop had voiced a demand for German colonies, the NSDAP party convention in September repeated his call, and Hitler himself alluded to it in a speech in celebration of the year's harvest.

And a collection for something called the Winterhelfswerk (Winter Aid

Fund) yielded 400 million marks. A fifth of that amount came from "sacrifices from wages and salaries," in other words, money withheld by the state from earned income. The dream of being a world power and the appeal to the Germans' willingness to make material sacrifices shaped the thinking of National Socialist Party members and sympathizers, and penetrated the people's day-to-day consciousness. They drowned out doubts and silenced well-founded objections. When in early 1937 Germany had officially withdrawn its signature from the debt articles of the Treaty of Versailles, the gesture had evoked hardly any surprise abroad. At the same time, Ufa newsreels showed pictures of work beginning on the West Wall and the fortification of Germany's eastern border. The Reich was becoming a bunker. Newsreel images that were supposed to waken trust and confidence in the government also inspired claustrophobic fears. In July 1937 the concentration camp at Buchenwald was built, a project that was certainly not unnoticed by the population. Shortly before, the pastor Martin Niemoller had been arrested after preaching a sermon protesting the Nazis' persecution of church members. Gustaf Gründgens was appointed general intendant of the Prussian State Theater in Berlin, and the government ordered the "sequestration" of "degenerate" German art for the purpose of an exhibition: the confiscated works of Expressionist, Cubist, and New Objectivity artists numbered in the thousands. The opening of a "House of German Art" with a "Great German Art Exhibit" in Munich on July 18 was intended to show Germany's turn away from the "decline of art, sculpture, and painting" experienced in the Weimar period, and "the passionate determination of the Third Reich and of the Führer to achieve a new, truly national art." The exhibit drew 420,000 visitors, but these numbers were far exceeded by the two million visitors to the simultaneous exhibit of "degenerate" art.

At a formal meeting of the Reich Guild of the Visual Arts on July 17, Goebbels noted that there was a "danger that the struggle against cultural Bolshevism could lead to the opposite extreme—a philistine, national kitsch closed to any kind of innovation."[9] His formulation betrayed latent reservations about the consequences of National Socialist policy in the arts and doubts about the real substance of what was being promoted; it also revealed, in Goebbels's case, the schizophrenia of the intellectual who had to bring these two extremes—"cultural Bolshevism" and philistine kitsch —into some kind of equilibrium in his own mind.

In the art guilds, in the "House of German Art," and, last but not least, the film factories under centralized state control, the regime had created monstrous propaganda citadels, but there were no mature concepts to give the ceaseless, overinflated Nazi ballyhoo real content. The dictatorship had created a political power structure built on empty forms borrowed from the academicism of the past century. The regime that wanted to create a new age was, despite its rhetoric, devoid of ideas.

The many attempts of Nazi ideologues to claim German films as part of their new "national culture" and to give a theoretical basis for the centralization of them were, to put it mildly, intellectually thin. They would not be worth our attention at all if the propaganda chiefs had not repeatedly and heatedly voiced their claim to leadership in the industry.

The contrast between verbal pretension and actual intellectual yield cannot have escaped thoughtful people in the film world, but the propaganda texts nonetheless have documentary interest for us today. Indirectly, they give us information about tendencies in the film industry that the regime regarded as counterproductive and that it continued to fight into the war years. Goebbels and his ideological lieutenants were combating forces that were still alive, especially in Ufa.

In his speech to the film guild in March 1937 Goebbels celebrated art for art's sake in the most inflated language and defended it against the principle of mere profitability. Like Ludendorff two decades before, though with far greater rhetorical finesse, he attacked the capitalists' egoism and commercialism. Here lay "the root of a disease that plagued German film like an insidious poison," so much so "that it is more accurate today to speak of a film industry rather than of film art."[10] But what he was really attacking was the lively unpredictability of a democratic entertainment culture that had indeed flourished in a democratic, profit-oriented economy. He hated the clever shamelessness of Weimar's uninhibited amusement industry, which, he thought, continued to work its mischief in the comedies and operettas of the Nazi years. He fulminated against the movies' "purely mercantile tendencies," but what he really abhorred was the quirky, "directionless," anarchistic urban culture that was still alive in some Ufa films; he abhorred the spirit in Curt Goetz's couplets and the petit-bourgeois insolence of the forbidden author Erich Kästner, the impudence of Reinhold Schünzel, and the ironies and invective in Erich Engel's comedies. In short, Goebbels detested the relics of Weimar; he detected a Semitic element in them, and he did not have to name it to denounce it.

In 1938 the "annual report" of the SS Security Service confirmed Goebbels's suspicions. Everywhere in the Reich and in all social classes, worrisome tendencies could be detected:

> The difficult periods in the year 1938 with its frequent crises have shown that breaking up liberal and pacifist organizations has not neutralized these opponents. The significance of liberalism lies not in its organizations but in the attitudes of individuals of liberal persuasion. . . . Liberal influence has increased in the arts. . . . Film and popular music degenerate more and more into the erotically oriented vapidity of the Weimar period.[11]

The very general standards that Goebbels set up against this ethos—a blend of draconian artistic judgments, middle-class genius worship, and aesthetic anti-rationalism—could inspire only confusion in his listeners. "The laws that have always been valid for art in general should now be applied to film," he said, "for these laws are eternal." Contemporary film was roughly in the same place "that German theater had been when Lessing wrote his *Hamburg Dramaturgy*." He, Goebbels, was "firmly convinced that somewhere and sometime in Germany a man would appear who would provide film, too, with its iron and immutable law and that this law would again provide a model that would remain valid throughout the world for centuries to come."

This will to subject film to undefined "iron" laws ran counter to another line of argument in Goebbels's speech, one that stressed the emotional values of cinema and evoked an almost anarchistic *élan vital*. Like all art, Goebbels said, film was a product not of reason but of emotion. The film artist's task was simply to "impart meaning to this emotion," "to capture life" and "to shape it according to the form dictated by his genius." If he remained close to life, Goebbels was willing to grant him the right to attempt "the boldest and most highly improvisational formal experiments." The "individual" had to make his own way; the "fertilization of the artistic element in film" had to originate in personality. Goebbels even went so far as to suggest that one had to have the courage simply "to start the motor and let it run, without worrying for the moment about where one wanted to go."

In 1942 Fritz Hippler, after 1939 chief of the film division in the Propaganda Ministry and later Reich Film Intendant, published *Observations on Film Production* in a series put out by the Reich Film Guild. This, too, reflects in its cynical and frighteningly primitive distortions the resistance that Goebbels's political pressure and ideological dictatorship continued to encounter even into the war years. Hippler devoted several pages of his brochure to the conflict with "freedom fanatics" who, "like rabbits terrified by a snake," stared at the institutions of the state as if paralyzed and "with martyrs' visages beatified by suffering" complained about their lack of artistic freedom. He advised them to use their intelligence and "to see things as they are and to work as rationally and purposefully as the enterprise deserved." It was obvious, Hippler said, that the oppression that enemies of the state were feeling was self-inflicted and that criminals would see themselves as persecuted.[12] Even in the middle of the war and almost ten years after the Nazis' assumption of power, resistance and open dissatisfaction had not died out in the film industry.

In the main body of his text Hippler does something that makes his pamphlet an interesting historical source: Using rejected scenarios as examples and acting as an advocate of "common sense," he analyzes typical plot patterns and narrative techniques to show up current German films as horrendous failures. From the passion invested in his polemic it becomes clear that the old Weimar vices, the suspect ambiguities of a democratic bohemian culture, were still showing through. This was particularly true for movies set in the Weimar period: "The film rendering of the inflationary and postwar period is usually very inadequate and poor . . . for example, degenerate bars with half-naked women, lascivious eroticism, and guttural Negro songs, also alcoholic drinks from champagne on down, and evening dress with white tie and tails."[13] Too much emphasis on "purely private love affairs"—an old standard—evoked Hippler's rage, too, especially if "a woman is an all too active partner" or if "a love story oversteps the limits of average understanding or shows no discretion in the portrayal of aberration."[14]

Hippler struggled against "the odd and the strange, the exceptional and the eccentric"—that is, against the very qualities in cinema that had made the medium such a joy for so many people, a vehicle for their yearnings. Totally in keeping with the National Socialist spirit, he wanted to repress sensuality. He hated eroticism in film and the eroticism of film. In the name of philistine normality he persecuted anything that refused to conform to the norms: any strange coincidence or bizarre happening, an overwhelming emotion or a sensual desire, insatiable longings or "eccentric" passions. But he was arraigning cinema itself. And his polemic involuntarily revealed that while Fascist rule may have threatened cinema and limited its further development, the medium was still very much alive.

23.

Sport on the Warship: Newsreels, Cultural Films, and Education for War

IN the political consciousness of the German people today, the film studios of the 1930s and 1940s, Ufa prominent among them, are seen simply as Nazi propaganda factories. "Nowhere else was the film industry so completely in the service of state propaganda; nowhere else was a state so obsessed with presenting itself in film."[1] And of course Ufa's founding in 1917 under military auspices and, even more important still, its political development under Hugenberg after 1927 did much to steer the company into being a propaganda instrument of the Nazi state. But the fact is that the same conservative, dyed-in-the-wool German nationalist board and management that in 1933 handed the company over to the National Socialist regime and in 1937 submitted to nationalization also resisted state pressure and the propaganda mission imposed on it. Given the political realities, Ufa's executives expressed their concerns primarily in internal and secret memos—but the documents clearly show what a struggle it was for the bourgeois, conservative mind to accept the bitter consequences of National Socialist control.

The difficulties were felt as early as mid-February 1933, two weeks after Hitler's assumption of power and six weeks before the Kaiserhof speech of the newly appointed Propaganda Minister, Goebbels. On February 18, Ernst Correll wrote a top-secret letter to Ludwig Klitzsch about a conversation he had had with Richard Schneider-Edenkoben, the director who a few months later provoked the ire of German farmers with his film *Thou Shalt Not Covet*.

Schneider-Edenkoben, a cousin of the prominent Nazi jurist Hans Frank, had noted "the key people who have been selected to reshape German culture in accordance with the views of the NSDAP."[2] And he had been interrogated himself and asked "whether he knew about Ufa's production plans and, in particular, about whether Ufa was now prepared to devote itself to purely German subjects, that is, folk subjects, and to abandon the international kitsch" that was good only for business abroad.

Correll assured Klitzsch that he had made Ufa's special situation clear to Schneider-Edenkoben, explaining that the public did not want either folk subjects or serious problem films, and that the "mentality of foreign countries" had to be taken into account, "for Germany alone could no longer pay for the films, especially when one considered the tax burden cinema was obliged to carry." Schneider-Edenkoben then told Correll that after the elections scheduled for March, the National Socialists would begin playing a different tune and resort to "radical measures." "Hitler had always had a great interest in film, because he had recognized its propaganda potential, and he knew how film had been used to influence people in Russia." The regime intended soon after the March elections "to place the film industry under state administration, to prescribe what kind of film could be produced, and to subject film production to total dictatorship," Schneider-Edenkoben said. The Nazi leaders realized that films with political messages were not popular, but the state would make up for the deficit, and a reduction in stars' salaries would help make up for the lost income.

Correll added here for his chief's information that Schneider-Edenkoben, no "lightweight," made an impression of "absolute integrity." He summed it up as follows: "I think we mustn't stick our heads in the sand. Rather, we have been forewarned."

Correll's secret memo not only suggests that the nationalization of the film industry was a foregone conclusion for the Nazis, but reflects in its content and conspiratorial tone the mixed feelings with which Ufa's conservative executives reacted to these plans. They were prepared to defend Ufa's market position and, with it, a production policy that had proved its worth for years, but Correll also hinted at how hard it would be, if not impossible, to withstand the new regime's pressure. He needed, he said, "clear guidelines." "It will be impossible to reject all the ideas they have suggested on the basis of the subject matter itself."

As we have seen, dissatisfaction with the state measures was voiced for a number of years, particularly by the producers. But the strong guiding hand of the government was a formidable problem for the distributors, too. In a statement prepared for the management meeting of July 12, 1935, Wilhelm Meydam made no secret of his bitterness. "The view of the Reich Film Guild that the production and distribution of films can be made to conform with generally applicable regulations handed down from on high continues to leave us with serious doubts about the viability of our business."[3]

Other sources of conflict had piled up that summer, too. Ufa had wanted to submit one of its prestige films, Reinhold Schünzel's *Amphitryon*, for the "Duce" prize awarded at the International Film Festival in Venice, but the Propaganda Ministry had decided on three others: Leni Riefenstahl's

Triumph of the Will; Hans Steinhoff's Prussian film *Der alte und der junge König* (*The Old and the Young King*, an Emil Jannings film produced by Deka-Film, 1934–35), refurbished in accordance with NSDAP ideology; and Terra's *Hermine und die sieben Aufrechten* (*Hermine and the Seven Honorable Men*, based on a novella by Gottfried Keller and directed by Frank Wysbar, with Heinrich George, Karin Hardt, and Albert Lieven in the leading roles, 1934–35). Ufa's movie was to be shown only in certain theaters in Venice on the periphery of the festival's main events. Ufa's executives were piqued and decided to withdraw *Amphitryon* altogether "because its drawing power would suffer considerably if it were shown outside the official competition."[4]

Shortly before this, in May, a meeting of newsreel directors at the Propaganda Ministry had given Ufa's managers other cause for alarm. Goebbels's lieutenant Hans Weidemann had told them that the government intended to draw all newsreel activities together into a "joint enterprise." The Deutsche Film-Nachrichten-Büro (German Film-News Office), Weidemann said, had been established for this purpose. Ufa's executives thought this threatened its independence, and established "on principle that in any further negotiations Ufa Newsreel's complete independence and freedom of action must be guaranteed and that any statements on this subject will be released only after prior discussion by senior management."[5]

But Ufa was clinging to an "independence" and "freedom of action" that now existed only on paper and that it had itself undermined with its overly eager compliance. From the National Socialists' point of view, the newsreel was the propaganda tool par excellence, and Ufa had already handed over this traditional political instrument to the eager hands of the new government in 1933.

Eberhard Fangauf, formerly in Ufa's cultural film division and since 1931 a member of the NSDAP, now the Propaganda Ministry's officer for film technology and film reporting, was supposed to coordinate the newsreel work and see that it served the interests of the state. When in 1933, after the Reichstag fire, the SA were sworn in as "auxiliary police" with white armbands, Fangauf, too, had done his part to promote the arbitrary exercise of state power: everyone working in newsreel reporting got a green ID card and a green armband with an eagle; their cars bore the legend "Officially Authorized Film Reporter." And, in a blatant usurpation of official power, Goebbels, then propaganda chief of the NSDAP and not yet a government minister, ordered all government agencies to help the newsreel teams with all possible practical support. Thus the newsreel business had long been an NSDAP instrument, its functions openly exploited by party interests.

Under Goebbels's direction, all the big public demonstrations staged by the party and the government were prepared for not just as major events in themselves but to be filmed: precise schedules were made up for the camera crews, locations were plotted, problems of lighting and sound pickup addressed and solved. The resulting "government-aligned" newsreels celebrated their first propaganda success early on: newsreels of events on March 21, 1933, the "Day of Potsdam," said the *Film-Kurier*, deserved the attention of everyone in the movie business, for they showed how documentary films, perhaps more than any other film form, could "honor the spirit of national awakening."[6] On May 1, the first "National Labor Day," which Goebbels made into a multimedia event with the help of Albert Speer and the radio, the first newsreel shots from an aircraft were taken. *Die Lichtbild-Bühne* had this to say:

> Ufa-Newsreel will send no less than four sound trucks equipped with 15 cameras and a staff of 30. Emelka-Newsreel will have 9 cameras operated by a staff of 24, and Fox, the major foreign newsreel that is permanently assigned to Germany, will send its entire staff. In addition, each newsreel company's special team will process the films immediately so that they will be not only developed and copied on the night of May 1 but also be ready for final editing that same night.[7]

By the time Ufa decided to build a copying plant, in 1936, on the Afifa grounds exclusively for newsreel purposes, its managers had given up any reservations they might have had about state interference in the company's affairs. Indeed, they were hoping to do lucrative business with army orders for the processing of secret military films. Also, in addition to newsreels, Ufa produced a monthly 8 mm "magazine," with selected coverage of important political events to be used at special showings for the party, the army, and the Arbeitsdienst (Labor Service).

While secretly preparing for the deployment of German troops in the demilitarized Rhineland in March 1936, the government recruited friendly press and film reporters with a surprise tactic. Barkhausen wrote:

> They had to wait for hours with no explanation. They were given beverages and sandwiches, but no official paid attention to them; the reporters wondered if they were in for a reproach. Not only the evening but the night passed in this way. Then early in the morning a bus took them to Tempelhof Airport, whence they were flown to Cologne. Meanwhile, also without being told why, cameramen were given instructions and railroad tickets for Cologne. There they were told that the Rhineland was being occupied by German troops, who were already crossing the Rhine and they were to cover this event for their respective companies. From their pictures we know with what joy the German troops were greeted as they marched into Cologne, Koblenz, and other cities. The reporters joined in the celebration.[8]

Similarly, for his triumphal march into Austria in March 1938 Hitler personally ordered from Ufa a documentary film of about twenty minutes, for which the government appropriated the noteworthy sum of 94,000 marks.[9] And in May 1938, when Hitler visited Italy, the Propaganda Ministry for the first time actually put all newsreel employees in uniform, "a completely neutral, uniform-like reporters' garb in blue gray."[10] Evidently the cameramen, sound crews, and their assistants had been able to resist the efforts to force them into brown shirts and thus to advertise their subjection to the state and the party.

None of these newsreels, monotonous propaganda vehicles for the government as they were, found favor with audiences. But to the distress of theater owners, Goebbels decreed in October 1938 that they had to be shown first in every movie program. The result was that many people deliberately arrived late and took their seats while the newsreels were running. Secret SS documents, which reported enthusiastic public response to the first wartime newsreels, nonetheless noted that public approval would be even greater "if the four German newsreel [companies] . . . differed more in their presentations."[11] In March 1941, the Propaganda Ministry ordered all theaters to have a five-minute pause between the newsreel and the main program (theater owners who disobeyed could be fined 10,000 marks); but audiences now simply waited for the newsreels to be over, crowding around in the lobby until the main feature began. Goebbels then took one more step in this petty war and ordered that the auditorium doors be locked once the newsreels had begun. In the last years of the war, the only way the moviegoers, now literally locked in the auditorium, could vent their frustration with the newsreels was to laugh, whistle, and boo.[12]

In November 1940, the four German newsreel companies were nationalized in one Deutsche Wochenschau. This marked the end of Ufa Newsreel, with its tradition reaching back to the time of Oskar Messter; its democratic spirit, almost eradicated under Hugenberg, disappeared entirely with the Nazi takeover.

It has to be said to the credit of Ufa Newsreels' editors and cameramen, sound men and film cutters, that they were motivated by high technical and artistic goals, devotion to their craft, and no little perfectionism. At historic moments, they turned in some amazing performances. In covering the Munich Conference in September 1938, for example, they managed to fly their film to the Afifa copying plant in Berlin-Tempelhof, cut and edit a master, produce the required number of copies, and deliver them to Ufa's Berlin theaters by nine o'clock that same evening.

Heinrich Roellenbleg, chief of the Ufa Newsreel Division from 1939 on, demanded "artistically presented documents of our time," and even if this aesthetic and journalistic concept was vague, it hinted at high ambitions. The producer had "to give dramaturgical form" to events in order to get "maximum impact." Film reports had to have an "inner dynamic." Newsreel work had progressed "beyond mere craft and reached a higher level of artistic creativity."[13] And indeed, Ufa newsreels were a major influence on film reporting for decades to come. Their "screenplays," montage, image presentation, and voice-overs left their mark on newsreels well into the 1950s and even on early television.

In its 1939 historical retrospective on the newsreel, Ufa declared that World War I had "demonstrated for the first time the propagandistic value of this most modern tool for reportage and education. Our present-day newsreel remains firmly committed to this same mission."[14] With the cultural film, that specifically German variation of the documentary, Ufa contributed something of its own to the National Socialist propaganda arsenal—and, at the same time, a model for the Nazi ideologues to admire. "Not only the aesthetic of the cultural film but the very concept of the 'cultural film' itself is a typically German phenomenon," Hilmar Hoffmann has written. "The makers of German cultural films demystify the creation and the cosmos."[15] No field of knowledge, nothing subject to empirical investigation, no phenomenon of the plant or animal world, no fact of natural history or technology was safe from their popularizing grasp, and everything they took in hand they subsumed under a "specific mode of elevated contemplation."

It was no coincidence that Ufa's "cultural division," established on July 1, 1918, wound up in the military hands of Major Ernst Krieger. Krieger was a regimental colleague of the Ufa executive Alexander Grau; this "old military tie"[16] outlasted the Weimar vicissitudes and guaranteed the continuity of a conservativism that was open to the sciences and technological progress, that was politically "value free" only on the surface, and that offered no resistance to the Nazis' totalitarian ideology.

The "theatrically viable short film" on virtually any subject readily assumed the task of political pedagogy in Hitler's state. No unbridgeable chasm yawned between the "insect optics" Ufa's cultural division had been developing since 1929 and National Socialism's macro- and microcosmically oriented social images. Technical achievements like slow motion and quick motion, telephoto lenses, and adjustable focus were susceptible to a scientific, Darwinian sociology "that systematically measures, analyzes, names, and explains societies"[17] the better to keep them under surveillance. The links were an obsession with technology, an affinity between biometry and sociometry, and a concept of work that could easily be transferred from films of popularized science, like *Der Ameisenstaat* (*The Ant State*, Ulrich K.T. Schulz, 1934), to populist propaganda in films like *Arbeitsdienst* (*Labor Service*, Hans Curlis, 1933) or *Deutsche Arbeitsstätten* (*German Workplaces*, 1940) by Svend Noldan (who had worked as a cameraman on the Ufa compilation film *The World War* in 1927). Nicholas Kaufmann, who had had a hand in *Ways to Strength and Beauty*, produced during the war *Das Sinnesleben der Pflanzen* (*The Sensory Life of Plants*), *Radium, Röntgenstrahlen* (*X-rays*), and *Können Tiere denken?* (*Can Animals Think?*). Hans Traub, chief of Ufa-Lehrschau (Ufa Instructional Visuals), summed up the mission this way: "The military-education film and the cultural film both stand completely in the service of the German struggle for freedom. . . . In recent years, the cultural film has been given over increasingly to subjects relevant to the state and the party."[18]

In November 1930, the NSDAP had founded its own Reich Film Office (as we have seen), and with party-produced films like *Hitlers Kampf um Deutschland* (*Hitler's Battle for Germany*, 1931), it had tested the documentary film as a propaganda tool. To produce a fifteen-minute film, Goebbels's Ministry budgeted the comparatively generous sum of 30,000 marks; they seemed to know how manipulable the medium was, how fluid the border between "objective" pictures of reality and demagogic presentation. The tendency to aestheticize social themes—a tendency that had reached a high point in Walter Ruttmann's *Berlin—Symphony of the City*—was now put to work aestheticizing the political, "taking flight into form"[19] but never losing sight of the propaganda mission. Ruttmann made for the National Socialist regime *Metall des Himmels* (*Metal of Heaven*, 1934), *Altgermanische Bauernkultur* (*Old Germanic Peasant Culture*, 1939), and *Deutsche Panzer* (*German Tanks*, produced by Ufa in 1941)—films that "educated for war," films for a culture of death and the willingness to kill.

The New Objectivity had encouraged a reification of montage, and this suited the new context of a reactionary aestheticizing of reality. According to Hartmut Bitomsky, who has analyzed many of the National Socialist cultural films, their montage "pulls together what it needs, but the resulting combination connects with nothing in the reality of the individual shots. . . . [A] uniform motion carries through each cut. It seizes each image it comes upon with rotating, thrusting gestures." The editing has separated images and put them back together again according to abstract, aesthetic criteria, but has destroyed the real "content," the wealth of meaning, in each image.[20] As with march rhythms in revue films, the point in movies about factory work or Germany's tanks was a new organization of social senses and feelings: "the adaptation of machine rhythms to the rhythm of the blood," as the National Socialist ideologues put it. *Sport auf dem Panzerschiff "Deutschland"* (*Sport on the Battleship "Germany"*) was inspired not only (as Bitomsky surmises) by Sergei Eisenstein's *Potemkin* but also by the Ufa operetta *Monte Carlo Madness* (Hanns Schwarz, 1931), where the sailors' choreographed athletics as cannon swing into position over their heads were perfectly prefigured.

In September 1940, a year after World War II began, the SS Security Service reported that all over Germany interest had increased in cultural films on non-political subjects, especially films about landscapes, animals, and scientific subjects. Movies about trees were a compensation for the daily experience of the war. Given expanded newsreel coverage of the war, the SS observers suggested having cultural films prior to the feature films. Matinees of this sort on Sundays, they pointed out, were for many people a kind of substitute church. "Developing them systematically into 'morning film rituals' would, some interested persons felt, add significantly to the wartime propaganda impact of film."[21]

The government had already, with major Ufa involvement, established the Deutsche Kulturfilm-Zentrale (Central Office for German Cultural Film) under Goebbels's control. In this one sector of film production at least, the Propaganda Minister was successfully realizing his hope for instruction subtly combined with political indoctrination, education for war with soothing entertainment.

24.

The Poisoned Kitchen: Propaganda and "Unpolitical Entertainment" before the War

IN 1938, the last year of peace, German movie houses had reported record attendance, with 440 million tickets sold. Domestic production was down compared with 1934 (114 films for the year, down from 147), but of the films distributed (152 all told) the great majority (95 full-length features) were German productions.[1]

After Hitler Germany's annexation of Austria, the situation in Vienna required, according to SS reports, "a special cleansing,"[2] for more than half of Vienna's 174 movie theaters were in Jewish hands. To counteract the "ill feeling among Austrian film people," Goebbels established a foreign office of the Reich Film Guild in Vienna, and with the assistance of Ufa and its Austrian offices and subsidiaries, Wien-Film was founded, its task to preserve for German film "the unique qualities of Austrian art . . . Viennese charm and élan."

1938: On the grounds at Neubabelsberg Goebbels dedicated the German Film Academy and set as its "ideal goal" the selection of thirty to forty young artists from a thousand applicants. "Anyone accepted at the German Film Academy in the future—regardless of what aspect of film he wants to pursue—must show signs of genius."[3] But even the SS observers urged more modest expectations: the new talent simply was not there.[4]

The SS spies also noted a broad popular dissatisfaction with movie reviews, for the press seemed to think it "had to glorify" all German productions—a consequence of Goebbels's ban on negative criticism. On the other hand, movies shown at NSDAP district film theaters found "universal approval," which was not surprising, since they were chosen from the "backlist" of older films.

On the whole, the SS observers thought they were seeing an upward trend in the movie business. The upswing could be attributed not only to Leni Riefenstahl's films about the 1936 Olympics but also to two major

Ufa feature films, *Urlaub auf Ehrenwort* (*On Leave but Still on Duty*) and *Pour le mérite*. From a National Socialist point of view, these two Karl Ritter movies were indeed shining examples of how one could successfully incorporate propaganda into a feature film. These well-received movies were key in establishing Ufa's reputation as an ideology factory of the Hitler regime. For a long time the quite small number of blatantly tendentious films obscured the truth that the vast majority of films produced under Nazi rule did not openly promote Fascist "principles." Goebbels relied more on insinuation and subtle suggestion, and most of the movies produced in this period were in fact "unpolitical" entertainment films. Of the 88 German productions from the period 1933–45 that Erwin Leiser considered in his study of this subject, 35 were made and distributed by Ufa; after the defeat of Germany, the Allied military governments banned 27 of them.[5] A number of representative propaganda films, among them a few major Prussian films, were made by other companies: Carl Froelich produced *The Anthem of Leuthen* in 1933, *The Old and the Young King* (Hans Steinhoff, 1934–35) was a Deka production, and *The Great King* (directed by Veit Harlan in 1942) a Tobis film. Harlan also made *The Ruler* for Tobis and, for Terra, the infamously anti-Semitic film *Jew Süss* (1940). Fritz Hippler's "documentary" *Der ewige Jude* (*The Eternal Jew*) was commissioned by the party's Reich Propaganda Office. Other anti-Semitic films were made by Tobis (*Robert und Bertram*, Hans Heinz Zerlett, 1939) and by smaller companies, such as Styria-Film in Vienna (*Leinen aus Irland* [*Linen from Ireland*], Heinz Helbig, 1939). Wolfgang Liebeneiner—chair of the artistic faculty of the German Film Academy and a producer for Ufa from 1942 until the end of the war—made movies promoting the "Führer" myth (*Bismarck* [1940] and *Die Entlassung* [*The Dismissal*, 1942]) and his "euthanasia" film *Ich klage an* (*I Accuse*, 1941) for Tobis, which also produced most of the heroic biographies that the National Socialists appropriated for their own purposes: *Friedrich Schiller*, for example, by Herbert Maisch (1940), Steinhoff's *Robert Koch, der Bekämpfer des Todes* (*Robert Koch, the Battler against Death*, 1939), and *Ohm Krüger* (*Uncle Kruger*, 1941). Maisch's film *Andreas Schlüter* (1942) was produced by Terra; Herbert Selpin's *Carl Peters* (1941) by Bavaria.

Even these few examples show us how the movie business organized itself around the principle of division of labor. Vertical "alignment" brought with it a horizontal "consolidation," and all decisions about production plans were of course made by the Ministry of Propaganda. Wherever political propaganda was on the agenda, it was attended to with technical perfection and aesthetic uniformity. Artistic individualism and cinematic originality were detrimental here. The distinctive "signatures" of directors and producers melded together in an ideologically prescribed uniformity. The "Ufa director" type, as embodied in Fritz Lang, Ludwig Berger, Joe May, Hanns Schwarz, and others, disappeared, replaced by politically compliant directors, many of whom had found their way to the NSDAP during its "period of struggle." In the following years, these serviceable men proved extremely versatile. Carl Froelich, Hans Steinhoff, Karl Ritter, and Veit Harlan functioned as authors, directors, and producers; they served on "artistic committees" and, like Liebeneiner, became "division leaders" or, like Froelich, presidents of the Reich Film Guild. They were commanders and accomplices of power; they functioned as executors of the all-powerful Minister Goebbels. In short, they were the indispensable middlemen between the source of political power and Germany's much ballyhooed "national art."

Hans Steinhoff, for example, had made a name for himself since 1921 as a craftsmanlike director with a preference for entertainment films sure to draw an audience, but also for nationalistic, conservative subjects (as in *Rosenmontag* [*Monday before Lent*], 1930). Then, with *Hitler Youth Quex* in 1933, he assured his rise to star director with a clear statement of allegiance to the new state. As a protégé of Baldur von Schirach (who wrote the lyrics of the Hitler Youth song "Our Flag Flies before Us" for this film), Steinhoff was decorated with the Hitler Youth golden Medal of Honor, was promoted to chief of the Reich Youth Leadership for Film, and was involved in the following years with the production of educational 16 mm films. Artistic and political functions, work in the studio and service to the government were inextricably woven together in his career.

With *Refugees, Das Mädchen Johanna* (*The Girl Johanna*, 1935), and *Homecoming* (1941), Gustav Ucicky made films for Ufa and Wien-Film that used all the clichés of nationalism and the "Führer" mythology. But at the same time, Ucicky was trying to save his reputation as an "unpolitical artist" with film versions of literary classics like *Der zerbrochene Krug* (*The Broken Jug*, Tobis-Magna-Filmproduktions, 1937) and *Der Postmeister* (*The Postmaster*, based on a story by Pushkin, Wien-Film, 1939–40). His pessimistic woodcutter drama *Am Ende der Welt* (*At the End of the World*, Wien-Film, 1943) was banned by the censors in December 1943.

Veit Harlan, who began during World War I as an extra with the silent-film pioneer Max Mack and worked as an actor after that, publicly espoused the NSDAP cause in 1933. He debuted as a director in 1935, but made his mark primarily as the author of emotional melodramas like *Jugend* (*Youth*, 1937–38), *Verwehte Spuren* (*Lost Traces*, 1938), and *Die Reise nach Tilsit* (*The Journey to Tilsit*, 1939), which he directed for Tobis, with Kristina Söderbaum in the lead and Bruno Mondi as his cameraman. *The Ruler* was his tribute to the National Socialist "Führer principle," and his Ufa comedy *Mein Sohn, der Herr Minister* (*My Son, the Minister*), made in that same year, was an infamous satire on parliamentary democracy. The Ufa color films *Die goldene Stadt* (*The Golden City*, 1942), *Immensee* (1943), and *Opfergang* (*Path of Sacrifice*, 1943–44) predestined Harlan to direct *Kolberg*, a megalomaniacal, death-hungry, fight-to-the-last-man production with which the Hitler regime took leave of film history in the last weeks of the war. Two years earlier, Goebbels had granted Harlan the title of professor and made him an Ufa producer. Among his permanent associates were the screenplay writer Alfred Braun and his assistant director, Wolfgang Schleif; all three began new careers in postwar West Germany.

Any film subject can be a National Socialist one "if it is envisioned and organized by a National Socialist personage for whom the laws and goals of the movement have become second nature."[6] When Wilhelm Müller-Scheld, president of the German Film Academy and former district propaganda chief in Hessen-Nassau, wrote that in a Festschrift for Hitler's fiftieth birthday in 1939, he may well have had in mind the Ufa director and producer Karl Ritter, a perfect exemplar of the virtues required by the regime who was also imbued with an unquestioning faith in the "Führer." In his mind, the public was raw material, and film was the machine for processing that material. "We do not want to see anyone sitting in our theaters who is not a convinced National Socialist. German film must be uncompromising in its service to the community, the nation, and the Führer."[7] Behind those convictions stood a monotone view of humanity that made Ritter the chief ideologue for the Fascist machinery of death.

It is an irony of film history that Ritter began his career as the director of a Karl Valentin comedy (*Im Photoatelier* [*In the Photo Studio*], Reichsliga-Film, 1932). A year later, this World War I major became an Ufa producer and soon made himself indispensable on *Hitler Youth Quex*. His inability to establish himself in civilian life during the Weimar Republic and his hatred of Weimar democracy, its cosmopolitanism, and its liberal culture led him to the NSDAP early in the 1920s. A producer of films directed by Frank Wysbar, Hans Steinhoff, Herbert Maisch, and others, Ritter became a director himself in 1936, and served intermittently as artistic representative on the Ufa board. He remained loyal to the film factory at Neubabelsberg until the end of the war. The National Socialist propaganda film, trademark Ufa, was largely his work.

It is impossible not to sense that many German films made before the war helped to create the psychological premises for Germany's aggression and to direct the public's hostility toward the "correct" enemies. The propaganda line required differentiations to be made, of course, some of which were dictated by the government's diplomatic maneuvers and some by the different attitudes that producers and directors had toward their subjects.

In the mid-1930s Ufa produced three films that dealt with England. In Gerhard Lamprecht's historical *Der höhere Befehl* (*The Higher Command*, with Lil Dagover, Karl Ludwig Diehl, Friedrich Kayssler, and Siegfried Schürenberg, 1935), a Prussian cavalry officer helps the British ambassador to Austria travel incognito from Vienna to London and form the European alliance against Napoleon. In the year when the Anglo-German Naval Agreement was signed, the National Socialists had an obvious interest in recalling the historic coalition that Prussia and England had formed to liberate Europe from Napoleon. Though the Prussian theme was a natural for Lamprecht, he was not a propagandist of the Goebbels breed, but in this case he won the Propaganda Minister's praise. Calling *The Higher Command* "a national and engrossing film," and gracing it with the rating "of special national political and artistic value,"[8] Goebbels recommended it to a populace who had just been told that universal conscription would be reintroduced and who were bracing for a harsher policy toward France.

Paul Wegener, too, director of the patriotic adventure *Ein Mann will nach Deutschland* (A Man Wants to Reach Germany, with Karl Ludwig Diehl and Brigitte Horney, 1934), turned a friendly gaze toward England. In this film, Willy Birgel plays a British officer who, early in World War I, balks at guarding a camp of German prisoners. But Karl Ritter's *Verräter* (*Traitors*, with Lida Baarova, Willy Birgel, and Rudolf Fernau, 1936) portrays England as the archenemy, alerting the viewer to the activities of the British Secret Service and inciting hatred toward traitors in their own ranks.

Der deutsche Film, the publication of the Reich Film Guild, called Ritter's "military films" "cinematic tanks that belong in the advance guard on the propaganda front."[9] The director himself spoke of them as "heroic films," and in 1937, when Hitler first revealed his war plans to the Wehrmacht leadership, Ritter as producer and director made three heroic epics in a row: *Patrioten* (*Patriots*, with Lida Baarova, Mathias Wieman, Hilde Körber, and Paul Dahlke), *Unternehmen Michael* (*Project Michael*, with Heinrich George, Mathias Wieman, Willy Birgel, and Hannes Stelzer), and *On Leave but Still on Duty* (with Ingeborg Theek, Fritz Kampers, Rolf Moebius, Berta Drews, René Deltgen, and Carl Raddatz in his first film role). The censors immediately awarded them high ratings. For all three Walter Röhrig did the sets and Günther Anders was the cameraman. The writer who worked most with Ritter was Felix Lützkendorf, who in 1936 had proclaimed the advent of the "literature of a new masculinity."[10]

In *Patriots* Ritter told, rather subtly, the love story of a French actress and a German pilot shot down behind enemy lines, but in *Project Michael* he renounced psychology altogether to glorify senseless death. The film relates an episode from the spring offensive on the western front in 1918. The commander of a battalion surrounded and hard-pressed by French and British troops orders his artillery to fire on his own position. "We shall not be judged by the grandeur of our victory but by the depth of our sacrifice" are his final words.[11] The mass deaths and sadomasochistic mysticism of the film evoked protest from high-ranking officers and set off a heated controversy between the army and the Ministry of Propaganda.

On Leave but Still on Duty, made at almost the same time, was a hymn in praise of "that damned sense of duty" that four combat soldiers on leave do not want to shed even in revolutionary Berlin of October 1918. It is the "leftist intellectual" among them, of all people, who lectures his pacifist friends of yore with patriotic sentiments: "We soldiers are dying for our country while you drink, hold meetings, and make love."[12] This sentence expressed perfectly the Nazi propaganda line against the "November criminals" of 1918, the democratic politicians who supposedly "stabbed" the troops in the back and sent Germany to its defeat. In Karl Ritter's films, Ufa offered a commentary on its own history: Germany's military situation in the last years of the war had led to the founding of the company, and the revolutionary "chaos" on the "home front" favored its development. Twenty years later, Ufa was returning to the fateful historic constellation from which it had risen; Ritter's films finally realized Ludendorff's legacy: "The longer the war lasts, the more essential the planned influencing of the domestic population becomes." A film like *Project Michael* showed that, in a psychological sense, the Second World War had already begun.

Shortly before Christmas in 1938, Hitler, the party leaders, and the Wehrmacht's entire general staff attended (at the Ufa-Palast am Zoo) the premiere of a Karl Ritter film that had been hailed a few days before in Himmler's press as a cinematic presentation par excellence of the party's program. *Pour le Mérite* was an encyclopedic and kaleidoscopic mirror for every conceivable Nazi distortion of history and "one of the most malevolent and mean-spirited representations of the Weimar Republic in Nazi film," as one critic has written.[13] Using 102 performers—among them Paul Hartmann, Fritz Kampers, Josef Dahmen, Elsa Wagner, Gisela von Collande, Paul Dahlke, and Wolfgang Staudte—Ritter spread out in forty episodes a panorama of recent history from the Nazi perspective. The film progressed from the "heroic deeds" of German fighter pilots in World War I to the sad fate of "decent" soldiers in the Weimar Republic and their struggle for illegal rearmament to the day in March 1935 when Goebbels announced universal conscription and the buildup of the armed forces "while cheering masses gathered at memorial monuments of the First World War. The old knights are wearing new uniforms, and the engines of the Third Reich's first fighter squadrons are bellowing out 'their heroic song in the spirit of *Pour le Mérite*.' "[14] (One of the "old knights" makes clear what he thinks of the Weimar Republic of "Jewish swindlers" and "Communist mobs," of "political corruption" and "moral degeneracy." "I wash my hands of this state, for I hate democracy like the plague. Regardless of anything you may do, I will undermine and sabotage it whenever I can. We have to create a Germany that is in keeping with the ideas of a combat soldier."[15])

Dorothea Hollstein, who in a study of anti-Semitic prejudice in Nazi films discovered a previously overlooked anti-Semitic sequence in *Pour le Mérite*, points out that Ritter, by way of his father-in-law—a "rabid National Socialist and fanatical anti-Semite"—had access to Richard Wagner's house, Wahnfried, in Bayreuth and, consequently, close contact with Hitler, who protected him from a certain "animosity" on Goebbels's part. Although Ritter was the only prominent Ufa director openly to embrace anti-Semitism, he does not seem to have had an interest in making blatantly anti-Semitic films. His focus was "the cultivation of an overbred nationalism and monumental heroism."[16]

Ritter's gifts became a subject of controversy in postwar film historiography. Francis Courtade and Pierre Cadars, French critics who could afford to judge Nazi films from an essentially aesthetic point of view, thought that *On Leave but Still on Duty*, apart from the "speculative" nature of its subject, was technically and artistically excellent.[17] Even the Polish film historian Toeplitz discovered something to praise: "If Karl Ritter had had better screenplays and if he had been more aware of the dangers of declamatory dialogue, his works would have gained immensely. They are lively and usually interesting but lack artistic profundity. They never go beyond rather loud, importunate propaganda."[18]

It was precisely this loud, importunate propaganda—together with ponderous, schematic dramaturgy, almost allegorical characters, and a lack of visual imagination—that characterized most National Socialist party-line films. Under Hitler and Goebbels, the aesthetic achievements of the old Ufa were forgotten or, indeed, fell into disrepute. And Ritter, who had pilloried the intellectualism of film in the Weimar period,[19] helped contribute to their demise.

Although Ufa's managers accepted the propaganda mission the Nazi regime imposed, clashes with the Propaganda Ministry and its unpredictable chief continued. In February 1938 in a memo for the files, Ernst Hugo Correll recapitulated the circumstances surrounding the banning of the anti-Communist film *Starke Herzen* (*Strong Hearts*).[20] His tone is objective, but the bitterness shows through.

In a November 1936 meeting with producers, directors, and actors, the Propaganda Ministry had demanded the production of anti-Bolshevist films. The timing was not coincidental: the regime was cranking up its "nation-without-*Lebensraum*" propaganda, and Hitler had observed that only two countries in Europe were standing firm against Bolshevism: National Socialist Germany and Fascist Italy.[21] The film people listened to the Ministry, and Ufa commissioned a film in keeping with its propaganda line, "with the best intentions of carrying the project through," as Correll put it. The projected *Strong Hearts*, Ufa optimistically announced, in 1937–38, would concern

> the fate of a city drawn into the witches' cauldron of a revolution in 1919. The struggle of a conspiracy against the messengers of Bolshevism. In this chaos, two human beings find their way to each other—bound by duty and a willingness to make sacrifices, these two hearts resonate in a stirring witness to the triumphant power of love over hatred and death.[22]

The new Reich film dramaturge, Ewald von Demandowsky, accepted this treatment and suggested only a few changes "that did not," Correll noted,

Triumph des Willens (*Triumph of the Will*), 1934–35

Morgenrot (*Dawn*), with (starting second from left) Rudolf Forster, Fritz Genschow, and Gerhard Bienert

Hitlerjunge Quex (*Hitler Youth Quex*), with Claus Clausen (center)

Propaganda Minister Goebbels awards the first state film prize to *Flüchtlinge* (*Refugees*), 1934: (left to right) Ernst Hugo Correll, Ludwig Klitzsch, Gerhard Menzel, Gustav Ucicky, Eugen Klöpfer, Goebbels, Undersecretary Funk

Refugees, with Hans Albers

Goebbels and Vittorio Mussolini visit the filming of *Preussische Liebesgeschichte* (*Prussian Love Story*): (from left to right) Goebbels, Undersecretary Hanke, Willy Fritsch, Mussolini

Amphitryon or . . .

. . . "Happiness Come Down from the Clouds": *Triumph of the Will*

Hallo Janine, with Marika Rökk

Hallo Janine

Frauen sind doch bessere Diplomaten (*Women Really Do Make Better Diplomats*), a typical Ufa operetta, with sets by Erich Kettelhut

Das Mädchen Irene (*The Girl Irene*), with Karl Schönböck, Lil Dagover, Sabine Peters, and Geraldine Katt

Glückskinder (*Children of Happiness*), with Lilian Harvey and Willy Fritsch in the pool

The same film again, with Harvey and Fritsch

A publicity shot for Lilian Harvey in *Glückskinder* (*Children of Happiness*)

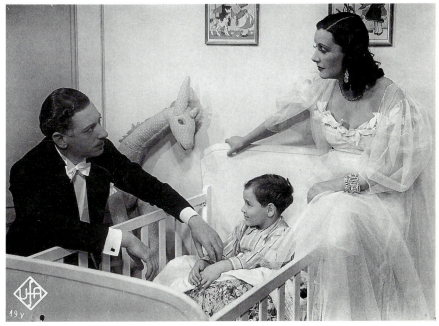

Schlussakkord (*Final Accord*), with Willy Birgel and Lil Dagover

Speer's "light cathedral," Berlin, 1937

Speer's model for the "Great Hall," 1939

Der Herrscher (*The Ruler*), with Marianne Hoppe and Emil Jannings

Der Mann, der Sherlock Holmes war (*The Man Who Was Sherlock Holmes*), with Heinz Rühmann
and Hans Albers

Unternehmen Michael (Project Michael), with Heinz Welzel

Urlaub auf Ehrenwort (On Leave but Still on Duty), with Elisabeth Wendt and Carl Raddatz

Pour le Mérite

Hitler Youth Quex, with Hermann Speelmans and Heinrich George

Oberwachtmeister Schwenke (Police Sergeant Schwenke), with Gustav Fröhlich (center)

. . . reitet für Deutschland (Riding for Germany), with Willy Birgel

Emil Jannings in *Ohm Krüger* (*Uncle Krüger*)

Goebbels awards the Goethe Medal to Emil Jannings in 1939; in the center, President Lehnich of the Reich Film Guild

Jud Süss, with Werner Krauss (right)

Ufa's twenty-fifth anniversary celebration at Ufa-Palast am Zoo in 1943, Goebbels at the podium

Kristina Söderbaum

Marika Rökk in *Kora Terry*

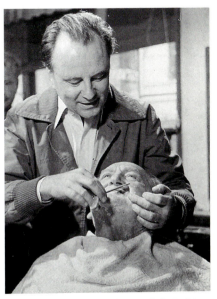

Kurt Gerron with Dolly Haas

Wolfgang Liebeneiner shaves Jakob Tiedtke

Der Weg ins Freie (Path to Freedom), with Zarah Leander and Hans Stüwe

Die grosse Liebe (The Great Love), with Viktor Staal and Zarah Leander

Wunschkonzert (Wish Concert), with Ilse Werner and Carl Raddatz

Annelie, with Luise Ullrich

Filming *Münchhausen*

Kora Terry, with sets by Erich Kettelhut

Kolberg

Filming *Die Mörder sind unter uns* (*The Murderers Are Among Us*) at Neubabelsberg in 1946; in the background, Wolfgang Staudte and Hildegard Knef

The Ufa-Palast am Zoo in 1945

Women cleaning up rubble in Ufa City, June 1945

"affect the scenario in any essential way." Ufa delivered a screenplay that met with his approval. Demandowsky was sometimes present in the studio during filming (Herbert Maisch directed; the singer Maria Cebotari, Gustav Diessl, and Walther Frank played the leads). Even the Propaganda Ministry had approved a plot summary. Correll summarized what happened next:

> In June 1937 the film was presented to the Propaganda Ministry, which requested various changes. Additional shooting was done, to the tune of 141,000 marks, and after the Ministry had been informed of how much the changes would cost. After the changes were made, the film was submitted to the censors, who suggested we retract our application because the film would be banned in any case. The film cost a total of 799,000 marks. Now it is on the shelf.

And in fact *Strong Hearts* was banned for good in November 1937 after several submissions to the censors. Friedrich Kahlenberg, in his reconstruction of its production history, could not conclusively determine why. He did, however, find a clue "in the substantially more cogent presentation of the position of the revolutionaries as compared with the portrayal of the representatives of the national cause."[23] After the war, sensitivity to Soviet feelings prompted the Allied Military Commission once again to suppress the film. Not until 1952–53, when anti-Communist sentiment became desirable in the Federal Republic under Konrad Adenauer, did the Voluntary Censorship Office release it, under the title *Starke Herzen im Sturm* (*Strong Hearts in the Storm*).

For the Nazis, the confrontation with Communism had many problems rooted in the social history of their own movement. Then, too, Hitler's 1939 non-aggression pact with the Soviet Union complicated the picture. With its two 1933 films—Steinhoff's *Hitler Youth Quex* and Ucicky's *Refugees*—Ufa established the direction anti-Communist agitation would take. In *Refugees* (as summarized by Oskar Kalbus), a group of Volga Germans finds its way "out of the hell of Russia into the purgatory of general war in China . . . buffeted by the storm over Asia—at their backs the Bolsheviks, before them Chinese rifle fire." Communism is represented here as a global danger bred in the depths of Asia. Its messengers have infiltrated the centers of civilization and brought Weimar Germany to the brink of disaster. The Volga Germans in this film, "full of inner dissension and pain, full of despair and weakness,"[24] are the Germans of the Weimar Republic, who in a state of deep humiliation are awaiting their leader.

Hitler Youth Quex shows the proletarian base that the National Socialist and Communist movements shared, and with perfidious intelligence uses the dramaturgical inventory, psychological patterns and atmospherics of such outstanding works of leftist cinema as Phil Jutzi's *Mother Krause's Journey to Happiness* and Slatan Dudow's *Kuhle Wampe*, as well as Heinrich George's tremendous appeal in the role of a Communist worker. As one analyst has put it, "the Communists are presented as the anti-types of National Socialist ideals, but the attributes ascribed to the Communists have their psychological roots in the character of National Socialists."[25]

The Hitler-Stalin pact of 1939 made any anti-Soviet or anti-Bolshevist impulse taboo and even brought about a ban on a prominent hit; *Hard Times in Friesland* by Peter Hagen (alias Reich film dramaturge Willi Krause) was not rereleased until after Germany attacked the Soviet Union in 1941 and then with a new and unambiguous title: *Dorf im roten Sturm* (*Village in the Red Storm*). Ufa did not make propaganda movies again about the Communist threat until Karl Ritter's inflammatory *GPU* (1942).

Hitler and his leading ideologue, Alfred Rosenberg, Goebbels's most determined opponent in the inner-party debate over the political "guidance" of cultural life, energetically promoted the political film and wanted to see it clearly distinguished from "unpolitical" entertainment. But Goebbels continued to think about insinuating the regime's "messages" into popular cinematic genres. And indeed, in the gray area between propaganda and entertainment many films kept the characteristic genre features and the ideological elements in equilibrium. Sometimes the harmless ambience seemed to have the upper hand, sometimes the covert political message overpowered the main text. In extreme cases, this led to differences in interpretation that have never been resolved. Was Herbert Maisch's *Friedrich Schiller*, with Horst Caspar's call for freedom and human dignity, a "flaming attack on a tyrant's oppression of the spirit"[26] and therefore obviously anti-Fascist? Or was it a heroic biography whose every detail fit perfectly into the genius and "Führer" cults (it had an official rating "of national political value")? The dialogue was clearly shaped to fit propaganda needs, and loyal nationalists clearly understood it in the National Socialist spirit in which it was written. But the film's ambiguity, its atmosphere of militaristic tyranny, and the appeal of the youthful Horst Caspar in his pose of freedom fighter reached those in the audience who thought differently, had different expectations and perceptions; they had the courage to oppose the regime by applauding at the "right" places.

In more than a few films the nature of the subject matter allowed for an ambivalence that nullified the intended indoctrination. In others, the desired contemporary meaning came wrapped in unambiguous historical or melodramatic material. Two Ufa productions of 1937 were classic examples of these diametrically opposed forms of political manipulation. In Herbert Maisch's *Menschen ohne Vaterland* (*People without a Fatherland*, with Willy Fritsch, Maria von Tasnady, and Willy Birgel), a German-Russian nobleman who in 1918 finds himself between the fronts in the Baltic provinces decides, after much hesitation, to support a German company; the enemy bullet that kills him at the end makes him a hero and consecrates his death in the eyes of the fatherland. Maisch was a career officer fixated on the mythology of war and violence. Like his patron, Karl Ritter, he was a "man of culture" given to chauvinism and old-boy clubbiness, and here he allowed no trace of ambivalence or ambiguity. The similarly structured plot of *Ritt in die Freiheit* (*Ride to Freedom*, directed by Karl Hartl, with Willy Birgel, Ursula Grabley, and Hansi Knoteck) gave the idea of freedom equal ranking with that of patriotism, and the subject, taken from the Polish struggle for freedom against Russian domination in the 1830s, excluded the possibility of any glorification of things Germanic. A Polish cavalry officer, whose hesitation at the beginning of the story endangers his comrades, saves them from the Russians at the end at the cost of his own life. Poles and Russians are portrayed as "fair opponents," equally inspired by patriotic feelings; the film lacks the "enemy" essential to Nazi propaganda. Ufa produced this film with the help of the Polish Ministry of War, which provided five Uhlan regiments for the outdoor filming at Ostroleka by cameraman Günther Rittau, and Poland's ambassador, Lipski, honored the premiere of *Ride to Freedom* in the Ufa-Palast am Zoo on January 14, 1937, with his presence. (From this Polish-German cooperation came other joint productions as well, such as *August der Starke* [*August the Strong*, directed by Paul Wegener, 1936] and *Abenteuer in Warschau* [*Adventure in Warsaw*, Carl Boese, 1937], both made by Nerthus-Film.)

A legend prevalent in film history is that the National Socialists succeeded in tainting with their ideological poison every cinematic genre, every film, and every subject, no matter how remote from politics. Eager as Goebbels and his subordinates were to achieve that goal, the state's various watchdog agencies often lost control over the material they wanted to regulate. The nature of film itself, with its unpredictability and its affinity for micrological structures, ultimately resisted the "macromanagement" of Goebbels's controlling machinery.

The clichés of the "unpolitical" adventure film, the melodrama, and even the social comedy obviously offered opportunities for ideological exploitation. "Masculine" virtues, misogyny, the family idyll, and the proscription of uninhibited eroticism fit in with Fascist concepts of the world and of humanity. But long before 1933 these motifs had crystallized out as standard items in cinema. Aware of the importance of "pure" entertainment in maintaining the system, the National Socialists let these genres flourish. Particularly after they had nationalized the film industry, they also realized that box-office success was crucial and that total control was achievable only within limits.

And so the entertainment film lived on, not altogether "unpolitical" but peripheral and hard to influence; occasionally it took positions contrary to the official friend-and-enemy doctrine. An example is Eduard von Borsody's *Caoutchouc*, a classic adventure made by Ufa. A perfect narrative and beautifully integrated documentary shots from the Brazilian jungle (Willi Winterstein and Edgar Eichhorn were the cameramen) made for a formally brilliant film, and even an unsophisticated eye can see that it is a panegyric on British colonial imperialism and the British spirit of exploration and enterprise.

Borsody had served in the First World War as an officer in the Austrian Army and had apprenticed to disparate cinematic masters. Like Karl Hartl, he started out working with Ucicky at Sascha-Filmindustrie in Vienna. He then joined leftist circles in Berlin and worked with Ernö Metzner as a cameraman (notably on the grimly realistic *Police Report: Hold-Up*). Working at Ufa as Ucicky's assistant director and editor after 1930, he began specializing in the adventure genre (*Brillanten* [*Brilliants*], 1937; *Sensationsprozess Casilla* [*The Sensational Casilla Trial*] and *Kongo-Express*, both 1939). Blithely disregarding political considerations and working with screenplays by the somewhat exonerated Rathenau assassin Ernst von Salomon, who went into "inner emigration" during the Nazi years and became a successful supplier of Ufa dramaturgy, Borsody competed with Hollywood action films and gave free rein to his Anglophile leanings. (So did Herbert Selpin in *Die Reiter von Deutsch-Ostafrika* [*The Horsemen of German East Africa*], Terra, 1934.) Like Karl Hartl, Borsody was one of those (conservative) scions of the Danube monarchy at Ufa who cultivated the genre of the patriotic adventure film without attaching importance to the "national political" implications. They formed a counterweight to the reactionary cinema sergeants like Karl Ritter.

> Neutrality was the only path available to anyone who could not make his peace with the regime yet wanted to continue working in film production. Not even in entertainment films could one entirely escape the authorities' commandments and recommendations, but one could modify and cut back on them. One could offer as an excuse that film reality took shape in dimensions of time and space beyond the territory of the Third Reich.[27]

Some stubborn types consciously exploited their neutrality to test the options open to them and to stick a few needles into the despised regime if they could. Reinhold Schünzel was good at this; he let his delight in subversion shine through in the quid pro quo of the sexes in *Viktor und Viktoria*, in the radically feminist film *The Girl Irene* (which Goebbels called "a really terrible, forced, and disgusting thing"[28]), and, most of all, in *Amphitryon*. Now, even though as a "half Jew" he was already operating on the outer limits of the regime's tolerance, he seemed to want to bet everything on one card with *Land der Liebe* (*Land of Love*). Following on his last films for Ufa (*Donogoo Tonka*, 1935–36, and *The Girl Irene*, 1936), Georg Witt-Film produced this film on commission from Tobis. Werner Bohne was the cameraman; Albert Matterstock, Gusti Huber, and Valerie von Martens played the leads. The film premiered on June 11, 1937, in the Tauentzien-Palast, but by then Schünzel had left Germany and settled in the United States.

Land of Love is constructed according to tried-and-true formulas for escapist fantasies. In an operetta kingdom, exploding firecrackers set off a
chaotic chain of events, police actions, and the arrest of a beloved poet;
the monarch flees, and his courtiers insist that his "assassin," of all people,
stand in for him; love and conspiracy, hullaballoo and court intrigues all
lead eventually to a happy ending complete with a double wedding—in
short, much ado about nothing. A revolution is merely temporary confusion in a country of dimwits. And yet this nothing is an extremely pointed
satire on the false pomp of Nazi politicos and their police state, on the
martial SA columns, on the gullibility of an endlessly duped people. Hans
Fritz Beckmann and Kurt E. Heyne wrote the lyrics. Curt Goetz (who
emigrated in 1939) helped with the screenplay but was not mentioned in
the credits.

The film was submitted to the censors in late April. When Goebbels saw
it, he raged in his journal: "Typical Jewish hogwash. Absolutely intolerable.
It can't come out like this. I'll clean up this rubbish." And two days later:
"Incredible trouble with the Schünzel film, which cost 1.3 million marks
and is completely unusable. That half-Jew did this on purpose."[29] *Land of
Love* was released only after more delays and major cuts. By then Schünzel
knew he was in disfavor and had left the country; Fritz Mainz, production
chief at Tobis, soon lost his job.

Arthur Maria Rabenalt, experienced as a director of "unpolitical" comedies, has described in his memoir how he and others used flights into the
past, costuming, and staging as "camouflage" and as a way of subverting
the imposed ideology. And he shows clearly that entertainment films had
to remain remote from life if they were to remain unpolitical. Thus was
generated the opera buffa peculiar to the National Socialist state, harmless
"operetta in a conversational mode, so to speak, with occasional hit tunes
thrown in." Many Ufa directors walked this vague borderline between "inner emigration" and resigned escapism. But satire and sophisticated irony
were likely to meet with incomprehension and mistrust from the Nazis, and
films that "elicited sheer delight from sophisticated audiences" in the
Gloria-Palast or Marmorhaus were received in "grave-like stillness" at the
Ministry of Propaganda.[30]

In 1937 the *Lichtbild-Bühne* touted the Ufa film *Der Mann, der Sherlock
Holmes war* (*The Man Who Was Sherlock Holmes*) as proof "that Germany
can produce a detective comedy that can hold its own with the best American films of this kind."[31] Sharing in this success were Karl Hartl as director,
Hans Albers and Heinz Rühmann as little detectives trying to fill the shoes
of Sherlock Holmes and Dr. Watson, Fritz Arno Wagner as cameraman,
and Hans Sommer as composer of the hit song "Jawoll, meine Herr'n"
("Yes, Indeed, Gentlemen"). Hartl hired his Austrian colleague Eduard von
Borsody as assistant director.

True, the tempo, parody, and comic effects of the Albers-Rühmann team were charming, but a comparison with sophisticated American comedy is hardly justified. By resolving all the grotesque complications of his plot with a brawl at the end, Hartl sacrificed elegance and resorted, with the appearance of the police, to a clichéd *deus ex machina*. Still, the movie is one of Ufa's most original comedies. The important people behind it were all "neutrals" who were trying to maintain a position between inconspicuous conformity and ironic distance, between opera buffa and parody. A year later Goebbels offered Karl Hartl the artistic direction of Wien-Film, and after considerable hesitation and at the urging of his Austrian colleagues, Hartl accepted the offer.

A co-author of the Sherlock Holmes screenplay was the theater and radio writer and cabaret artist R(obert) A(dolf) Stemmle, who had been a leftist sympathizer in the Weimar Republic. After 1936 at Ufa, a classic example of a "neutral," he tried his hand at a gangster film, set in a carefully observed milieu (*Gleisdreieck* [*El-Track Triangle*], 1936–37); an exotic adventure film (*Das Geheimnis um Betty Bonn* [*The Mystery of Betty Bonn*], 1937–38); and a denunciation of "crooked Jewish capitalists" (*Am seidenen Faden* [*By a Silken Thread*], 1938). But his attempt to conform failed. Nazi reviewers complained that the portrayal of individual fates in this last movie prevented the "idea" from coming through.[32] Like many of his colleagues, Stemmle oscillated between his own desire to educate, the concessions to public taste demanded by the industry, and occasional collaboration with the political goals of the government. This "neutral" experienced the peculiar fate that after the war the Allied Military Commission banned almost all his films, no matter how harmless.

Even in the last years before the war Ufa did not rid itself of contradictions. Management's decision to cooperate with the Nazi regime in all important political respects was unambiguous, and the propaganda films of Karl Ritter, Herbert Maisch, and others left no room for doubt. But the contingent of convinced National Socialist Party adherents was small, and even in their presence criticism was repeatedly voiced. There was open unhappiness with the military tone of command that had become the official mode of communication and with the general insecurity that the censorship system imposed on production.

Goebbels was no great fan of Ufa. Whenever he spoke of the sad state of German film or complained about the persistence of profit-oriented thinking and other tendencies "inimical to art," it was Ufa he had in mind. He knew that while the officer's style of command and address was acceptable at Ufa, the Hitler salute was considered crass and was quietly avoided. He knew that the company was still employing unreliable types capable of equivocation. Until 1937, the brilliant moralist, ironist, and language virtuoso Curt Goetz had continued at Ufa. He wrote his irreverent, sparkling dialogue not only for Schünzel's *Land of Love* but also for Paul

Martin's comedies *Children of Happiness* (1936) and *Sieben Ohrfeigen* (*Seven Slaps on the Face*, 1937), which rivaled American screwball comedy; and shortly before he emigrated he directed for Tobis the film version of his play *Napoleon ist an allem schuld* (*Napoleon Is to Blame for Everything*, 1938), a film that paid homage to the tradition of musicals before 1933, that was as Anglophile as it was Francophile, and that made no concessions to the Prussian spirit and its imitators.

Still another avant-gardist and obvious outsider who found temporary work with Ufa was Werner Hochbaum, who had begun in the 1920s as a film critic for a Social Democratic newspaper and as a pioneer of proletarian cinema. The National Socialists considered him suspect because of his leftist sympathies and possibly because of his homosexual leanings. After the Nazi assumption of power he was often subjected to police interrogation. The anti-militaristic character of *Vorstadtvariete* (*City-Outskirts Variety*, based on Felix Salten's play *Der Gemeine* [*The Free Man*], with Luise Ullrich, Mathias Wieman, and Oskar Sima, 1934), earned him the disapproval of the censors, who would not release it until cuts were made. After Hochbaum scored an international success and drew praise even from American critics with the Austro-Swiss co-production of his melodrama *Die ewige Maske* (*The Eternal Mask*, 1935), Ufa engaged him to direct its first Marika Rökk film, *Leichte Kavallerie* (*Light Cavalry*, 1935). In October 1934 at the Circus Renz, Ernst Hugo Correll had "discovered" the Hungarian dancer for German film. Produced for Ufa-Verleih by Fabrikation deutscher Filme, *Light Cavalry* was one of those circus-and-artiste films that, as Rabenalt put it, flourished "in their own ghetto," in a milieu hermetically sealed off from National Socialist reality.[33]

Two other films Hochbaum made for Ufa ran into difficulties. *Ein Mädchen geht an Land* (*A Girl Goes Ashore*, 1938, based on a novel by Eva Leidmann; with Elisabeth Flickenschildt, Günther Lüders, and Heidi Kabel) chronicled depressing lives in the seamen's milieu of Hamburg. Here Hochbaum stood Nazi clichés on their heads. In this film, strong women are contrasted with psychically weak, socially uprooted men with fragile egos. "Certain scenes, dialogues, and psychological developments" offended the reviewer in Goebbels's publication *Der deutsche Film*.[34] After its September 1938 premiere in Hamburg's Lessing Theater, *A Girl Goes Ashore* was recensored and cut by sixty meters.

With his final Ufa film, *Drei Unteroffiziere* (*Three Noncommissioned Officers*, 1938–39), Hochbaum took on a commission from the Ministry of Propaganda. The subject matter—a conflict between love and the imperative of military duty—was well suited to the spirit of "education for war." According to the critic Ulrich Kurowski, Hochbaum succeeded in turning the film's message into a subversive protest "against the adult world's annexation of youth."[35] National Socialist reservations about this film—and perhaps Hochbaum's homosexuality—assured his exclusion from the Reich

Film Guild in June 1939. (The reason given was his trial in 1923 for high treason on charges of spying for France, even though he had been acquitted.)

"Vagabonds with no attachment to the fatherland," cosmopolites, highly paid transients with their bags packed, were constantly jockeying with Ufa's executives for movie assignments, eternally on call for their chance in Hollywood—for more than a decade they had been Ufa's artistic and intellectual avant-garde. They created the films that stand out, and it was to them that German cinematography of the Weimar Republic owed its international status. Lang, Lubitsch, Berger, Pommer, E. A. Dupont, Murnau, and their best co-workers—Ufa's first generation—had long ago left Germany. Under Hugenberg it had still been possible—against the mainstream of politics and the reactionary spirit of the time—to bring Pommer back to Berlin and to attract Josef von Sternberg, an international star, as a guest. The Propaganda Ministry longed mightily for international recognition, but at the same time made it impossible with every measure it took. Schünzel had been in the United States since 1937, Detlef Sierck since 1938. Anyone who remained in Neubabelsberg and wanted to survive conformed and experimented cautiously with the possibilities that "inner emigration" offered.

25.

Soldiers of Art?
The Stars of Ufa

WHEN a film close-up lets "the play of facial muscles appear as fully exposed suffering, joy, hope,"[1] it is the star whose aura colors those emotions with ingratiating eroticism. Every successful film is filled "with the ups and downs of daydreams and pipe dreams," but it is the "micrologically trained" mimetic language of the star that indicates in what direction the dreams and wishes should flow.

Stars are of course synthetic products of a cultural industry, but they would not be stars if they had not mastered the "micrology of the incidental" that the camera's capacity for subtlety offers. Every good suspense film, Bloch says, is loaded with mimetic impulses from the subconscious and the prescient. And the "trivial film" may well be the most effective vehicle for those finely articulated oscillations between awareness and premonition. The star's complex erotic appeal is an elixir that nourishes the audience's dreams, encouraging either identification or a pleasant yearning for the unattainable.

Germany's top stars were always scaled-down versions of Hollywood's international stars. Even in the period of its keenest competition with American companies Ufa had not achieved global rank, and after 1933 the path of dreams down which the German movie idol could lead his audience narrowed. The restrictions on dreams put limits on the hero's image, too. Cinema could not freely give shape to the public's unconscious impulses. "Stars as manifestations of the collective mentality of a period could have undermined the political authorities,"[2] so stars embodied either authority or petit-bourgeois acquiescence to it. Here, too, of course, the obstinacy of cinema could not be totally controlled. Even the established norms of Nazi cinema were not immune to unpredictable deviations that showed the weakness of state authority or suddenly changed acquiescence into the courage to resist.

The "film reviewing" that Goebbels had commanded in place of genuine criticism was blind and deaf to cinema's "dream movements" and indifferent to the specific aura of leading performers. In keeping with the jargon of the Propaganda Ministry and the companies aligned with it, reviewers spoke only of "first-class films" and labeled the stars' performances merely as "outstanding dramatic achievements." Acting was seen primarily as a vehicle for a message to which the reviewer then gave a positive or negative evaluation.

Still, the highest levels of government appreciated the value of Germany's international stars. Given Goebbels's partiality to American film, it is not surprising that he wanted desperately to acquire top foreign actors for his companies. He tried in vain to retain Asta Nielsen for German film. In late June 1935 Ernst Hugo Correll reported to his fellow Ufa executives that at the behest of the Propaganda Ministry negotiations were under way to engage Greta Garbo for a film version of Knut Hamsun's novel *Pan*; Ufa's executives instantly fell in line with Goebbels's wishes.[3] (A film based on Hamsun's *Pan* was in fact produced two years later. It was made not by Ufa, however, but by Olof-Fjord-Film, and it did not star Greta Garbo. Marieluise Claudius and Hilde Sessak played the leads.)

The big companies were willing to grant their stars concessions and privileges above and beyond salary considerations. When Ufa hired Hans Albers (no great favorite of Goebbels) to make four "first-class films" in 1935–36 for a minimum of 100,000 marks per film, Ufa's executives took into account Albers's antipathy for historical subjects: without his consent, no more than one of the four would be a historical film. A further significant concession gave Albers right of refusal over subject matter, directors, and editing. Ufa's managers thus yielded indirectly to the actor's well-known reluctance to work on National Socialist propaganda films. The Propaganda Ministry no doubt held that concession against them, but had to put up with it anyway, because Albers numbered among Germany's few internationally recognized stars.[4]

Willy Fritsch, whose contract for the same period was renewed at 200,000 marks a year, had in the meantime come to be seen almost as an Ufa trademark. The contract gave him to Ufa exclusively, and also stipulated that Fritsch had to have Ufa's approval to use his name or photographs or other likenesses, "to be photographed for commercial or advertising purposes" or to "participate actively in any public gathering."[5] The actor, his name, his image, and his personal habits were literally Ufa's property.

Given his beginnings and his development as an actor, Fritsch hardly represented the classic type of glamorous star. His training at the Max Reinhardt School and in the German Theater predestined him for a career playing traditional roles—from the young lover to the young hero to the character actor. It was film, however (more precisely, Pommer's *The Farmer from Texas* in 1925), that tapped into his essential quality: the casual, carefree charm of a spirited go-getter that became the essence of the Fritsch aura.

Willy Fritsch and Lilian Harvey were the "dream couple" who dominated German film in the 1930s. This sometimes devil-may-care, sometimes sweetly sentimental alliance of souls was rooted partly in operetta and partly in the careworn everyday experience of a petit-bourgeois public. The Fritsch–Harvey dream couple evolved into one of those film constellations that seem to hover above the earth and acquire international glitter. Lilian Harvey could be coquettish, naïve, libertine, and melancholic—in short, she was an adaptable and versatile figure for the late Weimar Republic. Around 1930 she put her varied talents to work for Ufa and within two years became a superstar, completely absorbed by her work. She could dance and sing, and, born in England, the daughter of English and German parents, she could do the English and French versions of her films herself. She went briefly to Hollywood, but that was a failure, and when she returned to Germany in 1935, Ufa cast frugality to the winds and invited film journalists to a "press tea" for her.

Paul Martin, Lilian Harvey's director and companion, evoked real dramatic emotion from her in *Schwarze Rosen* (*Black Roses*, 1935) and the giddiness of screwball comedy in *Children of Happiness*. In Karl Ritter's crude opera parody, *Capriccio* (1938), she excelled in a *Junker* role: lithe, agile, and immensely spirited. In 1939, before war broke out, Lilian Harvey went to France, protesting a breach of her contract that stipulated that part of her salary would be paid in foreign currency. She made two more films, but her movie career was essentially over, a career that like few others was linked to Ufa's goodwill, ambition, and capital.

According to Mathias Wieman's definition, the stars of the 1930s and 1940s like Willy Fritsch and Lilian Harvey should have seen themselves as "soldiers of art." In their lighthearted, frivolous film *Children of Happiness*, they could not have been further removed from that function. Their films showed that the "American" star cult, which continued in some form in Ufa under National Socialism, was difficult to shape into an instrument of the regime; the two had nothing in common. To serve the goals of propaganda, the star had to be reshaped to fit the proper ideological patterns, but the German film industry under Hitler and Goebbels could not accomplish that.

In the case of Hans Albers, for example, we can see that after he played the role of a Teutonic leader in *Refugees* in 1933, he converted from a Weimar film idol to a German man of action. With the Ufa adventure film *Gold* (Karl Hartl, 1934) Albers's qualities were reshaped: he played "an engineer, inventor, and man of determination; once again he turns in a performance that will put an end to the view that Hans Albers is merely a natural jack-of-all-trades [for he is, rather,] the bearer and the symbol of the German idea of a man."[6]

Despite his dislike of the regime, Albers had to accept some National

Socialist propaganda roles, such as that of the chauvinistic and anti-Semitic colonial pioneer Carl Peters in Herbert Selpin's Bavaria film of that title. Aloof, audacious, and not without a touch of cynicism, Albers lost no sleep over the question of who commissioned his films, and he brought to his National Socialist roles the unmistakable Albers touch—with its mixture of devil-may-care adventure and sentimentality, of rough-and-tumble elegance and magical invincibility. In 1932, Herbert Jhering speculated that Albers was Germany's most popular actor "because he brings together folkish kitsch and modern roles, because he incorporates into his acting a bit of Henny Porten and a bit of Mackie Messer, a bit of Vicki Baum and a bit of Bert Brecht."[7] Albers and the roles he played kept this explosive combination intact, and it was his artful ambivalence that kept him, one of the few authentic folk stars of the NS cinema, from becoming a Fascist figurehead.

"The victor is victorious at the price of his own happiness," one critic has said.[8] As early as Karl Hartl's science-fiction film *FP 1 Does Not Answer* (1932), which made Hans Albers a star, signs of melancholy and resignation were already visible "in the weatherproof stucco of his heroic façade," and a (perhaps apocryphal) unhappy love affair left the battle-tested roué and clever pirate of the skies with a broken heart. With Albers it was always difficult to distinguish between pose and biography. He incurred Goebbels's enmity because he refused to abandon his Jewish girlfriend and colleague, Hansi Burg. Goebbels is said to have been outraged that "this blue-eyed, blond man," this physiologically perfect incarnation of Germanic culture, was living with a Jewess. Hansi Burg emigrated to England and returned to Albers after the war. Her father, Eugen Burg—Albers's partner in Richard Eichberg's film *Der Greifer* (*The Grasper*, 1930)—died in a concentration camp.

Heinz Rühmann, Albers's unequal partner in *Monte Carlo Madness* and *The Man Who Was Sherlock Holmes*, attained the status of "state actor" in 1940 by a different route. Rühmann began his film career playing the role of an aggressive draft resister (*Das deutsche Mutterherz* [*The German Maternal Heart*], directed by Geza von Bolvary for Ewe-Film, 1926). By 1939 he had become supportive of the regime and on orders from on high been classified as unavailable for military service. However, in 1941 he volunteered at the Rechlin Air Station for pilot training and then appeared in German newsreels as a prize example of a patriotic courier pilot, a role that (like his friendship with the air ace Ernst Udet) increased his favor with the regime, as did his successes in the Terra films *Quax der Bruchpilot* (*Quax Makes a Crash Landing*, directed by Kurt Hoffmann, 1941) and *Quax in Fahrt* (*Quax Under Way*, directed by Helmut Weiss, 1943–44).

Not until he began working with Ufa did Rühmann find vehicles suitable to the development of his "blond gentleness of nature"[9]—underlaid by a certain combative balkiness and suppressed rebelliousness—films like *The*

Three from the Filling Station, Hanns Schwarz's "musical comedy of marriage" *Burglars*, and Kurt Gerron's comedies of the crisis years, *Meine Frau, die Hochstaplerin (My Wife the Confidence Woman*, 1931) and *There'll Be a Turn for the Better* (1931–32). In 1931 he said, "The task of film as I see it is to cheer up our contemporaries, who are burdened with heavy cares, and to liberate them from an atmosphere of pessimism and discouragement by giving them fresh hope and new energy—those important weapons one needs to emerge victorious in the struggle for existence."[10] It is easy to see between the lines of this credo the opportunism that made his humor a standard ingredient in the affirmative entertainment of the "Strength through Joy" state.

The Ufa directors under whom Rühmann had begun as an edifying jokester and "predecessor of the Nazi fellow traveler," as the film historian Ulrich Kurowski dubbed him, had all emigrated long since or were locked out of the profession when their hero celebrated his triumphs in the late 1930s in Terra's Heinrich Spoerl films and, in 1940, contributed his song "Das kann doch einen Seemann nicht erschüttern" ("That Can't Bother a Sailor Any") to Eduard von Borsody's fight-to-the-last-man *Wish Concert* (Cine-Allianz/Ufa). Rühmann's vacillation between cringing timidity and rebellion did not contain those subversive qualities Goebbels thought he detected when he classified *Die Feuerzangenbowle (The Mulled Punch*, directed by Helmut Weiss, Terra, 1943) as hostile to authority and refused to approve it. Rühmann contacted Hitler personally and managed to have the film released.

In German films of the 1930s, Rühmann and Willy Fritsch, Gustav Fröhlich and Hans Brausewetter saw the star reduced to being the common man that urban anonymity and late Weimar "objectivity" had formed. In the roles they played, the "man in the street" became the hero of grotesquely complex plots and sentimental dramas in which the emotions were no more than quotations—reflections from a now defunct culture with richer, deeper feelings than this one. Most of the plots revolved around money and love, and in most cases money—or the social order regulated by financial arrangements—prevailed.

The man-in-the-street type who finds himself, more or less by accident, in drawing rooms, bogus affairs, or exotic adventures is clever, but he lacks the Hollywood star's sensuality and artificial radiance. And he is equally lacking in the features that would make him a "blond hero" in Alfred Rosenberg's sense, a style-setting figure for the Nazis. This everyday man is a simple philistine, and he is far from adaptable. He worships authority but is not fanatical. His ideals ultimately turn out to be no more than guidelines for living an inconspicuous life that permits occasional rambunctiousness but no profound or far-reaching change. Ufa's man-in-the-street star was the obedient German citizen who accepted Fascist rule without considering the consequences and who, when the consequences could no longer be ignored, retreated into his inner life. The more insecure he felt, the more anxious he was to protect that life.

In Gustav Fröhlich, the pose of the sentimental or pleasure-seeking but always moderate cavalier had an element of puerile simplicity, which may well account for why he became the idealized figure of the "direct, honest, and sympathetic German man"[11] with whom a politically immature movie-going public could identify. The simplicity of the idealistic youth, the quality that had made Fröhlich a star in *Metropolis* in 1927, stuck with him for a long time, and in Joe May's *Asphalt* (1928), in which he played a young German policeman who succumbs to the charms of a beautiful confidence woman, it took him to the verge of gentle imbecility. He later compensated for this with his performance as *Oberwachtmeister Schwenke* (*Police Sergeant Schwenke*, directed by Carl Froelich, 1935). Both Fröhlich and his precise contemporary Mathias Wieman had "classless" man-in-the-street faces with not much individuality, and they could take on many and varied roles, provided, of course, that they did not have to overstep the limits of middle-class respectability and virtue. Wieman, a "state actor," also had a well-modulated voice, so he could provide the right tone for a "noble soul" as well as the metallic pathos of military officers in Karl Ritter's films.

His aristocratic counterpart was Willy Birgel, whom Correll "discovered" for Ufa in 1934. Paul Wegener, too, thought Birgel's performance in Paul Joseph Cremer's war play *Marneschlacht* (*Battle of the Marne*) so convincing that he offered him an important supporting role in *A Man Wants to Reach Germany*. Birgel was forty-three at the time, and the bon mot "a Marne miracle of an actor" found ready circulation among the critics.

With a stoic nobility that could take on soft and unctuous overtones, Birgel was ideally suited for the role of the distinguished patriot in films by Karl Ritter, Herbert Maisch, and Karl Hartl, and that ultimately made him—in Arthur Maria Rabenalt's . . . *reitet für Deutschland* (*Riding for Germany*, 1941)—the "noble horseman of German cinema." The critic Thomas Brandlmeier points out, however, that this cliché actually hid this actor's real theme.[12] Behind the respectable rigidity of his figures "the doubts of the socially superior, the weaknesses of the strong" were palpable. In Sierck's *Final Accord* (1936) and *Zu neuen Ufern* (*To New Shores*, 1937), he played introspective high-society characters who were divided in themselves and hid their weaknesses behind a sovereign pose. Birgel was not really suited for the role of National Socialist hero, but his style ingratiated him with conservatives who were disappointed by the National Socialist state and who mourned the destroyed or abused values of an old tradition.

It was characteristic of the Ufa star, wrote the journalist Walter Kiaulehn, that the public made him into a "societal substitute."[13] Different classes selected from among the stars faces that satisfied their particular desires: faces "of an authority the public dreamed of, dreams become reality in the flesh." The Hitler regime exploited the public's need for authority and for

idols to admire "by inviting film stars to state receptions, by having beautiful actresses form a reception line for Mussolini," and by having the stars
act as an enthusiastic chorus at Goebbels's Sportpalast speech on "total
war."

In their memoirs, the actors of these years offer stereotypical protesta-
tions to the effect that they went to great lengths to avoid obligations of
this kind and accepted invitations to state receptions only when hard-
pressed and always against their will. And they frequently relate anecdotes
intended to show how disrespectful of power they were, even in power's
parlor. But repression and self-deception often distort what actually happened. Many stars did not find social trafficking with high Nazi officials
any imposition. Some used their influence—usually unsuccessfully—to
plead the case of colleagues who had been banned or were in difficulty.
(Heinrich Fraenkel says that Henny Porten, Hans Albers, Käthe Dorsch,
and Brigitte Horney were among those who were courageous enough to
speak up for persecuted colleagues.[14]) And in one respect the state remained almost a total failure: from among the significant number of well-
trained actors who were popular with the public, it was never able to
produce the homunculus of the "new era," the prototype of the "National
Socialist man."

There were, of course, actors, like Emil Jannings, who were "men of
action" and natural leaders and who satisfied their ambition by adapting
to the National Socialists' master-race cliché. In the early days of Ufa,
Jannings had risen to superstardom in potentate roles under Lubitsch's
direction. In the mid-1920s, in Murnau's *The Last Laugh* and Dupont's
Variety, he had portrayed, with great sensitivity, the feelings of society's
failures, the will to live of the downtrodden and the insulted. In 1926, at
the depths of Ufa's financial crisis, the company lost its most popular star
to Hollywood, where in 1928 he won the first Oscar in film history for two
of his American films. After his return to Germany, Jannings was overshadowed by Marlene Dietrich at the 1930 premiere of *The Blue Angel*, which
made Dietrich a world star overnight.

Now, under the National Socialists, he starred in roles of tyrannical authoritarian figures, fully conscious of his own authority and the aura of the
roles he enacted. After the Deka film *The Old and the Young King* came
the Tobis series *The Ruler; Robert Koch, the Battler against Death* (Hans
Steinhoff); *Uncle Krüger* (Hans Steinhoff); and, finally, the Bismarck film
The Dismissal (Wolfgang Liebeneiner). Granted special privileges by his
political patrons, Jannings enjoyed unprecedented freedom in his productions at Tobis. As a member of the Tobis board of directors in 1936 and,
in 1938, its chair, Jannings assumed "overall artistic control" and, later,
total control of production for his films. With the one exception of *The
Broken Jug*, they all took their places in the front ranks of National Socialist
propaganda films.

Heinrich George, too, specialized in portraying "Führer" figures, implacable men of power, harsh fathers, and strong individuals who, as Ibsen put it, are most powerful when they are alone. George, of all people—who had come to film after breaking a theater contract, who had tried in his youth to be an artist immune to commercial temptation, who had worked at Erwin Piscator's Volksbühne (People's Stage), who in 1931 had played Franz Biberkopf in Allianz-Film's *Berlin Alexanderplatz* directed by the leftist Phil Jutzi, who in Richard Oswald's *Dreyfus* (1930) had played the militant Emile Zola with great verve, who had been a supporter of the Volksfilmverband (People's Film Association) as late as 1928—this Heinrich George was one of the first leading actors to go over to the National Socialist camp. He played major parts in Steinhoff's *Hitler Youth Quex* and in Harlan's *Kolberg*, Ufa's first and last "first-class" propaganda films. In between, he developed to perfection his talent for portraying ranting authoritarians—or, as he put it, his ability to enter into a "controlled trance"—in films made for Ufa and other companies: *Stützen der Gesellschaft* (*Pillars of Society*, based on Ibsen, directed by Detlef Sierck as a Robert Neppach production of Ufa, 1935), *Project Michael, Ein Volksfeind* (*An Enemy of the People*, based on Ibsen, directed by Hans Steinhoff for Terra, 1937), *Heimat* (*Homeland*, directed by Carl Froelich for Ufa, 1938), *Das unsterbliche Herz* (*The Immortal Heart*, directed by Veit Harlan, Tobis, 1938–39), *Jew Süss* (Veit Harlan, Terra), and *Andreas Schlüter* (Herbert Maisch, Terra, 1941–42).

The German "original geniuses" were susceptible not so much to the bacillus of Fascist ideology as to their own desires and the illusion that Goebbels would fulfill them. Their ambition as artists made them politically compliant. It was not agreement with the philosophy and politics of the NSDAP that prompted internationally recognized stars of stage and screen like Jannings, George, and Werner Krauss to become character actors of "national political value" and thus half-witting half-unwitting collaborators. It was, rather, the temptation, succumbed to in massive disregard of the political facts, to develop "freely" their artistic potential.

Then, too, there were material and social privileges. George became intendant of the Schiller Theater in Berlin in 1937, where he was able to assemble an artistic ensemble of high caliber. In addition to his work in film, Krauss acted in Vienna's Burgtheater and Berlin's Staatstheater, had personal contacts in the highest government circles, and was appointed vice president of the Theater Guild by Goebbels. German silent film had cast him as a demon of the Caligari era, but with the introduction of sound film, he had shifted to the fatherland genre in Ucicky's Ufa films *Yorck* (1931) and *Man without a Name* (1932), and he also made himself available to Ufa for films of a National Socialist stamp such as *Annelie*. In Harlan's *Jew Süss*, he played the role for which he would stand trial after the war: five different versions of the "eternal Jew," five characters in which Krauss could "realize" his mimetic genius; five Jewish masks which, in Harlan's view, all "ultimately derived from the same root."[15]

Although Jannings and George were able in some of their roles to project the image of the "Führer" type or the Teutonic he-man, and though Krauss's opportunistic distortions of the anti-type (the Jew, the intellectual, the "subversive forces") were sometimes effective, there were no "Aryan models" who could show the people the way into the future as envisioned by the Nazis' race state. Weimar and Fritz Lang had already "used up" young Siegfried, and the National Socialists could not bring him back for a return engagement. The Moravian Viktor Staal, with Ufa from 1935 on, was a perfect "Nordic" type, but he was firmly entrenched playing masterful lovers in entertainment films. Only newsreels could show the "home front" audiences that the Germanic myth of the victor glorified by a heroic death was exemplified by the heroes of the Stuka squadrons and the mountain troops of Narvik, by naval desperadoes like U-boat Captain Günter Prien. (At the beginning of the war, newsreel cameramen were instructed to photograph German soldiers, when possible, in impressive poses, and the press willingly showed "the clear and noble image of the German soldier who, even in the thick of the fray, was always honorable, optimistic, and confident of victory."[16])

A Kriemhild was lacking. The typology of the female star seemed immune to National Socialist clichés of the young maid, the contentedly prolific German mother, the brave comrade. Even Luise Ullrich and Ilse Werner only approximated the ideal image of the German woman; it was Marlene Dietrich, Lilian Harvey, and Zarah Leander that German men dreamed of. Their international flair and worldly eroticism held sway over Germany's emotions and triumphed elegantly over the Reich Film Guild's guidelines and Rosenberg's doctrine of the Aryan type.

The Swedish-born Kristina Söderbaum, whose success in a 1936 Ufa contest for young performers brought her a film debut in Erich Waschneck's *Onkel Bräsig* (*Uncle Bräsig*, Fanal-Filmproduktion), was promoted as a blond angel of innocence by Veit Harlan, and she soon became the tragic heroine of his melodramas as well as of his propaganda films. But her director and writers often maneuvered her into conflicts that drove her characters to suicide—gloomy waters or brackish swamps often swallowed up her buxom white body—and she soon won the sobriquet of the "Reich's drowned rat." Image of the Teutonic vestal virgin that she was, the film industry offered her up on the altar of tearjerkers and potboilers, and so she, too, failed as an inspiration for the National Socialist state.

That was also true, in a different way, of Marika Rökk, who thanks to Ufa's promotion strategy and her own hard work became a revue star, but her film performances as a dancer and singer never measured up to international standards. Try as she would, she remained a somewhat rustic, frighteningly bouncy, excessively mugging Hungarian circus rider. "A miracle of vitality, a volcanic performer," she called herself.[17] But she lacked the skills needed to adapt her robust physique and skills to film's subtle demands or the nuances of a complicated story.

Although Correll had admired Rökk's acrobatic feats in the Circus Renz and "discovered" her for Ufa, senior managers were soon watching her development skeptically. After the only moderate success of the early films she made with Ufa's other revue star, Johannes Heesters, their initial enthusiasm gave way to sober reassessment. The weight-loss regimen prescribed for her was no great success, and the experiments of her cameraman Konstantin Irmen-Tshet, "who even made holes in the studio floor so he could shoot her legs from below,"[18] did not make her look slimmer. She may have won over lovers of military music with her energetic, rhythmic style and snappy body language, but she could not act, and her performances lacked the qualities that appeal to emotions and empathic impulses. Although Rökk underwent "constant variations on her basic type," she remained "the stage star who makes her way through an insipid plot full of banal intrigue, mistaken identity, or misunderstandings until she can shine in an overpowering production number at the end and win her partner for life at the same time."[19] It did not take long for this pattern to go stale.

What Ufa's managers refused to grant Marika Rökk and Lilian Harvey in 1939—payment of part of their salaries in foreign currency—they had willingly and generously granted to Zarah Leander. When the Swedish actress came to Germany in the fall of 1936, Ufa and the National Socialist propagandists saw a unique opportunity to make up for Marlene Dietrich's departure for Hollywood and Greta Garbo's refusal to act in German films. Zarah Leander would consign the "divine" Garbo and the irresistibly depraved vamp to history. She would stimulate the public's dreams anew.

A nature that moved between antithetical poles—the appeal of the exotic along with "German loyalty" and German repression; the broad horizons of a world of adventure and an acceptance of happiness in one's own small corner; utopia and the everyday; chaotic desires and a longing for order—accounts for the "inscrutability" of this actress. She could become a star only under a National Socialist Ufa and only because she filled gaps that others had left:

> She had Garbo's melancholy and accent; she had Mae West's figure and bearing. And like Dietrich and West, she played singers and courtesans. But instead of becoming a vamp, Leander wound up as a soldier's wife, a conversion that made Die grosse Liebe [The Great Love, 1942] the greatest success of the war years.[20]

Only Zarah Leander could have managed to make a National Socialist "war-education film" a box-office hit.

The great success that Leander celebrated in September 1936 in the Vienna premiere of Ralph Benatzky's musical comedy Axel an der Himmelstür (Axel at the Gates of Heaven) prompted Carl Froelich and Hans Weidemann, vice president of the Reich Film Guild, to contact her. The director of this theatrical success was none other than Max Hansen, who had left Germany for Austria in 1933 after allegedly "insulting the Führer." He had discovered Zarah Leander on a trip to Scandinavia and had immediately engaged her for the Benatzky operetta, thus delivering her—surely against his will—into the hands of the talent scouts from Berlin. Correll negotiated on behalf of Ufa in Vienna and, thanks to his courtesy and generosity (200,000 marks for three films), reached an agreement. Leander was granted the right to read screenplays and decide on material she considered suitable for her. Fifty-three percent of her salary, the contract stipulated, would be paid in Swedish kronor and deposited to her account in her Stockholm bank.

In late 1936, Ufa launched a major advertising campaign about their new star in a style that only it could have pulled off. Advertising chief Carl Opitz gave the Reich's central press offices information and stories about the "new Garbo." Press conferences were held ad infinitum. Photo opportunities became world-class events. Through the many channels of a centralized press, word of the new star reached the public in weeks, a star whose aura had been created before the first take was made in Neubabelsberg. And for the next few years Ufa marketed Leander vigorously. Every last detail of each of her appearances was carefully planned.

> When she went on extended publicity trips abroad, not she but the costume department at Ufa decided what she would wear when, where, and how. To make sure she made no mistakes, the costumers gave her long lists that prescribed in great detail the composition of her outfits and the accessories appropriate for each occasion.[21]

The most important person in this work was Franz Weihmayr, cameraman for Leander's ten Ufa films. Weihmayr made the lighting of her strong-boned face with its languorous eyes an arcane science; it required several hours to prepare a close-up so that it would reveal the mystery and melancholy that became the incarnation of her "ineffable sadness." In the prewar years and even more so during the war, Germans of the Nazi state found in her sadness the romanticism that was denied them in their everyday lives, and a strength they desperately needed. Her dark voice did its part, too, to ennoble and romanticize the sublimations that underlay her songs.

Detlef Sierck, the director of her first two films, helped create the Zarah myth, too. He had already made four films for Ufa, among them *Final Accord* with Lil Dagover and Willy Birgel. Now he focused on the screenplays, the lyrics, the costumes and makeup.

> Using flattering clothes, a lot of makeup, and decorative hats, he diverts attention from Zarah Leander's figure problems. He gives full play to her classic, theatrical beauty and stresses her femininity, adding, whenever the plot allows for it, plenty of glamour, too. He thus imparts to Zarah Leander the attractive, worldly sensuality of an earlier era.[22]

In the 1937 films *Toward New Shores* and *La Habanera*, Sierck brought the Ufa melodrama, with its underlying melody of longing and renunciation, to a level of maturity that has moved the critic Jon Halliday to observe that it demonstrated what German film after 1933 could have achieved. "Despite the political situation, Sierck succeeded in building on the cultural traditions of Germany before Hitler."[23] As in *Final Accord*, his visual imagination and instinct for mirror effects and complicated camera movements broke insipid screenplays wide open. As the film historian Thomas Elsaesser noted, his "psycho-symbolic realism" undermined not only the murky ideology of the sentimental plots but also his own social criticism —of nineteenth-century British imperialism in *Toward New Shores* and of colonial capitalism in *La Habanera*. These films show the double nature melodrama is capable of, its ability to blend contradictory elements together in a convincing unity: the "potboiler" and the artful chamber play, a reactionary plot with an avant-garde sense of form, sentimentality with irony. And through them ran Zarah Leander's songs, which reduced many people in the premiere audiences to tears: "I'm Standing in the Rain," "Yes, Sir," "The Wind Sang Me a Song." Measured against Sierck's achievements, Ufa melodrama in Leander's later films was mere kitsch, preachy pieces meant to console women on the "home front" and encourage them to accept their fates and losses gracefully.

Ufa producer Bruno Duday and cameraman Weihmayr, the composers Ralph Benatzky and Lothar Brüne, the writers Bruno Balz and Franz Baumann—these were the members of Zarah Leander's artistic court on her two Sierck films. Willy Birgel and Viktor Staal played opposite her in *Toward New Shores*; Ferdinand Marian and Karl Martell in *La Habanera*. Marian turned in a brilliant performance as the unscrupulous seducer and psychopathic tyrant Don Pedro, and after this success he was type-cast as an elegant villain in anti-British films like *Uncle Krüger*. In 1940 he finally yielded to Goebbels's massive personal pressure and played the title role in *Jew Süss*.

The outdoor shots for *La Habanera* were made on Tenerife from mid-August to the end of September 1937. (Warships and armed clashes in the harbor related to the Spanish Civil War dispelled the sense of a subtropical idyll remote from the rest of the world.) The premiere on December 18, 1937, in the Gloria-Palast, was a great triumph for Zarah Leander, but before the year was out, Detlef Sierck had emigrated to Rome with his Jewish wife. *Dreiklang (Triad)*, based on motifs from Turgenev and Pushkin and for which Sierck had already done the casting and prepared the sets, was taken over by Hans Hinrich.

The drastic decline in the quality of Zarah Leander's next films troubled her and raised doubts among her employers as well. After Carl Froelich's *Homeland* (1938) Ufa produced one artistic flop after another: Viktor Tourjansky's *Der Blaufuchs (The Blue Fox*, 1938), *Es war eine rauschende Ball-*

nacht (*It Was a Lovely Night at the Ball*, directed by Carl Froelich, with Marika Rökk, 1939), *Das Lied der Wüste* (*The Song of the Desert*, Paul Martin, 1939), and *Das Herz der Königin* (*The Heart of the Queen*, Carl Froelich, 1940). Uninspired direction went hand in hand with mindless plots, and the staging, costuming, and musical direction interfered with the star's aura. And because Leander's songs were less and less appealing, Ufa's managers went on the lookout for a new director in hopes of rescuing their star attraction from an ignominious end.

Leander herself insisted on Rolf Hansen, but he had drawn Goebbels's displeasure. Froelich's assistant director until 1938, Hansen took over in that year the direction of a film titled *Ultimo*, based on a play of the same title by Jochen Huth. The film title underwent many metamorphoses, all ideologically colored. *Ultimo* first became *Ein Mensch wird geboren* (*A Man Is Born*), then *Glück auf Raten* (*Happiness in Installments*), and later still *Das Leben könnte so schön sein* (*Life Could Be So Beautiful*); the subjunctive in that title presented problems, and the final version was *Das Leben kann so schön sein* (*Life Can Be So Beautiful*). But before the film could premiere, at a meeting on February 3, 1939, Ufa's executives noted that Goebbels had banned the film "because it tended to sabotage the government's population policy."[24] In truth, Hansen and his author, Jochen Huth, had, in the realistic style of the New Objectivity, used the marriage of a young couple to criticize economic and social distress in National Socialist Germany. With a sixth title, *Eine Frau für's Leben* (*A Wife for Life*), the film finally premiered, but not until 1950.

Zarah Leander could hold on to Rolf Hansen as her director, even against Goebbels, because even he knew he had to make concessions to keep Ufa's most expensive star in Germany. Her salary had risen to 400,000 marks, and her films numbered among the few that could be sold internationally. In the melodrama *Der Weg ins Freie* (*Path to Freedom*, 1941), which picked up on the success of Sierck's melodramas, Leander plays an opera singer and the wife of a landowner (Hans Stüwe) who can break out into freedom only in suicide. *The Great Love*, which premiered on June 12, 1942, was Leander's greatest triumph, also Ufa's most effective contribution to stabilizing Germany's crumbling home-front morale. Just two weeks before, the first major British air raid had reduced Cologne's central districts to rubble in ninety minutes.

Leander's last film was called *Damals* (*Back Then*, Rolf Hansen, 1942–43), the story, related in artful flashbacks, of a passionate love, a threatened marriage, and a suspicion of murder. It did not last long in the theaters. Six weeks after its premiere, Zarah Leander left Germany and her bombed-out house in Berlin-Dahlem for her estate in her Swedish homeland (where, however, no very warm feelings awaited her). From then on, she was *persona non grata* in the Nazi state, her films dismissed as regrettable errors.

This was all preceded by a disagreement with Ufa that escalated into a conflict with Goebbels. The shooting for *Back Then* had been in progress when she learned that Ufa had not honored the clause in her contract that required the company to transfer 53 percent of her salary to Sweden. She broke off filming to force the transfer of the money, but Goebbels took this as a personal challenge. He tried to persuade her to forgo the foreign currency, and offered her as compensation German citizenship, a country estate, a significant retirement pension, and the prestige of being a "state actress." She declined—either to avoid betraying Sweden (as she later claimed) or to save herself and her valuable personal property from bombing raids.

Zarah Leander perfectly exemplies the selfishness and cynical pragmatism of Ufa's stars in the Nazi period and the dead end they found themselves in. She had entered the service of Ufa because she realized that she could rise to the top in an industry drained by the exodus of its best talent. Allegedly lucrative offers in the United States and England did not offer such assurance. She did not hesitate to accept the connection with a regime hostile to humanity, and she continued to harbor the illusion that she could protect her art, like some delicate and noble plant, from the vulgar touch of politics and keep herself free of political entanglement. When Ufa's managers took her to task for her homosexual friends and she insisted on her right to choose her private contacts as she saw fit, she revealed the vast self-deception of the Third Reich's celebrated stars. They refused to see that their private lives had long since become part of the Nazis' public world and were partially responsible for its horrors.

26.

Ufa Goes to War

ON August 31, 1939, one day before the German invasion of Poland, the *Film-Kurier* informed its readers why the latest edition of the weekly newsreel, which usually appeared every Thursday, was not available: It would be delayed until September 3 so that it could be guaranteed to be up to the minute on the latest events.[1] The Propaganda Ministry was clearly preparing a surprise.

Ufa was forewarned by August 29 at the latest. On that day, complying with a "ministerial directive," Ufa's managers ordered that the Marika Rökk film *Hallo, Janine*, which had just been completed, as well as a number of other new productions, be supplied with Polish subtitles.[2] It was surely not just the film industry alone that regarded Poland as already conquered before the first shot was fired.

Five years earlier, at a meeting in November 1934, Ufa's senior managers had thought about preparations for war and had approved an expenditure of 34,000 marks to build an "artificial mountain" on the grounds at Neubabelsberg; it could serve for outdoor shots, they said, and they even considered putting an air-raid shelter in it.[3] After the construction of the "sound cross," Ufa-City started to evolve into a bunker complex, which was now extended underground.

When the Wehrmacht invaded Poland, the filming of Georg Jacoby's *Women Really Are Better Diplomats*, Ufa's first major color film, had been in full swing for a month. With a sure instinct for the mysterious link between war and cinema, the cast adopted as their slogan: "When the film is done, the war will be over, too." Even though the movie took longer to produce than any other in Ufa's history, the prediction was still foolishly optimistic. Two years later, when the film premiered on October 31, 1941, in the Capitol am Zoo, Hitler had attacked the Soviet Union, and for three and a half more war years, the "film that never ends," as Marika Rökk put it, would offer "strength through joy" to German moviegoers. By November 1944 it had earned 7.9 million marks, almost three times its production costs.

"This act of creation required light, light, and more light," Marika Rökk said of this major production. "The technicians continued tinkering on improvements for color film shooting while we valiantly filmed on" (and while the first German armored units mowed down Polish villages). "If we thought we had successfully completed a scene, some revoltingly gifted technician would come up with an idea for improving it."[4]

In these days and weeks gifted German technicians were working on many fronts at perfecting their skills. Some changed their jobs or underwent special training to be able to meet the demands of changing times. Leni Riefenstahl, for example, decided in early September to form a film team for reporting from the front. Together with her cameraman Sepp Allgeier and her sound technician Hermann Storr, she had an army major instruct her in the use of gas mask and pistol.[5]

For Karl Ritter, the convinced National Socialist and specialist in films that "educate for war," the outbreak of war was, ironically, a disaster. With the Luftwaffe General Wilberg as a consultant, he had begun shooting a Spanish Civil War film, *Legion Condor*, on August 9. (Felix Lützkendorf had written the book; Günther Anders was the cameraman; Paul Hartmann had the lead; Albert Hehn, Herbert A.E. Böhme, Karl John, Wolfgang Staudte, Fritz Kampers, Josef Dahmen, and other well-known Ufa actors were included.) At the end of August, Ufa discreetly informed its star director that there would be censorship problems because of the Hitler-Stalin pact, and after the invasion of Poland filming was stopped and never resumed. (In his *Deutscher Spielfilm-Almanach*, Alfred Bauer claims that the shooting "broke off because of the outbreak of war and the need to employ the Luftwaffe in the war."[6] That is unlikely. Even in the last weeks of the war Goebbels and Veit Harlan showed with *Kolberg* that it was possible to use an already defeated army as extras in a propaganda film extolling "total war.")

Ritter's documentary *Im Kampf gegen den Weltfeind: Deutsche Freiwillige in Spanien* (*At Battle with the Enemy of the World: German Volunteers in Spain*), also made with the help of the armed forces and based on a book by Werner Beumelburg, was withdrawn from distribution in late August 1939, too. Once Nazi Germany had made its pact with Stalin's Soviet Union, Bolshevism was no longer the enemy of the world. But these were not the only blows Ritter suffered: his *Kadetten* (*Cadets*, with Mathias Wieman and Carsta Löck) had been chosen for a gala showing at the eleventh NSDAP party convention in Nuremberg on September 5, but it, too, was withdrawn for the same political reasons. Not until the end of 1941, after the invasion of the Soviet Union, did this film become appropriate again, and it premiered in Danzig.

Fall 1939: The film industry, though possessed of current information, had difficulty in adapting its cumbersome organization to new ideological demands, but the German people accustomed themselves to the changed situation relatively quickly. People grew used to reading obituaries for soldiers killed in action, though there were complaints, the SS spies noted, about "the rather undignified placement of the notices in the papers' layouts,"[7] meaning the proximity of the notices to entertainment ads. Westphalia's innkeepers complained merely that the introduction of a midnight curfew was costing them the trade of many affluent customers who were patronizing instead the nearby Rhineland inns and restaurants, which could stay open until 2 a.m.

To supply the provinces with films sensitive to the military situation and to the film activities of the Nazis' mass organizations was to encounter major logistical problems. In its report on the domestic political situation at the end of November, the Security Service noted that a film hour planned for Hitler Youth groups throughout Germany had run into problems: In Stuttgart, for example, twelve- to fourteen-year-old boys and girls had simply been shown whatever happened to be in the current film program, and this included films like *Gern hab ich die Frauen geküsst* (*I Liked Kissing Women*, directed by Georg Zoch, Majestic-Film, 1934) and *Andalusische Nächte* (*Andalusian Nights*, directed by Herbert Maisch, a co-production with the Spanish company Hispano-Film that Goebbels forced on Ufa, 1938). "The Hitler Youth leaders' . . . complaints fell on deaf ears, for the theater owners said they had not received any other films from Berlin."[8]

Only two weeks later, however, propaganda successes were reported. The cultural activities of the NSDAP were evoking lively interest, it was said, and the rural population was grateful for increased efforts made by the NSDAP's district film offices. War films like *Dreizehn Mann und eine Kanone* (*Thirteen Men and a Cannon*, directed by Johannes Meyer, Bavaria, 1938), *D III 38* (Herbert Maisch, Tobis, 1939), Ritter's *Pour le Mérite*, and Ucicky's old Ufa film *Dawn* were popular; Hans Steinhoff's *Robert Koch* was "a positive experience for almost the entire nation."[9]

Special mention was made of the popularity of shorts featuring the figures "Hoarder" and "Complainer." That was good news for a government troubled by a wave of hoarding that had swept through Germany. Wartime regulations threatened imprisonment for anyone who "destroys, stores away, or keeps back" raw materials or necessities.[10] According to the SS's observations, many Germans doubted that accumulating goods for later use could be construed as "storing away," and behaved accordingly. The "Hoarder" comedy strips were intended to show them, in an entertaining way, the seriousness of the situation.

For the first time, a German government was trying to effect—in "a time saturated, overfed, and disgusted with propaganda"[11]—a comprehensive strategy that integrated the conduct of war with ideological influence over the populace; the strategy required communications technology as well as domestic political measures to stabilize the "national body politic." The domestic political advantages of a centralized state film industry were obvious, but for diplomacy, too, film was a highly effective instrument, the versatile employment of which the Supreme Command in World War I had not even begun to appreciate.

In an essay published in 1944, the émigré avant-garde critic Hans Richter pointed out a striking pattern in the National Socialist warmakers' use of the film medium. In early 1938, the German Embassy in Vienna invited the Austrian government to a showing of *Triumph of the Will*; "a few weeks later Schuschnigg made a quick trip to see Hitler, and a few days later Austria was occupied."[12] Similarly, shortly after a festive showing of German films for members of the Czechoslovakian government in the Prague embassy in early 1939, the "Protectorate of Bohemia and Moravia" was annexed to the Reich. The attack on Poland was preceded by a gala film evening in the German embassy in Warsaw. In the German embassies in the capitals of Romania, Norway, Holland, and Belgium, government members were invited to watch German films about the Polish campaign before their own countries were attacked. When Germany set out to occupy Greece and Yugoslavia in 1941, it used the film *Sieg im Westen* (*Victory in the West*), about the war in France, as a threat and means of extortion. And only nine days before the attack on the U.S.S.R., members of the Soviet government were invited to a showing of *Über den Feldern im Balkan* (*Over the Balkan Fields*). "This is how the Nazis used film as an instrument of their political demagogy," Richter wrote. "But we have to grant them that they did it thoroughly and thoughtfully. They made film into a sharp weapon and established its role as an instrument of propaganda."[13]

Ufa-Newsreel was in charge of the centrally controlled war reporting for theaters at home and in occupied countries. Shortening the showing period of each weekly newsreel from sixteen to four weeks and, more important, increasing the number of copies in circulation from 400 to 1,700, most of which Ufa had to pay for, meant that Ufa's expenditures for newsreel copies alone rose to 5.3 million marks per year.[14]

In German newsreels, the news was exclusively about events of the war, but at the same time newsreels were expanded from twenty-minute to forty-minute "totalitarian panoramas," movies that treated the souls of German moviegoers "like prisoners of war," as Kracauer put it.[15] In National Socialist war reporting, the fanaticism of the Wehrmacht's Supreme Command blended with Goebbels's vision of influencing the masses as "creative art." The army had established as early as August 1938 "propaganda companies" for each of its general headquarters. With the outbreak of war, these were responsible for ensuring the "coordination of propaganda and combat activities in the theaters of operation." An Agreement on the Utilization of Propaganda in War that Goebbels and General Keitel had reached in the winter of 1938–39 affirmed that propaganda was "a means of conducting war equal in importance" to field operations.[16]

The personnel of the propaganda companies—reporters, photographers, cameramen, radio journalists, and artists—were trained for combat in brief military courses. Military confrontation became, as the French theoretician Paul Virilio put it, a "war of perceptions," and the camera eye subordinated itself to the delusions of the regime, which in its Blitzkrieg had begun to make laws of destruction and conquest the only measures to be used in the world of time and space.

> The cinematic eye is able to see life filled to the brim with death, land-scapes spectrally illuminated with torches, space spread out in endless paths, ghostly vehicles rolling forward with guns blazing. Action, attack, will, rapid motion and fierce energy, the human and the kinetic fantastically blended—all this had found form here in a way that had as its goal to represent the moving force, the spirit, that set all this in motion.[17]

Although pictures of dead German soldiers were forbidden in film reports and though newsreels that spoke of the destruction of the enemy literally achieved a "pictorial abolition of death,"[18] the "heroic deaths" of German war correspondents were explicitly mentioned. In 1940 the Propaganda Ministry told the foreign press that since the beginning of the war twenty-three members of propaganda companies had been killed.

The integration of "propaganda" and "combat" was an element of a "modern," totalitarian strategy of conquest that in relation to the world beyond Germany's borders knew potentially no limits in geographical space and in the domestic realm was directed at the "deepest levels of the national soul," as Goebbels put it. "Power based on guns may be a good thing; it is, however, better and more gratifying to win the heart of a people and to keep it."[19] The image of the film camera that "goes in within rifle range" and "is carried by the same hand that in the next instant reaches for a weapon"[20] became the emblem of a propaganda machine that declared war on actual facts, on the laws of perception, on the consciousness of a nation.

Reality offered a much more sobering sight. The reporter Hans Ertl, who had been cameraman for Leni Riefenstahl's Olympics films, testified that it was impossible "to capture optically the danger as it really is."[21] War reporters with weapons in their hands—like tailgunners in a bomber, for example—were the exception, not the rule. The emotional image of the armed cameraman, however, added an aesthetic intensification to events of war. This emotionalizing was directed at the "whole nation" and recognized the individual "hero" and the individual death only as an emblem of a theatrical scenario culminating in "ultimate victory."

> On this moribund stage there is no room for heroes as individuals. They are swallowed up in a sea of extras and disappear in Hitler's anonymous

statistics of the doomed. The stage magic of a battlefield in enemy territory gives the heroic struggle of destiny's community a mystical flair of irreality that conveys to the spectator at home in his theater seat the feeling that stage and audience belong together.[22]

With the founding of Deutsche Wochenschau at the end of 1940, the army's propaganda companies, responsible agencies in Goebbels's Ministry, and the film companies' newsreel divisions came together in a monolithic complex that destroyed any distinctions between civilian and military staffs, between commercial and political interests. The entire machine was in the service of war, and its gears functioned flawlessly as long as the army's victories seemed to be fulfilling the propagandists' promises. Ufa's significant role in National Socialist war reporting was in keeping with what Traub pompously called its "historical stature." Ufa's historical stature was now reduced to the function that military strategists had envisioned for it in 1918. In a publication celebrating twenty-five years of Ufa newsreels, an Ufa cameraman wrote this report of his first bomber flight over Poland:

> From the nose turret I filmed everything my camera could pick up. Enemy fighters tried to turn us away from our target. Their action prompted a quick exchange between spotter and pilot, and a bold maneuver took our plane beyond the reach of enemy fire. Flying over burning villages and often above the clouds, we sought out the enemy, ready to make the last sacrifice and armed with the knowledge that, like us, everyone on this mission was prepared to lay down his life.[23]

The feature-length "documentaries" *Feldzug in Polen* (*Campaign in Poland*) and *Feuertaufe* (*Baptism of Fire*, both 1939–40), compiled from newsreel material, were followed by *Victory in the West* after the capitulation of France. They were all products of the military command and the Propaganda Ministry, but they could not have been made without the experienced cameramen, sound engineers, and film technicians of Ufa and Tobis, artistic specialists and passionately dedicated craftsmen. Ufa's cult of perfectionism, its "work ethic" and sense of mission, the "pride in the firm" —these were key psychological factors that partially account for the almost total failure to reflect critically on what was actually happening.

As an émigré in America in 1942, Siegfried Kracauer wrote an analysis of National Socialist newsreels and the films compiled from them; it is still exemplary, and his conclusions have never been refuted.[24] The sham of Nazi war documentaries simulated a reality intended to fill the vacuum of exhaustion which the same propaganda had created in the minds of Germans. The "superb orchestration" of the material by means of montage, music, and commentary was a sleight-of-hand that hid the facts in order to leave the way open for "enthusiasm" (Goebbels) and hysteria. Magical campaign strategies were shown on maps; huge geographical realms were divided into temporal and spatial concepts over which the strategic genius of the Führer exercised control. The epic structure of the heroic saga films gave life to the myth of German infallibility and invincibility.

For obvious reasons, Kracauer, a lone researcher in American exile, could not assess the effects of Nazi war propaganda; his surmise that they "served to transform German audiences into a chain-gang of souls"[25] could be no more than a hypothesis. But he noted an observation made by the American journalist William Shirer, who attended the victory parade in Berlin on July 18, 1940, after the capitulation of France. "I mingled among the crowds in the Pariserplatz. A holiday spirit ruled completely. Nothing martial about the mass of the people here. They were just out for a good time."[26]

Numerous private journals and the "Germany Reports" written by Social Democrats who had gone into exile document that the attitude of the German people in the first days of the war was anything but martial, and that apathy and depression were not uncommon.[27] Even the SS spies could not completely ignore this, and their reports on the reception of the war newsreels frequently noted unsettling mood swings in some segments of the population. A report of May 14, 1940, dealt extensively with critical responses from all parts of the country to *Baptism of Fire*. Many viewers criticized the tendency in Nazi propaganda to show the advance of the German Army and the superiority of the German Luftwaffe but to convey no impression of the Polish defense. The authors of the report observed, with a hint of resignation, that "a uniform reaction simply cannot be expected from all viewers, no matter how the film is designed." Women in particular expressed sympathy with the Poles, and some viewers expressed "not a mood of heroic pride but a depressed and frightened reaction to the horrors of war."[28]

No doubt the initial successes of the Wehrmacht in Poland and France increased support for the regime, but the optimism was superficial, a kind of equivocal *joie de vivre* to forestall depression. Germans were not prepared to change their patterns of consumption for the sake of a war and a government intent on "ultimate victory." Unlike the British government, the Nazi regime cut back on the production of consumer goods only slightly. (In 1945, it was only 7 percent below the 1938 level.) Even in 1943 the demand for attractive fashions, unrationed delicacies, and liquor was in keeping with "the dictatorship's strategy of maintaining continuity with the values of the prewar years and of the future peace."[29] If the soul of the people was enchained, terrorized by the propaganda of destruction and advertisements for death, their eyes were still searching hungrily after things that spoke to them of the urge to live, of peaceful pleasures. As late as February 1945, when Germany lay in ruins, a mortgaging company was still using the slogan "Save in wartime—build later."[30]

This ambiguous state of mind—enthusiasm and anxiety, patriotic fervor, consumerism, and longing for an unspoiled world—fed right into the Germans' new interest in film. Young people, the government was troubled to see, were especially susceptible to movies. In April 1940 the Security Service reported that in cities like Chemnitz, Halle, Dortmund, and Breslau young people were regularly turning up for films banned for juveniles. In Stuttgart, it noted that ever since the war began, increasing numbers of young people were "thronging into showings of mysteries and love stories forbidden for youth."[31] Gangs of "young people of dubious character" were seen at a theater in Gelsenkirchen. Evening shows in the Upper Silesian cities of Oppeln and Neisse were attended mostly by teenagers. In Chemnitz the police raided theaters in March 1940 to clear out adolescents when *Weltrekord im Seitensprung* (*World Record for Adultery*, a "Rhenish comedy of mistaken identity" forbidden to minors, directed by Georg Zoch, produced by Deka, 1939–40) and *Ehe in Dosen* (*Marriage in Small Doses*, directed by Johannes Meyer, Cine-Allianz, 1939) were shown. In Breslau, SS spies said, "a downright addiction to film" achieved epidemic proportions among adolescents, and in Halle the Hitler Youth recommended stricter measures against theater owners and the young addicts. Its patrols, helping the police in their raids, were pleased to discover that "only a small percentage" of the arrested movie fans belonged to the Hitler Youth or the Bund deutscher Mädel (League of German Girls). But too few films, they noted, were "suitable for youth," and "significant incorporation of film into the cultural work of the Hitler Youth" was not possible.[32]

The Propaganda Ministry was sensitive to the need for diversion. A new wave of carefree entertainment films began appearing on German screens. Once again, as Arthur Maria Rabenalt wrote, comedies of love and marriage "indulged in merry antics in a world of glass."[33] At the high point of a war supposedly already won, "the German entertainment film . . . was supposed to . . . support the Reich's efforts to attain political hegemony . . . to have European appeal, to form taste and set an example, both for fashion and for elegant and worldly style." Understandably, many entertainers saw in love stories set in exotic locales or worldly interiors a chance to escape the Strength-through-Joy and Blood-and-Soil culture of Nazi aesthetics. Understandably, too, the public was more than willing to be transported into weightless, seductive, glittering worlds outside time.

Goebbels decreed, not for the first time, at the convention of the Reich Film Guild in February 1941, that film was an "educational tool." It had to have "a national moral thrust" and help to "educate and enable the nation to achieve its goals."[34] But a year later he said just the opposite. Not every firm was obliged "to produce one great film after another and one heroic blockbuster after another." He would personally commission major films of "national political character." They should comprise not more than 20 percent of total production. The remaining 80 percent would be "good, high-quality entertainment." "I do not mean to appear purely didactic about film but, rather, in times so filled with tension, to see to it that art provides relaxation."[35]

German film production, which Goebbels so carefully divided into percentages, had by this time—the second and third years of the war—shrunk. In 1941, seventy-two full-length German feature films premiered, in 1942 only fifty-three. Ufa's share (not including the production of Wien-Film) was about 20 percent for both years. In the four years 1939–42 Ufa produced sixty-three full-length feature films, eighteen of which unambiguously displayed a "national moral thrust." In short, Ufa more than fulfilled the quota Goebbels set for the industry. But a closer look at the figures changes the picture. In 1941–42, total production decreased markedly while the number of "state commissions" increased just as markedly.

In 1939, Ufa produced nineteen entertainment films but only three that ever tried to satisfy "national political" requirements in the strict sense: *Three Noncommissioned Officers*, Werner Hochbaum's unsuccessful hymn of praise to military duty; Robert Stemmle's *Man for Man*, which turned out to deviate so much from the ideology of the German Work Front that it drew a harsh review from the Goebbels journal *Der deutsche Film*; and K. G. Külb's *Der Stammbaum des Dr. Pistorius* (*The Family Tree of Dr. Pistorius*), which was supposed to make the idea of a "folk community" plausible and which, judging from the box-office returns, was a flop. In the year the war began, Ufa did not book a "war-education film" to its account, but in 1940 that changed with the *Wish Concert* and Erich Waschneck's anti-Semitic *Die Rothschilds*; on the other side of the ledger were twelve vacuous entertainment films.

The war years 1941–42 show a totally different picture. In 1941, Germany opened the front in southeastern Europe with an attack on Yugoslavia and the occupation of Greece. The Wehrmacht invaded the Soviet Union in June with spectacular initial success, but when its tanks came to a standstill before Moscow in the winter, Goebbels had to retract his solemn promise that the Red Army would be defeated within a few weeks. In the occupied countries, notably in France and Czechoslovakia, resistance to the German occupation increased. Toward the end of the year, the Japanese attack on Pearl Harbor drew the United States into the war. Now, apart from Italy, Japan, and the unreliable satellites in southeastern Europe, Hitler had the whole world against him. Roosevelt and Churchill held their first talks about what the new order of the world would be after the collapse of German Fascism.

In 1942, marginal states like Panama, Luxembourg, Brazil, and Abyssinia declared war on Germany. By the end of the year the Wehrmacht's Sixth Army on the eastern front was hopelessly encircled by the Red Army. Albert Speer was appointed Reich Minister for Arms and Munitions; and as Inspector General for Highways, Water, and Energy, he was supposed to shore up the shaky logistical operations on all fronts of this already lost war. As a reprisal for an assassination attempt against the "Reich Protector of Bohemia and Moravia," SS-Führer Reinhard Heydrich, German gangster troops eradicated the village of Lidice and its inhabitants. At the same time, what Hitler and his confederates at the Wannsee Conference called the "final solution" was set in motion—the eventual murder of 6 million Jews in Auschwitz, Maidanek, Treblinka, and other death camps.

During these two years, amid ongoing squabbles with the Propaganda Ministry, the political and moral destruction of Universum-Film AG was completed. Germany's leading film company produced only twenty-six full-length features in 1941 and 1942. Twelve of them fulfilled to the letter the requirements of all-out war propaganda. Karl Ritter's 1941 contribution to the requested bully-boy patriotism was the episodic film *Über alles in der Welt* (*Above All Else in the World*; book, Felix Lützkendorf; camera, Werner Krien; music, Herbert Windt; starring Carl Raddatz, Hannes Stelzer, Marina von Ditmar, and Fritz Kampers). That same year, again with Raddatz and Stelzer in lead roles, he made *Stukas*, a panegyric on the Luftwaffe. In 1943 his crude, hyperemotional agit-cinema rose to new heights with *GPU*, a political melodrama about the Soviet secret police (with Laura Solari, Will Quadflieg, and Marina von Ditmar).

Günther Rittau, one of Ufa's leading cameramen ever since *Metropolis*, celebrated the struggle and "heroic death" of German sailors in the Atlantic in *U-Boote westwärts* (*U-Boats Westward*, with Ilse Werner, Herbert Wilk, and Heinz Engelmann, 1941). In 1941 in *Boys* (with Albert Hehn, Bruni Löbel, and Hilde Sessak; camera, Robert Baberske; Werner Egk had a hand in the music), even Robert Stemmle was propagandizing on behalf of Hitler's "folk community." And Arthur Maria Rabenalt made his Ufa film *Riding for Germany* with Willy Birgel, the story of a cavalry officer wounded in World War I who succeeds in restoring German honor.

There was no lack of patriotic tearjerkers like *Annelie—Die Geschichte eines Lebens* (*Annelie—The Story of a Life*, 1941, directed by Josef von Baky, with Luise Ullrich, Werner Krauss, Karl Ludwig Diehl, and Käthe Haack). The theme of Germans abroad struggling "to make their way home to the Reich" against all obstacles put in their way by a hostile world, immensely popular since 1933, was revisited in Gustav Ucicky's *Homecoming* (book: Gerhard Menzel, with Paula Wessely, Peter Petersen, and Attila Hörbiger, 1941). Produced by Wien-Film at the explicit command of Goebbels, this film (in which gore-laden scenes portrayed Poles as "subhuman") earned the highest possible rating: "Film of the Nation." And then anti-Soviet films held back for political reasons began to appear, some in revised versions. Among them were Karl Ritter's *Cadets* and Fritz Kirchhoff's *Anschlag auf Baku* (*Attack on Baku*, with Willy Fritsch, René Deltgen, Fritz Kampers, and Aribert Wäscher, 1942).

A counterweight to war propaganda was supplied by escapist films about the "elegant world," artists, or folksy peasants. The "musical comedy of mistaken identity," typified by *Tanz mit dem Kaiser* (*Dance with the Kaiser*, directed by Georg Jacoby, with Marika Rökk and Wolf Albach-Retty, 1941), was offered with many variations. The lifestyle of the imperial Habsburg monarchy, as portrayed in Erich Engel's *Hotel Sacher* (with

Sybille Schmitz and Willy Birgel, 1941), provided dreamy excursions into a lost world, one still very much alive in the German psyche. And Sudermann—not only in *Hochzeit auf Bärenhof* (*Wedding at Bärenhof*, directed by Carl Froelich, with Heinrich George, Paul Wegener, and Ilse Werner, 1942)—was an inexhaustible reservoir of motifs. The nineteenth century became a paradise for Ufa and the German cinema. Films like *Die Hochzeitsreise* (*The Wedding Trip*, directed by Karl Ritter, 1939) or the coach-and-four eroticism of Fritz Peter Buch's *Das leichte Mädchen* (*The Fast Girl*, 1941) conveyed the melody, the glow, and the freedom from care of a time that never existed; people consequently longed for it all the more passionately.

Broad humor, local color, dirty stories, and "full-blooded" *joie de vivre* were also popular, as in *Hochzeitsnacht* (*Wedding Night*, directed by Carl Boese, with a script by Richard Billinger, 1941) or Johannes Meyer's *Männerwirtschaft* (*Bachelor Life*, with Volker von Collande and Karin Hardt, 1941). And Ufa could draw on all the organizational and technical experience it had acquired over more than two decades. Setting up a jewelry robbery (for *12 Minuten nach 12* [*12 Past 12*], directed by Johannes Guter, 1939) was as routine as building tropical sets for a mythical Africa on the Hannover-Celle railroad line (for Eduard von Borsody's *Kongo-Express* with Marianne Hoppe, Willy Birgel, and René Deltgen). The young Ilse Werner—the "daughter of a good upper-middle-class family" type, endowed with the treasured German virtues of "naturalness" and "sweetness"—rapidly advanced to stardom, playing leads in Erich Waschneck's *Fräulein*, Carl Boese's *Drei Väter um Anna* (*Three Fathers for Anna*), and Josef von Baky's *Ihr erstes Erlebnis* (*Her First Experience*), all made in 1939. Throughout the coming war years, these films sang to German moviegoers in city and country an old song of love and love's pain, of errors of the heart, of the joys of marriage.

For a public having to cope with everyday wartime life, the bohemian milieu of artists, publishers, and theater people, with their supposedly loose morals and libertine ways, exerted a particular attraction, as in Georg Jacoby's mystery *Der Vorhang fällt* (*The Curtain Falls*, with Anneliese Uhlig and Hilde Sessak, 1939), Ritter's *Bal paré* with Ilse Werner, Paul Hartmann, and Pamela Wedekind (1940), Viktor Tourjansky's sensitive psychological study *Illusion* with Johannes Heesters and Brigitte Horney (1941), and Haral Braun's musical comedy about the theater world, *Hab' mich lieb* (*Love Me*, with Marika Rökk, Viktor Staal, and Hans Brausewetter, 1942). In *Mädchen im Vorzimmer* (*Girl in the Front Office*, based on a book by Walter von Hollander, 1940), Gerhard Lamprecht even managed to introduce everyday experiences and insights about social reality into an ambience of subdued bohemianism and contained erotic anarchy. Lamprecht was among the Ufa directors who were always trying to subvert the ideological structure of the Nazi film and to break through the established clichés (*Diesel*, with Willy Birgel, 1942).

Marika Rökk danced on, and the production histories of her films contain some interesting and revealing incidents. The flight of the actor Karl Stepanek after the completion of Women Really Are Better Diplomats was not the only event to cause Ufa embarrassment. At about the same time, during the production of Kora Terry (1940), Ufa again found itself squabbling with Goebbels over questions of dramaturgy. Ernst Leichtenstern, formerly a ministerial councillor in the Propaganda Ministry, was now Ufa's production chief for feature films. Correll left Ufa for good in February 1939, and after that the Propaganda Ministry fared badly in trying to fill his place. The reasons for his departure were perhaps more professional than political. But because Correll had been an outspoken critic of the cumbersome political machinery and a strong advocate for production independence, the Propaganda Ministry probably considered him a troublemaker. His successor, Alfred Greven, from Terra, was considered competent, but he had to go after only a few weeks because his politics and ideas on how to do the work were viewed as unacceptable. In May 1941, at the urging of Reich Film Commissioner Max Winkler, even the politically reliable Leichtenstern was forced to resign because of obvious incompetence; he was succeeded by Otto Heinz Jahn.

The production department's final report on Kora Terry gives us some insight into Ufa's disagreements with Goebbels and its efforts to maintain an independent production policy. The report indicates that Marika Rökk was originally supposed to play a double role:

> Filming had already begun when the Propaganda Ministry raised objections to the double role. But because the plot depended entirely on this device, Mr. Leichtenstern decided to make two versions and after completion leave the final decision to the Ministry. Thus it was that many scenes had to be filmed twice, which involved considerable loss of time, and the synchronization and mixing of two separate versions used an unusually large amount of film. . . . Personnel problems brought about by the war slowed the pace of production, and a lack of construction crews often brought shooting to a standstill. On several days no filming could be done because the dance stage was being used by others. . . .[36]

(As it turned out, production costs for Kora Terry exceeded the original estimate of 1.4 million marks by very little, and within a few months the film easily earned it all back.) We do not know the reasons for Goebbels's objections to Marika Rökk's double role. According to a perhaps apocryphal story related by the film composer Peter Kreuder, a stand-in was needed for Rökk for some shots, and Ufa found a suitable double in a concentration camp, "borrowed" her, and, after the shooting was completed, effected her permanent release.[37]

The German film industry of course had to adjust itself to the war economy. Leichtenstern willingly gave information to Filmwelt in early May

1940 on the political and economic limitations with which Ufa had been coping since the beginning of the war. While essentially maintaining the prewar program, Ufa had dropped a number of projects now considered "undesirable or impossible in the context of the war," for example, films set in foreign countries, "especially in countries now hostile to us but also in neutral countries at those times when there was risk of injuring feelings that ran understandably high in times of crisis and war." But, he went on, the war had also opened the way for new themes that took it "into account, first, by showing the people experiencing the war and doing their part for the war effort; second, like all propaganda instruments, unmasking the enemy; and, third, improving morale with light and entertaining subjects."[38]

War, the "father of all things," wiped the slate clean and created clarity—or such was the view of Leichtenstern and his National Socialist colleagues, as he called for "extreme frugality" throughout the film industry. In place of materials no longer available, Leichtenstern recommended using "German synthetics . . . of equal quality or even better." Wherever possible, "German fabrics" should be used for costumes and interior decoration. "The acquisition of rationed goods requires the approval of the competent authorities. Everything that is purchased new for a film should be stored in the prop room, where it will be available for reuse after appropriate alteration." While the German people were collecting old clothes, paper, tin cans, and used materials of all kinds for the Winter Aid program and for the front, Ufa's prop department was doing its part for the wartime economy by recycling rococo costumes and fairy-tale uniforms.

According to the reports of the Security Service, the entertainment films of the war years drew widely diverse responses. In early 1941 the spies were effusive in noting the "extremely enthusiastic reception" of *Operette*, which Willi Forst had directed for Wien-Film and Tobis-Verleih, a musical "picture of an era" that used a film plot to tell the story of the beginnings of Viennese operetta (Forst collaborated with Axel Eggebrecht on the book): "Here again at last was truly light entertainment untainted by vapidity, staleness, and trivial eroticism."[39] The language of this report echoed the Goebbels press, of course, but the dissatisfaction of many moviegoers with run-of-the-mill entertainment is all but audible.

A few days before, on February 17, the SS had also reported "enthusiastic approval for" *Wish Concert*, directed by Borsody and produced by Cine-Allianz for Ufa in 1940. The popularity of the radio-broadcast wish concerts, the report said, had been helpful in the advertising campaign. The movie successfully integrated events of the war into the plot and inserted well-known clips of the Olympic Games, the Legion Condor in Spain, and the Polish campaign into its fictitious context. This "satisfied amply the desire of a large part of the population for variety and contemporaneity."[40]

The radio program *Wish Concert* was broadcast every Sunday afternoon during the war. As a "promoter of community feeling" it was supposed to forge a close bond between "the battling and victorious front" and the home front.[41] This Sunday program was an hour of prayer for Germans, an orientation point for emotions in need of equilibrium. Dramaturgically simple but psychologically sophisticated, the program appealed to the "harmony of hearts" and played skillfully with sentiment and sentimentality, with genuine and manipulated feelings. Performances by Marika Rökk and Heinz Rühmann, Paul Horbiger and Hans Brausewetter, Josef Sieber and Weiss-Ferdl, Wilhelm Strienz and Albert Bräu blended together the pain of separation and the grief of the lonely, heroic pathos and foxhole humor, the death cult and help for the living—all this in a sticky stew of emotions whose common source—the "German spirit"—was evoked in folk songs and the velvet voice of the MC, Heinz Gödecke.

In Borsody's film, Wish Concert becomes the central switchboard for a pair of storybook German lovers (Ilse Werner and Carl Raddatz) who become acquainted at the Olympic Games in 1936 and then, separated by political events, find their way back together again after years of anxious waiting, after air sorties, wounds, recovery in a military hospital, and any number of misunderstandings. The happy ending that unites a sharp Luftwaffe lieutenant with his brave "partner for life" reflected the "harmony"of front with home front and at the same time anticipated "ultimate victory," that constantly evoked goal in all Nazi propaganda. Fritz Hippler, later Reich Film Intendant, in this case a reliable source, had this to say:

> We have here . . . an example of a genuine commissioned work that was spelled out in some detail in advance and imposed upon film production by the state. The elements of the film, established beforehand, were that it would begin at the Olympic Games and end during the ongoing war and with a tie to the Wish Concert programs.[42]

By the end of Nazi rule, 26.5 million people had seen this movie, and with box-office returns of 7.6 million marks, it was among the most profitable productions of the war years.

It was bettered slightly in 1942 by Zarah Leander's triumph in The Great Love, Ufa's most successful "war-education film." Entertainment and propaganda melded together here, as they had in Wish Concert, in that emotional amalgam that Goebbels's philosophy of mass manipulation had always striven to attain but rarely did. The original cost estimate had been for a little over 1.5 million marks; the actual cost was 3.1 million, but by November 1944 the film had brought in 9.2 million; by the end of the war almost 28 million people had seen it.[43]

Walter Bolz was responsible for overseeing production of The Great Love, which took from September 1941 to March 1942; Rolf Hansen directed; studio scenes were done in the Carl Froelich sound-film studio in Vienna and outdoor shots in Rome. Ufa supplied its top talent. The book, written by Peter Groll and Rolf Hansen, was based on an idea developed by Alex-

ander Lernet-Holenia, a story of love and renunciation between a Luftwaffe
first lieutenant and a cabaret singer. The cameraman was the Leander specialist Franz Weihmayr. Michael Jary wrote the music; Bruno Balz the lyrics
for Leander's songs. Of equally high caliber was the supporting cast. Along
with Leander herself, Grethe Weiser, Viktor Staal, Paul Hörbiger, Wolfgang
Preiss, Hans Schwarz, Jr., Victor Janson, and Paul Bildt gave the movie its
outward glow and melancholy passion. The screenplay pulled together war
theaters in Africa, France, Italy, and Russia in an emotion-laden scenario.
"Eroticism repressed for the sake of the mission at the front also imposed
deferred satisfaction on the home front," wrote the critic Karsten Witte in
summing up the underlying structure, though in Leander's performance an
irritating, "neurotically colored sensuality" overshadowed the propaganda
message.[44] It was impossible to tell from the lyrics of her songs—"That's
Not the End of the World," "I Know a Miracle Will Happen Some Day,"
alluding to the paradise that would come after "ultimate victory"—that
Bruno Balz had written them in a Gestapo prison. Michael Jary is said to
have won his release.[45]

On February 18, 1943, seven months after the gala premiere of *The Great
Love* at the Ufa-Palast am Zoo, Goebbels declared Germany's commitment
to "total war" in a speech at the Sportpalast. On July 8, the SS reported
that "fear of air raids in western Germany . . . was making many citizens
depressed and nervous," and signs of a shift in attitude were appearing—
listening to foreign radio stations, increased receptivity to "enemy propaganda," failure to use the "Heil Hitler" greeting, and a widespread "critical
attitude toward national and party leadership." "Even the most inane and
malign rumors about leading figures in the party and in the government"
spread with lightning rapidity. The rumor that the Hitler Youth leader
Baldur von Schirach had been shot while attempting to escape to Switzerland, for instance, spread from Bavaria to Danzig in two weeks. "Crass jokes
demeaning to the state and even jokes about the Führer himself" were
circulating. It was taken for granted "that anyone could tell a joke these
days without fear even of rebuff, much less of being reported to the
police."[46]

A joke that the Security Service cited as a particularly heinous example
used lyrics from *The Great Love*. Zarah Leander is summoned to an engagement in the Führer's headquarters where she then has to sing: "I Know
a Miracle Will Happen Someday."

27.

Survival Is All That Matters

WHEN Ufa celebrated the twenty-fifth anniversary of its founding in the winter of 1942–43, the course of the war was taking a decisive turn. Surrounded at Stalingrad, the Sixth Army under General Paulus surrendered. Almost 150,000 German soldiers died in the Soviet offensive; 90,000 became prisoners of war. In February, during the preparations for the Ufa celebration that was to culminate in the March premiere of the film *Münchhausen*, the situation on the eastern front overshadowed every other event and totally dominated the popular mood. On the afternoon of February 3, a special news announcement reported that the German forces at Stalingrad had given up further resistance. Then the radio played the song "Ich hatt' einen Kameraden." According to the SS, the music had "sublimated" the oppressive emotions of helplessness and grief that the people were feeling and transformed them into "respect for the heroic struggle of the men at Stalingrad." But the eulogy—delivered by Hans Fritzsche, the chief of National Radio—evoked mixed responses: many people thought his speech too "smooth and glib."[1]

These dark days nonetheless saw the premieres of "marriage comedies" like E. W. Emo's *Zwei glückliche Menschen* (*Two Happy People*), society films like Ucicky's *Späte Liebe* (*Late Love*), both produced by Wien-Film, romances from the artistic life like Tourjansky's *Liebesgeschichten* (*Love Stories*, Ufa), and musical comedies like Hubert Marischka's *Ein Walzer mit Dir* (*A Waltz with You*, Berlin-Film); meanwhile, the number of people deported to concentration camps since 1933 reached 10 million. On January 26 Hitler Youth members were detailed to auxiliary duties with the Luftwaffe. A day later the Reich Defense Commissioner Fritz Sauckel ordered the "enrollment of men and women for tasks of national defense": the government was mobilizing the nonworking population, women in particular, for war-related duty on the home front. Many women evaded the order, and the agencies responsible for carrying it out were reluctant to enforce it for fear of provoking "mass dissatisfaction."

On May 1, 1934, Ufa and all its subsidiaries had sworn an "oath of loyalty based on the statute for the organization of national work." Its more than 5,000 white- and blue-collar workers had convened solemnly to pledge themselves as vassals to their leader. By 1940 the war saw to it that Ufa experienced a reduction in force: technical workers especially—lighting men, stagehands, and "men from the workshops"—had been drafted in large numbers "or detailed to special duties," Leichtenstern announced in May. "However, immediate compensatory measures were completely successful. Employees are doing significantly more work. A lighting man who once worked two or three spotlights now tends five or six. The workday has been extended." From management's perspective, a side effect of the wartime economy was a welcome, perhaps even overdue rationalization of production. Ufa sorted through its performers carefully, too. Only a few "well-known actors who as stars or in supporting roles could sustain a film were declared exempt from military service."[2]

The war lifted the German film industry and Ufa, its leading company, out of the doldrums and onto a peak of prosperity that no one could have foreseen even as late as 1939—no one except, perhaps, Dr. Max Winkler, who had effected the nationalization of the film companies in 1937 and worked tirelessly ever since to consolidate the business into a single, monolithic state enterprise. While the Third Reich was hastening toward disaster, Ufa enjoyed unexpected prosperity and made a qualitative leap to the rank of a film colossus towering over half of Europe. But this colossus had clay feet and would not survive the downfall of its political directors.

In 1938 Germany's state film companies were still having difficulty amortizing their products. There was no export income, and production costs were averaging more than 600,000 marks per film. By 1942 they had risen to 1.38 million, but in the meantime the war had improved the business climate. The territories Germany had occupied and annexed raised the number of established theaters from 5,446 (1938) to 7,042 (1942). Box-office sales doubled between 1938 and 1941 from 441 million to 892 million and passed the billion mark in 1942. The gross income of movie theaters in this period climbed from 353 to 894 million marks.[3] The organized film events put on by the government and party and an increased need for information (then for diversion from the information received) partially account for the increased movie attendance, but shortage of consumer goods and excess household cash also played a part. From 1939 to 1940, Ufa's total gross income rose from 142 to 166 million marks, and profits grew astronomically from a modest 35,000 marks to 1.7 million. Like other state concerns, Ufa made grateful use of loans from the Reich Film Bank, but it was able to manage on its own and live in plenty.

Reich Commissioner Winkler, whose Cautio Company held the majority of stock in the four big movie companies on behalf of the state, wanted to increase their wealth, but he also wanted to wean them away from their reliance on the state treasury. Spiker correctly emphasizes that these economic considerations gave a "crucial impetus for the organizational perfecting of the National Socialist film monopoly."[4] Thanks to the bureaucracy of the Reich Film Guild and the authority of the Reich film dramaturge, political control had long been in place. Now Winkler wanted to find "investment opportunities that would enable [the film companies] to bring the film business of Continental Europe under their control."[5] His goal was a holding company that could unite under one roof the entire potential of the industry and at the same time shelter individual firms from critical losses through state taxes, war payments, and taxes on profits.

Winkler was fascinated by the organizational structure of Ufa and its wide network of subsidiaries in all sectors of the film industry. It was his ideal in prototypical form; only Ufa, in his view, could form that one roof he wanted. Ufa's administration was an exemplar of a holding company's hierarchy, and the commercial experience of Klitzsch and his administrators guaranteed "smooth functioning" on an even higher level of organization.

Winkler's enthusiasm for Ufa was not universally shared, of course. The Propaganda Ministry's finance section had grown accustomed to Cautio, which was for all practical purposes already functioning as a holding company, and Goebbels's reservations about the unreliability of certain "elements" in Ufa were no secret. Tobis, Terra, and Bavaria had a natural aversion for their traditional rival, and Klitzsch drew their special disfavor with his tendency to thrust himself into the limelight at every opportunity and play the *praeceptor Germaniae* in film matters. The Finance Ministry, too, wanted to see this dominant company stripped of its powers, and it was with this Ministry that Winkler had primarily to deal.

Still, Winkler managed to have his way in important matters. He first pushed for the founding of Film-Finanz as a holding company for the production companies of Ufa, Tobis, Terra, Bavaria, Wien-Film, and Berlin-Film (the last was formed to absorb the remaining private production companies). And his organizational by-laws stated "that the administration of film production would be handled directly by the holding company. Economic and technical functions in support of film production and marketing would be handled indirectly through Ufa."[6] In other words, the "old" Ufa would put production in the hands of the new holding company and consolidate under its weatherproof roof all other branches of the industry (including the copying plants, the Ufa subsidiary for technical equipment, the book and music publishing houses). A word from Hitler tipped the scales in favor of Winkler and against the resistance of the Finance Minister and the finance department of Goebbels's Ministry. The planned holding company would be called Ufa-Film, and the worldwide reputation and the achievements of Ufa "as representative of the German film industry had to be reflected in the business's structure."[7]

Film-Finanz—Winkler's short-lived but successful interim company—met on January 10, 1942, increased its capital stock to 65 million marks, and renamed itself Ufa-Film. From one day to the next, a massive structure united the old Ufa, the Tobis group, Terra, Bavaria, and Wien-Film. Ufa-Filmkunst was formed a week later to effect the formal withdrawal of Ufa's production branch from the old Ufa and its incorporation into the new organization. The upshot was that the German film industry now comprised two super-organizations: the old Universum-Film AG as an umbrella organization for all film activities exclusive of production and Ufa-Film as a gigantic production company. The name "Ufa" was now a synonym for German film; just as the swastika symbolized Hitler's Germany, so the Ufa rhombus symbolized everything that had to do with cinema in the Reich and in the countries it conquered.

The new Ufa-Film soon became known by the abbreviation "Ufi," and Ufi became, as Hans Traub wrote in 1943, "the administrative organ of the Reich commissioner for the German film industry as well as of the newly established institution of the Reich Film Intendant."[8] Goebbels appointed to this latter position his division chief Fritz Hippler, who in his "Observations on Film Production" (1942) had written a model polemic against "freedom fanatics" in Germany's film industry. According to a decree of his master, the Reich Film Intendant was "responsible for general production planning, overall artistic oversight of production, the supervision of artistic personnel, and the development of new talent."[9] Because Hippler stayed on as chief of Ufi's film division, his assumption of the new position simply shortened the chain of command leading from Goebbels's desk to the studios.

In the final years of the war, Ufa-Filmkunst, under the Ufi umbrella, continued to produce feature films. The old stock company remained responsible for newsreels and cultural, industrial, and scientific films. It also took over the distribution and marketing of all films at home and in occupied or neutral foreign countries. In the course of this centralization, the Deutsche Filmvertriebsgesellschaft (German Film Marketing Company) and the Deutsche Filmtheatergesellschaft were formed as Ufa subsidiaries. Thus, one year before the twenty-fifth anniversary of its founding, Ufa expanded its empire to include seventy-six German and foreign companies as either its subsidiaries or as companies in which it had part interest. By the end of May 1942, Ufa controlled 159 theaters in sixty-nine cities with a total seating capacity of over 160,000, and owned outright 17 theaters in Berlin and 98 throughout Germany.[10]

Gross income in the anniversary year reached a quarter billion marks, and the administrative staff grew correspondingly large. By Traub's count, Ufa had 10,354 employees. Its administrative building on Dönhoffplatz, which the company had occupied since the early 1930s and bought in 1935, was supplemented with neighboring buildings on Krausenstrasse. Traub estimated movie attendance in the anniversary year at a billion. (Before Hit-

ler's assumption of power, it had not ever reached 250 million.)
"Filmmakers are fully aware of the great significance of film in this war.
They have taken their place in the ranks of German warriors at the front
and at home. And in the vanguard of German film production in this
struggle for the future of our nation stands the world-renowned name of
Ufa."[11] With these sentences, Hans Traub concluded his deluxe anniversary
history two years before his film colossus went down with the Reich.

Spiker points out that Ufa's board of directors and senior management
displayed remarkable continuity in personnel from 1933 on, indeed from
before that. "Manager capitalism" had produced a financial and administrative elite whose "ideological interests, shared with the National Socialist
regime, made any serious disturbance or interruption of production and
marketing activity impossible."[12] In ideological matters, there were no fundamental disagreements between state and company leaders. Jewish executives had had to leave the company's top offices by 1933 at the latest.
(The only exception was distribution chief Wilhelm Meydam, whom the
government classified as a "half Jew." Though after the beginning of the
war he was no longer permitted to work, he remained a nominal member
of Ufa's senior management until late March 1941.)

In March 1943, chief executive Ludwig Klitzsch was named chairman of
Ufa's board of directors—"kicked upstairs," as Spiker puts it, because he
no longer fit into "the system of limited competencies within the Ufi
trust."[13] Because the boards of the film companies had in fact already lost
their influence in 1937, Klitzsch's promotion did amount to a loss of power.
He had never been politically troublesome to the Nazis, but his instinct for
power and his dictatorial manner were no longer appreciated. His successor
was Fritz Kaelber, a successful distribution manager for Terra before he
took over direction of the Deutsche Filmvertrieb in 1942. Kaelber, an
NSDAP member since 1933, though his personnel file noted that he had
been illegally active for the party before that, was among those who fell
out of favor in March.[14] For Winkler and presumably for Goebbels, too, his
professional competence was of primary importance, not his political
merits.

When Klitzsch gave his anniversary speech at the celebration on March
2, 1943, he still spoke in his capacity as Ufa's chief executive. Swastika flags
covered the façade of the Ufa-Palast am Zoo (and of the other Ufa theaters
where parallel celebrations were taking place), and the elite of the Nazi
film industry arrived with several thousand guests for a "company gathering." State, government, and party were represented by Goebbels, the
Reich Finance Minister and Reich Bank president Walther Funk, the Reich
party chief of the NSDAP and chief of the Labor Front Robert Ley, and Undersecretary Leopold Gutterer, since 1942 chair of Ufi's board and former officer in charge of demonstrations and state holidays for the Propaganda
Ministry. Alongside the protagonists of the new era stood an inconspic-

uous, now gray-headed, and still deeply wounded man who had in the past set Ufa out in the direction that had brought it to this point: Alfred Hugenberg. (Several prominent figures who had been invited were not present—Emil Jannings, for example, who supposedly did not want to make the long trip from his home on Wolfgangsee, and Zarah Leander, whose last film, *Back Then*, premiered on this same day; her conflict with Ufa and Goebbels had just occurred. Wilhelm Furtwängler, who was supposed to direct the Ufa orchestra in Beethoven's *Leonora Overture III*, had excused himself, too.)

As was to be expected, Klitzsch's retrospective slid into flowery declarations of devotion to the Hitler state. He recalled the low status of war propaganda in the First World War until "Ludendorff put an end to this sorry state of affairs with his demand that the economic, artistic, and technical branches of filmmaking come together in an influential enterprise under state leadership." Now, after long years of "political and economic instability" during which Ufa "was at the mercy of Jewish and financially irresponsible influences," the "fruitful marriage between the times and film" had been consummated under the sign of National Socialism.[15]

Then Goebbels added still another to his long series of "film speeches." It was no secret to any of the people in his audience that German film was now totally isolated internationally, but Goebbels claimed it was regarded as an international force, its reputation firmly established in all the countries of the world. And after his speech, he staged a show perceived by many in attendance as a farce that those involved could submit to only bitterly. For his service to German film, Hugenberg was awarded the eagle medal of the German Reich; Winkler and Klitzsch were both given the Goethe medal for art and science; the oft-disciplined director Wolfgang Liebeneiner was given a professorship, as was Goebbels's favorite, Veit Harlan.

Once again, the speeches followed an honoring of the war dead, but no one memorialized the many whom the people of Berlin were then mourning. On the night of March 1, for the first time Allied planes had penetrated into the air space over downtown Berlin, and the heaviest air raid to date had reduced parts of the capital to rubble. While the celebration was going on in the Ufa-Palast, many Berliners were picking their way through the bombed parts of the city, assessing the damage, inquiring after friends and relatives, criticizing the work of the fire department. Crowds of the curious gathered in front of ruins and discussed learnedly the different effects of incendiary and explosive bombs. "Workers of non-German background," the SS reported, exploited the situation to break store windows and to loot.[16] It was rumored that foreign spies supported the attack from the ground and made possible the bombardment of arms factories; rocketlike signals perhaps directing enemy planes to their targets had been spotted. Berlin was stirred up and its inhabitants torn by contradictory feelings—

fear and relief, deep depression and wild hopes, curiosity, sadness, and glee at the misfortune of others. In Germany's movie cathedral, meanwhile, in the midst of this reality but far removed from it, the past was celebrated and a doomed regime praised.

Forgotten and condemned to oblivion, too, on this day were hundreds of Ufa employees who in the past ten years—and some before 1933—had been driven from Germany for political reasons. No one inquired into the fates of the less prominent ones; the names of well-known artists, who had sought work and survival abroad against great odds and often under wretched living conditions, may have evoked pleasure among some audience members and only half-acknowledged pangs of conscience among others. The few Germans who had succeeded in building new careers in London or Hollywood were now *persona non grata* in Germany, while to the international film community they represented the history and spirit of the "different" Ufa which during the Weimar Republic had contributed to the diversity and flowering of a cosmopolitan, democratic culture. By 1943, this part of Ufa's history had been eradicated, and to name the names associated with it meant risk.

This same year Robert Siodmak, after some failures in France and routine jobs in Hollywood, was awarded a seven-year contract with Universal through the good offices of his brother Curt. Together with other émigrés like Billy Wilder, William Dieterle, Max Ophuls, and Edgar Ulmer, he was to initiate the greatest contribution that the "old" Ufa and German film made to the history of Hollywood: the American *film noir*. His last German film, *Brennendes Geheimnis* (*Burning Secret*, based on a novella by Stefan Zweig and produced by Tonal-Film for Deutsche-Universal-Film) had started its run after the Reichstag fire, the event that set off mass emigration. A month later, in the *Völkischer Beobachter*, Goebbels had attacked Siodmak as a corrupter of public morals and forced him to flee to Paris.

Kurt (Curtis) Bernhardt, director of the Ufa success *Die letzte Kompagnie* (*The Last Company*, 1930), made the thriller *Conflict* for Warner Brothers in 1943 from a book Siodmak and Alfred Neumann had worked on. Since 1939 Bernhardt—along with Dieterle, Conrad Veidt, the producer Gottfried Reinhardt, and the authors Bruno Frank, Erika Mann, Walter Reisch, and Salka Viertel—had been a steering-committee member of the European Film Fund. An idea of the emigrants Ernst Lubitsch, Salka Viertel, and Paul Kohner, the fund was organized in the Hollywood home of operetta star Fritzi Massary to aid European film artists who had fled from Hitler.

Billy Wilder, Siodmak's collaborator on *People on Sunday*, had had great difficulty establishing himself in Hollywood. "On the verge of starvation, he shared a room with Peter Lorre for a while and lived on a bowl of soup a day."[17] Teaming up with the writer Charles Brackett, he specialized in screenplays for sophisticated comedies and by 1943 was about to make a breakthrough as a director. Wilder's start in the United States in 1934 had been a film made by Ufa emigrants: with Robert Liebmann he wrote the book for the Fox film *Music in the Air,* produced by Erich Pommer and directed by Joe May.

Wilhelm (William) Thiele, the pioneer of the Ufa sound-film operetta, had been in Hollywood for ten years by the time his former company celebrated its twenty-fifth year. Under contract with RKO, he was working on his second Tarzan film with Johnny Weissmuller: *Tarzan's Desert Mystery.* Although he had introduced the "American" style of musical film to Germany, he would never direct a musical in the United States.

Many far less prominent personal histories have not been recorded in film annals, histories of "second-class" film artists whose destinies showed the dreary oppressiveness of life in Hitler's Germany and the ups and downs of the average émigré existence. An example is the Czech director Gustav Machatý, who came to America in the mid-1930s and had to make his way on Hollywood's Poverty Row, where shabby little studios cranked out cheap productions. He had made a name for himself in Europe in 1932 with his Austrian-Czech joint production *Ekstase* (*Ecstasy*), a story of adultery noteworthy for its emotionally evocative photography and for a scene in which the lead actress, Hedy Kiesler-Lamarr, appears naked. The National Socialist censors banned it in February 1933 and released it again in October 1934 under the title *Symphonie der Liebe* (*Symphony of Love*) only after extensive cutting. To everyone's surprise, it won the prize for best direction at the Venice Bienniale that same year. On January 8, 1935, the cut version premiered in Germany, and on the same day Machatý's name suddenly appeared in the minutes of Ufa's management meetings. Ufa planned to hire him for a production with Lida Baarova and had already paid him an advance of 20,000 Czech crowns. Vice President Grieving expressed distress "over attacks on Machatý in the press regarding his ancestry, his former political activities, and other personal matters."[18] It was decided that the contract should not be finalized until Machatý "clarified these matters" and the Reich film agencies certified they had no reservations about him. These conditions were not met, and Ufa determined ten days later that he should pay back his advance. Negotiations continued. Then Ufa, "in view of the possibility that the director may yet be granted a work permit," booked the advance as an option on future directorial work. That work was never done. Machatý went to the United States a little later. His only success there was with his 1945 film *Jealousy.* Several years later, he took his vengeance on the National Socialists in a screenplay for G. W. Pabst's film about the failed assassination attempt on Hitler, *Es geschah am 20. Juli* (*It Happened on July 20,* produced by Arca/Ariston, 1955).

But did any of the illustrious guests at Ufa's birthday party think about Machatý or all the actors and actresses who had helped build Ufa's reputation and who had left Germany long since? Who thought about Conrad

Veidt and Albert Bassermann, about Felix Bressart, Siegfried Arno, and
William Dieterle, about Hertha Thiele, Dolly Haas, or Blandine Ebinger,
about Franz Lederer, Elisabeth Bergner, Marta Eggerth, or Grete Mosheim?

Ufa's former production director Günther Stapenhorst, then in Switzerland, may have thought about the emigrants from his firm with especially
mixed feelings. He had worked closely with Robert Liebmann, Walter
Reisch, and Emmerich Pressburger, with Erich Pommer and Reinhold
Schünzel. In 1935, after his last production, Amphitryon, he emigrated to
England and, along with the cameraman Sepp Allgeier and the actress Lilli
Palmer, worked for Gaumont-British, then later for Alexander Korda's film
company. When the war broke out, he was a production director in Switzerland and applied through the German consulate in Berne for reinstate-
ment in the German Navy. It does not seem to have been granted him, for
he remained in Switzerland. Because of his continuing contact with Berlin,
the Berne government suspected him of espionage, and his possibilities for
work were limited. This highly talented but politically indecisive man fell
between all the chairs, though he may have received financial support from
Berlin. Between 1941 and 1943 he applied three times for a management
position with Ufa and was refused three times. Nazi Germany had not
forgiven him his "desertion" to England and his "collaboration" with the
"Jewish businessman" Alexander Korda. In 1949, Stapenhorst founded
Carlton-Film in Munich and in the next ten years produced movies with
his former colleagues Josef von Baky, Arthur Maria Rabenalt, Willi Forst,
Gerhard Lamprecht, Viktor Tourjansky, and G. W. Pabst.[19]

And then there were the internationally recognized stars to whom Ufa
(or the companies that it had absorbed) owed its early successes and whom
the Nazis deceived, censured, put under pressure, or forbid to work. Asta
Nielsen, deeply antagonistic to the National Socialist regime, had refused
Goebbels's offer to produce films independently and had left Germany in
1937. Unmögliche Liebe (Impossible Love, directed by Erich Waschneck for
Märkische Film, 1932) was her first and last German sound film. The Propaganda Ministry had, for all practical purposes, forbidden Henny Porten
to work because she had refused to separate from her Jewish husband, the
physician Wilhelm von Kaufmann. Persecuted by Goebbels, adored by Hitler and Göring, she became an apple of discord among the Nazi elite.
Thanks to the Chancellery's protection, her husband went unharmed, and
she was occasionally offered minor roles. In 1941, Porten, Käthe Dorsch,
and Hilde Krahl acted in Pabst's Bavaria film Komödianten (Players), a story
revolving around Caroline Neuber and the beginnings of the modern
German theater in the eighteenth century. Axel Eggebrecht and Walter
von Hollander had written the screenplay.

In the anniversary year of 1943 Henny Porten returned to Neubabelsberg
under the direction of Carl Froelich to make Familie Buchholtz and its
sequel Neigungsehe (A Love Marriage), stories of Berlin around 1880. The

star pulled out all the stops, displaying to the full the qualities that had made her a national legend for three decades. Once again she showed "common sense" and "native wit"; once again she showed that "her heart was in the right place":

> It is no accident that Porten's great comeback took place in the very worst of times, when bombs were falling all over Germany, when no one knew if he would live to see the next day, and when no one had time or interest for high art anymore or was in the mood for amusement. Porten was, in 1944 as she had been in 1914, the great consoler.[20]

But before the premiere in January 1944 even her admirer Göring advised her to divorce her husband; Kaufmann could emigrate to Switzerland or Sweden. Henny Porten would not budge. A month later her house was destroyed by a bomb. She and her husband witnessed the end of the war under Soviet artillery fire in Joachimsthal, in Brandenburg.

Renate Müller—a favorite of moviegoing audiences in the early 1930s, "the clean-cut German girl" in Wilhelm Thiele's *Die Privatsekretarin* (*The Private Secretary*) and in several Schünzel films—had been dead for almost six years in 1943. Goebbels had bullied her when she refused to break off her relationship with a young Jewish friend, who later emigrated to England, and continued to persecute her even after her sudden death in October 1937, spreading rumors through the press that she had been a drug addict and a suicide. (She had actually suffered from a serious illness, probably some kind of epilepsy. In 1935 she had had to be hospitalized. Ufa's managers requested medical certification that she *could* work and made her re-employment contingent on her health being good enough for her to be insurable. Her doctor was released from his obligation of confidentiality.[21])

In March 1943 the actor Robert Dorsay, who specialized in portraying good-natured chauffeurs and eccentric secretaries, was denounced by a Gestapo informer for telling political jokes in the refreshment room of the German Theater. His mail was subsequently opened, and the Gestapo intercepted a letter in which Dorsay made fun of the NSDAP and expressed his bitterness over the "idiocy" of the war. He was arrested, condemned to death for "ongoing activity hostile to the Reich and serious undermining of the German defense effort," and executed on October 29, 1943. His name was removed from the credits of all his films; his numerous shorts were withdrawn from distribution and disappeared as if they had never been produced.[22] Dorsay had worked for Ufa or for its distribution organization on six films: Carl Lamac's *Flitterwochen* (*Honeymoon*) and *Ein Mädel vom Ballet* (*A Ballet Girl*), both 1939; Alwin Elling's *Karussell* (1937); Detlef Sierck's *To New Shores*; Georg Jacoby's *Spiel auf der Tenne* (*Fun on the Threshing Floor*, 1937), and Eduard von Borsody's *Caoutchouc*.

On July 30, 1942, the director Herbert Selpin (*The Green Domino*, 1935) was in a Gestapo prison. While he was doing the outdoor shots for his

Tobis film *Titanic* in Gotenhafen, he had gotten into an argument with his screenplay writer, Walter Zerlett-Olfenius, and had said insulting things about the Wehrmacht; Zerlett-Olfenius had then denounced him. Hans Hinkel, SS-Obergruppenführer in the Propaganda Ministry and later Reich Film Intendant, tried to shrug the incident off, but Zerlett-Olfenius knew he had hit home when Goebbels called Selpin onto the carpet. Selpin refused to take back his spontaneous remarks, and was expelled from the Reich Film Guild and arrested. On the night of August 1, he committed suicide in his cell. Hinkel may have wanted to save Selpin, but he soon drove the actor Joachim Gottschalk, his Jewish wife, Meta Wolff, and his son Michael to suicide in November when he refused Gottschalk's request to accompany his family on their deportation to Theresienstadt, the concentration camp in Bohemia.

The highly successful Ufa actor and director Kurt Gerron wound up in Theresienstadt after the Gestapo had arrested him in Amsterdam, where he directed the Jewish theater. On orders from on high, Gerron supervised production of a propaganda film, *Der Führer schenkt den Juden eine Stadt* (*The Führer Presents the Jews with a City*), which was supposed to convince the Red Cross and the international community that Theresienstadt was a "model ghetto" with first-rate living conditions and culture. Once the film was completed, Gerron and others who had worked on it were sent to Auschwitz and murdered.

Others who died in concentration camps were Curt Alexander, screenplay writer for Max Ophüls; Rudolf Bamberger, Ludwig Berger's set designer; Hans Behrendt, co-author of the four-part *Fridericus Rex* of 1922[23]; the actors Eugen Burg, Fritz Grünbaum, and Otto Wallburg; the screenplay writers Max Ehrlich and Paul Morgan; the musician Willy Rosen, a colleague of Kurt Gerron's in Amsterdam; and many others whose names are lost and are not mentioned in any film history or eulogy. Even when a spectral afterlife was breathed back into Ufa after the war, the company never remembered its dead, and later attempts to count its emigrants, its murder victims, and its missing persons were incomplete and full of gaps.[24]

The high point of the company party of culprits, opportunists, and "inner emigrants" on March 3, 1943, was the premiere of *Münchhausen*, produced specifically for the celebration. Once again Goebbels had ordered a "first-class" film to convince the international audience, or at least the audience subject to German occupation at the time, of the "top quality" of National Socialist film. The upper limit on production costs on Ufi films was a million marks, but for this movie the sky was the limit. Goebbels explicitly ordered that no expense should be spared and that it should be a color film.

In the early 1930s Ufa had developed its own two-color process (Ufa-color), and had premiered the first German color film, *Bunte Tierwelt* (*The Colorful World of Animals*) on New Year's Eve of 1931. It took several years of expensive experiments after that before the laboratories of I. G. Farben developed the three-color Agfacolor process to the point where color filming of features was possible. Ufa and Agfa signed a contract of cooperation in 1938, and a state-of-the-art color-film lab was installed in Neubabelsberg, where the inventive talents of its specialists were allowed free rein. Still, the production of the first German color feature, *Women Really Are Better Diplomats*, dragged on for a very long time while the chemical labs improved the color quality virtually from day to day, making constant retakes necessary. At the tenth Biennale in Venice in 1942, Ufa's second color film, Veit Harlan's *The Golden City*, won the prize of the president of the International Film Guild (created by Goebbels) for its exceptional color quality.

In the selection of a screenplay writer for *Münchhausen*, Ufa squeezed a special dispensation out of the Propaganda Minister: it was permitted to commission Erich Kästner, whose books had gone up in flames in the Nazi book burnings of 1933. According to Hembus, the production director Eberhard Schmidt had suggested the banned author,[25] and Riess[26] reports that even Reich Film Intendant Hippler backed the choice. Goebbels, who secretly admired this "rootless writer" and enjoyed quoting his antimilitaristic poems,[27] insisted, however, that Kästner use a pseudonym, and the press was instructed not to reveal who the screenplay writer "Berthold Bürger" really was.

Direction of the film fell to Josef von Baky, a Hungarian who had come to Berlin in 1927 and until 1936 worked as an assistant director with his countryman Géza von Bolvary. He had made three films for Ufa: the young girl's story *Her First Experience* with Ilse Werner, the comedy *Der Kleinstadtpoet* (*The Small-Town Poet*) with Paul Kemp (1940), and the patriotic family chronicle *Annelie*. In the final weeks of the war, the censors would ban his Ufa film *Via Mala* because of its "dreary atmosphere."

Jobst von Reiht-Zanthier, in charge of casting for Ufa since 1931, was faced with the most important task of his career (to the extent that Goebbels did not, as he had so often in the past, take charge here, too, and decide himself who was to play which roles). Hans Albers as Münchhausen in his legendary travels—from Bodenwerder on the Weser River to Russia and from there to Turkey, Venice, and finally to the moon—meets not only Prince Potemkin (Andrews Engelmann) and Tsarina Catherine II (Brigitte Horney), but also the magician Cagliostro (Ferdinand Marian), Sultan Abdul-Hamid (Leo Slezak), Princess Isabella d'Este (Ilse Werner), and other figures from real and imaginary world history. Käthe Hack played the Baroness Munchhausen; Gustav Waldau, Casanova; Michael Bohnen, Duke Karl of Braunschweig; and Hubert von Meyerinck, Prince Anton Ulrich. Fritz Thiery, Ufa's sound-film pioneer, was in charge of dialogue direction. Georg Haentzschel wrote the music; Emil Hasler and Otto Gülstorff built the sets. The cameraman was Werner Krien. Special effects were in the hands of a Russian named Konstantin Irmen-Tschet, who had made his mark as a cameraman for Marika Rökk's revue films. Irmen-Tschet, a distant relative of Stanislavsky, had come to Ufa in the early 1920s; as an assistant to Günther Rittau, he specialized in special effects and filmed the models in *Metropolis* and *Woman in the Moon*. In the 1930s, he moved easily between both the entertainment and "fatherland" genres, working on Schünzel's *Viktor und Viktoria* after *Hitler Youth Quex* and *People without a Fatherland* after *Children of Happiness*.

(For *Münchhausen*, the expensive special effects—Albers riding on a cannonball, his horse perched on top of a church steeple, the balloon trip to the moon—and more than eight hundred extras in brand-new costumes made Ufa famous for having produced a movie that could be described only in superlatives—a special-effects machine and a "masterpiece of fantasy" that, as Hembus writes, the company permitted itself in a massive "act of denial"[28] two years before its collapse. But there was not a trace of *self*-denial. Ufa's managers had the support of the Propaganda Ministry; the performers and technicians loved recalling their achievements in the heyday of Ufa's magic kitchen; and the summer weeks they spent on location in Venice, floating about in gondolas on the closed-off Grand Canal in front of palaces with Gobelins hanging at the windows, evolved into a company party staged in a consumer's paradise, remote from the war and far from the home front's daily cares and nights of bombardments.

The magic of old Russia, fairy tales from *A Thousand and One Nights*, dreams of flight and immortality, stories of duels, pursuit, and romantic love—all these were woven together in a children's picture book for childish adults. The few allusions to the invasion of Poland and to National Socialist delusions of power and grandeur remained politically harmless: small truths smothered by overwhelming opulence. "Time is broken," says Albers-Münchhausen when his servant Kuchenreuther (Hermann Speelmans) suggests that his watch may not be working. For Albers and for many of his colleagues in 1943, it was perfectly clear that "time" was now beyond repair. "Things will turn around again. All we have to do is survive"—that was the consolation that Reiht-Zanthier routinely offered Albers and the other Ufa stars who—in the surrealistic atmosphere of Neubabelsberg, surrounded by Goebbels's errand boys and spied on by the Gestapo—were showing signs of exhaustion. Reiht himself had experienced the treachery of the times: in 1935 Ufa's managers had discussed "grounds for suspicion" that he "might be acting in accordance with the abnormal tendencies of his nature" and had considered firing him "in the interests of cleanliness."[29] Survival is all: in 1943 that was the secret (or openly embraced watchword) in Ufa-City, for the stars and for the rank and file, for the outspoken and for the silent, for the opponents and, increasingly, even for the adherents of the regime.

28.

German Film Policy
in the Occupied Countries

WHEN Adolf Hitler, accompanied by his architect Albert Speer and other members of his staff, inspected the conquered city of Paris early one morning in 1940, he saw from the terrace of the Trocadéro a ghost city:

> The Führer is visiting the conquered European capital—but is he really its guest? Paris is as quiet as a grave. Except for a few policemen, a worker and a solitary priest hastening out of sight, not a soul is to be seen at the Trocadéro, the Etoile, the huge Concorde, the Opéra and the Madeleine, not a soul to hail the dictator so accustomed to cheering crowds. While he inspects Paris, Paris itself shuts its eyes and withdraws.[1]

This is a sequence in a German newsreel described by Kracauer. The inhabitants of Paris had retreated to their homes and left the stony husk of their city to the occupier. What the masters of death saw there was themselves. The deserted streets mirrored "the vacuum at the core of the Nazi system." The ghostly reality exposed a hidden truth, and the newsreel camera that looked out on a lifeless Paris with the same fixed stare as the Führer's saw its own impotence. "Nazi propaganda built up a pseudo-reality iridescent with many colors, but at the same time it emptied Paris, the sanctuary of civilization. These colors scarcely veiled its own emptiness." In the occupied countries, the German virtuosos of propaganda operated in a huge vacuum.

German film production outside the Reich took place under the protection of the SS and the Gestapo. In the final years of the war "lighthearted" revues and operetta films were made in the shadow of death, in the deep silence of a siege. When Géza von Cziffra, an ambitious buffoon of the German-Austrian film industry, was making a "comedy of marriage" called *Hundstage* (*Dog Days*) in Prague's Barrandov studios for Wien-Film in

1943, he and and his German performers (among them Maria Holst, Wolf Albach-Retty, Walter Lieck, and Grethe Weiser) worked in an "icy atmosphere," it was said.

> The Czech workers tended their equipment in silence. The light crews worked without a word, and the stagehands went about their work just as silently. They made it clear they would have nothing to do with us. It was impossible to initiate a conversation with them. They all acted as if they understood not a word of German. The dreary atmosphere understandably affected the performers. They spoke their lines without animation. Punch lines had no punch. All efforts to cheer the cast failed.[2]

Cziffra, the new magician from Hungary who had just directed a successful ice show, *The White Dream*, sank into depression, convinced he was making the "saddest comedy of all time."

Ufa and Germany's other film companies had been operating in foreign countries since before the war. As early as 1938, "after the uniting of the Reich and Austria, the liberation of German territories from the bonds of the Versailles Treaty, and the victorious struggle for Bohemia and Moravia," numerous "efforts to establish German film production" abroad were crowned with success. Such, at any rate, was the view of Hans Traub.[3] Before 1938 Ufa had distributed its feature films and newsreels in Austria through the Viennese Ufa Film and Ufa-Ton-Kino. The Ufa theater in Vienna was in the eyes of Austrian republicans and democrats a "Nazi headquarters," and the press launched massive attacks against it on occasions such as the Vienna premiere of the Tobis film *The Old and the Young King*, which was attended by the staff of the German embassy.

When the Nazis murdered the Austrian Chancellor Engelbert Dollfuss in 1934, public outrage was vented on Ufa and its films. Occasionally, censorship was exercised against National Socialist propaganda films, and for a while Jewish emigrants were able to work. In 1936, reviewing the presentation of German newsreels, the Chancellor's office ordered that sequences be cut in which Hitler appeared "more often than the subject matter calls for and if his appearance is used for National Socialist propaganda purposes."[4] Austria under Schuschnigg was still defending itself effectively against "affiliation" with Germany, and Ufa was still operating on hostile terrain.

But after the annexation of Austria in March 1938, after German troops marched into the Sudetenland, and especially after the conquest of Poland, the SS noted that the "propagandistic and cultural possibilities" for German film "in the territories won back in the East" deserved special attention, and SS spies again fanned out to obtain the urgently awaited reports of success.

In July 1940 they were quick to note that the war newsreels were not only "awaited with particular eagerness by ethnic Germans in the East" but were making a great impression on the Poles.⁵ The reports also suggested a German-Polish cinema apartheid: "The announcement that the Poles, too, would be admitted to all showings elicited resentment from the German population," which wanted "to be separated from the Poles through some appropriate arrangement, either by means of separate showings or separate seating." The war against the conquered Slavs was continued not only on movie screens but also by humiliating them at the box office.

But the Security Service also reported some problems. The available choice of films was slim and could "in no way satisfy the cultural needs of the German population" in conquered Poland in the summer of 1940. The showing of the Terra thriller *Der Polizeifunk meldet* (*Police Radio Reports*, directed by Rudolf van der Noss, 1939) in Hohensalza came in for criticism because it "encouraged economic espionage for foreign powers," and was both dangerous and inappropriate for Poles, who "immediately interpreted [its plot] in terms of their struggle against German influence."⁶ Such negative propagandistic effects should be avoided, and the movies should have "educational value for the ethnic and Baltic Germans and strengthen their ethnic bonds as well as progagandistically encompass the Polish population." "Strengthening the ethnic bonds" of people of German background living in Poland meant increasing their allegiance to Germany. As for the Poles, "propagandistically encompassing" them meant using propaganda, however brutally and simplistically, to break their moral backbone.

There was no lack of failures either in Poland or in other occupied areas. The SS reported from Holland in October 1940 that Germany's film propaganda effort was faring poorly there because the public's "taste was geared to French, English, and, especially, American films."⁷ Movie audiences in Holland, spoiled by foreign products as they were, responded favorably only to elegant and witty comedies like *Viktor und Viktoria*, melodramas of artistic merit like *La Habanera*, and well-made adventure films like *Gold*. A report from Groningen noted that German newsreels were "not well received"—unless they produced "pro-English demonstrations," as they had in Maastricht, where shots of British troops boarding transport ships evoked "clapping and stamping of feet."⁸ As in the showings of *Fridericus Rex* in Ufa theaters in the early 1920s, applause contests broke out between opposing factions in audiences: "When German soldiers in the audience applauded scenes showing the bombardment of London, the other spectators demonstrated against them." SS observers in Norway noted with apparent astonishment that the people there responded with "special sensitivity" to pictures of the destruction German troops had caused in their country.

German film propaganda met with no great success in Luxembourg either. The general tendency "to resist the spread of German influence" was reflected in low attendance at German films.⁹ While *Jew Süss* had been very well received and even "evoked demonstrations against the Jews," the

Luxembourg population responded to German newsreels "with icy silence," and the authenticity of information presented in them was often questioned.

The reception of German films in the occupied territories did not improve as the war wore on. The initially extensive reports the SS made on the behavior of movie audiences shrank as the fortunes of war turned against Germany and by the fall of 1943 had dried up entirely. There were no more outbursts of enthusiasm over the German Army's rapid advances, and approval was muted even for films "of national political value" and "pure" entertainment ones. An SS report from Belgium in April 1944 noted that the Catholic clergy there had mounted a "planned propaganda campaign" to discourage attendance at German films.[10]

Film distribution in the occupied countries displayed that high level of organization which the National Socialist administration always achieved when it came to "encompassing" large populations and subjecting them to unified patterns of thought and behavior. And film policy in the conquered territories was part of Germany's political and military strategy. It was successful in exploiting the foreign infrastructure and expanding beyond Germany's domestic market, but the attempt to exert a lasting influence on subjugated people was doomed to failure.

The Nazis' annexation policy solved the amortization problems in the German movie business almost at one stroke. Behind the military fronts the German film empire spread out, installing production and distribution networks on the same model that had been so successful at home. But the ideological gains were minimal. As in the First World War, the goals were dictated by the general staff, and they all derived from a usurpatory philosophy well expressed in newsreel clips of the Führer surrounded by his officers and bending over a map table: the point was to win territory. The *people* in the occupied areas were secondary, a purely economic factor, a resource to be exploited. So rapacity and a fetish for organization dictated how the film markets in the subjected countries of both Eastern and Western Europe were acquired and reordered. The "vacuum at the core of the Nazi system" spread out, but it was still a vacuum, a gigantic hollow, superbly equipped in technical terms and endlessly subdivided.

In the territory now under the "general government" of Poland, the Germans confiscated all the movie theaters and placed them under a trustee they appointed. Whatever they had not destroyed they seized without paying compensation: production studios, equipment, film stores, and copying labs. Under the supervision of the former Ufa vice president in Budapest, Fliegel, the film and propaganda center in Cracow became a kind of depot for everything they thought useful for producing their own newsreels and propaganda films. Poland was culturally leveled. Any independent cultural impulse among the Poles was crushed, and the people themselves were confined in an intellectual ghetto whose needs for entertainment were rated at best of a "low order." Of Poland's 123 movie houses, 17 were reserved "for Germans only" (this was the cultural apartheid that the "ethnic Germans" had demanded); 62 showed films for both Germans and Poles but at separate screenings; the rest were for the Poles and were supposed to help pay for the cheap fare the German companies produced.[11]

The Reich commissariat followed a similar policy of confiscation in the conquered areas of the Soviet Union after 1941. All movie theaters, production facilities, and copying facilities that fell into German hands were placed under the Zentralfilm-Gesellschaft, whose capital stock was held by Cautio and the Reich Ministry for the Occupied Eastern Territories under Alfred Rosenberg. Winkler, the financial genius of National Socialist film politics, pulled all the strings in the occupied territories, too. At his urging and with Goebbels's support, an Ufa-Sonderproduktion Company (Ufa-Special-Productions) was set up within Ufi to serve the specific needs of the NSDAP and the army; among its responsibilities was the production of films in the occupied areas of the Soviet Union—a project that soon disappeared into thin air with the collapse of the eastern front and the advance of the Red Army.

In the West, notably in France, where cinema was highly developed, the German occupation decided on a less radical strategy. Faced with demanding French movie audiences, the Germans suffered from a justified if unconfessed inferiority complex. "Taking French law and the French mentality into account,"[12] Winkler argued for caution and suggested cooperating with French middlemen and trusted negotiators in either seizing the more important French theaters or bringing them under German control. Continental-Films was formed in Paris and charged with consolidating all production and commercial cinema operations in occupied Western Europe. Its leader was the former Terra production chief Alfred Greven. Greven took orders from Winkler and thus, in effect, from the National Socialist government, but the 15.5 million marks at his disposal came from Ufa, Tobis, and Terra, and it was they that stood to benefit from profits generated in France, Holland, and Belgium. Just as the Ufa board in the First World War divided up its millions to buy movie theaters all over Europe in June 1918, so now—in accord with a very similar scheme—the capital of Continental-Films was apportioned for investments in France (12.5 million), Belgium (1.5 million), and Holland (1.3 million).[13]

Continental-Films was also in charge of producing films in French, and it controlled France's cinemas through its subsidiary companies. Distribution was divided initially between Ufa's and Tobis's distribution companies; after 1942 Ufa took it over completely. A highly organized and widespread production and distribution system seemed now, after twenty-five years, finally to have realized Ludendorff's dream of German cinema hegemony in Europe, but the imposing structure was a house of cards. The National Socialists' cultural offensive was carried into the occupied countries on the point of a bayonet while the SS and the Gestapo covered its political flanks.

Measures taken in Czechoslovakia document with particular clarity that film policy under occupation law was nothing but ruthless colonial policy in the interests of the German film industry. And from 1942 on, the only end it served was the further expansion of the Ufi trust.

On October 1, 1938, the German Army marched into the Sudetenland. In April 1939, when a civilian administration replaced the military government, a cultural department was established in the office of Konstantin von Neurath, Reich Protector for Bohemia and Moravia, modeled—with its offices for press, theater and film, radio, music, literature, and the visual arts—on the Ministry of Propaganda in Berlin. Anyone who believed German statements could come away with the impression that the Czechs' national culture and their quite advanced cinema would retain freedom. But in reality the German administration intended to destroy the economic basis of the Czech film industry and sought cooperation with willing parties to do so.

The "Germanizing" and "Aryanizing" of the entire film industry were declared political goals from the outset. At one blow, German cinema had acquired more than a thousand theaters, and "required" German films were soon introduced. Those "of national political value" like *Andreas Schlüter*, *Bismarck*, *Diesel*, *Robert Koch*, *The Great Love*, *The Great King*, *I Accuse*, and *Jew Süss* had to be shown in every Czech movie house. Leni Riefenstahl's Reich party convention film and Olympic film, as well as Ritter's *Traitors* and *Project Michael*—all of which the Czech republic had previously banned—appeared in Prague theaters.

From one day to the next, newsreels proclaimed the blessings of Germany's annexation policy and the separation of Slovakia. In 1940 Ufa newsreels replaced Fox and Paramount ones, and together with the "aligned" Czech newsreel Aktuality, served up propaganda for Hitler's war. But the Ufa newsreels repeatedly evoked protest and noisy anti-Fascist demonstrations. Slides were projected before the newsreels began, warning the audience to remain quiet, but they did no good. The Protectorate supplied the theaters with monitors empowered to identify and arrest "troublemakers." Anyone who was caught could get a week in jail, but when this measure, too, failed, the occupation government threatened to close any theater where a protest took place. Czech moviegoers who were committed to resistance responded by boycotting the newsreels. In some cases, the theater owners cut offensive sequences out of their copies; sometimes they destroyed entire films and hindered their distribution. The Protectorate, suspecting this sabotage, threatened harsh action against "guilty individuals and organizations."[14]

The primary goal of the Nazi measures was absolute economic hegemony. As early as the spring of 1939, all Soviet films were banned in the occupied parts of Czechoslovakia; once war broke out, a ban on English and French films followed. The importation of American films went through Berlin now and was cut in half. Films starring Hans Albers were supposed to replace the entertainment and adventure films from Hollywood that had been so popular with Czech audiences. At the same time, laws to Germanize the film industry were promulgated. Film companies had to adopt German names. Office and studio personnel had to take language exams in German.

And then there was Aryanization, too: repressive measures against Czech Jews and expropriation of Jewish capital. Even before 1938, the National Socialists had tried to drive Jewish artists out of Czech film production: Czech production companies that took commissions from German firms had to abide by National Socialist quota regulations that forbid Jewish participation. Now, any business whose senior management included a "non-Aryan" was considered "Jewish." German trustees were put in charge of such businesses and empowered to nullify all existing laws and regulations. Hand in hand with expropriation went the stripping away of civil rights. From September 1939 on, Jews were not allowed to leave their residences after 8 p.m. They could not move or use public transport, and cinemas as well as hotels, restaurants, and theaters were closed to them.

A classic example of the forced appropriation of Czech property by means of the Aryan laws was the case of AB-Filmfabrikation and its modern, well-equipped studios on Barrandov Hill, in Prague. A straightforward confiscation of the company as Jewish property was not possible: the president and major stockholder was a non-Jew, the well-to-do film entrepreneur Milos Havel (uncle of the writer and later President of Czechoslovakia, Václav Havel), and the only Jew in the company's administration had been Oswald Kosek (until the occupation). A week after Neurath published his decree on Jewish property, Government Councillor Hermann von Glessgen—chief of the film office of the Protectorate, SA member, and former member of Ufa—informed Milos Havel that AB's Barrandov studios were Jewish property. Glessgen advised Havel to sell his 51 percent of the company's stock to the Reich; if he did not, a trustee would be appointed. Havel declined, even after Glessgen offered him 150,000 marks in "retirement compensation" in addition to the purchase price. The National Socialist film administrator thereupon officially declared the Barrandov studios a "Jewish company," even though Kosek held only 5 percent of the stock and had not been a director after March 16, 1939.

In July, Karl Schulz, formerly a film businessman and production chief for Bavaria, was appointed trustee. The chamber of commerce annulled the company's by-laws, the Protectorate raised capital stock from 1.5 million to 4.5 million Czech crowns, and Havel finally sold his shares, having been both forced and wooed with offers such as permission for his Lucerna-Film to continue independently.[15] In the Barrandov studios, he was stripped of all power. The studios became the property of the German Reich, represented by Cautio. Two years later, thanks to flourishing production, the capital stock amounted to 30 million crowns (6 million marks).[16]

In 1942 Karl Schulz wound up in court, convicted of forgery, embezzlement, and deriving personal profit from former Czech property. His successor was the Ufi business manager, Josef Hein.

The takeover of Barrandov and, a little later, of Czechoslovakia's second-largest studio in Hostivar put the two most important Czech production studios in German hands. The Protectorate's assurance that Czech production would retain priority was an empty promise, and Czechs were given production time only if no German movie was under way. The German film business lost no time in moving part of its production into the film factories of the Protectorate. Indeed, Barrandov became the most important bridgehead of German production outside the borders of the Reich. In November 1941, a general meeting of the old AB-Filmfabrikation voted to change its name to Prag-Film. Havel's studios were now officially part of the Ufi trust, and their top management made that clear: Bank president Friedrich Merten from Berlin, one of Winkler's most important colleagues, was president; other senior managers were SS-Sturmbannführer Martin Wolf; Josef Hein as studio chief executive; production chief Carl Wilhelm Tetting, SA and NSDAP member and former production chief at Bavaria; and Hermann Burgmeister, ministerial councillor in the Reich Finance Ministry. Added to the management team shortly before the end of the war were Hans Hinkel, at this point Reich Film Intendant; Karl Ott, an official from the Propaganda Ministry; and, as new production chief, the director Emmerich W. Emo.

Before he ran into trouble with the law, Karl Schulz was able to expand the Barrandov studios into a "bunker" for German film production, which was suffering more and more from Allied air raids. On Schulz's initiative the studios were enlarged significantly. The Czech contractor engaged for this work did not spare building materials, and was so extravagant with copper, a metal crucial to the war effort, that the Germans plausibly suspected sabotage. The National Socialists did not hire the architect Novak, who had designed modern glass-walled studios, because they thought his work was too like the "Jewish-Bolshevist" architecture of the Weimar Bauhaus, and used instead a Berlin architect whose drawings were more in line with their aesthetic sensibilities.

Within its walls, the Barrandov studio housed the most modern equipment from Berlin and occupied France, facilities for color-film production, and a copying facility capable of supplying the entire Reich. The technical apparatus in the laboratories came from Cinecittà near Rome, the center of Italian cinema, confiscated after the Badoglio putsch had toppled Mussolini's government in 1943 and opened negotiations for surrender to the

Allies; German troops had seized control of many of Italy's principal cities. Barrandov became, after Neubabelsberg, the largest film city of Europe; Goebbels, during a visit in November 1944, only six months before the collapse of his regime, declared it a German film metropolis of the future. The Czech firms and their specialists hired to do installation work were as a rule the most conscientious of saboteurs, but in this case they conscientiously fulfilled the terms of their contracts, knowing that the days of the Nazi regime were numbered and that the Barrandov studios would soon be in Czech hands again.

Prag-Film began production in August 1942 with Peter Paul Brauer's *Himmel, wir erben ein Schloss* (*Heavens, We're Inheriting a Castle*), based on a novel by Hans Fallada and starring Anny Ondra and Hans Brausewetter. The cameraman was a Czech, Václav Hanus. (Brauer, a "dedicated party activist,"[17] had been relieved of his post as production chief for Terra in 1940 because of incompetence.) The company's production chief, Tetting, ordered a number of Czech directors to work on German films, and when they refused, the German management used threats to force them to sign the contracts presented to them. A few directors, like Otokar Vávra and Vladimir Slavinský, were able at least for a while to avoid fulfilling the terms of those contracts. They went to work for Havel's Lucerna-Film and dragged out their shooting schedules as long as they could, hoping the war and German occupation would soon end. An order from Goebbels obliged Czech artists forced to work for Prag-Film to adopt German or German-sounding names, and behind several German names in Alfred Bauer's *Spielfilm-Almanach* are Czech directors, actors, and cameramen. "Otto Pittermann," who made the comedy *Die schwache Stunde* (*The Unguarded Moment*) for Bavaria in the Barrandov studios in 1943, was really Vladimir Stravinský, and the real name of his cameraman, Josef Strecher, was Strecha.[18]

In the last two years of the war Prague became a comfortable refuge for German cinema. Air raids had made working in Berlin and Munich dangerous, and as the situation rapidly worsened, the Czech studios were utilized to the full. Ufa, Tobis, Bavaria, Wien-Film, and other companies under the Ufi umbrella were now producing in the "Prague bunker." In March and April 1945, the Barrandov and Hostivar studios were busy full-time. While the Red Army was closing in on Berlin and National Socialist leaders were preparing to take their leave from the stage of history, Willi Forst was making a musical, *Wiener Mädeln* (*Viennese Girls*); Hans Steinhoff a thriller, *Shiva und die Galgenblume* (*Shiva and the Gallows Flower*, with Hans Albers, Aribert Wäscher, and Elisabeth Flickenschildt); Robert A. Stemmle a "Bavarian comedy," *Geld ins Haus* (*Money Comes into the House*); and Géza von Bolvary a musical comedy of love and mistaken identity, *Die tolle Susanne* (*Crazy Susanne*).

Bolvary and Steinhoff could not finish their movies. Steinhoff summoned his crew together one day and threatened to have anyone arrested who contemplated leaving Prague to avoid the advancing front; the next day, April 20, he himself flew to Berlin. From there he intended to fly on to Spain, but Soviet fighters shot down his plane. Steinhoff's body was found near Luckenwalde, in Brandenburg.[19]

29.

Blood Red in Dreadful Beauty:
Goebbels and Melodrama

"THE longer the war lasts, the more difficult the problem of newsreels becomes," Goebbels noted on May 25, 1943. "It's hard to know what to offer anymore."[1] He was unquestionably in a quandary: the German war machine was no longer turning out victories; or, more precisely, the pictures the German film-propaganda machine had to offer, especially those from the eastern front, could no longer be falsified into documentary evidence of German invincibility. A few months later, the situation would become still more desperate. On the night of November 22 and on the following nights, Allied bombers visited the heaviest air raids yet on major German cities—Berlin, Frankfurt, Bremen, and Leipzig. In Berlin alone (to some extent because adequate air-raid shelters had not been built) three thousand people were killed and more than half a million left homeless. Marauding bands plundered the bombed-out parts of the city in the following days and nights, and many, the SS reported, concluded that only the Führer "could deal with the difficult situation at this point and solve future problems." Other National Socialist leaders no longer enjoyed the "unconditional trust" of the people.[2]

The SS reports allowed that in view of the bombing raids Goebbels's speech at the "opening of the film program for youth" was excellent, displaying "the will to victory, unbroken confidence in German strength, and fanatical hatred," though it "failed to satisfactorily answer the question of retribution, which was preoccupying everyone."[3] And indeed, as rumors spread throughout Germany about the massive extent of destruction that Berlin had suffered, the "retribution" which the regime kept talking about but never delivered was fast becoming a "major issue undermining the people's confidence in the government." Most Germans were willing to fight on as long as they believed in the "miracle weapon" that Hitler and Goebbels had promised them. But as the SS noted, they found it hard to accept that only a few days after the bombing raids Berlin's theaters and cinemas were open for business again.

The Propaganda Ministry on Wilhelmstrasse had hardly been damaged. Employees had to replace window glass with cardboard, but they could continue their work in familiar surroundings, work deemed important to the war effort because it prolonged the war. Goebbels fancied himself directing "the defense of Berlin" from his "command post" in the air-raid cellar, and he published political poetry tinged with Nazi death mysticism. The sky over Berlin glowed "blood red in dreadful beauty." Never had he "loved the capital as much as now, when its face is gashed with deep wounds."[4]

But newsreels were a problem. "The newsreel pictures I have seen of Berlin are beneath criticism. One sees only images of frightful misery and nothing of the measures taken to alleviate the situation." Goebbels was still determined "to make a heroic saga of the battle for Berlin."[5] However, German Newsreel's production headquarters, Ufa's main building on Krausenstrasse, had been badly damaged. Work had to relocate in the cellar and in neighboring buildings until June 1944, when newsreel production was moved entirely into barracks in Buchholz, outside Berlin.

Ufa's feature films, too, made Goebbels ever more watchful, and he often had to step in to handle delicate situations. Marika Rökk recalls in her memoirs that he took offense at the "supple, sensuous movements" of her Spanish dance in *Die Frau meiner Träume* (*The Woman of My Dreams*): a German woman should not dance so provocatively and shamelessly.[6] The filming for this seventh German color film began in March 1943. Direction and supervision of production were entrusted to Georg Jacoby. The other stars were Wolfgang Lukschy, Walter Müller, Georg Alexander, and Grethe Weiser. The film was completed in September, but creating a version that would pass the censors took until August 1944: Goebbels's objections necessitated more shooting, which led in turn to major problems in the final shaping of the film. Sets and color coordination, lighting and editing all worked at cross purposes. The set designer, Erich Kettelhut, voiced his protests, and Ufa-Filmkunst kept changing the delivery date. But following its premier in the Marmorhaus the plagued production became one of the biggest revue successes of the 1940s. A few weeks after the assassination attempt on Hitler in July 1944, when Germany's major cities were in rubble, *The Woman of My Dreams* (production costs: 2.36 million marks) took in 8 million marks, even though the Reich Film Intendant had issued secret instructions to the press declaring that it was "not suitable" for public review.[7]

The fate of this movie reveals an odd dichotomy, and not only within Goebbels, who, though hardly averse to worldly elegance and erotic liberality, repeatedly felt obliged to insist on moral rectitude. This ambivalence was symptomatic of a central dilemma in the entire regime: faced with an increasingly hopeless military situation, it promulgated entertainment, diversion, and "high spirits," but at the same time saw in every ditty or dance, no matter how harmless, in every décolleté no matter how innocent, the danger of subversion and infiltration of Germany's "national body."

The reverse was also true. Day after day Nazi propaganda dwelt on the seriousness of the situation and on the "tragedy" of a decisive, historical struggle that had been forced on the German people. Still, it was obvious that most Germans were sinking into apathy and resignation. Goebbels and his aides mistrusted the people, but they also mistrusted their own slogans, and every day they lost confidence in the political and military developments they had themselves set in motion and now needed to trump up as a Nibelungen drama. They also knew that the people were essentially immune to their lie and could be whipped into line for the final siege only with vague promises of happiness and carefully measured doses of good cheer. Ufa films like *The Woman of My Dreams* walked a fine line: promoting strength through joy, though the *joie de vivre* should not get out of hand and interfere with loyalty to the regime and, ultimately, willingness to die.

The global vacuity in which the imagination of Goebbels and others took refuge was the inverse of their astonishingly limited understanding of everyday life and the people's needs. Pathos-laden talk of fateful destiny and bureaucratic narrow-mindedness, a yearning for destruction and the mentality of a vice-squad cop bred foggy confusion in the minds of the regime's leaders, allowing them to see the bombardment of Germany and hundreds of thousands of deaths in a "larger context" and at the same time to concern themselves in minute detail with Marika Rökk's dance steps and the cut of her costume. This obsession with petty detail is the mark of a bunker mentality that has lost contact with reality and masks itself with talk of geopolitics, miracle weapons, and decisive retaliatory strikes.

In short, Nazi film propaganda was moving, as one writer has put it,

> ever closer to the point of absurdity, for it became increasingly questionable from week to week whether the films produced would ever reach the public whose will to make a last-ditch stand they were meant to strengthen. On the one hand, Ufi's production machinery was working at top capacity despite all the obstacles in its way; on the other, the shortage of raw film limited distribution of its products.[8]

And not only war-related reduction in raw-film manufacture at Agfa caused problems. Cutbacks had to be made in every area, in administration and in the studios. On the one hand, Goebbels seized every opportunity to proclaim the film industry's "crucial role in the war effort." And on the other, he decreed cutbacks in personnel; without further ado the dismissed people were dispatched to the front, to support units, and to the arms industry. The war was on the verge of swallowing up the propaganda

establishment meant to aid it. By 1944–45, the heroic image of the prop-
aganda-company man who put his camera aside to pick up his rifle was
transformed into an all too real absurdity.

These measures affected an industry that had been enjoying a prosperity
never before achieved in Germany or indeed in any film-producing country
in Europe. Almost 1.12 billion people went to the movies in 1943 in the
"Greater German Reich" (including Luxembourg, Alsace-Lorraine, and the
Warthegau but not the Czech areas).[9] Statistically, that meant more than
fourteen film attendances per person, a record not even approached in any
other war year, much less any peacetime year. Ufi's gross income rose to
near astronomical proportions: 155 million in 1942–43, 175 million in
1943–44.

Taxes and special war-related taxes of course trimmed away the greater
part of this gross income, and in both those fiscal years Ufi was left with
net profits of only 18 million marks after taxes. Film Commissioner Winkler battled tenaciously against these painful consequences, but even he
could not prevent the high taxation from seriously affecting his expanding
industry, and the situation was aggravated when the Finance Ministry demanded a retroactive tax on profits for 1940 and 1941. "Winkler's dream
of a German monopoly with a strong capital base that could compete with
the American film industry after the war and bring Europe's entire market
under German control proved utopian even before Germany's collapse."[10]

Winkler's accomplishments were impressive, nonetheless. With Ufi, he
had brought the old Ufa to a state of hypertrophy and, structurally at least,
made optimum use of the German talent for efficiency But given the economic conditions during the war, even this powerful organization could
not fulfill Goebbels's demand to raise production to 110 films per year. In
1943, 78 films were made; in 1944, only 64.[11] Expensive movies like *Münchhausen*, *The Woman of My Dreams*, and *Kolberg* tied up the studios, editing
rooms, and copying facilities, and the increased British and American
bombing brought many a production to the verge of chaos. From one day
to the next, Berlin's studios were reduced to rubble. Carefully prepared
outdoor shots could not be completed because a dramaturgically important
bridge, building, or, indeed, entire street had been destroyed.

The last senior managers of Ufi, Ufa-Filmkunst, and the old Universum-
Film AG were sailing sinking ships. Their mood was in part defeatist, but
they also maintained the pose of men in command who refused to believe
that the collapse of Hitler's Reich would end their film empire as well.
Among them were a few genuine professionals and people who could be
called pioneers of the German film industry. One of them was Heinz Zimmermann, who as president of the Deutsche Filmvertrieb belonged to the
last senior management team of Ufi. A distribution man par excellence, he
had represented Fox in Berlin in the 1920s and had joined Ufa's distribution department in 1927, at the beginning of the Hugenberg era. Not until

1941, when he was appointed to senior management, did Zimmermann enroll in the NSDAP.

Friedrich Merten, who was president of Ufi until the end of the war, differed from Zimmermann in being neither a film expert nor a party member. Perhaps his expertise as a banker and his close ties with Max Winkler allowed him to avoid joining the party. Merten had been part of Winkler's staff since 1933, and owed his position in Ufi to the confidence Winkler placed in him. From late 1943 on, he shared the business leadership of Ufi with the Tobis manager, Karl Julius Fritzsche.

Not all of Ufi and Ufa's high functionaries kept their posts to the bitter end. Leopold Gutterer, board chairman of Ufi and after April 1944 the Propaganda Ministry's representative in Ufi's administration, was relieved by Goebbels of all his jobs at the end of that year and sent to the collapsing front. Even Goebbels's prize protégé, Fritz Hippler—NSDAP member since 1927, in 1938 Propaganda Ministry official responsible for newsreels, in 1939 chief of the Ministry's film division, in 1941 SS-Obersturmbannführer, and in 1942 Reich Film Intendant—even he was removed from all his posts over minor differences of opinion with Goebbels. Max Winkler could not keep his deputy, Bruno Pfennig, legal counsel and insurance expert for Ufa since 1930 and Ufi president since 1942, after it became known that he had been dealing on the black market.

In addition to Klitzsch's successor, Fritz Kaelber, and his distribution chief, Heinz Zimmermann, the management of the "old" Ufa stock company kept several Ufa veterans until 1945, among them the chief of the technical division, Hermann Grieving; the chief of bookkeeping, Fritz Kuhnert, who had joined the firm back in 1919; the chief of the theater division, Max Witt, an Ufa vice president since 1937; the Norwegian Agnar Hölaas, in charge of operations in Neubabelsberg; and, last but not least, Berthold von Theobald, who as a major on Ludendorff's general staff had come to Ufa highly recommended in November 1918 and in 1927 assumed direction of Ufa's foreign marketing. Few of these were members of Hitler's party. Goebbels's curse fell on the "just" and the "unjust" alike, just as his benevolence often seemed unrelated to whether one was a loyal "retainer" or ideologically unreliable.

There is no better example of the divided soul of the reluctant conformist—or conforming dissident—in the final years of the Nazi regime than Wolfgang Liebeneiner, "state actor," acclaimed director, professor by the grace of Goebbels, director of the artistic department of the German Film Academy, and after April 1943 production chief of Ufa-Filmkunst. Winkler had recommended Liebeneiner to Goebbels; he had directed the Bismarck films and the "euthanasia" film *I Accuse* for Tobis. It would be Liebeneiner's job to raise the artistic level of Ufa productions, and Goebbels agreed to the appointment, even though—or perhaps because—he knew that Liebeneiner, who was far from loudly supportive of the regime, indeed quietly skeptical of it, occasionally summoned the courage to voice criticism of production methods in the "aligned" film industry.

Liebeneiner was not eager for the new job, but he did not take the opportunities he had to wriggle out of the appointment. The war and the production difficulties it caused did not make the job very attractive, and it would have been easy to take advantage of Göring's protection and seek refuge in theatrical work or work at the Film Academy. And it is unlikely that Liebeneiner was dazzled by the prospect of power. More probably, he was tempted, as were so many other film artists favored by Goebbels, by the illusion that with the hated power of the state behind him he could encourage artists, advocate new talents and interesting material, and reform production methods. Also, Liebeneiner had—though without taking any risks himself—shielded colleagues who were in disfavor with the regime and protected them from the Gestapo; as Ufa's production chief he used his new powers to continue this protective function. And so it came about that at a time when Germany's still most prominent film company was pouring its energies into Harlan's Kolberg, Ufa's last but also most expensive hymn to the Nazi regime, artistic oversight was in the hands of a man who had garnered almost all the available state honors but was still regarded as a quiet opponent of the National Socialist state.

In the two years that Wolfgang Liebeneiner was production chief at Ufa-Filmkunst, several young directors had the chance to make their first long feature films. Among them was the stage director Hans Weissbach; his Jan und die Schwindlerin (Jan and the Confidence Woman, 1943–44), with a screenplay that Per Schwenzen had written based on his stage comedy of the same title, was one of many productions banned for reasons that no one can as yet determine or reconstruct.[12] Max Pfeiffer's experienced team was in charge of production, and Weissbach's cameraman was the veteran Franz Weihmayr. Nonetheless, poor quality may have accounted for the film's "temporary" rejection at the Reich Film Intendant's office in August 1944. As a rule, that verdict was the equivalent of an outright ban.

More spectacular still was a ban that once again affected that star of Nazi propagandists, Karl Ritter, this time in his capacity as producer for Erzieherin gesucht (Governess Wanted). Ufa's advertising releases called this a "humorous film comedy about love and all the hilarious complications that lovers can experience." Thea von Harbou wrote the screenplay, and Ulrich Erfurth directed for the first time. Along with the Tobis comedy Eine kleine Sommermelodie (A Little Summer Melody, directed by Volker von Collande), Governess Wanted was "temporarily banned" in August 1944; again no reasons were given. Several editorial changes failed to produce a lifting of the ban before the end of the war. After the war, Karl Ritter said the movie had been "cooked up by Ufa dramaturges," and that "assigning this worthless material" to him was typical of the "chicanery" Goebbels had directed against him.[13]

As a director, too, Ritter had to do battle with judgments passed down by Goebbels's censors, and as in the case of his earlier anti-Soviet films, the verdicts reflected the changed political and military situation. In 1942, Ritter developed his idea for *Besatzung "Dora" (Crew of the "Dora"),* a heroic epic about German aerial reconnaissance.

> After the scenes on the western front had been filmed, the team took a short break in Berlin and then set out in mid-October to do the shooting on the eastern front. Four weeks later, they were ready to go to Africa to shoot the parts of the film that took place there. But by then the military situation had changed so drastically that all the scenes set in Africa had to be filmed in Ostia. After late December 1942 part of the film was made on Ufa's grounds in Babelsberg.[14]

Everything was done by January 1943, but in February the Sixth Army surrendered at Stalingrad, and in April the Propaganda Ministry offered no support for Ritter's film. Attempts to salvage it with cuts were foiled by further military developments. In May General Montgomery's tanks drove German troops out of their North African positions. Mussolini's capture in July made another episode in the film ridiculous; in November the Reich Film Intendant's office banned it. Only members of the Luftwaffe were allowed to see a special showing in February 1945.

Growing shorter of breath by the minute, Ufa struggled on. It was demonstrating, unintentionally, that Germany's battle against reality was an absurd adventure doomed to failure; and the miracle weapon *Kolberg,* the most expensive propaganda film of all time, which never even reached its audience, marked an ironic end to all illusion.

The censorship decisions at this point seem little more than displays of bureaucratic whim. Film bans often struck Ufa like bolts out of the blue. In 1939, for example, Carl Junghans's comedy *Altes Herz geht auf die Reise* (*Old Heart Goes Wayfaring,* produced by Georg Witt-Film) had been withdrawn from circulation after word got around that Hitler disliked it. The patriotic army movie *Der 5. Juni [The 5th of June],* directed by Fritz Kirchhoff (1941–42), was banned despite its excellent cast (Carl Raddatz, Karl Ludwig Kiehl, Joachim Brennecke, Otto Gebühr) and large cost overruns caused by changes requested by the army. And in the Ufi era, too—that is, in the last three years of Nazi rule—the film censors continued to play inscrutable games. Even "unpolitical" subjects were not immune to their caprice. Banned movies now included E. W. Emo's marriage melodrama *Freunde (Friends),* a Wien-Film production (1943–44); a comedy of mistaken identity called *Die heimlichen Bräute (The Secret Brides,* Berlin-Film, directed by Johannes Meyer, 1943); and the erotic comedy *Intimitäten (Intimacies)* directed by Paul Martin (Berlin-Film, 1943–44, with Viktor de Kowa, Gretl Schörg, and Harald Paulsen), on which changes continued to be made into the last weeks of the war—as late as January 1945 the Reich film dramaturge recommended in a note to Goebbels "shortening or cutting entirely the kiss scene de Kowa–Schörg [from mouth to ear]."[15]

In 1944 Gustav Ucicky and his writer Gerhard Menzel, recognized specialists in the fatherland genre ever since their 1933 film *Dawn*, were the targets of truly incomprehensible decisions. The year before, Wien-Film had produced their *At the End of the World* (with Brigitte Horney, Attila Hörbiger, and Trude Hesterberg). Difficulties arose with the book because of "the minister's demand" that the role of a banker "had to be played by a Jew,"[16] and approval of the Czech actor Gottlieb Sambor (i.e., Boguslav Samborsky) selected for this role was slow in coming. Announcements described the film as the story of "a primitive woodsman from the Bohemian forest who, because of his love for a mysterious woman, is drawn into crime in the city."[17] Perhaps the theme struck Goebbels as too gloomy. In the summer of 1944 the film was banned.

For the same reason, Ufa-Filmkunst initially had to cancel its project of filming John Knittel's novel *Via Mala* in 1942 (direction, Josef von Baky; screenplay, Thea von Harbou) after it had paid a considerable sum for the rights. But soon an Ufa production team under Eberhard Schmidt worked at a version of it that won Goebbels's approval; the authorities' demands for retakes dragged shooting out into April 1944 and drove the budget sky-high. "Editing; the synchronization of music, sound effects, and speech; the ensuing mixing as well as difficulties in copying under wartime conditions"[18] delayed delivery until the end of the year; in March 1945 the censors' judgment only confirmed Goebbels's 1942 verdict. In spite of a generally favorable evaluation, *Via Mala* was "temporarily withheld from circulation because of its dreary atmosphere," and released only for distribution abroad.

The other companies under the Ufi umbrella encountered censorship problems, too. Peter Pewas, a graduate of the Film Academy who had Liebeneiner's backing, made his debut in 1943 as a director with Terra-Filmkunst. His *Der verzauberte Tag* (*The Enchanted Day*), a love story presented in a fairy-tale style, starred Winnie Markus, Hans Stüwe, and Ernst Waldow. Pewas and his cameraman, Georg Krause, achieved remarkably sensitive, poetic visual compositions, effecting what Herbert Jhering later called a synthesis of French and Russian film art. The censors rejected it. In early July 1944 Goebbels ordered that it be shown, with no previous announcement, to the air-defense team in his building. The report has been preserved:

> The response . . . was essentially negative. The male members in particular rejected the film out of hand. . . . A number of female viewers accepted it uncritically, while others rightly asked what exactly it was meant to convey. . . . Only a few employees in supervisory positions recognized the dangerous tendencies implicit in this film.[19]

These "dangerous tendencies" were manifested in the "demimonde milieu" of many scenes, in the "unfortunate portrayal" of a German official devoted to his duty, and in the "coquettish performance" in a supporting role of Eva-Maria Meinecke. Terra's production chief, Alf Teichs, personally intervened with Goebbels on behalf of Pewas, his protégé, but *The Enchanted Day* was banned and considered lost, until a copy turned up in Switzerland in 1947. It did not receive its first public showing until the Berlin Film Festival of 1984.

Another Terra film became the most widely publicized censorship case of the National Socialist period, and was also a dramatic illustration of the working conditions in an industry scraping out its last products under devastating bombing raids. The shooting of Helmut Käutner's *Grosse Freiheit Nr. 7* (*Great Freedom No. 7*, with Hans Albers, Ilse Werner, Hans Söhnker, Gustav Knuth, and Günther Lüders) began in early March 1943 in the Ufa studios in Neubabelsberg and continued in the summer in Tempelhof. The indoor scenes had not been finished when the Ufa complex in Tempelhof was destroyed by bombs. Production had to move to the Barrandov studios in Prague, where the sets were rebuilt. In the fall the team was in bombed-out Hamburg for outdoor shots: "It took no little adroitness on the part of the director and cameramen to present the viewer with the impression of an intact port."[20] When the movie was finally finished, the damage done by the air raids made the staging of a "gala premiere" difficult. In the Reich Film Intendant's view, a Hamburg theater was the only appropriate place: "If as a consequence of the bombing attacks there is no elegant film palace available, then the movie will be shown in five or ten provisional theaters so that the Hamburg population, so hard hit by the enemy's campaign of terror, will be the first to see their movie."[21]

However, Goebbels torpedoed his own fight-to-the-last-man strategy. He felt that the movie, made with such difficulty and costing Terra a few million marks (over and above Albers's salary of 400,000 marks), could be improved by further cuts. Terra responded with all due obsequiousness: "The synchronization material for this film is in Prague. Teichs and Käutner are currently investigating how the changes desired can be made quickly and practically. I would estimate—but cannot guarantee—that the changes can be made within two to three months."[22] Because no objections had been raised to the version intended for distribution abroad, the film premiered in Prague in December 1944, but it was not shown in Germany before the war ended. In March 1945, six weeks before the collapse of the Nazi regime, Goebbels decreed that *Great Freedom No. 7* could "not be released at this time."

"Germany as locale, Hitler as producer, Goebbels and his officers as director and stars, Albert Speer as set designer, and the rest of the people as extras"—the historian Anton Kaes begins his reflections on "images of Germany" in the movies with this fantasy.[23] Paul Virilio goes even further in his essay "War and Cinema" when he says of the German population during the Allied bombings: "The mass of German survivors became extras in a pan-cinema that was as total as the war itself. The population perceived the war as a show that became increasingly spectacular all the time and that could not be outdone even by Hollywood superproductions with their biblical cataclysms."[24] The fascination of the film medium has clearly seduced later interpreters into equating the picture world of cinematography with the real situation. Kaes is aware of this danger; he quotes the appeal that Goebbels directed to Ministry employees on April 17, 1945: "Gentlemen, in a hundred years someone will show a beautiful color film about these dreadful days that we are living through. Don't you want to play a role in this film? Stay the course, so that those spectators a hundred years from now won't whistle and boo when you appear on the screen."[25]

Such was the movie atmosphere pervading Germany's real world in 1944–45. With disaster looming before them, disaster they had themselves created, the Nazi leaders, and Goebbels in particular, gave themselves up to a delirium of preening, and they called upon reality to abdicate to aesthetics, as it were, to disappear in tableaux, in poses, in stage sets. It must have been a most unusual exorcism—a mad notion that one could ban reality from history and put illusion in its place—that prompted Goebbels to write this message to the Ufa director Veit Harlan on June 1, 1943: "I hereby commission you to make a major film titled *Kolberg*. The purpose of this film will be to demonstrate through the example of the city that gives the film its title that a policy supported both at home and on the front can conquer every opponent." Goebbels authorized Harlan "to request, where necessary, help and support from all agencies of the army, state and party and to point out that the film I have commissioned here is in the service of our intellectual warfare."[26]

A remarkable shift had taken place. Propaganda, whose task was to serve the party, the state, its policies, and the army, had now become an absolute in itself which party, state, and military agencies were obliged to serve, yielding to fiction's claim to power. In its final, lethal stage, Fascist pseudoproduction revealed its basic nature, its tendency to form a mythic blend of historical memory and present experience and to elevate it into a mad transcendence that bore the name of "ultimate victory." What Goebbels called "intellectual warfare"—war conducted within the mind alone, war as a scenario concocted by a delirious imagination cut off from reality— won the upper hand over real war, which seemed less real the nearer it came and became quite specifically a pretext, a backdrop, and ultimately a set of props and a locale for products of fantasy. Goebbels declared "intellectual war," and the army put its last regiments at his command.

Goebbels and Veit Harlan, an obsessive propagandist and no less obsessive maker of melodramas, worked together with a common goal, but they defined it differently. Where the Nazi politician saw an already defeated Germany as a shabby reality that he wanted to annul with a megalomani-acal theater of emotion, the politically naïve German Nationalist film director sought to obliterate everyday reality with melodrama. "In genre films narrative often makes a double leap, ignoring the need for transitions and every tie with its subject matter and hence with reality," the critic Norbert Grob[27] wrote in his description of how cinema melodrama achieves its effects. "The result is a confusion of attitude and perspective. With description, composition, and rhythm left behind, all that remains is the formulation of emotions conveyed directly to the viewer." Grob made a sound overall evaluation of Harlan, who, though often pilloried as "the devil's director," was really no more than a "shrewd artisan" from the Nazi milieu, "an opportunist who thought only about filmmaking and about enjoying his art," a specialist "with a sure instinct for mythical stories and emotional effects" and for the means, sufficient unto themselves, of creating magic in film.[28] In this unscrupulous preoccupation with effects that ignore "every tie with subject matter," the master of propaganda and the virtuoso of emotion came together to produce a movie that for the few people who saw it before Nazi Germany collapsed could only have seemed a bitter mockery.

Kolberg, using some historical facts from Prussian history, gives them a new meaning and incorporates them into the mythology of the "greater German struggle for freedom." Prussia, 1813: General Gneisenau (Horst Caspar) urges the hesitant Prussian King to assume leadership of his people, who are eager to take up arms against the French. "A king has to lead his people. That is a natural duty willed by God." The film opens with panoramas that show the people of Breslau marching in ranks. The rhythm of the montage is attuned to the tramping columns and their chorus: "The people rise up; the storm breaks!" (a "roaring" mass echo of the end of Goebbels's Sportpalast speech on total war). The beginning of *Kolberg* not only makes a leap of 130 years but also falsifies historical action by inserting the mass hysteria of 1943 into it. Goebbels had different members of his staff tinker endlessly on the screenplay, which Harlan and Alfred Braun had written, supposedly with some assistance from Thea von Harbou. Finally, he went to work on it himself, cutting and adding. He kept his hand in this work of futility right down to the final editing in December 1944.

A flashback follows Gneisenau's appeal to the King. The scene is Kolberg during the Franco-Prussian War of 1806–7. A civilian, the city council member Nettelbeck (Heinrich George), forms a citizens' militia against the wishes of the military, represented by the city commandant Loucadou (Paul Wegener), who is counting on Prussian reinforcements. Under Nettelbeck's supervision, the citizens of Kolberg build fortifications and a moat; the city and citadel are saved after the "folk" unite as "one man" behind their new "Führer," Gneisenau.

Shooting lasted from October 1943 until August 1944, with Bruno Mondi as cameraman and Wilhelm Sperber in charge of production. Indoor scenes were filmed in Neubabelsberg; outdoor ones in Kolberg, Königsberg, and the outskirts of Berlin. While the army was falling apart in the east, Goebbels and Harlan recruited more than 185,000 men as extras. Four thousand sailors were detailed to the film, too, over the protest of Admiral Karl Dönitz, and the army provided 6,000 horses. Ufa's numbers megalomania—an Ufa trademark ever since Lubitsch and Lang—celebrated new triumphs here; production costs went up to 8.5 million marks.

> While Berlin was being destroyed by bombing raids, Ufa reconstructed on its outskirts parts of Kolberg, so that Napoleon's cannons could destroy them. Six cameras, one of them on a boat and one in a tethered balloon, simultaneously recorded the destruction of the city. Thirty pyrotechnicians were in charge of the innumerable explosions, and to stage a flood a small stream was redirected into canals dug specially for the purpose. Remote controls set off charges of underwater explosives.[29]

Build and destroy—this production principle that Fritz Lang had first tried out in his Mabuse films Harlan now carried to a new extreme. Editing the final version was, however, taken out of his hands. Riess reported that Goebbels instructed Wolfgang Liebeneiner to revise *Kolberg* according to a detailed plan.[30] Harlan later claimed Goebbels had all the scenes removed that evoked "the horror of total war."[31]

The symbolism of the whole *Kolberg* project and its tendency toward self-parody were epitomized in the premiere, which Goebbels was determined should take place on January 30, 1945, the anniversary of Hitler's seizure of power, in the fortress of La Rochelle, the last position that the Germans still held on the Atlantic. Because La Rochelle was now behind enemy lines, the only way to make this heroic farce possible was to have a plane drop the film there by parachute. Goebbels addressed a radio message to Vice Admiral Scherwitz, the commander at La Rochelle: "May this film document for you and your brave troops the unshakable steadfastness of a people who, in these days of world conflict, are at one with our men at the front and who are prepared to follow the great examples in our glorious past." Scherwitz obediently replied:

> Profoundly moved by the heroic stand of the fortress at Kolberg and by this artistically unsurpassable rendering of it, I convey to you along with my thanks for sending this film for January 30 a renewed vow to emulate the heroic struggle of those on the home front and not to lag behind them in endurance and commitment.[32]

The simultaneous premiere in Berlin went off with less fanfare. The Ufa-Palast am Zoo, since 1919 the company's cinematic castle royal, was already rubble; guests were invited to the Tauentzien-Palast (later also destroyed by bombs). According to witnesses, Harlan's epic left the audience feeling "abandoned and cold."[33] Only with great difficulty had Ufa been able to arrange a cold buffet after this screening: it was "consumed in haste by a worried public eager to get home before the next air raid."[34] Hitler's thousand-year Reich was twelve years old to the day and on the verge of collapse.

30.

The End of Universum-Film AG

D URING the last years of the war, Ufa-Filmkunst moved its production out into the country. The provinces, the Bavarian Alps, and especially the rural areas of Mecklenburg, Pomerania, and East Prussia
seemed relatively safe from bombing attacks, and in the forests and mead-
ows, in idyllic villages, in sports hotels, and on extensive country estates,
war-weary directors and performers found their way back to their
tried-and-true material. In 1944 Ufa again presented its famous lighthearted movies in all their variants. The "society film" flourished; in Carl
Boese's comedy *Das Hochzeitshotel* (*The Wedding Hotel*, with René Deltgen
and Karin Hardt), artists and dashing journalists arranged trysts to indulge
in entertaining amours. The country-estate milieu and the horsy set came
back into style, too, as in Hans Deppe's *Der Majoratsherr* (*The Master of
the Estate*, with Willy Birge), and in Fritz Kirchhoff's *Warum lügst du,
Elisabeth?* (*Why Are You Lying, Elisabeth?*, with Carola Höhn and Paul
Richter), a comedy about an inheritance. For *Eine Frau für drei Tage* (*A
Wife for Three Days*, with Hannelore Schroth, Carl Raddatz, and Ursula
Herking; screenplay by Thea von Harbou) Kirchhoff chose romantic corners
of the Havel River landscape near Berlin, which also served as the locale
for Boleslaw Barlog's love story *Junge Herzen* (*Young Hearts*), though the
indoor scenes were shot in Neubabelsberg and in the Hostivar studio in
Prague. Harald Braun went to the Baltic coast to make *Nora*, based on
motifs from Ibsen, with Luise Ullrich and Viktor Staal in the leading roles
and Franz Weihmayr as cameraman. For *Sommernächte* (*Summer Nights*),
a comedy of mistaken identity, Karl Ritter chose the East Prussian lake
district, which was still untouched by the war.

In 1944 only two films deviated from this pattern of light entertainment
in holiday or society settings: Veit Harlan's melancholy *Path of Sacrifice*,
the sixth German color film, and Harald Braun's *Träumerei* (*Dream World*),

about the lives of Clara and Robert Schumann (with Hilde Krahl and Mathias Wieman; camera, Robert Baberske). It seemed as if most of Ufa's artists had gone off for country vacations after Germany's defeat at Stalingrad. The company released only one propaganda film in 1944, Alfred Weidenmann's *Junge Adler* (*Young Eagles*), a hymn in praise of the Luftwaffe and the manly "religion of flight" addressed to young audiences. The idea came from Herbert Reinecker, who later became a successful television writer. And until the last days of the war, German film companies continued turning out lighthearted films full of holiday cheer. Only a few of these ever premiered, however; most of Ufa's production consisted either of films that were never even completed or of movies banned by Nazi censors and released only after the war, which were called "deserters."

The best known of the "deserters" was Helmut Käutner's *Unter den Brücken* (*Under the Bridges*, with Hannelore Schroth, Carl Raddatz, and Gustav Knuth), a love story told in a poetic-realist style that was filmed in the summer of 1944 by Walter Ulbrich's production team. In quiet spots on the outskirts of Berlin, at the Glienicke Bridge, in Havelwerder, and in Potsdam, at a remove from the centers of Nazi power, Käutner's film focused on the everyday lives of two Havel boatmen and unpretentiously succeeded in capturing the "flow of life," with its "timeless" emotions and changing moods; it was a tender poem about experiencing life in the present moment, a gentle antidote to hollow pathos, and the last contribution to international film art that Ufa made before its ignominious end. *Under the Bridges* passed censorship in March 1945 and premiered in Locarno in September 1946; its first German showing was as a film from Gloria-Filmverleih in 1950 in Hamburg.

The directors, performers, and artistic and technical crews of the final National Socialist films were exempted from military duty. But many of them were subject to conscription once their work was completed. That they had been ordered to provide "diversion" may be a psychological explanation for the vacation mood prevalent in many of their films. But by October 1944, when the Red Army reached East Prussia, no exempted film team could work anywhere within the borders of the Reich without danger to life and limb. Käutner, his cameraman Igor Obergerg, and his performers—among them the new young talent Hildegard Knef, who had just turned eighteen—filmed on idyllic Havel waterways while the thunder of artillery could be heard to the east and Berlin braced itself for the "final struggle." "We lived in a dream state outside of time, and our work diverted our attention from all the horrors," Käutner said later,[1] and Igor Obergerg recalled, "We had to learn to film motifs we found as quickly as we could, because often they would be 'erased' before we could get back to them."[2] Carl Raddatz remembered these days as—

an idyllic, almost romantic period of filming while bombers streamed toward Berlin above our heads. Then a few minutes later mushroom clouds of smoke rose far away on the horizon; the sky darkened; we heard a rumbling, and the ground shook slightly; and all around us frogs were croaking; wind rustled in the reeds; the Havel flowed blithely on as if nothing had happened. We exchanged worried looks and went on with our work. At night, near the electric works in Potsdam, we often had to stop working: air-raid siren, spotlights off, on the double to the shelter at the Stern brewery, all-clear signal, and we kept on shooting until morning. Our work was a source of great happiness to us then.[3]

The entire country was now a battlefield, and the horizons of the Germans, in constant fear of their lives, narrowed as more and more of the country's infrastructure was destroyed.

Even different parts of the same city are cut off from each other after a heavy air raid, and that is so to an even greater extent between different parts of the country. The loss of transportation connections makes them ever more remote from each other. This constant shrinking of one's horizons, this restriction to one's own territory, is very strange. One can't help thinking of the collapse of the Roman Empire in late antiquity.[4]

Oscar Fritz Schuh wrote in his account of the filming of *Ein toller Tag* (A *Crazy Day*) in Neubabelsberg:

There were air-raid alarms almost every day. As a rule we could work for only an hour or two in the morning before sirens started wailing. The raids usually lasted a few hours. Because Ufa had only trenches for protection against shrapnel but no regular air-raid shelters, we were driven out into the country somewhere where it was less dangerous. We usually returned about three in the afternoon and shot a few scenes, often unusable because the strain of the raids showed too much on the actresses' faces.[5]

The same could have been said, presumably, for the actors as well. But Schuh's remark about the actresses indicates that even under these appalling conditions the beauty and youthful freshness of the female star's face remained, in the producer's mind, the obvious measure of her appeal. He also mentioned that for everyone it was "not only wise but also a matter of survival" to slow down the work and drag out production in the interest of avoiding military service. Movies became a "bunker" where one could avoid conscription into front-line combat units or into the "Folk's Storm."

In 1943 high levels of government began experimenting with a new organization of cinema geography, the "Flatland Action." The mass exodus from Germany's bombarded cities and industrial centers, the evacuations and the swelling streams of refugees from the east caused a shift not only between city and country but in the traditional distribution system. Large segments of the urban population were seeking refuge in rural villages that had never had cinemas. In the view of Reich Film Commissioner Max Winkler, the growing demand in the provinces should have been met with an increase in 16 mm production, but this plan was doomed to failure for lack of raw film and copying facilities. The "Flatland Action" became pointless, however, when the provinces, too, were drawn into "total war" and people were concerned less with movies than with self-preservation.

Leisure time had become extremely scarce anyhow. While Ufa was making its last entertainment and holiday films, a 72-hour work week was introduced in several branches of the arms industry. Because workers often had to travel several hours to reach their factories, free time was reduced to a minimum. In June 1944 SS observers noted not only the negative effects on the physical condition of the work force but also "the disappearance of any possibilities for relaxation, e.g., going to the theater or to a movie."[6] The public for whom films like *Summer Nights* or *The Wedding Hotel* were made—members of a "national community" who carried the entire burden of the war economy in the arms factories—were the last people in a position to enjoy them.

Also, by the final months of the war, an oddly ambivalent state of mind predominated among Germans, who found themselves confronted on the one hand with Goebbels's propaganda for "total war" and, on the other, with these frothy movies about high society or comedies of mistaken identity. When Goebbels spoke on the radio or wrote an editorial in the weekly *Das Reich* calling for "a more rigorous conduct of total war," he met with widespread approval, but his demands for cutbacks on consumption and a lowering of the living standard were not well received. The "common man had been obliged long since to cut back," though the upper levels of society, state, and party had shown no willingness to do without their usual amenities.[7] SS observers were distressed to note, after twelve years, this revival in the working population of the idea of class conflict.

Uppermost in everyone's mind in the summer of 1944 were the "retaliatory strikes," much ballyhooed by the Reich government, to be directed against London and southern England using Germany's "miracle weapon," the V-1. Most people did not set much store by it, and it was often jokingly referred to as *Versager Nr. I* (failure no. 1). But at the same time a great deal of hope was placed in the development of later generations of technically innovative weapons. In their imaginations, the Germans counted as far as the magic number 7. The V-6 and V-7, so rumor had it, would deliver the final, crushing blow to the enemy on the eastern front. Reports about the "retaliatory fire" on London were greeted with skepticism, however. When a provincial paper reported at the end of June 1944 that movie houses in London had remained empty because of a V-1 attack, many readers joked that the V-1 could not be such a big deal after all: everyone knew that Allied bombardment of German cities had not exactly improved movie attendance.[8]

Speculation about the technical nature of the V-1 displayed a bizarre mix of Germanic Walter Mitty fantasies and science-fiction visions inspired by the movies. The weapons, some people thought, were "simple gliders" that were "hauled aloft by motorized aircraft and then guided by remote control." The V-2 was pictured as a miniature submarine that could easily evade enemy detection devices;[9] this submarine mythology, suggested more by movies than by reality, was strong toward the end of the war, when most of Germany's submarines had been destroyed.

Discussions and decisions by Ufa's senior managers focused on completely different issues. The minutes of management meetings read like detailed reports of a crisis moving inevitably to a fatal conclusion which the managers nonetheless attended to with great bureaucratic care and conscientious attention to detail. Fastidious precision, rigorous logic, and foresight in the face of inevitable disaster—that was the unspoken motto of Ufa's managers; the underlying attitude, preoccupied with facts and measures, gives to the language of the minutes its technocratically dilute quality. Fritz Kaelber was now Ufa's chief executive; his predecessor, Klitzsch, once omnipotent "general" and now chairman of the board, still took part but only, it seems, for the sake of tradition, for he no longer exercised his old powers as initiator, preceptor, and authoritarian super-ego to the assembled vice presidents but attended the meetings as a stone-faced guest, judging in silence the maneuvers his colleagues undertook to rescue what was beyond rescue.

Those colleagues' full attention was absorbed by the problem of sheer physical survival and by retaining the ability to function from one day to the next. They had to identify which cinemas in Germany had been destroyed in air raids and look for substitute quarters in theaters, schools, or other public buildings. An incendiary bomb had destroyed the roof of their own central administration building on Dönhoffplatz, and repairs took months. Plans were developed for protecting flammable film material, compensation for employees who had been bombed out was discussed, as well as how to give due recognition to employees who had distinguished themselves in firefighting. After the heavy raids on Berlin in November 1943, management ordered that the building "be defended against further attack with all available means." The night crews for air defense were enlarged. Women employees were detailed to be telephone operators, messengers, and fire wardens.[10]

While the bombing raids were decimating its theaters, Ufa kept on buying up more land, cinemas, and studio complexes as if it were still enjoying a boom. The point was to compensate for losses and maintain capacity, all in the hope that after the war the company could sail ahead into a financially successful future and win back the markets it had lost. Given the prevailing conditions, it was not surprising that odd things happened. In November 1943 Cologne threatened to bring suit against Ufa when it refused to pay for a lot it had bought on Hohestrasse which, right after the contract had been signed, had been totally destroyed in an air raid. (Management decided, "in view of this altered situation,"[11] to solicit the opinions of the Reich Commissioner for Film and the Finance Ministry.)

In another case, the bombing raids uncovered clearly questionable business practices in the past. In March 1944, Vice President Theo Quadt, chief executive of Deutsche Filmtheater, reported on a 1935 contract between Ufa and Mannheim, which obliged the city "not to build any film theaters" except Ufa ones and to use municipal authority to stop the establishment of others, in return for an annual payment of 17,000 marks. Quadt, concerned for the well-being not only of Ufa but of the entire film business, was offended by this bribe tactic; he thought the contract was "invalid,"[12] and added that because of the war, the theater situation in Mannheim had changed so radically "that the so-called commercial situation on which the contract was based no longer existed."

An accounting on September 15, 1944, showed that of the total of 249 theaters affiliated with Deutsche Filmtheater 87 had been destroyed or taken out of service for war-related reasons; many of the remaining 162 theaters were making do with temporary quarters.[13] Shortly before this, Goebbels, "in his capacity as deputy in charge of the total-war effort," had implemented a plan to convert 270 stage, variety, and Strength-through-Joy theaters into cinemas and to detail their "ensembles to the arms industry."[14] Many legitimate theaters were indeed converted to cinemas in the last months before Germany's capitulation, an action that allowed Goebbels to triumph over his long-term rival, Hermann Göring, a theater patron.

But Ufa's managers did not fail to see positive aspects from the air war, whose consequences they recorded week by week. In March 1944, Agnar Hölaas, a producer at Babelsberg, thought it "extremely desirable" to make film records of the bomb damage, technically flawless clips that could then be used for backdrop projections in films calling for such scenes, and got official permission for the idea. "These shots should be made in color so that they can then be used later in either color or black-and-white."[15] Management granted his request for 10,000 meters of film and 30,000 marks; filming would be done "through the mediation of, and in communication with, the Gauleitung [District Direction] of Berlin." Goebbels himself was by now Gauleiter of Berlin; he may well have been the originator of this dramatic suggestion. But as the situation "on the home front" worsened, the originality and appeal of the idea evaporated. In June management considered moving the Tempelhof studio to Breslau. In early December Kaelber had to tell his colleagues that a bomb had destroyed important elements of the Afifa copying facility in Tempelhof.[16]

Delays caused by the censors continued to be a problem, and Kaelber had to intervene with Government Councillor Frowein in the Propaganda

Ministry.[17] Vice President Kuhnert complained about the reduced gasoline rations for film transport and offered the vague prospect that a "passenger car adapted to wood alcohol" might alleviate this situation.[18] Day-to-day problems within Ufi multiplied. Thefts increased because the use of personnel for air-raid defense left the entrances to the administration building unguarded.[19] There were also political setbacks. In November 1944 it became clear that "the mandatory reissue of films of national political value" had made cinema attendance plummet."[20]

Ufa was beating a retreat that paralleled the retreat of the German Army on all European fronts. In early February 1944 Berthold von Theobald, vice president for foreign marketing, reported that the Ufa subsidiary in Rome had closed down and everything stored there had been moved to Venice.[21] In May, management noted a gratifying improvement in business in Italy "despite the significant reduction in the territory brought about by the turn of events." Harlan's *The Golden City*, for example, had brought in twice as much income as projected.[22] And as late as January 9, 1945, Theobald reported the surprising success of *The Woman of My Dreams* in the Ufa theater Cinasio in Lisbon and in Basel.

But the overall situation was not cheerful. By September 1, 1944, Ufi's central administration and all provincial subsidiaries in France (with the exception of Nancy and Lille) were "in enemy hands."[23] Films stored in France were given up as lost. "It appears doubtful that those in power there now will tolerate the continued distribution of our films." There was no word from Ufi vice president Reinegger, a Swiss citizen, who had remained in Paris after the Liberation to represent Ufa's interests. The only "Reich German" in the French Ufa firms had been drafted and was now serving as an army cook. The situation in Romania was equally unclear. "We are currently unable to communicate with our subsidiary in this territory, and we remain ignorant of the fate of our managers there,"[24] though business had remained "very satisfactory up to this point." But still, management calculated Ufa's probable losses in France, Belgium, Romania, and Bulgaria at 17.5 million marks.

With no show of emotion and with a stiff upper lip (if we take the minutes of these meetings at face value), Ufa's managers witnessed not only loss of territory but an ongoing destruction of Ufa's fixed capital. Fortunately, the company could depend on some if not all of its employees. In January 1945, at the penultimate management meeting before the collapse of Ufa, Max Witt, vice president in charge of theaters, rendered an account of "brave conduct" on the part of a clerk who had distinguished herself in rescuing equipment from a local Ufa theater: despite sometimes heavy artillery fire, she had gotten the equipment to safety "in accordance with instructions." Management voted to reward her with a bonus of 300 marks and "recommend her for the War Merit Cross or the War Merit Medal."[25]

No doubt even Ufa's managers endured moments of helplessness and deep depression that no one admitted to. The records reveal nothing of what people thought when Fritz Kaelber opened a routine meeting on April 14, 1944, with the announcement that "the press chief of Terra-Filmkunst had been sentenced to death by the People's Court for subversive statements particularly hostile to the army."[26] Kaelber asked his colleagues to maintain tight discipline within Ufa and "to deal strictly with any derogatory remarks or irresponsible talk, especially if directed against the party, state, or army." (Failure to report such talk, Kaelber said, was a punishable offense.) Ufa, as a firm affiliated with the Reich, had to be spared such incidents.

Despite such incidents and even though the military situation was hardly encouraging for long-range planning, Agnar Hölaas nonetheless announced in mid-November 1944 production plans for 1945: three or four films in Tobis's studio in the Grunewald, and, despite the danger, twenty-six in the Ufa studios in Neubabelsberg.[27] Events prevented the realization of these plans. Ufa's production teams continued to work until the bitter end, but on May 8, 1945, when National Socialist Germany surrendered, the final hour also struck for Ufa and for the strategic dreams of its masterminds, from Ludendorff to Goebbels.

In the last days of March 1945, even the SS observers adopted a new, unusually warmhearted tone. With the German people, whose slightest move and thought they had been duty-bound to report, facing defeat, the observers saw them in a different light. Like no other people in the world, they had worked to the limits of their physical strength and demonstrated loyalty, patience, and willingness to sacrifice. Even intellectuals, the report said, had not been defeatist, but now they could not help drawing bitter conclusions. It was all too understandable why people were living solely for the moment:

> They seize on any pleasure that offers itself. Any trivial occasion is excuse enough to drink that last bottle they had been saving to celebrate victory, the end of the blackout, the return of husbands and sons. Many are considering putting an end to it all: demand is large for poison, pistols, and other means of suicide. . . . Things that no one dared to think a few weeks ago are now openly discussed on public transportation and with utter strangers.[28]

This remarkable report, only fragments of which have been preserved, closes with a long look at a humiliated people. They have endured everything, the report says. They are accustomed to discipline. In maintaining their traditional respect for the police, they have gone beyond what could fairly be expected of them. These people feel spied on from all sides by the "party's widespread network." They have "put up with everything," but now they have had enough. "Even people who burst out cursing are usually ones who do their duty, have lost relatives or have fathers and sons at the front, who have lost their homes and have been up all night fighting fires and doing rescue work." These were the overdue insights of an intelligence organization whose functionaries were discovering their own true mood and feelings in the moods and feelings they were charged with observing.

There is no question that most Germans rejected the scorched-earth policy that Hitler was demanding but that some Nazi leaders were successfully boycotting. "No ear of German grain will nourish our enemies, no German tongue give them information, no German hand offer them help. They will find every bridge destroyed, every road blocked. They will encounter nothing but death, destruction, and hatred."[29] With these words, the Völkische Beobachter of September 7, 1944, beat the drum for the strategy of organized self-mutilation. Not only Germany's industrial facilities and power plants were to go up in flames or fall to dynamite but its communications network, its administration and its documents and records, its foodstuff and farms, even its remaining monuments of art and culture. The Führer, who had meant to imitate Alexander, Caesar, and Napoleon, was now adopting the pose of Nero, but his powers of command were crumbling; his subordinates were pulling away from him; the core was collapsing. National Socialist centralism, which had always been more appearance than reality, suddenly developed an incredible centrifugal energy. Only Goebbels stood by his idol. The details of his death are well known, for he organized them with the careful attention of a film producer confident of his powers and determined to garner the acclaim of posterity. But by then his entire production staff had deserted him.

In Neubabelsberg in mid-April, work was in full progress. In the south studio, Alfred Weidenmann was filming a disaster scene with Carl Raddatz and Karl Dannemann from the mining film *Die Schenke zur ewigen Liebe (The Inn of Eternal Love)*, which it had been impossible to complete at the original locale in Silesia. Soviet air raids on Potsdam on April 14 and 20 damaged parts of the Ufa compound, too, and drove artists and camera crews, technicians and sound men, office workers and building crews into the 1,000-person shelter. Stragglers from the German Army wandered in and decked themselves out in civilian clothes taken from Ufa's costume rooms. Then, on April 24, Soviet troops occupied Europe's largest film-production center. "Soviet tanks are making their way over torn-up pavement and along streets dotted with dead horses and made almost impassable by toppled lighting towers. This street had been constructed for the film *Refugees*. Back then, this was all props; now it is a horrible reality."[30]

By the time the Red Army rolled into Berlin, all of Ufi's senior executives and administrators had long since left. In the shelter at Neubabelsberg and in the cellars of the Ufa building at Dönhoffplatz and at the Krausenstrasse office and workshop, personnel hunkered down to await their fate. A middle manager made the following journal entries while in an air-raid shelter:

April 25. The cellars are overcrowded. About 200 are huddling together here with fifteen of us from Ufa. April 26. Some SS men have fought their way through to us. They intend to defend the Ufa building at all costs. The Propaganda Ministry apparently issued them that order. If they obey it, that will be the end of us civilians. April 28. The SS commander has said the Russians will not take him alive. Our building is under fire. May 1. The building is on fire and has been in flames for six hours. I don't know how much longer we can stay in the cellars. Fire is coming in from three directions. May 2. Tanks rolled into Dönhoffplatz this evening and fired into the cellars and bunkers. Many of our soldiers are wounded. Negotiations with the Russians are under way. The SS commander blew himself and a comrade up with a hand grenade.[31]

No sooner had the Soviets arrived than they began to dismantle Ufa's administration and production facilities, and at the same time a cold war broke out between the Americans and Soviets over the assets and files of Ufi and its subsidiaries. While the Red Army in Neubabelsberg was cleaning out the equipment, cameras, spotlights, editing tables, cranes, emergency lights and generators, the office employees at Dönhoffplatz concealed from Soviet troops the existence of the safe with Ufa's administrative files, money, and securities; in the next few weeks, these were secretly transported to Tempelhof, which was in the American sector. Whatever was not destroyed in the bunker fire in Neubabelsberg made its way to the Soviet sector and from there to Moscow. Newsreel material and many of the war clips made by the propaganda companies were lost when an attempt in late April to ship the negatives (stored at the limestone quarries in Rüdersdorf) to Schleswig-Holstein on an Elbe freighter failed; fighter bombers attacked and sank the boat. Barkhausen assumes that whatever of the highly flammable material was left in Rüdersdorf was either destroyed by the SS or accidentally burned by Soviet soldiers.[32]

After filming of *The Inn of Eternal Love* was broken off in late April, Carl Raddatz and another Ufa star, Viktor Staal, were detailed to the "Folk's Storm." Raddatz's colleague Karl Dannemann shot himself when the Soviets invaded Berlin. On April 28, Harry Liedtke, one of the most popular devil-may-care charmers of German film since the days of Ernst Lubitsch, was killed by Soviet soldiers at his home in Saarow-Pieskow. The next day Hans Brausewetter, a stereotypical "nice guy" in Ufa's stable, died of shrapnel wounds received during the battle for Berlin.

On the morning of May 2, Helmuth Weidling, commander of the German troops still resisting the Red Army in and around Berlin, issued an order to cease hostilities. The battle for the capital, which Goebbels had wanted to transform into a heroic epic, was over, and the Red Flag was flying above the shattered Reichstag. On this same morning, a young Dutchman, Petrus Bartelsman, a sound engineer specializing in amplification technology who had been with Ufa since the early 1940s, traveled on his bicycle from his home in Charlottenburg to his work in Neubabelsberg for the last time. He had been using the bicycle since the bridge over the Havel at Kohlhasen had been destroyed and elevated-train service interrupted. Bartelsman had had frequent run-ins with the security guard, Krüger, a robust SA man who had tried to keep him off the Ufa lot on the grounds that his bicycle was a security risk. On this May 2, the strutting rooster Krüger was no longer in his gatehouse. The sound engineer passed unhindered. But he had no more workplace. A Soviet soldier checked his papers and told him to go home. Bartelsman's amplification equipment had disappeared along with the rest of Ufa's technical gear. The Universum-Film AG—Ludendorff's Golem, Hugenberg's election-campaign machine, Goebbels's recalcitrant toy, retort of all German dreams and miracle of the European media industry—was no more.

Trailer
The Dismantling and the New Founding

"MARIKA Rökk is taking her baby out for walks in a baby carriage. Leni Riefenstahl has just arrived from Kitzbühel," Erich Kästner noted in his journal for May 4, 1945. The writer, outlawed and banned by the Nazis, spent the last weeks of the war in Mayrhofen, in the Tirol, as an illegal member of an Ufa team, and watched this formerly idyllic summer spot turn into a transportation junction for people and matériel. Trucks of the retreating Wehrmacht drove through town; Russian officers, stragglers from the staff of the Vlassov army, which had fought on Germany's side, passed by before gaping peasants, followed by Serbo-Croatian "foreign workers" returning home. "Tirolean freedom fighters with armbands, nettle-picking Berliners, strolling high society from Budapest—the scene is unmistakably international here."[1]

The "nettle-picking Berliners" belonged to a sixty-member Ufa team which, equipped with papers from the Propaganda Ministry, had arrived in the Zillertal Alps in March, ostensibly to do the outdoor shooting for *Das verlorene Gesicht* (*Lost Face*). Kästner was not allowed to leave Berlin, but the production director, Eberhard Schmidt, had entered his name in the pre-signed blank forms and attended to the rest of the paperwork. In Mayrhofen, Schmidt headed up a first-class team and had at his disposal the latest in Ufa technology, from cameras to sound pickup equipment to lighting gear. The director was Harald Braun, with Ufa since 1937 and much in demand since his debut in 1941–42 with *Zwischen Himmel und Erde* (*Between Heaven and Earth*). The screenplay was by Herbert Witte, with whom Braun continued to work after the war. The cameraman, Robert Baberske, had been with Ufa since the early films of Fritz Lang and Murnau, and no less experienced was the set designer, Emil Hasler. Hannelore Schroth and Ulrich Haupt had the leading roles.

But it was all bluff. To avoid conscription for a four-week "militia course" conducted by the local Gauleiter, the entire Ufa crew, Kästner wrote in his entry for April 19,

> set out through the village and into the countryside with their made-up actors in the lead and filmed for all they were worth. The camera hummed; light reflectors flashed in the sun; the director directed; the actors acted; the cameraman bustled about; the makeup man overpowdered already powdered faces; and village kids gawked in amazement. How astounded they would have been if they had known that the cameras had no film in them. Unexposed film is expensive. Appearance is enough.[2]

Not until 1948—and with a different cast—would Kurt Hoffmann actually film *Lost Face*. But with the aid of this bluff and under Ufa's wing, Kästner was able to sit out the end of the war in a picturesque landscape and in reasonable certainty of having enough to eat. He scrupulously recorded in his journal the rumors that seeped through to this "alpine fortress" from the collapsed Reich. For example, on May 18, 1945: "A city council has been convened in Berlin, and Sauerbach is one of the councillors. Thirty movie theaters are operating again, and others will reopen soon."[3]

However, in the first two months after Germany's surrender, cinemas were closed to the civilian population—in the American and British occupation zones, at any rate. An American order stated that the entertainment needs of the Allied forces had priority over those of the defeated population. Not until the end of July were undamaged or restored theaters first opened to the general public.

For the great majority of Germans the entire system that had held everyday life together had collapsed: that tightly woven psychological fabric of official lies and self-imposed denial, of autosuggestion and repression, of flight from reality, of turning inward, of emerging doubt, and of daily renewed submission. They had been cheated of the victory which Hitler and Goebbels had promised them. "The total war mounted by a totalitarian regime ended in total loss."[4] The political collapse was followed by a fall into a psychic vacuum, the inevitable price to be paid for a freedom not fought for oneself but imported by the victors into a destroyed country. Material deprivation only reinforced collective apathy, repression, and yearnings for harmony. Once again movies became a kind of anaesthetic—a mild drug that helped to maintain the torpor to which many Germans had yielded.

At the end of 1944, the number of theaters in Reich territory (which was then defined to include the Saar, Austria, the Sudetenland, the Neman region, and Danzig) was estimated at 6,484, with about 3,000 of those in what would shortly be the American, French, and British occupation zones. In May 1945 there were 1,150 operable theaters in those zones and in West Berlin.[5] This was the legacy that Allied officers responsible for the reconstruction of arts and entertainment had to administer. Among those officers was Henry Alter of the Information Control Division of the American military government, who concluded that there were primarily two kinds of theaters in defeated Germany: "real" Ufa theaters and "so-called" Ufa theaters, the latter being theaters owned by the company and others that "had been requisitioned from Jews or other undesirable owners." In addition, some theaters were still owned by National Socialists and "remained in the hands of private owners."[6]

The lack of clarity in the theater sector initially hampered the Allies' efforts to establish clear guidelines for the reconstruction of the film and theater industry. For the Americans in particular, the Ufa rhombus was the symbol of German film, of the political collaboration with the National Socialist dictatorship of an enormous economic monopoly. But the division of labor in the highly organized American military administration was equally complex. The Property Control Division was supervising the confiscation of Reich and National Socialist property; other divisions were screening and, later, "de-Nazifying" cinema owners and managers; the film, theater, and music office of the Information Control Division was in charge of relicensing cinemas. In short, very different divisions were dealing with the same problem from different perspectives—a situation that brought little clarity and raised false hopes.

Justified and unjustified hopes also blossomed in the production sector, which had temporarily shut down in the Western occupation zones. A number of facilities were still partially intact. The Ufa studios in Neubabelsberg and Tempelhof were not completely destroyed, and of the sixty Berlin theaters twenty-two were still operable. The Soviet dismantling had left major gaps in the stock of equipment—on July 8 Henry Alter noted that only one 35 mm camera had escaped the Russians, for they had "removed" the entire stock of technical equipment, film copies stored in Tempelhof, and 1,250 million meters of unexposed film—but the Tobis studio in Johannisthal was undamaged; it was being used primarily for synchronizing Russian films.[7]

Among those who had a part in the cold war over the remains of the Reich's film assets were Ufa employees who succeeded in the first weeks after the war in transporting to the American sector some of the inventory from the main administration building, located in the Soviet sector. According to a report by Hans Borgelt, building materials, cinematic equipment, office machines, parts of the telephone system, files, and film material all made their way across the sector border bit by bit.[8]

"The Dismantling of the Dream Factory" was the title Helmut Käutner gave an essay he wrote at the time that focused on the various obstacles standing in the way of a reconstruction of German film production. Apart from the Allied ban on production, the problems were mainly material ones, such as lack of film. The factories of Zeiss-Ikon in Berlin and Perutz in

Munich had been severely damaged. Agfa, Germany's major manufacturer of film, was in the Soviet zone.

> Deliveries from there are infrequent and inadequate and can be offset for the time being only by the military government. The exchange rate makes importation impossible for now. Increased availability of film will not become possible until the economic unity of Germany is reconstituted and an equable—perhaps even regulated—distribution of raw film is instituted. Or until German exports reach a point at which foreign currencies are not used entirely for the purchase of food and might be available for buying film abroad.[9]

These hopes came to naught. There would be no economic unity for Germany for more than four decades; tension between the United States and the Soviet Union increased; very soon the military administration in the Soviet zone established terms for German film production there, but in the Western zones German producers, directors, and performers were condemned to inactivity or substitute work. Such was the case for a group of artists assembled by R. A. Stemmle that received permission in June 1945 to "entertain the troops." "They are relying primarily on artists whose effects are optical. The entire opera ballet along with a few very good soloists is working with them. For the rest, a few less well known actors perform sketches in more or less (mostly less) good English."[10]

Helmut Käutner and Wolfgang Liebeneiner found work with the Hamburg Chamber Players, founded by Ida Ehre in December 1945. Harald Braun worked as intendant of the Heidelberg Chamber Players until 1947, when he was once again able to produce and direct films. Heinz Rühmann, whom the Americans mistrusted for political reasons, toured the Soviet zone with a theater group before he founded the Comedia-Filmgesellschaft in 1947 with Alf Teichs. Ufa artists went on tour, entertained the occupation troops, or recited German poems and literature in the studio of Northwest German Radio, in Hamburg, which was licensed by the British.[11]

As in earlier periods of crisis, a founding fever spread rapidly and affected both old hands and newcomers, experts and laymen, soldiers of fortune and outsiders infatuated with the arts. New firms, Henry Alter reported to the Information Control Division in late July 1945, were "popping up out of the ground like mushrooms." No sooner was the war over, tyranny overcome, and the Goebbels thought-control bureaucracy swept away than German movie people were eagerly knocking on the Americans' door.[12]

The companies of the National Socialist propaganda factory still existed, on paper at any rate. Tobis, for example, grandly rented out its facilities to new firms, completely ignoring the fact that its staff in Johannisthal was working on Russian synchronizations and renting to anyone else was impossible. One hand did not know what the other was doing, and whatever was done was done on paper only; the Americans' blanket ban on production remained in effect. Ufa, Tobis, and Terra technicians "who wanted to pool their talents and some equipment they had salvaged" founded Deutsche-Film, and in December 1945 the Americans registered, to their astonishment, nine more new firms, behind which were some prominent names: the Ufa director Werner Hochbaum and the Terra producer Alf Teichs, Wolfgang Staudte and Heinz Rühmann, Boleslav Barlog and the cameraman Georg Krause, who was expressly listed as an NSDAP member. Back in July Alter had predicted this trend, but had also added that none of these new companies could "be regarded as truly serious enterprises."[13]

Chaos, red tape, sound and fury signifying nothing. With no guidelines, all the Americans could do was receive German applications and immediately deny them. But paper that has been written on has documentary value. When the director Werner Klingler, whom the National Socialists had forced out of work, applied for a license for his Kollektiv-Film, he wrote that he wanted to make "films of reconstruction that in their choice of subjects will speak to people in our time and will influence them in the gentlest possible way, so that they will leave the theater truly redeemed." He envisioned a new era: "German film must undergo complete liberation from the ideas of the past and at the same time absorb new sociological and philosophical content. With carefully selected personnel and clear leadership, it may in the future contribute greatly to the reconstruction, education, schooling, and inner convalescence of the national community."[14]

All over the country German idealism, both conservative and progressive, called for recognition and acceptance. The Americans were clearly overwhelmed. They and the other occupying powers agreed that first the Reich's film assets, under Max Winkler's Ufi construct, must be confiscated. Working on this assumption, the Americans, British, and French pursued a policy of "disentangling" and "reprivatizing" Ufi. The Soviets took just the opposite course, in 1946 utilizing the potential that had fallen into their hands to form a new centralized structure, the Deutsche Filmaktiengesellschaft (DEFA). Ufa and DEFA—the ideological abyss between them was unbridgeable, but the new company carried into the future at least the memory of the magical workshop of the past.

Because Germany's most important film studios were located in the Soviet zone, the Soviets controlled no less than 70 percent of Ufi's assets, estimated at about 450 million marks at the end of the war—not only studios, production facilities, and cinemas, but also copying facilities, distribution organizations, and music publishing houses, real estate, bank accounts, securities, and contract rights. The victorious powers agreed that "excessive" concentration of economic potential, "represented by cartels, syndicates, and other monopolistic associations," should be liquidated.[15] Each Allied military government went about this in keeping with its political and cultural goals, but they shared a consensus on opening the fallow German film market—so long isolated by the National Socialist policy of autarky—to foreign films, especially American, British, and French ones.

American policy struck a propagandistic note: film would help the Germans to be politically "re-educated" into being members of a democratic society. American information and cultural policy had several goals: The German people should come "to understand and accept the program of the American occupation forces"; be held to the task of "developing a stable, peaceful, and viable governmental system" for representing their own interests; be fully aware of the totality of their defeat, the impossibility of rearmament, and the "responsibility every individual German bore for the war and the atrocities committed in it." Through "work and cooperation," the German people would earn the opportunity "to be received again into the family of nations."[16]

In each of the occupation zones, the military government appointed German trustees to register the regional inventory and assets and administer them. In subsequent years, the Americans enacted laws and regulations for "decartelization" and "deconcentration" that would have splintered the movie business into small companies, while at the same time the German trustees seized what commercial opportunities they could, buying up movie houses, for example, to "maintain and concentrate the overall potential of the West German film industry with the ultimate goal of re-establishing the organizational concept of the 1930s."[17]

A number of regulations were issued in 1945—but there was still no overall law making decentralization compulsory. The West German movie people favored the privatization of the former Ufi assets, but the trustees, who wanted to see the company structures maintained in the interest of a "re-establishment of a healthy German film industry," objected to the decentralization trend. In July 1949, Hermann Pünder, chair of a two-zone administrative council, suggested that the military governments should limit themselves to issuing guidelines and leave all further measures to the future German federal government of the three Western zones.[18]

On September 7, 1949, the day on which the West German Bundestag gathered for its constituent meeting, the American and British military governments finally enacted law No. 24, which in German film history is known as the Lex Ufi. "To promote a healthy German film industry based on democratic principles and held in private hands," the law ordered the immediate dissolution of Ufa-Film (Ufi). The Reich's film assets were to be transferred to a liquidation commission made up of the German trustees, who within eighteen months would offer the assets "for public sale to the highest bidder among those persons entitled to bid." Ufa was on the block—and so were Tobis, Terra, and Bavaria.[19]

The most important provision of the Lex Ufi stipulated that no interested party could buy more than one film studio or three movie theaters.

Furthermore, anyone who had held a leading position in National Socialist state companies, whether politically incriminated or not, would not be allowed to buy a studio. "The bidder may not at any time during the ten years prior to May 8, 1945, have been a member of the board or senior management or an official of a motion-picture enterprise belonging to the German Reich."[20] And, finally, the law forbade the use of the abbreviations "Ufa," "Ufi," or similar-sounding designations in connection with any film-related activity.

The Lex Ufi encountered resistance from the newly re-formed Spio Council of the German Film Industry and from the government of the Federal Republic, which had just begun its first legislative session. West Germans had their own ideas on what should be done with Ufa, and they claimed sovereignty. In 1970, Rudolf Vogel, a Christian Democrat and chair of the film committee in the first Bundestag (later film commissioner for the Federal Republic), explained the government position in a television interview with the journalist Reinhold E. Thiel:

> The basic German goal at that time . . . was to get out from under the control of the Allies. We saw how national productions were succeeding on the international market, especially in Italy, France, and England, and we wanted to achieve the same thing. We felt that Germany, in view of its film tradition, should have the same opportunity the others had.

Vogel thought the banning of the Ufa designation was an affront to German national dignity. "The name Ufa had the highest international value in terms of goodwill. It would have been foolish not to revive something like that."[21] For conservative German politicians of the postwar years, the question of Ufa was still a question of national prestige and national sovereignty, though language had changed since Ludendorff, Hugenberg, and Goebbels. Vogel did not want to recognize that Ufa's glorious name had been totally compromised by National Socialism, that the company had squandered that international "goodwill" and good reputation it had had in the 1920s. His view was matched by an equally one-sided view on the left, which Thiel expressed well in the same broadcast: "The name Ufa had global significance only as a symbol of German nationalism, and Ufa enjoyed a dominant position in the German market only when Germany occupied half of Europe." This statement, understandable as a response to Vogel's narrow-minded nationalistic view, is clearly false.[22]

A phase of stagnation followed on the Lex Ufi. The occupation powers limited themselves to control functions, while the German trustees worked to maintain the value of the Ufa legacy and, where possible, increase it (by renting studios, for example). The West German film entrepreneurs and Spio claimed the legacy for their own entrepreneurial purposes, but they were much too short on capital to be in the running as buyers. Finally, the federal government suggested in June 1950 that decentralization might proceed in accordance with West German law. It agreed to the concept of "decartelization" but had reservations about dissolving the vertical structures (i.e., about separating the production, distribution, and theater-ownership chain). On July 20 the Allies responded with a second Ufi law, which simply expanded the application of the first to the entire territory of the Federal Republic, that is, to the French occupation zone and West Berlin.

The Federal Republic busied itself with suggestions for decentralizing the Reich film assets, but oddly enough, all its ideas pointed in the direction of a new monopolistic development, and the Allies rejected them. Dissatisfied with the slow pace of progress, the Allied High Commission took implementation of its law into its own hands in November: In Hall 3 of the Afifa studio in Wiesbaden, nine Ufi feature films were put on the auction block. With the exception of the Terra comedy *Kornblumenblau* (*Cornflower Blue*), directed by Erich Pfeiffer (1939), they were all Ufa productions: the love comedy *Wie könntest du, Veronika* (*How Could You, Veronica?*) by Milo Harbich (1940); the village comedy *Three Fathers for Anna*; Werner Hochbaum's *A Girl Goes Ashore*, which had been reviled by the Nazis; Herbert Selpin's *The Green Domino*; the comedy *Ich bin gleich wieder da* (*I'll Be Right Back*) by Peter Paul Brauer (1939); Richard Schneider-Edenkoben's comedy of mistaken identity *Incognito* (1936); Josef von Baky's *The Small-Town Poet*; and, finally, the marriage comedy *Liebesbriefe* (*Love Letters*) by Hans H. Zerlett (1943).[23]

The auction was a major fiasco. Only three distributors turned up as bidders. *Der Spiegel* detailed how and why this remarkable auction was such a flop:

> *Cornflower Blue* came on the block first. The film had been rerun in the British zone. . . . No bids. Ten minutes of silence. *Love Letters* ran until May 1950 and earned a colossal 1,800 marks after the war. No bid. *Three Fathers for Anna* was distributed from 1939 to 1942 and earned 137,000 postwar Reichsmarks as a rerun. No bid. *The Green Domino* had not been shown yet after the war. Max Freund from Hamburg Sternverleih took it for the minimum bid of 5,000 DM. Likewise with *Incognito* at the same price. Then there were no more bids.[24]

Apart from dismantling the former state companies, innumerable applications to start new firms required attention. The Allies insisted on licenses for all activities relating to film production; anyone who wanted to make movies or be involved in film production had to fill out three questionnaires, which served the purpose of political screening. The American process produced very erratic results, depending on whether advocates of the "soft" or the "hard" line made the decision, that is, on whether the applicant's experience and artistic qualifications or his political history was the decisive factor. The guidelines for licensing were as idealistic as they were abstract. The occupation powers wanted to exclude not only the senior managers of Nazi companies but also film artists and technicians who had cooperated with the National Socialists in any way. This proved impracticable. Even if it was not the case that "almost all the directors, writers, actors, cameramen, and technicians had been more or less active members of the NSDAP,"[25] it was certainly true that a great number of them had identified with the Nazi state and party and, in the interest of their careers, had supported the system.

On the whole, the Americans' questionnaires did not achieve the democratic ends they were meant to serve. They contributed almost nothing to "de-Nazification," and evoked bitterness and divisiveness among those affected by them. "Because no actor could work without being registered, examined, and approved, a long period of anger, hatred, injustice, denunciation, mistrust, and envy began in the film industry, all of it aggravated by endless red tape."[26]

In the offices of the Information Control Division, some realistic—and skeptical—assessments were voiced. Robert Joseph, in charge of film, theater, and music, warned against the unrealistic expectation "that German filmmakers who stayed in Germany will come up with movie ideas overnight that are not influenced, colored, or shaped by the nightmare of the past twelve years. The Germans are having a hard time learning the new grammar of democracy in their everyday lives. Can we really expect them to grasp instantly the democratic syntax of film the minute we issue them a license?" Anyone for whom Siegfried had been the model of a film hero for twelve years, Joseph thought, could not understand that the world was full of little people who looked like John Garfield, thought like Spencer Tracy, and acted like James Cagney. "We're not looking for just anybody," Joseph added, but for people "with originality and ideas. Run-of-the-mill hirelings are easy to find." It was not enough to make films "that will make people laugh. We want films that will make them think as well."[27]

The Information Control Division did not grant any production licenses until early 1947. According to Billy Wilder, who worked there briefly, no resources were available for new German production in any case. The material resources had been either destroyed or stolen; the required political screenings delayed the formation of teams and dampened enthusiasm. "I do not think there will be any new German films in the next eight to ten months." That was Wilder's cautious and accurate assessment in August 1945.[28]

The upshot was that the first production license was granted not by the Western powers but by the Soviet military administration, on May 17, 1946, and that DEFA, in East Berlin, and not a de-Nazified Ufa producer, promptly took over the legacy of the Ufi empire. The first German feature film made after the war, Wolfgang Staudte's *Die Mörder sind unter uns*

(*The Murderers Are among Us*) may have stood in the aesthetic and stylistic tradition of the Ufa workshop (some top people from the "old" Ufa, like the cameraman Friedl Behn-Grund and set designer Otto Hunte, worked on it), but its perspective on the present met the American demand for films that would "make the public think," while at the same time it fit seamlessly into the "anti-Fascist, democratic reconstruction" which the Soviets made the guiding principle for development in their occupation zone. A few days later, the British military government issued licenses to Helmut Käutner's Camera Film and to Studio 45, founded by some of Käutner's colleagues. In the late summer of 1946, the French issued their first license to Artur Brauner in Berlin for his Central Cinema Company, which still exists today.

The Americans were still waiting for the right Film Control Officer with the necessary background, knowledge, and overview to make sound professional and political judgments on license applications. The job description called for a highly qualified individual: an American citizen of German birth, completely fluent in German and thoroughly familiar with the German film industry until 1937 and preferably until 1939; active in the film industry or, better still, "a recognized and respected producer or director from Hollywood"; and willing to stay in a bombed-out Germany "for six months or a year . . . to take charge of the situation and move it forward."[29] In short, this was a job for a leading Ufa emigrant, and among the names considered were those of Curtis (Kurt) Bernhardt, E. A. Dupont, William (Wilhelm) Dieterle, and Eric (Erich) Pommer.

Pommer came. High time "to roll up one's shirtsleeves," Erich Kästner wrote after meeting the prominent homecomer in Munich in the summer of 1946.[30] The chief sorcerer of Ufa's great era of 1922–33 was now chief of the Motion Picture Branch in the Information Service Division of the American military government. He was responsible for rebuilding the German film industry in the American zone, and he was also to keep track of film-industry activities in the British, French, and Soviet zones and coordinate his efforts with them where possible. The producer of *Caligari*, whom Hugenberg's Ufa had fetched back from America once before, whom Hitler and Goebbels had wanted to keep in Germany despite his Jewish ancestry, was now a kind of general intendant of the new German cinema, an entity that still did not exist.

Pommer found himself falling between many stools. He felt hemmed in by the politicians in Washington who had given him his charge, and he was besieged by German applicants, among whom were many former colleagues but also a number of adherents of the Nazi regime. "Pommer knows he will have to make enemies," the journalist Paul Marcus wrote. "The archives are open to him. He knows who did or did not do what in the Hitler years."[31] He stood "between two fronts," *Der Spiegel* wrote in a series on Ufa. "The Germans suspected him of coming back as an enemy of

German film who wanted to 'destroy everything' here. The Americans criticized him for acting against instructions if he helped to rebuild the German film industry."[32]

Pommer tried to make the best of his uncomfortable but influential position. Käutner said, in February 1947, "I think everything Pommer is doing is very solid. He wants to put an end to improvisations and put things on a sound, organized basis."[33] According to Pleyer, Pommer played a "more supportive than controlling role." He "saw to it that the film assets formerly owned by the Reich were not routinely confiscated by the American military government but used instead to reconstruct and reoutfit the studios in Munich-Geiselgasteig and Berlin-Tempelhof."[34]

Pommer's "more supportive" activity benefited from the increase in tension between the Americans and the Soviets in 1946. The Paris conferences held in the spring and summer showed that there was no agreement among the four victorious powers for a common policy on Germany. The gap between East and West opened further. "This gradually brought the victors to the point of seeing Germany differently. Could the Germans not take a part in the conflict that was dividing the victors?" A speech given by Secretary of State James Byrnes in September in Stuttgart marked "the end of the punitive period of the occupation and opened the prospect of a less dreary future for the Germans."[35]

This change of course in American policy had its repercussions on measures affecting information and culture and led to considerable liberalization in the licensing process. Starting in early 1947, production licenses were granted with American blessings, and several prominent Ufa producers and directors founded film companies: Günther Stapenhorst registered Carlton-Film in Geiselgasteig; Fritz Thiery, the able sound engineer of the early musical and operetta films, became a trustee of Bavaria and at the same time founded Helios-Film; Josef von Baky registered Objektiv-Film in Berlin, and Harald Braun, together with Jakob Geis, Neue Deutsche–Film in Munich; the documentary filmmaker Curt Oertel founded Filmstudien in Wiesbaden-Biebrich.

The first feature film to be produced under a Western-powers license (a British one in this case) was based on one taken over from Ufi's assets. *Sag die Wahrheit* (*Tell the Truth*), a comedy of love and marriage, had been almost finished in the Terra studios by the end of the war. Helmut Weiss completed it in 1946 as a production of Studio 45, with a new cast (including Gustav Fröhlich, among others); the premiere was on December 20 in West Berlin. The first German film made under an American license was, in its staff and cast, a high-quality Ufa film. Produced by Objektiv-Film and distributed by Schorcht, *Und über uns der Himmel* (*And Above Us the Sky*) was the story of a homecomer who retains his integrity among racketeers, speculators, and black marketeers in postwar Germany. Direction was by Josef von Baky, with Hans Albers starring. Theo Mackeben wrote the music, and Werner Krien was the cameraman. Otto Gebühr, star of the *Fridericus* series, had a supporting role.

Film historiography has stressed repeatedly that the "seamless" continuity of Germany's film production from the 1930s to the 1950s was essentially the result of the Allied, especially American, licensing policy.[36] The Americans thought they had hardly any choice but to work with people who had offered no resistance to the Nazi regime and afterward displayed remarkable talent for repression and self-exoneration. In view of the political constellations of the Cold War and in the interests of quickly reconstructing a shattered industry, it seemed much more practical to work with the available personnel than to increase efforts to recruit emigrants or search out performers and production crews who had kept their distance from the Reich Film Guild.

The Ufi empire awaited its dismantling. Real estate, studios, movie theaters, copies of films, and equipment were to be auctioned off, or such was the intent of Lex Ufi, at any rate. In short, Ufa was considered dead, and if the victors had their way, it would never rise again. But the twenty-eight West German films of the years 1946–48 were almost without exception produced and directed by former employees of the National Socialist Ufa or of other Ufi companies: Helmut Weiss, Rolf Meyer, and Helmut Käutner; Josef von Baky, Harald Braun, Werner Klingler, and Gustav Fröhlich; Heinz Hilpert, Ulrich Erfurth, and Carl Boese; Herbert B. Fredersdorf, Heinz Rühmann, and Günther Rittau; Arthur Maria Rabenalt and Rudolf A. Stemmle. Among them were both the "politically incriminated" and the "unincriminated," former partisans of the regime and quiet dissidents, unenthusiastic followers and convinced opponents of the Hitler dictatorship. But one thing they all shared was the desire to make films again, "unpolitical" films that would help an impoverished, demoralized people forget their cares for a few hours.

For critics of German postwar cinema, these films were products of a "late Ufa style," which followed from National Socialist film and carried its bad traditions forward. "If one was to draw an analogy in the field of the visual arts, this would be the equivalent of allowing Professor Ziegler to continue exhibiting his boring nudes or Professor Thorak his outsized heroic busts," one critic has written.[37] But the analogy is not convincing. For one thing, the German movies of the early postwar years avoided any and all heroic portraits and instead picked up the tradition of the Ufa films that had focused on personal happiness, the friendly idyll, and satisfaction with a modest way of life. And for another, film, unlike other visual arts, responds to the intellectual and emotional needs of a mass public, and it formulates popular solutions for the obvious problems and deficits of the times. Because most Germans were not ready to unsettle their hard-won equilibrium—earned by repression and by shutting out bad memories—

continuity was an appropriate response to a spiritual emergency. The "rubble films" of 1947–49 fit in with that down-to-earth, positivistic model for "coping with the past" that the Allies offered to the Germans; they relieved them of the task of radical self-analysis and thoroughgoing revisionism.

The end of obligatory licensing in 1949 saw a significant rise in production. In that year, 62 German films were produced; in the following year, 82. The production boom in the early years of the Federal Republic lasted for almost a decade, but it properly belongs to post-Ufa history, still under the spell of the Ufa tradition.[38] The company no longer existed, but its virtuoso perfectionists, its character actors and set designers held the newly flourishing West German film industry firmly in their hands. The restorative climate of the 1950s even encouraged the Federal Republic to exercise unobtrusive economic influence and political control. The millions of marks in indemnifications that the federal government guaranteed to some producers between 1950 and 1955 enabled its Ministries (by way of the Deutsche Revisions- und Treuhand) to examine screenplays, casting plans, and cost estimates; the Reich Film Credit Bank no longer existed, but the conservative force's habit of exerting political pressure by means of economic mechanisms was unchanged.

The second phase of Ufa's decentralization—more exactly, the sale of film assets previously owned by the Reich—went more rapidly than the first. The unsuccessful attempt of the trustees to auction off the Bavaria company set off the second round of activity. The Federal Republic was just two years old, and in both legislative and movie circles the talk was of a new and "German" decentralization law. The Bavaria complex, estimated at 16 million DM, was up for sale at a minimum price of 8 million, but the film people hesitated. Producers and distributors lacked cash, and the banks held back, too; other industries, developing rapidly at that time, were safer places to invest in. Both politicians and film entrepreneurs were hoping that a new decentralization law would create a more favorable business context, since the federal government "shared the view of leading representatives in the film industry that vertically organized enterprises could better absorb production and marketing risks and were more attractive investments for German banks."[39] Among those "leading representatives" were old hands well versed in vertical management: Ludwig Klitzsch, for example, and Max Winkler.

Soon the efforts of various legislative committees were crowned with success. In December 1951 the High Commissioners approved the German government bill. A version passed the Bundestag in July 1952 but failed in the Bundesrat; a compromise bill was passed by the Bundestag on March 25, 1953, and went into effect on June 6. The Allies' Lex Ufi had been replaced.

Still, the text of the new law retained the old substance. Cautio and Ufi were to be dissolved. Privatization, to be completed within two years, would preclude a film industry owned directly or indirectly by the state, or an "excessive concentration of power in the film industry."[40] The federal government, the states, political parties, and de-Nazified individuals were forbidden to acquire film assets. Ufi's assets were to be sold privately. Missing, however, was any requirement that properties had to go to the highest bidder. The Allied rule that no one party could acquire more than one studio and its copying facility or more than three theaters was retained, but an exception was allowed: "The decentralization committee can, given compelling economic grounds, make exceptions for the acquisition of motion-picture theaters."[41] The name Ufa was no longer forbidden, nor was renewed centralization once the sale had been effected.

Seventeen years later, Rudolf Vogel frankly summarized the law's true intent, which was hidden away in unobtrusive amendments and exceptions:

> My idea was to achieve the greatest possible concentration for the simple reason that the available film assets of 80–90 million, seen in international terms, did not seem large enough to divide. I therefore felt that if it was impossible to form one large company, the film assets should be divided between no more than two companies.

Thiel's concluding remarks, never contested, remain valid today:

> The goal was to keep the concern as intact as possible; hence the exceptions allowed in the law, which read almost like a recipe for recentralization; hence the elimination of the ban on recentralization after the sale; hence the elimination of the ban on the use of the name Ufa.[42]

Thiel suspected, too, that the federal government—at that time under the chancellorship of Konrad Adenauer—was dreaming of setting up a new Ministry for Information and Propaganda," and wanted "to maintain the prospective new concern's sphere of influence." Arno Hauke, general trustee of Ufi in the British zone in the early 1950s, confirmed this hunch:

> The federal government at that time—that is, in the years 1950–53—had made it clear to the trustees, or at least to me, that it was very much interested in a workable concept for public-relations activities. I would not venture to claim that Mr. Lenz actually had in mind for me to commission an *Adenauer Youth Quex* straight off, but it certainly was the case that . . . the federal government had a lively interest in newsreels, in informational material, in influencing opinion.[43]

That interest must have been lively enough to seduce everyone involved into enacting a law supported and hailed from all sides, only to quietly circumvent it and ultimately annul it. A decentralization committee in the fall of 1953 appointed former trustees, like Fritz Thiery for Bavaria and Arno Hauke for Ufa, as "decentralizers," but then it decided in January

1954 that there really was not anything to decentralize. The Ufi subsidiaries—Ufa, Bavaria, and the Afifa copying facilities—kept their old legal status.

The pace of non-decentralization—the revival of companies pronounced dead but in fact dead only in appearance—now picked up. During the last six months of 1955, the old Bavaria-Filmkunst became a new Bavaria-Filmkunst, and Ufi joined forces with the "old" Universum-Film AG and several theater companies to form Ufa-Theater, with capital stock of 9 million DM and forty-eight theaters. "Whether the consolidation of forty-eight motion-picture theaters conformed with the terms of the German decentralization law was debatable."[44] Ufa's Berlin production facilities and those of Afifa in Berlin and Wiesbaden were consolidated in Ufa-Anlagen (which soon bore the name Universum-Film AG again) and Film-Anlagen.

The liquidation strategy became even clearer when the time came for the sale of the newly consolidated Ufi assets. Private buyers or applicants from the industry—such as the director William Dieterle, who was interested in Bavaria—did not stand a chance because "the buyer had already been determined. It was the German Bank, which had founded Ufa back in 1917 at the government's request; and the condition for purchase outlined in the sales literature was tailor-made to fit this buyer: the two Ufa companies were to be acquired together."[45] (A counter-bid from a consortium of Mosaik-Film, Artur Brauner's Central Cinema Company, and Ilse Kubaschewski's Gloria-Filmverleih exceeded the German Bank bid of 12.5 million marks by 1.5 million marks, but to no avail.)

The German Bank, which had not only founded Ufa but assumed the government's shares in it after World War I and engineered Hugenberg's takeover at a loss to itself—this same German Bank was now, once again, decades later, the crucial institution in the reconsolidation of Germany's largest film factory. In an interview with Reinhold Thiel, its executive Hans Janberg tried to explain:

> The German Bank did not step in on its own initiative but was drawn in, primarily through connections to the board of the old Ufi, through the liquidators, and, we assumed, through government circles. . . . Our assumption, which later proved correct, was that the bank was drawn in because we seemed to be predestined by tradition . . . to help bring about reprivatization. The motive was to depoliticize Ufa. We were to find a solution that was essentially commercial, and with its help—though this was in a sense at cross-purposes—use German film to export culture, civilization, and German prestige abroad and at the same time reestablish respect for German film at home.[46]

Private initiative—but also (limited) state control. Commercial solutions—but not entirely without culture and civilization. Promotion of German prestige abroad—but also success in the domestic marketplace. Janberg

tangled himself up in the old contradictions, contradictions that are perhaps inherent in cinema. In Germany, attempts were repeatedly made to
reconcile these contradictions by means of political administration—from
the founding of the Deutsche Lichtbild-Gesellschaft in World War I to
Ludendorff's vision of a state company dressed in private clothing to Hugenberg and Goebbels, and finally to Adenauer's failed attempt to have a
film industry loyal to a democratic government. The German Bank contributed its expertise and threw its influence into the balance; sometimes
it worked against its own business interests and lowered the quality of
cinema by doing so. Self-deception was all too often involved. In 1956 Ufa
was only a shadow of its former self, and the hopes it wakened in government officials, old-guard producers, and new investors quickly came to
naught.

What no serious historian would contest today was clear to critical observers then: Ufi's assets were not sold to the German Bank at their actual
value but were "thrown away for political reasons." Thiel presented the
following figures: Bavaria, whose net worth was estimated at 14.5 million
marks, went for 6.8 million. Ufa's theaters, valued between 25 and 30 million, went to the bank consortium for 9 million. Ufa's studios in Berlin-
Tempelhof, valued at about 10 million, were sold for 3.5 million. Assuming
Ufa's total assets amounted to a little less than 90 million, the loss to the
Federal Republic was between 30 and 45 million. *Film-Echo* spoke openly
at the time of a "political sale," and the commissioner for decentralization,
Vogel (who, incidentally, had to resign his posts in 1953 because of his
Nazi past), admitted in 1970 that the entire transaction had been "an
outright violation of the regulations of the federal budget office."[47]

No sooner had Ufa been "decentralized" than Curt Riess announced to
the world, "Ufa is back in the game."[48] Not only was it back in the game,
but it seemed to be what it always had been: Europe's largest film company.
Ufa and Bavaria together controlled "about 60 percent of West Germany's
studio capacity, two major distributors (Schorcht and Herzog), and in Ufa-
Theater had a large showing capability, especially since most Ufa theaters
were large, flagship theaters. Finally, for penetrating foreign markets, there
was Ufa-International.[49]

Ufa's new chief executive, Arno Hauke, was an experienced hand. As a
trustee in the British zone, he had realized such high returns from old Ufa
films that he could found Capitol-Film in West Berlin in 1953 and with
monies from Ufi's assets buy up Prisma-Filmverleih, founded by the French
occupation forces. ("The point of founding this company was to circumvent
the still existing ban on Ufa production."[50]) The new company attracted
prominent directors, among them Wolfgang Liebeneiner, Erich Engel, and
Helmut Käutner, but the ten Capitol films made in 1953–55 lost 5 million
marks and landed the company in bankruptcy. (A Bundestag committee
later investigated whether, and if so to what extent, the founding of Capitol

had violated the decentralization law. But the federal finance minister at the time, Ludwig Erhard, would not allow Ufi trustees to testify.)

Arno Hauke had no luck as chief of the "new" Ufa either. The third phase of the decentralization and miraculous revival dragged on into the 1960s and ended in death throes. Hauke had taken over the new bogus empire when the postwar West German film boom was at its peak: figures show 817.5 million admissions in 6,438 theaters for the year 1956.[51] But only a year later business dropped off, admissions fell, theaters had to close, and for the first time since 1945 there was talk of a dangerous "film crisis." At the same time, the number of television sets was showing a marked increase, and the added buying power, motorization, and mobility of large segments of the West German population had fundamentally changed the way people were spending their leisure time.

Moreover, the German Bank was making life difficult. For Ufa's first three years, Hauke later reported, relations were characterized by an "almost classic harmony between stockholders, credit consortium, management, and board." But "when the first drops of rain began to fall, the banks naturally wanted to have their umbrellas back."[52] The German Bank imposed an interest rate of 10.5 percent on its Ufa loans; foreign competitors, the Americans in particular, were exerting increasing pressure on West German film producers; and the movies Ufa made were enjoying no success abroad. The twenty feature films made through 1961–62 by the new Ufa, alone or in co-production,[53] had to return their investments on the domestic market, where they encountered increasing apathy. The older generation preferred to spend the evening in front of the television screen, and among younger ones, "films in the traditional, long-outmoded Ufa style"[54] were not in demand.

None of the Ufa directors seemed to have the energy and originality to strike out on new paths, to depart from the aesthetics of the 1930s and 1940s. The premises for a fresh start were, of course, totally absent, given the prevailing economic conditions and the backward-looking political and cultural climate of the Adenauer years. Helmut Käutner, who admitted himself that he had gone from the frying pan into the fire after the war, that is, from a system of political oppression to one of economic constraints, made *Die Gans von Sedan* (*The Goose of Sedan*) for Ufa in 1959, an "antiwar film" that did no more than offer ironic comment on a militarism that was already a thing of the past. In *Schwarzer Kies* (*Black Gravel*, 1961), one of the last films made by the postwar Ufa, Käutner at least dealt with a contemporary subject: the conflict-laden situation in an Eifel village dominated by an American military base.

Along with the repertoire of traditionally insipid comedies, Ufa made lots of inanely ingenuous "problem films" having to do with the petit-bourgeois struggle to attain peace of mind—Alfred Weidenmann's *Solange das Herz schlägt* (*As Long as the Heart Beats*, 1958, with O. E. Hasse and Heidemarie

Hatheyer)—or family films like *Ist Mama nicht fabelhaft?* (*Isn't Mama Fantastic?*, 1958). Here the director Peter Beauvais, who a little later would direct thematically more interesting and aesthetically more sensitive television films, had at his command a crew assembled from the stable of the old Ufa: Igor Obergerg as cameraman, Norbert Schultze as composer, Luise Ullrich and Paul Klinger in the leads. An exception was Bernhard Wicki's *Das Wunder des Malachias* (*Malachi's Miracle*, 1960–61), which was well received by critics and successful with the public. Working with images at once allegorical and realistic, it pilloried the materialism of the West German "economic miracle" and its idolizers.

In 1960 Hauke and the German Bank parted ways. Hans Janberg recalled the situation ten years later: "Mr. Hauke had lost the confidence of the stockholders and board, and the company's governing bodies felt that as captain he had steered their ship into heavy seas and could not steer it out again."[55] The bank hoped to have found a better captain in Theo Osterwind, chief of the distribution company Deutsche Film Hansa, which now became Ufa-Film-Hansa, with Osterwind the chief executive. Using the same navigation system that had left Ufa high and dry for Americans to salvage in 1925, Osterwind ran the foundering ship aground, never to sail again; this time, forty years later, there were no rescuers either at home or abroad.

> Osterwind produced many more movies than a reduced market could possibly absorb. Film-Hansa sustained such tremendous losses that it filed for bankruptcy; its application was rejected for lack of adequate assets. In January 1962 the stockholders voted to withdraw from production and distribution. Thus, barely six years after the sale to the German Bank, the federal government's concept had proved a failure. . . . It had long since abandoned its political interest in maintaining a major film company. All that remained was for the German Bank to extricate itself as quietly as it could.[56]

Ufa's second death was simply the end of an ultimately anachronistic attempt to revive what had already died in 1945. But even though the company was now irretrievably gone, its name remained, and the Ufa rhombus is still a familiar symbol in German cities today. It will probably continue to be until the last movie house in Germany closes its doors. The myth remained, and the last chapter in the history of Ufa chronicles the squandering of that legacy.

In 1963 the German Bank sold Ufa's remaining assets. Becker and Kries bought up the Berlin studios together with the copying facility and all associated buildings. The Bertelsmann publishing group in Gütersloh acquired title to the company (including its name), rights to its films, the Ufa music publishing house in Munich, Ufa-Werbefilm (advertising film),

Ufa-Fernsehproduktion (television production, founded in West Berlin), and Ufa-Theater. By this time, Bertelsmann already held a dominant position in the book and record market. With the acquisition of Ufa's assets, it was on its way to becoming Europe's leading media concern.

A major consideration for Bertelsmann was the tax advantage it gained from the Ufa acquisition. Janberg confirmed this in his interview with Reinhold Thiel: "I daresay Bertelsmann never would have considered the purchase if the Ufa companies had not had a collective tax debt of about 26 million DM that Bertelsmann could offset over five years. It made the purchase price appear quite attractive."[57]

It was a typical deal of the early 1960s. The boom of West Germany's "economic miracle," achieved with the help of the Allies, set the stage for the growth of large-scale monopolies that were ready to compete on a global level. The Federal Republic's tax laws worked to the advantage of rising companies and accelerated the demise of dying firms and industries. It was clear that a film business producing solely for cinema screens was a thing of the past but that respectable results could be achieved if a company planned and operated on a "multimedia" basis. By 1970 Bertelsmann reported sales of 712 million DM and employed 14,000 people (about as many as Ufa had in 1943). It stopped producing feature films and reduced the Ufa theater chain to the still profitable premiere theaters. Its Ariola company absorbed the two music publishers Ufa-Tonfilm and Wiener Bohème, and sold back Ufa-Newsreel to the government (which had been its major stockholder at one time in the 1950s but had sold its shares to the new Ufa). Second German Television leased from Becker and Kries the old Ufa's original studios on Oberlandstrasse in Tempelhof, the ones that had evolved out of the glass pioneers. Ufa-Werbefilm and Ufa-Fernsehproduktion continued to operate. In the 1960s and early 1970s, television production was located on the old Ufa grounds on Viktoriastrasse, in Tempelhof. Film production resumed again in 1981 with the founding of Ufa-Filmproduktion, a subsidiary of Ufa-Fernsehproduktion, but the company lasted only long enough to produce three films starring Didi Hallervorden.[58]

Bertelsmann had also acquired the rights to about 3,000 of Ufa's feature and cultural films, but copies of only about half of these had been saved. (The federal archives controlled whatever newsreels and documentaries had been preserved from the Nazi period.) Bertelsmann was on the verge of selling these rights to Seven Arts, an American company, for 6 million DM when the government stepped in and, with a loan from the Ufi liquidation fund, offered a better deal. The Friedrich Wilhelm Murnau Foundation, formed expressly for this transaction, wound up paying the obviously excessive price of 13.8 million DM for Ufa's film stock (and some of the old Bavaria films).

Reinhold Thiel has investigated in detail[59] the complex transactions involving Ufa's film stock, an artistic legacy which of course spanned virtually all of German film history. "And so," Thiel observed in 1970, "the government squandered Ufi's assets, which were by law supposed to go to the film industry."[60] From the perspective of today, however, it is clear that the money made from liquidating the Ufa assets could not have rescued the West German film industry anyhow.

Ufa-Film still exists today as a legal, bankrupted entity, which is to say that it is still in the process of being dissolved. This leaves the botched distribution of its legacy unclear, and the film industry itself has never asked for an accounting of the sums due it under the law. The history of the Ufi liquidation is, as Thiel says, "shameful," characterized by "incompetence, bureaucracy, and evasion of the law." Behind this lay "the intertwined interests of capital and government."[61] One can hardly argue with this judgment, and with its condemnation of an infringement of democratic principles. Indeed, these flawed political and moral premises worked against a new flourishing of film in postwar Germany.

It is, however, essential to look at the economic factors involved. The resurrected West German film industry found itself "in a state of crisis from the very beginning." Production slid into "permanent crisis" and was never able to emerge from it.[62] The Allied anti-cartel laws and licensing practices were surely one important reason for this. American film capital had no interest in encouraging strong competition in Europe and was eager to exploit the market that had opened up there after the war, especially in West Germany. The constellations had not fundamentally changed since the 1925 Parufamet agreement, except that the Americans had grown considerably stronger. With the "breaking up of the film industry into small, barely viable production groups"—a development Enno Patalas noted in the Federal Republic as early as 1950[63]—the Americans achieved the goal they had dreamed of back in the 1920s.

In short, "the permanent deficit in German film production is visible like a red thread . . . throughout its history."[64] The Federal Republic was caught between Scylla and Charybdis: in the interests of its Western partners it had to "set an example in liberalizing exchange of goods" and drop import tariffs (it was the only government in Western Europe to do so); on the other hand, it felt obliged "to support . . . crisis-ridden German film production."[65] Its vacillation between these two positions laid the foundations for the debacle which West German film policy created for itself over the next two decades.

Orientation to the domestic market was one disastrous consequence. In the view of the young directors and producers, who in the 1960s declared war on "Grandpa's cinema" and struck out on their own, German film, in "taking its cue from Ufa" and choosing autarky, had isolated itself from the world market and a cosmopolitan public. "This direction, characteristic of the 1930s, has not been corrected to this day. . . . Even when German film was faring well in the 1950s, it did not try to win back a place in world-class cinema."[66]

But the last place to lay the blame for this failure is on Ufa's doorstep. As long as the company could expand commercially and be free to develop artistically, it had guaranteed German film access to the world market; it was Germany's answer to Hollywood. Well into the late 1930s and even under the Nazi policy of autarky, Ufa still produced for foreign markets, and it was Ufa's producers who advocated internationally successful "prestige films," even under the difficult conditions of those times. It was the management not of Klitzsch or Correll but of the Reich Propaganda Ministry that was responsible for Germany's retreat from the world market. Yet German film had to struggle with the consequences of this policy well into the 1970s.

Epilogue

T HE squandered legacy of Ufa is part of the economic and cultural history of the Federal Republic, a history in which obsolete modes of filmmaking were perpetuated. It also is a variation on the old theme of the healing power of scandal in a democratic society. However, only scandals exposed early on can have that healing effect. The Ufa scandal came to light belatedly, and at a point in time when overly simplified conspiracy theories were current. The view that Ufa was from beginning to end a reactionary, nationalistic, militaristic monopoly dedicated to manipulating public opinion fit neatly into the leftist theory that a permanent conspiracy joined state power and capital. This cliché perpetuated itself, and in time grass grew over it, gradually covering the ruins of the Reich's film assets.

"Young German film"—the "departure from yesterday" that Alexander Kluge, Edgar Reitz, Peter Schamoni, Volker Schlöndorff, and others initiated in 1966—was a spectacular, highly idealistic, and highly necessary initiative. It had been preceded in 1962 by a declaration, the Oberhausen manifesto, which had been a kind of funeral oration for Ufa's culture. "The old film is dead. We believe in the new one." This faith seemed for a while to move mountains. Preoccupation with the domestic market ceased, and in a context of general social change many original talents found the means to develop a new film language that soon won international success. In the 1970s, German films directed by Wim Wenders, Werner Herzog, Rainer Werner Fassbinder, and others once again drew acclaim and prizes at the world's major film festivals.

The arrival of the Oberhauseners was accompanied by new efforts to support and promote movies, efforts that generated many new distribution modes, set large amounts of money in motion, created innumerable undercapitalized companies, produced a flood of mediocre films, and, on the whole, had a devastating effect on film culture in Germany. Now, in the

1990s, seventy-five years after the founding of Ufa, Germany's film market is once again in a shambles, and those who have brought about its downfall are suddenly harking back to familiar old solutions. They are calling for centralization, for a general intendant of German film; they dream of organizational forms of a "national" order; they probably dream as well of the old Universum-Film AG.

After the collapse of the Berlin Wall and the reunification of Germany, the empire of the cinema czar Heinz Reich (who bought the Ufa theater chain from Bertelsmann in 1971) is expanding into the five new federal states on the other side of the Elbe River. And with it the Ufa rhombus is returning to the region of its origin: to Berlin and Brandenburg, which once provided the outdoor locations for Joe May's and Lubitsch's monumental films. In the West, in the theater districts of Hamburg, Munich, Cologne, Essen, and Dusseldorf, the old Ufa trademark is now an accessory of the postmodern city, where anything is possible. One possible thing is that a company that died decades ago will live on in its emblem and as a myth.

But in the age of the "new media," of television, of Bertelsmann, of new cinema empires and big-time rights brokers, of video stores and CDs, there will be no more national, vertically structured film companies. Anarchy in production and distribution is flourishing globally, spurred on by the "multis." The need to expose film and distribute picture stories, where possible even to movie theaters, is only a secondary motive in their larger economic enterprises. An Ufa of today would have to compete with Sony, and what it produced would have to be as devoid of history and profile, as colorful and insubstantial as a television ad.

In 1987 Ufa made headlines on the sports page of daily newspapers: Ufa-Film- and Fernseh, the Ufa holding company in the Bertelsmann concern, paid the German Soccer Association 135 million marks for the broadcasting rights to the games of the national league. Ever since, it has been selling those rights at a profit to both commercial and public television channels. Sports can be turned into money more quickly than film can. Sports are cinema, too, and cinema is television. From the moneymakers' perspective, it's all one: "marketing" is the magic incantation of an age that has no need of magicians. The Super Cup is the prestige film of today.

Potsdam-Babelsberg, 1991: In the central complex of the "Great Hall" that Ufa built here in 1926, DEFA is making a feature film about the Stalin era. In this same studio sixty-five years ago, Fritz Lang was making *Metropolis*, investing four painstaking weeks in constructing a model of a factory hall that he would then blow up in a single shot lasting ten seconds. Create and destroy: the law of cinematography. Now the DEFA stagehands are constructing a Stalin era for the purpose of deconstructing it as quickly as possible in people's minds. This film factory has to come to terms with its own past quickly enough to keep up with the West and not to fall behind. But the construction work is being done in the old tempo of hand-made work, as DEFA's painters paint Stalin's oversized portrait on the transparencies, lovingly, in the service of a perfectionism they have inherited from Ufa.

On Germany's oldest and largest film lot the decentralizers meet once again. Eighty years of Babelsberg, seventy-five years of Ufa, forty years of socialist film production—all to the greater glory of an idea that once moved the world but was ultimately a pathetic failure. The Berlin Trust Institute commissioner in charge of DEFA, Peter Schiwy, has suggested expanding Babelsberg into a media center for Berlin and Brandenburg. Nine hundred and fifty DEFA employees—all that are left of 2,500—hope to escape the decentralization process. The Trust Institute is looking for solutions "that will do justice to Babelsberg's significance in cultural and cinematic history," prepared in principle to create television production possibilities in the old studios. The television people can produce images of a technical quality that does not quite equal that of an Ufa 35 mm film, but it comes close.

Fade Out

A VIEW of the lot of the old Ufa city. A surrealistic movie landscape overgrown with vegetation. The melancholy aesthetics of coincidence have left German armored reconnaissance trucks from World War II, which figured in a DEFA war film, parked among the bushes near barracks dating from the 1940s. Hitler's methods reduced the accelerations of the industrial age to a sociological and political denominator. His war of conquest was an exercise in cost-benefit analysis: How many people had to die so that the largest possible territory could be tied into the modern economy and its new tempo?

The Trust Institute is searching for more civilized solutions in its effort to tie Neubabelsberg, Ufa Strasse 99 to 103 (later: August-Bebel-Strasse 26 to 53) into the tempo of the media era. Ufa today: *une nature morte*. But as Alexander Kluge says, it is a mistake to assume that the dead are dead. They are alive among us in reincarnated form.

NOTES
AND SOURCES

BA = Bundesarchiv (Federal Archive), Koblenz
BA/MA = Bundesarchiv Militärarchiv, Freiburg

FADE IN

1. As cited in Arthur Rosenberg, *Entstehung der Weimarer Republik* (Frankfurt, 1970), 229.
2. As cited in Friedrich von Zglinicki, *Der Weg des Films* (Berlin, 1956), 394.
3. Sebastian Haffner, *Von Bismarck zu Hitler* (Munich, 1987), 126.
4. Paul Virilio, *Krieg und Kino* (Munich and Vienna, 1986), 74.
5. Hermann Glaser, *Maschinenwelt und Alltagsleben* (Frankfurt, 1981), 10.
6. Wolfgang Schivelbusch, *Lichtblicke* (Munich and Vienna, 1983), 56ff.
7. Hugo von Hofmannsthal, "Das Reinhardtsche Theater," in Heinz Herald, *Max Reinhardt* (Hamburg, 1953), 103.
8. As cited in Glaser, 63.
9. As cited in *Mythos Berlin*, catalogue to an exhibition of the same name (Berlin, 1987), 42.
10. H. D. Heilmann, "Fürstenberg und Rathenau," in *Berlin um 1900: Ausstellungskatalog der Berlinischen Galerie e.V.* (Berlin, 1984), 171.
11. Jerzy Toeplitz, *Geschichte des Films 1895–1933* (Munich, 1987), 33.
12. Ibid., 32.
13. Oskar Messter, *Mein Weg mit dem Film* (Berlin, 1936), 29ff.
14. Zglinicki, 273.
15. Virilio, 30.
16. From a memorandum Dr. Duisberg sent to the Foreign Office on October 26, 1917. The memorandum was occasioned by D. W. Griffith's film *Intolerance* and entitled "Uber die Revolution in der Filmkunst." See Hans Traub, "Aktenauszuge uber Filmpropaganda wahrend des Weltkrieges," Berlin, 1938 (unpublished manuscript), 157; BA/R 146/95.
17. Toeplitz, 70.
18. See Urban Gad, *Der Film, seine Mittel—seine Ziele* (Berlin, 1921).
19. Toeplitz, 76.
20. Ibid.
21. Zglinicki, 500f.

22. Figures from Rachael Low, *The History of the British Film 1906–1914* (London, 1949), 19 and 22, and from Toeplitz, 106.
23. Toeplitz, 110.
24. Cited in Hans Barkhausen, *Filmpropaganda für Deutschland im Ersten und Zweiten Weltkrieg* (Hildesheim, 1982), 7.
25. *Die Schaubühne*, October 2, 1913, as cited in Ilona Brennicke and Joe Hembus, *Klassiker des deutschen Stummfilms 1910 bis 1930* (Munich, 1983), 241.
26. Figures from Brennicke and Hembus, 239 and 241.
27. Emil Jannings, *Theater/Film: Das Leben und ich* (Berchtesgaden, 1951), 119 and 121.
28. As cited in Brennicke and Hembus, 24.
29. Barkhausen, 21.
30. *Der Kinematograph*, August 26, 1914, as cited in ibid.
31. Barkhausen, 75.
32. Ibid., 127.
33. Ibid., 108.
34. Ibid., 29.
35. Ibid., 17.
36. Minutes of the meeting of the committee charged to investigate the possibility of propaganda abroad through film and slide lectures held on April 6, 1916, BA/MA, RM 3/v.9901.
37. Barkhausen, 43.
38. Jürgen Spiker, *Film und Kapital* (Berlin, 1975), 23f.
39. Ludwig Klitzsch in a letter of October 17, 1916, to the president of the Zentralverband Deutscher Industrieller (National Association of German Industrialists), as cited in ibid., 23.
40. Title of notes taken at a discussion of the Voluntary Association to Promote Film as a Means to Serve the Common Good and Patriotic Ends, September 11, 1916, BA/MA, RM 3/v.9901.
41. Barkhausen, 47.
42. Ibid., 140f.
43. Ibid., 48.
44. Ibid., 50.
45. Hans Traub, *Die Ufa. Ein Beitrag zur Entwicklungsgeschichte des deutschen Filmschaffens* (Berlin, 1943), 28.
46. As cited in Barkhausen, 169.
47. Text of a Merkblatt für Kinematographen-Theater (Notice to Movie Theaters) issued by Bufa, as cited in Zglinicki, 393.
48. Memo from the DLG to the Naval Board, May 18, 1917, BA/MA, RM 3/v.9901.
49. Memo from Bufa to the publicity department of the Admiralty Staff of the navy, ibid.
50. Barkhausen, 120.
51. Ibid.
52. Ludendorff's letter to the Ministry of War is quoted here from Wilfried von Bredow and Rolf Zurek, *Film und Gesellschaft in Deutschland* (Hamburg, 1975), 102ff.
53. Barkhausen, 133.
54. Hans Traub, *Die Ufa*, 31f.

PART ONE

CHAPTER 1. LUDENDORFF'S GOLEM

1. The Reich's influence was guaranteed in a secret agreement whose points are spelled out in a memo of April 18, 1918, from the Ministry of War to the Reich Chancellor.

In this memo the shareholders Frenkel and Wassermann are listed explicitly as "strawmen" whose subscriptions "disguised" 7 million marks of government capital, the founders agreed "to vote against all measures the Reich representatives who have to be invited to the meetings disapprove of." See Wolfgang Mühl-Benninghaus, "Zur Rolle des staatsmonopolistischen Kapitalismus bei der Herausbildung eines Systems von Massenkommunikation zwischen 1900 und 1933" (diss., Humboldt University, Berlin, 1987), document volume, 99f.

2. Rita Lipschütz, *Der Ufa-Konzern* (Berlin, 1932), 6.
3. Traub, "Aktenauszüge," 223.
4. Traub, *Die Ufa*, 33.
5. Notes of the January 1, 1918, meeting of Ufa's executive committee, BA/R 109 I/2421.
6. Ibid.
7. Ibid.
8. Traub, *Die Ufa*, 34.
9. Ibid.
10. Barkhausen, 134.
11. Ibid., 135.
12. Traub, "Aktenauszüge," 219.
13. Ibid., 206.
14. Circular sent by Ministry of War to the Reich Ministries, August 31, 1918, unsigned, BM/MA.
15. Secret notes taken by Kiliani in the Foreign Office, September 4, 1918; see Traub, "Aktenauszüge," 206.
16. Bufa report 93, October 7–13, 1918; see Traub, "Aktenauszüge," 211.
17. Barkhausen, 137.
18. Heinrich Fraenkel, *Unsterblicher Film* (Munich, 1956), 85ff.
19. Toeplitz, 140.
20. H.-B. Heller, *Literarische Intelligenz und Film* (Tübingen, 1985), 117.

CHAPTER 2. THE ROOFLESS HOUSE

1. Ernst Bloch, "Blick von 1917 auf Deutschland," in his *Durch die Wüste* (Frankfurt, 1964), 22.
2. Lotte H. Eisner, *Die dämonische Leinwand* (Frankfurt, 1979), 73.
3. Ernst Bloch, "Der undiskutierbare Krieg," in his *Durch die Wüste*, 11.
4. Glaser, 166.
5. Jürgen Kuczynski, *Geschichte des Alltags des deutschen Volkes*, Studien 4, 1871–1918 (East Berlin, 1982), 450.
6. As cited in Brennicke and Hembus, 241.
7. *Lichtbild-Bühne*, May 10, 1913.
8. Gert Selle, *Kultur der Sinne und ästhetische Erziehung* (Cologne, 1981), 101.
9. Figures from Toeplitz, 138ff.
10. Ibid., 138.
11. Oskar Kalbus, *Vom Werden deutscher Filmkunst* (Altona-Bahrenfeld, 1935), vol. 1: 21.

CHAPTER 3. THE END OF THE WORLD

1. Fraenkel, 395.
2. Magnus Hirschfeld and Andreas Gaspar, eds., *Sittengeschichte des Ersten Weltkriegs*, reprint of the second, revised edition (Hanau, n.d.), 53.
3. Eisner, 48.
4. Zglinicki, 401.
5. Spiker, 27.

6. Peter Bächlin, *Der Film als Ware* (Basel, 1945), 177.
7. Oscar Geller, "Filmkrankheiten," in *Der Kinematograph*, January 16, 1918.
8. Fraenkel, 81.
9. Curt Moreck, *Sittengeschichte des Kinos* (Dresden, 1926).
10. See also Hirschfeld and Gaspar, 37.
11. Béla Balázs, *Der Film: Werden und Wesen einer neuen Kunst* (Vienna, 1961), 307ff.
12. *Lichtbild-Bühne*, June 14, 1913.
13. *Lichtbild-Bühne: Sonderausgabe 30 Jahre Film* (1924), 28.
14. Guido Seeber in *Filmtechnik—Filmkunst*, 3 (1930).
15. Richard Hamann and Jost Hermand, *Stilkunst um 1900* (East Berlin, 1967), 531.
16. Minutes of a special members' meeting of the Reichsverband deutscher Lichtspiel-theaterbesitzer (Association of German Motion Picture Theater Owners), in *Der Kinematograph*, March 13, 1918.
17. *Der Kinematograph*, March 13, 1918.
18. Heller, 87.
19. Peter Warthmüller, "Paul Wegener—dämonischer Koloss," in Knut Hickethier, ed., *Grenzgänger zwischen Theater und Kino* (Berlin, 1986), 79.
20. Heller, 90.
21. Ibid.
22. As cited in Hans Helmut Prinzler and Enno Patalas, eds., *Lubitsch* (Munich and Lucerne, 1987), 113.
23. Ibid., 114f.
24. As cited in Brennicke and Hembus, 180.

CHAPTER 4. LAY DOWN YOUR ARMS!

1. Egon Jacobsohn, "Neuheiten auf dem Berliner Filmmarkte," in *Der Kinematograph*, January 15, 1919.
2. Harry Kessler, *Tagebücher 1918–1937*, ed. Wolfgang Pfeiffer-Belli (Frankfurt, 1982), 18.
3. Lotte H. Eisner, *Murnau* (Frankfurt, 1979), 190.
4. Jacobsohn, "Neuheiten."
5. As cited in Brennicke and Hembus, 245.
6. Minutes of the board meeting of January 21, 1919, BA/R 109 I/2421.
7. Fritz Lang in an "autobiography," cited here from Michael Töteberg, *Fritz Lang* (Reinbek bei Hamburg, 1985), 18.
8. Siegfried Kracauer, *From Caligari to Hitler: A Psychological History of the German Film* (Princeton University Press, 1947), 82.
9. Kuczynski, *Geschichte*, Studien 5, 30.
10. Mierendorff's call for change appeared in November 1918 as No. 65 in a series of leaflets published by the group Die Dachstube. See *Expressionismus 1910–1923*, exhibition catalogue of the Deutsche Literaturarchiv im Schiller-Nationalmuseum (Marbach, 1960), 261.
11. *Der Kinematograph*, November 20, 1918.
12. Kracauer, 38.
13. Ibid., 37.
14. Ibid., 32.
15. *Film Yearbook 1* (1922–23), *Chronik der Jahre 1908–1923* (Berlin, 1923), 28.
16. Ibid.
17. As cited in Peter Gay, *Die Republik der Aussenseiter* (Frankfurt, 1987), 26.
18. Erich Steingraber, ed., *Deutsche Kunst der 20er und 30er Jahre* (Munich, 1979), 24.
19. As cited in Gay, 27.
20. Kurt Tucholsky, "Wir Negativen," in his *Gesammelte Werke*, eds. Mary Gerold-Tucholsky and Fritz J. Raddatz, vol. 2 (Reinbek, 1975), 52 and 57.

21. Gay, 10.
22. Ibid., 15.
23. Kracauer, 11.
24. Ibid., 52.
25. Eisner, *Dämonische Leinwand*, 75.
26. As cited in Prinzler and Patalas, 107.
27. Frieda Grafe, "Was Lubitsch berührt," in Prinzler and Patalas, 84.
28. Enno Patalas, "Ernst Lubitsch: Eine Lektion in Kino," in Prinzler and Patalas, 80.
29. Stefan Grossmann, "Reinhardt, Ufa und Berlin," in *Das Tage-Buch* 1:32 (August 21, 1920).
30. *Lichtbild-Bühne*, October 9, 1920.
31. Prinzler, in Prinzler and Patalas, 26.
32. Kracauer, 48f.
33. Ibid., 47.
34. Kessler, 108.
35. Ibid., 79.
36. Ibid., 89.
37. Ibid., 94.
38. Prinzler and Patalas, 30.
39. *Film-Kurier*, October 1, 1920.
40. From Paul Eipper's *Tagebuch: Ateliergespräche mit Liebermann und Corinth* (1971), cited here from *Hätte ich das Kino!*, exhibition catalogue of the Deutsche Litaraturarchiv im Schiller-Nationalmuseum (Marbach, 1976), 320f.
41. *Das Tage-Buch* 1:51 (October 1, 1920).
42. *Der Kinematograph*, August 14, 1921.
43. Kessler, 243.

CHAPTER 5. UFA GOES ABROAD

1. Minutes of the executive committee meeting of April 12, 1918, BA/R 109 I/2421.
2. Minutes of the executive committee meeting of June 13, 1918, ibid.
3. Minutes of the executive committee meeting of November 4, 1918, ibid.
4. Minutes of the board meeting of November 5, 1918, ibid.
5. Minutes of the executive committee meeting of December 30, 1919, ibid.
6. Lipschütz, 12.

CHAPTER 6. EARLY MONUMENTALISM

1. Mierendorff's piece was published as vol. 15 of the *Tribüne der Kunst und Zeit* (Berlin, 1920) and is here cited from *Hätte ich das Kino!*, 405.
2. *Reichlichtspiel-Gesetz vom 12. Mai 1920, fur die Praxis erläutert von Dr. jur. Ernst Seeger* (Berlin, 1923), 7.
3. This document is reprinted, without further identification, in the document volume of Mühl-Benninghaus's dissertation, 143ff.
4. As cited in Zglinicki, 409.
5. *Film Yearbook*, 29.
6. Ibid.
7. Ibid., 31.
8. Ibid., 29.
9. Rudolf Oertel, *Filmspiegel* (Vienna, 1941), 129.
10. Ufa had acquired all shares of May-Film in February 1918 but sold them back to Joe May one year later. In the following years May produced independently but was, because of a credit contract, dependent on Ufa. See file at the Ufa-Revisionsabteilung on May-Film, 1918–19, BA/R 109 I/531.
11. *Phoebus-Magazin*, 27 (Berlin, 1926).

12. Kracauer, 48.
13. Kalbus, 44.
14. Curt Riess, as cited in Brennicke and Hembus, 192.
15. Minutes of executive committee meeting of December 30, 1919, BA/R 109 I/2421.
16. Lipschütz, 9.
17. Zglinicki, 402.
18. OMGUS (Office of Military Government for Germany, United States Finance Division, Financial Investigation Section), *Ermittlungen gegen die Deutsche Bank, 1946–47* (Nordlingen, 1985), 45.
19. Ibid.
20. Ibid., 46f.
21. Kessler, 746.
22. Jost Hermand and Frank Trommler, *Die Kultur der Weimarer Republik* (Frankfurt, 1988), 261 (author's italics).
23. See file on the founding of Decla-Bioscop by Ufa, BA R 109 I/122.
24. Kracauer, 35.
25. As cited in Kalbus, 64ff.
26. *Die neue Schaubühne* 2 (1920), 104f.
27. Leopold Schwarzschild, "Die Vertreibung der EFA aus dem Paradies," in *Das Tage-Buch*, 3:46 (November 18, 1922).

CHAPTER 7. THE ALLURE OF DISTANT LANDS

1. Zglinicki, 402.
2. Stümke's article appeared in the evening edition of the *Berliner Tagblatt*, October, 1919; the response in *Der Kinematograph* (1919), 667.
3. Harry Count Kessler, "Die Kinderhölle in Berlin," in his *Künstler und Nationen: Aufsätze und Reden 1899–1933* (Frankfurt, 1988), 214.
4. Ibid., 217.
5. Lipschütz, 9.
6. Ibid.
7. Toeplitz, 211.
8. Gay, 101.
9. Kessler, *Tagebücher*, 215.
10. Ibid., 220.
11. As cited in Gay, 39.
12. Lipschütz, 18.
13. Ibid., 19.
14. Ibid.
15. Ibid., 20.
16. Ibid., 21.
17. Gerhard Lamprecht, *Deutsche Stummfilme*, published by Deutsche Kinemathek e.V. (Berlin, 1968ff.)
18. The Engel and Jhering quotes are cited in Brennicke and Hembus, 61f.
19. Kalbus, 49.
20. Ibid.
21. Kracauer, *From Caligari*, 57.
22. Norbert Jacques, *Im Kaleidoskop der Weltteile* (Berlin, n.d.).
23. Hanns Heinz Ewers, *Von sieben Meeren: Fahrten und Abenteuer* (Berlin, 1928).
24. Ibid., 345.
25. Jacques, 18.

CHAPTER 8. THE DEMOCRATIC DEPARTMENT STORE

1. Hermand and Trommler, 69.
2. Siegfried Kracauer in *Frankfurter Zeitung*, April 4, 1926.

3. Hermand and Trommler, 70.
4. Ibid., 73.
5. Erwin Panofsky, "Stil und Stoff im Film," as cited in Christoph Bignens, *Kinos: Architektur als Marketing* (Zurich, 1988), 19.
6. Thea von Harbou, *Legenden* (Berlin, 1919).
7. Hermand and Trommler, 71.
8. Thomas Nipperdey, *Wie das Bürgertum die Moderne fand* (Berlin, 1988), 37.
9. Eisner, *Dämonische Leinwand*, 51.
10. Kracauer, *From Caligari*, 79.
11. Eisner, *Dämonische Leinwand*, 116.
12. As cited in Kracauer, *From Caligari*, 79.
13. Fritz Lang on July 25, 1964, in *Frankfurter Rundschau*, as cited in Töteberg, 37.
14. Kessler, *Tagebücher*, 185.
15. Norbert Jacques, *Dr. Mabuse, der Spieler* (Munich, 1979), 216.
16. *Das Tage-Buch* 3:1 (January 7, 1922).
17. *Der Kinematograph*, as cited in Brennicke and Hembus, 234.
18. *Das Tage-Buch* 3:5 (February 4, 1922).
19. Herbert Jhering writing in 1921 in *Berliner Börsen-Courier*, as cited in Brennicke and Hembus, 228.
20. Hermand and Trommler, 193 and 196.
21. Ibid., 200.
22. Ibid., 207.
23. Eisner, *Dämonische Leinwand*, 75.
24. Hermand and Trommler, 69.
25. *Phoenix*, 1926, as cited in Hans-Michael Bock, Wolfgang Jacobsen, and Jörg Schöning, eds., *Reinhold Schünzel* (Munich, 1989), 53.
26. Gerhard Schoenberner, "Das Preussenbild im deutschen Film," in Axel Marquardt and Heinz Rathsack, eds., *Preussen im Film* (Reinbek, 1981), 15.
27. Wilhelm von Kampen, "Das 'preussische Beispiel' als Propaganda und politisches Lebensbedürfnis," in Marquardt and Rathsack, 174.
28. Walter von Molo, in *Vorwärts*, 41, 357 (July 31, 1924).
29. *Filmprogramme*, vol. 5: *Die grossen Preussenfilme*, assembled and introduced by Eberhard Mertens (Hildesheim and New York, 1981), vi.
30. Gay, 119.
31. Ibid., 157.
32. *Filmprogramme*, x.
33. Ibid., v.
34. Hans Feld, "Potsdam gegen Weimar oder Wie Otto Gebühr den Siebenjährigen Krieg gewann," in Marquardt and Rathsack, 72.
35. Toeplitz, 232.
36. *Vorwärts* 39:55 (February 2, 1922).
37. *Die Weltbühne* 19:13 (March 29, 1923).
38. *Die Glocke* 9:1 (April 2, 1923).
39. *Filmprogramme* "Fridericus Rex" (Berlin, 1922).

CHAPTER 9. THE BUILDERS' GUILD

1. Erich Pommer, "Geschäftsfilm und künstlerischer Film," in *Der Film* 50 (December 10, 1922).
2. Gay, 131.
3. Mendelsohn and Gropius quotes as cited in ibid., 131.
4. Zglinicki, 343.
5. *Film-Kurier*, May 11, 1920.
6. *Lichtbild-Bühne* (Tagesdienst), May 17, 1923.
7. Lothar Schwaab, "Der wohltemperierte Sonnenaufgang," in Uta Berg-Ganschow

and Wolfgang Jacobsen, eds., . . . *Film* . . . *Stadt* . . . *Kino* . . . *Berlin* (Berlin, 1987), 176.

8. Hans-Michael Bock, "Berliner Ateliers," in Berg-Ganschow and Jacobsen, 179.
9. *Reichsfilmblatt*, December 22, 1926.
10. A. Kosowsky, "Die Berliner Ateliers," in *Film-Kurier*, September 25, 1924.
11. Siegfried Kracauer, "Kaliko-Welt," in his *Das Ornament der Masse* (Frankfurt, 1963), 271ff.
12. *Der Kinematograph*, July 29, 1923.
13. As cited in Gay, 133.
14. Helmut Weihsmann, *Gebaute Illusionen* (Vienna, 1988), 147.
15. Lamprecht, *Deutsche Stummfilme* (1923–26).
16. Frank Warschauer, as cited in Brennicke and Hembus, 231.
17. As cited in Brennicke and Hembus, 220.
18. Kracauer, *From Caligari*, 139.
19. As cited in Brennicke and Hembus, 186.
20. *Berliner Tageblatt* (December 9, 1926), 581.
21. John Russell Taylor, *Die Hitchcock-Biographie* (Munich and Vienna, 1980), 58.
22. Lamprecht, *Deutsche Stummfilme* (1923–26), 504f.
23. Weihsmann, 140.
24. As cited in ibid., 104.
25. Kracauer, *From Caligari*, 76.
26. Ibid., 68n.
27. Eisner, *Murnau*, 90.
28. As cited in ibid., 95.
29. As cited in Weihsmann, 148.
30. As cited in Eisner, *Murnau*, 104.
31. As cited in Weihsmann, 135.
32. Ibid., 127.
33. As cited in ibid., 128.
34. *Film-Kurier*, October 3, 1932; see also Lotte H. Eisner, *Ich hatte einst ein schönes Vaterland* (Heidelberg, 1984), 119.
35. See Klaus Kreimeier, "Der Schlafwandler," in Berg-Ganschow and Jacobsen, 105ff.
36. As cited in Weihsmann, 146.
37. Ibid., 149.
38. Karl Freund, "Die Berufung des Kameramannes," in *Lichtbild-Bühne*, January 23, 1926.
39. Eisner, *Murnau*, 94.
40. Ibid., 94f.
41. As cited in Rolf Hempel, *Carl Mayer* (East Berlin, 1968), 150.
42. Eisner, *Murnau*, 97.
43. Weihsmann, 146.
44. Eisner, *Murnau*, 98.
45. Karl Woermann, *Geschichte der Kunst aller Zeiten und Völker*, vol. 4 (Leipzig, 1927), 488.
46. Gay, 130.
47. As cited in ibid., 131.
48. As cited in Toteberg, 42.
49. F[rieda] G[rafe], "Die Technik als Allegorie," in *Neue Zürcher Zeitung*, August 3, 1968.
50. Facsimile of the script for *Nosferatu* published in Eisner, *Murnau*, 402.
51. Gay, 142.
52. Ibid., 102.
53. See Klaus Kreimeier, "Das Drama und die Formen," in *Friedrich Wilhelm Murnau*,

1888–1988, published in conjunction with an exhibition of the same name (Biele-feld, 1988), 95.

CHAPTER 10. THE AESTHETICS OF THE GRANDIOSE

1. Joseph Roth in *Frankfurter Zeitung*, November 19, 1925.
2. Kracauer, "Kult der Zerstreuung," in his *Das Ornament der Masse*, 315.
3. As cited in Bignens, 26.
4. Dieter Bartetzko, *Illusionen in Stein* (Reinbeck, 1985), 170.
5. See "Fassadenkultur und Materialfilm," in *Reichsfilmblatt*, March 19, 1927.
6. Bartetzko, 160.
7. Ibid., 149 and 157.
8. Figures from *Film Yearbook 1923–25*, 189.
9. Kracauer, *Ornament der Masse*, 315.
10. Ibid., 311.
11. Bartetzko, 170.
12. As cited in Berg-Ganschow and Jacobsen, 30.
13. Brennicke and Hembus, 198.
14. Curt Riess, *Das gab's nur einmal*, vol. 2 (Frankfurt, 1985), 67.
15. *Das Tage-Buch* 6:40 (October 3, 1925).
16. Joseph Roth in *Frankfurter Zeitung*, November 19, 1925.
17. Bartetzko, 147.
18. Ibid., 165.
19. Siegfried Kracauer, "Die kleinen Ladenmädchen gehen ins Kino," in his *Ornament der Masse*, 284.
20. Bartetzko, 165.
21. As cited in ibid., 164.
22. *Reichsfilmblatt*, July 24, 1926.
23. Siegfried Kracauer, "Kult der Zerstreuung," in *Ornament der Masse*, 316.
24. *Reichsfilmblatt*, July 24, 1926.
25. Ibid., March 16, 1929.
26. Berg-Ganschow and Jacobsen, 39f.
27. Kessler, *Tagebücher*, 232f.
28. Ufa's program booklet for *Tartüff* (Berlin, 1926).
29. Ibid.
30. *Der Kinematograph* (1926), 989.
31. *Lichtbild-Bühne*, October 15, 1926.

CHAPTER 11. THE BALANCE AFTER LIQUIDATION

1. Wolfgang Jacobsen, *Erich Pommer* (Berlin, 1989), 55.
2. Stefan Grossmann, "Erich Pommers Sturz," in *Das Tage-Buch* 7:5 (January 30, 1926).
3. Gay, 206.
4. Ibid., 207.
5. Bächlin, 45.
6. Ibid., 47.
7. Spiker, 38.
8. Figures from Bächlin, 50.
9. Spiker, 40.
10. Ibid., 41.
11. Ibid.
12. "Tagebuch der Wirtschaft," in *Das Tage-Buch*, 5:52 (December 27, 1924).
13. See Lipschütz, 11.
14. Benjamin B. Hampton, *History of the American Film Industry* (New York, 1970),

349ff. and 361. Hampton's book was first published in 1931 under the title A *History of the Movies.*

15. Jacobsen, 70.
16. Traub, *Die Ufa,* 60.
17. Lipschütz, 12.
18. Jean-Luc Godard, *Einführung in eine wahre Geschichte des Kinos* (Frankfurt, 1985), 204.
19. As cited in Jacobsen, 76.
20. Spiker, 43.
21. Draft of annual report for the year 1925–26 (appendix to the minutes of Ufa's board meeting of December 10, 1926), BA/R 109 I/2421.
22. Ibid.
23. Ibid.
24. Toeplitz, 395.
25. Zglinicki, 425.
26. See Jacobsen, 75.
27. *Berliner Tageblatt,* 581 (December 9, 1926), 107 (March 4, 1927), 152 (March 31, 1927), and 188 (April 22, 1927). Also, *Das Tage-Buch* 8:14 (April 2, 1927). The article "Am Wrack der Ufa" was written by Leopold Schwarzschild.
28. Minutes of meetings of the executive committee of the Ufa board, March 24, 28, and 29, 1927, BA/R 109 I/2421.
29. Minutes of the executive committee meeting March 29, 1927, ibid.
30. Minutes of the board meeting March 30, 1927, ibid.

CHAPTER 12. MIND AND POWER

1. Heller, 203.
2. *Die Weltbühne,* April 26, 1927.
3. Ibid., May 10, 1927.
4. Toeplitz, 219.
5. Heller, 168.
6. Hugo von Hofmannsthal, "Ersatz für die Träume," in *Das Tage-Buch* 2:22 (June 4, 1921).
7. As cited in Heller, 197.
8. E. G. Lowenthal, "Die Juden im offentlichen Leben," in Werner E. Mosse, ed., *Entscheidungsjahr 1932* (Tübingen, 1965), 53.
9. The firing of Jacob gave rise to attacks on Ufa in the press and continued to pre-occupy the management and the board throughout 1928. See, for example, minutes of the executive committee meeting June 21, 1928. BA/R 109 I/2421.
10. See Lowenthal, 72.
11. Ibid., 52.
12. Ibid., 64f.
13. As cited in *Hätte ich das Kino!,* 222.
14. Ibid., 229.
15. Ibid., 235.
16. Carl Zuckmayer, *Als wär's ein Stück von mir* (Frankfurt, 1966), 439.
17. As cited in *Hätte ich das Kino!,* 179.
18. Ibid., 180f.
19. The controversy between Hauptmann and Ufa is documented in ibid., 262ff.
20. As cited in ibid., 171f.
21. Julius Sternheim, "Der Filmautor—gestern und morgen," in *Das Tage-buch* 1:35 (September 11, 1920).
22. As cited in *Hätte ich das Kino!,* 216.
23. Ibid., 217.
24. Ibid., 223f.

25. Ibid., 237.
26. See Jacobsen, 81f.
27. As cited in *Hätte ich das Kino!*, 244.
28. Heller, 192f.
29. Reinhold Keiner, *Thea von Harbou und der deutsche Film bis 1933* (Hildesheim, 1984), 36.
30. Ibid., 35.
31. As cited in ibid., 41.
32. See the Harbou bibliography in ibid., 248ff.
33. Ibid., 71.
34. See Arthur Maria Rabenalt's piece and Hans Feld's statements in the appendix in ibid., 277ff.
35. As cited in ibid., 119.
36. Hempel, 91.
37. Ibid., 68.
38. Ibid., 75.
39. Ibid., 77.
40. Ibid., 107.
41. Ibid., 83.
42. Heller, 209.
43. Cf. Lamprecht, *Deutsche Stummfilme* (1923–26), 198.
44. As cited in Hempel, 84.
45. Ibid., 86f.
46. Eisner, *Murnau*, 239.
47. Ibid., 223 and 247.
48. Jannings, 144.
49. As cited in Hempel, 88.
50. Herbert Jhering in *Berliner Börsen-Courier*, December 24, 1924.
51. As cited in *Hätte ich das Kino!*, 368.
52. Cf. Hempel, 91.

Chapter 13. Was There an Ufa Style?

1. Transcripts no. 13 (management meeting, April 22, 1927) and no. 24 (May 5, 1927), BA/R 109 I/1026a. The quotations that follow are taken from transcripts nos. 32 and 48.
2. Selle, 161.
3. Ibid., 163.
4. Cited in ibid., 169.
5. Ibid.
6. Roland Barthes, "Die Römer im Film," in his *Mythen des Alltags* (Frankfurt, 1964), 46 and 43.
7. Barthes, "Strip-tease," *Mythen des Alltags*, 68f.
8. Barthes, "Das Gesicht der Garbo," *Mythen des Alltags*, 73.
9. Ibid., 71f.
10. Carlo Mierendorff, "Die Romantik des Kapitalismus," in *Theorie des Kinos: Ideologie der Traumfabrik*, ed. Karsten Witte (Frankfurt, 1972), 302f.
11. Enno Patalas, *Stars: Geschichte der Filmidole* (Frankfurt and Hamburg, 1967), 9f.
12. As citte in *Hätte ich das Kino!*, 296.
13. Patalas, *Stars*, 50.
14. The *Lexikon zum deutschsprachigen Film*, ed. Hans-Michael Bock and published by Cine-Graph (Munich, 1984ff.) lists *So sind die Männer*, directed by Georg Jacoby and produced by Europäische Film-Allianz GmbH, as Dietrich's first film. However, the premiere did not take place until November 29, 1923; that is, several weeks after *Tragödie der Liebe*.

15. Patalas, *Stars*, 50.
16. Herbert Holba, Günther Knorr, and Peter Spiegel, *Reclams deutsches Filmlexikon* (Stuttgart, 1984), 68.
17. As cited in *Hätte ich das Kino!*, 277.
18. Rudolf Arnheim, "Helden fürs Herz," in his *Kritiken und Aufsätze zum Film* (Munich and Vienna, 1977), 116.
19. Cf. *Hätte ich das Kino!*, 280.
20. As cited in Jacobsen, 74.
21. Ibid.
22. *Fritz Lang—Metropolis*, publication of the Münchner Filmmuseum and the Münchner Filmzentrum e.V. (Munich, 1988), 3.
23. Kracauer, *From Caligari*, 164.
24. George W.F. Hallgarten, *Hitler, Reichswehr und Industrie* (Frankfurt, 1962), 66.
25. Kracauer, *From Caligari*, 163.
26. As cited in *Fritz Lang—Metropolis*, 27.
27. *Presseheft der Ufa zu "Metropolis"* (Berlin, 1927).
28. From Erich Kettelhut's unpublished memoirs as cited in *Fritz Lang—Metropolis*, 19.
29. Günther Rittau in *Deutsche Filmwoche*, January 28, 1927.
30. See Otto Hunte in *Presseheft der Ufa zu "Metropolis"* and Günther Rittau in *Fritz Lang—Metropolis*, 24.
31. As cited in Jacobsen, 74.
32. As cited in *Fritz Lang—Metropolis*, 31.
33. Ernst Bloch, *Erbschaft dieser Zeit* (Frankfurt, 1979), 66f.
34. Brennicke and Hembus, 141.
35. *Presseheft der Ufa.*
36. Transcripts 3 and 4 (April 7 and 8, 1927), BA/R 109 I/1026a.
37. Enno Patalas, "Metropolis in/aus Trümmern," in *Fritz Lang—Metropolis*, 17.
38. Transcript 48 (June, 3, 1927), BA/R 109 I/1026a.

CHAPTER 14. THE GENERAL IN CIVVIES

1. Otto Kriegk, *Hugenberg* (Leipzig, 1932), 36.
2. Willi A. Boelcke, ed., *Krupp und die Hohenzollern in Dokumenten* (Frankfurt, 1970), 187.
3. Peter de Mendelssohn, *Zeitungsstadt Berlin* (Berlin, 1959), 87.
4. Klaus Wernecke and Peter Heller, *Der vergessene Führer* (Hamburg, 1982), 95.
5. Riess, 26.
6. Ibid., 25.
7. This description of Ufa's restructuring is based primarily on Lipschütz, Spiker, and Traub, *Die Ufa*, and the material cited in their works.
8. As cited in Wernecke and Heller, 136.
9. Transcript 1 (management meeting, April 5, 1927), BA/R 109 I/1026a.
10. The documents in the document volume of Mühl-Benninghaus's dissertation, esp. 171–80, are especially valuable.
11. Transcript 80 (July 12, 1927), BA/R 109 I/1026a.
12. Transcript 92 (July 26, 1927), ibid.
13. Transcript 6 (April 11, 1927), ibid.
14. Transcript 64 (June 23, 1927), ibid.
15. Transcript 105 (August 10, 1927), ibid.
16. See Wernecke and Heller, 210, n. 492.
17. See Toeplitz, 395ff.
18. Transcript 58 (June 16, 1927), BA/R 109 I/1026a.
19. Kessler, *Tagebücher*, 557f.
20. Transcript 85 (July 18, 1927), BA/R 109 I/1026a.

21. Transcripts 87 and 88 (July 20 and 21, 1927), ibid.
22. Tucholsky, 5:361.
23. Transcript 15 (April 25, 1927), BA/R 109 I/1026a.
24. Transcript 20 (April 20, 1927), ibid.
25. Tucholsky, 5:217.
26. Transcript 60 (June 18, 1927), BA/R 109 I/1026a.
27. Transcript 15 (June 25, 1927), ibid.
28. Transcript 74 (July 5, 1927), ibid.
29. Transcript 98 (August 2, 1927), ibid.
30. Transcript 48 (June 3, 1927), ibid.
31. As cited in Brennicke and Hambus, 173f.
32. Rudolf Schwarzkopf, "Unser Ziel und unser Weg," in *Film und Volk* 1, no. 1:5.
33. Willi Münzenberg, "Film und Propaganda," in *Film und Volk* 2, nos. 9/10:5.
34. *Film und Volk* 1, nos. 3/4:18ff.
35. Ibid., 2, nos. 11/12:16.
36. Ibid., nos. 9/10:9.
37. Kracauer, *From Caligari*, 176.
38. As cited in Brennicke and Hembus, 202.
39. Ilya Ehrenburg, *Menschen—Jahre—Leben* (Munich, 1962), 662ff.
40. Transcript of the management meeting of March 30, 1928, BA/R 109 I/1026a. The political attitude under Hugenberg is also revealed in the conflict between Fritz Lang and Ufa's board. In June 1928, in connection with the production contract of *Woman in the Moon*, the board declared that Ufa had "the right to object to the manuscript on the basis of political, religious, and moral considerations." Supplement I to the minutes of the executive committee of the board, June 21, 1928, BA/R 109 I/2421.
41. See Jacobsen, 83.
42. As cited in ibid., 144.
43. In an article for *Film-Kurier*, 1928, as cited in Jacobsen, 88. See also Mühl-Benninghaus, document volume, 183.
44. In an article for *Film-Kurier*, as cited in Jacobsen, 86f.
45. Kessler, *Tagebücher*, 599.
46. As cited in Wernecke and Heller, 144. See also BA/R 109 I/1026b.

CHAPTER 15. GERMAN MUSICALITY

1. Hallgarten, 91.
2. Hugenberg in his inaugural address as new party chairman of the DNVP; cited in Wernecke and Heller, 146.
3. As cited in Hans Richter, *Der Kampf um den Film* (Frankfurt, 1979), 74.
4. Ibid., 72. These collective needs of the movie public made it difficult to accomplish Ufa's "spiritual restructuring," as it was called in nationalistic circles. An internal paper of the DNVP reports: "Spiritual restructuring did not progress as rapidly as economic restructuring. We will simply have to experiment. If Ufa showed only films that live up even halfway to your . . . and my standards, the Ufa theaters would be empty, because the general public unfortunately has no interest in such films. All we can do is to periodically sneak in a better film and the rest of the time show popular movies. . . . Educating the public to appreciate better films will be an extremely slow and difficult process." Mühl-Benninghaus, document volume, 197.
5. Hermand and Trommler, 162.
6. Richter, 74.
7. Hermand and Trommler, 120.
8. A. Kraszna-Krausz in *Filmtechnik—Filmkunst* 7 (1927).
9. See Bloch, *Erbschaft der Zeit*, 66.

10. *Der Lehrfilm*, published by the cultural division of Universum-Film AG (Berlin, n.d. [1919]), 75.
11. "Mustervorführung von Lehrfilmen der Kultur-Abteilung der Ufa in Hamburg am 6., 8., und 9. Dezember 1919" (promotional pamphlet without pagination issued by Ufa's cultural division).
12. Ernst Moritz Häufig in *Die Weltbühne*, cited in Brennicke and Hembus, 233.
13. *25 Jahre Wochenschau der Ufa*, published by Ufa-Lehrschau in collaboration with the publicity department of Universum-Film AG and Ufa-Wochenschau (Berlin, 1939), 7.
14. Ibid., 19.
15. Transcript no. 7 (management meeting, April 12, 1927), BA/R 109 I/1026a.
16. Richter, 95.
17. Traub, *Die Ufa*, 82.
18. Ibid.
19. Ibid., 82f.
20. Spiker, 50.
21. Traub, *Die Ufa*, 84.
22. Ibid., 85. The contract between Ufa and Klangfilm of April 8, 1929, stipulated that Ufa could lease two stationary and one mobile sound-film recording unit for a fee of 4,500 Reichmarks per month, with a lease period of four years, after which Ufa could buy the equipment "under especially favorable conditions." Important for Ufa's distribution policy was Klangfilm's permission, included in the contract, that Ufa could show films not made with Klangfilm equipment. This clause also applied, without restrictions, to films made by Paramount and MGM, which were run in German cinemas "on the basis of existing contracts." (See Mühl-Benninghaus, document volume, 212f.)
23. Ibid., 85.
24. Jacobsen, 90.
25. Figures from Brennicke and Hembus, 257.
26. The figures are derived from material in Traub, *Die Ufa*, and in Spiker.
27. Hugenberg in a programmatic article in *Lokal-Anzeiger* (August 1928), as cited in Wernecke and Heller, 144.
28. Helmut Heiber, *Die Republik von Weimar* (Munich, 1966), 206.
29. Kessler, *Tagebücher*, 630f.
30. Traub, *Die Ufa*, 78.
31. Figures from Spiker, 55.
32. Traub, *Die Ufa*, 73.
33. Ibid., 74.
34. Ufa's management was less restrained. In two confidential memos, dated May 22, 1928, Grieving noted that two lighting crew members working in Tempelhof and four stagehands working as foremen in Neubabelsberg had participated in the strike and should "be fired immediately." (See Mühl-Benninghaus, document volume, 200.)

CHAPTER 16. REVUE AND DECLINE

1. Heiber, *Die Republik*, 226.
2. Ibid., 220.
3. Cf. Jacobsen, 110.
4. Heiber, *Die Republik*, 231.
5. Rudolf Arnheim, "Hans Albers," in his *Kritiken und Aufsätze*, 292.
6. Ibid., 293.
7. Report in the DNVP publication *Unsere Partei*, as cited in Wernecke and Heller, 167.
8. Ibid., 169.
9. Hallgarten, 42.

10. Toeplitz, 733.
11. Joe Hembus and Christa Bandmann, *Klassiker des deutschen Tonfilms 1930–1960* (Munich, 1980), 18.
12. Toeplitz, 733.
13. As cited in Jacobsen, 95.
14. Both Sternberg and Jannings claim credit in their memoirs for having "discovered" Marlene Dietrich in a production of Georg Kaiser's *Zwei Krawatten*. Of course, Sternberg also claims to have been the sole author of the screenplay for *The Blue Angel*, denying any collaboration with Zuckmayer and Vollmoeller. (See Josef von Sternberg, *Ich, Josef von Sternberg* [Velber near Hannover, 1967], 156.)
15. Robert Siodmak, *Zwischen Berlin und Hollywood*, ed. Hans C. Blumenberg (Munich, 1980), 44.
16. As cited in Jacobsen, 99.
17. Kracauer, *From Caligari*, 218.
18. As cited in Toeplitz, 734.
19. As cited in Jacobsen, 98.
20. Ibid., 99f.
21. Traub, *Die Ufa*, 95.
22. *Kino* 4 (January 1931):58.
23. Cf. Spiker, 69.
24. Ibid., 77.
25. Traub, *Die Ufa*, 89.
26. Spiker, 71.
27. Ludwig Klitzsch in his radio talk "Bekenntnis zum deutschen Film" in July 1932, cited in Spiker, 72.
28. Spiker, 73.
29. Spiker's reconstruction of the Spio Plan is reconstructed from commentaries in Hugenberg's *Kinematograph*. See ibid., 77.
30. Figures from Toeplitz, 731.
31. Traub, *Die Ufa*, 80.
32. *Mitteilungen des Deutschen Städtetages* 8 (1932).
33. Lipschütz, 17.
34. Traub, *Die Ufa*, 91.
35. Figures from Toeplitz, 732.
36. Siodmak, 44ff.
37. Toeplitz, 735.
38. Jacobsen, 107.
39. Heiber, 235.
40. Hallgarten, 94.
41. As cited in Jacobsen, 107.
42. Bloch, *Erbschaft dieser Zeit*, 107, 114, 112, and 386.
43. Toeplitz, 741.
44. *Der Kinematograph*, July 20, 1932.
45. As cited in Kracauer, 550f.
46. Ibid., 551. In a confidential note of April 12, 1932, to Klitzsch, Correll went beyond this and argued that Ufa-Film should, in order to enhance its export potential, adopt international standards and take into account the needs of non-German audiences.

    To achieve this it will be necessary to accommodate to the wishes and demands of other countries and races. We will therefore sometimes have to tailor our subject matter to a foreign mentality and work with foreign actors. The repeatedly voiced accusations that we buy foreign material and employ foreign, non-Germanic actors have to be countered by pointing out that we are obliged to do so for the sake of greater profitability and, indeed, from a broader national point of view.

    (Mühl-Benninghaus, document volume, 240.)

47. Alfred Bauer, *Deutscher Spielfilm-Almanach 1929–1950* (Berlin, 1965), 143.
48. Joseph Goebbels, *Vom Kaiserhof zur Reichskanzlei* (Munich, 1934), 67.
49. Kessler, *Tagebücher*, 745f.
50. Transcripts 882 (management meeting, January 6, 1933), 885 (January 13, 1933), and 888 (January 25, 1933), BA/R 109 I/1029a.
51. Kessler, *Tagebücher*, 746.
52. Transcript 889 (management meeting, January 31, 1933), BA/R 109 I/1029a.

PART TWO

Chapter 17. Rituals of Death

1. Goebbels, 258.
2. *Illustrierter Film-Kurier*, no. 1920 (1933).
3. Goebbels, 236f. I quote from the politically edited popular edition of Goebbels's journals, which appeared in 1934, because its language accurately reflects the tone of Nazi propaganda.
4. Joachim Fest, *Hitler—eine Biographie* (Frankfurt, 1973), 699f.
5. Kalbus, *Vom Werden*, vol. 2, 122.
6. Ibid., 123.
7. Ibid., 120.
8. Bauer, 190.
9. Goebbels, 294, and Kalbus, *Vom Werden*, vol. 2, 119.
10. Goebbels, 282.
11. Ibid., 263.
12. Riess, *Das gab's nur einmal*, vol. 2, 207ff.
13. As cited in Gerd Albrecht, "Filmpolitik im Dritten Reich," in *Der Spielfilm im Dritten Reich* (Arbeitsseminar der Westdeutschen Kurzfilmtage Oberhausen, 1966), 39.
14. Wernecke and Heller, 187.
15. Goebbels, 289.
16. Barkhausen, 196.
17. Transcript 890 (management meeting, February 3, 1933), BA/R 109 I/1029a.
18. Transcript 900 (management meeting, March 10, 1933), ibid.
19. Transcript 905 (management meeting, March 29, 1933), ibid.
20. Ibid.
21. As cited in Joseph Wulf, *Theater und Film im Dritten Reich: Eine Dokumentation* (Gütersloh, 1964), 390f.
22. Habakuk Traber and Elmar Weingarten, eds. *Verdrängte Musik* (Berlin, 1987), 259.
23. Hans-Michael Bock, ed., *Cine-Graph: Lexikon zum deutschsprachigen Film* (Munich, 1984ff.), article on Robert Liebmann.
24. Riess, *Das gab's nur einmal*, vol. 2, 214f.
25. In a television film broadcast by ARD, John Pommer gave a very similar account of these events. "Das Kabinett des Erich Pommer," by Hans-Michael Bock and Ute Schneider, aired August 17, 1989.
26. Jacobsen, 121.
27. Heinrich Fraenkel and Roger Manvell, *Goebbels: eine Biographie* (Cologne and Berlin, 1960), 204–5. The authors base their statement on an account by Boris von Borresholm and Karena Niehoff.
28. Töteberg, 78.
29. Eisner, *Ich hatte einst ein schönes Vaterland*, 127.
30. Kracauer, *From Caligari*, 272.
31. Kessler, *Tagebücher*, 755.

32. As cited in Frank Grube and Gerhard Richter, *Alltag im Dritten Reich* (Hamburg, 1982), 66.
33. Cf. Bauer.
34. Toeplitz, 1190.
35. Ufa's program for *Flüchtlinge*, 1933.
36. Kalbus, *Vom Werden*, vol. 2, 104.
37. As cited in Wernecke and Heller, 187.
38. Ibid., 189.
39. Ibid., 190.
40. Ibid., 194.

Chapter 18. Converting Ufa

1. Marian Kolb, "Die Lösung des Filmproblems im nationalsozialistischen Staate," as cited in Bredow and Zurek, 151.
2. The *Illustrierte Film-Kurier* printed Goebbels's speech in non-verbatim form in its April 27, 1933, issue; here cited from Wulf, 268.
3. Documented in, among other places, Curt Belling's *Der Film in Staat und Partei* (Berlin, 1936), 31ff.
4. Spiker, 98.
5. Kurt Wolf, dissertation, "Entwicklung und Neugestaltung der deutschen Filmwirtschaft seit 1933," partially reprinted in Bredow and Zurek, 155ff.
6. Figures from ibid.
7. Management report for fiscal 1932–33 prepared for the executive committee of Ufa's board October 25, 1933, BA/R 109 I/2424.
8. Letter from management to Dr. Emil Georg von Stauss, vice chair of the board, November 23, 1933, ibid.
9. As cited in Spiker, 110.
10. Ibid.
11. From an internal memo by the production department, from which Klitzsch and Lehmann quoted extensively to supplement the fiscal report of August 10, 1934; BA/R 109 I/2420.
12. Figures from Spiker, 143.
13. Production contracts included in Supplement III to the annual report for 1932–33; cf. fn. 48.
14. *Frankfurter Zeitung*, September 27, 1936.
15. Transcript 1033 (management meeting, October 10, 1934), BA/R 109 I/1029c.
16. The data in the following paragraphs are taken from a memo prepared by the Ufa management to inform the board about the press campaign the Food Ministry was waging against Ufa, BA/R 109 I/2424.
17. *Rheinisch-Westfälische Filmzeitung*, January 9, 1937.
18. Spiker, 134.

Chapter 19. The Censorship Machine

1. Spiker, 106.
2. Act on the Establishment of a Temporary Film Guild, par. 3; cf. *Der Kinematograph*, July 26, 1933.
3. *Lichtbild-Bühne*, February 3, 1934.
4. Supplement to the fiscal report of August 10, 1934; cf. fn. 52.
5. Management report for the fiscal year 1934–35, BA/R 109 I/2420.
6. Wolfgang Theis in Bock, article on Reinhold Schünzel.
7. Transcript 1047 (management meeting, December 11, 1934), BA/R 109 I/1029c.
8. Bandmann and Hembus, 102.
9. Helga Belach, ". . . als die Traumfabrik kriegswichtig wurde," in *Wir tanzen um die*

Welt: Deutsche Revuefilme 1933–1945, ed. Helga Belach (Munich and Vienna, 1979), 139ff.
10. Ibid., 152.
11. Ibid., 142.
12. Rökk, *Herz mit Paprika* (Berlin, 1974), 132.
13. Ibid., 157.

CHAPTER 20. BACCHIC CHAOS

1. Wilhelm Reich, *Massenpsychologie des Faschismus* (n.p., n.d.), reprint of the 2nd edn., 106.
2. Hans Dieter Schäfer, *Das gespaltene Bewusstsein* (Frankfurt, 1981), 149.
3. See illus. 15 in Schäfer. The ad is for Rühmann's film *Die Umwege des schönen Karl*, directed and produced by Carl Froelich (1937–38).
4. Schäfer, 154.
5. Ibid.
6. Axel Eggebrecht, in *Die Weltbühne*, November 1, 1927.
7. Selle, 175 and 186.
8. Karsten Witte, "Gehemmte Schaulust: Momente des deutschen Revuefilms," in *Wir tanzen um die Welt*, 7.
9. As cited in ibid., 11.
10. Ibid., 21.
11. Ibid., 49.
12. Selle, 175.
13. Transcript 1350 (management meeting, January 17, 1939), BA/R 109 I/1033b.
14. This presentation of the facts is based on Schäfer, 168ff.
15. *Berliner Tageblatt*, January 2, 1937.
16. As cited in Fraenkel and Manvell, 272f.
17. George L. Mosse, "Schönheit ohne Sinnlichkeit," in *zeitmitschrift*, special issue "1937" (Düsseldorf, n.d.), 98.
18. Ibid., 108.
19. Transcript 1053 (management meeting, January 15, 1935), BA/R 109 I/1029c.
20. Heinz Boberach, ed., *Meldungen aus dem Reich 1938–1945: Die geheimen Lageberichte des Sicherheitsdienstes der SS*, vol. 2 (Herrsching, 1984), 273 and 271.
21. Schäfer, 184.
22. As cited in ibid., 179.
23. Fraenkel and Manvell, 230.
24. Helmut Heiber, *Joseph Goebbels* (Munich, 1965), 251.
25. Ibid., 253.

CHAPTER 21. ARCHITECTURE, FILM, AND DEATH

1. As cited in *zeitmitschrift*, 93.
2. Susan Sontag, "Fascinating Fascism," in her *Under the Sign of Saturn* (New York, 1980), 91.
3. Goebbels, 306f.
4. As cited in Bartetzko, 88.
5. Schäfer, 183f.
6. As cited in Bartetzko, 63.
7. Walter Benjamin, "Das Kunstwerk im Zeitalter seiner technischen Reproduzierbarkeit," in his *Schriften*, vol. 1 (Frankfurt, 1955), 395 and 397.
8. Joseph Peter Stern, " 'Der teure Kauf': Opferbereitschaft und Erlösungshoffnung," in *zeitmitschrift*, 89.
9. Albert Speer, *Erinnerungen* (Frankfurt and Berlin, 1969), 28, 174, and 175.
10. Bartetzko, 79.

11. Speer, 49.
12. Weihsmann, 177.
13. Bartetzko, 267.
14. Ibid., 270.
15. Ibid., 55.
16. Speer, 75.
17. Ibid., 151f.
18. Bartetzko, 148.
19. As cited in Speer, 71f.
20. Illustration in Anne Paech, *Kino zwischen Stadt und Land* (Marburg, 1985), 75.
21. Bartetzko, 171.

CHAPTER 22. UFA UNDER STATE OWNERSHIP

1. Ufa program 1937–38, p. 4, in status reports, BA/R 55/651.
2. Riess, *Das gab's nur einmal*, vol. 3, 39.
3. Minutes of the meeting of the executive committee of the board, December 14, 1936, BA/R 109 I 2420.
4. Figures from Spiker, 120.
5. Ibid., 172.
6. Ibid.
7. As cited in ibid., 174f.
8. Figures from ibid., 174f.
9. As cited in *Stationen der Moderne*, exhibition catalogue of the Berlinische Galerie (Berlin, 1988), 280.
10. This and the following quotes are taken from Goebbels's speech as it appears in Bredow and Zurek, 181ff.
11. Boberach, 71.
12. Fritz Hippler, *Betrachtungen zum Filmschaffen* (Berlin, 1942), 5f.
13. Ibid., 86.
14. Ibid., 49.

CHAPTER 23. SPORT ON THE WARSHIP

1. Anton Kaes, *Deutschlandbilder: Die Wiederkehr der Geschichte als Film* (Munich, 1987), 12.
2. A copy of Correll's letter is contained in the document volume of Mühl-Benninghaus's dissertation, cf. fn. 1 of Part II.
3. Transcript 1094 (management meeting, July 12, 1935), BA/R 109 I/1030b.
4. Transcript 1091 (management meeting, July 2, 1935), ibid.
5. Transcript 1079 (management meeting, May 14, 1935), ibid.
6. Barkhausen, 195.
7. *Lichtbild-Bühne*, April 29, 1933.
8. Barkhausen, 201.
9. Transcript 1322 (management meeting, May 20, 1938), BA/R 109 I/1033a.
10. Barkhausen, 204.
11. Boberach, vol. 3, 690.
12. Richard Taylor, *Film Propaganda* (London and New York, 1979), 164.
13. *25 Jahre Wochenschau der Ufa*, 33.
14. Ibid., 41.
15. Hilmar Hoffmann, *"Und die Fahne führt uns in die Ewigkeit": Propaganda im NS-Film* (Frankfurt, 1988), 113.
16. Oskar Kalbus, *Pioniere des Kulturfilms* (Karlsruhe, 1956), 27.
17. Hartmut Bitomsky, "Der Kotflügel eines Mercedes-Benz: Nazikulturfilme," pt. 1, in *Filmkritik* 322 (1983):456.

18. Traub, *Die Ufa*, 112.
19. Hoffmann, 142.
20. Bitomsky, 451.
21. Boberach, vol. 2, 1578f.

CHAPTER 24. THE POISONED KITCHEN

1. Figures from Bandmann and Hembus, 254, and Boberach, vol. 2, 116.
2. Boberach, vol. 2, 116.
3. As cited in Bandmann and Hembus, 254.
4. Boberach, vol. 2, 116.
5. Erwin Leiser, *"Deutschland, erwache!"*: *Propaganda im Film des Dritten Reiches* (Reinbek, 1968).
6. As cited in Wulf, *Theater und Film*, 348.
7. As cited in Toeplitz, 1201.
8. As cited in Friedrich P. Kahlenberg, "Preussen als Filmsujet in der Propagandasprache der NS-Zeit," in Marquart and Rathsack, 150.
9. As cited in Bock, article on Karl Ritter.
10. As cited in Joseph Wulf, *Literatur und Dichtung im Dritten Reich* (Gütersloh, 1963), 320.
11. As cited in Leiser, 26.
12. As cited in Bock, article on Karl Ritter.
13. Julian Petley in Bock, article on Karl Ritter.
14. As cited in Leiser, 46.
15. Ibid., 45.
16. Dorothea Hollstein, *"Jud Süss" und die Deutschen* (Frankfurt, 1983), 45f.
17. Francis Courtade and Pierre Cadars, *Geschichte des Films im Dritten Reich* (Munich and Vienna, 1975), 124.
18. Toeplitz, 1201.
19. Cf. Bock, article on Karl Ritter.
20. Appendix 9 to transcript of the meeting of the board committee on business affairs, February 18, 1938, BA/R 109 I/2420.
21. *Denkschrift Hitlers zum Vierjahresplan 1936*, excerpted in Reinhard Kühnl, *Der deutsche Faschismus in Quellen und Dokumenten* (Cologne, 1980), 287.
22. "Das Ufa-Programm 1937–38," 20, in status reports, BA/R 55/651.
23. Friedrich P. Kahlenberg, " 'Starke Herzen': Quellen-Notizen über die Produktion eines Ufa-Films im Jahre 1937," in Kraft Wetzel and Peter Hagemann, *Zensur: Verbotene deutsche Filme 1933–45* (Berlin, 1982), 121.
24. Kalbus, *Vom Werden*, vol. 2, 104.
25. Leiser, 35.
26. Rudolf Oertel, *Macht und Magie des Films* (Vienna, 1959), as cited in Karlheinz Wendtland, *Geliebter Kinotopp—Jahrgang 1939 und 1940* (Berlin, n.d.), 157.
27. Toeplitz, 1209f.
28. Journal entry by Goebbels for October 17, 1936, as cited in Jörg Schöning, *Reinhold Schünzel: Schauspieler und Regisseur* (Munich, 1989), 60.
29. As cited in Schöning, 61.
30. Arthur Maria Rabenalt, *Film im Zwielicht* (Hildesheim and New York, 1978), 43, 53f., and 56.
31. *Lichtbild-Bühne*, July 16, 1937.
32. According to the magazine *Der Deutsche Film*, as cited in Wendtland, *Geliebter Kinotopp—Jahrgang 1937 und 1938*, 193.
33. Rabenalt, 44.
34. As cited in Wendtland, (1937–38):195.
35. As cited in Bock, article on Werner Hochbaum.

CHAPTER 25. SOLDIERS OF ART?

1. Ernst Bloch, *Das Prinzip Hoffnung*, vol. 1 (Frankfurt, 1967), 471.
2. Patalas, *Stars*, 107.
3. Transcript 1090 (management meeting, June 28, 1935), BA/R 109 I/1030b.
4. Appendix 7 of the annual report 1934–35 of August 28, 1935, BA/R 109 I/2420.
5. Ibid.
6. Kalbus, *Pioniere*, 110.
7. As cited in Joachim Cadenbach, *Hans Albers* (Frankfurt, 1983), 15.
8. Hans C. Blumenberg in *Der Spiegel*, 1989, no. 34.
9. As cited in Bock, article on Heinz Rühmann.
10. Ibid.
11. Herbert Holba, Günter Knorr, and Peter Spiegel, *Reclams deutsches Filmlexikon* (Stuttgart, 1984), 104.
12. See Bock, article on Willy Birgel.
13. Walther Kiaulehn, *Berlin: Schicksal einer Weltstadt* (Munich and Berlin, 1958), 409.
14. Cf. Cadenbach, 88.
15. As cited in Bock, article on Werner Krauss.
16. Hoffmann, 210.
17. Carla Rhode, "Leuchtende Sterne?," in *Wir tanzen um die Welt*, 123.
18. Ibid., 122.
19. Ibid.
20. Patalas, *Stars*, 95.
21. Cornelia Zumkeller, *Zarah Leander* (Munich, 1988), 100.
22. Elisabeth Läfer, *Skeptiker des Lichts: Douglas Sirk und seine Filme* (Frankfurt, 1987), 55.
23. As cited in Bock, article on Detlef Sierck.
24. As cited in Wetzel and Hagemann, 90.

CHAPTER 26. UFA GOES TO WAR

1. Cf. Toeplitz, 1218.
2. Cf. *Wir tanzen um die Welt*, 156.
3. Transcript 1044 (management meeting, November 27, 1934), BA/R 109 I/1029c.
4. Rökk, 155f.
5. Leni Riefenstahl, *Memoiren* (Munich and Hamburg, 1987), 349f.
6. Bauer, 471.
7. Boberach, vol. 2, 334.
8. Ibid., vol. 3, 478.
9. Ibid., 527.
10. Ibid., vol. 2, 336.
11. Hans Richter, "Der politische Film," in Karsten Witte, ed., *Theorie des Kinos: Ideologiekritik der Traumfabrik* (Frankfurt, 1972), 71.
12. Ibid.
13. Ibid., 73; cf. also Kracauer, *From Caligari*, 275f.
14. Figures from Barkhausen, 214; Traub, *Die Ufa*, 110, mentions an increase from 900 to 1,900 copies.
15. Kracauer, *From Caligari*, 291.
16. Barkhausen, 206 and 212.
17. As cited in ibid., 227.
18. Kracauer, *From Caligari*, 305.
19. As cited in ibid., 299.
20. Barkhausen, 227.
21. As cited in ibid., 219.
22. Hoffmann, 214.

23. *25 Jahre Wochenschau der Ufa*, 47.
24. Kracauer, *From Caligari*, 275ff.
25. Ibid., 276.
26. As cited in ibid., 304.
27. Cf. Schäfer, 189.
28. Boberach, vol. 4, 1132.
29. Schäfer, 193 and 194.
30. Ibid., 195.
31. Boberach, vol. 4, 977.
32. Ibid., 978.
33. Rabenalt, 41.
34. As cited in Wendtland (1941–42), 81.
35. Ibid., 82.
36. As cited in *Wir tanzen um die Welt*, 182f.
37. Cf. Ibid., 225.
38. As cited in ibid., 179f.
39. Boberach, vol. 6, 2049.
40. Ibid., 2007.
41. *Filmwelt*, 1941, as cited in Bandmann and Hembus, 140f.
42. Hippler, 34.
43. Figures from *Wir tanzen um die Welt*, 184f.
44. Karsten Witte, "Revue als montierte Handlung," in *Wir tanzen um die Welt*, 228.
45. See Wendtland (1941–42), 103.
46. Boberach, vol. 14, 5445.

CHAPTER 27. SURVIVAL IS ALL THAT MATTERS

1. Boberach, vol. 12, 4764f.
2. As cited in *Wir tanzen um die Welt*, 179f.
3. Figures from Spiker, 196f.
4. Ibid., 195.
5. Ibid., 200.
6. Ibid., 210.
7. Ibid., 211.
8. Traub, *Die Ufa*, 113.
9. As cited in Spiker, 196.
10. Figures from Traub, *Die Ufa*, 157ff.
11. Ibid., 116.
12. Spiker, 227.
13. Ibid., 30.
14. Ibid., 294.
15. As cited in Wulf, *Literatur und Dichtung*, 321.
16. Boberach, vol. 13, 4889.
17. John Russell Taylor, *Fremde im Paradies* (Berlin, 1984), 75.
18. Transcripts 1051 (management meeting, January 8, 1935), and 1055 (January 22, 1935), BA/R 109 I/1029c.
19. Bock, article on Günther Stapenhorst.
20. Riess, *Das gab's nur einmal*. vol. 3, 202.
21. Transcript 1087 (management meeting, June 17, 1935), BA/R 109 I/1030b.
22. Bock, article on Robert Dorsay.
23. Cf. *Von Babelsberg nach Hollywood: Filmemigranten aus Nazideutschland*, exhibition catalogue of the Deutsche Filmmuseum Frankfurt am Main (Frankfurt, 1987), 81.
24. As, for instance, in the index of *Die Ufa—auf den Spuren einer grossen Filmfabrik*, exhibition catalogue of the Bezirksamt Tempelhof (Berlin, 1987), 62f.
25. Bandmann and Hembus, 146.

26. Riess, *Das gab's nur einmal*, vol. 3, 171.
27. Heiber, *Joseph Goebbels*, 231.
28. Bandmann and Hembus, 145.
29. Transcript 1078 (management meeting, May 7, 1935), BA/R 109 I/1030b.

CHAPTER 28. GERMAN FILM POLICY IN THE OCCUPIED COUNTRIES

1. Kracauer, *From Caligari*, 307.
2. Géza von Cziffra, *Es war eine rauschende Ballnacht* (Frankfurt and Berlin, 1987), 195f.
3. Traub, *Die Ufa*, 108.
4. As cited in ibid., 108.
5. Boberach, vol. 5, 1368.
6. Ibid.
7. Ibid., 1701.
8. Ibid., 1702.
9. Ibid., vol. 6, 1803.
10. Ibid., vol. 16, 6462.
11. Figures from Spiker, 191.
12. As cited in ibid., 193.
13. Figures from ibid., 193.
14. My presentation of the events in occupied Czechoslovakia is based on an as yet unpublished manuscript by the Czech film historian Zdenek Stábla generously made available to me by the author. I am indebted to Hermina Marxová of Prague for the translation.
15. Cf. Spiker, 189.
16. Ibid.
17. Ibid., 291.
18. Cf. Bauer, 592.
19. Riess, *Das gab's nur einmal*. vol. 3, 230f.

CHAPTER 29. BLOOD RED IN DREADFUL BEAUTY

1. As cited in Barkhausen, 238.
2. Boberach, vol. 15, 6064f.
3. Ibid., 6091f.
4. As cited in Heiber, *Joseph Goebbels*, 309.
5. Barkhausen, 238.
6. Rökk, 133.
7. Cf. *Wir tanzen um die Welt*, 190.
8. Spiker, 237.
9. Ibid., 230ff.
10. Ibid., 235.
11. Ibid.
12. The following presentation of censorship in the last years of the war is based primarily on the work of Wetzel and Hagemann, cf. n. 176.
13. Ibid., 64.
14. Ibid., 61.
15. Ibid., 77.
16. Ibid., 60.
17. Ibid., 59.
18. Ibid., 144.
19. Ibid., 138.
20. Ibid., 72.
21. Ibid., 73.

22. Ibid.
23. Kaes, 11.
24. Virilio, 110f.
25. As cited in Kaes, 11.
26. As cited in Riess, *Das gab's nur einmal*, vol. 3, 206.
27. Bock, article on Veit Harlan.
28. Ibid.
29. Virilio, 113.
30. Riess, *Das gab's nur einmal*, vol. 3, 208.
31. As cited in Bock, article on Veit Harlan.
32. As cited in Riess, *Das gab's nur einmal*. vol. 3, 210.
33. Friedrich Kahlenberg in Marquardt and Rathsack, 162.
34. Riess, *Das gab's nur einmal*, vol. 3, 211.

Chapter 30. The End of Universum-Film AG

1. As cited in Norbert Grob, "Die Vergangenheit, sie ruht aber nicht," in Helmut Prinzler, ed., *Das Jahr 1945: Filme aus fünfzehn Ländern* (Berlin, 1990), 34.
2. As cited in Jan Schütte, "Die Viererbande," in Prinzler, 172.
3. As cited in ibid., 171.
4. Felix Hartlaub in a letter to his family, late December 1944, in his *Das Gesamtwerk* (Frankfurt, 1959), 465.
5. As cited in Karsten Witte, "Die Überläufer ausliefern," in Prinzler, 154.
6. Boberach, vol. 17, 6585.
7. Ibid., 6627.
8. Ibid., 6629.
9. Ibid., 6642.
10. Transcript 1547 (management meeting, November 24, 1943), BA/R 109 I/1716.
11. Transcript 1546 (management meeting, November 9, 1943), ibid.
12. Transcript 1560 (management meeting, March 2, 1944), ibid.
13. Transcript 1573 (management meeting, September 15, 1944), BA/R 109 I/1716a.
14. Transcript 1572 (management meeting, September 1, 1944), ibid.
15. Transcript 1561 (management meeting, March 18, 1944), BA/R 109 I/1716.
16. Transcript 1569 (management meeting, June 28, 1944), ibid., and 1578 (December 7, 1944), BA/R 109 I/1716a.
17. Transcript 1555 (management meeting, January 26, 1944), BA/R 109 I/1716.
18. Transcript 1573 (management meeting, September 15, 1944), BA/R 109 I/1716a.
19. Transcript 1579 (management meeting, January 9, 1945), ibid.
20. Transcript 1577 (management meeting, November 16, 1944), ibid.
21. Transcript 1556 (management meeting, February 2, 1944), BA/R 109 I/1716.
22. Transcript 1567 (management meeting, May 26, 1944), ibid.
23. Appendix to the minutes of the management meeting of September 1, 1944, titled "Kurze Übersicht über die derzeitige Lage der Auslandsgebiete," BA/R 109 I/1716a.
24. Ibid.
25. Transcript 1579 (management meeting, January 9, 1945), ibid.
26. Transcript 1563 (management meeting, April 14, 1944), BA/R 109 I/1716.
27. Transcript 1577 (management meeting, November 16, 1944), BA/R 109 I/1716a.
28. Boberach, vol. 17, 6735ff.
29. Cf. Speer, 412.
30. Riess, *Das gab's nur einmal*. vol. 3, 246.
31. Hans Borgelt, "Schicksalswende in Berlin," in *Wissen Sie noch? Ein DnF—Tatsachenbericht vom Zusammenbruch und Neubeginn des deutschen Films* (Wiesbaden-Biebrich, 1955), 7.
32. Barkhausen, 242.

TRAILER

1. Erich Kästner, *Notabene 45* (Berlin, n.d.), 130.
2. Ibid., 96.
3. Ibid., 157.
4. Alfred Grosser, *Geschichte Deutschlands seit 1945* (Munich, 1976), 41.
5. Figures from Johannes Hauser, *Neuaufbau der westdeutschen Filmwirtschaft 1945–1955* (Pfaffenweiler, 1989), 362, and Michael Dost, Florian Hopf, and Alexander Kluge, *Filmwirtschaft in der BRD und Europa* (Munich, 1973), 101.
6. Brewster S. Chamberlin, *Kultur auf Trümmern*, Schriftenreihe der Vierteljahreshefte für Zeitgeschichte 39 (Stuttgart, 1979), 73.
7. Ibid., 33.
8. *Wissen Sie noch?* 18ff.
9. The ms. is in the Helmut Käutner archive, Archiv der Akademie der Künste, West Berlin, folder 133.
10. From a letter by the film director Victor Becker to Helmut Käutner, June 26, 1945, in the Helmut Käutner archive (see note above), folder 49.
11. Presentation based on Hauser, 383.
12. Chamberlin, 74.
13. Ibid. The list of film companies, along with some further details given in the wording of the American report, is reprinted in Hauser, 385f.
14. As cited in ibid., 391 and 393.
15. Cf. ibid., 313f.
16. The original American text is reprinted in Peter Pleyer, *Deutscher Nachkriegsfilm 1946–1948* (Münster, 1965), 25.
17. Dost, Hopf, and Kluge, 102.
18. Cf. Hauser, 315.
19. Ibid., 316.
20. As cited in ibid., 317.
21. Reinhold E. Thiel, "Was wurde aus Goebbels' Ufa? Eine Untersuchung," in *Film aktuell*, Mitteilungen der Arbeitsgemeinschaft der Filmjournalisten e.V. 3 (1970), 3.
22. Ibid., 4. It should be pointed out here that at that time all "leftist" film critics in West Germany shared Thiel's assessment of Ufa—including the author. See Klaus Kreimeier, *Kino und Filmindustrie in der BRD* (Kronberg, 1973).
23. Cf. Hauser, 322f.
24. *Der Spiegel*, November 22, 1950.
25. Henry P. Pilgert of the U.S. High Commission, as cited in Pleyer, 29.
26. In *Wissen Sie noch?*, 26.
27. Chamberlin, 229 and 231.
28. Ibid., 103.
29. As cited in Hauser, 442.
30. As cited in Jacobsen, 145.
31. As cited in Hauser, 443.
32. *Der Spiegel*, January 17, 1951.
33. From a Käutner letter in the Helmut Käutner archive (see n. 9), folder 45.
34. Pleyer, 42.
35. Grosser, 106.
36. For example, Hans-Peter Kochenrath, "Kontinuität im deutschen Film" (1966), in Bredow and Zurek, 286ff.
37. Ibid., 287.
38. For recent literature on this, see Hilmar Hoffmann and Walter Schobert, eds., *Zwischen Gestern und Morgen: Westdeutscher Nachkriegsfilm 1946–1962*, exhibition catalogue of the Deutsche Filmmuseum Frankfurt am Main (1989).
39. Hauser, 326.

40. As cited in ibid., 329.
41. As cited in ibid., 330.
42. Thiel, 4f.
43. Ibid., 5f.
44. Hauser, 334.
45. Thiel, 6.
46. Ibid., 7.
47. Ibid., 8.
48. Riess, *Das gibt's nur einmal* (Hamburg, 1958), 14.
49. Dost, Hopf, and Kluge, 106.
50. Ibid., 105.
51. Figures from Hauser, 342.
52. Thiel, 11.
53. Cf., for example, the almanac *Die deutschen Filme*, published annually by the Export-Union der deutschen Filmindustrie, each volume of which contains an alphabetical list of all the films produced in West Germany since January 1, 1946, including names of the production companies.
54. Thiel, 11.
55. Ibid., 12.
56. Ibid., 13.
57. Ibid., 14.
58. Cf. Hauser, 344.
59. Thiel, 14ff.
60. Ibid., 15.
61. Ibid., 1.
62. Hauser, 581.
63. Enno Patalas, "Vom deutschen Nachkriegsfilm," in *Filmstudien*, ed. Walter Hagemann (Emsdetten, 1952), 17.
64. Adrian Kutter, as cited in Hauser, 582.
65. Hauser, 586.
66. Dost, Hopf, and Kluge, 9.

INDEX